D0955384

MAKING CITIZEN-SOLDIERS

MICHAEL S. NEIBERG

Making Citizen-Soldiers

ROTC and the Ideology of
American Military Service

HARVARD UNIVERSITY PRESS

Cambridge, Massachusetts, and London, England   2000

Library of Congress Cataloging-in-Publication Data

Neiberg, Michael.
   Making citizen-soldiers : ROTC and the ideology of American military service /
   Michael S. Neiberg.
       p. cm.
   Includes bibliographical references and index.
   ISBN 0-674-54312-2 (alk. paper)
   1. United States. Army. Reserve Officers' Training Corps.
   2. United States. Air Force ROTC.
   3. United States. Naval Reserve Officers Training Corps.
   4. United States—Armed Forces—Officers—Training of.   I. Title.

U428.5.N45 2000
355.2'232'071173—dc21   99-044354

To the memory of Ethel Neiberg and
Renee Saroff Oliner

Acknowledgments

In completing this book I have accumulated debts that I cannot hope to re-pay. The deepest of these debts is to my wife, Barbara, who has had to live with this project almost as long as she has had to live with me. I will be for-ever grateful for her patience and understanding. She also read the manu-script in its entirety. Thanks are also due to our families, Larry, Phyllis, and Elyssa Neiberg, and John, Sue, and Brian Lockley, for their support while I ran around the country.

This project began as a doctoral dissertation, and I must acknowledge the debt I owe to those who helped me at Carnegie Mellon University and else-where. My dissertation committee of John Modell, Peter Karsten (of the University of Pittsburgh), and Edward W. Constant III top this list. Professors Mary Lindemann, Steven Schlossman, and Peter Stearns also served as im-portant informal advisors along the way. The more I talk to graduate stu-dents about their experiences, the more grateful I am to these professors for both their intellectual and their personal support. Other friends and col-leagues at CMU, including Etan Diamond, Gail Dickey, Dan Holbrook, David Jardini, and Montserrat Martì Miller, gave help and advice (and wonderful Catalan food), for which I am grateful. John Shy at the University of Michi-gan got me started and helped along the way. I must also thank Walter Harrison; Robben Fleming; Richard Jessor; Elvis Stahr; Captain Michael Riordan, USN; William Snyder; Mark Grandstaff; Maggie McCaffery; and Richard Kohn for going above and beyond the call of duty.

At my new home, the United States Air Force Academy, I wish to thank Brigadier General Carl Reddel (Ret.); Colonel Mark Wells; Elliott Converse; Lieutenant Colonels Lorry Fenner and Tony Kern; Jeanne Heidler; Major Edward Maldonado, USA; Captain David Arnold (who read the entire manuscript); Jacob Abadi; and John Jennings. Dennis Showalter of Colorado College, a frequent visitor here at USAFA, was kind enough to read the manuscript on short notice, and I am grateful for his comments. I would like to thank the entire history department, but space forbids it. My colleagues there, to a person, have been helpful and supportive of both my teaching and my research efforts. I thank them.

I wish I had the space to thank all the archivists and librarians who helped me find the materials that allowed me to write this book. They were all wonderful. In the interest of brevity, let me single out Carnegie Mellon's Sue Collins, Michigan's Francis Blouin, the Air Force Historical Research Agency's Archie DiFanti, and the University of Illinois's John Straw. Pat Mazumdar of the University of Kansas and Josh Silverman and David Wolcott, both of Carnegie Mellon, provided research assistance and friendship and read part or all of the manuscript. The United States Army Center of Military History, the Mark C. Stevens Travel Fellowship at the University of Michigan Bentley Library, and the Spencer Foundation all saw enough merit in this study to fund it. Jeff Kehoe at Harvard University Press and two anonymous reviewers helped me to make this a much better book. Jeff's support of this manuscript made the final revisions a joy instead of a burden. If any errors remain, they are my own. Portions of this work have previously appeared in *New Interpretations in Naval History: Selected Papers from the Twelfth Naval History Symposium* (Annapolis, Md.: U.S. Naval Institute Press, 1997) and Elliott Converse, ed., *Forging the Sword* (Chicago: Imprint Publications, 1998).

Since I began this project I have lost two people who were very special to me. I dedicate this book to the memory of Renee Saroff Oliner and Ethel Neiberg. I wish with all my heart that I could be handing you a copy of this book instead of dedicating it to you.

Contents

Tables

MAKING CITIZEN-SOLDIERS

Introduction

> We must train and classify the whole of our male citizens, and make
> military instruction a regular part of collegiate education.
>
> —Thomas Jefferson

In the summer of 1996, the University of Connecticut requested that the
army reassign the head of its ROTC unit because the colonel "allowed classes
to be run like a boot camp." At first glance, the idea of dismissing a military
officer for running a military training program like a boot camp seems paradoxical if not ludicrous. Rather than treat the issue as such, however, the
army quickly acceded to the university's request and transferred the officer.
Both parties agreed that the transfer was in the best interest of both the
army and the university, because the colonel, according to one University of
Connecticut official, "just didn't realize what a university was like, and he
tried to impose a structure on it that just didn't belong here."[1]

That same summer, Massachusetts Institute of Technology officials made
strident efforts to defend ROTC in the face of objections from student groups
who contended that ROTC, bound by the military's "don't ask, don't tell,
don't pursue" policy toward homosexuals, violated the nondiscrimination
policies of the university. MIT responded in a fashion similar to that of other
universities faced with the same controversy. It pledged to keep ROTC, in
large part because of "its contribution to the important goal of preparing 'citizen-soldiers.'" Rather than expel the program, it sought, in the words of the
MIT faculty chair, to "remake it in our own image."[2]

These cases are contemporary examples of a process of remaking military
training (and thus the military itself) in the universities' image that has been
ongoing since the inception of military training on civilian campuses in the

1

nineteenth century. Indeed, when seen in historical context, the controversies at Connecticut, MIT, and elsewhere have roots that reach back as far as the eighteenth century, when the fledgling American military inherited its traditions from the English army. These controversies also have more recent precedents in the visible conflicts between universities and the military seen in the 1930s and the Vietnam War era, as well as in the less visible conflicts of the 1950s and 1970s. In this study I examine those roots and the evolution of ROTC training on civilian campuses, from the creation of the Reserve Officers' Training Corps in 1916 through the solidification of the current all-volunteer force (AVF) by 1980. I argue that the creation of ROTC just before America's entry into World War I, the confrontation that characterized ROTC in the 1960s, and the reform of ROTC in the 1970s are all rooted in a deeply held and enduring American belief, shared by educators, politicians, and college students alike, in the importance of populating the military with nonprofessional officers produced outside the traditional military academies.

Civilian colleges and universities, not the armed services, led the way in creating on-campus military training programs. From the early nineteenth century to the present, the administrators of American higher education have believed firmly that the national defense requires skilled young officers, but that these young men should not be prepared exclusively by the military itself. As the universities were taking the lead in preparing young Americans for other professions, they also assumed the task of preparing military officers, sometimes without the active cooperation of the formal military establishment. The officers so produced, however, were never supposed to be mere additions to the body of junior officers being produced at the insular military academies at Annapolis and West Point.

The officers produced through on-campus training programs were designed to counterbalance, not complement, the professional officers coming out of the academies. Many Americans, including many educators and administrators of the nation's colleges and universities, viewed the elite military academies as a "bastion of aristocracy" whose graduates were increasingly "isolated from [their] civilian contemporaries." Educators also derided the "uneven" education of the academy-trained officer. Formally mandated boards of visitors described it as "so dogmatic [that the curricula] discouraged initiative."[3]

By contrast, university and college administrators believed that civilian-educated officers would bring to military service a wider and more rounded background. They would also bring to the military a value system more consistent with American society, by virtue of having lived in a civilian environment. These officers were thus close to the "citizen-soldier" tradition that Americans have idolized in the icon of the minuteman. Furthermore, cooperation with the military offered university communities a means of contributing to the nation's well-being.

At first these citizen-soldiers were trained to serve in state militias (later the National Guard), but as the United States took on global military responsibilities after 1950, it was a natural and easy next step to use thousands of ROTC graduates in the active-duty forces. Academics and educational administrators judged that these new officers should play a dual role: they should serve the interests of national security abroad by joining the armed forces, and they should protect the freedoms of American society against encroachment by the very military system they were joining. In other words, training citizen-soldiers allowed the United States to have a military large and professional enough to protect the nation from without while avoiding the dangers of heightened militarism, which, if unchecked, could destroy the nation from within.

Lawrence Cress has argued that two English intellectual traditions have dominated American thinking about the military since the colonial period.[4] The "Radical Whig" tradition "opposed professional armies as invariably dangerous to liberty and civic virtue."[5] Radical Whigs preferred a militia system composed of men whose primary livelihood did not derive from their military service, even if such a military system would be less organized and less reliable. A militia, they argued, correctly placed the responsibility for national defense in the hands of men who would fight for property and family, not for a wage. Radical Whigs argued that "military service should be the obligation of every citizen and the profession of none."[6] In their eyes, a military populated by professionals threatened to become an instrument of ministerial power in the hands of an Oliver Cromwell or a William III.

Conversely, "Moderate Whigs" argued that while the military possessed the "means for the subversion of the political order," it would not destroy republican values if proper safeguards were created. Moderate Whigs like Adam Smith and George Washington understood that the complexities of eighteenth-century warfare necessitated a division of military labor and the creation of a professional soldiery.[7] For Smith, military professionalism was nothing more than a positive expression of the complexity of contemporary European (and, increasingly, American) society. In other words, soldiering had become too complex for part-time militiamen; national security had to become the responsibility of professionals. American experiences after Bunker Hill proved this point to Moderate Whigs like Washington, who became convinced of the need for a professional American military.

Furthermore, Moderate Whigs believed that a standing military was necessary both to protect civil liberties from foreign threats and to project the state's interests abroad. They argued that the military would not threaten republicanism if legal controls existed to take the army out of the exclusive control of the executive branch. To that end, both English and American Moderate Whigs supported the right of citizens to bear arms, legislative control of the power of the purse for all military requests, and limits on gubernatorial power to appoint militia officers. They understood the power that a professional military could bring to bear in the protection and projection of civil liberties but demanded that that very power be constitutionally controlled.

While the idea of the militia remained central to republican ideals of citizenship, the Radical Whig position faded—although it never disappeared.[8] As a result, the dominant Moderate Whig ideology greatly influenced the creation of the professional American officer corps. This ideology held that standing armies were not antithetical to individual liberty so long as "proper constitutional safeguards existed."[9] As American ideas about military service evolved, Moderate Whig ideology remained dominant.

ROTC has survived and received support from military officers, educators, students, and politicians in large measure because it is consistent with an American consensus that favors an updated and modernized version of the Moderate Whig position. ROTC allows for an acceptable level of civilian control of the military through the influence of civilian colleges and universities. In this way, it plays a critical role in creating an American military firmly rooted in the Moderate Whig tradition.

College and university administrators have thus seen ROTC not as an example of the military in the university but as an example of the university in the military. ROTC's staunchest and most important critics have been in uniform, not on campus. The military has often resisted diverting resources toward programs that it has perceived as citizenship programs, not essentially military programs. Local and national politicians have often thrust upon the military the responsibility of teaching civic virtue and patriotism through programs like the Civilian Conservation Corps (CCC) of the New Deal era. Before World War II, ROTC looked more like the CCC than a realistic program for developing junior officers. Despite the military's occasional dislike for, and indifference to, ROTC, educators have believed in it stridently enough to defend it against threats from the military itself. University administrators have also challenged the services to make changes that have enabled the program to keep pace with changes in American culture, military technology, and university dynamics.[10]

This book, consistent with much recent scholarship, argues that military systems are not institutions that act according to their own dynamic by virtue of ancient traditions, sacrosanct ceremonies, and a distinct mission. Rather, they are extensions of the societies that produce them.[11] The military officer, in the words of John Keegan, is now understood to "act as a man of his time and place."[12] The traditional Western military academies at Annapolis, St. Cyr, Sandhurst, and West Point all developed monastic pedagogical styles designed to reduce as much as possible any civilian influence on prospective officers. Nevertheless, as Keegan and others have demonstrated, even officers so produced reflect the values, beliefs, and interests of their society.

Since the beginning of the Cold War, the United States has relied heavily on the active cooperation of civilian institutions of higher learning to produce the majority of its active-duty officers through the Reserve Officers' Training Corps program. ROTC is one part of a system for developing junior officers that is consistent with the localized, federal structure of American government and society. The program has evolved and changed in character since 1916, but the relatively incremental change that had characterized the program before World War II yielded to revolutionary change with the onset of the Cold War. In 1950, ROTC was primarily composed of white male students from private eastern schools and land-grant universities nationwide. These students took a curriculum of 480 contact hours that included heavy doses of drill and military ceremony. The program, mandatory for two years on most campuses for all physically fit males, served largely to populate the reserve component of each service.

I chose 1980 as an endpoint for this book because in that year, incoming President Ronald Reagan's support for the concept of the all-volunteer force made ROTC an entrenched part of the American military system. By 1980, ROTC, voluntary almost everywhere, had jettisoned its heavy military emphasis; the curriculum included as few as 180 contact hours and included courses taught by regular civilian faculty. Its students were now primarily from the South and the Midwest, and they included large numbers of women and minority students. Furthermore, ROTC had become indispensable as a means of populating the active-duty officer ranks.

These and other remarkable changes over a relatively short (thirty-year) period were the result of changes to the ROTC program itself, combined with developments in the two institutions primarily responsible for its oversight: American higher education and the military. Like those institutions, and American society more generally, ROTC became more specializd, differentiated, and open to persons of all ascriptive categories. Understanding ROTC, then, has importance beyond understanding officer procurement and training. In this book I use ROTC as a lens through which to examine the evolution of the military as well as higher education's relationship to the military.

My work complements and expands on recent scholarship on both higher education and the military. For the field of higher education, studies by Roger Geiger and Julie Reuben are helping a new history of higher education in America to develop beyond individual case studies and an antiquated narrative style.[13] Adam Garfinkle's *Telltale Hearts* and Kenneth Heineman's *Campus Wars* provide fresh examinations of the working dynamics of American universities in the tumultuous and often misunderstood 1960s.[14] These books take serious and probing looks at the goals, ideologies, and achievements of the various actors on American campuses during that decade.

Scholars concerned with the military have recently begun to focus more attention on the people that the military recruits and how they affect the function and operation of the American military system. Christian Appy's *Working-Class War* is a fine example of such scholarship for the Vietnam period.[15] My book thus represents, along with Appy's and others, an effort to examine more carefully the origins and preparation of the American officer. Most important, these studies look carefully at the beliefs and values of men and women before their entry into the military and how those values affect the military as an institution in American society.

Studying ROTC therefore presents an opportunity to examine the history of military personnel procurement, American higher education, and American beliefs about the military. Despite the potential value of this subject, ROTC has been the subject of just five book-length studies, all now at least fifteen years old and all of limited utility for the purposes just described.[16] These studies, while informative, share three important flaws. First, they all focus exclusively on the military side of ROTC, exploring the effectiveness of the program in producing and training military officers. The most influential of these studies, Gene Lyons and John Masland's *Education and Military Leadership: A Study of the ROTC*, published in 1959, explored ways to reposition ROTC to meet the challenges of the Cold War era. In doing so, however, it focused exclusively on changes to the military curricula and an argument against unification of the army, air force, and navy programs (the Marine Corps receives officers through the navy's ROTC program). It did not address the university-military relationship in any substantive detail.

Their second flaw is that their attempts to examine ROTC historically generally consist of a short chapter or two devoted to an undocumented (and rather uninteresting) narrative. None of these studies has attempted to place ROTC within the American cultural, social, and political context. Nor have they placed ROTC within the context of American military traditions. Only Victor Hirshauer's 1975 study uses primary materials to examine changes to ROTC, and his materials consist solely of army and Pentagon records.[17] Four of these studies examine only one service, further narrowing their utility. These studies make no effort to examine events within universities themselves or the interaction of military and civilian officials. As this book will show, the quality of that relationship has been a critical variable.

The first two flaws contribute to a third: all of the previous studies assume that universities have acted as units of the military services, following orders just as any other component of the military would. One study argues that ROTC was administered "virtually the same way . . . at all Air Force detachments."[18] These studies examine only the military side of ROTC, and they assume that only those issues of concern to the military were significant to ROTC's development. Therefore they contain such erroneous statements as "the method of designating officers for ROTC duty and the fact that the military curriculum was determined in Washington did not become important issues at most colleges and universities participating in the ROTC program."[19] As the following chapters will make clear, both of these issues have been hotly debated outside Washington since at least 1950. To understand ROTC, one has to understand it as it has operated in places like Ann Arbor, Urbana, Seattle, New Brunswick, and Austin.

Past studies have overemphasized top-down leadership and high-level decision making. I argue that decisions made on local levels contributed significantly to the course and direction of ROTC between 1950 and 1980, and I demonstrate that the ROTC program was necessarily dependent on both the military and higher education for its survival. Both of these institutions, in turn, rely on the support and confidence of American society.

When Americans lose or gain faith in education or the military, ROTC feels the effects, if at times indirectly.

For many people, when they think of ROTC, they think of the time in the late 1960s when radical student groups on American campuses questioned connections between the university and the military. The images of burning ROTC buildings and campus protests have remained powerful. The years between 1968 and 1972 were indeed a time of rapid, fundamental change for ROTC, but it was only one such period, and the student movement was only one cause. The introduction of curricular reforms in the late 1950s, the 1964 implementation of the ROTC Vitalization Act, and the introduction of the all-volunteer force in 1973 also brought about important changes in the program. In short, this study looks at several periods of controversy and reform.

Despite such controversy, the ROTC program has survived two world wars, the Cold War, intense scrutiny from academics, violent opposition from a small but dedicated group of students in the Vietnam War era, and the end of the draft. It has survived because it was (and is) consistent with fundamental American values and ideas about the place of the military in American society. ROTC allows Americans to support a large standing military without the fear that the military will develop a value system alien to their own.

This book covers four chronological phases of ROTC development. Chapter 1 deals with the roots of the Moderate Whig position and the evolution of civilian officer education programs before 1950. Those programs had a modest quantitative impact on the active-duty American officer corps, but they laid the groundwork for the development of a regularized ROTC program that later produced officers for the active-duty military. Chapters 2 and 3 cover the years 1950 to 1964, which I refer to as the Cold War period.[20] This period was marked by relatively slow, incremental changes within the context of global international crisis. Nevertheless, even amid a general consensus that civilian institutions had to cede latitude and power to the military, the Moderate Whig position still dominated discussions of the role of military training and the proper role of civilian authority in officer preparation.

Chapters 4 and 5 cover the years of most intense reform, between 1964 and 1972. As fears about the growth of a military-industrial complex spread, educators stressed their desire to retain their role in officer production. The war in Vietnam did not lead most administrators, faculty, or even students to argue that ROTC should be expelled from the campus. Rather, the academic community reached a consensus that ROTC, properly reformed, could reinforce civilian influence over the military and that in this way, the worst excesses of the Vietnam experience might be avoided in the future.

Chapters 6 and 7 cover the years 1972 to 1980, when no conscription legislation existed to coerce men into military service. With the elimination of conscription (for the first time since the Cold War began), many Americans believed that the nation might return to the citizen-soldier concept, which had been lost when the draft took a disproportionate share of the nation's soldiers from those at the bottom of the society's social and economic scales. For both ROTC and the all-volunteer force to survive, the very definitions of citizenship and soldiering had to be changed. Throughout all of these changes, the Moderate Whig argument, rooted in fears of excessive military influence in civilian affairs, held considerable sway over the course of ROTC's evolution.

National-level changes, such as the end of the draft and the growing technological sophistication of military officers, affected all ROTC units. The ROTC program itself, however, evolved from school to school with variations to account for university traditions, the desires of local faculty and administrators, and the particular strengths of a given institution. I have therefore relied heavily not only on military archives but also on the archives of ten different schools. I chose these universities both for the availability of records in their archives and for the range of schools that they represent. The Universities of Colorado, Illinois, Michigan, Pittsburgh, Texas, and Washington, and Georgia Tech, Kansas State, Kent State, and Rutgers, are all large, public universities, but they offer a variety of geographical settings and relationships to ROTC.[21] This sample includes five land-grant universities, six charter Army ROTC (AROTC) units, two charter Naval ROTC (NROTC) units, and five universities that had significant student movements in the 1960s.

No clear distinction emerged between land-grant and other public universities in their treatment of ROTC issues. Rather, I found that public universities of all kinds reacted similarly. In all ten cases, the university communities under study demonstrated a willingness to work out problems relating to ROTC in order to be assured that the program would continue to serve as one of the "safeguards" that Cress argued were critical to Moderate Whig ideology.

Of course, ROTC exists in a much larger variety of settings, including private schools and military academies like Virginia Military Institute (VMI), Norwich, and the Citadel. However, my approach—focusing on public universities—provides three distinct advantages: first, public school administrators understood that their taxpayer-supported institutions had a distinct responsibility to deal seriously with ROTC; second, these schools have a remarkable ability to preserve and document their own history, and to make that documentation available (many private schools close their archival records for as long as fifty years); and third, faculty and administrators from such institutions served on national organizing bodies and advisory committees.

Several umbrella organizations also paid careful attention to ROTC, including the National Association of State Universities and Land-Grant Colleges (NASULGC), whose papers I examined at the University of Illinois, and three joint civilian-military advisory boards. Because of its prominence and its long history of hosting military training programs, the NASULGC served not only as a representative of its own interests but also as a conduit for the interests of schools outside the land-grant system. The Air Force Historical Research Agency at Maxwell Air Force Base (AFB) in Montgomery, Alabama, the United States Army Center of Military History in Washington, and the Suitland Federal Records Center in Suitland, Maryland, were invaluable resources for understanding the military side of ROTC.

This study uses ROTC to gain insight into the nature of American attitudes toward the military, reforms within the military itself, and the nature of the American public university's commitment to service. Antiwar protest has often been simplistically interpreted as a rejection by university communities of all things military. Such an analysis reduces to black and white a picture that is full of color. It certainly was possible for an individual to hate the war in Vietnam, hate the military, and, at the same time, be a firm supporter of ROTC. This position was entirely consistent with eighteenth-century beliefs that "the condemnation of the army as an agent of ministerial influences did not include an outright denunciation of military professionalism."[22] Dominant Moderate Whig ideology demands civilian controls on the military, not a sharp delineation of military and civilian spheres.

I would like to reiterate what this study does *not* do. I did not undertake an exhaustive study of private institutions or of state military schools like the Citadel and VMI. Public universities, whether involved in the land-grant system or not, act under a different dynamic than private ones. Like Kenneth Heineman in his book *Campus Wars,* I have chosen to limit my analysis to those schools that rely heavily on public funding and have to answer to publicly elected state legislatures and, in some cases, publicly elected trustees. Of course, such a choice of schools does not limit the importance of private universities to the overall story.

Furthermore, I have not attempted to deal with the issue of class dynamics in ROTC. It is surely possible that the services have used ROTC to gain access to men and women from less privileged socioeconomic backgrounds than their academy counterparts. It is also possible that ROTC students, generally less privileged than their non-ROTC peers at the same school, have used their military scholarships as a way to gain entrance into schools otherwise out of their financial reach. ROTC's role in "bluing" both the officer corps (witness Colin Powell) and the student body is fascinating, but beyond the purview of this study.

Although the service academies produce more senior leaders and generally attract more attention than does ROTC, the accomplishments of the Reserve Officers' Training Corps ought not to be ignored. ROTC permitted the first large-scale introduction of college-educated men into the officer corps. It also was the first significant means of entrance into the officer corps for women and African Americans.

This book covers a period when both higher education and the military became increasingly important to American society in a wide variety of overlapping realms. The interactions of the two institutions at the time of their growing centrality to the American identity deserves careful attention. As these two very different institutions have evolved along occasionally congruent paths, they have often tried to use each other for their own improvement and that of the nation. Part of this process has been the quest to find a middle ground between the academic world and the military.

CHAPTER 1

ROTC and the American Military Tradition

They come to us at the supercilious and sophomoric stage of their development and seriously need restraint and guidance such as the Army is so well equipped to render.

—Dean of Men Fraser Metzger, Rutgers University, March 15, 1944

The buildup of the large, peacetime military force that began in earnest in 1950 is an exception to the rule in American history. Traditionally, American beliefs about the military from all points along the ideological spectrum have been characterized by suspicion, charges of elitism, and vigorous efforts to place limits on both the size and the power of the professional military. The pressures of war and internal security in the twentieth century have led to a general consensus in favor of an increased standing military, but not to an increased desire to turn that military over to a professional elite.

Even in the Cold War era, when the American military's prestige and influence were at a historical peak, questions arose regarding the wisdom of placing the military in the hands of a small, careerist clique. Scandals involving the encroachment of career military officers on civilian authority include West Point graduate Douglas MacArthur's challenge to President Truman's authority during the Korean War and Annapolis graduate Oliver North's subversion of congressional intent during the Iran-Contra affair. Both of these men had a vocal public following, but, notably, neither was able to use his military career to propel him into a successful political career.[1] In the words of Professor Samuel Huntington, "While the American people like their political candidates to be military heroes, they want their military experience to be an interlude in, or a sideline to, an otherwise civilian career."[2]

The American polity has consistently rejected professional officers who cross a firm, if not always visible or definable, line separating proper conduct from improper conduct.

The American dilemma, then, has been to support a military strong enough to achieve the nation's political and economic goals without being so strong as to threaten the civil liberties and civilian oversight consistently valued by the Moderate Whig tradition that Lawrence Cress argues characterizes American military attitudes.[3] Over the course of the twentieth century, ROTC came to encompass a large share of the solution to achieving that delicate balance. ROTC offered the means to produce nonprofessional officers sufficiently civilian to assuage the fears of Moderate Whigs. At the same time, however, these officers could be professional and competent enough to fill the company grades of the officer hierarchy, with a relatively small percentage of such officers moving on to field grade and general grade.[4]

To understand ROTC, one must understand the nature of America's distrust of standing armies as well as the role that universities and colleges played in shaping the military before the onset of the Cold War. These two traditions created historical forces that operated on the decision-making process involving ROTC in the Cold War era and beyond. Campus protesters, university presidents, and secretaries of defense alike were operating in an environment whose roots had been established centuries earlier. While the actors in the ROTC debate were rarely cognizant of the context within which they were operating, that context nevertheless set the terms of debate and made some courses of action, such as the abolition of ROTC, impossible. ROTC played a critical role in fulfilling a powerful American belief: that the military must be subservient to civilian interests for it to truly represent and defend the interests of the society it serves.

Newburgh and the Anti–Standing Military Tradition

The American dilemma of relying for national defense on a military populated by large numbers of nonprofessionals was inherited from a similar British dilemma. Virtually all of the men who shaped early American military beliefs were trained in the British system. In the eighteenth century, Britain's military shared with other European systems an emphasis on fighting low-intensity wars for limited political goals. Unlike many of its European counterparts, however, the English system firmly emphasized civilian control over the military, even at the tactical and strategic levels; only civilian leaders decided what political goals were worth fighting for and how much force to use in trying to achieve those goals. Consequently,

> an eighteenth-century British or American general might admire a Caesar or a Frederick. But he knew that he would never have the kind of military and political power that such men possessed. He knew that he could not alone decide how to wage war—that his government would determine not only when to go to war but also what kind of war the people could and would support. An Anglo-American general would have to receive instructions from or at least discuss his plans with his government before embarking on any campaign.[5]

Despite the triumph of the American army in the War for Independence and the popularity of its commander, General George Washington, the end of hostilities did not produce a desire to elevate the place of the military in the new American state. Rather, it yielded a desire to return to a "traditionally antimilitary" society that treated its returning veterans poorly and remained suspicious of professional soldiers.[6]

American fears of a military takeover seemed entirely justified in 1783. A group of senior officer veterans of the Revolution led by General Horatio Gates opposed what they saw as an excessively moderate government under Washington and the alleged indifference of that government to their own financial problems. They envisioned a more centralized and aristocratic social and political system. Their plan to wrest control of the government from civilians was, according to Richard Kohn, "the closest that an American army has ever come to revolt or coup d'état." General Washington had to intervene personally at a meeting in Newburgh, New York, to prevent the officers from, in Washington's words, "sowing seeds of discord and separation" between the military and its properly constituted civilian overseers.[7]

Public awareness of the details of the Newburgh conspiracy reinforced Americans' "real fear" of a revolt from the professional standing army.[8] It convinced many civilians, Thomas Jefferson among them, that a large standing military was the greatest threat to the personal freedoms so recently won. It also "positively reaffirmed Anglo-American tradition: the first national army in American history explicitly rejected military . . . independence from civilian control."[9] That civilian control, many came to believe, was all that stood between American liberty and totalitarianism.

Constitutional controls over the military, traditionally favored by Moderate Whigs, appeared in the Articles of Confederation and in all state constitutions as well as in the U.S. Constitution. All thirteen governors served as commander-in-chief of their state's militia, while state legislatures retained the power of the purse and the power to mobilize. The Constitution maintained firm civilian control over all aspects of the national military as well. The president had ultimate authority as commander-in-chief, Congress held the power to declare war and controlled all military funding (the Constitution forbids Congress to provide military funding for more than a two-year term), and a civilian secretary of the navy and secretary of war headed up the military departments themselves. While the new United States made conscious efforts to break away from English traditions in some realms, the tradition of firm civilian control over military activities not only did not substantially change but, as a result of the Newburgh conspiracy, probably intensified.

After 1783 Congress pared the United States Army down to a single regiment. Because civilian fears of a standing military "remained strong in all regions of the country," Congress preferred to rely on "distance and foreign forbearance alone" to protect the nation from overseas enemies. Similarly, Congress did not judge any internal enemies to be sufficiently strong to merit the risks of creating a professional military. Native Americans on the frontiers were left to "the sheer weight of an advancing population" and whatever actions local and state military forces deemed just.[10]

One of the proposals that emerged in the wake of Newburgh foreshadowed later solutions by proposing cooperation with civilian colleges to ameliorate the excesses of a professional military. In 1783, New York governor George Clinton proposed that one civilian college in each state in the union offer military training to selected male students. Graduates of these programs would then serve brief stints as officers in the national army.[11] Clinton hoped that his plan, which Congress chose not to fund, would staff the professional military with men who were not professional soldiers. As civilians, well-schooled in the need to protect and preserve American freedoms, they would work against the tyrannical and aristocratic elements believed to exist among military professionals.

James Madison shared Clinton's fears of a standing military. Such a force, he argued, could be "dangerous," even "fatal," to the liberties of a free people. A strong federal union, Madison contended, had the virtue of making a standing military unnecessary. "The distance of the United States from the powerful nations of the world gives them the same happy security," he said, that Great Britain enjoyed by virtue of its "insular situation." The British monarchy had "never been able, by real or artificial dangers, to cheat the public into an extensive peace establishment." A strong federal union, combined with America's distance from Europe's internecine warfare, would eliminate quarrels between the states and therefore obviate the need for a standing military.[12]

Americans from most political perspectives preferred local militias as the solution to the problem of how best to defend the nation. Under this scenario, Americans could avoid the threats to civil liberties inherent in a standing army by localizing national defense and relying on individual state militias to complete the tasks expected of a national military. The Constitution guaranteed the rights of states to operate and staff local militias, and these units assumed much of the constabulary role that otherwise would have fallen to the national army. Acquiescing in the development of state militias also permitted Congress to reduce the funding for an army it did not trust. According to Harry Coles, "leaders in both parties had reason to suspect that money spent on the army was soapsuds down a rat hole."[13]

Strong local authority had the additional benefit of taking a large federal army out of the hands of potentially despotic civilians. Colonial politicians argued that a strong federal army in the hands of a civilian such as George III was every bit as dangerous as an army whose officers planned a coup d'état. The only reasonable course of action that these men saw involved reducing the power and authority of a central, professional armed force in favor of citizen-soldiers. The minuteman who beat his plowshares into swords became the model of the future American soldier.

In 1784 Congress explicitly stated that "standing armies in time of peace are inconsistent with the principles of republican government, dangerous to the liberties of a free people, and generally converted into destructive engines for establishing despotism."[14] The congressional plan in the event of foreign invasion, then, was for a small professional navy and army to delay the arrival of an invading force just long enough for latter-day Paul Reveres to rouse latter-day minutemen into action. By 1785 the Congress had further weakened the professional military by selling almost all its naval vessels (the navy had one combat-ready frigate to fight the "quasi-war" with France in 1798) and by directing that regular officers be assigned only to West Point and Fort Pitt (at the site of present-day Pittsburgh, then still considered the frontier).

Furthermore, Congress was willing to permit the states to develop militias or not, according to local wishes. Without professional leadership or direction, these militias rarely developed into respectable fighting forces and were often beaten badly in combat with Native American nations. Federalists such as Washington and Alexander Hamilton argued that in the absence of a reliable militia system, the professional army needed to be strengthened, but Congress did not agree to create a military academy at West Point until 1802, and then it was limited to a cadet class of ten engineers and run by a superintendent with no military background. West Point was fifty-six years old before it created a Department of Tactics.[15]

The ideal of a small standing military served the nation well in peacetime, but in times of war the weaknesses of a disorganized and unprofessional military became glaringly evident. During the War of 1812, a small fraction of the British army (most of which was busy fighting Napoleon on the Iberian Peninsula) moved at will, burning most of the public buildings in Washington, D.C., forcing the president to flee into the countryside, and threatening Baltimore and New Orleans. Some New England states refused to allow their militias to leave their state. These units drew the scorn of professionals for their amateur leadership; officers tended to be businessmen and politicians who had achieved their position based on their popularity back home. The hero of the war was, of course, Andrew Jackson, a nonprofessional who owed his fame to the commonly held perception that his Tennessee volunteers (also nonprofessionals) were primarily responsible for the American victory over the British near New Orleans. Despite its evident disfunctionality, the volunteer/militia system continued to capture the imagination of the American people.

The strength of the militia system lay not in its mastery of tactics and operations but in its ability to mobilize men for war and keep them highly motivated. The system received much of the credit for the isolated military successes of the war (such as New Orleans). Americans continued to prefer that their military units be constituted of local men and officers, not part of a federal army. The military failures of the War of 1812 did nothing to diminish Moderate Whig fears of a large federal force, and the immediate postwar years did not produce an enduring movement to strengthen the national army and navy.[16] After a brief period of attention to military matters, traditional anxieties returned. An economic slump in 1819 and the general indifference that Congress showed toward the army in the absence of a foreign threat resulted in a reassertion of traditional antimilitarism. In 1821 Congress cut the army in half, from 12,000 officers and men to 6,000 officers and men, and ordered that only one major general (then the highest rank) be retained.[17]

In typical American fashion, the problems and tensions that resulted from the humiliation of 1812 produced a desire to provide better training and preparation for the militia officers before it produced enduring efforts to improve the preparation of professional officers. Recalling George Clinton's plan, these efforts focused on civilian institutions of higher learning. Before the war only the University of Georgia had offered military training, but after the war other schools soon developed ideas for military training programs independent of West Point.

In 1819 the American Literary, Scientific, and Military Academy (now called Norwich University) began military training to produce, in the words of the school's founder, Alden Partridge, officers "identified in views, in feelings, [and] in interests with the great body of the community."[18] Partridge resigned his army commission after serving as West Point's third superintendent in order to create a new academy that would help to build "a balance between the militia and the Regular Army, a balance that would bring the popular support and allegiances of the militia system into harmony with the training and discipline of an efficient army."[19] This solution, Partridge hoped, could walk the tightrope inherent in American military attitudes. With civilians trained in the skills needed of military officers, the nation could avoid another disaster like 1812 as well as another threat to civil liberties like the one so narrowly averted at Newburgh.

Other schools developed similar programs in the years between 1815 and the Civil War. In 1820 Thomas Jefferson directed that the University of Virginia require military training for all students, in the hope of creating officers for a national militia and, perhaps, making military science an academic field of study. By 1840 the University of Tennessee and Indiana University were also requiring military training.[20]

The programs at civilian colleges also helped to counterbalance changes occurring at West Point. During the 1820s, John Calhoun led a determined effort to reform West Point and make it the principle source of entry into the officer corps. Part of the reformation involved guaranteeing that the cadets came from a narrowly defined social background. As a result, West Point "increasingly restricted access to the officer corps to established old-stock families."[21] In an era of Jacksonian egalitarianism, the military became one institution to which access could be restricted by virtue of its relatively small size and the aristocratic traditions it had inherited from Europe.

While the reform of West Point gave it, and the army, more respect and prestige, it also led to increasing charges of elitism. The socialization process at the Military Academy produced "a distinct military subculture . . . subtly apart from the expansive individualism which permeated contemporary civilian society." The army responded to antimilitary attacks by developing antipathetic attitudes toward the civilian world and by creating an increasingly separate "band of brothers." Officers often married daughters or sisters of other officers, and loyalty to the army grew more intense.[22]

A resulting tension emerged regarding the militia and the citizen-soldier. As the professional military grew more insular and more protective of its role, its members came to feel "notorious contempt" for nonprofessionals.[23] Similarly, as they derived more identity from their status as officers, they grew more suspicious and distrustful of the enlisted men. As William Skelton noted, "Increasingly, the officer corps consisted of long-term, West Point–trained careerists who identified strongly with the army, especially their particular branches, and who viewed the civilian world with suspicion."[24]

The formation of the United States Naval Academy at Annapolis in 1845 intensified these patterns. Naval officers had even more elite backgrounds than their army contemporaries. Annapolis midshipmen came disproportionately from affluent manufacturing, commercial, and professional backgrounds. The naval officer corps quickly became, in the words of Peter Karsten, a "naval aristocracy" that socialized, married, and interacted with other navy families.[25]

Before the Civil War, then, two trends dominated decisions regarding American military personnel. The first was a perceived functional need, consistent with the prevailing social structure, for a small, highly professionalized officer corps drawn from an increasingly small group at or near the top of the American social structure. The second, contradictory, trend was a cultural preference for citizen-soldiers, ill-prepared and unprofessional though they were, to act as a counterbalance to the antidemocratic tendencies Americans feared in their own officer corps. Relying on local forces also allayed antifederal fears that another Cromwell or George III would use his civilian authority to command a large army for the purpose of removing democratic freedoms. The crisis of the Civil War and its aftermath brought these two ideas together and eventually produced the modern antecedent to the twentieth-century ROTC program.

The Morrill Act

In 1861 the Union army estimated that it would need about 20,000 officers to lead its units in the initial phase of the war against the South. Loyal West Point cadets and Norwich graduates could provide at best only 1,500 officers.[26] Faced with such a tremendous shortage of officers, leadership of the Union army fell to civilian officers in charge of local units. Many of these men lacked any formal training in military matters and relied on their familiarity and authority at home to command. Some, like Robert Gould Shaw and Joshua Chamberlain, performed their tasks very well, but on the whole, the nonprofessional officers were often overwhelmed by the responsibilities of command.[27]

The professionals did not perform much better. Throughout the war, West Pointers drew a great deal more scorn than praise. Few career officers had had any sustained experience in commanding large units, and many quickly found their academy training in the teachings of Baron Antoine-Henri de Jomini outdated in an era of rifled weapons, telegraphs, and railroads.[28] The Union army went through a series of military commanders, such as George McClellan, Joseph Hooker, and Ambrose Burnside, who failed to achieve victory and were frequently humiliated in battle by smaller Confederate units. The two most popular Union generals were the distinctly unaristocratic Ulysses Grant, who wore a private's coat instead of a general's uniform, and William Sherman. Both were West Point graduates, but they were of a different breed and were comfortable with civilian dominion; notably, both had experienced problems fitting in with their Military Academy colleagues.

The initial inability of American officers, however trained, to provide leadership on any level impelled considerations of reforming the military system. Few people considered expanding the military academies, both because of their aristocratic reputation and because the performance of West Point graduates in the Union army did little to inspire awe or confidence. Instead, within a year of the outbreak of the war, Americans had already begun to look to the nation's civilian colleges as the solution, just as they had after the War of 1812.

In the Jacksonian period, Whigs and Democrats had debated the federal funding of state universities and colleges. Whigs had consistently favored the use of funds from the sale of government-owned lands to create public academies to teach Latin, Greek, mathematics, and other subjects. Democrats had either opposed the idea as elitist or favored the creation of these schools as institutions to teach what they contended were more practical subjects, such as farming and mechanics. Before the Civil War, comprehensive action on either plan had failed to come to fruition.

The formation of the Republican Party, which picked up the Whig banner on the issue, and the departure to the Confederacy of several key southern opponents of the Whig plan opened the way for the public funding of colleges to be considered anew. Vermont Representative Justin Morrill led the fight to get the public colleges created. Morrill was a friend and neighbor of Norwich founder Alden Partridge and was particularly impressed with the level of preparation and competence of Norwich graduates serving in the Union army. Morrill's bill proposed that 30,000 acres of public land be sold in each state to generate funds to create public colleges. These colleges could teach any other subjects they wished, but they had to offer courses in agriculture, mechanical arts, and military tactics.[29] Congress approved the Morrill Act in July 1862.

Morrill had envisioned that his plan would produce more men trained in the Norwich model, men who had military knowledge but were not military professionals. "Like Partridge, [Morrill] offered the alternative of military training in civilian educational institutions as a means by which a democratic people could gain a competent officer corps . . . without endangering their basic liberties."[30] Men trained at these land-grant colleges were to be citizens first and soldiers second. Furthermore, the Morrill Act left decisions on the amount, intensity, and regularity of military training to the discretion of local officials at the new schools.

The Morrill Act was consistent with many traditional American beliefs about the proper way to commission officers for the army: it localized training and offered a civilian alternative to West Point graduates, yet it did not compel individuals actually to serve in the military if they chose not to do so. The Morrill system attracted significant support in Congress after the war, and supplementary acts quickly followed. Between 1866 and 1890, Congress passed acts authorizing the War Department to dispatch a total of 20 (later 100) officers to teach military classes, to supply small arms and equipment for training purposes, and to provide on request both men and material to schools outside the land-grant system (as well as to "separate but equal" black schools created by the land-grant system).

By 1900, forty-two colleges and universities had military training programs in operation that received support from the War Department. Several other programs received support from the hosting institution, usually in the form of finding Civil War veterans to conduct drill sessions. The army's own support of on-campus military training was "lukewarm" between 1870 and 1910, while the army's leadership focused its energies on wars against the American Indian nations of the West. The army was often reluctant to assign officers higher in rank than lieutenant to college campuses; in one noteworthy case, it assigned an eighty-year-old major to North Dakota Agricultural College.[31] Between 1898 and 1902 it assigned no one to Kansas State; the unit was commanded by a cadet selected by the school's board of regents.[32]

Like militia units in the era between the Civil War and World War I, campus military training programs had no standard uniforms (indeed, Kansas State cadets did not even have uniforms until 1885) and no systematic access to modern equipment, and they did little except teach men how to march in straight lines. Nevertheless, the militia system's main supporter, the National Guard Association, secured a doubling of federal funds in 1887 and kept up the pressure on Congress to make the National Guard and local militia units the primary means of guaranteeing national security from within and without. Localism and nonprofessionalism remained powerful.

Thus, until World War I military programs on campuses remained quite informal and inefficient. These programs had no connection to the system of appointing and commissioning officers for either the active-duty forces or the National Guard. However, the groundwork for such a system had been laid. A loose connection between the War Department and civilian institutions of higher learning had been established, and a preference for nonprofessional officers had become a consistent feature of American culture. These factors formed the background for the creation of the ROTC program in a form that is still recognizable today.

The Birth of a Formal ROTC Program

The preparedness movement that preceded World War I argued for a more formal connection between officer training programs and the larger military system, which was itself under review. Progressive emphasis on efficiency and rationality had already created a "virtual revolution" in the army and the navy between 1890 and 1910.[33] The reborn military had more modern weapons, a streamlined promotion system, a General Staff to centralize decision making, and war colleges to study the problems of wars past, present, and future.

This movement also led to the passage of the 1916 National Defense Act (NDA), which created the three components of the American military system still in use today: the active-duty forces, the organized reserves, and the National Guard. The active-duty forces are composed of men in uniform and under the direct control of the army, the navy, the marines, and, after 1947, the air force. The reserves, also under the direct control and supervision of federal authority, were intended to be composed largely of veterans of tours of duty with the active forces, supplemented by men recruited with bounties and other incentives. As the name implies, it is a force "in reserve," subject to periodic rudimentary training and, if need be, emergency call-up to active duty.

The reformed National Guard was the result of a compromise between local officials who wanted a militia organizationally distinct from the federal government and national military officials who saw the state militias as little more than militarily inept social clubs, unreliable should the United States be drawn into war. The former group fits Cress's "Radical Whig" position: they wanted the militias to remain structurally and functionally independent of the regular army so that they might stand guard against the tyrannical potential inherent in a professional, federally controlled army. Regular army officers, however, had long been suspicious of the National Guard and militia units for their lack of formal training, their election of officers, and the familiarity between those officers and the enlisted men they led.

Despite its inefficiencies, eliminating the National Guard altogether or absorbing it into the army reserves would have been impossible. The 1898 Spanish-American War, the "splendid little war," had been largely fought by local units, commanded by locally elected officers who often allowed their men to address them on a first-name basis. The units had had "few hours given to serious training, almost none to long marches," but had made significant contributions to victory.[34] The national hero of the war, Theodore Roosevelt, was a nonprofessional whose soldiers, the Rough Riders, were also nonprofessionals.[35] This evident success, fresh in the minds of Americans, produced wide support for keeping the militia system basically intact.

As a result, the NDA dictated that the new National Guard units were to grow in size from 100,000 men to 400,000 and remain under the control of the states in which they served. They were, however, to be subject to mandatory training periods directed by regular military officers and to federalization in the event of a national emergency. Discipline, quality of leadership, mission, and supply were to be roughly the same across the three components of the reconfigured military, although in reality, patronage and local popularity continued for many years to dominate the process of awarding National Guard officer commissions.[36]

To professionalize the officer corps of the reserves and National Guard, the NDA also called for the creation of a Reserve Officers' Training Corps to absorb and build on military training programs already in existence at land-grant schools and many other large universities. The army's General Staff saw the creation of ROTC as the "only foreseeable option . . . to a greatly expanded military academy." Such an expansion would have been prohibitively expensive, and the staff knew that it would have required a massive effort to convince a majority of congressmen to vote for an increase at any cost.[37]

ROTC served as an effective compromise that offered something to all interested parties. The program allowed the War Department to standardize curriculum and equipment, thereby regularizing the type of military training young men received. Standardization also pleased military educators, who had been lobbying since 1913 for the army to institute minimum standards so that military training would do more than teach men how to march.[38] The ROTC plan also pleased proponents of the National Guard, because the graduates would be primarily available to them, not the regular army. Since the vast majority of students, especially those in the land-grant system, attended colleges close to home, ROTC reinforced the localized nature of the National Guard system and remained consistent with traditional beliefs in the value of the militia.

The initial number of ROTC units was limited, due to the relatively meager funds the War Department made available for the new program; therefore intense competition developed among schools that wished to acquire a unit. Professors Lyons and Masland argued that patriotism and a sense of public responsibility were the primary motivations for university officials seeking a unit for their campus.[39] Students seemed to share these sentiments. At many private eastern colleges, for example, students demanded that their school be included in the ROTC system along with the land-grant schools, so that the latter would not have a monopoly on patriotism. Students at Bowdoin, Williams, Harvard, Princeton, Yale, and Dartmouth all circulated petitions asking to have an ROTC unit; all were approved.[40]

In 1916 at the University of Pittsburgh, administrators and students, like their peers nationwide, began military training to prepare for American participation in the Great War. The Pittsburgh trustees authorized such training, without support from the War Department, in May. At the same meeting, they authorized the chancellor to apply for one of the new ROTC units.[41] Pittsburgh officials told the army that they were "extremely anxious" to get a unit and offered to pay as much as $80 per month of an active-duty officer's salary, if one could be assigned to conduct training programs.[42] Chancellor S. B. McCormick then sent one of the university's deans to Washington, D.C., to solicit the help of Pennsylvania's two senators, "in order that we may not only get ROTC, but that we may get it in a short time."[43] Georgia Tech's president and the chairman of the board of trustees made a similar trip to Washington to make a personal appeal for an ROTC unit at Tech.[44]

Collegiate administrators and faculty believed in the university's responsibility to serve society, and they "volunteered to help in whatever ways they could during World War I."[45] Working with the army provided universities with several benefits. Princeton's Edward Corwin argued that working with the army gave university professors "self respect by giving us some useful work to do while drawing our salaries."[46] Such work also protected one from undue suspicion. In 1917 the American Association of University Professors (AAUP) Committee on Academic Freedom in Wartime stated that faculty could legitimately be fired because of their "attitude or conduct" related to the war.[47]

Support for the war and ROTC thus imparted patriotism and shielded one from allegations that could lead to dismissal. With enthusiastic support from trustees, administrators, and faculty, the land-grant system alone provided 28,000 officers (including 43 generals) and 51,000 enlisted men to the army, navy, and marines during World War I.[48] Schools outside the land-grant system contributed as well. The University of Washington opened special programs to train navy and marine officers and ran the Student Army Training Corps program for the army.[49] Washington produced more naval officers for the war than any other school except Annapolis.

These experiences demonstrate the desires of students, faculty, and administrators to participate formally in military training programs. To the university communities, such participation represented a visible demonstration of patriotism and national service, even given the army's great difficulty in meeting the universities' demand for equipment, instructors, and guidance. In 1918 the army suspended the entire ROTC program for the duration of the war in favor of the Student Army Training Corps, which prepared men for enlisted service. After the war, however, enthusiasm for ROTC remained high. A 1919 student report at the University of Pittsburgh argued that ROTC "promises much for the future of higher education in America."[50] The *Kansas State Collegian* said in the same year that ROTC "gives promise of being a great thing for college men."[51]

One hundred thirty-five institutions had been granted ROTC units by the end of 1919. These institutions all agreed to offer a two-year basic course, mandatory at many schools, of at least three hours per week, and a voluntary two-year advanced course of at least five hours per week. Students who completed the latter could receive a reserve or National Guard commission. The War Department agreed to pay the salaries of the instructional staff, the cost of books, and the stipends of advanced cadets. In return, the host schools agreed to provide classrooms and office space and to give senior officers the title of professor of military science and tactics and junior officers the title of assistant professor of military science and tactics. By January 1922, 57,419 students were enrolled in 131 units.[52]

Administrators devoted considerable resources to their quest for ROTC units. University of Washington president Henry Suzzallo donated ninety-eight acres of the campus in the hope of attracting a navy ROTC program to train navy and marine reserve officers "exactly as the university is now training army reserve officers." Suzzallo was the first official to suggest such a program, but he would have to wait until the 1926 creation of the Naval Reserve Officers' Training Corps for his suggestion to become a reality.[53] Georgia Tech's president was no less enthusiastic. He credited ROTC with raising the athletic standards and "manly bearing" of students at Tech; in 1919, 90 percent of Tech's male students were enrolled in the program.[54]

While World War I provided the immediate impetus for these campus communities to seek an ROTC unit, other, more subtle, processes had been at work for decades. Julie Reuben has recently argued that the period from 1915 to 1930 in American higher education represented an "extracurricular" phase that followed religious and scientific phases. In the late nineteenth century, conflict between the traditional religious orientation of American colleges and universities and a more secular, Darwinian approach revealed "religion's intellectual marginality" to a generation of university reformers at prominent schools like Harvard, Johns Hopkins, and Michigan. By 1910, the reformers' scientific approach had won out. That approach, however, failed to give the campus the emotional and moral organization that religion had formerly provided. As a result, reformers "began . . . to emphasize secular sources for moral development."[55]

Reuben was primarily concerned with an intellectual history of the notions of truth and science, not with a study of moral guidance in the curriculum. Carrying her argument a small step further, however, one can easily see how the military came to be one of the institutions to which the universities turned for much of the secular guidance that the reformers believed had fallen away. The army, with its focus on discipline, patriotism, and the building of "men," fit in almost perfectly. The military thus stepped into a sort of moral guidance vacuum on the nation's campuses.

In this vein, the president of Rutgers University welcomed ROTC because he believed that it "was good physical and moral training for the student."[56] Devotion to country, symbolized by the availability (in many places the requirement) of military training, came to serve as a substitute for devotion to God and "the unity of truth," symbolized by chapel attendance and theology courses that had earlier been mandatory at some of the same schools that required ROTC. ROTC was not, of course, the only such program (intramural athletics, begun at the University of Michigan in 1912, offered another sort of structure), but it did provide the secular moral guidance that reformers sought while simultaneously fulfilling the desires of educators to provide service to the nation.

In response to military needs and the requests of educators, the army standardized the ROTC curriculum and mandated that military instructors teach map reading, military history, military law, basic tactics, camp sanitation, drill, and marksmanship. It did not take long, however, for serious problem areas to develop. Since the program produced Reserve, not active-duty, officers, "a sense of urgency and immediacy was often absent." As budgets tightened, the War Department resisted assigning high-quality officers to campuses. It also assigned fewer and fewer instructors, until by the mid-1920s, officer-to-cadet ratios in the basic course often fell as low as 1 to 100.[57] Furthermore, the General Staff quickly realized that patriotism alone would not provide the numbers of advanced cadets that they had hoped to attract. An early proposal by the General Staff to provide scholarship authorizations for selected students failed to get congressional approval, but the proposal itself acknowledged that financial incentives would be necessary for the program to have the quantitative impact it was designed to have. Moreover, differences between the military's subject matter and civilian aims for higher education created friction. In the interwar years "there developed a good deal of antagonism between military men and educators on the problem of accepting the ROTC courses as legitimate educational programs . . . Basically, the ROTC courses had two lessons to teach, the techniques of soldiering and the obligations of citizenship and neither was academically appealing."[58] These problems all intensified as a result of the overlapping system that managed ROTC problems. No single agency in the War Department had direct oversight for ROTC matters, and as a result no single office existed to regularize policy or even to meet with educators who came to Washington to discuss ROTC.

This friction was symptomatic of the secondary importance of ROTC to the active-duty forces in the immediate postwar years. The program primarily existed to provide officers for the Reserves or, in some cases, the National Guard. The addition of a Navy ROTC program in 1926 (inaugural units were established at Harvard, Yale, Georgia Tech, Northwestern, Washington, and California) made the nation's civilian colleges an indispensable source of reserve officers for all arms of the military. A limited number of ROTC graduates received active-duty commissions, but the American officer corps of the 1920s and 1930s remained small enough for it to be trained by the service academies; therefore, the best jobs went to the graduates of Annapolis and West Point. In 1935, fifty-two of the army's sixty-four generals and sixty of the navy's sixty-one admirals had graduated from the academies. Only five of the generals and none of the admirals had graduated from civilian colleges or universities.[59] The sole interwar attempt to open pathways for ROTC officers, the 1935 Thomason Act, made available 1,000 one-year active-duty appointments. However, no more than fifty of those men would receive permanent commissions at year's end. Even future U.S. Air Force chief of staff Curtis LeMay was unable to obtain an active-duty commission, because there "just weren't any vacancies" when he finished ROTC training at Ohio State in 1928.[60] This policy remained in effect until World War II.

It is unlikely that these advancement restrictions caused too much consternation among cadets. Most men who joined the advanced ROTC course did not desire an active-duty military commission.[61] Rather, they saw ROTC as a means to prepare themselves as citizen-officers for future emergencies. ROTC was designed to produce men who would go on to serve their country in myriad civilian occupations, from lawyer to farmer to architect. Their skilled presence in the organized reserves or the National Guard would allow the active-duty military forces to be kept at appropriately small levels.

ROTC's early years thus established it in good stead on the nation's campuses. Both the army and the navy supported it as an appropriate means to train young men for military service outside the traditional academies and such less formal arrangements as the prewar Plattsburg training camps and locally run National Guard training programs. By 1940 ROTC had become responsible for producing 80 percent of the organized reserves' officer corps and had commissioned more than 100,000 men.[62]

For the campuses, ROTC demonstrated patriotism in a bold and evident manner. Within twenty-four years of its creation, 220 colleges and universities had successfully acquired a unit, and many more sat anxiously on waiting lists.[63] The young men who took the classes were often ROTC's biggest supporters, creating military honor societies and campus traditions like military balls. For some of the large number of students who did not desire military training, however, mandatory ROTC classes became a symbol of the potentially perilous influence that the military could wield over civilian institutions. For most of those who shunned or ignored it, ROTC was just another campus inanity.

ROTC in an Era of Isolationism

The most important pre–World War II challenges to ROTC occurred in the environment of isolationism in the 1920s and 1930s. In the wake of reconsiderations about the wisdom of the U.S. involvement in World War I came concerns over the influence of military ethics and manners on civilian life. Traditional American fears of a standing military reawoke and helped to kill a postwar conscription plan proposed by the army. Pacifist groups on American campuses sought to change university policies regarding the military as a step toward removing militaristic elements from American society generally.

The two-year compulsory nature of ROTC at land-grant colleges, called for in the 1916 National Defense Act, attracted the most attention on campus. Representatives of the American Friends Service Committee, the Young Men's Christian Association (YMCA), the Women's International League for Peace and Freedom, and other secular and religious groups formed the Committee on Militarism in Education in 1925 to eliminate the compulsory military training required of students at land-grant colleges. Requiring military training of young men, they argued, developed a habit of warfare that was not instinctual but learned. "If the habit were broken, humanity would make some other response besides violence when the causes of conflict appeared."[64]

The University of Wisconsin was the first land-grant college to challenge compulsory training in 1923. The Wisconsin state legislature interpreted the Morrill Act as calling for schools only to offer military instruction to interested students and voted to make all military instruction elective.[65] Private schools were not mandated by the Morrill Act to offer military instruction, and therefore they had more latitude to change their policies. Most of these schools had initially chosen to adopt the compulsory two-year program in existence at land-grant schools, but by the mid-1920s several were reconsidering. By 1927 ROTC had been made voluntary at such schools as Johns Hopkins, the University of Pennsylvania, and Princeton.[66] In 1930 the U.S. attorney general voiced his support for Wisconsin's move, and in 1934 the Supreme Court ruled in favor of a voluntary ROTC.[67] By the mid-1930s, twenty-one schools had made the program voluntary, including another land-grant school, the University of Minnesota.[68]

The anticompulsory forces never focused their efforts on removing ROTC itself; their primary goal remained the elimination of ROTC as a graduation requirement. They objected to the imposition of military training, not its existence for students who desired it. The navy and the war departments held conflicting views on the issue. Higher officials opposed the change, arguing that removing compulsory ROTC might serve as a first step toward eliminating the program altogether. ROTC instructors themselves, however, often argued that the army could gain by acquiescing. Requiring men to participate in ROTC was unpopular, but ROTC itself was not. Requiring the program, then, served only to give ROTC a bad reputation and to bring thousands of disgruntled and unmotivated men into the units.

The army was uninterested in managing the character-building aspects of ROTC thrust upon it by Congress and college administrators. Congress had also put the army in charge of a high school version of ROTC and the Civilian Conservation Corps, neither of which served any direct military role. Congress put an unwilling army in control of both programs, because of the military's perceived ability to turn boys into men. To the extent that the collegiate ROTC program could provide officers, it had the army's support. But the army consistently tried to separate that role from what it argued was the discrete role of instilling patriotism in college men. Mandatory ROTC was, of course, also uneconomical. In a typical year, the army had to train, equip, and outfit 150,000 young men to produce just 3,500 reserve officers.[69]

The 1930s' controversy over compulsory training resulted in the first wave of required programs that elected to go voluntary. A second wave, discussed in Chapter 2, would play out along almost identical lines in the early 1960s. In both debates, the vast majority of educators and students either supported the ROTC *status quo* or supported it as an elective course of study. Indeed, the universities supported ROTC much more intensely than the army did. By 1936, as international tensions were increasing, educators warned the army that it needed to begin to prepare ROTC for the role it would have to assume should the United States get drawn into war. The Land-Grant Association told the army that "no . . . explanations or alibis can persuade anyone that the Army is not indifferent toward ROTC . . . [W]ith the all-time high appropriations in peacetime, there is no evidence of sincere and vigorous effort to provide for ROTC."[70]

The compulsory debate, then, should be read not as evidence of academic unwillingness to participate in military training but as evidence of an unwillingness to continue those programs as a requirement for graduation. Nor were all universities interested in abandoning compulsory ROTC. No anti-ROTC movement developed at schools where the program was voluntary. Kansas State won a 1935 lawsuit brought against the college by a student who refused to participate in military training activities.[71] Seventeen schools switched to voluntary programs in the 1930s, but a national bill to make ROTC programs entirely voluntary failed in 1936. The failure of the bill, combined with the rise to power of Nazi Germany, effectively ended the movement.

Most educators and students in the 1930s believed in the program enough to support it and keep it operating in the face of challenges from isolationists and pacifists, but few campus officials showed the enthusiasm for it that they had shown in the years after World War I. Moreover, rearmament programs under President Franklin Roosevelt focused primarily on technology and materiel, not personnel. As a result, ROTC's purpose was ill-defined. Most men completed their required training and quickly tried to distance themselves from the program. Robert McNamara recalled his ROTC training at the University of California, Berkeley: "What I learned was that nobody took the military seriously. My classmates and I saw [ROTC] as a pointless ritual, irrelevant to our world. On the day of our final parade, when we had to march before the president of the university, we threw our rifles down as soon as we were done—the hell with it!"[72]

The School of the Soldier

World War II was as a watershed in American attitudes toward the military and the military model of social organization. Prewar isolationism and anti-militarism disappeared almost overnight. After the war, hundreds of thousands of men and women returned from military service to direct corporations, run universities, and use their GI Bill benefits to attend college. Many brought with them a belief that some, if not all, of what they had learned in the military could be profitably incorporated into their civilian lives.

They also learned that "the army as a whole is a vast school."[73] To convert civilians into soldiers, sailors, marines, and airmen, the military ran a wide array of schools and programs, including the navy's V-12 program and the army's Advanced Student Training Program, which built on the infrastructure of prewar ROTC programs. As they had done during World War I, the services suspended ROTC for the duration of the war in favor of faster, more specialized training programs. The University of Colorado hosted a V-12 unit and navy language-training programs in Japanese, Malaysian, Russian, and Chinese.[74] A shared consensus that the World War II experience had been a "school for the soldier" helped legitimize the military's reconstruction of ROTC on college campuses beginning in 1946. "Just as school colors the war," noted Paul Fussell, "the war colors school."[75]

Military leaders credited ROTC, rudimentary though it sometimes was, with having played a critical role in the early days of mobilization following Pearl Harbor. More than 100,000 ROTC-trained men served as officers in the wartime army and navy. The power of nonprofessionalism remained strong; American soldiers in Europe derived great satisfaction from the fact that a "bunch of soda jerks and grocery clerks" were beating the best professional soldiers in Germany and Japan.[76] These men were, by most measures, qualitatively inferior to academy-trained officers, but they provided a reservoir of nonprofessional men with at least some military knowledge at a time when few Americans had any serious or sustained experience with the military. General George Marshall was particularly impressed: "Just what we would have done in the first phases of our mobilization without [ROTC graduates] I do not know. I do know that our plans would have had to be greatly curtailed and the cessation of hostilities on the European front would have been delayed accordingly."[77]

The propaganda value of Marshall's observation notwithstanding, the high regard that respected military men like Dwight Eisenhower, Chester Nimitz (himself a former NROTC instructor), and Marshall had for the wartime contributions of the ROTC program helped to legitimize its reemergence after the war. Moreover, many university presidents pointed with pride to the contributions of their alumni in the war effort. More than 100 members of the University of Colorado faculty in 1950 (including a future CU president) had served in the navy during the war.[78] Georgia Tech provided more naval officers than any school except the Naval Academy and provided more ordnance officers to the army than West Point.[79]

Furthermore, the universities' largely favorable experience with the military during the war inclined them toward participation in the years that immediately followed. Wartime training programs of all sorts "brought succor" in the form of higher enrollments to institutions of higher education that had been crippled by the Great Depression. Educators' fears that the end of the war would mean the return of lean times proved unfounded, in large measure because of the one million veterans who attended colleges and universities on the GI Bill.[80] To many academics, then, the military experience in World War II had meant a return of good times and a chance to contribute to a common cause. These experiences greatly aided the process of reestablishing ROTC.

The military, too, was satisfied with its World War II experience with the nation's colleges and universities and hoped to continue that association in the years to come. The 1948 Gray Committee recommended to the army that ROTC be renamed the Army Officer Training Corps and that it become the primary source of active-duty army officers. ROTC, in the opinion of the committee, was "the best available means of producing enough officers of the right type to lead America's Cold War Army. The need for a college-educated leader capable of understanding and employing increasingly sophisticated military technology, *the predilection for an officer corps reared in the citizen-soldier tradition* and the pressure to keep the costs of officer production as low as possible all played a part in creating this sentiment."[81] The Gray Committee's report assured not only that ROTC would remain a fixed institution on American campuses, but also that its roles and functions would become more central to the overall national defense structure than had been true before the war.

The creation of ROTC in 1916 and its full implementation after World War I marked the fruition of at least a century of informal military training on civilian college campuses. Although enthusiasm for such programs waxed and waned throughout the interwar years, enough support for the idea of civilian training programs existed to keep them operating through the isolationist era of the 1930s. Indeed, educators supported the idea of ROTC much more stridently than did the War and Navy Departments. To educators, these programs represented an opportunity to have a critical *civilian* impact on the operation and staffing of the professional military.

Thus from 1819 to 1949 military training on civilian college campuses came quite a long way: it became a regularized way to expose men to the rudiments of military instruction for the navy, the marines and the army; it became a recognized and respected institution in all regions of the country; and it evolved a semistandardized and semicentralized structure—a remarkable achievement in itself, considering the intensely diverse and decentralized structure of American higher education. These changes prepared ROTC to earn a national reputation among many military officers and civilian educators during World War II. That success, in turn, validated the re-creation and expansion of ROTC on civilian campuses in the years immediately following the war.

A Favored Position on Campus: The Military and Higher Education in the Cold War Era, 1950–1964

> Let it not be thought that objectives of communism and the Soviet Union are new, mysterious, exotic, and omniscient. Present Soviet actions are former Russian expansionism writ large—only a historic continuum of the expansionism of Peter the Great, Empress Catherine, and the ancient principalities of Kiev and Moscow from whence began the conquest of lands now idealized as "Mother Russia."
>
> —1953 Air Force ROTC textbook

Because they had been dismantled during World War II in favor of faster training programs, ROTC units had to be created anew on college campuses after the war. By 1950, as this process was completed, Americans faced a new global environment of Cold War in Europe, hot war in Asia, and atomic war in the American psyche.[1] The role of ROTC in producing large numbers of reserve and, eventually, active-duty officers became significantly more important than it had been before World War II. As ROTC units became more central to the American military system, they also became more of a factor in campus life. As Americans were adjusting to the new role of the military in American social, political, cultural, and economic life, Americans on college campuses were searching for ways to adjust to an increased role for military training programs. The belief that associations with the military during World War II had brought colleges much more good than ill greatly facilitated this adjustment.

The ROTC programs of the 1950s had two components: a basic course for freshmen and sophomores and an advanced course for juniors and seniors. The former carried with it no after-graduation military obligations, but participants obtained no benefits other than completion of the prerequisite for the advanced course and exemption from conscription. The 1916 National Defense Act, which created ROTC, required men seeking commissions to have enrolled in the program for all four of their undergraduate years (see Chapter 1). Therefore, student decisions about ROTC had to be made early on. The decision to enroll in the advanced course was more serious, since it entailed military service after graduation. Most men who entered the advanced program, which was mandatory only at military colleges, did so to further defer their draft obligations or, if the student desired military service, for the chance to serve with the prestige and higher income of an officer.

By 1955 the Reserve Officers' Training Corps program existed on 313 campuses in all 50 states, the District of Columbia, and Puerto Rico. Thirty-two schools, mostly large state universities, hosted air force, army, and navy programs; most schools hosted just one. Virtually all of the land-grant schools hosted ROTC units, but the ROTC program was not limited to public schools; many prestigious private schools, including all of the members of the Ivy League, Johns Hopkins, Stanford, and Georgetown, also had ROTC units.

The army, navy, and air force (and, through the navy, the marines), by virtue of a 1949 agreement, ran organizationally separate but quite similar programs, with the important exception of the navy's Holloway Plan, which provided scholarship support to selected NROTC students.[2] The army and air force had no scholarship authorization and no plans to pursue such authorization. Instead, they counted on congressional passage of universal military training (UMT) legislation or some other conscription policy to entice men into ROTC.

For the most part, ROTC units were popular and often eagerly sought by administrators, faculty, and students for many of the same reasons that they had been popular after World War I. Many academics argued against UMT on the grounds that "traditional higher education had more to offer toward [national security] than did military training."[3] ROTC allowed both to exist; students could participate in military training while pursuing their civilian education. Former Harvard University president Nathan Pusey recalled the consensus of his fellow educators in the 1950s: "ROTC provided an acceptable way of attracting college men with leadership potential into the military services . . . Furthermore, these units gave the students who joined an opportunity to discharge their military obligation without interrupting their education. It is not surprising, therefore, that they were sought often by many institutions, and where awarded, were welcomed by administrators and students alike."[4] Nevertheless, ROTC would have remained marginal to the development of active-duty officers had the United States not opted for a massive expansion of the military in the 1950s. This expansion involved both men and machines. Ultimately, the army mobilized 2,834,000 men to fight in Korea and to guard against the possibility that the Soviets would use the cover of America's preoccupation with Korea to strike at Western Europe.[5] Indeed, the events of the early Cold War convinced American military and political planners of the need for a much larger standing military than had been planned in the years immediately following the end of World War II. This new military would need men who could handle the ever more complex tasks of the military officer in the atomic age.

The services wanted high-quality men with diverse skills and abilities. The nation's colleges and universities, where a system for training officers, albeit mainly reserve officers, already existed, were the logical places for the military to find and train these men. The other two officer production methods were inadequate for this task. A sufficiently large expansion of the service academies would have been prohibitively expensive and consequently was never seriously considered. The World War II–era Officer Candidate Schools had been valuable for turning out large numbers of immediately employable candidates, but not always high-quality officers. The services in the 1950s sought not only swift training, but also officers with a diverse body of general military knowledge. ROTC offered access to university-trained men at virtually all of the best schools in America and therefore became the primary means of producing large numbers of active-duty officers in the years following the outbreak of hostilities in Korea.

From the universities' perspective, civilian participation in military training programs reinforced two traditional and generally agreed-upon principles that had also influenced ROTC in the prewar years. The first was that civilian participation would serve as a critical check on the growth of a professional military. This position was consistent with academic opposition to UMT on the grounds that the best way to prepare the citizen-soldier was first to ensure that he had a firm grounding in the demands and nature of his citizenship. Here, of course, the universities believed that they could play a great role.

Second, and perhaps more important, the universities took great pride in preparing young men for all walks of life. Why, they asked, should the military be an exception? As American interests became increasingly international in scope and as the military became a more important profession in America—in many respects, becoming like any other profession—why shouldn't the universities take an active role in the preparation of junior officers? The military fit in nicely with how Nathan Pusey understood the mission of universities in the 1950s:

> It was our national policy in the postwar years to endeavor to ensure peace through the creation of a world order built on cooperation in many fields of activity and on enlarged international understanding. The nation's colleges and universities had a role of fundamental importance to play in this, for only they could prepare the highly trained people, specialists and laymen . . . needed in the public and the private sector, in government and in business, for the implementation of the policy.[6]

Few administrators could find logical reasons to exclude the military profession from this policy. Instead they welcomed the chance to participate in the education of military officers in much the same way that they welcomed the chance to influence the development of doctors, engineers, and bankers.

ROTC thus represented a joint partnership between the military and higher education to train officers for the national defense needs of the postwar era. As such, its character would necessarily be dependent on changes in the nature of the two institutions themselves and changes in the nature of the relationship between academe and the military. Neither of these institutions, of course, existed in a vacuum; as national and international contexts changed, so did the quality and character of the academic-military relationship.

ROTC is a rather lackluster case of the increasing scale of military-academic relationships in postwar America when compared with the development of organized scientific research for the military; the latter involved more money, more faculty, and more university energy than the officer training programs. Despite differences of scale, however, national-level economic, political, social, and cultural changes affected organized research and ROTC in similar ways. In both cases, the military understood that each university was different and that some flexibility had to be introduced to account for institutional variance. Just as the Office of Strategic Research and Development and the Office of Naval Research were willing to operate under decentralization, so too did ROTC evolve with variation from school to school.[7] Such a pattern fit in nicely with the traditional authority structure of the military, especially the navy, where Vincent Davis has described a "commitment to decentralization."[8] As with captains on a ship at sea, NROTC unit heads had a great deal of latitude with which to command their units.

For all the similarities, however, the financial arrangements of ROTC were much less lucrative for the schools involved than were those of the organized military research system. While the universities profited immensely from organized research, ROTC was, if anything, a losing financial proposition for the university communities of the 1950s and early 1960s. All three services paid a twenty-seven-dollar monthly stipend to cadets in their junior and senior years, but as noted above, only the navy (the smallest program, existing on only fifty-two campuses) paid scholarship money to selected students. As had been true before the war, the services paid the salaries and benefits of the uniformed staff, but the universities were responsible for providing classroom and office facilities, maintenance of those facilities, and secretarial support. Additionally, some universities paid the full cost of new facilities to house ROTC classes and offices. In 1955 the University of Texas paid all of the $1 million needed to construct a new ROTC armory, for example.[9] Although academics found plenty of reasons to support the existence of ROTC, direct financial benefit was not one of them.[10]

A Quest for Harmony

Differences between the military and university culture, values, and mission manifested themselves often in the debates over the goals and character of ROTC. The military preferred an officer preparation program that emphasized *training,* teaching the practical knowledge a man needed to have to become a junior officer the day after his graduation from college. The obvious person to conduct such training was, of course, a uniformed officer. University administrators, while conceding that some training was necessary, came to argue for *education* as the model of officer preparation. By education they meant the teaching, by civilian faculty, of courses such as psychology, history, engineering, and other fields relevant to the military profession. The two institutions also disagreed on issues of university oversight and the exact place of ROTC on the campus.

Still, while acknowledging these differences, leaders in the military and higher education firmly agreed on the importance of ROTC to the nation and the campus. Both institutions considered ROTC sufficiently important to devote considerable resources to monitoring the progress of officer training and keeping an eye toward reform and improvement. For the military, support for ROTC was a function of several factors:

1. A belief that the military needed a place on campus if it was to compete successfully with industry for talented men.
2. A more subtle desire to maintain good relations with higher education—the locus of critical military research.
3. A belief (especially prevalent in the army) that ROTC instilled civic awareness and patriotism;
4. The great cost-effectiveness of ROTC, especially in comparison to the service academies.
5. A desire to please members of Congress, most of whom were firm supporters of an on-campus military instruction program.

University administrators and faculty had their own reasons to support, or at least tolerate, ROTC:

1. A firm belief, especially among the highest officers of universities (themselves often ardent supporters of the Cold War), that American higher education had an obligation to assist in the prosecution of the Cold War as a service to society.
2. A desire to keep the military happy in an era in which, at several large research universities, government contracts were worth many millions of dollars. Total Department of Defense (DOD) outlays to universities for basic research alone equaled $105.7 million in 1958, and they continued to climb into the late 1960s.[11]
3. A fear that any negative statement about the military could be construed as "un-American" and lead to marginalization or dismissal.
4. A belief that ROTC contributed to good order on the campus and good citizenship in the undergraduate population.
5. A belief that training officers via ROTC would "civilianize" the military by infusing it with ideas from the universities. Concurrently, ROTC would prevent the creation of a military caste composed of officers trained at the service academies.
6. A desire to please groups with influence over the university, such as alumni, trustees, and state legislators, most of whom were staunch supporters of ROTC.

These reasons were sufficiently compelling to overshadow many areas of concern and disagreement. ROTC was important enough to attract the personal attention of university presidents, who attended ROTC honor ceremonies and balls, wrote letters to incoming freshmen encouraging their participation in ROTC, and corresponded with the admirals and generals in charge of the military administration of ROTC.[12] The program enjoyed strong support from those in charge of its welfare and rarely had to deal with vocal or sustained opposition. When asked in 1954 to communicate the most serious problem university administrators had with ROTC, Russell Thackrey of the American Association of State Universities and Land-Grant Colleges (AASULGC) stated that it was the "lowering of morale among students" because the end of the Korean War (and the subsequent reduction in the need for officers) would delay their entry into the active-duty armed forces.[13]

The quest for harmony meant that areas of dissonance, especially during the height of the Cold War, were muted. The universities and the services worked out problems through an informal process of congenial reform and compromise that allowed each side to defend its position on the patriotic grounds of better preparing the American officer. Dissent rarely made it into the public discourse because of a shared understanding that the health of the overall program and public perception of military-academic unity was more important than disagreement over any single issue.

The Cold War Background: "The Supreme Contest of Our Times"

A 1960 Army ROTC pamphlet made a case for ROTC:

> The educational systems of the Iron Curtain countries train their men as soldiers of the state first, and then as scientists, technicians, even painters and poets, as part of their over-all plans for world domination. From the privileged sanctuary of our campus quadrangles, laboratories and study halls, dare we forget for whom the bell tolls? It tolls not for the murdered students of Prague, Riga, and Warsaw, but for those now bent to the task of the extinguishment of man's hopes. It tolls for those who "don't have the time," for those who cynically ask "what's in it for me?" It tolls for all who fail to realize the nature of this supreme contest of our times.

Publications like these argued for the importance of ROTC to national and international security. Against the backdrop of global struggle, this pamphlet and others challenged students and administrators alike to place a heavy emphasis on the importance of ROTC: "It is inconsistent to admit an obligation to country in principle and to deny it in practice on the grounds of interference with academic freedom or competing demands for the student's time. The Communist threat calls for realistic thinking in terms of survival, or there can be no freedom, academic or otherwise, only time for remorse."[14] Such tough talk was intended to remind those connected with ROTC of the critical need for unity and cooperation against the perceived monolithic Communist threat.

These publications reflected much more than military propaganda. The Cold War was a war of ideology; many Americans, civilian and military, believed that "the moral and democratic traditions" of America were under assault from without and within.[15] The only way to assure victory, many believed, was to teach American youth good civic virtue and moral values. The schools and the military were the obvious places to inculcate such values, and many believed that the latter was better positioned to do so. As Michigan State University president John Hannah said, "Teaching such fundamentals should be done at home and in school but it is not being done, and the services provide the 'last chance' for society to do the job . . . [Without such training] there is no assurance that our country will come out right in the end."[16] Beliefs such as these implied that the universities needed to give the military sufficient latitude to conduct training programs whose importance was central to national security and survival.

ROTC was particularly well suited to do the training that Hannah advocated, since it was both educational and military and it allowed military training to take place within a civilian environment. The civilian environment was a special concern of many Americans as the nation moved from the immediate postwar years (when most Americans looked forward to rapid, large-scale demobilization of the armed forces) to the early years of the Cold War (when a large standing army looked increasingly necessary). A 1950 presidential committee warned that to avoid military dominance of American society, it was critical "to preserve within the military as much of [the soldier's] civilian life as possible."[17] ROTC training, conducted as it was at civilian colleges and universities, fit the bill quite well.

The Cold War environment of the 1950s thus buttressed ROTC's position on campus by giving supporters a patriotic justification for their position and opponents an incentive to remain quiescent. The years before World War II had been marked by considerable controversy over the place of the military on such college campuses as Johns Hopkins, Princeton, Wisconsin, and California. No such controversy existed in the 1950s, when supporters could more easily defend their support for ROTC as being in the national interest than they could in the isolationist 1930s.

Furthermore, the military argued that modern weapons systems, such as long-range bombers and intercontinental ballistic missiles, necessitated increased attention to national preparedness. "We've got to be ready when the bell rings," said Air Force ROTC (AFROTC) commandant Brigadier General M. R. Deichelmann, "There will be no time to train pilots after the enemy strikes." Many university administrators agreed. Note the juxtapositions in Wheaton College registrar Enock Dyrness's 1954 address to a meeting of the Association of Higher Education: "[ROTC] is a recognized and respected part of the curriculum on each campus where it operates. The world situation makes it imperative that the United States maintain an adequate active military force backed by a strong body of reserves in all branches, adequately trained and prepared to meet any emergency which might arise. Because of modern weapons, the ROTC program has taken on new significance."[18] This environment of cooperation and agreement on the national security justifications for ROTC represented a significant departure from the environment of the 1930s.

As important as the changed national and international contexts were, McCarthyite fears inspired a loyalty oath at Berkeley and the investigation of more than one hundred professors by the House Committee on Un-American Activities. Thirty-one University of California faculty members lost their jobs in 1950 for refusing to sign the oath, and the University of Michigan fired two professors for alleged anti-American activities, despite the recommendations of a special faculty committee that they not be dismissed. Loyalty oaths were the result of a movement by "American Legionnaires, frightened parents, and many other narrowly patriotic citizen groups" to "censor textbooks and curricula in schools and colleges, and, where they did not already exist, to pass laws requiring loyalty oaths of all teachers." Nathan Pusey described this era as an "agitated and difficult time" in which accusations were leveled at teachers on all levels "as a special class" because of their influence on the young.[19]

As important as the forced signing of oaths and the actual purging of professors with views critical (or believed to be critical) of American military and foreign policy were "the incalculable effects of intimidation, which encouraged acceptance of the status quo and avoidance of politics."[20] Those faculty unconvinced by the merits of arguments in favor of ROTC therefore had reason to keep their objections to themselves. All faculty could make a visible demonstration of their patriotism by supporting ROTC, even if they had their own privately held convictions. The worst excesses of McCarthyism were over by 1954, but uncertainties over the possibility of its return and memories of the purges worked on people's minds and actions for years afterward. Moreover, issues of patriotism reemerged periodically; in 1958, for example, the National Defense Education Act required that all federal grant winners sign an oath of allegiance to the United States.

For administrators, the Cold War environment meant that decisions about ROTC had to be made on patriotic as well as curricular grounds. The comments of Harvard College dean John Monro are representative:

> An abstract case could be mounted—out of ignorance, to be sure—that military training has no place in the college and that such training should be moved out to summer cruises and camps, or post-graduate OCS [Officer Candidate School] . . . The powerful reason why the ROTC should stay in the colleges is that our national defense requires it . . . We may, indeed we must, argue about what subjects our military officers teach our students, about how much of our students' time they are to have, and how much credit we will finally allow for their training effort. But no responsible college administrator of my acquaintance argues that we should deprive the armed services of their most-favored recruiting position on our campuses.[21]

Similarly, most military and higher-education officials believed that college-educated men, privileged as they were by virtue of their education, had a responsibility to serve their nation through military service as an officer. In June 1951, the army, with the support of President Truman, took advantage of the crisis in Korea to assure passage, finally, of the Universal Military Training and Service Act. Several prominent Americans, including the president of Columbia University, Dwight Eisenhower, testified before Congress as early as 1948 to argue for universal military training for all physically fit males. As we have seen, many academics had reservations about UMT, but Truman's proposal received wide support in the end, despite loopholes that offered deferment from active-duty military service to more than two million men, including 333,000 in ROTC or the reserves.[22] Indeed, since it contained a proposal to allow local draft boards to grant students deferments, the Truman plan held out the potential to dramatically increase college enrollment.

While the act hardly lived up to its name by making military service universal, it reasserted the principle that every man owed his nation military service. It also encouraged men to join ROTC so that they might have more power over when and where they entered military service. For example, if one wanted to avoid conscription into the army (the navy and the air force relied exclusively on volunteers) one could sign up for Naval or Air Force ROTC, thus assuring that if military service was likely or desirable, it would at least be on one's own terms. Enlisting could also help a man get the kind of military training or overseas assignment he desired. The Universal Military Training and Service Act therefore served to boost ROTC enrollments by providing cadets immediate deferments and more pleasant military service in the officer corps.

Service as an officer may not have been a young man's first career choice, but national and international contexts forced him to think seriously about it. The 1950s were a time of Cold War, but they were also, as Vincent Davis, Elaine Tyler May, and others have noted, an extended period of normalcy. Thus the Cold War held a peculiar place within the traditional American pattern of pacifism in peace and bellicosity in war. While the perception of a Soviet threat drove some men into ROTC so that they might be prepared should war arise, for many others the lure of good jobs in a growing economy loomed large. For these men, military life seemed "uncongenial." Though he may have been "suspicious of . . . professional military men," conscription nonetheless forced the typical college student to rethink his relationship to the military. [23]

The draft held an important place in the minds of young American men at a time when the logic of universal military participation was at its height; the air force directed internal studies in the early 1950s that concluded, to its great dismay, that UMT, not the chance to fly, was the primary reason men signed up for AFROTC.[24] The conscription of celebrities like Elvis Presley and Willie Mays made universality visible.[25] If the lives of these public icons could be disrupted, there was little reason for a college student to hope to be able automatically to avoid service. "They'll get us anyway," said one Georgia Tech student in 1951. "I'd rather be in the Air Force than the infantry."[26] The power that selective service had over college men is evident in the words of one student-poet:

> Today in college
> To gain more knowledge
> More and more I strive.
> A student deferment

Is my preferment
'Til I reach thirty-five.
But Selective Service
Has me nervous
They grant but one degree.
Despite my plea
For a Ph.D.
They offer me P.F.C.[27]

In this vein, the army executive staff argued that "it would be a waste of [the college-educated man's] knowledge and leadership potential to serve in an enlisted capacity even though that enlisted service might be in the field of his academic major."[28] In other words, it was more important for educated men to be officers and leaders than to be in a position suited to their technical talents, in part because having educated men in the officer corps demonstrated that the "best" sectors of American society were doing their part. After all, as the army argued, "It cannot be repeated too often that Man, Communist or Free, is the ultimate weapon. It behooves us to make certain that he is given the best leaders possible."[29]

The military's Cold War policy of insisting on the accession of college graduates as junior officers is consistent with the shifts described by sociologist Morris Janowitz in *The Professional Soldier.* Janowitz argued that the growing complexity of military technology and the ever-expanding links between the military and the civilian worlds necessitated by technological change greatly accelerated the military's movement away from arbitrary discipline and toward group consensus. Because of this growing technological and logistical complexity, fewer men were serving in the combat arms (the military's "tooth") and more were serving in highly specialized support roles (the "tail"). Thus the junior officer ceased out of necessity to be "the raspy-voiced cavalry officer" and became more like "the junior executive" found in civilian industries. The latter role called for more "competence and technical ability" to manage the specialized information of the new military "without resort to arbitrary and ultimate sanctions."[30]

In other words, the military now needed to recruit large numbers of experts in such diverse fields as public relations, engineering, and financial administration, in both the enlisted and officer ranks. Such men were no longer the typical laborer or foot soldier "assumed to be ignorant." They needed, in the words of a 1961 University of Washington committee, "academic skills not even dreamed of by their predecessors."[31] Having college-educated men in the officer corps, it was assumed, would create a corps of leaders familiar with a diverse body of knowledge and technical skills.

"Leadership" to the military planners of the 1950s meant something more akin to management based on psychology and group dynamics than what Janowitz called the hero model of the past. With this shift in leadership definitions came a concurrent shift away from authoritarianism as a means of structuring the military; instead, military leaders were expected to invoke a sense of "solidarity" among the men they led. Successful manager-officers therefore needed to be more sophisticated than the old "hero" types. The universities were the obvious training ground for the sort of well-rounded, educated men the military believed it needed to manage the increasingly complex and technical men and machines of the Cold War military.

The focus on education had relatively little to do with soldiering, flying, or sailing; many fine military officers lacked traditional degrees. Rather, education would help the military attain legitimacy and prestige by countering "the image of the military as something apart from and alien to civilian society."[32] In the words of Vance Mitchell:

> While academic education offered no guarantee of either intelligence or competence, it, along with experience, provided the foundation for the future growth of the individual. Experience and education constituted personal potential that, with maturation and the proper stimulation, could translate into achievement. High academic achievement also indicated individual ambition, a will to overcome obstacles, a capacity to solve problems, a capacity to deal with adversity, and the ability to get along with people. Further, college-educated officers would likely have better perspectives on and insights into the complex issues of civil-military relations, leadership, management, and America's role in the post-war world.[33]

The military was not alone in its drive to increase its legitimacy through formal education. In 1951 fewer than half of America's lawyers had college degrees.[34]

The Cold War also changed the focus of ROTC production from the reserves to active-duty forces. Prior to the Korean War, the *R* in ROTC correctly denoted its central function as producing officers for the reserves. Very few "distinguished graduates" became eligible for regular commissions in the immediate postwar years; the majority of officers produced through ROTC before 1952 entered the reserve component of their commissioning service. With the national defense buildup that accompanied the outbreak of hostilities in Korea, however, ROTC began increasingly to provide and retain officers for the active-duty forces. The American military needed more officers on active duty; one solution to this problem was simply to assign ROTC graduates directly to active duty instead of to the reserves.

In this vein, in November 1952 the assistant secretary of defense (manpower and personnel) directed that "the Reserve Officers' Training Corps program will be based upon the needs of the active-duty Armed Forces and upon a policy that all graduates will be called to active duty for a minimum of twenty-four months."[35] The percentage of AFROTC graduates assigned to active duty rose from 34 percent in 1951 to 79 percent in 1953 and peaked at 91 percent the following year. The policy of assigning ROTC cadets to active duty survived the Korean War intact; throughout the 1950s the services assigned 80 percent or more of their ROTC graduating classes to active duty, denoting the central place ROTC had assumed in the military's plans for active duty officers.[36]

The place of ROTC became even more central as academy graduates began to leave the services in increasing numbers. In 1958 *Look* magazine described what it called a "military manpower scandal" wherein unusually high numbers of academy graduates were completing their required tours of duty and then leaving. These men were resigning in larger numbers due to the strong job prospects available to them in private industry and the stress that military life placed on their families. As a result, *Look* noted, ROTC officers were becoming even more critical to staffing the American officer corps.[37]

This shift from reserve to active duty production meant fundamental changes. Previously, men could leave ROTC secure in the knowledge that, since they were entering the reserves, they could concurrently begin their civilian career. Now men completing their ROTC courses faced the real prospect of immediate active-duty service and time away from their chosen profession. In the 1920s and 1930s, ROTC had allowed a man to train for military service as a complement to his mostly civilian career. After Korea, ROTC represented a conflict between one's civilian pursuits and one's military obligations.

Sources of Tension

Despite a consensus on the importance of ROTC to the nation, fundamental philosophical differences between the military and university communities created disagreements. Despite occasional tensions, the quest for harmony was never abandoned; disagreements never produced a desire to remove ROTC from the campus or even to introduce significant structural reform. Nevertheless, four issues were argued nationwide: the place of ROTC on the campus; the appropriate level of communication between the services and the host schools; the importance of ROTC to national and campus life; and the compulsory nature of ROTC training at many colleges and universities.

The Place of ROTC on the Campus

Unlike instructors in most civilian college programs, ROTC faculty did not possess Ph.D.s, seek tenure, nominate candidates for degrees, or serve on university-wide committees. ROTC instructors rarely remained at a single school for longer than a three-year tour of duty.[38] Nevertheless, ROTC programs were set up as full academic departments to make military instruction more respectable in the eyes of students and to encourage civilian faculty to treat the uniformed officers as peers rather than interlopers. Furthermore, ROTC officers owed their first allegiance to an outside agency that paid their salary and with whom they had taken an oath of service. All of these characteristics distinguished ROTC from other academic departments, yet the universities rarely challenged the elevated stature of ROTC during the height of the Cold War.

As McCarthyism faded in the late 1950s, academics became more assertive in addressing these distinctions. The anomaly of departmental status was one concern, because it pointed out the need to clearly define the relationship between the services and the universities. Russell Thackrey, executive secretary of the AALGCSU, like virtually all administrators of this period, firmly believed that the universities, especially the public universities his organization represented, had an unwavering responsibility to the nation to cooperate with the services in producing officers. He was dismayed, however, by what he saw as an increasingly separate military program with very few intellectual links to the remainder of the university community. In writing to University of Illinois president David Henry, he said, "I doubt if we can any longer say with conviction, as we once could say, that the ROTC is wholly an integral part of the academic program of the institution, run on the basis of full cooperation and joint participation by the institution and the Armed Services. There are an increasing number—not large as yet but growing—of requirements that are non-academic and related wholly to the military, not the university." Among the strictly military issues of concern to

Thackrey was the military's policy of running security checks on advanced ROTC cadets, a policy created within the context of McCarthyite Cold War anxieties and consistent with drives at many schools, including many ROTC hosts, to require loyalty oaths from faculty.[39]

David Henry, for his part, agreed with both of Thackrey's propositions: that the universities, especially the land-grant schools required by the Morrill Act to offer military instruction, had a responsibility to assist in the national defense, and that universities "should classify the ROTC program, not as an academic program completely integrated with the university [read: department], but as a cooperative program for which we have limited responsibility."[40] These men envisioned a place for ROTC units analogous to that occupied by postwar research institutes like the University of Michigan's Institute for Social Research and MIT's Lincoln Labs. Such facilities received support exclusively from outside funds, had faculty who did not teach classes in the general university, "had extra academic origins and were products to some extent of federal interest." Like ROTC, these institutes were not frontally academic in nature and therefore "presented new problems to university administrators."[41]

A move to institute status for ROTC would separate it from the larger educational mission of the university and amount to a declaration that ROTC was not an educational program. As Thackrey and Henry must have known they would, the services viewed the proposal as a denigration of ROTC and rejected the idea. During this period, no university administrator tried to remove, or even challenge, ROTC's status as a department, but the notion that the universities should formally acknowledge the differing missions of ROTC and the academic departments had been advanced and would return.

Communication between Service and School

The universities and the services also debated the appropriate level of communication between service and university. The services designed and managed the training of their massive World War II and Korean War OCS programs and the curricula of the three service academies without interference from civilian educators. They assumed that they could operate ROTC programs in much the same manner. Indeed, for much of the 1950s administrators seemed willing to acquiesce to allowing the services to train officers as they saw fit. By the end of the decade, however, the universities were asserting their desire to have a voice in the running of ROTC.

University presidents like Michigan State's John Hannah were especially disturbed that the services were imposing changes without consulting the schools affected. In 1957, as a representative of the AALGCSU, whose schools then accounted for 55 percent of all ROTC graduates, he told an Armed Forces Policy Board how "seriously concerned" he and his colleagues were about the worsening relationship between the services and higher education.[42] Harvard's John Monro observed three years later, "I know of no program of comparable size and importance where regular communication could be so valuable, and is in fact so poor."[43] Serious problem areas were beginning to develop, and with relatively few open channels of communication, those problems did not receive the attention they deserved.

The comments of Thackrey, Henry, and Hannah reveal that some educators, while not questioning the value of ROTC, nevertheless desired to see military control of the program somewhat diminished. They wanted more input on key decisions and a voice in directing a program that was, they argued, populated by students for whom they had ultimate responsibility. They were willing to acknowledge and accept "limited" responsibility, not to yield all responsibility.

The Importance of ROTC to Campus and National Life

During the years of the Cold War, university presidents and the service ROTC staffs developed different understandings of the importance of ROTC. The presidents, conditioned by their early compromises with the military and their own Cold War ideology, saw ROTC as crucial to national security and, closer to home, as a vital instrument for maintaining civic virtue and order on campus. The University of Texas, for example, permitted students to count one semester of ROTC training as a substitute for the university's American government requirement, on the assumption that ROTC served as a kind of laboratory in American civics.[44]

The services, however, saw ROTC as an extension of the military, subject to fundamental change without consultation of the hosts if national and international events necessitated. An incident from the early 1960s demonstrates this difference in definition. The army, faced with chronic ROTC budget shortfalls, decided to save money by asking all host units to reduce AROTC enrollments to 85 percent of their previous year's freshman enrollments. To Major General Frederick Warren, the highest ranking army officer with direct oversight of ROTC, the plan seemed sensible enough, but university presidents and chancellors sent a barrage of sharp and angry letters to the army in protest both of the substance and the execution of the order. This incident is important because of how it exposed the poor channels of communication between those responsible for ROTC and for its demonstration of the high level of support ROTC enjoyed among university presidents.

Warren had erroneously assumed that Army ROTC units were detachments of the larger army and could therefore be ordered to comply with changes in army policy. In fact, he had created a policy that stood in direct conflict with university policies and, in some cases, state laws that university administrators saw as superseding any directives from the army. Furthermore, the universities interpreted his order as weakening ROTC and thus also the national defense. Campus officials saw themselves as defending the integrity of national security against the erosion proposed, ironically enough, by the United States Army.

Those institutions that required men to take ROTC to qualify for graduation opposed the army's order because, in the words of University of Kentucky president Frank Dickey, "By imposing a ceiling on the number of freshmen who can enroll in the Army ROTC you are, in effect, abrogating this college requirement."[45] Furthermore, such states as Illinois, Kansas, Maine, and West Virginia had laws requiring male underclassmen at land-grant colleges to take ROTC. The Morrill Act of 1862 that created the land-grant colleges required them to offer military instruction, and the state legislatures had interpreted the act as requiring all male students to take ROTC. In his letter to Warren, West Virginia University president Paul Miller told him flatly, "We will not be in a position to effect the modifications delineated in your letter" because they would violate the laws of West Virginia.[46]

To exempt men from military service in order to save money seemed foolish to many administrators. The Right Reverend Wilfrid Nash, president of Gannon College in Erie, Pennsylvania, wrote to Warren: "The future of the United States depends, in great part, on the caliber of men who select the Army as their career. As soon as Military Science becomes limited I fear that many qualified boys will not have the opportunity to learn from experience the value of the Army . . . I fear that the cut-back will greatly lower the standards of the ROTC in the years ahead."[47] R. H. Woods, president of Murray State College in Kentucky also felt that Warren was proposing a diminution of national defense. "I feel that Military Science is important in college life and important to our national well-being and the program needs to be stable," he wrote. "If this [reduction] is done, the result may be very harmful to the future of the ROTC program."[48]

In the midst of this debate, a Duquesne University student wrote an editorial in the student newspaper questioning the "wisdom, not the right" of the university to impose compulsory ROTC.[49] Duquesne University president Henry McAnulty responded with a personal letter to the author: "This administration feels that the required basic ROTC course for all non-veteran, male students is, at this time, to the best interests of the nation and Duquesne University . . . Perhaps you might be happier at another school more in conformity with your personal philosophy of education and life."[50] University officials had their own views of the contributions ROTC made to national defense, the development of civic responsibility, and the quality of campus life. These views were not necessarily in conflict with those of the military, but neither did they overlap perfectly. Their differences would manifest themselves again in the debate over the value of compulsory ROTC in the nation's universities (see below).

Warren's attempt to order the universities into compliance with a policy decision made without their consultation failed. Within two weeks of the first responses to Warren's letter, Secretary of Defense Robert McNamara approved additional funding so that 106,000 freshmen could be enrolled, as opposed to the 84,500 Warren had originally envisioned.[51] Warren again wrote to the presidents, to tell them that his order was rescinded "because of great concern evidenced by institutions in this matter."[52] University administrators felt strongly that ROTC was critical to the security of the nation and the quality of campus life, and they were willing to fight a two-star general to prove it.

This debate reveals the differing goals and directions that the military and officers in higher education had for ROTC. For the former, ROTC represented a cheap, reliable method for meeting annual officer production requirements. For the latter, ROTC represented a training program for both military and civilian pursuits. Most academic administrators believed that ROTC taught civic responsibility, discipline, and morality. For all these reasons, then, they hoped for continuance of what they understood as an implied agreement by the military to pay for mandatory ROTC. They thus angrily read Warren's order as being "in direct violation of a pledge [by the DOD] to maintain required ROTC at institutions desiring it."[53] In fact, the military was trying to move away from required ROTC, setting up another debate over the meaning and rationale for supporting officer education programs on civilian campuses.

Compulsory ROTC: A Military Necessity?

The furor caused by Warren's letter occurred in the midst of a debate over the national security justifications of compulsory ROTC. University administrators, as we have seen, objected to Warren's order on the grounds that it abrogated university and state requirements that all male freshmen and sophomores take ROTC and that it had the potential to undermine the national security contributions of on-campus military instruction. Even as they made the argument, however, virtually all compulsory programs were reconsidering the issue of compulsory ROTC in light of discussions with DOD and service officials that indicated, paradoxically, that those in the defense establishment saw no military reason for compulsory ROTC and, indeed, many were strongly opposed to it. Ironically, the university administrators, not the military, were the champions of compulsory ROTC.

ROTC was compulsory throughout the 1950s on more than half of the campuses hosting the program and at more than two in three land-grant colleges. As noted earlier, some of these schools had experienced controversy over the issue of compulsory military training in the 1920s and 1930s, in debates rooted in post–World War I pacifism and isolationism, but most schools had held to their compulsory programs. By the mid-1950s, few people were arguing for the abolition of compulsory ROTC on isolationist grounds; instead, the dominant arguments held that compulsory ROTC was too costly and too burdensome on the schedule of the contemporary college undergraduate. As college curricula became more demanding and student time more precious, the issue of compulsory ROTC became visible on enough campuses to compel the National Association of State Universities and Land Grant Colleges to address it.[54]

In 1957 Troy Middleton, president of Louisiana State University and chairman of the NASULGC Committee on National Defense, wrote to Secretary of Defense Charles Wilson to get clarification on the legal basis for compulsory basic ROTC programs. Most administrators were firm supporters of compulsory ROTC and expected the DOD to return an unequivocal statement of support that they could use as ammunition against the minority among them pushing for reform. They felt surprised and betrayed by the responses from the DOD. The army reported that it could find no federal authority requiring ROTC and no army policy in the history of the program to justify support of compulsory military education.[55] The secretary of the army's general counsel found that "the Army Staff has stated that ever since the establishment of ROTC in 1916, the Department of the Army has consistently held that the question of whether basic ROTC shall be compulsory or elective is purely a matter of individual institutional prerogative."[56]

If no law or policy could be found that required or compelled compulsory ROTC, the institutions next asked if the services believed that the mandatory military education of male underclassmen contributed to the defense of the nation. The air force and navy returned a quick "no." The navy, which offered the most scholarship aid to its ROTC students and therefore ran the most expensive ROTC program per capita, used the scholarship application process as a primary recruitment and selection base; therefore it did not need to select advanced midshipmen from a large population of basic midshipmen. The heart of the air force's program, flight training, was simply too expensive for the air force to expend resources on instruction and uniforms for thousands of students taking ROTC only because they were forced to do so.[57] An internal air force study conducted in 1959 showed that AFROTC taught twenty cadets for every officer produced.[58] Senior air force officials argued that dropping required basic ROTC would have no appreciable impact on advanced enrollment and, therefore, on officer production, because the cadets who were "lost" to the program were unmotivated to begin with.[59] In other words, the air force saw no value in paying the costs to educate, clothe, equip, and train men who did not want to become officers. As a professor of aerospace studies at Rutgers University noted, "There is no place in the cockpit for a man who is not a volunteer."[60]

The army, however, always concerned with numbers, argued that it needed the compulsory basic course to attract enough students to sign up for the advanced course.[61] The army also contended, in accord with the arguments of educators, that ROTC training should be compulsory because of what it did for those who did not seek a commission:

A vital secondary mission of the Army ROTC program is to impart valuable citizenship training, develop leadership potential, stimulate and motivate the student for future service in behalf of the nation, his community, and his fellow man. This training is upheld by the Army as valuable beyond calculation in the development of healthy, public spirited citizens, aware of their responsibilities of American citizenship, willing through self-sacrifice to assume the responsibilities of American citizenship in whatever professional pursuit the college student may elect to pursue.[62]

The army wanted its ROTC policy to be consistent with its support of the draft, partly on the basis of its ability to promote "moral welfare" and "character guidance."[63]

Officials in all services agreed, however, that compulsory ROTC had several drawbacks: it was expensive, unpopular with most students, and inefficient. Several student newspapers had opposed mandatory ROTC for years; the *Targum* at Rutgers had been arguing for a voluntary ROTC program since 1949. Like most campus newspapers, the *Targum* did not oppose mandatory ROTC on philosophical or moral grounds, but because it "imposed an unnecessary academic burden on freshmen."[64] It also acted to create a group of "cynical upperclassmen who can effectively recite drill field traumas and classroom incidents."[65]

For all of these reasons, the air force favored making all units elective. The official Air Force ROTC history for 1964 reads:

> Corollary to changing the public image of AFROTC, we pressed for elimination of mandatory attendance in basic ROTC . . . Such a requirement, while imposed by the institution, was generally believed by the student to be a service imposed requirement and for those not initially motivated for AFROTC, the requirement simply generated discontent that spread throughout the class and school, further impairing the desired image of AFROTC and the desirability of a career as an Air Force officer.[66]

The DOD emphatically agreed: "Compulsory basic ROTC is not needed to meet quality standards nor is it needed to produce the number of officers required. Surveys of the academic standings of ROTC officers in the Service Schools following commissioning do not furnish conclusive evidence as to whether elective or compulsory programs produce the higher quality officers."[67]

These responses frustrated university administrators who believed in the value of compulsory military education. John Hannah, president of Michigan State, complained, "We are now seriously concerned because of the repeated and continuing evidence that the Armed Services and the Defense Department no longer regard the ROTC programs as worthy of vigorous support by them."[68] Russell Thackrey, the NASULGC's executive secretary, wrote, "As to required ROTC: I think it fair to say that most of our Presidents feel it is a lost cause . . . With few exceptions, [university administrators] still believe that the elimination of required ROTC would be a costly mistake from the standpoint of the Department of Defense, but that it is not up to them to fight this battle."[69] Given the DOD's inability to identify a military need for compulsory basic ROTC, the administrators began to rethink fundamental assumptions. Thackrey told a reporter from the *New York Times* that the land-grant schools were now willing to consider a change. "College Trustees, faced with meeting rapidly rising enrollments and increasing costs, naturally are inclined to re-examine their responsibility for requiring a program which the Department of Defense itself does not consider of real importance to national security."[70] In 1960 the NASULGC decided on a policy of indifference toward whether its members required basic ROTC for graduation. The former policy of strong preference for compulsory basic ROTC "was chiefly predicated on the theory that the Department of Defense considered the requirement of Basic ROTC as a distinct contribution to the national defense program." Such a theory no longer being defensible, a policy of indifference now seemed appropriate.[71] The army held to an official policy of support for compulsory basic ROTC, but Warren's 1962 debacle over the 85 percent enrollment order undermined that policy's legitimacy by demonstrating that the army believed that it could operate optimally with significantly less than 100 percent enrollment.

Without a strong statement of support from the DOD and with civilian curricula becoming more demanding, many universities abandoned compulsory basic ROTC. Even at the University of Illinois, where the program had been compulsory since the school's opening in 1868 and had produced more senior army officers than any school except West Point, a 1960 poll of University of Illinois students found 71 percent against continuing the program on a compulsory basis. Later that year a faculty committee recommended changing to voluntary ROTC because of the absence of a national need for the required program.[72] In 1961 Illinois president David Henry informed the DOD that he expected university enrollment in the coming years to increase by 50 percent and that he could not ask the state to pay for facilities for the military training of all of the males if the DOD could not defend that training as necessary for national defense.[73]

Most administrators were displeased with the change. University of Arizona president Richard Harvill told Major General Warren that he believed compulsory basic ROTC to be vital to creating a large pool of men from which the services could choose their officers, but that "it is very clear that the efforts of those of us who have believed strongly in compulsory basic ROTC and have opposed relaxation of this requirement have been fighting a losing battle and did not have the support of top-level military officials in this country."[74] Those military officials were more interested in keeping ROTC inexpensive than in using it as a citizenship-training program.

The Illinois state legislature removed the law requiring basic ROTC for graduation from the University of Illinois in time for it to open the 1963–64 academic year with a voluntary ROTC program for the first time.[75] Other schools converting to voluntary programs in this era included Ohio State, Washington, Michigan State, Kansas State, Missouri, Connecticut, Rutgers, Colorado State, Texas A & M, Nebraska, Iowa, Iowa State, Oregon, Florida State, Maine, and Idaho. Between 1961 and 1965, sixty Army ROTC units and fifty-nine Air Force ROTC units switched from compulsory to voluntary. Thirty-nine of the army units and thirty-two of the air force units were at land-grant schools or their satellites.[76] Even as early as 1963 the air force had benefited from the switch to voluntary training by saving fifty-seven officer positions and $572,375 in uniform costs.[77] For the first time since its creation in 1916, compulsory basic ROTC had become the exception, not the rule.

Students across the nation rejoiced. The Rutgers student newspaper ran an extra edition to celebrate "a day that should become memorable in the history of Rutgers."[78] As expected, ROTC enrollments quickly fell at many schools (though, ironically, not at Rutgers). Enrollment in the basic AROTC program at the University of Illinois fell from 2,195 in the final mandatory year, 1963, to just 350 in the first voluntary year, 1964—a drop of 84 percent. Advanced enrollments there fell as well, though not as sharply, from 243 to 206.[79] Of greater concern to the services, predictions that the production of commissioned officers would not suffer proved to be inaccurate (see Chapter 3). Certainly much of this drop was to be expected, and some of it was welcomed in the interests of economy, but the shock of the drop and concern over where it might bottom out led to further changes to make the program "salable," to attract men freely into the program.

The ROTC of the 1950s was not the same ROTC that had existed in the 1930s. ROTC changed to meet the needs of the Cold War–era American military. It took on renewed importance because it produced active-duty officers instead of the reserve officers it had produced before the Korean War. The Cold War provided a national context of urgency—and for many, fear—that permitted the military to take almost sole control of the program until the very end of the 1950s. University administrators shared the national sense of urgency and acceded to military control, in large part because they believed it to be the best way to prepare the American officer for the tasks he would face. Tensions, however, existed over the value of ROTC and the exact character that it should assume. Throughout this period, educators and officers agreed on the value of ROTC but disagreed significantly on how it should look, act, and operate.

CHAPTER 3

The Origins of Postwar Dissatisfaction

> It is important that ROTC units should be more adequately inte-
> grated into the life of the university than they are at present. Certain
> aspects of the curricula, the preparation of teachers, appointments,
> and promotions are items on which we do not at the present time
> have common practices.
>
> —Dean of Arts and Sciences W. F. Dyde, University of Colorado, 1956

The Cold War forced the ROTC program into the new and uncharted territory of preparing large numbers of active-duty officers for an increasingly
complex and diffuse military. The very definition of ROTC was in flux, as
was the relationship of the military to American society. In many realms, including education, the military's influence far exceeded what it had been in
the years immediately before World War II. The re-formation and re-creation of ROTC on campus, then, led to a ten- to fifteen-year period of debate
about what kind of program ROTC ought to be to prepare junior officers for
the Cold War world. These questions had a direct impact on the relationship
between universities and the military and, of course, on the daily life of the
officer candidates themselves.

Because the services assumed that "in an age of atomic weapons, the next
attack would be fast, a surprise, and would strike the homeland," the life of
the ROTC cadet in the 1950s and early 1960s revolved around training in
strictly military subjects designed to prepare him to be immediately useful
to the armed services.[1] The services were primarily concerned with using
ROTC to produce men who could step directly from their college graduation
into a junior officer position. That responsibility notwithstanding, the Cold
War represented an era of what Samuel Huntington has called "fusion" between civilian and military expertise that demanded that "military leaders

incorporate political, economic, and social factors into their thinking."[2] The Cold War thus represented a tension between the need for immediate availability (which implied a narrow training focus for officer candidates) and fusion (which implied a broader, more general education).

At the same time, American higher education was beginning to adopt a much more international focus. Universities developed several new courses and concentrations in area studies, humanities, and social sciences that were designed to better inform American undergraduates about the world to which the United States now found itself inexorably tied. Ironically, the tight professional curriculum of ROTC programs meant that military training programs stood apart from these changes. Academic thinking and fusionist ideals were thus moving in the same direction, toward a more well-rounded collegiate education for ROTC candidates. As a result, by the end of the 1950s many academics came to argue for an increased presence of civilian courses in the ROTC curriculum in order to include cadets in the new areas of instruction.

Furthermore, the ROTC curriculum became a point of contention with academics who disliked the increasing presence of vocationally based courses in American universities. ROTC, they argued, was not only vocational but also exclusively geared to producing workers for a single employer. To defenders of a more classic liberal arts model of higher education, ROTC represented one manifestation of a growing and disturbing trend. Notably, the strongest calls for reform came from academics in liberal arts colleges, while those in professional programs, such as engineering schools, were more satisfied with the status quo.

While academics were willing to cede to the military some latitude, in acknowledgment of the severity of the military and political crisis of the Cold War, they were not willing to be silent partners. In keeping with their traditional desire to be active participants in the process of educating military officers, they lobbied the military to include courses from civilian offerings that were relevant, they argued, to the military profession. Throughout the Cold War, Moderate Whig beliefs remained powerful, resulting in a push for a "civilianization" of the ROTC curriculum and closer links between the professional military curriculum and the regular civilian curriculum.

ROTC and the Campus: The Wright Stuff

In 1950 the army introduced an illustrative comic book–style recruitment ad that followed the college career of a character named Ted Wright, a freshman at "State" who lacked "what it takes to step up and introduce himself."[3] Ted, on the recommendation of his faculty advisor (an ROTC grad himself), joins ROTC, and we follow him through his classes and collegiate adventures. Ted's activities are limited to strictly military events, like parades and planning the military ball. The advantages of ROTC are clearly spelled out: "ROTC men looked mighty sharp in the officer type uniform that's issued to them! Free of charge, too!"; "This training, with it's [sic] emphasis on teamwork and coordination was a help in football and other sports"; "Squeezing the trigger on the rifle range trains the eye and steadies the nerves"; and ROTC provides "self-confidence and leadership."

"Ted found that ROTC paid off in other ways, too," when a coed asked, "Ted, you're getting so many decorations, are you a General or something?"[4] Throughout the ad, there is an unmistakable message that ROTC cadets had access to the campus's most respected women, who existed as trophies for the successful cadets. In recalling his experiences as a cadet, Ted's faculty advisor remembers a woman telling him, "You remind me of the song 'There is something about a soldier.'" Ted finds the same rewards. At the annual military ball, his date says, "I wouldn't have missed this for anything." "Yes you would if you weren't going steady with an ROTC man," he replies. A 1960 booklet, *You and the Army ROTC,* told prospective students that "at most colleges and universities, the Annual Military Ball is one of the outstanding campus social events of the year—one the girl you're dating won't want to miss."[5] ROTC thus took on a peculiarly masculine air, deriving a share of the rationale for its existence from its presumed ability to make men out of boys.

The military had long played a role in "making men" in American society, including via the army's management of the Civilian Conservation Corps in the 1930s. But ROTC did not assume a large role in carrying out the military's new policy of racial integration. In a telling example of the power of localism in ROTC management, the program focused almost exclusively on fostering white manhood, despite its traditional presence on some historically black campuses. Although de jure integration of the armed forces occurred in 1948 and de facto integration began during the Korean War, ROTC still operated in keeping with the campus's segregated local environment.[6] Formal desegregation of the armed services brought little change to ROTC units, especially in the South. Because ROTC existed as a partnership between the military and higher education, it had elements of both institutions. While the military was quite clearly still dominated by whites, it had received a formal mandate to become more inclusive. Higher education, especially in the South, had no such mandate.

Academia, like the military, could be said to have some generally unified interests, but neither institution could be said to be monolithic. The interests of northern and southern universities were sometimes at odds, especially on the touchy issue of integration. In 1961, the Presidential Civil Rights Commission, headed by Michigan State University president John Hannah, called upon President John Kennedy to complete the integration of the national defense establishment by ending the enduring segregation of National Guard and ROTC units in place in "most Southern states."[7] The problem of segregation was a serious one for many educators, including Hannah. The Air Force ROTC Advisory Panel of 1963 noted that sixteen AFROTC units, including such large units as those at Auburn, Louisiana State, Louisiana Tech, Mississippi State, Baylor, and Southern Methodist, practiced segregation.[8]

Acknowledging the existence of segregation did not necessarily imply swift action, however. The air force noted that those segregated schools produced 297 officers in 1962, about one in eleven of that year's AFROTC graduates. The air force argued that it could ill afford to lose these graduates, nor did it wish "to change institutional policy that is based on state or local laws or is fixed by institutional governing bodies."[9] Several key members of Congress, most significantly House Democrat F. Edward Hébert of Louisiana, opposed the integration of ROTC. As a result, the desegregation of these units was not a high priority for either civilian or military officials until American society and law were transformed by passage of the Civil Rights Act of 1964. Substantial integration of ROTC did not begin until the 1970s (see Chapter 5).

ROTC was most popular among white male students, and it carried some distinct advantages, such as visibly demonstrating one's patriotism. A 1950 survey of 1,503 students from twenty-six schools across the nation showed that even among the half of the survey population not enrolled in ROTC, more than 90 percent believed that ROTC should be offered, though only one in three thought that training should be compulsory. Three in four of the students who were enrolled in basic ROTC courses reported that they planned to continue on to advanced ROTC, although a somewhat smaller proportion actually did so.[10] The ROTC students surveyed noted that the program conveyed prestige and the possibility for career advancement.[11] The popularity of ROTC also derived from a shared sense among college students that ROTC was "a worthy and valuable institution, vitally necessary to the defense of our country."[12]

Students joined ROTC for various reasons, but in the Cold War era many joined because the military had become a highly respected American institution and an attractive (if, for most, temporary) employer, particularly when compared to the military job environment in the years before World War II. Mark Grandstaff argues that between 1945 and 1955 the military conducted a successful public relations campaign to convince middle-class Americans that a "modern military career was similar to other middle-class careers" and that it "offered youth a respected occupation that placed self-sacrifice above profit and was rewarded with educational and promotion opportunities, good pay, fringe benefits, and retirement pensions."[13] Whether due to this public relations campaign or not, the military enjoyed a great deal of prestige in the 1950s. In a 1955 survey, male teenagers listed "officer in the armed services" as their fifth most highly esteemed occupation, above even "minister or priest."[14]

The improvements in American attitudes toward the military were combined with real improvements in the nature of the military job environment. The Officer Personnel Act (OPA) of 1947 rationalized and streamlined officer promotions, more systematically basing them on merit rather than seniority. In fact, the OPA probably increased the control that academy graduates had over the field grades, but it made the system of military promotion appear more equitable. Two years later, Congress approved an 18.8 percent military pay raise (another large pay raise would come in 1958) and introduced a twenty-year retirement plan that was, in Grandstaff's words, "more lucrative than many companies' retirement plans."[15] In 1956 Congress approved the extension of medical benefits to dependents. In short, as the military became a more attractive military career, ROTC became a more attractive—and popular—college activity.

Still, careerism remained rare among ROTC graduates. Given the importance of the draft in student decision making, it is not surprising that few ROTC cadets expressed a great desire to make the military their life's work. In 1958 only 39 percent of AFROTC graduates stated that they had an interest in making the service their career.[16] Most ROTC graduates "looked toward a more lucrative civilian job market for their (long term) career choices."[17] Table 3.1 demonstrates the lack of commitment of ROTC officers, especially in comparison to academy graduates and graduates from the army's Officer Candidate School and the air force's Officer Training School (OTS).

The figures in Table 3.1 were borne out in reenlistment rates. In the late 1950s, 70 percent of all air force officers contracted to serve beyond their obligation, but only 28 percent of AFROTC-trained officers did so.[18] Samuel Huntington summed up the military's officer accession dilemma nicely when he wrote: "Academy graduates have education and commitment but not numbers; ROTC men have numbers and education but not commitment; OCS men have numbers and commitment but not education."[19] The services showed their desire for education over commitment by consistently preferring ROTC graduates to OCS graduates and by sharing President Eisenhower's mandate that all officers needed "a background of general knowledge similar to that possessed by graduates of our leading universities."[20] With ROTC, Eisenhower's mandate was fulfilled to the letter.

Lack of career commitment notwithstanding, the large population of students on which ROTC could draw meant that the overall quality of cadets was high. Entrance into the advanced program was dependent on a formal application process and the approval of the instructional staff of the unit. The very worst students could therefore easily be kept out of the advanced portion of ROTC. A 1952 air force survey found that 46 percent of senior cadets and 40 percent of junior cadets were in the top third of their academic class. Only 4 percent of the ROTC juniors and seniors were in the lowest third.[21]

Educators and military officers understood ROTC cadet quality to be vital. "Think of the fighter-bomber pilot with a megaton weapon," the air force chief of staff observed at a 1959 meeting with educators. "The responsibility of a second lieutenant has never been exceeded in history."[22] The preparation of that second lieutenant, then, became paramount to military officials. They argued that modern military technology had greatly increased the responsibilities of junior officers, necessitating increased attention to their

Table 3.1   Percentage of officers stating "high career commitment," by commissioning source, 1961

Commission source	Army	Air Force
Service academy	62%	65%
OCS/OTS	78%	78%
ROTC	31%	37%

Source: Samuel Huntington, "Power, Expertise, and the Military Profession," *Daedalus* 92 (Fall 1963): 792.

training and their roles in the contemporary military. According to one study, ROTC cadets underwent a total of 1,128 hours of training (and all that *before* military service actually began), compared with the 1,050 hours of training received by draftees.[23]

According to Morris Janowitz, the daily life of the junior officer was characterized by progressively less discipline after World War II. Such does not appear to have been the case for the training of the junior officer, however. ROTC classes were well known for strict, sometimes arbitrary discipline. The University of Pittsburgh's *Standard Operating Procedure for Cadets* outlined typical infractions that could provoke demerits (earning 25 demerits led to dishonorable dismissal). Some of these are listed below.

Unauthorized absence: 5
Failure to carry out specific instruction: 5 (first offense)
Failure to carry out specific instruction: 10 (second offense)
Failure to carry out specific instruction: 25 (third offense)
Failure to wear uniform: 3
Drill infraction: 1
Uniform discrepancies: 1–2
Needing haircut badly: 2
Wearing disreputable, unclean attire: 1–3
Failure to salute on campus: 3

Rules regarding the wearing of the uniform read as follows: "No civilian decorations, watch chains, pencils, fountain pens, or other jewelry will be exposed on the uniform."[24]

One cadet handbook from 1956 told ROTC students that "discipline is considered an essential part of successful military service as it is in any ordered and civilized life" and outlined the behavior expected of ROTC cadets:

Cadets will come to attention when any member of the staff enters a classroom . . . *Members of the section will remain until dismissed by a member of the department staff. When on duty as such, cadet officers are required to correct breaches of discipline, and, if circumstances warrant it, report these infractions to the Military Department.* Cadet officers are directed to observe members of the Corps and to correct any mistakes noted. It is only by doing so that a high standard may be maintained in the Corps and self-confidence and firmness of character, so necessary to a leader, may be developed in the cadet officer."[25]

Several university deans, presidents, and chancellors across the nation supported the implementation of this regimen as beneficial to the development of good character and order on the campus. Military officials, for their part, saw it as preparation for the regimented climate of the military. To assure a firm grounding in the basics of such regimentation, ROTC detachments spent considerable time on such subjects as "personal appearance, wearing the uniform, military courtesy, military discipline, leadership, drill, and customs and courtesies of the service."[26] Success in mastering these subjects largely determined one's success and advancement in the ROTC program. University of Texas Army ROTC cadets received their grades based on the following criteria:

(a) *Appearance.* Neatness, clean and properly fit clothing, shave and haircut, military bearing, standing and sitting erect, cleanliness.

(b) *Demeanor.* Calm, poise, confidence, and enthusiasm.

(c) *Courtesy* and *cooperation.*

(d) *Aggressiveness.* Voluntary, constructive participation.

(e) *Grammar.* Ability to phrase questions and answers clearly, concisely, and to the point.

(f) *Voice.* Volume, clearness, and pronunciation.

(g) *Honesty.* In answering questions. Bluffing will be penalized.[27]

Drill (also known by the euphemistic name Leadership Laboratory) served as the quintessential example of military regimentation and discipline on the campus and was usually conducted in a visible public space like a quadrangle or an open athletic field. Proponents of drill contended that it was the only way to turn individuals into a true corps—a body of men acting in concert toward the same goal. Opponents of drill, most often those men subjected to too much of it, have seen it differently. Drill would surely fall under the definition of what Paul Fussell called "chickenshit," which he defined as "behavior that makes military life worse than it need be: petty harassment of the weak by the strong; open scrimmage for power and authority and prestige; sadism thinly disguised as necessary discipline; a constant 'paying off of old scores'; and insistence on the letter rather than the spirit of ordinances."[28]

ROTC cadets sometimes spent as much time drilling and being drilled as they spent in the classroom. In 1956, University of Texas ROTC cadets described a typical day thus: "Up at 6:15. Weekly shave. Name tag, collar stay. 7:00 Drill. Breakfast. Go to Eng. 601a [Freshman Composition]. Go to [Air Science] 403a— '. . . so while I was in Bangkok, never forget that night, I'd flown in a P-38 and . . .' 12:00 Drill. 'Your OTHER left foot, mister!' Lunch. Class—7:00 Lecture: 'The Geo-Politics of Southeastern Manitoba.' Hang uniform reverently in closet. Study. Sack time."[29] At the University of Texas and elsewhere, all demerits a student had accumulated from infractions like those listed above had to be worked off by the end of a semester by participating in still more drill. Furthermore, all Texas cadets were required to join an ROTC cadet organization "to enhance the prestige of the Army ROTC and make it an organization in which every cadet can take pride." Several of these organizations were precision drill teams, necessitating further training in drill.[30]

Despite its obvious differences from other educational methods, drill encountered little opposition in the Cold War era. For most passersby it was more likely to arouse patriotic feelings than cause unease. To civilian administrators, it symbolized discipline, maturation, and good order, all values they hoped to nurture in young men. To the cadets, it was either another requirement to be borne with the best face possible or an activity that they believed instilled useful values. In a 1963 survey, 84 percent of recent AFROTC graduates said that leadership lab "served a good purpose" at their school.[31] Of course it is impossible to estimate the number of people who felt unease but did not express it out of a fear of being labeled unpatriotic.

ROTC was, then, a preprofessional program of an unusual sort. While engineering, nursing, and fine arts programs could also be called preprofessional, they prepared students for a field, not for one exclusive employer.[32] Here was yet another difference between ROTC and other university programs. Since ROTC training was geared for one employer, the training was not only preprofessional but also specifically geared to the needs of the service (and sometimes to the specific branch of that service) with which the student had contracted. In the 1950s this training included indoctrination into the customs of the military profession: discipline, courtesy, and care of the uniform. It also meant a technical curriculum designed around strictly military courses, to meet the needs of the services.

From Specialized to General Military Training

In the Cold War era the military updated the ROTC curriculum to fit the rapidly changing and increasingly complex responsibilities of the junior officer. The same conditions that argued for a professional curriculum argued also for preparing officers to fill a wider variety of roles and giving them a wider understanding of the military. As a result, the first post–World War II changes to the military curriculum sought to make military training less specific to individual branch skills than it had been before the war.

Educators largely agreed with the military's stated goals but saw the problem slightly differently. They argued that the junior officer needed a wider range of civilian courses to complement the military courses and expose officer candidates to new fields in the humanities and social sciences as well as traditional civilian courses relevant to the military. Curricular changes in the civilian world, they argued, should be a part of total educational and professional preparation of officer candidates. By the late 1950s, as the specter of McCarthyism faded and as academics reached rough consensus on their ideas for the inclusion of civilian courses, civilian faculty and administrators began to lobby the services for the inclusion of civilian courses relevant to the military in the ROTC curriculum.

The first step in postwar curricular reform aimed at separating military training from the specific functions of the branches. Army ROTC training had, since World War I, been tied to the twelve branches of that service: Armor; Army Security; Artillery; Cavalry; Chemical; Engineering; Infantry; Military Police; Ordnance; Quartermaster; Signal Corps; and Transportation. The air force, sprung from its army parents in 1949, also began its training of ROTC cadets with a branch-based system that offered preparation in eight air force areas analogous to the army's branches: Administration and Supply; Comptroller; Armament; Aircraft Maintenance Engineering; Air Installations; Communications; General Technical; and Flight Operations. The branch system was a product of World War I, when weapons and logistics had grown sufficiently complex to merit formal specialization. Branch-oriented ROTC curricula in the Cold War era had the advantage of producing immediately employable junior officers who possessed knowledge of a particular branch. As noted in Chapter 2 and earlier in this chapter, the military assumed that if the Cold War turned hot, mobilization would need to take place much more quickly than it had in 1917 or 1941.[33] The specialized training system, many believed, made the assignment and use of recently activated reserve officers more rational.[34]

To many army, air force, and DOD officials, such a system of training officers was antiquated and irrational for several reasons. First, it hampered recruitment. Schools like the University of Colorado, which offered ROTC only for the Engineering branch of the service, effectively disqualified all of its nonengineering students from serving. Second, some branches were less appealing than others, the University of Missouri, which offered only artillery training, thereby "lost" students who might have wanted to join the army but not as an artillerist. Third, it made the assignment of instructors difficult, because the army and air force needed to staff ROTC units with officers who possessed the specialized training taught at that unit. Fourth, the branch system created shortages in some areas and too many officers in others and, to make matters worse, produced officers incapable of working outside their branch. The imbalances created were therefore difficult both to predict and to correct.[35]

Finally, many senior uniformed officers and two important civilian analysts believed that the training was too specialized. The mobilization exercises for the Korean War had demonstrated that technical knowledge was either not mastered or had quickly become obsolete in the "complicated and intricate" world of the modern military.[36] The army and air force needed a system that taught men how to be military leaders and well-rounded officers, not just branch specialists who knew how to operate equipment that was often replaced within a short time, rendering training that irrelevant.[37] According to a 1959 study of recent trends in ROTC by Gene Lyons and John Masland, the post-war military officer needed "a rich store of general knowledge as well as specialized knowledge of military affairs."[38] In the words of the branch system's most important uniformed critic, Major General Hugh Milton, "It is more essential to develop leadership qualities in these students and provide them with a broad base of military knowledge than to give them predominately branch specialized training."[39]

This was not, of course, to argue that a military officer did not have need of specific knowledge for his occupational specialty. Rather, it was an argument for keeping on-campus training general enough to give the officer sufficient knowledge of the rest of his service and to prepare him for specialized training once he was in service at one of the various professional military facilities, such as Ft. Benning for Infantry and Ft. Hood for Armor. Lyons, Masland, Milton, and others were, in effect, making the case that the military officer needed more than just the specialized knowledge taught under the branch curriculum and, further, that on-campus time was too valuable to spend on matters that could be easily taught to men in uniform who possessed a good general military education. Men were therefore asked to develop, as cadets and as junior officers, a knowledge of *both* their specialty and the more general world of the military.

General Milton played a large role in devising a new system, the army's General Military Science curriculum, or GMS. The army designed GMS without significant input from civilian higher education, and it had strictly military goals. The military was able to eschew significant civilian advice on GMS due to its sole intellectual ownership of the ROTC curriculum during the height of the Cold War. The GMS curriculum had three main goals: to reduce the production fluctuations of the branch system; to permit the assignment of a wider field of officers to ROTC duty; and to broaden the recruitment base by accepting students from all majors.[40] It reflected a change in the emphasis of the military environment more generally from the more heroic (to paraphrase Janowitz) military of years past to the more managerial and technologically complex world of the contemporary military.

The GMS curriculum and a concurrent air force equivalent, the General Military Course, aimed to make military training less technical and specialized, representing an important shift in the understanding of what an officer needed to know. These new curricula implicitly acknowledged that regular university courses such as psychology, political science, and communications had relevance for the junior officer. As such, they opened the door to changes that occurred in the late 1950s (see below). They did not, however, make any attempt to upgrade the academic quality of conventional ROTC courses. The motivations of the GMS curriculum were strictly and explicitly military. ROTC cadets, whether trained under a branch or a general system, continued to take courses understood by civilians to be of marginal academic value, taught by men without traditional academic qualifications.

The general absence of civilian input into ROTC curricula meant that the courses ROTC students took, whether at summer camps and cruises or on campus, were strictly military in their subject matter and quite squarely professional in their application. In the early 1960s the army described the goals of the national ROTC curriculum model thus: "the ROTC curriculum is not designed to educate the student, but to train him in the basic skills required of a second lieutenant."[41] NROTC students at the University of Colorado in 1953 described their classes thus: Naval History and Orientation; the Uniform Code of Military Justice; "a maze of ordnance and navigation"; "customs of the Navy"; the "innermost workings of the Navy's ordnance equipment"; "the art of pin-point navigation"; and "sea stories."[42]

This view, of course, stood in opposition to traditional modes of instruction in higher education, especially in colleges of liberal arts. So long as the Cold War seemed sufficiently threatening to national security, however, higher education officials by and large accepted the military's argument that cadets and midshipmen needed to use on-campus time to learn the nuts and bolts of military service in order to be immediately useful upon commission. Over time, however, the dissonance between pedagogical goals resulted in conflict.

Whenever possible, the services worked within the diversity of American higher education. They gave the senior unit officers (known as professor of military, air, or naval science) tremendous latitude and discretion in shaping the ROTC program to meet, within reason, the demands of local officials. In the air force only three officers, the chief of staff, the deputy commandant, and the commandant, could sign a letter denying a request by a professor of air science (PAS).[43] ROTC staff officers created a standard national curriculum that allowed local officers to make changes, but few officers strayed very far, out of the fear that their graduates would fare poorly in postcommissioning tests, which were designed to assess officer mastery of the material in the standard ROTC curricula.

The national army curriculum model, which predated the introduction of GMS in 1953 and had been virtually unchanged since World War II, required 480 hours of "academic" contact over four years and 264 hours of contact in two summer camps before the junior and senior years. Although the army sold part of the curriculum as academic, it was more technical and less reflective than the curricula of most liberal arts colleges and many engineering colleges as well. The official list of ROTC courses is shown in Table 3.2.

These courses did not follow a liberal arts pattern of reflection and analysis and often taught very different material than civilian classes, even in analogous subjects. The army course in military history stressed "the history of the Army and leadership as inspirational and integrating factors."[44] Summer camp courses were even more martial in orientation. In the first camp, after the student's sophomore year, courses included: Drill, Military Customs and Organization of the Army; Bayonet and Hand-to-Hand Combat; Field Sanitation and Inspections; Weapons and Marksmanship; and Basic Tactics. After the junior year, courses included: Drills, Parades, and Ceremonies; First Aid; and Field Problems.

Ted Wright, the hero of the comic book discussed earlier, first learned how to shine his shoes ("only an officer and a gentleman shines the heels"), then he learned hygiene, first aid, drill, and the use of crew-served weapons. Once in the advanced program, he learned how to set a road block, fire the new 57mm recoilless rifle, conduct a court martial, and, as we have seen, deal with women.[45] These, then, were the subjects the army saw as most vital: weapons training, drill, and how to dress and act like an officer.

Real ROTC students took courses similar to Ted Wright's. Army ROTC cadets at Kent State in 1952 took courses titled Military Organization, First

Table 3.2 Standard army curriculum, 1950s

Year	Courses	Contact hours
Military Science I (freshmen)	Introduction	5
	Weapons and Marksmanship	25
	Leadership Lab (drill)	30
	Military History	30
Military Science II (sophomores)	Role of the Army	10
	Map and Aerial Photo Reading	20
	Crew-Served Weapons	30
	Leadership Lab	30
Military Science III (juniors)	Leadership Lab	30
	Branches of the Army	30
	Tactics and Communications	55
	Leadership	10
	Military Principles	20
	Pre-Camp	5
Military Science IV (seniors)	Operations	50
	Logistics	20
	Leadership Lab	30
	Administration and Military Justice	30
	Service Orientation	20

Source: Gene Lyons and John Masland, *Education and Military Leadership* (Princeton N.J.: Princeton University Press, 1959), p. 182.

Aid, Drill, and Marksmanship. In their junior year they took Infantry Tactics, Field Fortifications, Gunnery, and (again) Drill. Their air force peers took such ambiguously titled courses as Applied Air Power (which taught desert, jungle, and arctic survival), Military Publications, and Flight Operations, along with the ubiquitous Drill.[46] Eight years later at the University of Pittsburgh, Weapons and Marksmanship, Leadership Laboratory, Operations and Tactics, Branches of the Army, Service Orientation, and Tactics formed the core of the ROTC curriculum.[47]

The description of the Kent State Air Force ROTC course Military Publications indicates the courses' strictly professional content:

Military Publications: The course provides a basic knowledge of military publications, their indices, filing, and use. The ingenuity of the instructor is relied upon to some extent in that he must present specific questions, which will require the students to be familiar with the procedures to be followed in using military publications in order to determine the answers. Publications covered will include Air Force Regulations, Air Force Letters, Manuals, Technical Orders, M & S Directives, T/O & Es, TMs, and TBs.[48]

While not questioning the national need for ROTC, or the university's obligation to sponsor ROTC classes, these courses seemed to many higher education officials to be out of step with the goals of higher education in general and liberal education in particular. ROTC, with its squarely professional classes based on repetition and memorization (symbolized by the automatonic drill) did not fit in with a careful reading of goals like those of the University of Pittsburgh's College of Liberal Arts:

> The School believes that liberal education is a life-time process of intellectual and aesthetic development and that, while it cannot and should not be a professional training program, it does provide the best foundation for one's future professional interests. The dynamic balance of observation and participation, of reflection and action, of free minds and a free society, is the essence of life itself and, in turn, of liberal education.[49]

If ROTC had a place in the curriculum, and few doubted that it did, it was surely not the same place as English, philosophy, or chemistry. University of Texas officials noted that ROTC "is not to be viewed as a scholarship program" but as a specifically military program.[50] It is illustrative, then, that at many schools, including the University of Pittsburgh, ROTC had the same curricular standing as physical education. Students could complete four semesters of either one to fulfill a graduation requirement.[51]

A tension therefore existed between the steadfastly acknowledged national need for officer training programs on civilian campuses and the awareness that the courses offered were tangential to the mission of many colleges and universities. The general support among those in higher education for the ROTC curriculum began to be undermined in the late 1950s by the desire of some faculty members to make the ROTC curriculum more compatible with civilian curricula. For the most part, however, top-level administrators preferred not to interfere too deeply with the military's decisions about what a junior officer should learn. Indeed, the universities formally approved the courses by awarding academic credit. At Kent State, army and air force ROTC cadets received two hours per quarter for the basic course and three hours per quarter for the advanced course.[52] Texas allowed ROTC courses to count for as many as 24 of the 120 hours needed for graduation.[53] The University of Pittsburgh's colleges of liberal arts and engineering permitted students to count 8 ROTC credit towards the 124 and 144 credits needed, respectively, for graduation.[54]

A Green Pasture

As with the content of ROTC courses, the universities by and large permitted the services to determine the qualifications of ROTC instructors. Although the qualifications of military faculty were quite different from those of civilian faculty, throughout the 1950s this variance produced little formal opposition. Cadre officers, despite the customary title of professor for senior officers and assistant professor or associate professor for junior officers, very rarely held or even sought an advanced degree; indeed, the military did not believe that such a degree was necessary to teach the professional subject matter of the ROTC curriculum. Nor was the need for such qualifications obvious to some university officials. When queried by the air force about its preferences for officers assigned, the University of Illinois replied in 1957 that "academic major, degrees beyond the baccalaureate, section of the country in which raised, and type of school from which graduated are not matters of importance in carrying out the responsibilities of the PAS."[55]

ROTC duty developed a reputation as a "pre-retirement sinecure" for officers who failed to qualify for promotion.[56] ROTC duty was often a terminal assignment, understood as signaling the end of the productive years of one's career. As early as 1950, the Association of NROTC Colleges complained to the navy that it had been "several years" since a professor of naval science had been promoted to rear admiral. The association noted that of the fifty-two professors on duty, only fifteen even had the qualifications to be considered for such a promotion.[57]

Many others saw an ROTC assignment as a reward after a long overseas tour of duty. One observer described ROTC duty as "a 'green pasture' where officers about to be retired took it easy."[58] Indeed, ROTC positions were understood to be among the safest posts in the military, they allowed an officer to establish a home, and the work was not particularly difficult. The services did not require the officers to have teaching experience, nor did they offer training programs to help them learn how to teach.

Although civilian faculty sometimes lacked teaching experience as well, their professional qualifications (measured by degrees earned) served as indicators to fellow academics that they had sufficient expertise to merit inclusion in the faculty. Few people argued that an officer needed a master's degree to teach logistics, but to many academics, giving faculty titles to men who had neither professional qualifications nor teaching expertise seemed irresponsible and a breach of academic protocol.

In theory, the universities had the right to reject candidates nominated by the services, and they did exercise that prerogative on occasion. More often than not, however, candidates recommended by the services and endorsed by the cadre were quickly approved. Since the officers applying for ROTC teaching positions rarely had publications or other standard academic materials to evaluate, there was little on which administrators could base a decision. In many cases, it was impossible for the cadre or university officials to interview or even meet the candidate, because he was assigned to an overseas post. As a result, personnel decisions were made on the basis of service records or some arbitrary criterion, such as the "neat military appearance," in one case, of an air force major who came to the University of Illinois for an interview in 1960.[59]

Sometimes the schools even accepted instructors with no college degree at all. In 1958 an air force captain with no college education and "little formal class room instructing" was nevertheless found to be "quite acceptable" to University of Illinois associate provost Royen Dangerfeld.[60] Of the seventy-eight officers assigned to ROTC duty at Duquesne and the Universities of Illinois, Pittsburgh, and Texas between 1957 and 1963 whose education could be determined, only twelve had a degree beyond the bachelor's; seven had no degree at all at their time of appointment. Further instruction from men without degrees came from cadets themselves, who were often called upon to teach freshmen classes, especially drill, as part of their training in leadership.

Attempts to rectify this situation faced several obstacles. In 1962 only 12.6 percent of all air force officers had an advanced degree, and nearly one in five lacked even a bachelor's degree.[61] Given these limitations, air force reforms were aimed at eliminating non–degree holders from ROTC duty and, somewhat ironically, lowering the age of the instructor. Between 1961 and 1964, the number of non–degree holders on the ROTC staff dropped from fifty-four to just four. Oddly enough, however, in the same period the number of full colonels on staff fell by fifty percent, illustrating a determined effort by the air force to put more young officers, particularly lieutenant colonels and majors, on campus. "These efforts have placed younger, more adaptable and ambitious Air Force representatives on campus, men with academic backgrounds compatible with those of other faculty members with whom they associate. All these measures have served to improve both the stature of the AFROTC on the campus and the rapport between its representatives and the college community."[62]

Surely the air force was being sanguine in expecting that eliminating non–degree holders would make the cadre's "academic backgrounds compatible with those of other faculty members with whom they associate." Nevertheless, the new requirement of the completion of some college education pleased educators. The universities were willing to accept somewhat lower qualifications for military instructors than for civilian instructors, provided that a minimum standard could be maintained.

Still, some administrators tried to address ROTC's reputation for poor instruction more systematically, and such attempts usually centered around standard academic indicators like advanced degrees. Demanding an advanced degree for all ROTC instructors would have been folly, since there were simply not enough officers with master's degrees. The University of Minnesota nevertheless tried to set higher minimum standards than the air force had done, as evidenced by this letter from President O. Meredith Wilson to Secretary of the Army (and future Indiana University president) Elvis Stahr: "We have had many fine officers here, but in some cases, the officers assigned have not met those standards which we attempt to meet for the remainder of the faculty. We therefore have decided that our minimum academic requirement for those officers nominated for duty in the ROTC units shall be that they be fully qualified for entrance into our Graduate School . . . We, of course, would prefer officers who already have graduate degrees, but we know that this is not now practicable."[63]

The debate over instructor qualifications indicated another area of dissonance that, throughout the 1950s and early 1960s, was acknowledged but, in the quest for harmony, not hotly contested. Once again, the perceived needs of national security took precedence over addressing ROTC's anomalous place in the university.

Substitution: The Coming Order of the Day

By the late 1950s, when the bipolarity of the early years of the Cold War was replaced by a more complicated understanding that included the Third

World, educators developed several ideas to integrate more fully the military and civilian instructional programs. Furthermore, the 1957 Soviet launch of the first *Sputnik* satellite reawakened an interest in officer education, just as it reinvigorated interest in American education more generally. Such an environment proved fertile for the development of civilian suggestions for changes in the ROTC curriculum.

Various ideas for the larger incorporation of civilian faculty into ROTC programs developed independently at several institutions nationwide. One such plan, developed in 1957 by the Association of Naval ROTC Colleges and Universities (ANROTCCU), a group constituted of the presidents and provosts of those schools hosting NROTC units, involved using civilian faculty as guest lecturers to broaden and supplement the instruction provided by uniformed personnel.[64] The use of civilian lecturers, the ANROTCCU argued, could upgrade the academic quality of instruction while playing on one of the traditional strengths of ROTC. Part of the value of officers from civilian colleges was in their exposure to civilian ideas. It made sense, then, to take advantage of civilian faculty who taught subjects relevant to the general education of the junior military officer. Rutgers University introduced guest lecturing on a broad scale in 1958 with "excellent" results.[65]

The most important military objection to such a plan, and to subsequent similar plans, was that, if carried out on too grand a scale, it would reduce the number of contact hours between officer and cadet or midshipman. Such contact was vital, some argued, for the officers to be able to determine the leadership potential of their students, as that potential is not easily measurable through papers and exams. Any reform that took time away from direct officer-student contact therefore met with resistance from many officers. Still, the idea of using civilian instructors was logical and consistent with the recent switch from branch training to GMS. If the goal was a broader general education, then an understanding of history, political science, geography, mathematics, and languages could only help to produce the better-educated officers desired by proponents of GMS.

Some universities were even developing plans to use civilian faculty to teach entire ROTC classes, not just selected lectures. At the same time that the ANROTCCU plan was developed, the Ohio State University AFROTC detachment began to work out a plan to have civilian instructors teach "such courses as International Tensions and Security Organizations, Fundamentals of Global Geography, Military Aspects of World Political Geography, Communicating in the Air Force, Problem Solving and Leadership Management."[66] In this pilot program, civilian Ohio State faculty taught courses that were military in their orientation but more reflective and academic than those courses taught by uniformed officers.

The Ohio State plan had the support of the air force, which also introduced the idea of asking universities to develop specific courses to be taught by civilian professors according to air force requirements. These courses would be offered as a joint military-civilian enterprise and open to any student.[67] Ohio State, for its part, was anxious to have other schools try what was becoming known as "substitution," the replacement of vocational, military courses by academic ones. Civilian faculties strongly resisted the idea of the joint courses because of the fear of outside influence on course design. They received the idea of substitution more favorably, as it involved the use of existing academic offerings. By 1960, 48 of the air force's 176 host schools used some variant of substitution.[68] To be sure, 128 schools still used strictly military curricula, but a strong alternative was emerging.

The localized nature of the ROTC curriculum meant that experimentation in the use of civilian faculty could be carried out at any school whose faculty and administration showed an interest. The University of Pittsburgh showed such interest early on and developed its own plan for substitution without significant input from Ohio State officials. A 1959 faculty senate committee's review of the Army and Air Force ROTC programs at Pittsburgh had found that what was known as the "academic" portion of the ROTC curriculum did not merit the credit awarded and that "the academic courses might profitably be replaced by courses already existing in our regular department offerings." The committee recommended that "the University should request the ROTC to consider a change in their curriculum which would recognize the suitability of regular departmental courses for credit toward military commissions . . . These courses would be taught by regular non-military university faculty" in the departments of political science and geography.[69]

The air force proved receptive to Pittsburgh's suggestions and responded with quick and enthusiastic approval. For the spring trimester of the academic year 1959–60 the air force authorized Pittsburgh to substitute two courses, International Relations and Political Geography, for air science courses. University of Pittsburgh military affairs coordinator Alan Rankin told the faculty senate that the changes in the air force curriculum, and discussions with the army for changes in its curriculum, had improved the academic legitimacy of ROTC:

Colonel Hills (the Professor of Air Science) and Colonel Wolff (the Professor of Military Science) join me in expressing appreciation to the Chancellor and the Senate for their interest in developing ROTC Programs which will enrich the educational experiences of the students and at the same time recognize the requirements of the Departments of the Air Force and the Army . . . In undertaking the study of the steps necessary to implement the Senate Committee's recommendations, we have found the Departments of the Air Force and the Army favorably disposed to change . . . The Army is hoping to give purely academic courses a greater emphasis, to reduce on-campus instruction in purely military subjects and to allow ROTC credit for courses in psychology, mathematics, and physics.[70]

A reduction in the teaching of military subjects on campus would be necessary to make time for the new substituted courses. Under most proposals considered for national implementation, those military subjects would be moved to the summer camps.

The same motivations that produced substitution produced coincident changes at the three service academies aimed at broadening the educational background of academy-trained officers. In 1957 the Air Force Academy became the first service academy to allow elective courses, thereby jettisoning the "straitjacket" curriculum formerly required of all cadets; West Point and Annapolis followed suit within two years. All three academies, arguing, in the words of the Naval Academy's superintendent, that "the time has passed . . . when it was simply enough to teach cadets and midshipmen how to shoot guns and run ships," sharply reduced time spent on "purely military training."[71] All three academies increased time spent in humanities and social science classes, "junking . . . hardware courses . . . in favor of studies of a fundamental nature which will not soon go out of date."[72]

Substitution in the ROTC curriculum succeeded both because it was consistent with similar changes at the academies and because it easily overlapped the interests of military and civilian officials. Substitution met the services' desire for more broadly educated students and higher education's desire to raise the academic standard for ROTC course instruction in the absence of highly qualified military teachers. The University of Pittsburgh's Alan Rankin attended a 1959 AFROTC conference and noted with pleasure the participants' warm reception of substitution:

The most interesting feature of the conference was the unmistakable sentiment on the part of both institutional representatives and the Air Force officials to liberalize the AFROTC program in exactly the same direction as the University of Pittsburgh is moving. Our regular academic courses taught by our regular faculty members is the coming order of the day, and I would anticipate little difficulty in getting approval from the Air Force headquarters for whatever modifications in our curriculum we might want to undertake.[73]

The following year, Pittsburgh introduced eighteen more hours of substitution for AFROTC. Freshmen took speech and one class in math, natural science, social science, language, or the humanities. Juniors took social psychology and either Technical or Expository Writing. Cadets still took a core primarily composed of military subjects, but these were now complemented by cognate civilian courses.

The army, too, moved quickly to substitute academic courses for purely military subjects, but it gave substitution less emphatic support than had the air force, out of a desire to maintain a high number of contact hours between cadre and cadet. Along these lines, the Army in 1960 rejected a proposal by the Army ROTC Advisory Panel to substitute 135 of the curriculum's 480 hours, but it did agree to reduce the amount of time spent on weapons and marksmanship by 45 hours.[74] The time freed up could be used to substitute civilian-taught classes in science, psychology, communications, and political science.[75] The army made it clear to schools that they were free to reject the idea of substitution. Not surprisingly, Pittsburgh chose to take the army's offer and introduced courses in four general groupings: effective communication; science comprehension; general psychology; and political institutions.[76]

The navy's ROTC program had, since 1946, used a scholarship program designed to produce officers "capable of going to sea" right after graduation. The navy therefore was hesitant to take any time away from its rigid curriculum for nonprofessional courses that might reduce its ability to turn a college senior into an immediately employable ensign. Nevertheless, by 1960 the navy had, at the insistence of its host schools, authorized substitution of two courses, General Psychology and Naval Engineering, across the curriculum. The navy also turned over the NROTC course on the history of sea power, which accounted for 60 of the first year's 120 contact hours, to civilian instructors at appropriate institutions. Naval officers in charge of NROTC stood firm, however, in saying that they would not authorize any substitution beyond those three courses, because "we just cannot see how it is possible to relinquish more time" to nonmilitary instructors.[77]

Substitution had the added virtue of making it easier for students to fit

ROTC into their increasingly demanding schedules. The services had long recognized time constraints as an important detriment to advanced ROTC enrollment. A 1950 study noted that students gave "too time consuming" as their most frequent complaint.[78] In 1961 the Army ROTC Advisory Panel noted in its report that "some educators are exerting pressure to further reduce on-campus military instruction. They consider that reduction is necessary in order to integrate student academic requirements and to reduce the impact of the pressure of time on the students."[79] An ROTC curriculum conference sponsored by Ohio State advocated the substitution policy by praising its ability to "reduce the overload on advanced students."[80] Basic-level cadets were under time constraints as well; at Georgia Tech the AFROTC program reduced classroom time for freshmen and sophomores from eighteen hours a week to six "in order that each student may have more time for academic activities."[81]

Substitution thus had many virtues: it made the program more appealing to a large minority of military officials, primarily in the army and air force, who wanted ROTC to move in the direction of education, not training; it pleased educators by injecting academic material from a wide variety of disciplines into the vocational curriculum; it pleased undergraduates by allowing them effectively to count some classes twice—once as credits for their diploma and once as requirements for their commission. This last advantage partly explains why the services were so quick to adapt substitution to their curricula. The army felt compelled to respond to air force plans that made it easier for students to enroll in and complete AFROTC training—especially on those campuses where both programs existed—lest it should lose potential cadets to the other service. Substitution was not widespread enough to allow the services to save money by assigning fewer officers to the ROTC programs, but it did bring all of the above advantages without any additional costs. Therefore the new programs steadily spread, making at least a portion of the ROTC student's curriculum more academic in nature and demonstrating the benefit of close working relationships between the two agents in charge of ROTC.

For all of substitution's virtues, the debate over the policy did point out that the military and academia had different, if sometimes compatible, goals for ROTC. Representatives of the military, especially those in the navy, wanted to focus on-campus time on strictly military (and less reflective) subjects, such as drill, courtesy, and the wearing of the uniform. The universities pushed to add required cognate areas to the curriculum, such as psychology, political science, and communications. While substitution proved to be an effective compromise, the military remained suspicious of ceding too much time to civilians at the risk of reducing its ability to judge leadership capabilities in their cadets. Meanwhile, university officials continued to contend that on-campus time was more properly spent learning group-dynamics theories than the rudiments of crew-served weapons.

Because virtually all of the civilian and military agents in charge of ROTC saw the program as an inexpensive, efficient means of expanding the talents and numbers of the officer corps without resorting to a larger academy-trained military elite, ROTC came to possess a highly elevated status on American campuses. It thus occupied a peculiar position in the university: it received the status of a department despite not sharing important qualities with civilian academic departments, its courses were accredited despite faculty reviews that found them substandard in content, and its instructors received the title of "professor" despite their having backgrounds very different from those of civilian faculty.

In spite of these anomalies, little sustained opposition to ROTC emerged. The period from 1950 to 1964, while witnessing some changes, was one of great continuity for ROTC. The quest for civilian-military harmony born of the Cold War led to a great deal of university acquiescence which in turn buttressed the elevated stature of the program. Beginning in 1964, however, ROTC began to experience rapid reform, first as a result of new legislation and then, more fundamentally, as the nation's shared sense of purpose during the Cold War gave way to the uncertainties and doubts of a new era that brought into question the role of the university in America's prosecution of the war in Southeast Asia.

CHAPTER 4

The ROTC Vitalization Act, 1964–1968

> These symbolic practices when viewed outside their context may appear unnecessary, and civilians sometimes express impatience or irritation with them . . . [but] ceremonies involving drill are practices in the [military], and the student will have to acquire some skill in performing these activities if he is to participate in them on active duty.
>
> —*ROTC Curriculum Handbook, 1968*

By the late 1950s and early 1960s, critics as diverse as radical sociologist C. Wright Mills and President Dwight Eisenhower began to argue that the military, and the industrial system to which it had become tightly connected, had gained too strong a hold on American society. With McCarthyism in remission and with the replacement of early Cold War hysteria with a more complex view of global affairs, critics could more confidently express their concerns about the militarization of American society. Mills decried the "military ascendancy" and the new role that the services had taken in many fields traditionally dominated by civilians, including education. "Some universities," Mills argued, "are financial branches of the military establishment, receiving three or four times as much money from the military as from all other sources combined."[1] He identified ROTC as one manifestation of this influence, noting that, while "prestigeful," ROTC linked the "pursuit of knowledge" in the American university to "the training of men to enact special roles."[2]

President Eisenhower sounded a less radical but no less concerned tone in his 1961 farewell address. The preeminent military hero sounded like the model Moderate Whig:

In the councils of government, we must guard against the acquisition of un-warranted influence, whether sought or unsought, by the military-indus-trial complex. The potential for the disastrous rise of misplaced power exists and will persist. We must never let the weight of this combination endanger our liberties or democratic processes. We should take nothing for granted. Only an alert and knowledgeable citizenry can compel the proper meshing of the huge industrial and military machinery of defense with our peaceful methods and goals, so that security and liberty may prosper together.

Eisenhower also warned against the unprecedented growth of the military into American higher education. "The prospect of domination of the na-tion's scholars by Federal employment, project allocations, and the power of money is ever present—and is gravely to be regarded."[3] Sentiments such as Eisenhower's and Mills's reflected a reemergence of Moderate Whig fears all along the American ideological spectrum after a period of notably more yielding attitudes toward the military at the height of the Cold War era.

Emerging concerns such as these may have sowed the seeds of later oppo-sition to the influence of the military on campus, but to judge from the cor-respondence and policy decisions of educators and the military, they had lit-tle immediate impact on ROTC in the early and mid-1960s. Military officials and educators alike were more concerned that the ROTC program was not well constructed to meet the future. Both the military and academia had ex-perienced significant recent change. Furthermore, the universities were ex-pected to expand dramatically to accommodate the large numbers of Ameri-can baby boomers that would be reaching college age. ROTC, many argued, had outlived its 1916 enabling legislation.

In 1964, as a response to declining ROTC enrollments (in an era of rapidly expanding collegiate enrollments more generally) and the increased de-mands that American higher education was beginning to place on its stu-dents, Congress passed the ROTC Vitalization Act to update the program and to prepare it for its future as the nation's primary source for active-duty officer procurement. The debate over the bill provides insight into ROTC's value to those agents responsible for its oversight—ROTC staff officers, the universities, service headquarters officers at the Pentagon, and Congress—and set the precedent for later negotiations. The debate also reveals what Congress and the services sought to gain from ROTC and what they thought the program could achieve.

Even as the Vitalization Act was being implemented, faculty and students at several universities nationwide, with Mills as an intellectual ancestor, were beginning to question American involvement in the widening war in Southeast Asia. The creation of Students for a Democratic Society (SDS) in 1962, itself not initially an antiwar organization, provided a national infrastructure on which opponents of the war would eventually build a significant and compelling movement.[4] While real, sustained opposition on the campuses did not arise until 1968, nascent student and faculty hostility to the Vietnam War affected ROTC, if only indirectly at first, as early as the 1965 teach-ins at the University of Michigan and subsequent teach-ins across the nation. Just as the Vitalization Act set the framework for later negotiations between the schools and the services, so were precedents set for how ROTC units would respond to campus disorder during the Vietnam era.

This period was also one of tremendous expansion for higher education as America strove to make college attainable for a larger percentage of the population (see Table 4.1). The 1960s were dynamic times for American universities, with the government, and the DOD specifically, funding much of that dynamism. The faculty and students of the 1950s had not expressed great concern about how such government influence could distort the mission of a university.[5] Many people in the 1960s, however, believed that the university would have to curb government influence if it was to remain objective and able to pursue truth. All of these dynamic changes of the 1960s would eventually play a role in the reform of ROTC.

Table 4.1   Growth of American higher education, 1960–1964

Factor	Growth
Number of faculty	30%
Undergraduate enrollment	38%
Expenditures	64%
Federal support	133%
Revenue from student fees	64%

Source: Bureau of the Census, *Historical Statistics of the United States, Colonial Times to 1970, Part 2* (Washington, D.C.: Government Printing Office, 1975), pp. 382–386.

The Genesis of the ROTC Vitalization Act

The 1916 National Defense Act, which initially authorized ROTC, had assumed that ROTC's role would be to provide officers for the reserve components of the armed forces. The Cold War, however, had forced a reexamination of that role as ROTC became the primary source of active-duty officers. Now the air force, for example, expected that one of every two active-duty officers commissioned in 1964 would come from ROTC; the army expected that figure to be three in four.[6] ROTC had therefore taken on a new role, but it still operated under legislation designed to help it fulfill an antediluvian one.

As early as 1960 the air force had called for new legislation to replace the "outmoded" 1916 law.[7] Colonel (later Brigadier General) William Lindley took personal charge of developing new legislation to bring AFROTC into line with the needs of the services for high-quality, active-duty junior officers. His goal was to produce a program that would be available to more male undergraduates, take up less of the student's time than the five hours per week mandated by the NDA, and shift the focus of ROTC training from drill and military ceremony to management and problem solving.

The army chief of staff shared the air force's concerns and ordered a review of the Army ROTC program in 1961 to "make the program more productive and appealing to students and institutions, and more compatible with Navy and Air Force programs, while still fulfilling Army requirements."[8] Those in charge of ROTC concurred that the program needed "an entirely new look." They also agreed that the first step in creating that new look was to repeal the 1916 NDA, which they deemed "inconsistent with current . . . requirements."[9] In the course of the ensuing debates among Congress, the ROTC staffs, and the Pentagon, each agency revealed its own goals and hopes for ROTC.

The task of reforming ROTC focused most urgently on numbers. As already noted, fifty-nine AFROTC and sixty AROTC units ended the compulsory feature of their programs in the early 1960s. While defenders of those decisions continued to insist that voluntary programs alone could produce enough officers, those at the top of the command structure had reason to be concerned. Despite predictions to the contrary, enrollments and, more important, commissions, were falling below established minimum standards.[10] In the fall of 1963, as the debate over compulsory ROTC was being settled, the Illinois AROTC unit expected 170 juniors to enroll in advanced ROTC; only 101 actually did.[11]

On a national level, the picture was much the same. The army failed to make its 1963 enrollment goal and the air force expressed concerns about its ability to meet future goals. Army ROTC enrollment fell "alarmingly" from 169,000 in the academic year 1962–63 to 158,016 in 1963–64 to 157,303 in 1964–65.[12] An air force survey of eighty-eight AFROTC units found fifty-one experiencing falling enrollments, many of these by as much as 20 percent.[13] The army noted, "This is a disturbing trend and if it continues it will have a serious impact on the readiness of the Army to fulfill its role in national defense."[14] Moreover, the need for officers was expected to become more acute in the coming years as the huge cohort of men who received their commissions during World War II and the Korean War retired after completing twenty years of service.[15] The army predicted that officer shortages could reach as high as 7,000 per year between 1963 and 1969.[16]

The services and educators primarily focused on four theories, in addition to the end of the compulsory programs, to explain the drop in enrollments. The first theory contended that a lessening of the national Cold War hysteria, beginning with the death of Josef Stalin and the end of the Korean War in 1953, had reduced the urgency men felt to join the military. The Geneva Summit of 1955 and the "Kitchen Debates" of 1959 served to further thaw, if not melt, some of the Cold War tensions. As the possibility for war seemed less imminent, this theory held, fewer men signed up for military training.

The second theory argued that the power of the draft as a motivating factor had waned, causing fewer men to look to ROTC as a means of evading conscription. A 1961 presidential order that placed married men "at the bottom of the [draft] call sequence" had given men another way to defer their military obligations. The order had been designed to reduce "an overabundance of young men" eligible for conscription. Similarly, the system encouraged automatic deferments for college students who passed their courses.[17] Many men continued to look for ways to deal with the capricious draft system, but by the early 1960s that system looked less threatening to some than it had been in the 1950s, when even national celebrities like Elvis Presley and Willie Mays were called to serve.

Third, some educators argued that increased demands on student time made ROTC, which required at least five hours per week, simply too onerous. Collegiate curricula were becoming more demanding, and adding ROTC made a student's schedule that much more hectic. And fourth, some observers believed that the college student of the 1960s was more interested in making money and less interested in serving his country than his predecessors had been. Philip Caputo noted that his fellow students in the early part of the 1960s "thought of joining the army as the most conformist thing anyone could do, and as the service itself as a form of slavery."[18] Similarly, a University of Illinois senior named Roger Ebert told *Newsweek* in 1964: "Most of us just want to get through school, get to work, get married, and get out to the suburbs."[19]

Of these four theories, the first reflected the military's autonomous effort to reposition itself in a world that it now saw as less bipolar than during the Cold War. The other three were related to manpower and recruitment issues. None of these explanations was directly connected to antimilitary or antiwar sentiment on the campuses, though they were all certainly connected to the new student indifference and unwillingness to join the program.

The services, especially the air force, hoped to address the enrollment drop by increasing the pool of men eligible to become ROTC cadets. To do so, the air force focused on "the restrictive features of existing legislation (that) inordinately limit the selection base for our commissioning program."[20] The 1916 NDA had required any man seeking a commission to serve in ROTC for all four of his undergraduate years. The services wanted this feature repealed and a two-year ROTC program created (for the student's junior and senior years) to take advantage of four groups of men barred from service under the NDA:

1. Transfers from senior colleges without ROTC units and the growing number of junior colleges, which accounted for 800,000 of the nation's 3.1 million undergraduates in 1963. Junior college populations, moreover, were expected to grow throughout the 1960s. The services especially targeted this group, which constituted 64 percent of the junior-year male student population in a 1962–63 sampling of AFROTC host schools.[21]

2. Students who attended schools that did not themselves host ROTC units but were located within an easy commute to an ROTC host.

3. Students who had to work to earn money for school and therefore could not afford to make a four-year commitment.

4. Students who decided late in their college career to join ROTC.[22]

University administrators, through the Army Advisory Panel on ROTC Affairs and the National Association of State Universities and Land-Grant Colleges, supported these ideas and favored "a bold move rather than . . . a creeping approach" to the enrollment problems.[23] They proposed that the air force and army lobby for legislation authorizing them to grant full scholarships to their ROTC students as the navy had done since the DOD's approval of the Holloway Plan in 1946. The educators believed that the Holloway Plan made the NROTC program less susceptible to enrollment fluctuation and better able to attract high-quality men. The new scholarships, the schools hoped, would "be made available to all cadets, without discrimination, whether enrolled at an institution conducting the four-year program, or the modified two-year program."[24]

The army and air force also hoped to get scholarship authorization, but they put less faith in scholarships than the universities did, knowing that Congress would give them only the *authority* to award scholarships (as it had done for the navy); it would not provide additional money to make the scholarships a reality. Consequently, the services believed that the initial impact of the scholarships would "almost surely be rather limited."[25] The services did, however, push to raise the monthly ROTC stipend, which had been at $27 per month since 1947, to $50 per month.[26]

Many military and civilian officials liked the idea of the two-year program so much that they proposed abandoning the four-year version altogether. The two-year program, they argued, would be less expensive and encourage wider student participation by reducing the time demands, allowing students with heavy academic commitments to fit ROTC more easily into their college schedule. The Air Force ROTC senior staff favored the elimination of the four-year program; the University of Illinois's Military Affairs Committee officially concurred in 1963.[27] An informal survey conducted by the air force found that 120 of the 182 schools hosting AFROTC units backed dropping the four-year program in favor of the proposed two-year program.[28]

The AROTC and AFROTC staffs strongly favored offering only the two-year program but promised to give schools the option of choosing to host the two-year program, the four-year, or both, depending on the desires of the school. Whatever their choice, the ROTC senior staffs told the schools that they could look forward to fewer ROTC contact hours. They had determined that they needed to reduce the students' "intolerable burden" of 480 contact hours, especially for the engineers that Secretary of Defense Robert McNamara coveted.[29] Therefore they proposed that much of the ROTC's technical preparation be moved to summer camps.

After coordinating its plan with the army and navy, the air force submitted a proposal to the Bureau of the Budget in 1962 that involved four major features: a raise in the ROTC stipend; a reduction of on-campus training in such technical subjects as drill and tactics; the opening of two-year programs (if desired by the host school); and the authority for each service to offer 8,000 scholarships annually.[30] Few expected that the army and air force would take immediate advantage of the scholarship authority, but the air force saw the opportunity to get such authority and have it securely protected from any future budget cuts.

The DOD and the Bureau of the Budget granted quick approval of the air force plan and sent it to the House Armed Services Committee, under the sponsorship of Louisiana Democrat F. Edward Hébert, in time for the 1963 legislative session. The bill, House Resolution 9124, had the unanimous support of educators, whose spokesman, NASULGC executive secretary Russell Thackrey, wrote to the committee: "I would like to *emphasize* that we are strongly in favor of the enactment of HR 9124 . . . Believe me, the ROTC needs the kind of revisions this bill provides. It has not been brought up to date since it was started and is beginning to suffer."[31]

Educators and military officers agreed on the important features that the new legislation should contain: scholarships in the existing four-year program *and* the proposed two-year program in order to include, among others, "the great development of 2-year institutions whose transfer students have not been eligible for ROTC"; a reduction of the teaching of military subjects such as drill on campus; and a raise in stipend for all cadets.[32] Such changes would halt the recent reduction in "the potential and actual effectiveness of the Reserve Officers' Training Corps programs" and create a "comprehensive program compatible with the educational objectives of the colleges and universities and adequate to assure meeting the qualitative and quantitative needs of the respective services."[33]

The general consensus that the highest officers of the military and academia had reached concluded nearly fifteen years of harmonious relations. Tensions certainly existed, but enough agreement on fundamental issues also existed to permit the two institutions to present a bill to Congress with one voice. The bill tried to create a program that met the educators' desires for a more educationally sound program and the military's desires for cost-effectiveness and greater participation from white undergraduate males. Despite this general level of agreement, however, the ROTC Vitalization Act ran into immediate difficulties with members of Congress, who had quite different goals for ROTC. The resulting legislation, instead of continuing the quest for harmony, set the goals of the military and the university at odds, unintentionally helping to create the crisis that would come at the end of the 1960s.

"More as a Means of Teaching Americanism"

The debates over the ROTC Vitalization Act lasted for two legislative sessions.[34] In the course of these debates, Congress altered or jettisoned many central features of the air force plan, which had focused on ways to make the program smaller, easier for students to fit into their schedules, and less technical. The congressional product focused more on citizenship training and visibility. The final Vitalization Act substantially altered the ROTC program in ways that solved some problems, left others unresolved, and created some unintended legacies for later years.

Congressional leaders took issue with certain features of the air force plan for the reform of the ROTC program. Representative Hébert argued that the program should be designed to provide good order on campus.[35] He therefore favored the full four-year program over the service's preferred two-year program. He also opposed the closing of "low-producing" units, as well as the conversion of units to voluntary enrollment, believing that the patriotic value of these units on campus justified their existence, despite their higher per capita costs. Similarly, he opposed the air force's plan to remove military training from campus on the grounds that more, not less, military presence on campus was desirable.

Hébert thus conceptualized the ROTC program as a large and visible program for all male undergraduates at participating institutions. As he said on the House floor during the debates, "As I envision this program, it is something which will bring about a resurgence in this country toward making our youth, not from the cradle, but certainly from the playground on up, conscious of their duty to their country and eager to perform in the service of their country and to be motivated by the highest ideals of citizenship."[36]

Some headquarters officers in both the army and the air force also opposed their ROTC staffs on the issue of on-campus military training. The staffs had hoped to remove such training to summer camps to free up time on campus for other subjects. To many ROTC officers, drill seemed antiquated; junior officers in the more managerial military environment of the 1960s did much less marching than their predecessors had done and were subjected to much less formal discipline. As a 1964 AFROTC report declared, "Today's Air Force has little time or need for yesterday's emphasis on drill."[37] Military managers, in Morris Janowitz's formulation, relied on "the technical proficiency of their team members" not the "formal authority structure" of years past.[38] As the new military was based much more on consensus than authority, devoting hours of valuable on-campus time to drill seemed wasteful. Moving the teaching of drill to summer camps could leave campus ROTC instructors with more time to teach military management, decision making, and critical-thinking skills.

Nevertheless, those at army headquarters pushed for such training to continue on campus "in order to preclude the loss of prestige for the ROTC program and its becoming an extracurricular activity leading to its possible discontinuance."[39] Some officers in the army also believed that to remove drill and other military subjects would marginalize the program: "It is felt that the importance of drill and ceremonies in the cadets' training is such that it must be a part of the curriculum . . . It is anticipated that morale and esprit of the cadets and, in turn, effectiveness of the training [are related to drill] . . . [Removing these subjects] may lead to the ultimate removal of the ROTC program from some campuses."[40] To these officers, abandoning drill meant abandoning the very heart of military training. These men were older, and almost all of them were veterans of the authoritarian military. According to them, removing drill meant eliminating the martial foundations of military training and risking irrevocable damage to the entire chain of command.

To emphasize the continued importance of the four-year program, Hébert authorized the 8,000 scholarships per service called for in the air force proposal, but he added a provision that these scholarships be made available only to students in the four-year program. A two-year program would be created, but its students would receive only a stipend, not the tuition assistance given to selected four-year students. The bill thus opened ROTC to transfer students and men who decided to join ROTC later in their career. However, the four-year program remained the heart of ROTC. Only ten AFROTC units and five AROTC units dropped the four-year program, because to do so meant abandoning access to scholarship money.[41]

The headquarters officers believed, like Hébert, in the principle of universal military service that had been the basis of the draft laws of the 1950s. ROTC service should be visible, they believed, because it was a badge of pride, indicating an individual's commitment to his country. As army headquarters stated: "Every young man has an obligation to contribute to national defense. The college-educated man can best serve his country and his personal interests by earning a commission and fulfilling his obligation as an officer."[42] Reducing the four-year programs, drill, and the visibility of ROTC seemed to threaten a denigration of the principle of military obligation.

The service headquarters officers in the Pentagon were also closer to Congress and more sensitive to broad budgetary issues. Because of this sensitivity and their ideology of universal service, they went against the advice of their ROTC staffs, who counseled them to keep the program small, efficient, and inexpensive. Instead they concurred with the congressional view of the program as a citizenship training course that had to be visible to serve as a model of loyalty and patriotism. The ROTC staffs were primarily interested in a program to produce junior officers. The Congress and the service headquarters wanted that and more.

The law as finally passed had five main features:

1. The addition of a two-year, nonscholarship program.
2. The authorization of 5,500 full scholarships per service for four-year students.
3. The increase of monthly stipends to $50.
4. The authorization of the "cross-enrollment" of students from nearby schools that did not have ROTC units.
5. The reduction of contact hours from 480 to 360.

Three other features of the legislation that were added almost as afterthoughts are illustrative of the difference discussed above between the ROTC staffs and the Congress. Congress required that all advanced ROTC cadets enlist in the reserves. Should the cadet leave ROTC before graduation, he would then become subject to immediate call-up to enlisted service in the reserves. This provision closed a loophole that had permitted students to accept a scholarship, then walk away from ROTC weeks before graduation. The bill also required that contracts with host institutions specify that the highest ranking ROTC instructor be granted the title of professor and, finally, that the institution award "appropriate credit" for ROTC classes. The ROTC staffs had not asked for these features in any of their proposals.

The final bill legislated twice the number of total contact hours in the four-year program than the air force plan had called for (360 as opposed to 180). Furthermore, the law did not specify, as the AFROTC planners had hoped, that the reduction in contact hours should come at the expense of technical military subjects like drill. Reduction of contact hours was at the discretion of unit commanders. Army headquarters recommended eliminating the substitution of civilian-taught courses for those taught by uniformed personnel (see below) and reducing the time spent on academic subjects such as military history, which, of course, contravened the desires of educators.[43] The new curricula, then, affirmed the centrality of technical, military subjects at the expense of liberal arts courses.

These alterations did not damage support for the bill among educators, who rallied to assure passage. University of Illinois president David Henry wrote to Brigadier General William Lindley, "We strongly share your hope that the new ROTC legislation, HR 9124, will be approved by Congress this session," and Kent State president Robert White wrote to Ohio senators to say that he "unreservedly hope[d] for enactment of so-called ROTC bill."[44] Their support was based on a patriotic expectation that the program would be improved by the new legislation, the possibility for greater student participation promised in the bill, and the hope that the new scholarships would mean more money coming from the DOD to the university community. Although the Senate reduced the scholarship authorization from the House's 8,000 per service to 5,500 per service, this was still a dramatic improvement from the previous authorization of 5,500 *total* scholarships, limited to the fifty-three schools with NROTC units.

Still, the bill demonstrated that Congress had different goals for ROTC from those of educators or even some military officers. These differences created a legacy of visibility and adherence to technical military subjects that neither educators nor many ROTC instructors desired. *Newsweek* summed up the debates over the Vitalization Act well when it reported that "some Congressional patriots view the ROTC more as a means of teaching Americanism than of turning out officers."[45]

The Impact of Vitalization

Hébert told the House that his bill would "be the salvation of the free world and a free nation as we know it."[46] While it may not have been exactly that, the Vitalization Act did give ROTC the "new order of battle" that it needed to bring it in line with the mission it had already assumed.[47] It was not, however, exactly what the services and the schools wanted. Those on Capitol Hill and in the Pentagon emphasized the visibility of ROTC and therefore were unwilling to reduce drill or compromise the four-year program, despite recommendations from the program's administrators. To the politicians and headquarters staffs, ROTC represented idealized patriotism and committed self-sacrifice among the nation's college students. They were therefore willing to reject the advice and recommendations of those senior officers directly in charge of the ROTC program.

Those officers wanted to make the program available to more students, and they also wanted a program that would be more acceptable to the university hosts. The hosts wanted to see less drill, both because of its visible contrast to other university programs and because even many ROTC instructors acknowledged that "close order drill in many instances drives men away from the program."[48] The high visibility that the Vitalization Act legislated was an important legacy because it established a priority that educators, and even some military personnel, did not share.

The services' desire to maintain high standards for on-campus technical military preparation meant that reduction in contact hours would have to come from academic subjects. This lack of priority for academic subjects influenced the 1964 ROTC curricula introduced by both the army and the air force. The new curricula deemphasized liberal arts courses and authorized the end of the substitution experiments of the late 1950s. The imminent reduction in the total number of contact hours meant that the services had to make some choices about what they wanted their cadets to learn. They chose to emphasize nonacademic military subjects because they believed that deficiencies in these areas made postcommissioning training more expensive. They also believed that academic subjects were only tangentially related to the military and to the successful completion of the mission of the American junior officer.[49] Before the Vitalization Act, the services had been willing to devote portions of the ROTC curriculum to academic subjects, but when the act mandated a reduction of contact hours, the services demonstrated their preference for nonacademic, military courses.

University administrators, however, were "highly disposed toward this idea of substitution" and were reluctant to give it up.[50] Michigan and Princeton officials argued that the kinds of cognate courses that had been substituted in the past were indeed military in that they were concerned with the political, cultural, technical, and social environment within which military officers operated. Substitution had the additional virtue of making ROTC "fit in with the 'social fabric' of the university campus." At Princeton, this fit meant that ROTC cadets studied such subjects as economics and non-Western societies. Princeton president Robert Clifford protested the end of substitution to Secretary of the Army Stephen Ailes by arguing that "the Army must allow a degree of flexibility in the implementation of the new program so that it may be adapted to individual campus conditions. Each college must be encouraged to participate in the teaching of such courses in so far as its faculty talents permit."[51]

University of Michigan officials also protested the end of substitution, saying that the program had been a "terrific boon" to Michigan ROTC students. Michigan had been in the process of negotiating the substitution of two more courses into the AFROTC curriculum, Aeronautical Engineering and Business Administration, when it was informed that all substituted courses would be removed from the curriculum. Michigan administrative dean Robert Williams told the air force, "Some years ago the Air Force was the leader in this move toward the utilization of one course for two purposes, and it is the judgment of our group that the discontinuance of this practice can result only in harm to our combined efforts."[52]

Their protests fell on deaf ears. The Vitalization Act mandated a drop in contact hours from five to three per week, and the services had decided that technical military courses were more important to their mission than the civilian-taught courses that schools such as Princeton and Michigan wanted to remain a part of ROTC. The original architects of the bill wanted to see the technical courses moved to summer camps in order to continue the substitution programs, but congressional intent promoted the teaching of these subjects on campus to give ROTC visibility and vitality.

The 1964 cancellation of substitution echoed the debates over the initial introduction of substitution in the late 1950s. Those debates had touched on the larger issue of whether ROTC instruction was to be based on education, the general preparation of the cadet's talents through instruction in subject areas with more ecumenical applications, such as non-Western societies and business administration, or training, the more narrow preparation of individual ability to perform such tasks as drill, marksmanship, and map reading. American universities had been moving away from training in undergraduate instruction, even in specialized areas such as engineering and architecture, preferring instead to focus on more general problem-solving and management techniques.

This broad trend had the support of philanthropic groups such as the Ford Foundation, which dispensed $100,000,000 in grant money in the early 1960s through its Special Program in Education. The goal of the Special Program was to encourage "the humanities, natural sciences, and social sciences in cultivating the thoughtful leadership and independent opinion essential in a free society." Five of the six largest recipients of Ford Foundation Special Program in Education grants hosted ROTC programs.[53]

Substitution had thus been extremely popular with educators because it inclined the ROTC program toward the education model they preferred. The termination of substitution demonstrated that the services, despite occasional rhetoric to the contrary, were still inclined toward military training as the heart of their program. This dissonance underscored ROTC's growing divergence from the general trend in higher education. Educators attending a joint army-civilian ROTC meeting at Ohio State University in 1965 warned the army of the growing conflict: "ROTC on the campus is a 'paradox' to many students, since it gives heavy stress to 'training' (drill, rifle practice, map reading, etc.) at the same time instructors in other subjects are attempting to develop the student's conceptual powers through liberal education."[54] Michigan administrative dean Robert Williams warned the ROTC instructional staff in Ann Arbor that ROTC programs could not continue to exist at variance with changes in the general development of higher education:

> I am fully convinced that in the foreseeable future educational philosophy in all areas will demand more and more emphasis on 'principles' and less on 'how to do it' courses. If this be true, the competition for the time of the undergraduate who may wish to secure a commission through ROTC activities will require, in my judgment, (1) full recognition of ROTC courses as general electives within degree requirements, and (2) the critical review of the course content which justifies full utilization of the courses for degree programs.[55]

Close observers of the ROTC program might have noted that in reducing contact hours and endorsing a two-year program, the services were acknowledging that the program was indeed of marginal quality. The services were in fact admitting that they could turn out the same quality product with significantly fewer contact hours. All three ROTC programs developed six-week summer camps to be attended before the student's junior year for men entering the two-year program. This meant, of course, that the services thought that they could teach the first two *years* of the ROTC program in just six *weeks.* And indeed the six-week camp proved adequate; by all accounts, the two-year cadets were every bit the peers of the four-year cadets by the time they reached their senior year.[56]

The addition of the two-year program proved to be a moderate success by providing "greater flexibility in meeting the needs of students interested in obtaining Air Force commissions."[57] The air force claimed that within two years of the Vitalization Act's passage, the new program had served to boost enrollments by attracting men from all four targeted areas. The air force had hoped that the majority of the two-year cadets would come from junior colleges, but air force data indicated that the biggest appeal of the two-year program was to nontransfer students who decided to join ROTC at some point in their freshman or sophomore year. Seventy percent of the AFROTC two-year cadets were nontransfers; only 15 percent came from junior colleges.[58] Evidence from individual units supports this conclusion; by 1966 all of the two-year cadets from Kent State's army ROTC unit were four-year, on-campus students.[59]

The two-year program was more important for schools like the University of Pittsburgh, which then had a system of four regional campuses. The addition of the two-year program allowed the many University of Pittsburgh students who transferred from a branch campus to the Pittsburgh campus to enroll in ROTC in their final two years. Between 1965 and 1967 Pittsburgh's Army ROTC enrollment jumped 50 percent and the instructional staff subsequently grew from six to nine. Pittsburgh professor of military science Lieutenant Colonel Benjamin Hollis credited the two-year program with the enrollment increase.[60] In the same time period, the University of Washington's Army ROTC enrollment rose from 334 to 696, the first rise since Washington had dropped compulsory ROTC in 1962.[61]

The Vitalization Act fulfilled its main quantitative task: in 1967 the air force predicted that ROTC would begin to overproduce by 500 officers and that only twelve units were still producing unacceptably low numbers of officers.[62] But the act also sent some uneasy messages to the careful onlooker. It reduced time spent in the academic cognate courses that civilian officials saw as central to the mission of higher education and maintained the emphasis on the technical, military showpiece courses that the universities saw as most antithetical to their mission. Moreover, the act did not address some important abiding concerns, such as instructor qualification and credit for ROTC courses. Nor did it address the widely held perception that ROTC was so out of step with the new American university that it could not attract men and keep them interested long enough to convince them to pursue military training.

The Life of the Cadet

The main goal of the Vitalization Act was to attract significant numbers of students from groups previously excluded from serving. Even as the ROTC programs were trying to attract new men, however, they were suffering a period of quiet crisis among the men they already had. On campuses nationwide, people concerned with ROTC noted that the enthusiasm of cadets was low and that the program was having trouble keeping students motivated. One observer noted that "quite a few ROTC units wear their uniforms and drill with the precision of fat ladies exercising at the YWCA."[63]

One analysis of this problem argued that the sagging enrollments and enthusiasm were a function of the program's not being sufficiently martial. In this vein, some Army ROTC units, including the one at Rutgers, created Ranger units.[64] Other army units, such as that at the University of Illinois, increased field training and introduced training in airborne and special warfare in order to add "challenge" and "realism" to the ROTC experience.[65] Similarly, the University of Texas AROTC unit added a counterinsurgency branch in 1966.[66] The Illinois unit also established a military counseling office to advise students on the options open to them if they chose a military career.[67]

Another interpretation argued that as graduation requirements increased, students simply had less time and energy to devote to ROTC. The logical solution, of course, would have been to encourage the greater use of substitution, which effectively allowed one class to count twice—once for ROTC credit, once for graduation credit. But of course the services' interpretation of the Vitalization Act discouraged substitution.

If the participants at the 1965 Ohio State conference were right, then many students were having trouble understanding the role of ROTC on the campus. As noted, ROTC was not keeping pace with the general pedagogical trend at American universities of developing student talents through liberal education models. Indeed, the subjects the military and Congress preferred, such as drill and marksmanship, were ill-fitted to such a model.

The ROTC cadets of this era fell largely into two groups. One group of students joined ROTC primarily out of a desire to join the military and perhaps to make the armed forces their career. For this group, ROTC was a means to a commission and, for some, a scholarship. They were particularly attracted to the airborne and special warfare programs started at Illinois, Rutgers, Texas, and elsewhere. A commission in a special warfare unit had become an extremely prestigious military accomplishment since President Kennedy's championship of the Green Berets.

The second group joined ROTC primarily to avoid the draft. By most measures, this group accounted for just under half of the ROTC cadet population.[68] While it is true that until 1970 a student in good standing received a virtually automatic draft deferment, the expanding needs of the American military for manpower owing to the war in Vietnam created uncertainty about the security of student exemptions. In 1952 only 210,693 men were exempted from the draft due to student deferment (known as a 2-S), but by 1965 the explosion of college enrollments meant that 1.8 million men (or 10 percent of the total draft pool) were 2-S. Selective service officials consistently considered the removal of the student deferments as a way to increase the draft pool and lessen the class-based inequities that student deferments implied. By 1967 many politicians, including Massachusetts senator Edward Kennedy, were advocating a random "lottery" system for the draft that would end all blanket exemptions.[69] And of course student exemptions were never permanent; they ended after graduation.

University of Pittsburgh professor of military science (PMS) Lieutenant Colonel Benjamin Hollis explained that the enrollment increase at his unit in 1966 was partially a function of "more sweat being put on the students" by local draft boards.[70] The draft boards, Hollis believed, were putting increasing pressure on students in the lower half of their class by making conscription seem to be a more tangible reality. Consequently, those in the bottom half hoped that ROTC would give them "an additional assurance that they [would] be able to finish college."[71] Such pressure had the paradoxical consequence of encouraging the best students to avoid ROTC while holding out ROTC to the remainder as a means of avoiding conscription.

This dual motivation for ROTC enlistment explains the seemingly contradictory situation of declining enthusiasm on the one hand and the introduction of special warfare training at some units on the other. At least among a portion of the ROTC cadets, interest in the military was not waning; membership in ROTC honor societies was at record levels.[72] Still, on most campuses, a large minority of cadets, many of them not among the best students, were in ROTC primarily because of an interest in *avoiding* military service. It was largely due to the insouciance of this group that outside observers noted increased sloppiness and apathy in ROTC training. This quiet crisis for ROTC was exacerbated by the inability of the universities and the military to resolve many of their abiding concerns over academic issues.

Sometimes the actions of ROTC units themselves reinforced negative stereotypes, confirming the antimilitary beliefs of some and driving some young men away. In 1966 the Army ROTC unit at Worcester Polytechnical Institute held a "mock invasion" of the town of Middleboro, Massachusetts. At dawn on a May morning, ROTC cadets in full uniform moved through the town carrying weapons. The unit, however, had failed to inform town officials, resulting in "a police switchboard jammed with calls from frightened residents reporting suspicious looking characters in the neighborhood."[73]

The Middleboro incident and an incident at the University of Washington in 1967 both made national news and created significant negative publicity for ROTC. Washington cadets had received a secret briefing (no notes and no outside discussion permitted) on "subversive" groups at the university, including SDS and the civil rights group the Student Nonviolent Coordinating Committee (SNCC). Then, in "an attempt to add realism to our Brigade Staff training," cadets were ordered to collect posters and information on the groups and any students or faculty who belonged to such groups.[74] One cadet refused to participate and may have been the individual who leaked the story to the American Association of University Professors (AAUP) and the American Civil Liberties Union (ACLU) in Seattle.

Once the story became public, Washington president Charles Odegaard ordered that the "spy" exercise be stopped. The Washington PMS at first denied that any such operation had been ordered, then recanted when a brigade S-2 (intelligence) file on "left wing activities" emerged. The ROTC file told cadets that persons or groups that opposed the war in Vietnam "were in fact our enemies." The PMS later refused to show President Odegaard the briefing materials on the grounds that they were secret, because the university was then in the process of removing credit for any course (including two NROTC classes) that used classified materials.[75]

Despite attempts by all parties to keep the scandal out of the spotlight, the case made national news, appearing in newspapers from San Francisco to New York. In Seattle, the fallout over what became known as the "duck scandal" proved to be quite damaging for ROTC.[76] The duck scandal produced the first serious challenge to military training in the University of Washington's history. Professors and students charged that ROTC had "violat[ed] the canons of academic freedom, especially the principle of free and open exchange of knowledge."[77] The controversy eventually blew over, but it left a shadow on ROTC at the University of Washington and elsewhere that contributed to an overall unease with military training on civilian campuses.

Abiding Concerns

Of the issues left unresolved from the Cold War era, academic credit and instructor qualifications were the two most often debated. ROTC instructors were not more formally educated than their counterparts from the 1950s had been, despite service protestations to the contrary, and they were not the "top flight" men the services needed in order to improve relations with the host schools.[78] The services assumed that "men who have discharged responsibilities successfully in other assignments will do so in this one."[79] Moreover, as information and education both grew more complex, the need for technically proficient and experienced instructors became even greater. After passage of the Vitalization Act, all three services added programs to teach their instructors how to teach, but these programs were usually perfunctory two- to three-week courses that hardly provided the academic credentials of collegiate teaching experience and advanced degrees.

Of the 196 officers assigned to AFROTC duty in 1964, only 36 (18 percent) had an advanced degree; this figure was actually much lower than the 27 percent of ROTC instructors already on assignment that year who possessed an advanced degree. The air force continued to hold to the idea that it was more important to assign young officers than to assign formally educated ones. No officer assigned to AFROTC duty that year was older than forty-eight; only one had attained the rank of full colonel.[80] The navy was only slightly more able to assign officers with advanced degrees; 28 percent of its instructors were so qualified in 1965.[81]

The services had taken great pains to advertise that ROTC duty was "definitely not a 'last assignment' before retirement," as it had once been.[82] Nevertheless, the services used ROTC duty as a reward for men who had recently completed an overseas tour of duty; volunteers for ROTC assignments continued to get priority. Eighty-five percent of AFROTC officers took their appointment while completing an overseas tour of duty, meaning that the universities were unable to interview the candidates and that factors other than qualifications and teaching experience determined assignments to ROTC units.

The services and the universities agreed that the assignment of formally educated officers was an important goal and would, if attained, improve military-university relations. Two successive University of Illinois professors of military science argued in their annual reports that the university should insist on men with master's degrees, as they would be "ambassador(s) for the United States Army."[83] They further argued that men with advanced degrees made the job easier by becoming more a part of the university and its value system: "Officer personnel should either possess graduate degrees or be qualified and interested in graduate study. It is essential to overcome the objection that our officers lack professional academic credentials. Those officers who possess graduate degrees are more acceptable to the professional academicians, and those officers who pursue graduate study are invaluable as intelligent advocates of the program on the academician's home ground."[84] Those at AFROTC headquarters, while not placing a priority on formal education, understood that the job of the PAS "takes them into areas of [the] academician while remaining a professional Air Force officer. This requires the utmost in background, interest and versatility to properly fit into this academic environment."[85]

But if a general consensus existed that formally educated officers made the ROTC-university relationship easier and instruction better, the services still made no determined effort to assign more ROTC officers with advanced degrees. Two problems inhibited such assignments. First, the services simply did not have many officers with master's degrees whom they could assign to ROTC units. While the 28 percent of NROTC instructors with a master's degree in 1965 may seem itself a small number, only 12 percent of all naval officers had a master's degree.[86] Simply put, the number of officers who had an advanced degree was very small, and many of them served in highly specialized areas from which they could not easily be reassigned. Thus even when the services and the universities could agree on the necessity and value of formally educated officers, personnel realities meant that, in the words of a joint university-navy board, "the achievement of this goal [was] going to take time."[87]

Second, the personnel assignment calculus, difficult under ideal circumstances, became even more chaotic as officers were assigned in greater number to Southeast Asia. The war changed officer assignment priorities and forced the universities to an initial position of lenience toward the services. If the services needed officers for the war, the universities could hardly insist that ROTC assignments take precedence over providing leadership for what was then seen by many as a war against communism. As the University of Illinois provost told the army in 1966, "While we normally expect that faculty nominees at the assistant professorial level possess doctoral academic credentials or, at a minimum, the equivalent of a Master's Degree, I am in agreement with our Professor of Military Science that an exception may be made at this time because of the severe personnel problems generated by the situation in Viet Nam."[88]

All universities had to deal with the limitations of the service personnel systems. The services genuinely wanted to assign "only officers of demonstrated competence, vigor, and initiative" to ROTC units, but they were constrained from doing so.[89] To compensate for the comparatively low level of instructor education, some schools began or expanded seminar programs that featured lectures by civilian faculty on issues relevant to global military systems. In 1966–67, the Illinois seminar program featured talks entitled "The Indian Army and India's Military Potential," "The Role of the United States in Southeast Asia," "Soviet Attitudes," "Military-State Relationships in Germany," "The Role of the United States in World Affairs," "Soviet Foreign Policy," "Military-Civilian Relationships in Latin America, and "Chinese Foreign Policy."[90]

Because instructor qualifications did not rise as the universities had hoped, resolution of the question of academic credit remained difficult. The services had also reduced time spent on academic subjects while maintaining the number of contact hours in courses, like drill, that the universities had determined were least worthy of credit. According to national ROTC curriculum models, drill and military ceremony were to constitute one-third of the cadet's total contact hours.

Academic opinion of ROTC course quality dropped significantly when the new curriculum models were introduced. A 1965 review of the ROTC programs at the University of Washington found the new programs "not rigorous in the usual academic sense." Washington officials pushed for NROTC instructors to audit civilian courses in order to "be introduced to new teaching methods." ROTC courses, they alleged, focused too much on "approved solutions" and "housekeeping chores." Cadets and midshipmen, they argued, were "indoctrinated," not taught. Their analysis found that ROTC graduates were "not capable of . . . sophistication of argument" and received inflated grades. In one quarter, 72 percent of ROTC grades were A's and B's, when the College of Arts and Sciences only awarded 44 percent A's and B's. That same quarter, only 2 percent of ROTC students received D's and F's; 16 percent of students in the College of Arts and Sciences received D's and F's.[91]

The new evaluations contrasted with the enthusiasm the services them-selves had for their curricula. The services advertised their courses as follow-ing the creative model of liberal education, not the "how to do it" model of the past. Still, the goals of ROTC were narrower than those of civilian edu-cational programs. The air force introduced its 1964 curriculum thus: "[AFROTC's] emphasis is on education—*professional education*. The basic goal of this professional education is to provide the military knowledge and skills needed by the cadets on the day they become Air Force second lieuten-ants."[92] The services nevertheless argued that their courses were enough like civilian courses to merit academic credit on the same basis.

The ROTC staff officers, however, were of mixed opinion as to exactly *why* it was important that the universities extend full credit to ROTC courses. On the surface, of course, it seemed intuitive that maximum academic credit would encourage more students to enroll and would also make ROTC a more central part of the school's general academic offerings. At the same time, insisting too forcefully on more credit carried with it the risk of offend-ing university faculties who jealously guarded their right to determine which courses merited credit, the ultimate stamp of official approval. Fur-thermore, both the air force and the army had conducted studies that ar-gued that the amount of credit awarded bore no relation to the quality of ROTC graduates produced and affected enrollment only in engineering pro-grams.[93]

The army's official policy, then, was for a PMS to press for more credit only if such a move would clearly benefit the program, although on a na-tional level the army still lobbied educators for credit as recognition of the ROTC curriculum's educational merit. The air force and navy, however, were more insistent. The air force had determined that only 50 of its 170 host schools awarded "full effective credit" in all degree programs, and it pressed for an increase nationwide at the 1966 meeting of the AFROTC Ad-visory Panel:

We believe that the Air Force has a responsibility to both the students and the institutions to offer courses that have academic substance and are pre-sented in a manner in harmony with the educational goals of the host insti-tution. We think that students taking ROTC courses on the campus should receive academic credit for these courses on the same basis that they would for other campus offerings. We recognize that academic credit is a matter for local faculty determination and we seek only to have our course offerings examined on their merit.[94]

With one-third of the AFROTC curriculum dedicated to drill and military ceremony, the air force's plea for evaluation of its courses "on their merit" made it easy for university faculties consistently to deny service requests to increase credit, although reductions in credit were also rare.

The universities continued to insist that if the services wanted their ROTC programs to carry more academic credit, they would need to be strengthened. The Army Advisory Panel on ROTC Affairs meeting in 1967 was almost wholly dedicated to the issue of credit. Educators told the army that to receive more credit, its courses would need to devote more attention to academic subjects, be taught by men with advanced degrees, and "serve an education need for future leaders, civilian as well as military." The panel suggested that the army fund programs in "team-teaching," classes taught by both civilian and military instructors, until enough officers with advanced degrees arrived on ROTC staffs.

Civilian faculties resisted giving ROTC credit for courses that they believed could be better taught in regular university departments. Thus, in 1965 the University of Texas College of Arts and Sciences Course Committee rejected a proposed basic AFROTC academic program that included courses that overlapped with offerings in the history and government departments: "The Committee does not consider that certain portions of the subject matter content of these courses should be taught by professional military officers. It is the contention of some members of the Faculty that the subject matter in question (Democracy, Communism, etc.) is purely academic and that an objective presentation of it could not be given by military personnel obligated to conform to establish[ed] Defense Department policy.[95] University officials proposed that the air force either return to substitution to allow civilian faculty to teach these courses or develop a purely technical curriculum for which the university would grant credit. The University of Texas was thus willing to give ROTC credit for teaching military subjects within the range of the instructor's expertise, but not for academic subjects generally understood to be outside their purview.

In other words, the universities, despite general official support, informed the services that if they wanted ROTC to receive more academic credit, they would have to improve the academic value of the program. The centrality of ROTC to national security warranted the program's survival, but it no longer provided sufficient justification to merit further university concessions to the program. These debates were unrelated to the growing, but still minor, opposition on campuses nationwide to the expanding war in Southeast Asia. Rather they were issues that remained from the Cold War. The war in Vietnam was, however, coming to occupy more of the nation's energy and drawing more attention from critics.

Vietnam's Early Impact on ROTC

President Lyndon Johnson's decision in August 1964 to ask for a congressional resolution to prosecute the war in Vietnam provoked few immediate negative reactions on American campuses. Congress passed the resolution with only two dissenting votes, and by all accounts the American people were in agreement. According to one poll, 67 percent of the American people supported Johnson in February 1965 after he ordered the series of punitive bombings known as Rolling Thunder in retaliation for a Viet Cong attack on an American airbase.[96]

By the end of 1965 American planes had flown 25,000 sorties and dropped 63,000 tons of bombs on Vietnam. In July President Johnson had promised General William Westmoreland 100,000 American troops, in addition to the 40,000 already in Vietnam, to allow Westmoreland to begin "search and destroy" operations against the Viet Cong.[97] These events still had no demonstrably negative impact on ROTC units nationwide. The University of Illinois Army ROTC unit even noted "a definite trend towards improved attitudes towards ROTC" in the fall of 1965.[98] The only immediate impact of the war may have been to boost enrollments; many analysts cited students' attempts to avoid being conscripted into the war, not the Vitalization Act, for the rising ROTC enrollments.

Still, as the war casualties and questions mounted, so did student opposition. ROTC instructional staffs endeavored to stay out of campus debates. In September 1965, when an antiwar poster was glued to an ROTC bulletin board at the University of Pittsburgh, Lieutenant Colonel Benjamin Hollis chose not to take any action himself; instead he handed the poster over to university police and told the chancellor that he hoped to "avoid publicity." Hollis argued that most members of the University of Pittsburgh community were either supportive of or indifferent to ROTC and that to seek a confrontation would only play into the hands of the antiwar students and faculty.[99]

The New Left, which led the antiwar movement, had not yet begun to oppose ROTC because of the program's connection to the war in Vietnam. At schools such as Kent State, ROTC cadets had the unenviable job of presenting colors to the next of kin of a local soldier or airman killed in Vietnam, but no other visible links yet existed. ROTC cadets had not yet begun to go to

Vietnam in large numbers, and few Vietnam veterans had returned from overseas to serve as ROTC instructors. Initial campus opposition to ROTC, then, was not focused, as it would be later, on ROTC's production of officers necessary for the war.

Instead, student opposition to ROTC focused on those traditional points of conflict that remained from the 1950s. A fall 1967 rally at the University of Pittsburgh featured signs that read "No Tenure for Sergeants" and "Intellectualism, Not Militarism."[100] Even Pittsburgh's most implacable ROTC foe, psychology professor James Holland, took his stand not because of the war but "because [ROTC] is so out of step with University policy."[101] Similarly, at Rutgers, student body president Ray Korona spoke out against ROTC's teaching methods rather than its link to the war in Southeast Asia.[102] While the war may have made ROTC foes more assertive, it did not initially provide new reasons to call for the program's reform or abolition. The principle objections to ROTC remained those based on the basic discrepancies between ROTC and other university programs.

Until 1968 the American people, including most of those in university communities, generally supported the war. As late as October 1967, 53 percent of Americans favored *escalation* of the war.[103] Most campuses were not hotbeds of activism during this early period of antiwar sentiment. For example, the Rutgers chapter of SDS received only five responses to its mass mailing of a student referendum on ROTC in 1967.[104] Still, a growing number of people were coming to challenge American intervention in Vietnam. The problem was not yet serious enough to cause ROTC staffs to address the problem on a national level, but ROTC unit heads were beginning to take note.

The question of the appropriate response to antiwar demonstrators was a topic of much informal conversation at the 1967 conference of professors of military science, held at Ft. Meade. Kent State's PMS expressed the consensus of the conference in a letter to Kent State president Robert White:

> To my knowledge no overt opposition to our programs has been evident [as a result of anti-Vietnam feelings]. My position to both my cadre and cadets is that we will avoid any confrontation with campus groups which might demonstrate or harangue against us—I would hope that we could totally ignore them . . . [Kent State] is not a military reservation or defense installation and groups have every right to their existence in order that each student and faculty member may have a wide range of ideas from which to

choose—the right to question is fundamental. Excuse the soapbox, but I want to do everything possible from my position to prevent, before it is even a possibility, any fracas between hotheads on both sides.[105]

The same year, the PMS at Rutgers defended the rights of twenty-seven demonstrators who blocked an ROTC drill period. He also supported the mild punishment (disciplinary probation) given by the university's disciplinary board.[106]

ROTC officers were caught in a difficult position. If they made statements deemed contrary to the aims of the military, they were in violation of the values of their profession and possibly faced sanction from above. If they remained silent or stuck to the rhetoric emanating from the Pentagon, they were accused of not tolerating academic freedom or objectivity. Most officers, anticipating that their futures were as military professionals, not academics, chose silence. This tactic was more than a product of self-interest; it was also intended to keep ROTC out of campus debates. Instead, however, it opened ROTC officers to new charges of anti-intellectualism. Military officers across the nation hoped to keep antiwar sentiment from affecting ROTC programs. Until 1968, they were largely able to do so. But after 1968 the visibility that the Vitalization Act mandated would contribute to the sternest challenge in the history of the program to the place and order of ROTC.

The debates over the passage and implementation of the ROTC Vitalization Act demonstrate two important points. First, serious problems in ROTC predated later challenges that were related to anti-Vietnam sentiment. Even without rising antiwar sentiment, the program was approaching a period of crisis in terms of the quantity and quality of cadets produced, its relations with the university hosts, and the direction of the ROTC curriculum. The problems that ROTC encountered after 1968, then, were not entirely new. They had roots that went back to the 1950s and were encouraged by major changes that accompanied the Vitalization Act of 1964.

Second, the Vitalization Act shows that the military, Congress, and higher education had different goals and directions in mind for ROTC. Several military officers lobbied for changes that reflected the civilization, innovation, and diversification that Janowitz has described. They argued that as the United States military began to assume a more constabulary role (both at home and abroad), junior officers would need to have a better understanding of politics, history, and management.[107] For the most part, educators were sympathetic to this view because it was more in line with their own understanding of how the on-campus portion of military training should be conducted.

This view, however, was at odds with an older position that emphasized military ceremony and drill as a means of achieving order and discipline. Proponents F. Edward Hébert and others were less interested in increasing the efficiency of the armed forces than they were in using the authority and hierarchy that they saw in the military to promote patriotism and civic virtue. Drill became a focal point in the debate, symbolizing either outdated, automatonic mindlessness or orderly ceremony.

The compromise between these two viewpoints delayed the implementation of an ROTC curriculum centered around problem-solving educational techniques similar to those used by civilian faculty. By maintaining an outdated image of the military, the Vitalization Act highlighted the most objectionable features of ROTC. Furthermore, by contravening or ignoring the wishes of the air force architects of ROTC reform, the bill also left several critical problems unresolved. As a result, ROTC was poorly positioned for the battles ahead.

CHAPTER 5

ROTC from Tet to the All-Volunteer Force

Those who fear the rise of an American Foreign Legion, loyal only to its own officers, must see that the fastest way of bringing such an organization about is to abandon the ROTC. For America's sake, let's strengthen the ROTC, not destroy it.

—Georgia Tech *Technique,* May 17, 1970

Before the 1968 Vietnamese lunar new year, known as Tet, the majority of Americans believed the proclamations of the American military and political establishments that the war, while not yet won, was clearly under control and that victory was certain. However, within hours of the start of what became known as the Tet offensive on January 30, millions of Americans had reason to doubt all that they had been told. On hearing early reports of the attacks, one of America's most respected journalists, Walter Cronkite, shouted, "What the hell is going on? I thought we were winning the war!"[1] As the bombing of Pearl Harbor had done a generation earlier, Tet changed the American approach to war almost overnight and, eventually, ended Robert McNamara's reign as secretary of defense, General William Westmoreland's position as head of American forces in Southeast Asia, and the Johnson presidency itself.

The Viet Cong used American overconfidence as well as the noise, heavy traffic, and thirty-six-hour cease-fire for the Tet holiday to disguise a series of well-coordinated attacks on five of South Vietnam's six largest cities, thirty-six of South Vietnam's forty-four provincial capitals, sixty-four of its district capitals, Tan Son Nhut Airport, the presidential palace in Saigon, and the headquarters of the South Vietnamese general staff. Nineteen Viet Cong soldiers even got inside the new American embassy in Saigon.

The Tet offensive created a psychological collapse in the United States and a dramatic shift in attitudes toward the war. Robert Kennedy argued that Tet had "finally shattered the mask of official illusion with which we have concealed our true circumstances, even from ourselves."[2] Some opposition to the war had been steadily growing throughout 1967 as the personnel needs of the army had forced the conscription of recent college graduates and as the financial costs of the war had ballooned to $33 billion per year, provoking inflation.[3] Tet, however, was the watershed; in March 1968, for the first time, the percentage of Americans calling themselves Doves exceeded the percentage calling themselves Hawks.[4] After Tet, support for the war fell sharply among Republicans, Democrats, and Independents alike.[5]

Of course, Tet alone did not create the "dissolution of consensus" on American campuses in the late 1960s.[6] Civil rights issues and questions of university procedures regarding defense contracts had already caused contention. But Tet marked a dramatic turning point that "breathed life into languishing American liberalism" and forced a complete reexamination of both the war and the place of the military in American society:[7] "What mattered to the American public what that this [supposedly] defeated enemy could attack anywhere and was attacking everywhere more fiercely than before. The winning of the war was not coming 'into view.' The war in Vietnam was never going to be won. Nothing had been achieved by the outpouring of lives and treasure and the rending of American society. The assurances the public had been given were the lies and vaporings of foolish men."[8] After Tet, the battles in Southeast Asia and the debates on American campuses took on a whole new dimension.

"Like an Embassy on Foreign Soil"

Just as the American public's response to the war changed sharply as a result of Tet, so too did university attitudes change toward ROTC. As noted earlier, ROTC's position on the campus had always been somewhat uneasy, but official approbation and the perception of ROTC's contribution to national security had provided it with, if not universal support, a general level of approval at best, indifference at worst. Tet cast a shadow of doubt on the national security justifications of the American military system in general and on ROTC as a manifestation of the military. On the campuses, this sentiment produced an air of suspicion and incertitude. By the end of March, ROTC officers were beginning to talk about their unit in words similar to the army's professor of military science at Michigan State, who likened his assignment to being at "an embassy on foreign soil."[9] The level of outright hostility and violence varied significantly from campus to campus, but on most campuses ROTC's prestige dropped significantly after Tet.

Tet also enlivened and accelerated the politicization of college students, many of whom were already active in such causes as the civil rights movement. Many radical students were, in Tom Hayden's words in October 1968 to the National Commission on the Causes and Prevention of Violence, "moving toward confrontation" as a means of protest, and many less radical students were paying increasing attention to controversial issues on campus and across the nation.[10] Political views on many American campuses were moving to the left, challenging the status quo and the nature of university links to the military, the intelligence community, and the giants of the defense industry, to name but a few.

As a manifestation of this sentiment, forty-five AFROTC units reported "verbal abuse, sit-ins, placards, pamphlets, and anti-ROTC articles in both official and unofficial campus newspapers" between February and June 1968.[11] Most protests against ROTC were peaceful; national events, such as the assassinations of Martin Luther King in April and Robert Kennedy in June, created heightened tension but no real violence. The ROTC cadre's policy of not getting involved in campus confrontations surely helped to keep protests nonviolent.

But just as some military officers had predicted, the visibility of drill and military ceremony legislated into ROTC through the 1964 Vitalization Act (see Chapter 4) made ROTC more of a target than it might otherwise have been by highlighting exactly the features of the program that were most objectionable to university communities. Outdoor drill sessions were the scene of virtually all of the anti-ROTC activities reported by AFROTC units to air force headquarters in 1968.[12] While these confrontations rarely provoked violence, they added to the tension and mutual mistrust that was building between on-campus military personnel and student protesters.

For the most part, ROTC officers and cadets remained apart from the protests. Only on rare occasions did they confront student protesters, and when they did the results were quite damaging to the already declining status of ROTC. To cite one example, in October 1968 an army master sergeant assigned to the University of Pittsburgh ROTC staff approached a protester who was wearing a jacket adorned with army medals he had purchased at a military surplus store. The sergeant demanded that the protester remove the medals. The protester refused but invited the sergeant to cut them off if he was offended; the sergeant did.

The incident seems minor enough in retrospect; there was no violence and it did not incite further action from either side. Still, the reaction of the university community gave ROTC units a sufficient reminder of why they should try to be nonconfrontational. The Pittsburgh student newspaper reported the incident as "ROTC versus 'Democracy'" and argued that the event served as a vivid example of why ROTC had no place on campus. "This blatant act of assault, without any legal authority to act, was shocking to everyone who witnessed it. But in effect, the action taken by [the] Sergeant . . . is a microcosmic example of the problem that ROTC presents to this university in particular, and to the entire higher educational system in general."[13]

Interestingly, Pittsburgh's PMS, Colonel David Clagett, did not defend the sergeant or try to justify his actions. Instead, he reiterated the position of his department: "The policy of the Department of Military Science has been and is that members of the department will not in any way interfere with students or student activities. This is the first time such an incident has occurred and it will not be repeated." That same day, the sergeant apologized to the student, saying that he had "acted *as an individual* and did exercise poor judgment."[14] The position of ROTC units, then, was clear. They would try, despite the visibility Congress had mandated into the program, to remain apart from antiwar activity. The mood on college campuses was becoming ever more hostile to the military; confrontations only aggravated the problem.

The air force also counseled its ROTC instructors not to use a "response of force" to protesters, but to try a "peace offensive" characterized by "curiosity, open-mindedness, and empathy." Through these actions, the air force argued, "we can contribute to the remodeling of the military image in the eyes of students, publicize the mission of the AFROTC, and in on our small way, help close the barrier between adults and youth in this critical generation."[15]

For many members of that generation, the link between ROTC and the war in Vietnam had come to symbolize the Faustian militarization of many American institutions, including the universities. For others, the war and attendant antimilitary feelings on campuses nationwide had dramatically reduced the prestige of the military and inclined many against pursuing a military career. Even those already in ROTC were chafing at the program's discipline more than they had in the past. Both by demanding a new approach and by simply staying away from the program, undergraduates were pushing for change.

Total ROTC enrollments fell dramatically, from 218,466 in October 1968 to 161,507 one year later, a drop of more than 25 percent.[16] After producing a record number of commissions in 1968 (largely as a result of the reforms introduced by the Vitalization Act) ROTC enrollments declined in 1969 at all but two schools nationwide, Kearney State (Nebraska) and Southern Colorado State.[17] The ninety NASULGC schools reported a 22 percent drop in ROTC enrollments among member institutions.[18] University of Michigan ROTC enrollments fell 31 percent from academic year 1967–68 to academic year 1968–69; in the same time period University of Illinois enrollments fell 38 percent.[19] Evidence from freshman enrollments portended even more serious problems in the future. One hundred seventy-four freshmen had enrolled in AFROTC at the University of Pittsburgh in the fall of 1968; only 34 freshmen did so one year later.[20] At Illinois, total freshman ROTC enrollments fell from 376 in 1968 to 182 in 1969.[21]

Some military officers tried to make a simplistic connection between the end of academic credit for ROTC at many schools and the lower enrollment levels, but it is clear that much more was happening. Enrollments dropped just as sharply at schools where the amount of credit awarded did not change. More important than credit, ROTC had ceased to carry the prestige it had in the past. Only one in four AFROTC cadets surveyed in 1968 described the prevailing attitude toward ROTC cadets on their campus as "highly favorable" or "mildly favorable."[22] The *Wall Street Journal* noted in 1968 that "a few college girls wouldn't be caught dead dating an ROTC cadet."[23] Once a badge of patriotism, ROTC had become a stigma. Even at Georgia Tech, where "anti-ROTC peer pressure was minimal," the army's PMS asked that campus security guards, not cadets, lower the American flag at the end of each day to "lessen the military profile on campus to the minimal reasonable level."[24]

Furthermore, after Tet, the character of the war in Southeast Asia itself changed. With the official goals of the war and sanguine proclamations of progress largely discredited (along with the beginnings of troop withdrawals in 1969) fewer men went to war because of an ideological belief in the purpose of American involvement. Many soldiers fought simply to remain alive, not to achieve murky military and political goals. After Tet the war became bloodier, racial tension among American forces became rampant, drug use among the men soared, and discipline in some units broke down entirely. In 1970 alone, 2,000 incidents of "fragging," attacks by enlisted men on their own officers, were reported.[25] As Neil Sheehan, a careful observer of the war from its outset, noted:

> The riflemen who had fought with Hal Moore in the valley of the Drang [in 1965] and at Bong Son [in 1966] would not have recognized the U.S. Army of 1969. It was an Army in which men escaped into marijuana and heroin and other men died because their comrades were "stoned" on drugs that profited the Chinese traffickers and the Saigon generals. It was an Army whose units in the field were on the edge of mutiny, whose soldiers rebelled against the senselessness of their sacrifice by assassinating officers and noncoms in "accidental" shootings and "fraggings" with grenades.[26]

Before Tet, many men had joined ROTC out of a desire to have some control over their military service, not to avoid it. After Tet, service in ROTC was seen to carry with it the possibility of assignment to the more brutal, less meaningful war of the post-Tet era.[27]

The introduction of the draft lottery in 1969 meant a further change in the quality and quantity of ROTC cadets. The lottery system ended the blanket service exemptions previously given to undergraduates in good standing. Instead, in December 1968 the selective service system randomly assigned a draft number to each day of the year and then to each man between age nineteen and twenty-six, based on his date of birth; thereafter an individual's chance of being drafted depended on his draft number. Men born on June 8, for example, no longer had anything to fear from conscription, for they had the highest number, 365.[28]

The lottery brought an end to much of the speculation that had characterized the draft. Now a man knew more precisely his chances of being drafted. For men with high draft numbers, ROTC no longer had to serve as a means of avoiding military service. One DOD study concluded that one-third of ROTC cadets nationwide dropped out after the lottery system was introduced and that the overwhelming majority of those men held high draft numbers.[29] In 1971 only 13 percent of AFROTC cadets had draft numbers higher than 280.[30]

For men with low draft numbers, conversely, ROTC could serve as a way to avoid conscription. In 1970, nearly half (46 percent) of AFROTC sophomores said that they had joined ROTC because "it was AFROTC or the draft."[31] One year later, 33 percent of AFROTC cadets had draft numbers lower than 80; that is, one-third of the cadets were among the one-fifth of males most likely to be drafted.[32] Enrolling in ROTC offered an option to those who found other means of evading the draft unappealing. ROTC might keep a man on campus long enough for the war to end, or, if military service was inevitable or desirable, at least give the man some say as to which branch of the service he entered. Army ROTC experienced the sharpest enrollment declines, partially because of the perception that the army and marines bore a heavier casualty burden than either the air force or the navy. To many, a commission in one of the latter two services seemed to offer a way to fulfill one's military obligation with less risk. As the saying went, "There ain't no Viet Cong submarines."

The services were certainly aware of the impact of the lottery system; the ROTC units often used it as recruitment tool "woo[ing] university students with promises of safe assignments and deferred enlistments."[33] The University of Pittsburgh Army ROTC unit even displayed a poster in 1969 that read, "Want to Beat the Draft? Enroll in the 2-Year ROTC Program."[34] The two-year program became especially popular with sophomores who had just drawn a low draft number and were therefore suddenly more vulnerable to conscription. Georgia Tech's AROTC program advertised that for two-year cadets, "a draft deferment is authorized and takes priority over a previously issued draft notice."[35] In other words, enlisting in ROTC could defer the draft notice that had arrived in a young man's mailbox the day before.

University officials, like Georgia Tech president Arthur Hansen, understood that "draft pressure is overwhelmingly the primary reason for ROTC enrollment."[36] Most studies concluded that anywhere from 35 percent to 60 percent of ROTC cadets were motivated by the draft. One study argued that only 31 percent of ROTC students from schools in the Northeast and 45 percent of ROTC students from schools in the South were "true volunteers" who would have joined ROTC in the absence of the draft.[37] Using ROTC to control the timing and nature of one's military service existed before this era, but now perhaps half of the cadets were using ROTC primarily to avoid the draft.[38]

Given that so many ROTC students enrolled primarily to avoid the draft, it is not surprising that the character of the program changed. Yale president Kingman Brewster argued throughout this period that a system of conscription with student exemptions had turned the nation's colleges and universities into a draft haven, thereby creating "sourness" toward both higher education and the military.[39] This sentiment certainly made it down to ROTC units. Just as the blanket student exemptions had caused many men to enter or remain in college to avoid the draft more than to learn, so did the draft cause significant numbers of men to join ROTC to avoid the war more than to satisfy a desire to be in ROTC. As more of these men joined ROTC units and as the prestige of these units on campus fell, cadets began to object to many ROTC requirements that made them stand out from their peers and thus made them easy targets for ridicule.

Not surprisingly, cadets focused on hair and uniform requirements as the two military regulations that most visibly separated them from their non-ROTC classmates. One study of AFROTC dropouts at the University of Massachusetts found that half of them left the program because of appearance requirements and their "unwillingness to wear the uniform on campus."[40] Similarly, University of California officials noted that uniform requirements were cited most frequently in cadet complaints about ROTC.[41] In 1970, two AFROTC cadets from Michigan State University wrote a seventy-four-page paper "challenging the morality, legality and practicality of Air Force regulations governing permissible coifs, mustaches, and beards," an act of recalcitrance unthinkable before Tet. Their report was intended to demonstrate that the military's insistence on crew cuts was not only irrational but also counterproductive: "The cadets cite evidence indicating that students with crew cuts are at a disadvantage with girls and that they are subject to the ridicule of fellow students and teachers. They also allege that the corps' image, which is under attack at Michigan State and many other campuses, would be improved if hair were left a matter of individual preference and that the recruiting of candidates would become easier."[42] Or, as the girlfriend of one University of Pittsburgh cadet warned his instructor, "Your stupid haircut regulations are going to break up our relationship!"[43]

"Those Which Are Hardest to Defend"

The most radical students and faculty held to a position, vocally espoused by groups such as the Students for a Democratic Society, that the goals of ROTC and the goals of the American university could never be reconciled. ROTC, they argued, "is not only antithetical to the ultimate purposes of higher education, but contrary to basic pedagogical principles as well [because of] the unquestioning submissiveness endemic in the rigidly hierarchical structure of military education."[44] They sought expulsion of ROTC, not reform, because in their eyes ROTC was "an island of indoctrination in a sea of academic freedom."[45]

The radicals also opposed ROTC because, they argued, the program turned the university into an "officer factory." SDS contended in 1970 that "ROTC . . . produces the officers essential for continuing the United States' genocidal war in South East Asia."[46] At a 1969 rally at the University of Washington, SDS members argued that "ROTC is as much a part of the exploitation in Latin America as the United Fruit Company. In order to help the liberation struggles in the Third World we must fight the military as well as the corporation."[47] The logical extension of this argument was that the universities were complicit in the immorality of the war in Southeast Asia (and elsewhere) by permitting the services to train future officers on campus:

> If the university's role in cooperating with ROTC is the production of officers, our universities have become, in part, mere extension schools of our government's military establishment . . . The university continues to provide the tools to make possible policies such as those which led the U.S. into war in Asia . . . The university has granted the government the same moral sanction that the Krupp Industries gave the German government during World War II when it supplied the Reich with arms and munitions.[48]

The radical position occasionally found violent outlets, especially in 1969 and 1970 (see Table 5.1). The number of AFROTC units reporting hostile activity rose from 45 in academic year 1967–68 to 131 in 1968–69.[49] Eighty-two units reported physical damage to their buildings in 1970.[50] The type and amount of anti-ROTC activity varied widely from school to school. Of

Table 5.1 Anti-ROTC incidents reported by AFROTC units, by type and academic year

Type of incident	1969–70	1970–71
Major damage/injury	55	16
Minor damage/injury	138	34
Disruptive demonstrations	37	4
Official studies	175	59
Threats of disruption or violence	90	54
Nonviolent demonstrations	180	74

Source: "AFROTC/Host Institutional Activities" (1972), University of Illinois Archives, President John Corbally Papers, Box 33, ROTC–Air Force.

the universities studied most systematically here, the University of Michigan experienced by far the highest number of violent disruptions. In 1969–70 alone, Ann Arbor ROTC units reported six major incidents, including a dynamite explosion, a fire, a three-day occupation of the ROTC building, severe damage to ROTC vehicles, and a night of demonstrations that left the ROTC building with forty broken windows.[51] At Kent State, protesters burned the ROTC building and cut the hoses of fire fighters sent to douse the flames, just two days before the Ohio National Guard shot and killed four KSU students, including, ironically, an ROTC student who was observing the demonstration. Georgia Tech, Kansas State, Pittsburgh, and Illinois, however, reported no incidents of similar severity. In fact, a "Smash ROTC" demonstration planned at Illinois in response to the Kent State shootings failed to yield enough students and was canceled.[52]

But as newsworthy and visible as radical student attacks were, the military and most university administrators paid little formal attention to them. Plenty of reliable evidence existed that the protesters constituted a small, if vocal, minority on all campuses. University of Michigan president Robben Fleming "never thought there were more than 20 or 25 really disruptive, violent people around campus."[53] Two polls taken at the University of Pittsburgh in 1968 showed 70 percent of undergraduates were in favor of continuing ROTC with credit.[54] Even at Kent State, a poll taken in 1970 *after* the shootings in May showed three in four students in favor of retaining ROTC and half in favor of its remaining accredited.[55] At only one of the ninety NASULGC member schools, State University of New York (SUNY)–Buffalo, did a student referendum show a majority of students opposed to ROTC's continuance.[56]

The University of Colorado experienced incidents of both student activism and sustained support for ROTC. In March and April of 1970, Colorado's ROTC unit was firebombed, a student sit-in aimed partly at ROTC attracted 1,000 people, another anti-ROTC rally attracted 300 people, and the faculty voted to end credit for ROTC classes in the College of Arts and Sciences. All of this turmoil and publicity notwithstanding, support for the idea of ROTC remained high. Table 5.2 shows the results of two Colorado referenda conducted just two weeks after the Kent State shootings, along with the results of a similar poll taken at Rutgers in March. At Colorado, 78.7 percent of the student body and 82.3 percent of the faculty favored keeping ROTC, though not all wanted ROTC to remain accredited. At Rutgers, an almost identical 80 percent of the student body wanted ROTC on campus.

Table 5.2   Results of student and faculty referenda at the University of
Colorado and Rutgers University

Type of referendum	No. of respondents	Abolish ROTC	Keep ROTC, remove credit	Keep ROTC, retain credit
Student referendum, University of Colorado, May 13–15, 1970	6,388	21.3%	39.3%	39.4%
Faculty referendum, University of Colorado, May 18, 1970	741	17.1%	29.0%	53.3%
Student referendum, Rutgers University, March 1970	1,949	20.1%	21.2%	58.7%

Source: "War and ROTC Related Events 1969–," (n.d.), University of Colorado at
Boulder Library, Archives, News Media Relations Office, Box 1, Student Disturbances,
Folder 2; "Students Favor ROTC," *Targum,* Mar. 18, 1970. Faculty numbers do not add
up to 100% because 0.6% of the faculty voted for ROTC to be compulsory for men.

On a national level, the picture was much the same. The 1969 National
College Poll found that "most students . . . are antiwar. They are not necessarily antimilitary. There is quite a distinction between the concepts."[57] Indeed, this distinction is crucial. The National College Poll found that 60 percent of the nation's undergraduates believed that America was wrong in
sending troops to Vietnam but that 80 percent (exactly the same percentage
as at Colorado and Rutgers) were at the same time in favor of voluntary
ROTC programs, and 59 percent were in favor of their receiving academic
credit.[58] Thus a considerable amount of evidence demonstrated two important points: that the student radicals did not speak for the vast majority of
the nation's undergraduates and that anti-Vietnam sentiment did not necessarily correlate to anti-ROTC sentiment.

The services devoted much more attention to the numerous formal investigations that faculty committees made into ROTC than they did to addressing the concerns of student radicals. As the Air Force ROTC commandant
told university representatives in 1969, "While the threats and actual incidents of violence are by far the most dramatic manifestation of the anti-
ROTC sentiment, the sixty-seven institutional investigations of the AFROTC

curriculum [in academic year 1968–69] are considered more significant by AFROTC."[59] By June 1970 forty-six of the ninety members of the NASULGC had formal studies under way to investigate ROTC and its place on campus.[60] Illinois, Kent State, Michigan, and Pittsburgh produced a total of nine such reports between April 1968 and September 1971.

These reports were either written by ad hoc faculty senate committees given the specific task of examining ROTC and its relationship to the university or by education and curriculum committees that had official supervision over university courses and faculty appointments but had not customarily exercised that authority over ROTC in the past. These reports represented the faculties' chance to reassert that leverage. They revealed that the central concerns of the majority of the university communities were the same concerns that had been expressed in the 1950s. In short, the turmoil accompanying the protests against the war in Vietnam increased the attention faculties focused on ROTC, but it did not fundamentally change the issues or even introduce new ones.

Rather, Vietnam gave the universities the motive and the opportunity to correct long-standing anomalies presented by the ROTC programs. Critics later charged that academics set conditions that were solely intended to make it impossible for ROTC to remain on campus; this was simply not the case. Instead, the faculties issued reports that challenged ROTC to reform itself to become more a part of the university according to the same criteria applied to other programs. When the dean of Rutgers College reviewed the report of the Rutgers faculty in 1968, he did not describe it as the first step of a program to eliminate ROTC; rather he said that the "faculty did everything it could *to bring ROTC into the mainstream of Rutgers College as a regular department.*"[61]

Sensitivity among the faculty to ROTC also reflected a growing tension in higher education between the image of the "multiversity" capable of fulfilling the vocational and nonvocational needs of the nation and the image of the university as a place for nonvocational liberal arts training for a variety of disciplines, such as that supported by the Ford Foundation in the early 1960s (see Chapter 4). The latter position favored, in the words of Yale president Kingman Brewster, "the squeezing out of vocational courses generally in university colleges of the highest standing. As knowledge becomes more complicated and more demanding, there is less room for the 'how to do it' courses in the best universities."[62] This trend had been accelerating on some campuses since the 1950s and had long been a source of contention among some civilian faculty. ROTC, they argued, focused on the "how to do it" model of instruction. One such critic opined that "the problem analysis and decision-making [of ROTC courses] can be learned in a brick-laying course."[63]

The most common feature of the faculty reports recommended that the university (especially liberal arts colleges) no longer sanction ROTC through the blanket awarding of academic credit. Engineering colleges presented a different situation because they received their accreditation from the Engineers Council for Professional Development (ECPD). This group, according to Michigan professor of engineering M. J. Sinnott, had a policy for "25+ years that engineering degree programs not be diluted by giving credit toward graduation for ROTC courses."[64] This system of accreditation, combined with the shared professional emphasis of engineering curricula and military education, rendered the question of academic credit in engineering colleges either moot or incontestable.

The recommendations of no academic credit in the colleges of liberal arts were largely related to the faculties' opinion of the quality and content of ROTC courses. As a common prelude to open discussion of ROTC, faculty subcommittees reviewed ROTC courses to determine how their quality matched up to those in the regular university offerings. They unanimously criticized ROTC courses for being, in the words of Michigan's 1969 Gindin Committee, "shockingly bad . . . simply inappropriate to a liberal arts education . . . appalling . . . conjectural, non-analytical, cheaply moralistic, and often blatantly propagandistic."[65] Pittsburgh's Student Affairs Committee further criticized ROTC as lacking "humanistic or political analyses."[66]

The reports also argued for the imposition of more university control over ROTC, whose faculty, they contended, were selected under different criteria from those that applied to civilian faculty. Furthermore, ROTC faculty had to answer to an outside agency and, the faculties charged, were therefore incapable of pursuing objectivity and freedom of inquiry. Princeton's 1969 Ad Hoc Committee on ROTC argued that "the ROTC courses of instruction are prescribed and conducted under procedures incompatible with those which normally govern the establishment of courses and the selection of faculty at Princeton."[67] Or, as the University of Illinois faculty senate argued: "It is clear that certain organizational and procedural aspects of ROTC on the campus presently are not closely parallel to those normal to other academic or professional programs."[68]

These reports argued that the ROTC courses were dissimilar enough from regular university offerings to warrant some formal distinctions, including the removal of credit for ROTC courses. In some cases the committees removed credit for any course connected to ROTC, but more commonly they demanded that ROTC courses receive credit only after passing faculty reviews. The University of Illinois Faculty Senate in 1970 recommended that credit be awarded only after "subjecting that course of instruction to our normal procedure of academic review and approval. To do otherwise would only intensify the growing concern of many members of the academic community over control of university functions and prerogatives by agencies outside the university."[69]

Given the most recent evaluations of ROTC courses by Illinois faculty, this recommendation was effectively the same as a blanket denial of credit, but it did leave open the possibility of credit restoration in the future. Michigan also left such a door open in 1970 when the Literature, Science, and Arts faculty removed ROTC credit for any course not cross-listed with an academic department. Therefore, if a regular university department could find disciplinary or interdisciplinary merit in an ROTC course, that course could receive credit. Similarly, a spokesman for the University of Pittsburgh committee that recommended denying credit to ROTC students in the College of Arts and Sciences declared that "if members of the faculty were to participate in restructuring the program's curriculum towards academic acceptability, ROTC might again receive academic credit."[70]

A university did not need to remove all credit to make a statement about its impression of the quality of ROTC courses. University of Texas officials told the air force that "as long as the ROTC courses contain material of University caliber and are taught at University level by properly qualified individuals, they will continue to receive our maximum support."[71] Nevertheless, the Texas faculty voted in 1969 to reduce credits given for ROTC courses from a maximum of twenty-four to a maximum of nine. They also voted to end a policy that permitted ROTC to serve as a substitute for the American history graduation requirement.

Many of the reports also recommended, in the words of the faculty of Rutgers University, "that courses not specifically military—e.g., history, political science—[should] be taught by appropriate civilian academic departments."[72] Such a recommendation recalled the substitution programs of the late 1950s that academics had lauded (see Chapters 2 and 4). Substituted courses, taught "under the auspices of one of the degree granting colleges or schools," would, of course, receive full credit.[73]

The reports also challenged the academic titles universities gave to military personnel. Titles are the closest academic parallel to military rank, and therefore, like degree credit, they are more than just a formality; they signify the faculty's approbation and formal sanction. As noted in Chapter 4, ROTC contracts stipulated that the head of an ROTC unit receive the title professor of air (or military or naval) science. Junior officers had customarily, although not contractually, received the title associate professor or assistant professor. Military instructors, however, were not professional academics, they rarely held advanced degrees, and they usually lacked teaching experience. The faculty committees, therefore, were generally united in arguing that the officers were unworthy of holding academic titles.

During debates at Boston University, one group of radical faculty proposed that the PMS be known by the title "Coach of the Back Bay Chowder and Marching Society."[74] Some of the more mild reports suggested qualifying the titles granted to ROTC officers. At Pittsburgh, the Student Affairs Committee recommended adding "clinical" or "adjunct" to the titles. At Princeton, the Ad Hoc Committee voted to change the titles of ROTC officers to "Lecturer with the Rank of Professor."[75] At Michigan, Harvard, and the University of Illinois at Chicago Circle, however, the faculties voted that officers should not have any academic title and thenceforth should be known only by their military title.[76]

The reports also argued for more civilian oversight of the program. Yale stated that the necessity of more civilian control was "almost beyond challenge. Military officers certainly listen to a different drummer."[77] The type of oversight varied from having civilian faculty serve as advisors to military courses to requiring that all ROTC courses be approved each semester by the faculty. At Kent State, supervision of the program changed hands from the faculty of the College of Arts and Sciences to the Provost Office, in the hope of assuring greater centralized control over ROTC appointments and course offerings.

At Cornell, Michigan, and Princeton, faculty committees also recommended changing ROTC from a department to a "program." The committees argued that the change would formally, and correctly, acknowledge ROTC's place on the campus. The Princeton committee said the change would end "what the Committee believes has been an inappropriate status for ROTC. Departments . . . characteristically have undergraduate concentrators and recommend candidates for degrees."[78]

The issues of drill and military procedure arose in several reports. Drill was singled out in many reports as being especially antithetical to the mission of the university and unworthy of credit because it had no "appeal to intelligent students."[79] Many faculties therefore wanted to remove drill from the curriculum or at least remove it from the visible public centers on campus. The University of Pittsburgh moved drill practice from a lawn in the heart of campus to the confines of nearby Forbes Field.[80] Kent State similarly recommended that all ROTC drill courses be conducted inside the campus football stadium and that "military courtesy procedures be eliminated on campus except in the formally designated drill and drill-related areas. No rifles, swords, or other potentially lethal weapons be permitted on campus at any time except in the drill and drill-related areas. Because KSU does not have a dress code, voluntary wearing of the uniform will not be restricted. However, *involuntary* wearing of the uniform on campus except in the drill and drill-related areas will not be permitted."[81] Princeton and the University of Illinois at Chicago Circle went a step further and voted to ban both drill and lethal weapons from the campus.[82]

These changes were designed to soften the most martial aspects of ROTC, but they were also a response to real questions of officer training and preparation. To some military and civilian leaders, Vietnam had demonstrated that tactical preparation alone was insufficient for American officers fighting a war of liberation. The war in Vietnam was as much a war for the "hearts and minds" of the Vietnamese people as it was a war for territory and tactical advantage. Substitution was the universities' answer, to reform ROTC and its officer preparation by introducing more understanding of the history, culture, and politics of the world's peoples.

As a package, then, these reports argued for consequential reform in the operation of ROTC. For all of the many changes recommended by these faculty committees, however, what is perhaps more significant is what the faculties did not recommend. Only one faculty report, that from Dartmouth College, recommended that ROTC be removed from the campus. Elsewhere, motions and petitions demanding that the university sever all ties to ROTC were routinely defeated by margins of five to one or more. Even recommendations that ROTC retain ties to the university but be moved off campus were soundly defeated. Furthermore, on some campuses, faculties recommended reform only for certain issues. In 1968, for example, Johns Hopkins faculty voted to deny credit for ROTC but to allow ROTC instructors to keep their academic titles.[83] Some individual faculty members saw these moves as a first step toward removing ROTC from the campus, but the faculty committee reports did not argue that ROTC was an all-or-nothing venture. They could, and did, make recommendations designed to make ROTC fit into the fabric of their campus community.

Indeed, despite the changes they recommended, the faculty committees remained firmly committed to their traditional support of ROTC. The NASULGC's Special Subcommittee on ROTC Policy rejected the idea that "the civilian academic community, public or private, is antithetical to association with national security affairs."[84] The Princeton and Pittsburgh reports explicitly supported ROTC because it prevented the formation of a military caste and infused the military with civilian ideas. At Colorado an initial motion for ROTC reform failed to pass a faculty vote. A rewritten version began: "ROTC should continue to have a place on the campus of the University of Colorado." The second motion passed easily.[85] These reports, then, argued not for abolition of ROTC but for reform. ROTC's traditional strengths continued to outweigh the faults academics saw in the program. Therefore they made a series of recommendations designed to bring ROTC in line with regular academic offerings and produce a program worthy of remaining on the campuses on its own merit.

The student movement had a mixed impact on these faculty reports. It would be erroneous to assume that the faculties considered these issues only because of pressure from students. As the previous chapters indicate, faculties since the 1920s had investigated the role of ROTC on the campus; at least in part, the post-Tet reports represented the fruition of years of inquiry. Faculties had their own sense of what did and did not merit inclusion in American colleges and universities, and their ideas did not necessarily overlap with those of students.

Radical faculty were less interested in ROTC per se than they were in using ROTC as a means of repudiating the military and university ties to the military. The faculty reports, however, did not share the logic of the radical formulation that an anti-Vietnam position necessarily equated to an anti-ROTC, or even an antimilitary, position. Richard Jessor, the most important faculty critic of ROTC at the University of Colorado, was "dismayed" to learn that students received credit for ROTC, but he did not view the ROTC problem as an antimilitary issue. The faculty Jessor represented and the student radicals had a "sharp difference of perspective despite having a common concern." Although he disagreed with the academic and procedural issues connected with ROTC, Jessor saw the civil-military connection that ROTC provided as "healthy" for both parties.[86]

Jessor's position was not unusual. Arval Morris, a professor of law at the University of Washington, argued on behalf of the Washington chapter of the AAUP that ROTC "is unquestioningly non-curious" and "corrosive of the ideal of the university as a community of scholars." Nevertheless, the

AAUP believed that ROTC was "clearly preferable" to a system of officer training directed solely by the military. ROTC, Morris argued, "must be preserved . . . It is no answer to say: 'Throw ROTC off campus and be done with it.'"[87] Faculty could, and did, argue for significant change for ROTC while concurrently supporting the concept of officer training on civilian campuses. Similarly, a Harvard faculty member elucidated his support for officer training but not the ROTC status quo when he said, "Some faculty members (including myself) do indeed believe that it is legitimate for students to participate in reserve officer training activities, while rejecting the notion that certain courses taught by military officers form a solid part of the educational process which we work hard at maintaining."[88] A vote against ROTC accreditation therefore did not necessarily equal a vote against military training.

Furthermore, the student movement pushed significant numbers of faculty, many of them senior faculty, to a hard-line position in opposition to student radicals. This position inclined many to support the ROTC status quo in order not to give in to the student radicals. The faculties, they argued, should not "placate a minority of yahoos on the left who had threatened confrontation unless [the university] cleansed itself of its infectious association with an ill-defined but presumably insidious military establishment."[89]

Although opinions and faculty declarations varied from campus to campus, a consensus emerged that ROTC should be changed, not expelled. An observer of Michigan's 1969 Buttrey Committee, which produced one of the harshest anti-ROTC reports, noted that "no member of the committee supported ROTC as it now exists throughout the nation. There was, however, no desire on the part of the committee to recommend abolition of ROTC."[90] The recommended reforms pertained to the long-standing anomalies inherent in the creation of ROTC as a vocational military officer preparation program that existed under different regulations from those that governed other university programs. The services received this flood of reports with concern because of the sheer weight of changes proposed therein, but many of the reports' key features were in accord with an officially stated position that emerged in 1969 from the new Nixon Pentagon.

The Benson Report

It would be misleading to assume that all of the initiative for reform of ROTC came from the universities. As indicated in previous chapters, many uniformed and civilian officials in the armed services had long agreed that reform of the ROTC program was necessary if it was to retain its vitality. Now President Nixon's support of a zero-draft military added greater urgency to the problem of ROTC. Many in the new Nixon administration believed that reform would be critical to ROTC's future if and when the draft, a major motivation for enrollment in the program, ended. In this vein the new secretary of defense, Melvin Laird, created the Special Committee on ROTC in the first few months of his tenure, to report on the most serious problems facing the program and to make recommendations for its reform.[91] George Benson, president of Claremont College, chaired the committee; the remainder of the panel, which became known as the Benson Committee, included administrators from Stanford, John Jay College, Tulane, Purdue, and Illinois, and the highest uniformed officer in charge of ROTC from each of the four services.

In September 1969 the committee produced the "Benson Report," a sixty-one-page exploration of the major issues connected to ROTC.[92] It made twenty-one recommendations to the secretary of defense, many of which argued for less change than the university faculty reports. For example, while acknowledging that credit was the exclusive prerogative of university faculties, the report recommended that "appropriate academic credit be given for ROTC courses" other than drill, that ROTC instructors should keep their academic titles, and that "uniforms and drill are a part of the military profession and should remain on campus."

The report did, however, recommend some changes. It advised that universities should assume more responsibility for the hiring and firing of ROTC instructors, encouraged greater use of substitution, and recommended the creation of "high level faculty-administration committee(s) to oversee and work with the ROTC programs."[93] The report argued that ROTC was "clearly in the national interest," and it strongly favored continuing the program, but with some changes in operating procedures. It rejected the radical position that ROTC had no place on civilian campuses, but it did acknowledge ROTC's dissonance from other college programs: "ROTC is the only instructional program on campus whose curriculum and method of instruction is largely determined by an external body, whose instructional staff is furnished by one external source, and which prepares young men for a single employer."[94] Consistent with a century and a half of university experience with military training, the report firmly argued that it was important to keep ROTC intact, even with its anomalies. "If ROTC were to be removed from the nation's campuses there would be grave danger of isolating the services from the intellectual centers of the public which they serve and defend."[95]

The report was endorsed by the DOD and most universities as an appropriate starting point for negotiations. The NASULGC noted that the Benson Report marked a "positive approach to the improvement of officer education programs."[96] A year later, the association's Council for Academic Affairs "commend[ed] the Benson Report of the Department of Defense regarding ROTC and urge[d] the implementation of the recommendations made therein," especially, the council noted, the recommendations to permit the host institution to "determine its own policies and procedures in educational matters, such as the amount of credit to be granted for the ROTC programs."[97]

The Benson Report provided general guidelines, not a boilerplate to be implemented nationwide. Still, it became the seminal document for ROTC policy in the Nixon Pentagon. The report's final recommendation was the creation of "an office in the Department of Defense to secure coordination of service ROTC rules which may affect the relationship of ROTC as a whole within the academic world."[98] The DOD responded by creating the office of assistant secretary of defense (education) in 1970 and naming Benson to the position. Through the Benson Report, the DOD made a commitment, as the universities had, to work to save ROTC. It is therefore worth examining in greater detail the motivations that both the universities and the services had for negotiating a re-formed place on campus for ROTC.

Why Save ROTC?

If ROTC was so out of step with the goals and procedures of higher education, why not, from the university perspective, throw out this distasteful manifestation of a sordid connection with the military? Or, from the service's perspective, why not abandon Michigan, Illinois, Pittsburgh, Colorado, Kent State, and any other campus that wanted to force reform and instead open larger, postgraduate Officer Candidate Schools where the services could run their officer preparation programs without the interference of interloping civilians?

The answer was that, for all its faults, ROTC provided real, tangible benefits to the campus and the services. These benefits overlapped in many cases. Both institutions had an interest in attracting the highest quality student possible. The ROTC host schools were some of the finest colleges and universities in the nation. ROTC thus provided an on-campus recruitment and training office that many in the services believed was crucial to attracting high-quality cadets. Due to the selectivity of the ROTC scholarship programs, ROTC had the potential to bring full-scholarship students onto the campuses who were at least the equal of their non-ROTC peers.

Furthermore, the services and the universities had legislative bodies to placate. All state legislatures, as well as the United States Congress, favored retention of the ROTC program. If the universities and the services could negotiate away the major problems surrounding ROTC, they could keep the elected officials who had oversight over the budgets of both institutions out of the reform process.

Two additional factors impelled the military to negotiate a reformed, but certain, place on campus. First, cost effectiveness played a considerable role. In 1969 the average ROTC officer cost $4,320 to produce. By contrast, officers produced through Officer Candidate School cost $8,406 each on average, and service academy graduates cost $47,136 on average. ROTC was a bargain even when one considered factors such as the higher attrition rates and post-commissioning training costs of ROTC-trained officers. One study of ROTC and Naval Academy graduates from 1962 found that total training costs per 100 officers still in service ten years after commissioning were $2.9 million for NROTC graduates and $8.9 million for Annapolis graduates.[99] Given that the services projected that ROTC would be relied on to produce as many as 80 percent of the post-Vietnam officer corps, ROTC represented potential for enormous savings.[100]

Second, not all military personnel believed that civilian criticism had harmed the program. Rather, many understood that most civilian academics were committed at least to the *idea* of ROTC. They recognized that much of the criticism of ROTC, such as that of course content, was directed at improving the program, not discarding it. Furthermore, some uniformed personnel had long agreed that some aspects of the program, such as the emphasis on drill, needed to be changed. To these officers, the faculty reports signified a genuine desire on the part of the universities to work to find ways to make ROTC stronger. The stereotype of the conservative, rigid military officer did not always fit the reality. Many ROTC commanders, such as Colonel Wayne Bridges at Georgia Tech, saw the demands for change as "justified" and believed that a fruitful, open dialogue with university administrators could prove beneficial to ROTC.[101]

Three major factors impelled university administrators to negotiate with the services, despite vocal protests on campus for the absolute removal of ROTC. Without question the most important of these considerations was a long-standing ideological belief in the importance of citizen-officers and the role of ROTC in assuring the supply of such officers. Administrators, especially those from state-supported schools, felt that higher education had an obligation to produce officers. Furthermore, they remained convinced that ROTC's greatest advantage was that it served as a hedge against the creation of a military elite exclusively trained at the service academies.[102] To these men, ROTC did not mean the military's presence in the university, but the university's presence in the military. Ralph Huitt of the NASULGC noted that his group "believe[d] that officers in the military should come from institutions all over the country, and that this diversity of background helps to maintain a democratic leadership in the military. This is a principle which we would not surrender lightly."[103]

Second, although many universities themselves lost money conducting ROTC programs, their students often depended on ROTC's scholarship authorization.[104] In 1966 NROTC, the smallest of the three ROTC programs, paid $93,500 in tuition to the University of Illinois.[105] In the 1968–69 academic year, ROTC meant close to $1 million to the University of Michigan; direct scholarship payments to Michigan students accounted for more than $400,000 of that figure.[106] More subtly, DOD research money was a significant source of income at these schools. Keeping the services happy had financial benefits beyond officer education.[107]

The third reason involved leaving a career option open for those students who desired it. Many young men (and, increasingly, young women as well) wanted to become military officers. The university had an obligation, many faculty and administrators argued, to assure that such a career option remained open. The NASULGC concluded in 1969 that "it is appropriate for institutions . . . to offer courses and programs of interest to those wishing to serve as officers in the Armed Forces, as they do for other occupational fields."[108]

For all these reasons university administrators supported the idea of ROTC, if not in the program's current form. Their view agreed, in broad outline, with the consensus of the faculty reports. The task at hand, then, was for the administrators—serving both as representatives of the individual schools and as faculty delegates—to build on their agreement with the services as to the necessity of ROTC reforms in a way that would serve the interests of both parties.

"A Disposition on Both Sides to Find Common Ground"

The reform of ROTC revolved around a dialectical process of negotiation, heretofore absent in discussions of the issue, that had formally existed between the schools and the military since the creation of regular ROTC advisory boards in the 1950s. Between August 1969 and November 1971, Michigan president Robben Fleming and vice president Robert Williams met several times with Secretary of Defense Melvin Laird, the uniformed heads of the NROTC and AFROTC programs, an assistant secretary of the navy, an assistant secretary of defense, two deputy assistant secretaries of defense, the head of the Navy Bureau of Personnel, and the chief of naval operations, always exclusively on the topic of ROTC. In 1970 the Association of American Universities surveyed its member schools on the issue of negotiations with the DOD and found "evidence of a disposition on both sides—the military and the universities—to find common ground on which ROTC programs can be continued . . . Most of the universities seem to be approaching the issue with a readiness to adjust and compromise with the services in order to preserve ROTC programs in some form."[109]

To be sure, this process was accelerated—but not created—by Vietnam and the attendant turmoil on the campuses. Without the student movement, it is unlikely that officials of such importance would have involved themselves personally in the issues. But these men did not bring a radical agenda with them to the negotiations. They aimed to reconcile basic inconsistencies and contradictions between the goals of military training and higher education. The discussions, between the highest academic and military officials in the country, kept the issue of ROTC reform alive until settlements could be reached.

With Nixon's reduction of American forces in Vietnam, the military began to prepare for fundamental changes.[110] During the Vietnam War era, many officers had received their commissions through Officer Candidate School, which had been expanded to meet the increased demands of the military for junior officers. While most of these officers performed their duty admirably, several university and military officials believed that the six-week crash preparation offered by OCS was markedly inferior to ROTC. As George Benson noted in 1970, "We cannot doubt the importance of a high degree of education for our officers. A half hour of immaturity on the part of one ill-educated junior officer can affect our whole national image adversely."[111] Benson's comment about the ill-educated junior officer is a thinly veiled reference to army Lieutenant William Calley, who was tried for the March 1968 massacre of 350 Vietnamese civilians in the village of My Lai.[112] One explanation of that massacre was that the services had accepted too many "substandard" men into OCS; only one of the eight officers charged as principals in the massacre had a college degree. Calley himself had had only one checkered year of junior college. He later told an interviewer that he left for Vietnam "with the absolute philosophy that the U.S.A.'s right. And there was no gray . . . there was just black or white."[113]

Many military men themselves argued that ROTC provided a humanistic counterbalance to OCS- and academy-trained officers. University of Colorado class president and ROTC cadet Glenn Porzak told an assembly of students that "ROTC is vital for keeping dissent within the Army by officers with a liberal education."[114] One American soldier told an interviewer in Vietnam in 1969, "Believe it or not, there're a lot of young officers, especially a lot out of ROTC, who really preach against the genocidal thing."[115] Many academics, students, and military officers believed that ROTC had the potential to infuse the services with better educated men who had been exposed to the diverse ideas of the modern university rather than more narrow ideas of OCS. A college education, they contended, imparted more of the maturity and refined, "gentlemanly" qualities idealized in military officers than did the six weeks of training in OCS.

To many academics, then, reform of ROTC, not abolition, held the potential to create a military that more closely shared the values of American society. To reject ROTC, they believed, would only serve to place the military out of reach of academic and civilian influence. Many academics thus took a keen interest in the discussions revolving around ROTC. In August 1970, the NASULGC senate met in a special session to discuss three issues related to the relationship between higher education and government, including "revision of the ROTC program to make it academically stronger." Such revisions, members argued, would assure that the primary means for academics to influence the military would survive.[116]

One year later, they forcefully reiterated this position in a resolution approved by the NASULGC member institutions and later by the Association of American Universities. Their statement captures the consensus of university administrators in this era:

Recently the desirability of civilian educational institutions participating in the education of those who may serve as officers in the Armed Services has been subject to question. Some charge that this involvement contributes to the "militarization" of our society. We believe that the opposite is true. The continued availability in substantial numbers of officers for the Armed Services from a variety of civilian educational backgrounds actually is one of the surest guarantees against the formation of a military caste or establishment . . . It would be highly undesirable for officer education to be restricted to the service academies, or to be carried on entirely in programs removed from college or university campuses.[117]

The military shared this view, but for slightly different reasons. Military officers viewed ROTC reform as a critical part of reestablishing good relations with American society in the aftermath of Tet and the graduated withdrawal from Vietnam. One way to replenish a diminishing fund of legitimacy was to create an officer corps that shared the values of the society it served. To many, ROTC played a critical role in this process, as cadets were exposed for four years to civilian peers and instruction from civilian professors. This pattern offered a better opportunity for the interaction of civilian and military ideas than the more isolationist pedagogical model of the service academies or OCS.

University administrators, usually provosts or vice presidents, had the job of relaying the major features of the faculty committee reports to the services and negotiating with the uniformed and civilian heads of ROTC programs to implement the faculty recommendations. In many cases, these recommendations violated the spirit or the letter of the 1964 Vitalization Act or existing university-service ROTC contracts. Additionally, where the recommendations of a faculty report violated the Benson Report, they also stood in opposition to the officially stated DOD position.

The administrators generally agreed with the recommendations contained in the faculty reports, which, after all, brought up many of the issues they had been dealing with for years. They shared the general goal of reforming ROTC, as Michigan president Robben Fleming demonstrated:

As to the larger question of whether ROTC ought to be on the campuses, I tend to favor it despite my own connection with civil liberties causes. My reasons are that I fear a professional army in a democracy; that I think the infusion of officer talent from non-professional ranks promotes the concept of a civilian army; that in twenty-two years on three campuses which have ROTC programs, I have yet to find the faintest hint that somehow the military is dominating the campus; and I believe that officer standing is a legitimate outlet for those students who must serve some time in the military anyway.[118]

Even in cases where the administration disagreed with the faculty, the diffuse nature of university administration and power distribution meant that there was little they could do. Issues of credit, for example, were in almost all cases the exclusive prerogative of the faculty. A university president could not simply order that credit be awarded, and in several cases, the administrators realized that trying to use political clout to sway a faculty vote ran the risk of producing a rogue outcome. Knowing all this, University of Pittsburgh chancellor Wesley Posvar, himself a West Point graduate and former Air Force Academy department chairman, told the Pennsylvania state legislature that he would not try to change his faculty's vote to drop credit for ROTC courses, despite the legislature's threats to cut funding to Pittsburgh by 25 percent and Posvar's belief that ROTC deserved elective credit.[119]

The academic authority structure, of course, was nearly the polar opposite of the military pattern. Administrators who assumed the job of negotiating with the services and state legislatures to implement reform often had a very difficult time explaining that they simply could not order faculties to change their recommendations. Threats from Michigan and Pennsylvania legislatures and Congress to cut funding to the universities if they dropped ROTC credit therefore put administrators in an awkward position. They obviously had to pay attention to real budget issues, but they could not circumvent faculty votes with which they disagreed.

Furthermore, presidents and their representatives had their own supervisors to consider. University trustees and regents commonly favored the status quo regarding ROTC programs and looked with great suspicion at any move that might call the university's commitment to the nation into question. Robben Fleming knew that at Michigan "there was not a single vote among the Regents for abolition of ROTC . . . Thus if the [Buttrey] Committee made such a recommendation, it would fail before the Regents. If I did not support the recommendation, the faculty would reject me. If I supported it, the Regents would nevertheless turn it down, and my influence with them would be greatly diminished, perhaps to the point where I should resign."[120] Of course, the committee made no such recommendation, but Fleming's words indicated the sensitive position sometimes occupied by university administrators.

Within this background, formal discussions about ROTC between the universities and the military began in mid-1969, soon after the Nixon administration had established itself at the Pentagon. In an interview shortly after he became secretary of defense, Melvin Laird said that he was willing to see military ceremony reduced and the substitution of regular academic courses for military ones broadened, but said, "We are not prepared to see the ROTC program degraded in any way."[121]

Similarly, the uniformed services were quite willing to discuss possible changes to the program, in large part because many of the faculty recommendations, such as the reduction of drill and the assignment of instructors with advanced degrees, were in line with suggestions they had made as early as 1960. They also understood that other changes, such as qualifying the academic titles used by ROTC instructors, need not affect the program unduly. AFROTC staff told their instructors that "even out of the turmoil, some good will come. Some legitimate needs for change will be made and even in some of the colleges where opposition has been the greatest we may find more faculty support and involvement after they examine our program and have an opportunity to input their ideas for an improved program."[122] These negotiations, then, were not always as acrimonious as the backdrop of faculty reports and student demonstrations might lead one to believe. To be sure, hard-liners existed on both sides, but most negotiators understood that both sides also shared the goal of finding a way to keep ROTC on the campuses.

Drill: "The Program's Worst Enemy"

The issues that were reformed most quickly and easily were those on which some general level of agreement already existed, such as the visibility of drill on campus. Other issues, such as the awarding of academic credit for ROTC courses and academic titles for ROTC instructors, were more contentious because the services saw changes in those areas as a threat to the status and quality of the program. In addition, general agreement existed on some issues, such as instructor qualification, but structural problems inhibited easy solutions. In these cases, the services and the universities worked to find creative temporary solutions until permanent ones could be implemented.

As noted, some military criticism of drill had been building since 1960. Observers in the late 1960s continued to criticize drill as outdated, irrelevant, mindless, and embarrassing to the student. Survey evidence suggested that drill was even unpopular among people who supported all other aspects of the ROTC program.[123] Reducing the importance of drill promised to reduce a source of tension for both supporters and opponents. "Leadership laboratory," noted one army officer, "may well be the program's worst enemy."[124] And as a navy officer argued, "It's the weapons and the drilling that get up their dander, so, hell, let's throw them a crumb."[125] This officer's casual willingness to abandon drill indicates that its training value was minimal, a mere "crumb." The services had few problems accepting the faculty recommendations for removal of academic credit for the drill portions of the ROTC curriculum, and some officers were willing to consider removing drill from the campus altogether.

At least initially, the services and the universities had to negotiate around the desires of powerful members of Congress, who held that the arguments against drill were "without merit." A House Armed Services Subcommittee, led by F. Edward Hébert, declared, consistent with the logic that had produced the Vitalization Act five years earlier, that it intended to see drill continued on the campus. Drill, the subcommittee determined, instilled leadership and "training in the ability to accept orders."[126] Nevertheless, negotiations between the universities and the services to reduce the amount of drill continued undaunted. The services did, however, begin to lobby Congress to explain the changes in ROTC policy and try to convince congressmen that drill did not form a necessary part of ROTC training.

Indeed, the congressional lobbying paid dividends. Meetings in March 1970 between F. Edward Hébert, Assistant Secretary of Defense Roger Kelly, and the three uniformed heads of ROTC convinced Hébert that the changes to the program, including a reduction of "some of the weapons and tactics orientation," were intended to strengthen ROTC. Army Brigadier General C. P. Hannum noted immediately after the meeting, "I consider the briefing with Congressman Hébert a total success . . . This effort should serve to finally clarify to the [House Armed Services] committee that what the Army is doing to revitalize the ROTC program is truly progressive change rather than 'knuckling under to the dissidents,' as some members of the committee now believe."[127] Hannum succeeded in convincing Hébert that the authoritarian military model the congressman so admired was not the direction that ROTC had gone in the recent past, nor was it the direction that it would head in the future. To succeed in the new American military system, ROTC had to focus less on drill and more on assuring its place on the campus through congruity with the goals of higher education.

Knowing that the consensus of informed opinion within the military had become decidedly receptive to a reduction of drill, University of Michigan vice president Robert Williams led off a meeting with the Bureau of Naval Personnel by saying, "Let us begin by dismissing the drills, spit and polish, corps activity, or whatever you care to call it as a vital [and] necessary part of the ROTC program."[128] In a similar vein, University of Illinois provost Dayton Pickett told a representative of the Army War College, "That portion of military leadership skills acquired through participation in drill is seen as a highly questionable component of a university curriculum."[129]

Because many uniformed and civilian military officials agreed that drill was overemphasized in the ROTC curriculum, they did not strenuously object to university desires to deny credit for drill or to reduce the number of hours spent on drill. Indeed, many military officials had opposed the changes of the Vitalization Act that made drill as much as one-third of the curriculum's total contact hours. Thus this issue became the easiest to resolve. The hours devoted to drill became the common target of military and educational officials who were pushing to reintroduce substitution.

Substitution and the "New York Plan"

As noted in earlier chapters, substitution had been a popular program from the late 1950s until 1964, when ROTC curricula returned to a more technical emphasis. The services reacted to initial substitution suggestions in the late 1960s by allowing the ideas to germinate on the individual campuses. The proposals varied significantly in scale and scope nationwide. MIT, for example, replaced drill with cadet presentations on aspects of engineering and physics relevant to the military.[130] Elsewhere, substitution ideas were more complex. In 1969 the army authorized all professors of military science to introduce substitution, encouraging the substitution of courses from the following areas: American military history, world military history, diplomatic history of the United States, political geography, American government, international relations, geopolitics, studies of developing countries, international trade and finance, psychology, sociology, group dynamics and human relations, calculus, chemistry, biology, physics, geology, foreign language, political philosophy, organization and management, computer science, and statistics.[131] "This is a forward move, in my judgment," noted Michigan's Robert Williams, "and it is my understanding that the departments concerned and the assistant deans in the college who work with the students and their programs are delighted about this movement."[132]

Most universities introduced some form of substitution, but the University of Michigan introduced the most elaborate series of curricular changes nationwide. Michigan introduced substitution for army and air force drill periods for the 1969 fall semester. Air force freshmen took political science, juniors took two courses in aeronautical engineering, and seniors took international politics and either two industrial engineering courses or two business administration courses.[133] Army cadets in their freshman year substituted political science and speech, and sophomores substituted geography and history. For the 1970–71 academic year, the navy agreed to require its midshipmen at Michigan to take American military history, national security policy, calculus, physics or chemistry, and computer science.[134] The air force also selected Michigan to be one of four campuses to test a new "alternate curriculum" that made more elaborate use of substitution ideas than had previously occurred anywhere. In place of Air Science 102 (United States Military Forces), freshmen cadets selected a course from the following list: Humanities 101 *(Iliad, Oedipus, Canterbury Tales)*, Humanities 102 *(Hamlet, Candide, Civil Disobedience)*, Freshman Composition, Shakespeare, Creative Writing, and Great Books. Introduction to International Politics replaced Air Science 201 (Introduction to Defense Policy) for sophomores.[135]

The services generally supported the idea of a limited amount of substitution, because they saw value in having junior officers with a broader education and a firmer grounding in areas like engineering, administration, and even the humanities. They did, however, urge that a significant amount of the corps training activity remain the sole preserve of uniformed officers. As the University of Pittsburgh PMS told the administration: "Although the Military Science Department could expand its use of the University courses provided they met the overall objectives, a course composed solely of University courses is not desirable," because the ROTC faculty needed to know their cadets well enough to evaluate their ability to succeed in the military. Pittsburgh's ROTC instructional staff proposed instead a "team" approach wherein civilian instructors would teach the academic portion of the curriculum and military instructors would teach the corps-preparation aspects.[136]

The University of Illinois also supported the team-teaching concept and introduced team-taught courses in the following areas: military map and photo analysis, United States defense establishment, American military history, principles of military instruction, military law, and principles of military leadership.[137] The services generally showed more enthusiasm for team teaching than for substitution because team teaching allowed the ROTC staffs to maintain more contact hours with their cadets. It also meant less fundamental change to the program; team teaching had already existed informally on some campuses in the form of guest lectures from civilian faculty.

Their utility notwithstanding, team teaching and substitution could not help the ROTC units respond to criticisms that their instructors were unqualified to teach at American universities. As noted earlier, the ROTC headquarters staffs had long desired to have master's degree holders assigned to ROTC units, but the personnel realities of the armed forces and the need for officers in Southeast Asia had constrained them from doing so. After 1968, the need for highly qualified officers became even more acute; having highly qualified officers could improve relations with host schools and increase the chances for restoration of academic credit. Furthermore, some schools, like the University of Texas, had established new criteria for accepting officers as ROTC instructors and had begun to reject candidates who failed to meet these criteria.[138]

Knowing that a permanent solution was still some time away, the universities and the services teamed up to create a temporary solution through New York University's National Security Information Center (NSIC). Beginning in May 1968, with funding from the private sector, the NSIC began to conduct an ROTC Enrichment Program that had three goals:

> To give added depth and perspective to instruction in politico-military subjects in the ROTC curriculum.
> To assist ROTC in maintaining standards of study that merit academic accreditation.
> To assist ROTC instructors in broadening the academic base of their teaching.[139]

The "New York Plan," as it became known, paid guest lecturers to give talks to ROTC cadets, most often at times formerly devoted to drill, to enrich the level of ROTC instruction. The original list of 233 lecturers included Zbigniew Brzezinski, Walt Rostow, and various university professors, as well as officials from Los Alamos National Laboratories, the RAND Corporation, the White House National Security Staff, and other national security organizations.[140] The NSIC designed the New York Plan to supplement ROTC instruction for a period of four years, by which time it anticipated that instructors with advanced degrees would be the norm. With the help of General Motors, the NSIC also sponsored two-day training programs in which a total of 263 ROTC instructors participated. Eventually, 11,000 cadets at 201 schools heard lectures supported by the NSIC.[141]

Some ROTC units drew inspiration from the NSIC and created their own programs. Georgia Tech's ROTC programs developed the Atlanta Forum on National and International Affairs (AFNIA), designed with ROTC in mind but open to all students from nine colleges and universities in the Atlanta area. AFNIA sponsored a conference on Sino-American relations in 1971 that featured speakers from the Brookings Institute, the State Department, the Japanese Embassy, Johns Hopkins University, Dartmouth College, and George Washington University.[142] The following year Dean Rusk gave the keynote address at an AFNIA conference on the Middle East.[143] Similarly, at the University of Washington the Carthage Foundation and Claremont College supported a program of ROTC guest lecturers on such topics as nuclear proliferation, Russia's relationship to Eastern Europe, the Berlin crisis, and American foreign policy. These seminars met in the time period formerly devoted to drill.[144]

With the New York Plan and local variants like the AFNIA helping to upgrade instruction, the services took their own steps to assure that they could assign officers with advanced degrees in the years to come. They ended the policy of giving volunteers priority in ROTC assignments and began treating ROTC as a regular assignment to assure that the quality of instructors would improve. One AFROTC instructor recalled: "The feeling I had was I wondered what I had done wrong to be selected [to teach ROTC] . . . Somewhere along the line I understood that it would be helpful to the ROTC program if they had someone who was competitive for promotion to general in the role of a detachment commander in ROTC."[145] Or, as Colonel Glen Watkins, University of Pittsburgh PAS, noted in 1969, "It's time for people with experience and motivation to come to the college campuses. The Armed Forces have always put their best men in Southeast Asia and the Pentagon."[146] Watkins was among the many ROTC instructors who were sent to their alma mater in the hope of further improving the standing of ROTC instructors and their relationship with the host schools.

The services still had to find a way to get around the structural problem of not having a large supply of men with master's degrees. The army demonstrated its commitment to solving this problem when it introduced the Civil Schooling Plan, under which officers would spend two years, on full salary, earning a master's degree, then three years teaching ROTC at the same school.[147] The assignment of formally educated officers was a special priority of Admiral Elmo Zumwalt, chief of naval operations, who instituted navy programs similar to the army's Civil Schooling Plan to assure that men with high professional qualifications were sent to NROTC campuses.[148]

By 1970, these programs had paid off. After that year, all ROTC instructors assigned to Michigan, Illinois, Kent State, Georgia Tech, and Pittsburgh had advanced degrees. This pattern was partly due to the increased assertiveness of the universities; Michigan turned down two candidates at this time because of their inability to qualify for admission to Michigan graduate schools.[149] But even on a national level the number of officers with advanced degrees was increasing. All but four AFROTC instructors assigned to a detachment in academic year 1970–71 had an advanced degree.[150] All four services stabilized the tours of duty of men with advanced degrees at three years to keep qualified instructors on the campuses.

Official Recognition and Meaningful Perquisites

While the formal qualifications of ROTC officers were improving, university faculty and administrators on some campuses continued to push for a change in the academic titles given to ROTC officers. At Michigan and the University of Illinois at Chicago Circle, the faculties voted to remove their academic titles altogether, while at Pittsburgh the faculty voted to add "visiting" to the title. They argued that military officers, having climbed a different career ladder than academics, did not merit professorial titles. Michigan astronomy professor and navy reserve captain Freeman Miller told Senator George Kuhn:

> Academic appointments are won by members of the faculty the hard way—year after year of teaching and scholarly study and research. It simply comes down to the fact that a promotion to lieutenant colonel or commander is earned by one kind of endeavor and a professorship by another . . . [H]aving traversed the two quite different routes to a navy captaincy and university professorship, I can testify that neither qualifies one for recognition by a title or rank in the other area.[151]

The services initially resisted this change but amended their stance after the civilian leadership of the DOD accepted the position that the titles themselves were not important but the status they conferred was. Secretary of Defense Melvin Laird told the Senate: "I would see no objection to calling an officer by his military grade if he had the official recognition and meaningful perquisites of the academic rank of professor—other than tenure, of course. If an institution does not agree to this, then it cannot have an ROTC unit on its campus."[152]

These perquisites included having the ROTC instructor "listed in the institutional catalog on the same basis as other professors and shar[ing] the same faculty voting and committee responsibilities as other professors."[153] In the Big Ten schools, of course, such perks also included access to the schools' two most precious commodities—parking spaces and football tickets.[154] The schools had never planned to remove the perks or status, just the titles. The maintenance of fringe benefits and listings in the course catalogs helped convince DOD officials that dropping the titles did not necessarily denigrate the ROTC programs. To them, the issue of titles was cosmetic if it did not affect the formal functioning of the officers on campus.[155]

The debate over changing the ROTC units from academic departments to programs followed similar lines. Michigan and Illinois at Chicago Circle faculty voted to remove ROTC's departmental status because "department [is] inappropriate due to [ROTC's] nonpreparation of its own budget, only nominal control over curriculum, exterior funding and nonrecruitment of its own staff."[156] As with individual academic titles, the universities proposed not a reduction in ROTC status but a change in its formal position to "recognize the distinction (in no way derogatory) between the typical University department and an ROTC unit."[157]

Again it was a high-level meeting, this one at Maxwell AFB, between Brigadier General Ben Cassiday and Robert Williams, that produced agreement. Williams "made clear in all statements that the University was in no sense 'downgrading' ROTC" in changing ROTC to a program. Michigan, he told Cassiday, simply wanted to acknowledge ROTC's distinctive nature. The change would not affect ROTC's listings in course catalogs, the ability of ROTC officers to participate in university administration, or the secretarial and custodial support the university provided to ROTC. Cassiday accepted the Michigan position, and thereafter the ROTC units at Michigan and Illinois-Chicago Circle became known as Military Officer Education Programs (MOEPs).[158]

Academic Credit

The services and the universities reached easy resolution on the preceding issues because of the general agreement that had already existed. Achieving resolution on other issues, however, proved to be more difficult. The arduous problem of academic credit remained the most hotly contested issue. Virtually all of the faculty reports discussed above recommended the removal of academic credit for ROTC courses in the colleges of liberal arts because, in the words of a University of Illinois committee, "The content of courses and the qualification of the instructors appear sufficiently marginal that such offerings are not commensurate with the College's traditional goals. The assignment of a limited number of hours or advanced ROTC course work for graduation credit seemed a dereliction of duty if the educational quality of the service programs are to be enhanced."[159]

In the 1960s, in an Illinois ROTC class on navigation, a cadet (who happened also to be an astronomy major) correctly identified a constellation as "Cassiopeia." The sergeant who graded the exam marked the answer incorrect, telling the cadet that the army manual called the constellation "The Big M" and that "no other response was acceptable." When the civilian academics in the astronomy department learned of the problem, they reacted by protesting against the "basic inflexibility and oversimplicity of the Army ROTC program."[160] Incidents such as these helped to produce a consensus among academics that the levels of credit awarded for ROTC classes were not at all justifiable.

Whereas the universities were in general agreement on this issue, three distinct military opinions emerged. One was that losing credit would adversely affect enrollment, since students would be less inclined to take ROTC classes. Lack of accreditation would therefore damage the program's ability to recruit and keep students. "Unless we can give credit where credit is due," noted Pittsburgh PMS David Clagett, "then our enrollment figure will continue to drop to such an extent that the university['s ROTC unit] will become non-productive. The possibility then arises that the unit could be removed."[161] This position was most common among ROTC unit heads, who saw their enrollments plummeting and looked to credit as a means to stop the flood of students leaving the program. Academic credit, they hoped, would make their recruitment task that much easier.

A second position, related to the first, was that a loss of credit would constitute "prima facie evidence that [the University] has downgraded the services."[162] The issue, then, was one of image not credit. Lack of credit, some argued, would demonstrate that the university, and especially the liberal arts colleges, wanted to put ROTC "on the fringe."[163] This argument implied that the problems created by the loss of credit would go far beyond enrollment; such a vote would indicate that faculties were repudiating the military and the military model for organization and authority. Traditionalists like Congressman Hébert and some in the civilian leadership of the navy held most adamantly to this position, fearing that any weakening of the military's authority would portend disaster both for good order on the campuses and for the good order they saw dissipating in society more generally.

The third position, subscribed to by those DOD officials most interested in finding a basis for negotiation with the universities, was that losing credit would not necessarily harm the program. Melvin Laird argued, "We have found over the years that many well-supported and highly productive programs have given little, and in some cases no, degree credit for military courses in the ROTC program. Where overall institutional support is strong, the issue of degree credit has not been a bar to a successful program."[164] Those who held to this position noted that engineering schools rarely gave any academic credit to ROTC, yet several engineering colleges, like Georgia Tech, supported strong and vibrant ROTC programs.

Obviously the third position left the most room for negotiation. Faculty and administrators were for the most part unconvinced by the first two arguments. They held to their positions that ROTC courses were the intellectual inferior of standard university courses and, if ROTC sought accreditation, it would have to improve the course quality. University of Pittsburgh professor Peter Karsten argued, "Other [students] may not come because we offer no credit for Cuban guerrilla warfare training, John Birch Society readings, or underwater polo. Those are risks we take when we construct . . . curricula that we believe has merit."[165] The services' arguments about enrollment declines also failed to convince most university officials. "I doubt whether the Army wants officers who entered the service merely because they could get a few hours of academic credit toward their degree," one provost told a trustee, calling it a "hardly defensible motivation."[166]

The DOD derived its official stand on the issue from Laird's argument that lack of credit was not necessarily a hindrance to a successful program and the Benson Report's determination that credit awarded should be the prerogative of the faculty. Lawyers from the DOD and the Association of NROTC Colleges and Universities had agreed that "appropriate credit" could legally mean no credit if so determined by the group with authority to make such a judgment—namely, the faculty.[167] The services (despite some initial resistance by the navy) thus concentrated their energies on upgrading their courses and instructors so that ROTC courses could receive accreditation on their own merits; such a course of action, if successful, would fully satisfy all parties. In 1971 the air force nominated Colonel Marvin Grunzke, who held a Ph.D. in experimental and industrial psychology from Yale, to the position of PAS at Michigan in the hope that he could attain an adjunct professorship in the psychology department (see Chapter 7). Such an appointment would thus accredit all courses taught by Colonel Grunzke.

The navy initially fought to retain all credit, but later modified its position. It threatened to pull its units out of Colorado, Michigan, and Illinois, as well as Minnesota and Northwestern, where faculties had made similar recommendations, and replace them with schools from its NROTC waiting list of sixty institutions. This threat failed, however, because Assistant Secretary of Defense Theodore Marrs and Secretary of Defense Melvin Laird were opposed to the navy's leaving any Big Ten school; also, the Navy agreed with DOD and Michigan officials that there was not "an equivalent to . . . any one of the institutions in the Big Ten with NROTC units" on that waiting list.[168] Nevertheless, in 1971 the navy directed that no NROTC scholarship student be permitted to enroll in a liberal arts college that had removed credit. This policy remained in effect for one academic year while an irate Association of NROTC Colleges and Universities successfully appealed the "mortmain" directive.

This debate over credit indicates that the services—even the navy, which fought hardest on this issue—preferred having no-credit programs at schools like Michigan and Illinois to having full-credit ones at less visible, less prestigious schools. The services continued to push for the restoration of credit (see Chapter 6) but never again threatened removal of a unit as ultimate sanction. Instead, they accepted the universities argument that to be accredited they needed to have the approval of an academic department.

The debates over these abiding issues reflected the general consensus between university and military officials that the ROTC program was indeed worth saving, but that it needed serious reforms to "place ROTC within the regular academic framework of the University and make ROTC much less an adjunct unit than it has been."[169] By the end of this period, working compromises had been reached to permit ROTC programs to exist with the frameworks laid down by university faculties. At the end of 1971, University of Illinois chancellor J. W. Peltason described the debates of the past few years thus:

Vigorous support of academic programs on the campus of any major university does not imply unquestioning allegiance to traditional modes of instruction and curricular patterns. The proposal recently considered and approved by our Senate represents a serious attempt at increasing the academic quality of our three ROTC programs without substantially diluting that measure of professional military officer contact with the cadet or midshipman absolutely necessary to programs of this type . . . I can tell you honestly . . . that these conversations [between administration and military], as well as others conducted in the same vein are designed not to weaken or degrade programs which we already consider to be good ones, but rather they are intended to strengthen our ROTC programs, and to place them more within the regular academic framework of the campus than has heretofore been the case.[170]

These resolutions were sufficient to placate most faculty and administrators. Whether the ROTC units could attract enough undergraduates to make the program viable, however, remained to be seen.

Resolution of some of these key issues did not mean that ROTC's continuance was assured. The military, while agreeing as an institution to many fundamental changes to the program, still had many members, such as the navy's director of educational development, who saw the compromises as "inexcusable" and "less than satisfactory."[171] Similarly, many in the universities remained suspicious of the military despite the conclusion of negotiations on favorable terms to academe. After his battles with the navy, Robert Williams told Admiral Kinney, "It would be appropriate during the coming year for each party to watch the other in the same manner that the American Navy and the Russian Navy are watching each other in the Mediterranean."[172] Furthermore, although working compromises had been agreed to in principle, they still had to demonstrate that they could provide a lasting harmony for ROTC on American campuses.

More fundamentally, the compromises would be rendered moot if enough undergraduates did not find the ROTC program sufficiently important and interesting to join. Even increases in the number of scholarships could not stop the plummeting enrollments. The army increased the number of scholarships it awarded from 4,759 in academic year 1969–70 to 5,500 (the ceiling established by the Vitalization Act) the following year.[173] Still, even many large universities were turning out far fewer officers than they had in previous years. Michigan, which had produced fifty-nine army, twenty-eight navy, and twenty-seven air force officers in 1969, produced only thirty army, seventeen navy, and nine air force officers in 1972.[174] Nationally, the figures were equally dramatic. In 1968, the freshman AFROTC enrollment had been 25,966; by 1972, it had fallen to 8,147.[175] After 1973, a zero-draft environment meant that a major force for sustaining ROTC enrollment levels was gone. For ROTC and the all-volunteer force concept to survive, the American military system would have to make fundamental changes in the education and training of American officers in the post-Vietnam era.

CHAPTER 6

ROTC in the Era of the All-Volunteer Force, 1972–1980

Margaret Snyder has a job waiting for her when she graduates: she is going to be a marine.

—University of Washington *Daily,* 1976

The antidraft pressures of the Vietnam War and traditional American anxieties over conscription combined in 1973 to produce a new "zero-draft" military environment; for the first time since 1948, the United States military would rely exclusively on volunteers. The draft had served as a primary motivator for recruitment in all branches and grades of the armed forces for a quarter century by giving men a way to control the nature and timing of their otherwise capricious military service obligations. Similarly, the draft had served to boost ROTC enrollments by offering men the possibility of service in the more prestigious and higher-paying officer grades. Nixon's jettisoning of the draft meant that the freefall in ROTC enrollments caused in large measure by the Vietnam War would not immediately correct itself after the withdrawal of American forces from Southeast Asia. The zero-draft environment portended fundamental change to ROTC and to the entire system of military personnel procurement.

Criticisms of the draft that led to its abandonment were twofold. One argument against the draft was that, with its system of deferments and exemptions, it was biased against young men from low socioeconomic backgrounds. The very poorest members of society were relatively infrequently drafted due to their tendency to do poorly on physical and mental tests, but "among those who were found to be qualified, the poor were more likely to be drafted than were men of higher social status."[1] Also, draftees were more likely than volunteers to see combat.

The second argument recalled traditional American anxieties over conscription. The draft, many said, amounted to a conscription of labor. Forcing an individual into military service had always been inconsistent with American cultural and economic beliefs, but in times of war and national emergency, such as the Cold War that had inspired the 1948 draft law, this inconsistency could be tolerated.[2] In the aftermath of a humiliating defeat, however, it could not. The 1970 Gates Commission, which was assigned by President Nixon to examine the concept of a volunteer force, began its report by arguing that "a return to an all-volunteer force will strengthen our freedoms, remove an inequity now imposed on the expression of the patriotism that has never been lacking in our youth, promote the efficiency of the armed forces, and enhance their dignity."[3] Higher wages and better working conditions, it argued, not conscription, would attract men into the American armed services.

After the Gates Commission issued its report, the all-volunteer force became a virtual inevitability, and the services began planning for the transition. Furthermore, because the Nixon Pentagon called fewer draftees for Vietnam after 1969, the AVF was functionally in place even before its official creation in 1973. Supporters of the all-volunteer concept argued that market incentives, such as higher pay, would keep the services supplied with enough highly motivated men. But for the AVF to work, the services would have to make some fundamental changes in the nature of the military to attract volunteers, including raising pay and improving the quality of military life.[4]

ROTC units faced the same dilemma. Without the draft to induce men to join, ROTC training had to be redesigned, in the words of George Benson, assistant secretary of defense for education in 1971, "to make [ROTC] attractive enough in an era of volunteer armed forces."[5] ROTC now had to induce men to volunteer in an absolute sense. This structural necessity, combined with movements in American society more generally, created changes in the program that did not result from faculty reports or student demonstrations. Eventually these reforms forced a change in the very definition of the groups in American society that were qualified to be military officers.

The AVF was the third major cause for declining ROTC enrollments in an approximately fifteen-year period. The first cause had been the conversion of many compulsory units to voluntary status in the late 1950s and early 1960s. The services had supported that drop because the draft, the foundation of ROTC enrollments, was still compelling enough to push many men into the program. The second cause for enrollment decline had been the consistent erosion of the power of the draft itself as a motivating factor, beginning with the 1961 exemption of married men. Throughout the 1960s, young men found other ways of beating the draft, most of them inspired by a desire to avoid the war in Vietnam.[6] The introduction of the lottery system in 1969 formally removed large numbers of men from the draft; a large subset of those men were concurrently able to eliminate ROTC as an option for evading conscription. The AVF represented the impetus for the third, and most essential, major decrease in ROTC enrollments.

As Table 6.1 indicates, ROTC enrollments were on the decline even before the abandonment of the draft was widely contemplated. Now, for the first time in the history of the program, a majority of units, some of them large units with long traditions of officer production, were unable to meet their contractual obligation of having seventeen juniors enrolled. In 1974 the army put 140 of its host schools on probation for failure to meet this minimum standard.[7] Even a school as large as Michigan spent much of the 1970s on probation for enrollment reasons. Similarly, total University of Illinois ROTC enrollments fell 82 percent from 1966 to 1974; total University of Texas ROTC enrollments fell 66 percent in the same period.[8]

ROTC thus faced a monumental challenge with the end of the draft. It also faced uncertain campus and political climates. The formal agreements dis-

Table 6.1   ROTC enrollments 1968–1975, by service

Academic year	Army ROTC	Naval ROTC	Air Force ROTC
1967–68	141,495	9,443	44,987
1968–69	125,126	9,063	40,533
1969–70	87,122	7,708	27,978
1970–71	62,647	6,528	23,070
1971–72	45,130	6,445	21,201
1972–73	34,773	6,898	18,724
1973–74	31,363	6,765	17,464
1974–75	38,228	6,546	15,993

Source: Department of Defense Manpower Statistics, various years.

cussed in Chapter 5 created a truce on those campuses that had most vocally
called for change in the 1960s, but the long-term success of that truce was
still in some doubt. ROTC had become less visibly distinct from the civilian
programs with which it coexisted, but even after 1972, it still had the distinction of being a vocational, military program. The *Princetonian* spoke for
many when it reported: "Students may have a right to learn the techniques
of warfare, but it is not the responsibility of the university to make such instruction available to them."[9] The truces and curricular changes to the program notwithstanding, ROTC's vocational and military emphases continued
to make it an anomalous, and therefore controversial, university program.

Universities also had to face an increasingly watchful federal government
in an era of what administrators experienced as "adversarial regulation."[10]
Universities had become the target of increasing federal attention through
the Buckley Amendment, which limited the universities' right to distribute
information about their students, and Title 9 of the Education Amendments
of 1972, which prohibited gender distinctions in all educational programs
and activities. The proponents of Title 9 did not consider ROTC per se, but
the law certainly implied that all educational programs would have to promote gender equality.[11] These new laws "proceeded from the conclusion
that universities were guilty of violating the public interest" by being too exclusive.[12] Through these and other laws, universities in the 1970s had to
deal with a significantly more intrusive federal government than they had in
the 1960s.

Furthermore, university and government budget concerns grew more serious in the 1970s than they had been in the 1960s. The level of public support given to higher education began to fall after the oil crisis of 1973, even
as inflation and the costs of computing, facilities expansion, and financial aid
programs were rapidly increasing.[13] These financial crises forced universities
to scale back commitments and focused attention on the cost-effectiveness
of university support for ROTC units. At the same time, military budgets
were tightened; the services opted to close unproductive training units and
spend the money saved on the creation of new units, fundamentally changing the nature of the ROTC hosts.

All was not gloomy for ROTC's future, however. As we have seen, formal
agreement existed on some of the most contentious issues, and support for
ROTC among university administrators was generally high. Furthermore,
American confidence in the military began to rise again after 1973, even as
faith in other institutions was waning. Between 1973 and 1976 the percent-

age of Americans expressing "a great deal" of confidence in military leaders rose from 33 percent to 42 percent, while the percentage of Americans expressing "a great deal" of confidence in educational leaders fell from a high of 50 percent in 1974 to 38 percent just two years later.[14] The degree of confidence expressed by college-age people was even more remarkable. Between 1973 and 1975 (the first three years of the AVF), the percentage of eighteen- to twenty-three-year-olds reporting "a great deal" of confidence in the military rose from 28 percent to 44 percent. The percentage of that group who reported "a great deal" of confidence in education grew much more slowly, from 34 percent to 38 percent.[15]

There was therefore some indication that the military as an institution still held the confidence of many Americans, some of whom were concurrently losing faith in other American institutions. That confidence might help the services reestablish good faith with the general public, but it would not in itself be enough to guarantee ROTC enlistments or good faith with university communities, whose values did not necessarily overlap with the public's on military matters.

Furthermore, some of the problems that had confronted ROTC in the Vietnam era were absent in the era of the AVF. If Kingman Brewster's argument that the draft created a feeling of "sourness" on the campuses was valid, it might then be presumed that without the draft that sourness and the concurrent threat to life and career patterns would produce far less campus opposition and disruption. Indeed the vocal, and at times violent, antiwar protests began to dissipate by 1971 and were totally absent the following year. Even at schools with radical traditions, such as Michigan, anti-ROTC rallies after 1972 failed to generate significant numbers of protesters.[16] The lower levels of visible protest on military issues led some observers to talk of a new "post-Vietnam" era of university-military relations even while American soldiers were still in Vietnam. "Remember the 1969–70 protest days on the American college campuses?" queried a 1973 Army ROTC publication nostalgically, "Indeed those were dreary days for Army ROTC."[17]

The desire to place Vietnam safely and squarely in the recesses of memory, combined with the rapid turnover among undergraduate populations, also led some observers to talk of a new kind of college student. In 1975 an officer reflecting on his four years' experience as an ROTC instructor noted, "The wild radical is gone. Replacing him is the serious-minded student who knows he is here for a purpose and wants to get as much out of his college education as possible."[18] Such widespread proclamations gave some observers cause for renewed faith and optimism, but the American college student had not changed quite so rapidly. What had changed rapidly was the nation's abandonment of conscription and the concurrent shift to market incentives as a means of military recruitment.

The volunteer environment of the 1970s meant a new challenge for officer procurement. Market incentives—such as higher pay, better conditions, and the inducement of a genuine, rather than half-coerced, patriotism—combined with a new sense of worth in the military as a profession, would have to replace the draft as the primary means for getting men into ROTC. The Gates Commission had optimistically (and erroneously, in view of the heavy role the draft played in determining enlistment rates) predicted that with such incentives and an improved public image for the military, ROTC could begin to overproduce officers by 1975; this judgment appears even more sanguine in retrospect, when one considers that the Gates Commission never seriously contemplated an expanded role for women or African Americans in the AVF-era ROTC program.[19] As we will see, however, market incentives were entirely insufficient to induce enough college students to sign up for ROTC, threatening the viability of the program so long as it continued to prefer white males.

The Gates Commission's rosy predictions notwithstanding, ROTC administrators and observers saw only steadily declining enrollments. "ROTC survived demonstrations, sit-ins, and trashings in the late sixties," noted Michigan's *University Record* in 1974. "Now it is on the verge of succumbing to something less dramatic—disinterest."[20] Instead of waiting for the better times the Gates Commission predicted, the services responded to the enrollment crisis with a series of new tactics. They expanded the pool of potential officers by responding to the desire of women to join the program and by making serious efforts to recruit higher numbers of African Americans into ROTC. These changes, while coincident with a growing sense of egalitarianism in higher education and in American society more generally, were themselves only partly its product. None of the faculty reports of the 1960s and 1970s had criticized ROTC for excluding women and African Americans, despite attempts by those faculties to seize the moral high ground. Universities in the Vietnam era expressed a great deal of concern over issues of credit and procedure, but not ROTC demographics. In the latter case, the interests of the military, which was itself moving (albeit slowly) toward equality, and the demands of the AVF pushed for a change that all parties could agree was the "right thing" to do.

Rather than being prompted by university communities, these demographic changes emanated both from a simple need to fill the junior officer ranks in an era of declining enrollment from traditional sources and from the desires of previously excluded groups to enter what they perceived as the advantageous job environment of the armed forces. Women and African Americans were also concurrently entering new sectors of the civilian economy in increasing numbers. To be sure, federal legislation and the complementary interest in equal opportunity programs emanating from the universities themselves provided a synergy that increased the potential success of these integrations. But the military embraced the idea of a broadened base for officer recruitment even in the absence of direct pressure from university administrators and faculty, because of its own belief in its wisdom and utility.

"The Intent and Spirit of National Policy"

The 1948 law that had made women a permanent, if auxiliary, component of the American military system had established that no more than 2 percent of the American officer corps could be female. Since the mandated percentage was so small, before 1969 American military planners had only once considered opening ROTC to women, in 1956. With the single exception of that failed experiment, the American military trained its women officer candidates at sexually segregated female officer candidate schools both to separate them from men and because the focus of women's training was administration, not combat. Once trained, women served in separate units—the army's Women's Army Corps (WAC), the air force's Women in the Air Force (WAF), and the navy's Women Accepted for Voluntary Emergency Service (WAVES)—which had separate promotion lists and a clear noncombat ideal.[21]

On most campuses, however, women participated indirectly in ROTC events through women's auxiliary units. As early as 1927 such an auxiliary existed at Kansas State, where sixteen women competed for the positions of honorary colonel and honorary major.[22] These auxiliaries sponsored teas, helped cadets type theme papers, served as hostesses for ROTC events, and helped to plan the annual military ball. They also existed to make "indoctrination a little more bearable, a little more appealing" for the men.[23] The air force female auxiliary, called Angel Flight, became a national organization in 1957, and within nine years it had more than four thousand members at 113 schools.[24] Membership in the University of Pittsburgh Angel Flight was a prerequisite for election as queen of the military ball; in 1961 there were twenty candidates for the honor.[25]

The explicitly feminine emphasis of these auxiliaries was in part a conscious attempt to emphasize by contrast the very masculine qualities that ROTC was designed to instill (Angel Flight selection criteria included "scholarship, personality, appearance, and leadership"[26]). In 1960 Army ROTC headquarters advertised that "the Army's primary job is to develop MEN, poised, alert and capable of taking full advantage of the progress thus far achieved in organization of units and development of materiel."[27] Indeed, the strong masculine emphasis of ROTC culture—as a reflection of the larger military culture—made the inclusion of women on anything but an auxiliary basis difficult. Official marching cadences (called "Jody Calls") at the University of Colorado in the 1950s included, "There ain't no use in looking down / There ain't no women on the ground" and "I don't know but I've been told / CU women are mighty cold."[28]

In 1956 ROTC had made a formal attempt to enroll women when the air force opened ten ROTC units to women on a trial basis in order to boost WAF officer ranks. Penn State, Butler, Miami (Ohio), George Washington, and the Universities of Maryland, Texas, California, Southern Illinois, Georgia, and Florida tested the new Women's Air Force Cadette Pilot Program, which was to commission ten WAFs per unit per year. Consistent with the auxiliary status of the WAFs, the conditions of ROTC training for women "cadettes" was designed to be unequal. The male and female programs were legally separate, and WAF commissions technically came not from ROTC but from direct commissioning.[29] The women received no scholarships, were not permitted to take weapons training, and enrolled with the knowledge that they could withdraw at any time without penalty, meaning they had a way out if they decided that they preferred raising a family to having a military career.[30]

The program did not last long, in part because it offered a clearly second-class (and nonscholarship) status to the prospective cadettes, thereby deterring enlistment, and in part because of the air force's insistence on separate training for female officers, necessitating the assignment of female instructors.[31] The program stirred some limited interest in the WAFs but commissioned only seven officers. It never got past the trial stage and was formally canceled in July 1960.[32] Thus the first attempt to enlist women in ROTC ended. To the extent that women were connected to ROTC before the 1960s, then, they served primarily as auxiliaries to men.

Shortly after the Cadette Pilot Program foundered, however, a fascinating process of militarization began among small groups of college women, altering the relationship between collegiate women and the ROTC program. One manifestation of this evolution is evident in the changing nature of the female auxiliaries. Careful observers of the ROTC program noted "the accelerating rate of participation by young women in collegiate military societies" in the early 1960s.[33] These societies were themselves becoming more martial in their orientation.

In 1960 two "girls drill teams" were among the twenty-eight teams that competed in the Twelfth Illinois Invitational Drill, marking the first time that women participated in the event.[34] Four years later the University of Illinois Angel Flight auxiliary had a fifty-woman drill team, led entirely by women, and in 1966 the University of Texas AROTC rifle team accepted its first female member.[35] To be sure, the traditional auxiliaries continued to exist, but elements of change were undoubtedly mixed in with the continuity. In 1967, for example, Kent State's female auxiliary, the Army ROTC Sponsors, changed its name to the less ancillary-sounding Coed Cadets (note also the 1960s' spelling of *Cadets,* compared with the 1950s' spelling, *Cadettes*) and purchased military-style uniforms; membership subsequently rose from eight to thirty-one.[36] Women's societies were taking a much greater interest in military matters on several campuses, and they were taking on responsibilities much more martial than typing the theme papers of their male peers. These changes foreshadowed an integration of women into ROTC that was vastly more successful than anyone in power had believed was possible.

Evolving definitions of women's place in America drove many of these changes. The "separate spheres" of the 1950s gradually began to yield to more complex gender definitions. Among the important events of the early 1960s were the publication of Betty Friedan's *The Feminine Mystique* and President Kennedy's establishment of a Commission on the Status of Women, both in 1963. Three years later the National Organization for Women (NOW) released its statement of purpose, endorsing "true equality for all women in America, and [movement] toward a fully equal partnership of the sexes."[37] Surely, not all women shared the goals and ambitions of groups like NOW, but across the nation the rebirth of feminism called into question traditional views of men's and women's roles.

Individual women reacted to these changes in a wide variety of ways. Many daughters of World War II veterans were coming of college age, and they took great pride in the accomplishments of their fathers and wanted to make some patriotic contribution of their own. They had grown up under-standing, in the words of Lynda Van Devanter, who entered nursing school in 1965, "the obligation we all had to be of service not only to our family, community, church, and country, but to all of mankind." The military seemed to her the way to fulfill that obligation and to answer the challenge of President Kennedy's call for the "chosen" generation to change the world.[38] From World War II to the AVF, women had consistently been more interested in joining the military than the military had been in recruiting women. On one level, the evolving nature of the military auxiliary societies, and the creation of organizations such as the gender-integrated Peace Corps in 1961, were reflections of this process.

More important to policymakers than the changing nature of women's military auxiliaries was a legislative change in 1967 (Public Law 90-130) that removed the 2 percent ceiling and promotion restrictions that had been imposed on female officers in 1948. The immediate impulse for the legis-lation was twofold. Since, in the words of the Marshall Commission on Se-lective Service, "women willing to volunteer for military duty exist in far greater numbers than the services will accommodate," lifting the ceiling might allow the military to relax the numbers of men who had to be in-ducted.[39] Also, the promotion restrictions had created a bottleneck of valu-able female officers who had joined the armed forces during World War II. Before Public Law 90-130 these women were significantly behind their male peers in terms of rank, and because their promotion possibilities were so constrained, they were leaving the services in high numbers.[40]

Public Law 90-130 meant that there was now no formal ceiling on the number of women whom the services could recruit. Informal ceilings, how-ever, still existed, since women were banned from all combat operations and therefore could not legally hold some military jobs. Still, the number of sup-port personnel the services needed was sufficiently high to permit women to qualify for a much larger number of jobs than they were then filling. In other words, after 1967 there suddenly existed a large number of jobs in the military for female officers and no ceiling to prevent them from taking those jobs. The services' initial response to these changes was mixed. Public Law 90-130 had lifted the legislative ceiling, but it had not required the services to take any action to raise the percentages of women in uniform. Because there was then no formal mandate for increasing the number of female officers, Public Law 90-130 need not have had an impact on ROTC units.

The ROTC staffs responded to Public Law 90-130 as early as 1968, when an air force feasibility study found "no insurmountable obstacles to the recruiting, selection, preparation, and commissioning of WAF officers at selected AFROTC detachments." Still, the air force initially found it "costly," due to anticipated low enrollments, and "undesirable," due to the need to assign a WAF officer to each detachment, to enroll women in AFROTC.[41] The air force, consistent with the logic of its Cadette program about a decade earlier, had assumed that women could not be integrated into ROTC on the same basis as men because of their auxiliary status, thus necessitating the assignment of a WAF officer to each detachment. The university representatives on the 1969 Air Force ROTC Advisory Panel gave the air force little encouragement to think otherwise, noting, "We are not convinced that a WAF ROTC program would settle any major problems for the Air Force."[42]

The problems of training and cost, however, would be rendered moot if ROTC opportunities were made available to women on the same basis that they were already available to men. Under this scenario, assigning WAF officers to all detachments would not be necessary; women could be trained under essentially the same procedures as men. Colonel Jeanne Holm, the WAF Director, believed that "coeducationalizing" AFROTC was "essential to expanding career roles for women," and she pushed for full gender integration of AFROTC.[43] Theodore Marrs, under assistant secretary of the air force for reserve and ROTC affairs, agreed with Holm, indicating that opening ROTC to women also had the benefit of being consistent with "the intent and spirit of national policy."[44] The air force's need for officers, its tradition of comparatively liberal attitudes toward female officers, the enrollment crisis in ROTC, and such legislation as Title 9 and the Equal Rights Amendment combined to produce an environment singularly congenial to reform rather than conservative retrenchment.

In 1969 the air force began a pilot coeducational, two-year AFROTC program, identical to the male program in curriculum, at Ohio State, Auburn, Drake, and East Carolina; if successful, the air force planned to expand the program to six more units in 1970. The air force further directed that the officers produced from AFROTC would count in addition to, not in place of, the 225 women officers produced annually from OCS.[45] No ceiling therefore existed on the quantitative success of the air force program.

Women responded immediately to the opportunity to experience ROTC training. Fifty Ohio State University women signed up for ROTC in the first year.[46] At Temple University, which was not part of the pilot program, eight women signed up for ROTC in 1969 in response to a "routine university announcement" that such courses could be used as a substitute for that university's physical education requirement. Because the program was unrelated to the air force integration experiment, the women could not qualify for a commission even if they desired one. Nevertheless, they took marksmanship and tactics courses along with the men.[47]

The surprising success of the pilot program caused the air force to abandon plans for a gradual expansion and immediately begin gender integration in the two-year and four-year programs at all units. In the fall of 1970, eighty-one AFROTC units enrolled more than five hundred women officer candidates—a modest 2 percent of the AFROTC total, but impressive for a trial program. The quantitative success of the Women in the Air Force Reserve Officers' Training Corps (WAFROTC) program was evident to the army and navy as well. "At a time when male disillusionment . . . ha[d] thinned the ranks," women represented a source of a rather large number of new cadets.[48] This is not, of course, to argue that women were any more or less disillusioned with the military or America generally than men, simply that the disillusionment itself argued for opening military service to the one-half of the American population theretofore clearly marginalized.[49]

The army and navy programs, lacking the active support of people like Holm and Marrs, were characterized more by acquiescence than action. The navy agreed to a test program on four campuses for women in 1972 "as a compromise," in the hope that the Naval Academy could remain all male.[50] The army was also hesitant, but due to "pressure generated by the other coeducational ROTC programs, particularly that of the Air Force," it also opened a test program in 1972.[51] Not surprisingly, the air force took a definitive early lead in the integration of women and thus began to see the most immediate positive effect on enrollment. In 1972 the navy had 17 female midshipmen on 4 campuses and the army had 212 female cadets on 10 campuses, but the Air Force already had 1,427 women enrolled on 156 campuses.[52]

While some men had difficulty responding to the dramatic expansion of women into ROTC, the success of female cadets could not be denied. At the University of Illinois, where female enrollments lagged behind national patterns for a few years, male cadets found that the biggest advantage of having women in the unit was "to make sure we have something more to look at than just the cadre when we attend AFROTC functions!"[53] These attitudes notwithstanding, women were proving themselves the equal of men in units nationwide, much to the surprise of some men, who had expected them to fulfill a quite different role.

The army gave the ten units selected to test the integration of women in 1972 "little guidance on whether or not to modify their program." The cadre at the University of Hawaii, assuming that women's roles would expand in the coming years, made no curriculum changes; women completed rappelling exercises and M-16 rifle training alongside men. Twenty of the unit's 69 cadets were female; 3 women joined Hawaii's arduous Ranger unit. The Hawaii women outscored the men in small-unit operations and behavioral sciences tests, and the senior cadets (all men) gave the outstanding cadet award to one of the women. The Hawaii cadre told the army that it was "extremely impressed with the enthusiasm demonstrated by the young women. At the outset they were much more inquiring, energetic, ambitious, and outspoken than their male counterparts."[54] The army understood the success of the female cadets to be a function of their exceptional dedication, suggesting that women who decided to join ROTC came from a self-selected group.

The air force, army, and navy all increased the pace of their integration programs faster than initially planned, largely due to the demand of women to sign up. The army found the response to its ten-campus pilot program "greater than expected and hundreds of women expressed their desire to enroll in Army ROTC at the [nonpilot] institutions offering the course."[55] By 1973 the Air Force ROTC Advisory Panel, which in 1969 had recommended against opening the program to women, had "wholeheartedly support[ed] long-range relationships between the Air Force and the academic community in regards to acceptance of ROTC on campuses and to the effective recruitment of women."[56] The increasing interest in, and commitment to, military life among a subset of American female college students provided the justification for a rapid expansion of women's place in ROTC.

At some schools, such as the University of Pittsburgh, women accounted for more than one-third of new enrollments and a large share of the high-quality enrollments.[57] In 1975, 42 percent of female Army ROTC cadets from the fourth region (the Northwest) were number one or two in their class. Only 15 percent of the men were so qualified.[58] Women cadets soon became heads of their units at several schools, including the army ROTC unit at Ohio State.[59] By 1976 women held three of the nine offices in the University of Illinois AFROTC honor society and the Outstanding Basic Cadet award at the University of Texas.[60] The following year women won battalion commander honors and the Army ROTC Gold Medal at Illinois.[61] These accolades indicate that women were not only interested in the financial benefits of ROTC but also sought to excel as female pioneers in a formerly all-male bastion.

Women's motivations for enlisting in ROTC ranged from the simple desire for a challenge or "to do something different" to the more practical reason that the military job environment offered equal pay scales to women within grades, a rare condition in the civilian economy.[62] ROTC also allowed women to break out of traditional roles in dramatic and visible ways, providing leadership opportunities and, for those who sought it, weapons and flight training. In a 1980 survey, four in five female ROTC cadets said that ROTC gave them more opportunities for personal growth than any other campus activity.[63]

As noted earlier, the success of women in ROTC units was coincident with a changing social and legislative environment. By early 1973, thirty of the necessary thirty-eight states had ratified the Equal Rights Amendment; the DOD assumed that the imminent passage of the amendment would force major changes in the nature of the American military system. A 1972 DOD task force noted that "it is likely that *after* the Equal Rights Amendment is ratified, all laws and Service policies which treat women differently than men will be challenged on grounds of unconstitutionality."[64] The services and the DOD hoped that if they were able to make changes "in an orderly way" they could avoid being forced to make drastic changes by the courts, which were already forcing gender equality in military family and benefits policies.[65] The integration of women was also helped along by the belief of some men, such as the PNS at the University of Washington, that opening training to women was the proper course of action. "Training military officers without regard to sex is an idea whose time has come," he noted. "The Navy needs female officers, and we have the facilities for graduating female officers. It's as simple as that."[66]

It may not have been quite as simple as that, but the surprising ease with which women were integrated into ROTC programs was critical to keeping the program viable. "Only the participation of women in ROTC," noted the DOD in 1980, "has been responsible for keeping enrollments on the increase."[67] By 1980, 2,080 women had been commissioned via the AFROTC program and almost 4,000 more women were enrolled in the program, including 1,102 scholarship winners.[68] The success of female ROTC cadets mirrored, and in turn contributed to, the success of military women more generally. Their ability to succeed in a previously all-male realm led to the gradual disbanding of the WAC, WAF, and WAVES auxiliaries between 1973 and 1978 and the integration of the service academies in 1976.

Two trends combined to create the reforms that made the integration of women into ROTC possible. First, the interest women were showing in ROTC was a reflection of their expansion into other previously male-dominated professional fields, such as engineering, where women's share of the profession rose from 9.1 percent to 13.4 percent between 1972 and 1978, and in fields analogous to the military, such as law enforcement, where in the same period women's share rose from 2.6 percent to 5.9 percent.[69] To be sure, the military was not alone in blazing new trails; other significant gender integrations included the Secret Service in 1970 and the New York City Police Academy in 1972. Women's own changing sense of appropriate careers, reflected both in the changing nature of the auxiliary societies and the trend of female employment nationwide, therefore increased the supply of qualified women for ROTC. Second, a change in the American personnel procurement system reduced the number of available male officer candidates and increased the demand for women to fill the void. The successful integration of women into ROTC depended on both of these changes.

"An All-Out Effort to Correct Such Inequities as May Have Existed in the Past"

The integration of African Americans into ROTC mirrored the integration of women in timing, causation, and outcome. The desire of more African Americans to enter the armed forces, changing legislative and social environments, and a structural change in manpower policies combined to produce reform. There were, however, two key differences between the integration of women and the integration of African Americans. First, African Americans had a history of greater rates of participation in the military than women. Thus the integration of African Americans built on an earlier tradition, and rising rates of participation by African Americans in ROTC represented an acceleration of an existing pattern, rather than the creation of a completely new one. Second, many charged that African Americans had borne disproportionately high casualty rates in Vietnam, in large part because of their overrepresentation among the enlisted ranks and underrepresentation in leadership positions.[70] The services thus hoped to use ROTC to increase African American representation in the officer corps, which stood at just 2.2 percent in 1971, compared with 10 percent among the enlisted ranks.[71] Therefore, the recruitment of more African American officers for ROTC received far greater institutional support from the military than had the integration of women in this same period.

All four services understood the racial integration problem to be serious, especially in light of racial violence on ships and bases worldwide in the early 1970s. In 1971 the DOD created the Defense Race Relations Institute at Patrick Air Force Base and set a goal of sending all air force personnel through the program in four years. The following year, the Marine Corps banned race as a consideration for housing or personnel assignments. According to historian Bernard Nalty, the program was more than just words. Marine Corps Commandant General Cushman enforced the new directives with a force sufficient to demonstrate "that he meant what he said."[72] In the hierarchical environment of the military, firm support from a commander can make a world of difference.

These programs and others like them reflected a recognition among many political and military leaders that old understandings of the place of African American soldiers had to be discarded. The notion that white southerners, who supposedly knew how to "deal with" African Americans, should be in command positions over them faded. The military came instead to understand that having African American noncommissioned officers (NCO's) and regular officers was critical to both the operational efficiency of the military and to the creation of the more just and equal environment that military leaders like Cushman and Admiral Elmo Zumwalt, chief of naval operations, wanted to create. To achieve this goal, however, the services would need to find a way to get more African American officers in uniform.

Production of African American officers had fallen by more than 50 percent between 1967 and 1972, largely due to the low prestige of the military among African Americans during the Vietnam era and the wider opportunities available to African Americans in the civilian sector as American corporations developed equal opportunity programs. In 1971 the navy, under Zumwalt, set a goal of raising the percentage of African American officers to 12 percent in five years.[73] The army and air force also set goals to increase the percentage of African American officers to a number commensurate with their representation in the service populations as a whole, but since the service academy classes were relatively small and were themselves only 2.2 percent African American in 1970, raising the percentage of African American officers required "an all-out effort to reverse [past] trend[s] and to correct such inequities as may have existed in the past."[74]

With the academies largely unable to make a dramatic impact on racial balance and with the OCS program on the ropes following the My Lai incident (see Chapter 5), ROTC emerged as the obvious solution. Universities, of course, were themselves undergoing a revision in racial composition, and they represented a source of high-quality minority officer candidates. The major currents of reform centered around two complementary approaches. The first approach focused on opening new ROTC units at historically black colleges and universities and other schools with high minority populations. In this period, the navy added units at Florida A & M, Prairie View A & M, Savannah State, and Southern University. The air force established units at Grambling, Mississippi Valley State, Fayetteville State, and Tennessee State. The army added units at Alabama A & M, Fort Valley State, Alcorn State, Jackson State, St. Augustine's, Benedict, Bishop, and Norfolk State.

The historically black schools already had some experience with ROTC programs. The twelve Army ROTC units created before 1950 had provided nearly 9,000 officers to date. Some of these schools were land-grant institutions and were therefore mandated to have military training programs. Schools such as Southern University (ROTC unit activated in 1916), Howard University (activated in 1921), and Tuskegee Institute (activated in 1941) had ROTC units that long predated the Vietnam era.[75] Their administrations saw access to military training as "a significant stride forward" for African Americans. While many civil rights leaders had bitterly opposed the war in Vietnam, they had not necessarily become antimilitary. African American leaders had traditionally seen the military as a means for African Americans to demonstrate loyalty, reliability, patriotism, and courage, as well as a place to gain valuable training and access to good jobs. The student bodies of these schools supported the establishment of ROTC units, indicating that they shared the view of the military as a means of advancement for the African American community, for themselves personally, or both.[76]

For African Americans, ROTC offered several important advantages. While the overall job environment in the United States appeared to be improving, the job market continued to offer fewer opportunities for African Americans than it did for whites. As a result, African Americans were "more willing to subject [themselves] to the demands of life in the armed forces in return for the combination of pay, allowances, and the promise of training and travel."[77] Enlisting in ROTC offered the additional benefit of a free or subsidized education and service in the officer corps. The military job environment was also one of the rare situations in America where African Americans could be in positions of authority over whites.

In a racist society the military can, at times, stand out as a model of racial harmony. When field and company grade officers took military directives on equal treatment seriously, military service was color blind. Authority in theory, often in practice, derived from criteria utterly unrelated to race. A reporter for *Ebony* magazine observed the high reenlistment rates of African American soldiers and commented, "The Negro has found in his nation's most totalitarian society—the military—the greatest degree of functional democracy that his nation has granted to black people."[78]

Over time, the military job environment improved for all employees in terms of pay and conditions. For African Americans, especially, however, the military job environment looked more appealing as racial animosity eased. Bernard Nalty argued that by 1973 "two or more blacks no longer constituted a potential riot in the view of whites" and that off-base encounters between African American and white service personnel were "no longer as overtly antagonistic toward each other as before."[79] This is not, of course, to argue that all of the racial tension of the past decades had suddenly dissipated; rather, it is to say that as volunteers replaced draftees and as the military made a genuine commitment to improve the lives of African American service personnel, the military became a less hostile working environment for African Americans. This improvement in the working conditions of the military helped ROTC recruit officer candidates at old and new units alike.

The new units to be hosted at historically black schools were selected according to a formal application procedure and a series of on-campus visits by military personnel. The services seem to have been particularly attracted to conservative schools such as Prairie View A & M, where the administration still enforced curfews and hair regulations for students; the administrators had also considered changing the sports nickname of the school from the Panthers after the confrontational Black Panther Party grew in popularity among African Americans at universities nationwide. However chosen, the success of these units was a high priority for the services. The first Prairie View PNS came to his post from a similar position at Harvard, and Secretary of the Navy John Chafee personally administered the oaths of service to the school's first group of NROTC graduates.[80]

The second approach to integrating the officer ranks centered around increasing the presence of African American cadets at existing ROTC units. The army understood that the most important step to be taken in this direction was improving the image of the military in the eyes of African Americans, both civilian and military. Nationally, the services ran advertisements in African American magazines such as *Jet* and *Ebony,* and they vigorously sought the support of African American leaders through lobbying the NAACP and the Urban League. On the campuses, improving the image of the military meant assigning more African American officers to ROTC units as instructors. The services especially tried to make such assignments at schools, such as the University of Pittsburgh, where the minority representation was increasing. In 1970 the army assigned Captain Alvin Officer to Pittsburgh. Provost Charles Peake noted that Officer's assignment would "be of considerable help in strengthening the rapport between the Military Science Department and black students."[81]

These efforts paid dividends almost immediately, especially for the army. In 1973, 12.9 percent of those attending ROTC summer camp were African American, up from 9.1 percent in 1972 and 4.9 percent in 1971.[82] Within ten years African American students accounted for 25 percent of AROTC cadets, 10 percent of NROTC midshipmen, and 18 percent of AFROTC cadets. By 1980 many of the historically black schools had become prolific producers of junior officers. Prairie View A & M's unit was the nation's second largest by 1982.[83] The twenty-one historically black schools that hosted Army ROTC units produced a total of 551 officers in fiscal year 1979; these units were responsible for 9 percent of the total Army ROTC officer production and more than half of the total minority officer production.[84] As was the case with the integration of women, the pressures of the AVF, the desires of African Americans to join the military, and a growing sense of a need for African American officers combined to create significant demographic change. Because of its role as the primary source for active-duty officers, ROTC was in a position to make a more immediate and dramatic impact on the demographics of the American officer corps than the smaller service academies could. The campuses felt this impact as well. In 1971 Duquesne University's graduating ROTC class chose as their motto: "Our numbers here at Duquesne are many . . . white and black . . . long hairs and short."[85]

The gender and racial integration of ROTC mirrored ideological trends in American higher education in the 1960s and 1970s. Roger Geiger has recently argued that the pressures of federal legislation were a relatively minor factor in assuring the success of affirmative action programs. As early as

1965 many schools had begun considering the admission of more women both as a way to stop losing qualified male students to coeducational schools and as a way "to have larger and academically more talented undergraduate student bodies while also alleviating their financial burdens with additional tuition."[86] In short, admitting women made sense both for the universities and for ROTC, because they offered a way to increase enrollments without reducing existing standards.

Furthermore, many schools had internal commitments to affirmative action that exceeded federal goals. For these schools, the addition of women and African Americans to ROTC fit smoothly into overall plans. The University of Michigan, for example, "established [affirmative action] goals for some departments that were not deficient and overall targets for minorities that were unrealistically high. The ascendant ideology and local coalitions of [faculty] activists induced universities to go beyond the legal minimum in implementing affirmative action . . . It was this internal conviction of the correctness of affirmative action that ultimately propelled university policy."[87] Thus, although university faculties did not demand demographic change in ROTC, such change nevertheless fit nicely into ideological currents in both the military and higher education. Academics thus received federal changes to ROTC demographics not as evidence of intrusion but as evidence of agreement.

Shifting the Geographic Balance of ROTC

To solve the problem of lower ROTC enrollments, the services also opened new units at schools that did not necessarily have significant minority populations. All three services had long waiting lists of colleges and universities that wanted to host an ROTC unit; in 1969, the army's list had 90 colleges, the navy's had 126, and the air force's had 116.[88] Until the AVF, however, enrollments had been high enough to permit the services to avoid trying something new; no new units had been added since the Korean War. The enrollment and financial pressures of the 1970s led ROTC headquarters in all three services to adopt a dual strategy of closing costly units (that is, those units producing too few officers) and opening a combined total of eighty new units at schools where they believed interest would be high enough to yield the contractual minimum of fifteen officers per year.

The new schools were decidedly different in character and specialization from those schools already in the program and those that were disestab-

lished. The closing of units at Ivy League schools received the most attention, but the services closed eighty-eight units in all during this era. To be
sure, the disestablished schools included Harvard, Yale, Columbia, Stanford,
and Dartmouth, where the services and the universities could not agree on
changes to the program, but much more numerous were small schools,
many of them liberal arts colleges like Franklin and Marshall, Grinnell, Davis and Elkins, and Denison, where the services initiated deactivation proceedings based on their inability to attract enough cadets without the coercion of the draft.

Thus ROTC units often closed for the undramatic reason of cost effectiveness. Historians Peter Karsten and Vance Mitchell agree that even without
the turmoil of the 1960s, the Ivy League schools "would probably have been
phased out within the next few years anyway" because they were "'self-
destructing' low producers," having accounted for less than 2 percent of
the total annual officer production for many years.[89] Harvard, Brown, and
Princeton each averaged fewer than seven AFROTC graduates per year in
the early 1960s.[90]

As long as the draft had existed, ROTC's "continued prolific production
was taken for granted."[91] Without the draft, the air force estimated that the
future viability of 40 percent of its ROTC units was in doubt. Many of those
schools, such as Case Western, Coe, and DePauw, had been low producers
for years; the AVF made them financially unsustainable.[92] Even large units
were suffering from the transition; in 1974, both the University of Michigan
and the University of Illinois AFROTC units dropped below the fifteen com-
missionees required by their contracts.[93] In such a climate, the services decided to finally disestablish chronic low producers and invest the money
saved into opening a new series of units based on hosts' "enrollment,
growth potential and student and faculty interest."[94]

Officials at one of the new schools, Columbus College, a public school in
Georgia first established as a junior college in 1958, saw the unit as a "wonderful opportunity" for the school and its students. The faculty committee
that investigated the acquisition of the unit noted the following benefits for
participating students: a monthly stipend; a paid six-week summer camp;
the availability of scholarships; and the opportunity to obtain an army commission. Columbus College thus agreed to pay the full cost of an 8,900-
square-foot building for the unit's classroom, storage, and office facilities.[95]
Columbus College was one of the new breed of ROTC hosts that was drastically changing the character of the program: it was public; it saw ROTC as a

point of pride; and its students supported the idea of having the program on campus.

The most immediately notable difference between the "old" units and the "new" ones was their location. As Table 6.2 indicates, the new units were disproportionately southern and midwestern, while the disestablished units were mostly eastern. The only significant variation among services occurred in the Midwest, where the army opened fifteen units and closed two; at the same time the air force closed seventeen while opening only one. This difference nicely illustrates the general tendency of the services to move away from private schools; the closed air force units were all at small, private institutions such as Otterbein, Grinnell, Kenyon, and St. Olaf. Conversely, the army opened four and five ROTC units on satellite campuses of the Oklahoma and Wisconsin systems, respectively.

It would be easy to argue that the services opened new units in the South and Midwest and at public schools because they could reliably expect that they would face much less of the student and faculty opposition that they had faced in the private schools of the East; this explanation alone, however, provides a rather limited view of the larger issue. Undoubtedly the expectation of more favorable treatment played a large role; all of the new units allowed academic credit for ROTC courses, for years a contentious issue on many campuses.[96] The services sought to establish units at schools that evinced a strong desire to become a host and where they believed student interest in the program would be high. As one navy observer noted, "Overall we wanted institutions who wanted us, irrespective of their program strengths."[97]

Table 6.2   Net gain or loss of ROTC units by region, 1968–1974

Region	Total units in 1968	Units closed	Units opened	Total units in 1974	Net change
East	123	43	13	93	−30
Midwest	115	19	16	112	−3
South	147	12	45	180	+33
West	88	14	6	80	−8
Total	473	88	80	465	−8

Source: Directory of ROTC/NDCC Units (Ft. Monroe, Va.: Headquarters, United States Continental Command, 1969 and 1974).

Not only were the new schools in the presumably more "promilitary" South and Midwest, many of these schools were also in or very near places with strong military communities and traditions: Old Dominion and Norfolk State are near both the Newport News naval complex and Ft. Monroe (home to AROTC headquarters); Fayetteville State is near Ft. Bragg; Alabama State is near Maxwell Air Force Base (home to AFROTC headquarters); and Benedict College is near Ft. Jackson, to name but a few. The director of development at Columbus College cited "close college ties with Fort Benning [also in Columbus, Georgia] and local interest in military affairs" when he announced that the unit would be "a great asset to the community as well as the college."[98]

Broadening the geographic focus of ROTC was consistent with a trend in DOD research funding as well. In an attempt to expand the base of scientific research in the nation's colleges and universities, the DOD awarded grants to 100 schools "well down the research university hierarchy."[99] These schools, too, were disproportionately in the South and Midwest. The shift in geographic representation of ROTC units therefore mirrored a larger trend of DOD cultivation of better relations with a larger number of schools beyond the traditional eastern colleges and universities. In large measure, the services hoped to compensate for the declining military presence on eastern campuses by substituting desire for institutional quality. In other words, the services sought new hosts based upon a logic analogous to that which informed the AVF: seek out motivated, eager volunteers.

Many of the new schools had specific technical emphases that the services found attractive; not surprisingly, some of these were military schools. The navy opened programs at the Citadel and Virginia Military Institute, which had long supported AROTC and AFROTC programs. These programs offered cadets at military colleges a faster path to the types of military training and jobs they desired. Similarly, the air force opened a unit at Norwich University, which in the nineteenth century had begun the tradition of training officers at the nation's civilian campuses (see Chapter 1). The services also instituted military training at schools that specialized in relevant civilian skills. In this vein, the navy opened units at Maine Maritime College and SUNY–Maritime College. The air force followed suit by establishing units at schools such as Embry-Riddle Aeronautical University in Florida.

The AVF sparked one other fundamental change to the nature of ROTC unit demographics. The 1964 Vitalization Act had authorized the establishment of so-called cross-enrollment agreements between ROTC host schools and nearby schools that did not host ROTC. These agreements permitted a student enrolled at a school without ROTC, or without the desired branch of ROTC, to commute to an ROTC host for his or her military training.[100] The cross-enrollment authorization had been used only sparingly before the AVF. In the era of the AVF, however, the services encouraged much wider use of cross-enrollment authority.[101]

Initially, ROTC hosts signed cross-enrollment agreements with schools of obvious qualitative value, such as Pittsburgh's AFROTC agreement with nearby Carnegie Mellon and Michigan's agreement with Western Michigan University, which had a degree program in aviation engineering.[102] Shortly thereafter, however, the services saw the advantages of rapidly expanding the cross-enrollment program for quantitative reasons, as it was inexpensive to do so and, especially in large cities, it dramatically increased the potential cadet pool. By 1975 the 156 Air Force ROTC hosts had signed a total of 316 cross-enrollment agreements, more than doubling the total number of campuses connected to AFROTC.[103]

Obviously, schools in areas with a high concentration of colleges and universities stood to benefit the most from cross-enrollments. The University of Pittsburgh signed seven such agreements with schools with a combined undergraduate enrollment of more than 16,000, and the University of Michigan signed three agreements with schools with a combined undergraduate enrollment of more than 27,000.[104] In 1976–77, cross-enrollees accounted for 32 percent of the University of Texas Army ROTC enrollments, including 75 percent of Texas's African American cadets. Cross-enrollments also had the advantage of allowing ROTC to target schools from specific categories, such as junior colleges or predominately female colleges; Smith, Wellesley, and Chatham all signed cross-enrollments agreements. Cross-enrollments also permitted students from recently disestablished host schools, such as Harvard and Amherst, to remain in the ROTC system.[105]

These changes in the nature of ROTC host schools and cadets mirrored geographic and other changes in the quality of academic institutions and their students more generally. Between 1960 and 1980 the number of public colleges and universities climbed from 700 to 1,500. Their total undergraduate populations rose from 2 million to 9.5 million, compared with the growth in private schools from 1.5 million undergraduates in 1960 to 2.5 million in 1980. ROTC, with "a move coincidental with the extension of college opportunities to this [southern and midwestern] segment of American youth," was going where the students were going.[106]

The integrations of women and African Americans into ROTC also reflected demographic changes in the American undergraduate population in the 1960s and the 1970s. Between 1960 and 1980 the percentage of all undergraduates who were female climbed from 37 percent to 51 percent. The percentage of all undergraduates who were African American rose from less than 4 percent to 10 percent.[107] ROTC units were therefore keeping pace with changes that affected their host schools.

The end of conscription thus forced the services to change the nature of their ROTC cadets and hosts. The AVF resulted in the addition of women and African Americans, as well as students from a much wider array of colleges and universities, both through the establishment of new units and through cross-enrollments. But widening the recruitment base alone could not save ROTC enrollments from continuing to fall. As was the case in the military more generally, conditions had to improve to attract men, and now women, to enlist voluntarily and remain in ROTC.

A More Humanized Approach

As noted, the architects of the AVF assumed that market incentives and a new, unforced patriotism would suffice to replace the draft as a major factor in enlistments. Chief among those incentives were higher pay and better conditions. For the American armed forces, better conditions meant a reduction in discipline and a change in many traditional features of military life, such as the disappearance of on-base, barracks-style housing. ROTC in the years immediately following the introduction of the AVF mirrored these changes. The "working conditions" of ROTC became less onerous as the services ameliorated many of the elements of ROTC training most distasteful to college students.

ROTC certainly benefited from renewed congressional attention in the early 1970s to improving military pay, benefits, and living conditions. To make the AVF work, Congress raised the average active-duty military salary 113 percent between fiscal years 1968 and 1974. In addition, Congress enriched the military health and pension systems, modernized military housing, and hired civilians for many of the more distasteful paperwork and clerical jobs formerly assigned to junior officers.[108] These changes benefited ROTC indirectly by improving the image of the military as an employer.

Increasing direct monetary compensation was one way for the services to quickly, if not cheaply, improve the recruiting environment for ROTC. As noted in Chapter 3, the army and the air force built up to their maximum authorization of 5,500 scholarships earlier than they had expected in an effort to curtail the falling enrollments of the late 1960s. Shortly thereafter, in anticipation of the end of the draft and with the expectation of further declines in enrollment, they pushed for an amendment to the Vitalization Act that would permit them to offer more scholarships and higher monthly stipends. In the early 1960s, the army and air force had responded to scholarship plans unenthusiastically; by the early 1970s, however, scholarships had become a critical part of their plan to save ROTC. The 1971 amendment to the Vitalization Act raised the scholarship authorization from 5,500 to 6,500 per service and increased stipends from $50 to $100 per month.

Pecuniary considerations were important, but changes in the daily life of the cadets were probably even more important. The services worked to introduce reforms that would permit college students to take ROTC without, in the words one Army ROTC instructor, making the cadet "walk around campus as a marked man."[109] ROTC instructors referred to these changes as "a more humanized approach" and "not much more than common sense."[110] They understood many of these changes to be only tangentially related to training issues. One PMS told an observer, "A lot of the meaningless things have been eliminated."[111]

Chief among these "meaningless things" were those elements of ROTC training that made the cadets visibly different from their non-ROTC peers. At most schools, hair regulations were substantially relaxed; African American students were allowed to wear Afros, and haircuts below the ears were tolerated as well.[112] "[W]e aren't so concerned about haircuts and that sort of thing," noted an army instructor. "It's not indicative of leadership."[113] The new hair policy was consistent with relaxations in hair regulations outside ROTC. The navy, prompted by a desire to raise reenlistment rates and convinced that "the conflict is not worth all the fuss," had already led the way in 1970, permitting beards, longer hair, and sideburns for its personnel.[114] While the service academies didn't go as far as ROTC, traditional crew cuts nevertheless gave way to "longer, thicker hair, with sideburns permitted down to midear."[115]

Uniform requirements were another target of reform. Some schools dropped uniform requirements altogether; students could attend ROTC classes in their civilian clothes if they wished.[116] The University of Pittsburgh ROTC staffs reduced time spent in uniform from three days per week to one. Other schools were also showing "less concern for the perfunctory" by permitting students to attend ROTC meetings (including one at Colorado with a major general) in civilian clothes and by becoming less exacting on the formal presentation of uniforms.[117] At Michigan, army cadets spent only one hour per week in uniform and NROTC students wore their uniforms only four times a year.[118] By the mid-1970s cadet yearbooks across the country began using candid photographs of students in civilian clothes instead of rigidly posed portraits taken in dress uniform. Compare these attitudes with those of 1963, when 97 percent of AFROTC cadets surveyed said that "care and wearing of the uniform" should be an important part of the precommissioning program and only 20 percent said that "students might be more interested in ROTC if there was [sic] no requirement for wearing the uniform on campus."[119]

The ROTC programs were now also characterized by significantly less drill, both because of its educational dissonance with civilian collegiate programs (as noted in Chapter 4) and because students themselves disliked it. After 1971 army cadets at Michigan spent just six hours per year in drill; Naval ROTC students spent only four hours marching in their entire ROTC career.[120] The reduction of the "spit and polish" elements of ROTC permitted substitution experiments to continue and appealed to undergraduates for the same reason that they were attracted to the new permission to keep longer hair: both changes made them less visibly distinct from their peers.

Similarly, ROTC instructors took great care to reduce the discipline that had marked ROTC in years past. They stopped issuing lengthy demerit lists and ceased using extra drill as punishment for misdemeanors. As a University of Texas PMS told an observer: "I consider my mission to balance the academia and the military. After all, we have students, not recruits. When a student rushes in late and out of breath after running over from the law school, we don't yell at him. And believe me, I've been in combat, so I know how to yell orders."[121]

Similar but less fundamental changes were also taking place at the service academies. While the academies retained "traditional military discipline" as a "basic ingredient," they nevertheless officially banned physical hazing and physical punishments such as "bracing" (standing rigidly at attention for long periods). They also broke down some barriers between first-year students and upperclassmen, as well as barriers between students and instructors.[122] Relative to civilian schools, the academies remained bastions of monastic dedication (Air Force Academy cadets were still not permitted to own a radio or watch television during their first semester), but they eliminated the "extremely childish and non-productive" harassments of years past.[123]

As with ROTC, changes at the academies were designed to increase the number of applications, reduce dropout rates, and improve the academic records of graduates. They were also designed to produce "a different breed of leaders for tomorrow's armed forces."[124] Those leaders took a curriculum that now included courses in Black studies, Roman classics, contemporary drama, music appreciation, and far eastern literature. As with ROTC, the changes reflected the military's general movement away from "crime and punishment" and toward the "development of leadership ability."[125]

Such reforms also kept pace with changes in the nature of the AVF-era officer candidate. Close observers of the ROTC program after 1972 identified a new "post-Vietnam generation" cadet who was much less concerned with the martial aspects of the program and much more concerned with the financial benefits and perceived advantages that ROTC and military service could provide for their postmilitary career. As a Pittsburgh reporter put it, "They think of the Reserve Officers' Training Corps as a door that will admit them into fields of their own choosing. Among the college students, the ROTC is no longer the symbol of a distant and despicable war."[126] ROTC had evolved from a mechanism for evading the draft to a pathway into the job market after an individual had fulfilled his or her service obligations. One cadet told a journalist, "I'm not in it [ROTC] for the war aspect, but for the growing up aspect." His interviewer noted that the cadet was

> one of those people who wouldn't have dared involve themselves in the military a decade ago, in the days of the anti-war movement when ROTC cadets were frequently objects of derision and hatred. He represents those students now joining ROTC for practical, calculated reasons—they like the idea of financial support and they like the idea of a job after college. These students sense a renewed respectability for ROTC on campus and want to take advantage of it . . . For most ROTC participants, the personal security motives are of such importance that the real purpose of ROTC—to prepare college-educated officers for military functions—is almost overlooked.[127]

In fact, the percentage of ROTC students desiring to make the military a career had always been small, and their propensity to leave the service after fulfilling their obligation had always been greater than that of academy graduates. What had changed was that the dominant definition of "calculated reasons" implied job market advantages in the 1970s, where it had meant draft evasion in the 1960s and the fulfillment of a moral obligation to serve the nation in the 1950s.

The ROTC advertisements of this era reflected this change. The ads of the 1950s that featured ROTC cadet Ted Wright had focused on the prestige in meeting one's contribution to the military, while the ads of the 1970s focused on job training and money. The students in the new ads explained why they had joined: "[ROTC] pays for all of my tuition, books and lab fees . . . it's really a good deal!" and "My reasons are basically selfish. Jobs are getting hard to get these days, and I know for a fact that a lot of employers think an ROTC guy's got a head start in management and things like that."[128] "Right now you may think Army ROTC will look small on your resume," read another ad, "but a lot of employers don't think so."[129] This line of recruitment reached full fruition in a 1985 army brochure, *The Margin of Difference: American Business and Industry Assess the Values of Army ROTC*, which featured testimonials on the value of ROTC training from the CEOs of thirty Fortune 500 corporations, including Xerox, Rockwell, Ford, and United States Steel.[130]

Ted Wright had been attracted by the chance to wear an army uniform and to participate in drill, ceremonies, and hours of physical and weapons training. The prospective cadets of the 1970s were told that "Army ROTC only takes up about three to five hours a week of your time while you're in college. No big thing."[131] Ted had also been drawn to ROTC as a way to fulfill his patriotic impulses and demonstrate his Americanism. By the 1970s, that mood had changed. "I've never considered myself especially patriotic," said one of the students in an ad. "With me, it all came down to one word," said another, "money. I needed a scholarship to go to college."[132] Little wonder then, with these being the advantages espoused by the military itself, that reenlistments of ROTC graduates beyond their obligation were so low. The services, looking for a quick fix for plunging enrollments, were selling ROTC as a temporary inconvenience, not a patriotic obligation as they had done with Ted Wright.

Many analysts have referred to military service as a trade-off of benefits and burdens; one gets benefits such as job training in return for the burden of potentially life-threatening service and time removed from the civilian job market. The ROTC ads of the Cold War era focused on the burdens; ROTC was arduous but necessary because of its centrality to the global struggle in which every American had a role. One's rewards came largely from the satisfaction of doing one's part. The same logic underscored ROTC's place on the Cold War campus. ROTC may have been a "burden" to collegiate faculties and administrators, but it was essential to national security and a sign that the campus, too, was doing its part. By the 1970s, ROTC ads stressed the financial and educational benefits of the program. ROTC became attractive because it made college possible for many and, for most, carried with it the presumption of a better place in the civilian job market after military service.

ROTC survived the AVF by reducing the ascriptive criteria for being an ROTC student and by making ROTC a less onerous course for students to take. Both of these steps had precedents in the era of the ROTC Vitalization Act, which expanded the pool of potential officers by including two-year cadets and transfers and also reduced the number of contact hours required in the ROTC curriculum. The changes brought about by the AVF followed similar goals but changed the quality and character of the program much more radically. With the incorporation of more African Americans and women, ROTC lost the white male focus that had characterized the life of Ted Wright. Furthermore, as one journalist put it, the AVF changed "the military's Spartan 'You will' doctrine on campus to an almost pleading 'Will you?' attitude," creating an ROTC program almost unrecognizable to those who had graduated from ROTC units in 1950 or 1964.[133]

These changes were indeed successful in bringing up enrollments, which began to rise by the middle of the 1970s (Table 6.3). All units did not share equally in the improvement, however; Michigan was on AFROTC probation from 1975 to 1978 due to low enrollment, and in 1978 it had the lowest Army ROTC enrollment of any of the state's eight units, despite being the

Table 6.3 ROTC enrollments 1976–1981, by service

Academic year	Army ROTC	Naval ROTC	Air Force ROTC
1975–76	44,363	7,016	14,589
1976–77	55,282	7,012	14,071
1977–78	57,910	7,095	14,660
1978–79	61,100	6,816	15,972
1979–80	66,212	6,685	18,387
1980–81	70,975	7,323	21,361

Source: Department of Defense Manpower Statistics, various years.

second largest university in the state. Still, even in Ann Arbor the picture was brighter from ROTC's point of view. The NROTC unit there reached its enrollment limit in 1978 for the first time in ten years, and student replies to the cards sent out to incoming freshman describing the ROTC program were up 25 percent from 1977.[134]

The dynamism that ROTC displayed in the 1970s was reflected in the fact that two schools that had disestablished their ROTC units, Princeton and Boston University, began negotiations for reinstatement and subsequently reopened their ROTC units. Indeed, even as ROTC demographics were changing, so was the ROTC curriculum. ROTC staffs answered the challenges laid out in faculty reports of 1970–71 to upgrade the quality of instruction as a precondition for reconsideration of academic credit. These curricular reforms set up new debates on much the same terms that had existed since the 1950s.

CHAPTER 7

A New Academic Program: ROTC, 1972–1980

The question of reestablishing ROTC credit . . . should be quashed now. The issue was decided satisfactorily two years ago and attempts to push it through the back door won't wash.

—Rutgers *Targum*, 1973

The war on the campuses, if not the ideological divisions, had conclusively ended by 1972; significant leftist elements remained after 1972, but they were much less confrontational than their predecessors had been.[1] As noted in Chapter 6, student demonstrations were by 1973 already being discussed as a quaint relic of an earlier time. The actions of student groups reflect this change. In 1974 the University of Michigan's Student Government Council rescinded its 1969 resolution calling for the abolition of ROTC, saying that the resolution "violated the rights of students desiring to be in ROTC."[2] Similarly, faculties had stopped assigning new ad hoc committees and faculty boards to study ROTC and recommend reforms. This changing climate led Assistant Secretary of Defense George Benson to announce in 1973 that "the troubled relationships [*sic*] between the military and academic world, which grew up during the university disturbances recently passed, is now pretty well resolved."[3]

ROTC's resurgence on some of the campuses that had earlier called for its abolition symbolized the change in climate and university attitudes. A 1972 survey at Princeton, whose trustees had voted two years earlier to sever all ties with ROTC, showed that 57 percent of the students and 73 percent of the faculty favored the return of ROTC.[4] Based on this evidence and pressure from the alumni, many of whom were proud ROTC graduates or military veterans, the trustees of Princeton voted to begin negotiations to reestablish its dormant ROTC program.[5] Boston University also reopened negotiations on ROTC after having requested discontinuance.

As had been the case at Michigan and other schools, ROTC gained support at Princeton from some of the same groups that had opposed it just a few years before. Furthermore, ROTC drew support at Princeton for many of the same reasons that schools like Georgia's Columbus College sought out new units.[6] The Council of the Princeton Community's Ad Hoc Committee on ROTC, comprised of students, faculty, and administrators, which in 1970 had voted to ban ROTC, argued three years later that ROTC courses were "pursued in an atmosphere conducive to open discussion and questioning." They further noted that ROTC was beneficial to the Princeton community because it permitted students a wider range of career choices, provided financial aid for select students, humanized the military, and supported the concept of national service.[7] Still, there was no consensus at Princeton for the return of the *status quo ante;* all the concerned groups at Princeton insisted that if ROTC were to return, it would have to do so without the sanction of academic credit. At Princeton and elsewhere, ROTC was experiencing a resurgence, but on terms heavily influenced by prewar and wartime concerns.

The resurgence of ROTC at Princeton occurred despite the notable absence of lobbying by service officials, who insisted that the decision of whether or not to keep ROTC was Princeton's alone.[8] Some army officials, including Professor of Military Science William Snyder, argued that it was not in the interests of the army to reestablish a unit at a school where the chances for meeting contractual enrollment minimums were slim; even before the Vietnam War, Princeton had been a low producer. Nevertheless, the army saw symbolic value in reestablishing a unit at a prestigious school that had so recently expressed a desire to sever relations with the military; it further hoped that "returning to Princeton would improve the image and status of ROTC at other institutions and with the public generally."[9] The army therefore agreed to the trustees' 1974 request to reopen the unit.

The return of ROTC to Princeton illustrates the prevailing compromises, directions, and terms of debate regarding ROTC in the post-Vietnam period. The unit returned, but not under the same conditions that had governed it before 1968. The reborn ROTC program included weapons and drill training (specifically banned by a 1970 Princeton report) alongside four classes, including military history, taught by regular Princeton faculty.[10] Only the civilian-taught courses received academic credit. These changes reflected the debates that had been a major feature of university-military relations since the 1950s and continued unabated into the 1970s.

As previous chapters have demonstrated, the significant changes to ROTC during the Vietnam era were more than a response to student, faculty, and administration dislike of the war. ROTC reform was much more than a way for university communities to "get" the military. Rather, they represented the fruition of years of study and concern about ROTC and its proper place on civilian campuses. Because all of these reforms had roots in an earlier period and because the reforms had many causes that were only indirectly connected to the war, they remained important for the shaping of ROTC even as the postwar era drew to a close in 1980.

The Changing ROTC Curriculum

As noted, ROTC courses had frequently been criticized as being intellectually bankrupt and devoid of contextual analysis or practice in decision-making skills. While most of these criticisms came from academics, several military officers had themselves come to question the academic value of much of the ROTC curriculum. Throughout the 1960s educators and military officers had worked together in a variety of ways, from sponsoring guest lectures to supporting the more elaborate National Security Information Center's New York Plan, in an effort to upgrade the quality of ROTC instruction and make the courses worthy of full admission into collegiate curricula. As a group, they understood that this would require the marginalization of some of the most martial of the ROTC courses. As one ROTC instructor noted, "Personally I do not believe that subjects we now teach, such as small unit tactics, tactical communications, and other fundamental military subjects, are college level courses. They are important and should be taught . . . but not [on campus] for academic credit."[11]

Much of the military and civilian motivation for improving the quality of the ROTC courses centered around making the nonmartial courses worthy of receiving academic credit on their own merit. Several military and civilian officials continued to hold to the position that without academic credit, ROTC programs would have a difficult time attracting quality students, especially if the all-volunteer force concept succeeded. Without quality students, they argued, the ROTC programs themselves were in jeopardy, and the services thereby ran the risk of being constituted of less than the best men and women available for the job.

To some civilian faculty, the continued denial of credit for ROTC in colleges of liberal arts ran the risk of isolating the military from sources of humanistic thought, undermining what for many was the most important justification for ROTC's existence: the university's ability to influence the military through the production of officers with a broad educational background. This debate, then, recalled issues that dated back to ROTC's creation and before. Academics remained on the whole committed to ROTC to assure that civilians would continue to influence the development of junior officers. To them, not having ROTC was a far greater danger than having it. A University of Michigan professor of astronomy argued:

> The . . . credit loss continues to pose a significant deterrent to students wishing to pursue ROTC, as such students are forced to carry effective overloads each term or add an additional semester to their undergraduate program to accommodate the non-credit military science courses. This imposes an undue financial and/or academic burden on those students formally pursuing ROTC and reinforces the general, if unfair, suspicion that ROTC courses are different from or less visible than standard elections in one of the undergraduate colleges of the university.
>
> The alternative to ROTC detachments on campuses such as the University of Michigan is the development of a professional military which does not have the sensitivity to the integrity of diverse ideas and various modes of thinking encouraged in the give and take of a liberal education. We . . . may have to face the concept of a professional military being developed apart from the intellectual and humane atmospheres of our great universities if steps are not taken to encourage the continuation of military officer training programs on campuses such as our own.[12]

By the post-Vietnam era, several civilian professors and military officers who were careful observers of the ROTC program were arguing that the courses had indeed been improved to the point where a discussion of the appropriateness of academic credit and other matters could begin anew. For others, the postwar period also offered a chance to discuss these issues more rationally than they believed had been the case during the war, when, according to the chair of the University of Pittsburgh's ROTC Study Committee, the academic issues had been "clouded over by anti-war sentiments." The clear message from these proponents was that the removal of ROTC credit had been "contrary to the wishes of the student body," the result of the administration's giving in to a vocal, but in their view misguided, minority.[13] With that minority no longer a force in campus politics, an opportunity existed to right the presumed wrong. This view contained some truth, but it completely ignored the long-standing debate over ROTC's place in the curriculum.

That debate had traditionally been centered around three interrelated concerns over ROTC: the quality of the courses; the quality of the instructors; and the degree to which their professional, military orientation (including their dependence on an outside agency for materials and guidance) conflicted with the overall mission of civilian colleges, especially liberal arts colleges. Still, to many professors and administrators the efforts of the military during the Vietnam War to upgrade ROTC courses had been successful. The dean of the University of Pittsburgh's College of Arts and Sciences, Jerome Schneewind, noted in 1972 that "The present ROTC program . . . is richer and more academically interesting" than it had been in 1968. This improvement, he believed, argued for a reexamination of the no-credit policy in place in the college.[14]

To judge from the changes in course descriptions and the proclamations of support from civilian faculty, the reforms of the Vietnam period had indeed produced ROTC courses that were less doctrinaire, that included more emphasis on the context within which military officers operated, and that involved much less rote memorization. ROTC course descriptions before 1970 reveal the dissonance of these courses from civilian counterparts. The description of the 1960 Military Science I course, taken by all AROTC freshmen, listed as some of its goals: "[To understand the] necessity for a large U.S. Army . . . To provide a thorough indoctrination in military discipline . . . [To instill a belief in the] necessity for discipline."[15] Similarly, a 1968 AFROTC course at the University of Illinois titled Freshman Theory Course was not focused on theory at all. Physical fitness and American citizenship were prerequisites for the course; half of the contact hours were devoted to drill.[16]

These nonintellectual, hyperpatriotic elements of ROTC courses were among the several features of the curriculum to which civilian faculty had objected in their numerous committee reports of the Vietnam era. As shown in previous chapters, steps taken by the services, including participating in the NSIC New York Plan, soliciting advice from civilian faculty in order to "incorporate recent research," and raising the academic qualifications of their instructors, yielded courses that were more like those offered by civilian faculty.[17] These courses dealt much more with problem solving and analysis of context, while still remaining focused on the military as an institution and an employer.

By 1973–74, course descriptions read less like those described above and more like this one for a University of Michigan AFROTC class called National Security Forces in Contemporary Society:

> Focusing on the Armed Forces as an integral element of society, this course provides an examination of the broad range of American civil-military relations and the environmental context in which defense policy is formulated. Special themes include: the role of the professional officer in a democratic society; socialization processes within the armed services; the requisites for maintaining adequate national security forces; political, economic, and social constraints upon the national defense structure; and the impact of technological and international developments upon strategic preparedness and the over-all defense policy-making process.[18]

To focus on one course's evolution as an example, Naval Science 101 had been known as late as 1968 by the title Naval Orientation and Sea Power and had drawn particular criticism for being anti-intellectual and narrow in scope. It was described in the 1968 University of Michigan undergraduate catalog as: "Introduction to basic Navy background, procedures, regulations, and organization, with emphasis on the junior officer['s] duties and responsibilities. The last third of the semester introduces Naval history and sea power."[19] By 1974 it had been redesigned and renamed Introduction to Naval Science and was described as "an introduction to structure and principles of naval organization and management. Practices and concepts lying behind naval organization and management are examined within the context of American social and industrial organization and practice."[20]

Courses had thus been redesigned and their emphasis changed in the direction that the faculty reports had suggested. They were now focusing on environment and context and had eliminated much of the memorization, drill, and corps activity. Furthermore, the services encouraged all students, even noncitizens, to take ROTC courses without an accompanying military obligation, to address ROTC's reputation as furtive and inaccessible to civilians; more than one hundred non-ROTC students at Duquesne University took advantage of that opportunity in 1976–77.[21] These changes reflected both the military's desire to become more acceptable to the students and administrators of civilian colleges and its own sense that military education after Vietnam had to be broadened.

Course descriptions provide only a limited sense of how a course has changed; authors can change the description without altering the substantive material of the course. However, as Jerome Schneewind's observation at Pittsburgh suggests, faculty and administrators who attended ROTC courses and examined the materials used were generally pleased with the new courses, with the notable exception of those courses that they understood to have no application outside a single profession.

In this vein, a 1974 faculty committee review of the ROTC courses at Michigan found that many courses could "stand on their own academic merit" and were "compatible with what we understand to be appropriate to the liberal arts curriculum." The committee recommended credit for all ROTC courses except Introduction to Small Arms, Conduct of Military Operations, Ship Systems II, Naval Operations, and Amphibious Warfare.[22] A separate subcommittee report recommended a reappraisal of the no-credit policy at Michigan, noting that "we found in the current course offerings none of those deficiencies that were found by the preceding ROTC sub-committee in the 1968–69 programs and which caused it to render the negative verdict leading to the withdrawal of all credit. The disparity between the earlier appraisal and the present one, we believe, is due not to different standards of evaluation or to a shift in academic values, but reflects a real change in the nature of ROTC courses."[23]

At several schools, many where the status of ROTC had survived the wartime period intact, the ROTC staffs redesigned curricula with the explicit intent of putting the ROTC courses up for review on the same standards as those obtaining for non-ROTC courses. The goal was "to provide a program compatible with the evolving environment of the academic community" and therefore fully capable of existing alongside other courses and making significant academic and intellectual contributions of their own.[24] At the University of Colorado, a Committee on Courses that investigated ROTC in 1976 found that "a serious review of the ROTC courses and of their conduct does not disclose an orientation in the direction of indoctrination or of the mastery of the mere techniques of military life." The committee was "favorably impressed by the willingness of the ROTC staffs to cooperate with [the College of Arts and Sciences] in modifying course content so as to make their curricula more acceptable to this College."[25]

These changes improved the standing of ROTC in the students' eyes as well. Although students lacked the perspective to compare ROTC courses to those of years past, cadets reported general satisfaction with the quality of

ROTC instruction. ROTC students and recent ROTC graduates testified at committee hearings at Michigan in 1975 that their courses were taught objectively and with critical presentations.[26] Three years later, an independent survey of AFROTC cadets found that four in five believed that the quality of instruction in their AFROTC courses compared favorably with the level of instruction in their civilian courses.[27]

Civilian faculties acknowledged that the ROTC instructors themselves were now better educated and more formally trained in educational methods. These qualifications, the schools believed, permitted the instructors to make substantive improvements in the courses and the presentation of material to cadets. After 1970, all military officers assigned to Kent State, Illinois, Michigan, and Pittsburgh had a master's degree, reflecting a trend nationwide, as shown in Table 7.1.[28]

The 1974 Army ROTC Advisory Panel noted that the new instructors were "one of the important factors in gaining faculty support" for reaccrediting ROTC courses.[29] The improvements in course quality and formal qualifications of the instructors thus created a paradox: there was a general sense that ROTC was of significantly higher quality than it had been before 1968, but despite these changes, it received less academic credit and status than it had previously enjoyed.

Furthermore, some changes to general university procedures made the sanctions imposed on ROTC look to some, in retrospect, more Draconian than was warranted. Several universities had introduced programs in the early 1970s through which undergraduates could teach their own courses in consultation with, but not under the supervision of, regular faculty. Such programs, military officers and some civilian faculty charged, undermined

Table 7.1   Highest degree attained by AFROTC officers, by year assigned

Year	Bachelor's	Master's	Ph.D.
1967–68	74%	25%	0%
1969–70	73%	26%	<1%
1971–72	26%	72%	1%
1977–78	1.5%	95%	3%

Source: Joseph Pearlman, "A Study Comparing and Contrasting Views of the Role of the Air Force ROTC in Relationship to the Role of the University, 1960–1978," Ph.D. diss., University of Denver, 1978, p. 83.

the faculties' demands that accredited courses be taught under the direct control of members of the faculty; accepting credit for these courses and denying credit for ROTC courses, they believed, amounted to a distinction that was certainly arbitrary, even if it was not directly aimed at the military. As Michigan president Robben Fleming told his Princeton counterpart, "The claim is made, probably with a good deal of justification, that the College is applying a double standard which is directed at the military."[30]

By 1975, then, a growing number of civilian faculty were arguing that ROTC was not what it had been in the Vietnam era and before, and that therefore it was time to revisit many of the sanctions imposed on ROTC during the war. For some, this reexamination was justified because the sanctions had been unwarranted even as they were being implemented. For most, the reexamination was needed because the program was qualitatively different from what it had been just a few years earlier.

"Under the Influence of an Outside Institution"

As noted in Chapter 5, the faculty reports of the Vietnam era did not mandate that ROTC courses be thereafter prohibited from receiving academic credit. Instead, they determined that to be accredited, ROTC would have to meet the same standards that civilian courses had to meet. At the University of Michigan's College of Literature, Science, and the Arts, this standard meant that ROTC courses would have to meet the following guidelines for accreditation: "Experiential courses involving work accompanying systematic learning under direct supervision of faculty of this College [or physical activities] accompanied by a conceptual framework furthering insights into concepts of culture within which performance is tested and interpreted."[31] The narrow professional courses that the 1974 faculty committee determined were unfit for credit failed to fit these guidelines because they lacked the conceptual framework that the guidelines described.

The efforts to reaccredit ROTC did not amount to a drive for a blanket restoration of academic status. Instead, ROTC staffs attempted to convince civilian faculty that many of their courses met the standards established by the colleges within which ROTC existed. The program's position in the national and international security apparatus no longer justified such concessions as blanket academic credit for causes that were, in the faculty's opinion, not always the intellectual equal of other programs.

In the 1970s, as a result of the growing sense that ROTC had indeed changed to become more academically respectable, civilian faculties again agreed to consider the issue of academic credit for ROTC courses. These reconsiderations took place in colleges of liberal arts, which had generally been quite critical of the services, and in engineering colleges, which had to this point largely avoided controversy over the issue of ROTC. The improvement of the courses notwithstanding, most of the liberal arts faculties of the postwar era upheld their bans against blanket ROTC credit. By contrast, engineering faculties, who for decades had seen ROTC as a dilution of the academic standards of their own curriculum, granted credit for ROTC courses, on some campuses for the first time.

The difference in the approaches of the liberal arts and engineering faculties can be only partially explained by a generally more hostile attitude among the former toward the military. As important as ideology was the long-standing aversion in liberal arts colleges to professional courses of all kinds. Faculty members in both engineering and liberal arts colleges agreed that the new ROTC courses were, by their standards, "better" and worthy of academic credit alongside civilian courses. However, the reforms were not enough for the liberal arts colleges, which continued to chafe at the outside control and professional emphasis that ROTC represented. In the engineering colleges, these issues were less urgent because of the professional orientation inherent in engineering curricula and the lack of a tradition of conflict with ROTC.[32] Therefore, by 1980 accreditation patterns on many campuses were the reverse of what they had been in 1950.

In the liberal arts colleges, faculties consistently either voted not to reconsider the issue of blanket ROTC credit or they voted against blanket restoration. Still, in some individual cases ROTC courses, with the support of a civilian department, were able to gain accreditation. The faculties continued to hold to the prohibitions on blanket credit, even while acknowledging the credit worthiness of several ROTC courses. Permitting blanket credit would, in the faculties' eyes, restore to ROTC the special privileges of the prewar era, which the faculties were loath to do.

The ROTC staffs themselves, while for the most part believing that some academic credit could be useful in bringing enrollments and cadet quality up, did not lobby civilian faculty for credit restoration. They understood, as their predecessors had, that if they pushed too hard they would risk producing ill will and antagonism. Instead civilian faculty who either saw ROTC as a means to civilianize the American military or believed that the ROTC courses were the intellectual equal of civilian courses introduced measures to reaccredit ROTC. ROTC instructors occasionally testified at faculty committee hearings, met privately with influential faculty members, and often opened their classes to faculty visitors (at Colorado, ROTC staffs invited the faculty to make unannounced visits whenever they wished[33]), but they did not press publicly for a reconsideration of academic credit.

Among the liberal arts colleges of the universities studied here, only the University of Illinois voted to restore substantial ROTC credit. In 1976 the Illinois College of Liberal Arts and Sciences, arguing that it was "educationally sound to enable our students to participate in [ROTC] programs," permitted students to count six ROTC credits toward graduation, far fewer than the fifteen credits of the prewar era but a clear change from the zero-credit policy passed in 1971. Illinois had, in effect, replaced the prewar blanket credit policy with a new policy that accredited only those courses, all above the freshman level, that the faculty believed merited consideration alongside civilian courses. Here, as elsewhere, the reconsideration of credit resulted from the faculty's belief in the genuine improvement in the quality of ROTC courses and the desire of the ROTC instructors to be a part of the campus community. As Illinois provost J. W. Peltason informed the army, "As important as the actual granting of credit, has been the *way* in which credit was granted—via a rigorous evaluation process. ROTC work is thus being viewed as it should be: a serious, academically legitimate program of pre-professional education."[34] At Illinois, ROTC's reaccreditation symbolized an acknowledgment of the improvement in the quality of ROTC and its appropriateness to the mission of the university.

Nevertheless, liberal arts faculties continued to express deep concerns over the wisdom of permitting an outside agency to determine the course content of an accredited offering. Most faculty members could agree that at least some ROTC courses were intellectually equal to accredited civilian courses, but ROTC's anomalous position and character argued against a reconsideration of blanket credit.[35] In 1972 a Pittsburgh College of Arts and Sciences faculty cabinet voted thirty-seven to nine to reject a proposal to reconsider the issue of academic credit for ROTC, arguing that ROTC materials were "under the influence of an outside institution and cannot be controlled by the University."[36]

Michigan's College of Literature, Science, and the Arts (LSA) faculty debated the issue of academic credit in 1975 and again in 1979; both times, ROTC came away without credit. In 1975 the faculty "overwhelmingly" rejected a proposal to reaccredit ROTC despite an executive committee report that argued for ROTC credit because military instructors "now teach courses our way."[37] The committee members had divided ROTC courses into four groups: history/political science, management, technical, and military. They argued that courses in the first three groups were professional but analogous to regular university courses in content and quality and therefore worthy of credit after a faculty review of the course materials and the instructor's qualifications. Those in the last category, however, were deemed to have no academic equivalent.[38] "Armies must salute, of course," said the executive committee's chairman, "but we don't want anything to do with that."[39]

Of course, the military itself was not asking for credit for courses like drill. The significance of the Michigan committee's report was its recognition that "technical" courses, like Navigation, and "management" courses like Principles of Leadership were on the same professional level as other vocational courses, which were themselves becoming a larger part of liberal arts curricula. As economics professor W. H. Anderson, a strong ROTC critic in 1969, argued, "LSA is getting more professionalized, and there isn't that great a distinction between these LSA courses and the ROTC courses which train for a different profession."[40]

Nevertheless, ROTC most clearly symbolized the sole-employer model that was anathema to many faculty members in colleges of liberal arts. As such, the Michigan executive committee added the stipulation that credit would need to be awarded anew every year after a faculty review of relevant materials. Thus it implicitly acknowledged the anomaly inherent in ROTC. Even if ROTC were the intellectual equal of civilian courses, it was different in ways important enough to warrant special supervision. Such supervision was necessary because without it an outside agency would have unchecked authority over accredited course offerings, a condition that did not exist anywhere in the university. The 1975 faculty vote to deny ROTC credit was based on these issues, not on the propriety of military training per se. The LSA dean observed that

> it was my sense of the meeting, confirmed by discussions since the meeting with a considerable number of faculty members, that the vote was not based primarily on political views or an effort to strike out at the Military Services. Rather, I think it was predominately based on broader academic issues, including unnecessary course duplication, methods of selection and certification of instructors in contrast to the selection of our own faculty, and *particularly* the propriety of permitting an outside agency to enjoy the

privilege of exercising special influence over any portion of the curriculum.[41]

The fact that the outside agency was the military did not help the case of accrediting ROTC, but neither did it make the negative votes a certainty. No outside agency had the special privileges that ROTC was requesting, and in the absence of a global crisis such as the Cold War, faculties could find no compelling reason to reinstitute them.

When the issue arose again at Michigan in 1979, the situation had changed only slightly. By then, some civilian professors were still arguing that the no-credit situation impaired the overall success of ROTC, but the officers themselves, while hoping for a restoration of credit, were emphatically stating that regardless of the outcome, ROTC was at Michigan to stay. They were also willing to consider further changes to their program to satisfy civilians. "We would appreciate your telling us what standards you have or want," one officer told a faculty subcommittee. "You name it; we'll do it."[42] ROTC looked in 1979 decidedly less threatened and less threatening than it had a decade earlier. Still, the faculty rejected by a large margin the request to repeal the no-credit policy. Again participants, such as LSA associate dean John Knott, observed that they were "satisfied that the discussion focused on academic questions":

> Two of the issues in particular strike me as likely to come up at [future] faculty meetings on the issue. The first argument is based upon credentials. The officers who teach the ROTC courses, although screened by a faculty committee, are likely to have a masters degree at best and this is not always in the subject that they are teaching . . . The second argument has to do with the fact that the officers owe their primary allegiance to an organization other than the University.[43]

The contested issues of 1979 were thus little different from those of 1969 or even 1959.

At the same time, engineering colleges were increasing academic credit for ROTC. As early as 1973, some schools began to anticipate a change in policy from the Engineers Council for Professional Development (ECPD), which accredits engineering programs. Illinois raised credit for ROTC classes from six to twelve hours in its College of Engineering, anticipating no resistance from the ECPD and anxious to acknowledge what it saw as the improved ROTC curriculum.[44] In 1977 the ECPD formally changed its policies to permit ROTC credit to count toward the sixteen hours of social science and humanities credits it required of all engineering students. Michigan initially responded by permitting four ROTC hours to count toward graduation, but within a year it had voted to award credit "as earned" for all courses except drill, meaning that Michigan engineering students could earn up to sixteen credits for ROTC.[45]

The change in engineering school policy was a reflection of three factors. The most important was an understanding, mirrored in the liberal arts colleges, that the ROTC courses themselves no longer diluted the curriculum. The second was an awareness that ROTC, especially Naval ROTC, was seeking to have more of its scholarship students enter colleges of engineering; given that the courses were no longer evidently inferior, it made sense to encourage the navy's efforts in this direction. Last, ROTC had fewer vocal opponents in engineering colleges. While this factor alone made little difference, when combined with the rise in course quality and military's desire to produce more engineers, it yielded a decidedly more friendly atmosphere among engineering faculty.[46]

The efforts to reaccredit ROTC by restoring the program's prewar blanket credit privileges failed at most of the campuses where the issue was contested. Civilian faculties in the colleges of liberal arts were simply unwilling to return ROTC to a status with which many had always been uncomfortable.

Having been denied its status quo ante, ROTC sought to restore its prewar curricular status through avenues opened after the implementation of the post-Tet faculty reports. Cross-listings (officially listing an ROTC course with the offerings of a civilian department) and joint appointments (gaining an adjunct appointment in a civilian department) offered guaranteed paths to accreditation without formal approval from a college's assembled faculty. But here, too, the ROTC units had little success. Civilian departments recognized only those ROTC courses that filled an obvious gap in that department's undergraduate offerings, such as when the NROTC executive officer at Michigan succeeded in securing a joint appointment in the department of naval architecture and marine engineering and cross-listings for aeronautical engineering and navigation courses.[47] Where the proposed ROTC course filled no departmental need, the departments rejected requests for both cross-listings and joint appointments. Engineering and liberal arts colleges rejected these requests with equal regularity, arguing that ROTC courses had little overlap with their own offerings except in such areas as political science, management, and military history, where the courses were taught satisfactorily by regular faculty. Furthermore, they argued, ROTC instructors were not interested in relevant research, a common (though not necessary) qualification for adjunct and visiting professorships.

Civilian faculties, with few exceptions, rejected formal associations with ROTC because the instructors were employed by an outside agency and the programs offered no courses that filled obvious gaps in regular civilian offerings. For both of these reasons, Michigan's history department rejected a proposal to use military officers as teaching assistants in a military history survey course run by a member of the history faculty.[48] The department argued that its graduate students, under the department's direct supervision, were sufficient for the job. Using the same logic, the College of Engineering at Illinois consistently rejected ROTC requests for cross-listings.[49]

The faculty reports of 1969 and 1970 represented more than a vehicle for some faculty members to lash out at what they perceived as an immoral and corrupting military establishment. They represented a prevailing belief among civilian faculty members, especially in colleges of liberal arts, that ROTC programs were not the intellectual and academic equal of regular civilian offerings. After 1972, when campus tensions had eased and some student groups were rescinding anti-ROTC proclamations, liberal arts faculties had the opportunity to restore academic credit and status to the ROTC programs. On most campuses they did not; in upholding the decisions they had made a few years earlier, they used many of the same arguments that their predecessors had used. ROTC, they contended, while beneficial in many important ways, was different enough from civilian academic programs to warrant special distinctions.

The Military and ROTC

Despite its inability to achieve a satisfactory conclusion to the question of academic credit, the military remained generally pleased with ROTC, especially as enrollments began to climb in the mid-1970s (see Chapter 6). Qualitatively, ROTC students were at least the equivalent of their non-ROTC peers, even at competitive schools such as Michigan (see Table 7.2). Nationally, the mean composite SAT score of entering college freshmen fell from 924 in 1974 to 878 in 1979. The mean composite score of ROTC scholarship students, however, rose by at least 100 points in all four services in the same period.[50]

Table 7.2   Mean composite SAT scores

Students	Score
AROTC scholarship students, 1978	1,285
NROTC scholarship students, 1978	1,246
AFROTC scholarship students, 1978	1,220
U.S. Naval Academy, 1976	1,220
College average, 1976	930

Sources: Rear Admiral Robert McNitt, Dean of Admissions, "Naval Academy Admissions" (1978), University of Michigan Archives, Bentley Historical Library, Vice-President for Academic Affairs Papers, Box 141, Navy Curriculum 1974–1980 Folder; Department of Defense, *Report on the Reserve Officers' Training Corps* (Washington, D.C.: Government Printing Office, 1980).

Even at some of the schools where ROTC-university relations were most tumultuous, the quality of cadet produced remained high. Furthermore, those schools were among the most popular choices for scholarship winners, because of their prestige and because the scholarship made the university affordable in an era of rapidly rising education costs.[51] During the 1970s, in-state tuition rose by 415 percent at the University of Illinois and 220 percent at the University of Michigan. Out-of-state tuition, usually three to four times more expensive, rose 298 percent and 188 percent at those schools, respectively.[52] ROTC thus became all the more appealing to students. Public schools commonly had half or more of their cadets come from out of state (in 1971, thirty-two of Georgia Tech's fifty-eight NROTC seniors were from out of state[53]). In-state students used ROTC to make their state's flagship institutions more affordable. In 1974, 40 percent of the Army ROTC scholarship winners from the state of Michigan used their scholarship to attend the University of Michigan. No other school accounted for more than 10 percent.[54]

The services were willing to accept the no-credit status in place at several schools because those schools continued to supply high-quality students. As cadet quality and enrollments reached acceptable levels, arguments that the no-credit situation impaired ROTC's mission became less germane. Nevertheless, the accreditation debates of the late 1960s and 1970s created an impression among some military officials that the actions of liberal arts colleges were "discriminatory," "demeaning," and "unfair" to the military.[55] As en-

gineering colleges concurrently increased academic credit, some officials began to argue that creating formal links between engineering colleges and
ROTC units might be an appropriate way to improve relations significantly
between the universities and ROTC. In this vein, the University of Michigan
PNS proposed having his unit "co-opted" by the College of Engineering.[56]

A general impression that liberal arts faculties were antimilitary coincided
in the middle of the 1970s with a shortage of junior naval officers qualified
to serve in the rapidly expanding and technologically complex nuclear fleet.
Admiral Hyman G. Rickover led a navywide effort to see that virtually all
officers were qualified to serve in the nuclear fleet that, in the late 1970s,
was quickly replacing the diesel and electric fleet as a result of Title 8 of the
1975 Defense Appropriations Act.[57] That act mandated that all major combat ships be nuclear powered, except by a special written directive of the
president.

In 1976, as a result of Title 8, the United States planned to build 41 new
nuclear-powered ships to complement the 114 already in the fleet.
Ironically, the navy's reputation for quality nuclear training made it difficult
to staff the new ships. By the navy's own estimate, former naval personnel
operated 60 percent of the nation's civilian nuclear industry. That industry
could offer significantly higher salaries than the navy. As a result, retention
problems compounded recruitment problems for the nuclear fleet.[58]

Consistent with these problems, the navy announced that beginning in
the fall of 1977, 80 percent of all NROTC scholarship students would be required to have an engineering or "hard science" major. The navy had always
been the most engineering-intensive service, but to some naval officers,
what became known as the 80-20 requirement seemed unnecessary.[59] The
NROTC curriculum, originally designed in 1947, had traditionally emphasized the accession of "outstanding young college men of diverse and superior educational background representing a wide and catholic range of interest, imposing and introducing a critical sense of values, frankly
unregimented in a professional sense."[60] As late as 1973 the chief of naval
education and training had informed a conference of professors of naval science that all academic majors were acceptable to the navy.[61] The new plan
thus represented a sharp break from NROTC tradition.

Additionally, the navy designed a new NROTC curriculum that more
closely resembled that of the engineering-intensive U.S. Naval Academy. All
NROTC students were now required to take two semesters of calculus and
physics and one semester each of math, chemistry, and computer science, in

addition to their NROTC courses and the courses required for the completion of their degree. In recognition of "the overload situation" created by the new curriculum, American Military History and National Security Affairs became optional courses for engineers.[62] Most engineering students would take the science and math courses whether or not they were also enrolled in NROTC, so the real effect of the new requirements was to discourage humanities and social science students from taking an NROTC scholarship. The navy's shift to engineers caused rapid changes. Whereas in 1974 only 41 percent of NROTC graduates nationwide had completed calculus and physics, by 1978, 79 percent had done so.[63]

While not intended as a snub to liberal arts colleges, the 80-20 requirement moved the NROTC program almost entirely into the presumably more friendly environment of the engineering colleges. Administrators and faculty in the liberal arts colleges were not, however, willing to surrender the principle that junior officers should come from a wide variety of educational backgrounds. The best example of such a viewpoint came from Adam Yarmolinsky, a former Pentagon official and professor at the University of Massachusetts, who argued that the post-Vietnam military's

> primary mission [will be] deterrence, rather than warmaking . . . A [military] that will probably spend all its time preparing for wars it may never fight needs highly sophisticated leadership, [with the] capability of resisting the tendency of entrenched bureaucracy toward either rot or rigidity and [the] ability to draw on inner resources to combat boredom and inertia. If this is the definition of a liberally educated person, perhaps a liberal education is necessary to produce him—or her.[64]

Yarmolinsky reflected the concerns of many academics who believed that a liberal education was critical to creating an officer corps that would be responsive to American society and to the many conditions that officers might have to face in as yet undefined missions.[65] Many educators thus believed that while the 80-20 requirement fulfilled a short-term, bureaucratic goal of producing more engineers, it threatened long-term harm to the military by creating a more narrowly educated officer corps. The Association of NROTC Colleges and Universities noted:

> In view of the historical role of the NROTC in the staff[ing] of the officer corps of the United States Navy with officers of equal abilities, but different academic traditions from graduates of the United States Naval Academy, the

members of this Association respectfully express their deep concern over the unilateral decision to state as a goal that 80 percent of NROTC scholarship students graduate from technical and/or scientific areas.[66]

The move to recruit more engineers also threatened to impair navy attempts to recruit more minorities and women, because those two groups remained underrepresented in colleges of engineering. Still, the top leaders of the navy saw the production of personnel qualified to serve in the nuclear fleet as critical to national security. Therefore, they told the association that "the 80-20 hard science requirement stands, and is not debatable."[67]

When placed within the context of university-ROTC relations since 1916, the ANROTCCU's defense of the place of liberal arts graduates in the NROTC program reveals the universities' fundamental desire to participate in ROTC training. Their "deep concern" over the 80-20 requirement stemmed from a genuine belief that the participation of men and women from "different academic traditions" improved the military and gave the universities an opportunity to influence—positively, they contended—the quality and character of the armed forces. As University of Minnesota president C. Peter Magrath told the navy, "We believe that [this policy] is not in the best interests of the Navy. Certainly it is not in the best interests of the nation to have most officers of the future educated in technical/scientific areas to the detriment of the liberal arts or humanities . . . I can only contemplate with alarm any proposal that would provide us with a single-minded, inflexible Navy. Like the nation, the Navy needs a variety of points of view."[68]

As such, the 80-20 discussions recalled debates in 1962 between universities and the army over the question of enrollment limits (see Chapter 2). In both cases, administrators were willing to fight for their own views about national security and the role of the educational system in producing junior officers. In neither case did university administrators seek disestablishment from ROTC; to the contrary, they actively sought the opportunity to participate in officer training, but they fought for their own vision of how such training should be conducted.

The universities tried to continue a policy, dating back to the 1950s, of actively participating in the determination of the ROTC curriculum. They paid careful attention to the evolution of the military curriculum and protested those changes that threatened a denigration of their basic principles. Thus their goal was not to keep the military out of the university but to ensure that the university would continue to exercise influence over the military through the production of officers on terms amenable to civilian educators.

In 1974 Michigan AFROTC professor of air science Colonel Marvin Grunzke failed to obtain credit for two air science classes, Concepts of Leadership and Principles of Management, despite the significant improvements made in them. The university also denied him a joint appointment in the department of psychology, despite his Ph.D. in psychology from Yale. Frustrated, he told the air force that "it must be concluded that there is insufficient interest within the University of Michigan representative structure to support a viable Air Force Officer Education Program as an integral part of the total educational complex encompassed by the University of Michigan."[69] The colonel was perhaps more astute than he knew; he had hit on exactly the point of faculty actions in the 1960s and 1970s. Similarly, when in the following year the Princeton trustees voted to readmit ROTC, they also voted in favor of a change in the wording of the part of the contract regarding ROTC's place on campus, from "an integral academic and administrative department" to "an integral element."[70] These changes and observations reveal a critical point: the faculties of the liberal arts colleges under study here were not at all interested in having ROTC as "an integral part of the total educational complex" on their campus. They were willing to accept or tolerate ROTC because of the benefits it provided to students, the university, and the nation, but they were unwilling to give it the same status, privileges, and rights as regular civilian departments.

The debates over abiding matters in the postwar era demonstrate that ROTC reform has to be seen through a much wider lens than one that encompasses only the turbulence of Vietnam. The refusal of liberal arts colleges to reaccredit ROTC after the Vietnam era—despite improvements in the quality of the courses and the people who taught them—argues for looking at the issue over a longer period of time. Faculty and administration opposition to ROTC had been consistently focused since the 1950s on the ways in which ROTC differed from civilian academic programs. The universities, as a body, could accept the logic that the ROTC programs served the public good and fit in with the service role of American universities, especially those supported with public money. They drew a line, however, at including these anomalous programs as regular intellectual and academic offerings on a par with their own.

Epilogue

Having taught navy and marine NROTC students at Carnegie Mellon as well as Air Force Academy cadets, I know the stereotypes that exist about both. To many Americans generally unfamiliar with the military, the service academies immediately call to mind an image of a hyperpatriotic automaton ready to subvert Congress if so ordered. As I prepared to leave Pittsburgh for Colorado Springs, one of my fellow historians told me to "watch out for the Oliver Norths" that were sure to be my students and colleagues at the Air Force Academy. North personified for many a problem seen by Moderate and Radical Whigs alike: as an academy-educated agent for the executive branch, he found a way around the "constitutional safeguards" established to prevent the military professional from acting without the legislature's knowledge.

ROTC, on the other hand, calls to mind a much more comfortable image, that of a competent and less threatening military officer entirely content with civilian oversight. As with all stereotypes, these images do not correspond exactly to reality; nevertheless, they exist. The citizen-soldier iconography is no less profound now than it was in the days of Paul Revere. Americans still prefer having soldiers who are not totally military, as the nightly "Joe in the field" interviews during the Persian Gulf War attest.

The survival of ROTC, even in the face of some serious crises, stands as a testimony to American values regarding its military officers. Even during the Vietnam War few Americans (influenced as they were by Moderate Whig ideology) were willing to surrender the idea that civilian education and influence served a critical role in preparing officers. As this book has shown, resistance to the American military and the wars it has fought has often had the ironic effect of *increasing* support for ROTC.

202

That support has never been in serious doubt in the minds of the faculties, students, and administrators of the nation's public universities. Almost since ROTC's inception, university communities and the military have debated details, but public universities have never wanted to turn the training of military officers exclusively over to the military itself. Neither has the military wanted (or been able to afford) to do that job itself. For all of its faults, ROTC fit almost everyone's idea of how to commission officers.

That fit, of course, has never stopped the push for important reforms. ROTC has had to change as American higher education and the military have changed. ROTC simply was not the same institution in 1933 (when none of the presidents from the nation's twenty-five largest public schools had served in the military or the State Department) as it was in 1950, when 40 percent of those presidents (including the presidents of six of the ten schools under study here) had a background of such service. Similarly, the end of the war in Vietnam and the concurrent end of the draft forced more changes. By 1980 ROTC no longer claimed that it stood on the line between freedom and a total communist takeover. It had become a part of campus life that was no longer so easy to distinguish. As the University of Washington's professor of naval science said in a *Washington Daily* article on October 14, 1980, "We're not saviors of democracy. We're just here."

Abbreviations

AALGCSU	American Association of Land-Grant Colleges and State Universities
AAUP	American Association of University Professors
AFB	air force base
AFROTC	Air Force Reserve Officers' Training Corps
ANROTCCU	Association of Naval Reserve Officers' Training Corps Colleges and Universities
AROTC	Army Reserve Officers' Training Corps
AVF	all-volunteer force
DOD	Department of Defense
ECPD	Engineers Council for Professional Development
GMS	general military science
JROTC	Junior Reserve Officers' Training Corps
MOEP	Military Officer Education Program
NASULGC	National Association of State Universities and Land-Grant Colleges
NDA	National Defense Act (of 1916)
NROTC	Naval Reserve Officers' Training Corps
NSIC	National Security Information Center
OCS	Officer Candidate School
PAS	professor of air science
PMS	professor of military science
PNS	professor of naval science
ROTC	Reserve Officers' Training Corps
SDS	Students for a Democratic Society
SNCC	Student Nonviolent Coordinating Committee
UMT	universal military training
USAF	United States Air Force
WAC	Women's Army Corps
WAF	Women in the Air Force
WAFROTC	Women in the Air Force Reserve Officers' Training Corps
WAVES	Women Accepted for Volunteer Emergency Service

Notes

Introduction

1. "ROTC Officer Transferred amid Charges of Coercion," *Chronicle of Higher Education,* July 12, 1996, p. A6.
2. Colleen Cordes, "MIT Tries a New Approach in the Battle over ROTC," *Chronicle of Higher Education,* May 31, 1996, p. A23. MIT's case is just one example; virtually all ROTC host universities have expressed some degree of discomfort with the "don't ask, don't tell" policy. Most have worked out a truce with the Department of Defense to open all on-campus ROTC classes to all students, regardless of sexual orientation. Some schools, like MIT, have pledged financial aid to any gay or lesbian ROTC cadet who loses his or her scholarship.
3. James L. Morrison, "Military Education and Strategic Thought, 1846–1861," in Kenneth J. Hagan and William R. Roberts, eds., *Against All Enemies: Interpretations of American Military History from Colonial Times to the Present* (New York: Greenwood Press, 1986), pp. 113–131, quotations from pp. 117, 121, and 120.
4. Lawrence Cress, *Citizens in Arms: The Army and Militia in American Society to the War of 1812* (Chapel Hill: University of North Carolina Press, 1982). See also William B. Skelton, "Samuel P. Huntington and the Roots of the American Military Tradition," *Journal of Military History* 60 (April 1996): 325–338.
5. Skelton, "Samuel P. Huntington," p. 328.
6. Cress, *Citizens in Arms,* p. 22.
7. Ibid., p. 60.
8. Ibid.
9. Ibid., p. 26.
10. There have, of course, been several military champions of the ROTC program, such as Admiral James Holloway in the navy and Brigadier General William Lindley in the air force.
11. I could cite several important studies here, but the best examples are found in the introduction and several essays in Peter Karsten, ed., *The Military in America from Colonial Times to the Present* (New York: Free Press, 1986).
12. John Keegan, *The Mask of Command* (New York: Viking Press, 1988), p. 2.

13. See Roger Geiger's *Research and Relevant Knowledge: American Research Universities since World War II* (New York: Oxford University Press, 1993) and *To Advance Knowledge: The Growth of American Research Universities, 1900–1940* (New York: Oxford University Press, 1986). Julie Reuben's *The Making of the Modern University: Intellectual Transformation and the Marginalization of Morality* (Chicago: University of Chicago Press, 1996) provides a wonderful analysis of the development of nineteenth- and early twentieth-century American universities.

14. Adam Garfinkle, *Telltale Hearts: The Origins and Impact of the Vietnam Antiwar Movement* (New York: St. Martin's Press, 1995); Kenneth Heineman, *Campus Wars: The Peace Movement at American State Universities in the Vietnam Era* (New York: New York University Press, 1993).

15. Christian Appy, *Working-Class War: American Combat Soldiers in Vietnam* (Chapel Hill: University of North Carolina Press, 1993).

16. They are: Maxwell J. Richards, "A Ten-Year History of Air Force ROTC, 1946–1956," master's thesis, University of Maryland, 1957; Gene Lyons and John Masland, *Education and Military Leadership: A Study of the ROTC* (Princeton, N.J.: Princeton University Press, 1959); Victor Hirshauer, "The History of the Army ROTC," (Ph.D. diss., Johns Hopkins University, 1975; Joseph Pearlman, "A Study Comparing and Contrasting Views of the Role of Air Force ROTC in Relationship to the University, 1960–1978," Ph.D. diss., University of Denver, 1978; Donald Cummings, "Army ROTC: A Study of the Army's Primary Officer Procurement Program," Ph.D. diss., University of California at Santa Barbara, 1982.

17. Hirshauer used ROTC institutional files that he obtained at Ft. Meade in Maryland. I was unable to locate these records.

18. Pearlman, "A Study Comparing and Contrasting," p. 87.

19. Hirshauer, "The History of the Army ROTC," p. 383. A focus on the Pentagon is all the more misleading because the key military agencies in charge of ROTC were not in Washington at all, but in Annapolis, Montgomery, Pensacola, and Ft. Monroe.

20. The Cold War, obviously, extended past 1964. I use the phrase "Cold War period" and focus on 1950 to 1964 to underscore the importance that the developing Cold War had for the concurrent development of an active-duty ROTC program.

21. To a lesser extent, I have also included Columbus College, Duquesne University, and Princeton. Their stories are interesting, but extant archival material limited the attention that I could devote to them.

22. Cress, *Citizens in Arms*, p. 39.

1. ROTC and the American Military Tradition

1. Contrast these officers with General Dwight D. Eisenhower, who successfully used his military career to attain the presidency. Unlike North and MacArthur, Eisenhower projected a distinctly unaristocratic image. As Paul Fussell noted,

"General Eisenhower [was] popular with the troops because [he was] in so many ways the typical Second World War American serviceman and thus sympathetic with their needs." See Paul Fussell, *Wartime: Understanding and Behavior in the Second World War* (New York: Oxford University Press, 1989), p. 145.

2. Samuel Huntington, *The Soldier and the State: The Theory and Politics of Civil-Military Relations* (Cambridge, Mass.: Harvard University Press, 1959), p. 159.

3. Lawrence Cress, *Citizens in Arms: The Army and Militia in American Society to the War of 1812* (Chapel Hill: University of North Carolina Press, 1982). Please see the introduction for a fuller discussion of Cress's arguments.

4. *Company grade* and *field grade* are army terms that divide the nongeneral officer corps into two groups. In the army, air force, and marines, the lieutenants and captains constitute the company grades, while the majors, lieutenant colonels, and colonels constitute the field grades. Equivalent navy ranks are ensign, lieutenant (junior grade), and lieutenant; and lieutenant commander, commander, and captain.

5. Ira D. Gruber, "The Anglo-American Military Tradition and the War for American Independence," in Kenneth J. Hagan and William R. Roberts, eds., *Against All Enemies: Interpretations of American Military History from Colonial Times to the Present* (New York: Greenwood Press, 1986), pp. 21–47, quotation from p. 29.

6. Richard H. Kohn, "The Inside History of the Newburgh Conspiracy," in Peter Karsten, ed., *The Military in America from Colonial Times to the Present* (New York: Free Press, 1986), pp. 79–91, quotation from p. 81. Kohn was talking here about New England, but his comments are equally relevant for other sections of the new United States.

7. Kohn, "The Inside History," pp. 80 and 89.

8. Richard Kohn, "Out of Control: The Crisis in Civil-Military Relations," *The National Interest* 35 (Spring 1994): 3–17, quotation from p. 15.

9. Kohn, "The Inside History," p. 90.

10. Russell Weigley, *The American Way of War* (Bloomington: Indiana University Press, 1973), p. 41.

11. Arthur Coumbe and Lee S. Harford, *U.S. Army Cadet Command: The Ten-Year History* (Ft. Monroe, Va.: Office of the Command Historian, U.S. Army Cadet Command, 1996), p. 7.

12. James Madison, "Federalist Number Forty-One," in Roy Fairfield, ed., *The Federalist Papers* (Garden City, N.Y.: Doubleday Anchor Press, 1966), pp. 118–126, quotations from p. 120.

13. Harry Coles, "From Peaceable Coercion to Balanced Forces," in Kenneth J. Hagan and William R. Roberts, eds., *Against All Enemies: Interpretations of American Military History from Colonial Times to the Present* (New York: Greenwood Press, 1986), pp. 71–89, quotation from p. 79.

14. Quoted in R. Ernest Dupuy and Trevor Dupuy, *Military Heritage of America* (New York: McGraw-Hill, 1956), p. 121.

15. Huntington, *The Soldier and the State*, p. 198.

16. Dupuy and Dupuy, *Military Heritage*, p. 139.

17. William B. Skelton, "The Army in the Age of the Common Man, 1815–1845," in Kenneth J. Hagan and William R. Roberts, eds., *Against All Enemies: Interpretations of American Military History from Colonial Times to the Present* (New York: Greenwood Press, 1986), pp. 91–112.
18. Alden Partridge quoted in Coumbe and Harford, *Cadet Command,* p. 8.
19. Gene Lyons and John Masland, *Education and Military Leadership: A Study of the ROTC* (Princeton, N.J.: Princeton University Press, 1959), p. 28.
20. Coumbe and Harford, *Cadet Command,* p. 8. This was also the period when southern military colleges like VMI and the Citadel were formed. While created partly to support the citizen-soldier model, they also owe their creation to the southern belief that military training was important to character development. As these schools were almost exclusively military, they do not fit the overall pattern being discussed here.
21. Skelton, "The Army in the Age of the Common Man," p. 97.
22. Ibid., p. 98.
23. James L. Morrison, "Military Education and Strategic Thought, 1846–1861," in Kenneth J. Hagan and William R. Roberts, eds., *Against All Enemies: Interpretations of American Military History from Colonial Times to the Present* (New York: Greenwood Press, 1986), pp. 113–131, quotation from p. 121.
24. Skelton, "The Army in the Age of the Common Man," p. 105.
25. Peter Karsten, *The Naval Aristocracy: The Golden Age of Annapolis and the Emergence of Modern Navalism* (New York: Free Press, 1972), chap. 1.
26. Coumbe and Harford, *Cadet Command,* p. 8.
27. Shaw and Chamberlain were educated at Harvard and Bowdoin, respectively. The classic study of nonprofessionals in the American Civil War is Gerald Linderman's *Embattled Courage: The Experience of Combat in the American Civil War* (New York: Free Press, 1987). See also Joseph T. Glatthaar, *Forged in Battle: The Civil War Alliance of Black Soldiers and White Officers* (New York: Free Press, 1990).
28. Jomini was the most widely read military historian and theorist at West Point in the antebellum years. In 1862, West Point curriculum developers wrote that "General Jomini is admitted by all competent judges to be one of the ablest military critics and historians of this or any other day." See Baron de Jomini, *The Art of War* (Philadelphia: J. P. Lippincott, 1862), p. 5. Jomini's studies of Napoleon and Frederick the Great led him to believe that successful strategy prescribed "offensive action to mass forces against weaker enemy forces at some decisive point." Between the time of Jomini's writings and the Civil War, however, rifled guns had replaced muskets, vastly increasing the range and lethality of defenders against massed forces. See John Shy, "Jomini," in Peter Paret, ed., *Makers of Modern Strategy from Machiavelli to the Nuclear Age* (Princeton, N.J.: Princeton University Press, 1986), pp. 143–185, quotation from p. 146.
29. The Morrill Bill, without the provision for military tactics, had been vetoed by President Buchanan in 1857.
30. Lyons and Masland, *Education and Military Leadership,* p. 30.

31. Coumbe and Harford, *Cadet Command*, p. 11. It should be noted that the "bottleneck" of officers who entered the army between 1861 and 1864 meant that some lieutenants had twelve or more years of service. Junior officers were often much more experienced than their ranks might indicate. See Peter Karsten, "Armed Progressives," in Peter Karsten, ed., *The Military in America from Colonial Times to the Present* (New York: Free Press, 1986), pp. 239–274.

32. Arthur Russell La Belle, "Kansas State Agricultural College Military Science and Tactics Department, 1863–1918," unpublished student paper, Kansas State University, May 1987, pp. 10–11.

33. Karsten, "Armed Progressives," p. 239.

34. Gerald Linderman, "The Spanish-American War and the Small-Town Community," in Peter Karsten, ed., *The Military in America from Colonial Times to the Present* (New York: Free Press, 1986), pp. 275–294, quotation from p. 278. See also the book from which this article was excerpted, *The Mirror of War: American Society and the Spanish-American War* (Ann Arbor: University of Michigan Press, 1974).

35. Of course, Roosevelt wielded a great deal of influence over the military, but he did so *as a civilian*. He served as assistant secretary of the navy until he joined the Rough Riders, but he was a product of civilian upbringing and education, not a graduate of West Point or Annapolis.

36. For more, see Russell Weigley, *A History of the United States Army* (New York: Mac Millan, 1967), pp. 347–349.

37. Lyons and Masland, *Education and Military Leadership*, p. 37.

38. Coumbe and Harford, *Cadet Command*, p. 13.

39. Lyons and Masland, *Education and Military Leadership*, pp. 42–43.

40. Barrow, *Universities and the Capitalist State*, pp. 135–136.

41. Procedure Preliminary to Inauguration of Military Training at the University of Pittsburgh [May 1916], University of Pittsburgh Archives, Hillman Library, Classification Number 2/10/1904–20, File Folder 40.

42. Chancellor McCormick to Adjutant General, U.S. Army, Dec. 12, 1917, ibid.

43. Chancellor McCormick to Senator Philander Knox, Jan. 8, 1918, ibid.

44. Robert McMath, *Engineering the New South: Georgia Tech, 1885–1985* (Athens: University of Georgia Press), p. 147.

45. Ronald Schaffer, *America in the Great War: The Rise of the War Welfare State* (New York: Oxford University Press, 1991), p. 127.

46. Quotation from ibid., p. 128.

47. Ibid., p. 146.

48. La Belle, "Kansas State Agricultural College," p. 15.

49. Charles Gates, *The First Century at the University of Washington: 1861–1961* (Seattle: University of Washington Press, 1961), p. 154.

50. Louis Marley, "The Civil Administration of the University of Pittsburgh as a Student's Army Training Corps Unit," Feb. 17, 1919, University of Pittsburgh Archives, Hillman Library, Classification Number 2/10/1904–20, File Folder 41.

51. *Kansas State Collegian*, Feb. 7, 1919, cited in Kansas State University Historical Index, Kansas State University Archives.
52. Ibid., pp. 148–149.
53. President Suzzallo to Commandant, 13th Naval District, Sept. 8, 1917, University of Washington Archives, Allen Library, W. U. President's Papers, 71–34, Box 129, Naval ROTC, 1917–1926 Folder.
54. McMath, *Engineering the New South*, p. 149.
55. Julie Reuben, *The Making of the Modern University: Intellectual Transformation and the Marginalization of Morality* (Chicago: University of Chicago Press, 1996), p. 5.
56. William H. S. Demarest, *A History of Rutgers College, 1766–1924* (New Brunswick, N.J.: Rutgers University Press, 1924), p. 520.
57. Coumbe and Harford, *Cadet Command*, p. 16.
58. Lyons and Masland, *Education and Military Leadership*, p. 44.
59. Morris Janowitz, *The Professional Soldier* (Glencoe, Ill.: Free Press, 1960), p. 106.
60. LeMay received an ROTC commission (to the reserves) that year from Ohio State, but he did not receive his degree, due to, in his words, "my own private course in 'Advanced Slumbering.'" See General Curtis E. LeMay with MacKinley Kantor, *Mission with LeMay: My Story* (Garden City, N.Y.: Doubleday and Company, 1965), p. 42.
61. It is also unlikely that the $9 monthly stipend given to advanced cadets made a significant difference in their decision making. But for some men, especially those outside of the prestigious eastern universities, the money played a small role. One future Marine Corps commandant, General David M. Shoup, noted that the money made his stay at DePauw College in the mid-1920s possible: "in all truth [the money] was the only reason I signed up for the senior ROTC." Shoup came from a poor farming family in Indiana. For more on Shoup, see Howard Jablon, "General David M. Shoup, USMC: Warrior and War Protester," *Journal of Military History* 60 (July 1996): 513–538, quotation from p. 514.
62. Coumbe and Harford, *Cadet Command*, p. 14.
63. Ibid.
64. Ronald Schaffer, "The War Department's Defense of ROTC, 1920–1940," *Wisconsin Magazine of History* 53 (Winter 1969–70): 108–120, quotation from p. 110.
65. See James Hawkes, "Antimilitarism at State Universities: The Campaign against Compulsory ROTC, 1920–1940," *Wisconsin History* 49 (Autumn 1965): 41–54.
66. Kathryn McKay, "The Debate over ROTC at the University of Delaware, 1920–1940," *Delaware History* 23 (Spring–Summer 1989): 232.
67. *Hamilton et al. vs. the Regents of the University of California*, 239 U.S. 245 (1934).
68. See Lyons and Masland, *Education and Military Leadership*, chap. 2.
69. Schaffer, "The War Department's Defense," pp. 110. The military itself had just 134,024 men and officers in 1932, a number significantly below the 280,000

authorized by Congress. Given the low number of men in uniform, many War Department officials argued that mandatory training simply had no understood purpose in an army that was already overpopulated with World War I veterans.

70. Lyons and Masland, *Education and Military Leadership*, p. 51.

71. F. D. Farrell to C. M. Harger, Jan. 17, 1935, Kansas State University Archives, President's Papers, 1934–1935, File Folder 43.

72. Robert McNamara, *In Retrospect* (New York: Random House, 1995), p. 6.

73. Ross Parmenter quoted in Paul Fussell, *Wartime: Understanding and Behavior in the Second World War* (New York: Oxford University Press, 1989), p. 61.

74. Clem Work, "ROTC Has Long History on CU Campus," *Rocky Mountain News,* April 21, 1969, p. 5. University of Colorado at Boulder Library, Archives, CU History (Departments), ROTC Folder.

75. Fussell, *Wartime,* p. 60.

76. Quoted in Peter Schrijvers, *The Crash of Ruin: American Combat Soldiers in Europe during World War II* (New York: New York University Press, 1998), p. 63.

77. Quoted in Danforth Eddy, *Colleges for Our Land and Time* (New York: Harper and Bros., 1957), p. 224.

78. Rear Admiral J. Cary Jones, Commander Ninth Naval District, to President Robert Stearns, Sept. 5, 1950, Archives, University of Colorado at Boulder Libraries, Central Administration, President's Office, Series I, Box 331, ROTC—Navy 1940–1977 Folder.

79. "ROTC Halves Tech Induction," *Atlanta Journal,* Jan. 11, 1951.

80. Nathan M. Pusey, *American Higher Education, 1945–1970* (Cambridge, Mass.: Harvard University Press, 1978), p. 9.

81. Coumbe and Harford, *U.S. Army Cadet,* p. 22. Emphasis mine.

2. A Favored Position on Campus

1. See Paul Boyer, *By the Bomb's Early Light: American Thought and Culture at the Dawn of the Atomic Age* (New York: Pantheon Books, 1985), and the film *The Atomic Café* (1982).

2. For more on the Holloway Plan please see James Holloway, "The Holloway Plan," *Proceedings of the U.S. Naval Institute* (Nov. 1947): 1299.

3. Nathan Pusey, *American Higher Education, 1945–1970: A Personal Report* (Cambridge, Mass.: Harvard University Press, 1978), p. 151.

4. Ibid., p. 152.

5. Russell Weigley, *The History of the United States Army* (New York: Macmillan, 1967), p. 508.

6. Pusey, *American Higher Education,* p. 45.

7. See Roger Geiger, *Research and Relevant Knowledge: American Research Universities since World War II* (New York: Oxford University Press, 1993), chap. 1.

8. See Vincent Davis, *The Admiral's Lobby* (Chapel Hill: University of North Carolina Press, 1967), chap. 2.

9. M. K. Deichelman to Logan Wilson, Apr. 12, 1955, University of Texas President's Office Records, VF 30/A.b, Air Science and Tactics 1954–55 Folder.

10. Nathan Pusey included a lengthy and detailed discussion of the finances of higher education in his book, but there is no mention of ROTC. Between 1940 and 1970 the operating costs of American higher education rose from $600 million to $24 billion. In this large picture, ROTC finances appear minuscule. See Pusey, *American Higher Education*, p. 7 and chap. 3.

11. Seymour Harris, ed., *A Statistical Portrait of Higher Education* (New York: McGraw-Hill, 1972), pp. 790–791.

12. For schools like Pittsburgh, Illinois, and Michigan, ROTC was important enough for the uniformed men at headquarters to merit access to that most prized of big-school perks—an invitation to a football game in the president's box.

13. Russell Thackrey, "Some Current ROTC Problems," in *Current Issues in Higher Education: Proceedings of the Ninth Annual Conference on Higher Education*, Chicago, 1954 (n.p.), pp. 294–296.

14. Army ROTC pamphlet, *Quality Is the Answer*, 1960.

15. Mark Grandstaff, "Making the Military American: Advertising, Reform, and the Demise of an Antistanding Military Tradition, 1945–1955," *Journal of Military History* 60 (Apr. 1996): 299–324; quotation from p. 315.

16. Quoted in ibid., p. 315.

17. Ibid., p. 316.

18. Enock Dyrness, "Recorder's Report, Group 37," in *Proceedings of the Ninth Annual Conference on Higher Education*, p. 301.

19. Pusey, *American Higher Education*, pp. 131–133.

20. Geiger, *Research and Relevant Knowledge*, p. 315.

21. John Monro, "Strengthening the ROTC Curriculum," in *Role of the Colleges and Universities in ROTC Programs* (Columbus: Ohio State University Press, 1960), p. 13.

22. George Flynn, *The Draft* (Lawrence: University of Kansas Press, 1993), pp. 135–137.

23. Davis, *The Admiral's Lobby*, p. 5.

24. Vance Mitchell, *Air Force Officers: Personnel Policy Development, 1944–1974* (Washington, D.C.: Air Force History and Museums Program, 1996), p. 59.

25. Mays was drafted in 1952, the year after he won the National League Rookie of the Year award.

26. "Colleges See Lean Pickings in the Fall as Draft Gains Force," *Atlanta Journal*, Jan. 5, 1951.

27. Quoted in Flynn, *The Draft*, p. 150. PFC stands for private first class, a low army enlisted rank.

28. Colonel Eugene Lee to Secretary of the Army, Jan. 27, 1958, Suitland Federal Records Center, Record Group 335, Box 798.

29. Army ROTC, *Quality Is the Answer.*

30. Janowitz, *The Professional Soldier,* p. 45. The "tooth-to-tail" ratio refers to the number of men in combat to the number of men in support. According to Janowitz, the percentage of army enlisted personnel in the tooth went from 93.2 percent in the Civil War to 36.2 percent in World War II to 28.8 percent in 1954. See Janowitz, *The Professional Soldier,* p. 65. This percentage continued to decline well into the Vietnam War era.
31. Report of the Ad Hoc Committee to Study ROTC Programs, Apr. 21, 1961, University of Washington Archives, Allen Library, W. U. Presidents Papers, 71–34, Box 52, Folder 18.
32. Samuel Huntington, "Power, Expertise, and the Military Profession" *Daedalus* 92 (Fall 1963): 785–807, quotation from p. 793.
33. Mitchell, *Air Force Officers,* pp. 50–51.
34. Huntington, "Power, Expertise, and the Military Profession," p. 805 n. 7.
35. Quoted in Maxwell J. Richards, "A Ten-Year History of Air Force ROTC, 1946–1956," M.A. thesis, University of Maryland, 1957, p. 55.
36. Ibid., p. 9.
37. J. Robert Moskin, "Our Military Manpower Scandal," *Look* 22 (Mar. 18, 1958): 27–33.
38. The head of an ROTC unit was usually a colonel (in the navy, a captain).
39. Russell Thackrey, Executive Secretary of AALGCSU, to David Henry, Jan. 23, 1957, University of Illinois Archives, President David Henry Papers, Box 26, ROTC–Air Science Folder. See also Russell Thackrey, "Financing ROTC Programs," in *Role of Colleges,* pp. 37–42, where he discusses the loyalty oath further. The American Association of Land-Grant Colleges and State Universities changed its name to the National Association of State Universities and Land-Grant Colleges in 1962.
40. David Henry to Russell Thackrey, Executive Secretary of AALGCSU, Feb. 8, 1957, University of Illinois Archives, President David Henry Papers, Box 26, ROTC–Air Science Folder.
41. Geiger, *Research and Relevant Knowledge,* p. 53.
42. John Hannah, Statement before the Armed Forces Policy Board, Oct. 1, 1957, University of Illinois Archives, President David Henry Papers, Box 26, ROTC Folder.
43. Monro, "Strengthening the ROTC Curriculum," p. 16.
44. University of Texas, *College of Engineering Catalogue,* 1954–1956; University of Texas, *General Information,* Main University, 1955–56.
45. Frank G. Dickey, President, University of Kentucky, to Major General Frederick Warren, Apr. 28, 1962, Suitland Federal Records Center, Record Group 335, Box 1227.
46. Paul Miller, President, West Virginia University, to Major General Frederick Warren, May 2, 1962, ibid.
47. Right Reverend Wilfrid Nash, President, Gannon College to Major General Frederick Warren, May 2, 1962, ibid.

48. R. H. Woods, President, Murray State College, to Major General Frederick Warren, May 1, 1962, ibid.

49. David Guerrieri, "Open Forum: Unreason at Duquesne," *The Duke,* May 11, 1962.

50. Henry McAnulty to David Guerrieri, May 18, 1962, Duquesne University Archives, ROTC Box 1, ROTC–Army Correspondence 1953–1965.

51. Elvis Stahr, Secretary of the Army to the Secretary of Defense, May 11, 1962, Suitland Federal Records Center, Record Group 335, Box 1227.

52. Major General Frederick Warren to University Presidents, n.d., ibid.

53. Christian Arnold, ed., *Proceedings of the National Association of State Universities and Land-Grant Colleges Seventy-sixth Annual Convention* (Washington, D.C.: NASULGC, 1962), p. 46.

54. As noted earlier, the NASULGC was known as the American Association of Land-Grant Colleges and State Universities until 1962. I am going to take the liberty of using NASULGC exclusively in this section to avoid confusion.

55. Colonel Josef Prall, Assistant Executive, General Staff, to Assistant Secretary of the Army (Manpower, Personnel, and Reserve Forces), Mar. 26, 1957, Suitland Federal Records Center, Record Group 335, Box 798.

56. Frank Millard, General Counsel, to Assistant Secretary of the Army (Manpower, Personnel, and Reserve Forces), Dec. 19, 1957, ibid.

57. As early as 1953, the Air Force Bureau of the Budget had internally proposed a switch to voluntary ROTC in the interests of economy. "A Study Leading to the Development of a Long Range AFROTC Program," unpublished Air University Study [1968], ROTC History Office, Building 78, Maxwell AFB, Montgomery, Alabama.

58. Mitchell, *Air Force Officers,* p. 161.

59. *History of the Air Force Reserve Officers' Training Corps,* Twentieth Anniversary Command Edition, 1966, Air University, Maxwell AFB, Montgomery, Alabama. These arguments proved valid in the end. Although basic enrollments did fall, AFROTC advance enrollments did not immediately fall. "The earlier fear of losing the selection base with the loss of compulsory ROTC was groundless since no appreciable decrease occurred in advance course enrollments due to the wholesale change from compulsory to elective ROTC," p. 33.

60. "ROTC Is Voluntary," *Targum* extra edition, Apr. 26, 1960, p. 1.

61. "Army Recommendations" [1958], University of Illinois Archives, National Association of State Universities and Land-Grant Colleges Papers, Series Number 10/3/57, Box 14, 1958 Folder.

62. Major General J. W. Bowen quoted in *Role of Colleges,* p. 50.

63. Eliot Cohen, *Citizens and Soldiers* (Ithaca, N.Y.: Cornell University Press, 1985), p. 159.

64. "The Battle Is Over," *Targum* extra edition, Apr. 26, 1960, p. 1.

65. "A Word about ROTC," *Targum,* Sept. 11, 1960, p. 1.

66. *History of the AFROTC,* Jan. 1, to June 30, 1964, vol. 8, appendix H, Air Force Historical Research Agency, Maxwell AFB, Montgomery, Alabama.

67. Charles Finucane to C. M. Hardin, President of AALGCSU, Feb. 15, 1960, University of Illinois Archives, Series Number 27/3/5, Box 1.

68. John Hannah, Statement before the Armed Forces Policy Board.

69. Russell Thackrey to Robert Thurston, July 24, 1959, University of Illinois Archives, National Association of State Universities and Land-Grant Colleges Papers, Series Number 10/3/57, Box 14.

70. Russell Thackrey, Executive Secretary, NASULGC, to Jack Raymond, Feb. 17, 1960, ibid.

71. Russell Thackrey to Colonel L. D. Farnsworthy, Apr. 25, 1960, ibid.

72. "Significant Elements in U.S. Army ROTC Program," Dec. 17, 1963, University of Illinois Archives, Series Number 4/2/14, Box 3.

73. David Henry to Carlyle Runge, Assistant Secretary of Defense for Manpower, Mar. 31, 1961, University of Illinois Archives, National Association of State Universities and Land-Grant Colleges Papers, Series Number 10/3/57, Box 14.

74. Richard Harvill, President of University of Arizona, to Major General Frederick Warren, Chief RROTC, Apr. 28, 1962, Suitland Federal Records Center, Record Group 335, Secretary of the Army General Correspondence, Box 1227.

75. Captain John Sibbald, "A History of the Military Department at the University of Illinois, 1868–1964," unpublished paper, 1965, Army ROTC Historical Files, University of Illinois Department of Military Science Library, 0.432.

76. "Army and Air Force ROTC," University of Illinois Archives, National Association of State Universities and Land-Grant Colleges Papers, Series Number 10/3/57, Box 15.

77. Transcript of Meeting of AFROTC Advisory Panel, Dec. 9, 1963, ibid.; *History of the AFROTC.* Uniform cost savings represent the period from 1960 to 1964.

78. "The Battle Is Over."

79. *The Army ROTC at the University of Illinois,* 1965, Army ROTC Historical Files, University of Illinois Department of Military Science, 0.432.

3. The Origins of Postwar Dissatisfaction

1. Mark Grandstaff, "Making the Military American: Advertising, Reform, and the Demise of an Antistanding Military Tradition, 1945–1955." *Journal of Military History* 60 (Apr. 1996): 299–324, quotation from p. 301 n. 7.

2. Samuel Huntington, *The Soldier and the State: The Theory and Politics of Civil-Military Relations* (Cambridge, Mass.: Harvard University Press, 1959), p. 351.

3. Grant Advertising, Chicago, Research Studies for ROTC, September–November 1950, Chief of Army Reserve General Correspondence 1948–1954, National Archives, Record Group 319, Box 50.

4. For Ted, the uniform served as an important identifier. He is shown wearing the uniform to all of his classes, civilian and military. As we will see, Ted's attitude toward his uniform would not be shared by later cadets and midshipmen.

5. "You and the Army ROTC" [1960], University of Illinois Archives, National As-

sociation of State Universities and Land-Grant Colleges Papers, Series Number 10/3/57, Box 15.

6. Leo Bogart's *Social Research and the Desegregation of the United States Army* (Chicago: Markham Publishing, 1969) convincingly argues that the experience of combat for integrated units in the Korean War was crucial to a general acceptance among military personnel of the idea of integration. See also Sherie Mershon and Steven Schlossman, *Foxholes and Color Lines: Desegregating the U.S. Armed Forces* (Baltimore: Johns Hopkins University Press, 1998); Bernard Nalty, *Strength for the Fight* (New York: Free Press, 1986); and Richard Dalfiume, *The Desegregation of the U.S. Armed Forces* (Columbia: University of Missouri Press, 1969).

7. Peter Braestrup, "Rights Unit Asks Congress to End Union Race Bars," *New York Times*, Oct. 14, 1961, p. 1. Recall that the National Guard units were legally under the control of state governors but subject to federal authority. Therefore the Guard units did not necessarily integrate as the rest of the military did. The Hannah Commission wanted the president to use his authority to force integration under threat of federalization.

8. Transcript of Meeting of AFROTC Advisory Panel, Dec. 9, 1963, University of Illinois Archives, National Association of State Universities and Land-Grant Colleges Papers, Series Number 10/3/57, Box 15.

9. Colonel R. W. Koontz, "Equal Opportunity and the AFROTC," presented to the AFROTC Advisory Panel, Dec. 9, 1963, ibid.

10. It should be noted that significant variation existed by region. The highest percentage of students who intended to continue on to advanced ROTC (94.3 percent) came from the Fourth Army area (Texas, Oklahoma, and Arkansas), followed by the Second Army area (including Pennsylvania, Ohio, Virginia, and Maryland) at 75 percent, the First Army area (New England and New York) at 61.8 percent, and the Third Army area (the Southeast) at 57.7 percent. The lowest percentages (39.7 percent and 49.1 percent) came from the Sixth Army area (California, Oregon, and Washington) and the Fifth Army area (Midwest), respectively.

11. Grant Advertising, Research Studies for ROTC. The schools from which students were sampled were: Yale, Fordham, Vermont, NYU, Carnegie Tech, University of Cincinnati, Ohio State, VMI, Howard, Emory, Alabama, Florida, North Carolina State, Oklahoma A & M, Henderson State, Texas A & M, Knox College, Kansas, Nebraska, North Dakota Agricultural, Iowa State, Wyoming, San Jose State, California, and Oregon. The survey can be found in Chief of Army Reserve General Correspondence 1948–1954, National Archives, Record Group 319, Box 50.

12. Associated Students of the University of Washington, "Compulsory ROTC at Washington," Feb. 1, 1961, University of Washington Archives, Allen Library, W. U. Presidents Papers, 71–34, Box 52, Folder 18.

13. Grandstaff, "Making the Military American," pp. 306 and 304.

14. Morris Janowitz, *The Professional Soldier* (Glencoe, Ill.: Free Press, 1960), p. 227.

This survey was conducted by Public Opinion Surveys, Inc. The four professions more highly esteemed by male teenagers than military officer were: physician, scientist, lawyer, and college professor. The national adult sample rated military officer seventh behind physician, scientist, college professor, lawyer, minister or priest, and public school teacher.

15. Grandstaff, "Making the Military American," p. 310.
16. Vance Mitchell, *Air Force Officers: Personnel Policy Development, 1944–1974* (Washington, D.C.: Air Force History and Museums Program, 1996), p. 159.
17. Ibid., pp. 182–183.
18. Ibid., p. 182.
19. Samuel Huntington, "Power, Expertise, and the Military Profession," *Daedalus* 92 (Fall 1963): 785–807, quotation from p. 792.
20. Quoted in Richard Abrams, "The U.S. Military and Higher Education: A Brief History," *Annals of the American Academy of Political and Social Science* 502 (Mar. 1989): 15–28, quotation from p. 24.
21. J. W. Bowles and Donald Torr, *An Attitude Survey of AFROTC Cadets*, Nov. 1955, Air Force Historical Research Agency, Maxwell AFB, Montgomery, Alabama.
22. "Report of the Institutional-USAF Conference on Air Force ROTC Affairs, 9–10 December, 1959, Maxwell AFB, Montgomery, Alabama, p. 16.
23. Russell Thackrey, "Some Current ROTC Problems," in *Current Issues in Higher Education: Proceedings of the Ninth Annual Conference on Higher Education*, Chicago, 1954 (n.p.), p. 299.
24. University of Pittsburgh Military Science Department, *Standing Operating Procedure for Cadets*, Sept. 1, 1954, University of Pittsburgh Archives, Hillman Library, Classification Number 35/2-B, File Folder 1. Recall the pledge pin from the film *Animal House*.
25. *Duquesne University Cadet Handbook: Learn Today, Lead Tomorrow*, 1956, Duquesne University Archives, ROTC Box 1, ROTC 1958–65 Folder. Emphasis in original.
26. *History of the Air University*, Aug. to Dec. 1952, Air Force Historical Research Agency, Maxwell AFB, Montgomery, Alabama, appendix 74, letter from Brigadier General M. K. Deichelmann, AFROTC Commandant, to all PAS, n.d.
27. University of Texas, Department of Military Science, *Army ROTC Cadet Regulations, 1962*. Emphasis in original.
28. Paul Fussell, *Wartime: Understanding and Behavior in the Second World War* (New York: Oxford University Press, 1989), p. 80. The possibilities for abuse were made more rampant by the practice of allowing advanced cadets to drill the basic cadets.
29. *Flight 56* (Texas AFROTC Yearbook), University of Texas Archives, UG 638.8 F5553 TXC 1955/56.
30. University of Texas Center of American History, Department of Military Science Papers, *Army ROTC Cadet Regulations*.
31. *History of the Air Force Reserve Officers' Training Corps*, July 1 to Dec. 31, 1963, Air Force Historical Research Agency, Maxwell AFB, Montgomery, Alabama.

32. The closest analogy in academic settings was engineering, where curricula were set by engineering societies, though those societies certainly had more faculty input than did ROTC curricula. As noted earlier, the professional orientation of engineering colleges helped to reduce levels of dissonance between engineering faculty and the military.

33. The same logic underlay the joint university-military creation of permanent research labs in the Cold War era. See Roger Geiger, *Research and Relevant Knowledge: American Research Universities Since World War II* (New York: Oxford University Press, 1993), p. 14.

34. Maxwell J. Richards, "A Ten-Year History of Air Force ROTC, 1946–1956," M.A. thesis, University of Maryland, 1957, p. 11.

35. "For Wider ROTC Plan," *New York Times,* Nov. 4, 1953, p. 25, col. 3.

36. Gene Lyons and John Masland, *Education and Military Leadership: A Study of the ROTC* (Princeton, N.J.: Princeton University Press, 1959), p. 12. This study was funded by the Carnegie Corporation as part of a large grant given to several schools to study international affairs. The authors were in Dartmouth's School of Government. The impact of Korea is noted in "A Study Leading to the Development of a Long Range AFROTC Program," unpublished Air University Study [1968], ROTC History Office, Building 78, Maxwell AFB, Montgomery, Alabama, pp. 52–53.

37. The number of specializations themselves grew from just 24 in the World War II–era Army Air Corps to more than 300 by the beginning of the 1960s. See Mitchell, *Air Force Officers,* chap. 11.

38. Lyons and Masland, *Education and Military Leadership,* p. 13

39. Quoted in Benjamin Fine, "Army Will Spread Change in ROTC," *New York Times,* May 10, 1953, p. 26, col. 3.

40. Lyons and Masland, *Education and Military Leadership,* p. 183.

41. [W. H. S. Wright], Headquarters, U.S. Continental Command, Ft. Monroe, Virginia, Senior Division Army ROTC Program, Jan. 27, 1964, Suitland Federal Records Center, Secretary of the Army General Correspondence, Record Group 335, Box 1228.

42. University of Colorado NROTC, *Knots and Fathoms,* 1953, University of Colorado at Boulder Library, Archives, 378.788 Un3PK 1953.

43. *History of the Air University,* Aug. to Dec. 1952, p. 48.

44. Quoted in Lyons and Masland, *Education and Military Leadership,* p. 180.

45. Grant Advertising, Research Studies for ROTC. The ad certainly seems patronizing and even insulting in retrospect, but Grant Advertising's research indicated that Ted was a hit. Their survey of 1,500 college men (half of whom were not in ROTC) from twenty-six schools nationwide showed that only 6.6 percent remembered not liking the ad.

46. *Kent State University Bulletin: The Reserve Officer Training Corps Program,* Aug. 1952, Kent State University Archives, Series Number 33.13.3.

47. Paul Wolff, Army PMS, to Alan Rankin, Oct. 10, 1960, University of Pittsburgh Archives, Hillman Library, Classification Number 55/1, File Folder 188.

48. "Transfer of Air Force ROTC Responsibilities," supporting document 33.

49. *The University of Pittsburgh School of Liberal Arts Bulletin*, 1961–1962, p. 1.

50. H. Malcolm Macdonald to Vice Admiral H. P. Smith, Oct. 27, 1958, University of Texas President's Office Records, VF 30/A.b, Naval Science 1958–59 Folder.

51. *The University of Pittsburgh College Bulletin, 1950–1951*, p. 81.

52. *Kent State University Bulletin*, 1952.

53. Agreement regarding Credit Applicable towards Graduation, Feb. 16, 1954, University of Texas President's Office Records, VF 20/A.b, ROTC General, 1953 Folder.

54. *The University of Pittsburgh School of Liberal Arts Bulletin*, 1961–1962, pp. 4–5; *The University of Pittsburgh School of Engineering and Mines Bulletin*, 1964–66, p. 32. By way of comparison, the freshman English composition course was worth 6 credits.

55. Gordon Ray to Colonel Howder, Aug. 27, 1957, University of Illinois Archives, President David Henry Papers, Box 26, ROTC—Air Science Folder.

56. "Rot-Cee Ranks," *Newsweek*, Feb. 24, 1964.

57. Report of the Executive Committee Meeting of the Association of NROTC Colleges, Oct. 30, 1950, University of Texas President's Office Records, VF 17/C.a, Association of NROTC Colleges Folder.

58. Hanson Baldwin, "The ROTC—III," *New York Times*, Aug. 27, 1960, p. 8, col. 2.

59. Royen Dangerfeld to Colonel L. J. Rohrs, Jan. 4, 1960, University of Illinois Archives, President David Henry Papers, Box 51, ROTC—Air Science Folder.

60. Colonel J. D. Howder to President David Henry, Jan. 30, 1958, ibid., Box 26, ROTC—Air Science Folder.

61. John Lisack, "Qualitative Educational Requirements for Air Force Officers," n.d., American Society of Mechanical Engineers Paper Number 63-AHGT-83, located in the James Shelburne Papers, Maxwell AFB, Montgomery, Alabama, 168.7036–32, vol. 5.

62. *History of the Air University*, Jan. 1, to June 30, 1964, vol. 8, appendix H.

63. O. Meredith Wilson, President, University of Minnesota, to Elvis Stahr, Secretary of the Army, June 15, 1962, Suitland Federal Records Center, Record Group 335, Box 1227.

64. E. R. Durgin, Secretary-Treasurer, Association of NROTC Colleges, to K. L. Nutting, Assistant, Director, Center for Naval Education and Training, Jan. 29, 1957, University of Illinois Archives, President David Henry Papers, Box 26, ROTC—Naval Science Folder.

65. Lewis Jones to H. F. Harding, June 9, 1958, Rutgers University Archives, Office of the President (Lewis W. Jones), Box 10, Air Force ROTC Folder.

66. H. F. Harding, Chairman, Air Science Department, Ohio State University, to President Henry, Apr. 10, 1958, University of Illinois Archives, President David Henry Papers, Box 26, ROTC Folder.

67. Major General T. C. Rogers, USAF ROTC Commandant, to President Henry, May 5, 1958, ibid.

68. Ray Hawk, "A New Program for the AFROTC," *Journal of Higher Education* 31 (Feb. 1960): 103–106.

69. Jerome Rosenberg, Secretary, Senate Educational Policies Committee, to Dr.

Edward Litchfield, Chancellor, Apr. 30, 1959, University of Pittsburgh Archives, Hillman Library, Classification Number 55/1, File Folder 186.

70. Alan Rankin, "Report on Progress in Implementing the Recommendations of the Educational Policies Committee of the University Senate with Regard to the ROTC Programs," Nov. 13, 1959, ibid.

71. "The Revolution at Service Academies," *U.S. News and World Report,* Dec. 2, 1963, pp. 75–77.

72. "Updating the Academies," *Time,* Sept. 7, 1959, p. 61.

73. Alan Rankin to Edward Litchfield, Dec. 18, 1959, University of Pittsburgh Archives, Hillman Library, Classification Number 55/1, File Folder 190.

74. Major General Frederick Warren to Russell Thackrey, Feb. 12, 1960, University of Illinois Archives, National Association of State Universities and Land-Grant Colleges Papers, Series Number 10/3/57, Box 14.

75. Telegram from Army ROTC Adjutant General [Major General Frederick Warren] to David Henry, Feb. 15, 1960, University of Illinois Archives, President David Henry Papers, Box 51, ROTC—Miscellaneous Folder.

76. Funari to Alan Rankin, May 12, 1960. University of Pittsburgh Archives, Hillman Library, Classification Number 55/1, File Folder 186.

77. Captain J. A. Lark, quoted in *The Role of Colleges and Universities in ROTC Programs* (Columbus: Ohio State University Press, 1960), p. 57.

78. Grant Advertising, Research Studies for ROTC.

79. Report of the Meeting of the Army Advisory Panel on ROTC Affairs, Apr. 25, 1961, University of Pittsburgh Archives, Hillman Library, Classification Number 55/1, File Folder 188.

80. "ROTC Proposals," *New York Times,* July 17, 1960, sec. 4, p. 7, col. 6.

81. "ROTC Presents New Curriculum," *The Technique,* Feb. 19, 1960, p. 1, col. 4; "Army, Air Force ROTC Reduce Hours to Afford More Academic Study Time," *The Technique,* Oct. 20, 1961, p. 6, col. 3. The Army ROTC followed the AFROTC's lead, reducing time in the freshman year by one-third. See "Army ROTC Unit Submits Proposed Major Change," *The Technique,* Nov. 18, 1960, p. 1, col. 1.

4. The ROTC Vitalization Act, 1964–1968

1. C. Wright Mills, *The Power Elite* (New York: Oxford University Press, 1956), p. 217.

2. Ibid., pp. 218–219.

3. Dwight D. Eisenhower, Farewell Address, Jan. 17, 1961.

4. SDS's early activities focused more on civil rights than on the Vietnam War, but many members quickly came to argue that American prosecution of the war overseas and racism at home were linked. For more on New Left origins, see Todd Gitlin's *The Sixties: Years of Hope, Days of Rage* (New York: Bantam Books, 1987).

5. Roger Geiger argues that the consensus of the 1950s was that government

influence did *not* greatly affect research and education missions. It should also be noted that the DOD's relative share of the federal dollars flowing to universities was declining due to the enlarging support coming from the National Science Foundation and NASA. See Geiger's *Research and Relevant Knowledge: American Research Universities since World War II* (New York: Oxford University Press, 1993).

6. *History of the Air Force Reserve Officers' Training Corps,* July 1 to Dec. 31, 1962, Air Force Historical Research Agency, Maxwell AFB, Montgomery, Alabama; Lieutenant General W. H. S. Wright, Chief Officer of Reserve Components, U.S. Army, to Harlan Hatcher, Nov. 18, 1963, University of Michigan Archives, Bentley Historical Library, Harlan Hatcher Papers, Box 37, Folder 11.

7. Mershon National Security Program, *Role of the Colleges and Universities in ROTC Programs* (Columbus: Ohio State University Press, 1960), statement of Colonel William Lindley.

8. Background Information to ROTC Information Plan, [1964], Suitland Federal Records Center, Secretary of the Army General Correspondence, Record Group 335, Box 1228. In 1949 the services and the DOD agreed not to merge the three ROTC programs into one large officer-training program. At the same time, they set compatibility as a goal to reduce competition among the programs.

9. *History of the Air University,* Jan. 1 to June 30, 1964. Air Force Historical Research Agency, Maxwell AFB, Montgomery, Alabama, Call Number K239.01, vol. 8, appendix H.

10. Lieutenant General W. H. S. Wright to Harlan Hatcher.

11. "Significant Elements in U.S. Army ROTC Program," Dec. 17, 1963, University of Illinois Archives, Series Number 4/2/14, Box 3.

12. Gordon Moon, "ROTC on the Rebound," *Army* (Aug. 1967): 46–55.

13. *History of the Air University.*

14. Lieutenant General W. H. S. Wright to Harlan Hatcher.

15. Robert Williams to Dean James Wallace, Nov. 6, 1962, University of Michigan Archives, Bentley Historical Library, Vice-President for Academic Affairs Papers, Box 39, ROTC General, 1957–1962 Folder.

16. "Proceedings of the 26 October 1962 Meeting of the Army Advisory Panel on ROTC Affairs," Duquesne University Archives, ROTC Box 1, ROTC—Army Correspondence 1953–1965.

17. George Flynn, *The Draft* (Lawrence: University of Kansas Press, 1993), p. 168.

18. Philip Caputo, *A Rumor of War* (New York: Ballantine Books, 1977), p. 7.

19. Ebert's lens on student life is located in "Rot-Cee Ranks," *Newsweek,* Feb. 24, 1964, p. 84.

20. *History of the Air University.*

21. "A Study Leading to the Development of a Long Range AFROTC Program," unpublished Air University study, ROTC History Office, Building 78, Maxwell AFB, Montgomery, Alabama. Benjamin Fridge, Special Assistant to the Secretary of the Air Force for Manpower, Personnel, and Reserve Forces, *Statement*

before Subcommittee no. 3, Committee on Armed Services, House of Representatives, September 1963, University of Illinois Archives, National Association of State Universities and Land-Grant Colleges Papers, Series Number 10/3/57, Box 15.

22. *History of the Air University.*

23. "Conclusions of the Army Advisory Panel on ROTC Affairs, 25 April 1961," Duquesne University Archives, ROTC Box 1, ROTC—Army Correspondence 1953–1965.

24. "Proceedings of the 26 October 1962 Meeting of the Army Advisory Panel on ROTC Affairs," ibid.

25. *History of the Air University.*

26. Association of State Universities and Land-Grant Colleges Circular Letter #5, Feb. 27, 1963, University of Illinois Archives, Series Number 4/6/26, Box 1.

27. "Report of the Military Affairs Committee," Oct. 1, 1963, ibid., Series Number 4/2/14, Box 3.

28. *History of AFROTC,* July 1 to Dec. 31, 1964.

29. Quotation from "Rot-Cee Ranks." In 1963, 23 percent of AFROTC cadets graduated from engineering programs. Shortly afterward, the air force set a goal of having 60 percent of its graduates come from engineering. *History of the Air University,* Jan. 1 to June 30, 1964, vol. 6.

30. *History of the AFROTC,* July 1 to Dec. 31, 1962.

31. Russell Thackrey to Oliver Meadows, Dec. 13, 1963, University of Illinois Archives, National Association of State Universities and Land-Grant Colleges Papers, Series Number 10/3/57, Box 15. Emphasis in original.

32. Christian Arnold, ed., *Proceedings of the Association of State Universities and Land-Grant Colleges Seventy-seventh Annual Convention,* Chicago, 1963 (n.p.), p. 60.

33. Christian Arnold, ed., *Proceedings of the Association of State Universities and Land-Grant Colleges Seventy-sixth Annual Convention,* Washington, D.C., 1962 (n.p.), p. 72.

34. Congressman Hébert forced the defeat of the bill in the 1963 session when he blocked the "Powell Amendment" from being added. The Powell Amendment would have denied federal funds to any ROTC host school that practiced segregation. By the time the bill came up in the 1964 session, Congress had already passed the Civil Rights Act, making the Powell Amendment superfluous.

35. Hébert was particularly interested in the development of the Junior ROTC program (for high school). He devoted much of his time on the bill to expanding the JROTC program nationwide. The Senate authorized fewer JROTC units than Hébert wanted, but the total program was nonetheless expanded dramatically. James D. Hittle, interview with the author, Aug. 5, 1997.

36. *Congressional Record* (June 23, 1964) vol. 110, p. 14686.

37. "The New Air Force Curriculum," May 29, 1964, Kent State University Archives, President Robert White Papers, Folder 14, Army and Air Force ROTC Correspondence, 1962–1964.

38. Morris Janowitz, *The Professional Soldier,* (Glencoe, Ill.: Free Press, 1960), p. 41.

39. Lieutenant Colonel G. A. Payne, Assistant Adjutant General to Chief of Office

of Reserve Components, Feb. 28, 1964, Suitland Federal Records Center, Secretary of the Army General Correspondence, Record Group 335, Box 1228.

40. [W. H. S. Wright], Headquarters, U.S. Continental Command, Ft. Monroe, Virginia, Senior Division Army ROTC Program, Jan. 27, 1964, Suitland Federal Records Center, Secretary of the Army General Correspondence, Record Group 335, Box 1228.

41. *History of the AFROTC*, July 1 to Dec. 31, 1964; U.S. Army Command Information Unit, *Army ROTC Newsletter*, June 1965, Duquesne University Archives, ROTC Box 1, ROTC 1958–65 Folder. Ninety-four air force and 213 army units chose to open two-year programs, maintaining their four-year programs as well.

42. *United States Army Command Information Fact Sheet #53*, May 25, 1966, United States Army Center of Military History, Washington, D.C., Decimal Number 326.6.

43. [W. H. S. Wright], Senior Division Army ROTC Program.

44. David Henry to Brigadier General William Lindley, May 8, 1964, University of Illinois Archives, President David Henry Papers, Box 123, ROTC—Air Science; Robert White to Ohio Senators, Sept. 18, 1964, Kent State University Archives, President Robert White Papers, Folder 19, Army ROTC Correspondence, 1964–1965.

45. "Rot-Cee Ranks," p. 84.

46. *Congressional Record* (June 23, 1964), vol. 110, pp. 14685–6.

47. "Rot-Cee Ranks," p. 84.

48. Clair Worthy, University of Illinois Professor of Military Science, to Royen Dangerfeld, Aug. 13, 1964, University of Illinois Archives, President David Henry Papers, Box 123, ROTC—Military Science.

49. [W. H. S. Wright], Senior Division Army ROTC Program.

50. Robert Williams to the Committee on ROTC Affairs, March 31, 1969, University of Michigan Archives, Bentley Historical Library, Vice-President for Academic Affairs Papers, Box 39, Advisory Committee on ROTC Affairs Folder.

51. Robert Clifford to Stephen Ailes, Secretary of the Army, Dec. 27, 1964, Suitland Federal Records Center, Record Group 335, Box 1228.

52. Robert Williams to Arthur Stone, Dec. 8, 1964, University of Michigan Archives, Bentley Historical Library, University of Michigan Vice-President for Academic Affairs Papers, Box 39, ROTC—Air Force 1964 Folder.

53. "Ford Grants to Liberal Arts Colleges," *School and Society* (Nov. 18, 1961): 388–389. The five grant recipients with ROTC programs were Brown, Johns Hopkins, Notre Dame, Stanford, and Vanderbilt.

54. *NASULGC Circular Letter #38*, Nov. 4, 1965, University of Michigan Archives, Bentley Historical Library, Vice-President for Academic Affairs Papers, Box 39, ROTC General, 1965 Folder.

55. Robert Williams to ROTC Staff, Nov. 19, 1965, ibid.

56. Moon, "ROTC on the Rebound."

57. *History of the AFROTC*, Twentieth Anniversary Command Edition, 1966.

58. *History of the AFROTC,* Jan. 1 to June 30, 1966. The percentage of transfers from junior colleges was lower than the air force had hoped despite several programs, including the assignment of ROTC units to recruit and publicize the two-year option at nearby junior colleges. This trend mirrored larger trend in American higher education: junior college students did not transfer to four-year schools in the numbers educators had anticipated.

59. Major John Rogers, Acting Professor of Military Science, to Harold Roskens, Dec. 13, 1965, Kent State University Archives, Robert White Papers, Folder 29, Army ROTC Correspondence 1965–1966.

60. Army ROTC Unit, University of Pittsburgh, to David Kurtzman, Mar. 1, 1966, University of Pittsburgh Archives 2/10 1966/67 Box 26, File Folder 243. The University of Pittsburgh system then included campuses in Bradford, Greensburg, Johnstown, and Titusville. See Robert Alberts, *Pitt: The Story of the University of Pittsburgh, 1787–1987* (Pittsburgh: University of Pittsburgh Press, 1986), p. 343.

61. *Annual Report,* Department of Military Science, Academic Year 1968–1969, University of Washington Archives, Allen Library, W. U. Reserve Officers Training Corps Program, Military Science, 95–289, V.F. 2457.

62. *History of the AFROTC,* July 1 to June 30, 1967.

63. "Rot-Cee Ranks," p. 84.

64. Colonel Rashid to Mary Helen Pendel, Mar. 6, 1964, Duquesne University Archives, ROTC Box 1, ROTC History Folder.

65. "Significant Elements in U.S. Army ROTC Program."

66. Lupe Zamarripa, "Commission Possible from ROTC Program," *Daily Texan,* Aug. 19, 1966.

67. "Significant Elements in U.S. Army ROTC Program."

68. Flynn, *The Draft,* p. 197.

69. Ibid., p. 199.

70. Quoted in Dan Booker, "ROTC Enrollment Up 70 Percent," *Pitt News,* Sept. 12, 1966, p. 1.

71. Booker, "ROTC Enrollment Up 70 Percent."

72. Interestingly, membership in female auxiliary societies was at even higher levels than those of the male honor societies. This subject is covered more fully in Chapter 6.

73. "Worcester Polytech Institute Conducts Mock Invasion of Middleboro, Mass." *New York Times,* May 2, 1966, p. 40, col. 6.

74. Frank Fischer, PMS, to President Odegaard, Feb. 1, 1967, University of Washington Archives, Allen Library, W. U. Presidents Papers, 71–34, Box 39, Folder 3.

75. Julie Emery, "Cadets Trained to 'Spy' on Left-Wing Groups," *Seattle Times,* Jan. 25, 1967, ibid., "Statement of George Smith, AROTC Senior," n.d., ibid; President Odegaard to Lieutenant General James Richardson, Nov. 3, 1966, ibid.

76. During the briefing, cadets had been shown a slide explaining how to identify

subversive groups. The slide read: "If it walks like a duck, talks like a duck, and lays eggs like a duck, then it is a duck." See "Army Makes Spies Out of Students; Cadets Snoop on SNCC, SDS," *Sunday Ramparts* [1966], ibid; "ROTC Topic for Program," *The Washington Daily,* Feb. 16, 1967, p. 5.

77. "ROTC Invited," *The Washington Daily,* Feb. 17, 1967, p. 2.

78. Clair Worthy to Royen Dangerfield, August 13, 1964.

79. "Working Paper from the Report from the Subcommittee on the Navy," Committee on Officer Education, July 1, 1965, University of Washington Archives, Allen Library, W. U. Presidents Papers, 71–34, Box 53, Folder 2.

80. *History of the Air University,* Jan. 1 to June 30, 1964.

81. Association of NROTC Colleges Minutes, Dec. 13, 1965, University of Illinois Archives, President David Henry Papers, Box 154, ROTC—Naval Science.

82. *History of the AFROTC,* July 1 to Dec. 31, 1965.

83. Clair Worthy to Royen Dangerfield, Aug. 13, 1964.

84. [Colonel C. E. Curran], "Recommendations of the PMS, 1965," University of Illinois Army ROTC Historical Files, Military Science Department Library, 0.432.

85. *History of the AFROTC,* Twentieth Anniversary Command Edition.

86. "Officer Training and Education," *Naval Training Bulletin* (Fall 1965), Air Force Historical Research Agency, J. C. Shelburne Papers, Call Number 168.7036–32, vol. 5.

87. Association of NROTC Colleges Minutes, Dec. 13, 1965. In some cases, the universities accepted advanced degrees from a service school, such as one of the war colleges, as a substitute for a Masters degree, but they did not wish to do so as a matter of policy.

88. J. W. Briscoe, Associate Provost, to Brigadier General Joseph Jones, Apr. 8, 1966, University of Illinois Archives, President David Henry Papers, Box 154, ROTC—Military Science.

89. *History of the AFROTC,* Twentieth Anniversary Command Edition.

90. Lieutenant General J. H. Michaels to David Henry, April 14, 1967, University of Illinois Archives, President David Henry Papers, Box 176, ROTC—Military Science.

91. "Working Paper from the Report From the Subcommittee on the Navy," and "Working Paper from the Report from the Subcommittee on the Air Force," Committee on Officer Education, July 1, 1965, University of Washington Archives, Allen Library, W. U. Presidents Papers, 71–34, Box 53, Folder 2.

92. *History of the AFROTC,* Jan. 1 to June 30, 1966. Emphasis in original.

93. "Awarding Academic Credit for ROTC Courses," Army Advisory Panel on ROTC Affairs, Oct. 26, 1967, University of Illinois Archives, National Association of State Universities and Land-Grant Colleges Papers, Series Number 10/3/57, Box 15.

94. "Credit for AFROTC Courses," Air University presentation to the AFROTC Advisory Panel, Dec. 5, 1966, ibid.

95. H. Malcolm Macdonald to Brigadier General William Lindley, Mar. 23, 1965, University of Texas President's Office Records, VF37/C.b, Air Force Science 1960–1968 Folder.

96. Leslie Gelb and Richard Betts, *The Irony of Vietnam: The System Worked* (Washington, D.C.: Brookings Institute, 1979), p. 130.

97. George Herring, *America's Longest War: The United States and Vietnam, 1950–1975* (New York: McGraw-Hill, 1986), p. 146.

98. "ROTC History: University of Illinois at Urbana-Champaign" [1965], University of Illinois Military Science Department Library, Army ROTC Historical Files, 0.432.

99. Benjamin Hollis to Dr. Crawford, Acting Chancellor, "Possible Subversive Activity," Sept. 27, 1965, University of Pittsburgh Archives 2/10 1966/67, Box 26, File Folder 243.

100. "Students Protest against ROTC," *Pitt News*, Nov. 3, 1967, p. 7.

101. Don Marbury, "University Professor Argues ROTC Should Be Abolished," *Pitt News*, Nov. 15, 1967, p. 3, col. 1.

102. "Korona Evaluates ROTC Course," *Targum*, Sept. 12, 1967.

103. Gelb and Betts, *The Irony of Vietnam*, p. 162.

104. "Korona Evaluates ROTC Course."

105. Colonel R. J. Jackson to Robert White, Oct. 26, 1967, Kent State University Archives, Robert White Papers, Folder 30, Army ROTC Correspondence, 1967–1968.

106. "Officer Says Sit-In Will Help ROTC," *Targum*, Nov. 13, 1967.

107. Janowitz, *The Professional Soldier*, p. 429.

5. ROTC from Tet to the All-Volunteer Force

1. Quoted in George Herring, *America's Longest War: The United States and Vietnam, 1950–1975* (New York: McGraw-Hill, 1979), p. 91.

2. Quoted in Todd Gitlin, *The Sixties: Years of Hope, Days of Rage* (New York: Bantam Books, 1987), p. 300.

3. Neil Sheehan, *A Bright Shining Lie: John Paul Vann and America in Vietnam* (New York: Random House, 1988), p. 717.

4. Gitlin, *The Sixties*, p. 301.

5. Leslie Gelb and Richard Betts, *The Irony of Vietnam: The System Worked* (Washington, D.C.: Brookings Institute, 1979), p. 163.

6. This wonderful phrase belongs to Roger Geiger. See *Research and Relevant Knowledge: American Research Universities since World War II* (New York: Oxford University Press, 1993), chap. 8.

7. Gitlin, *The Sixties*, p. 300.

8. Sheehan, *A Bright Shining Lie*, pp. 717–718.

9. "ROTC under Fire," *Wall Street Journal*, Mar. 22, 1968.

10. Quoted in Gitlin, *The Sixties*, p. 285.

11. Ileana Brown, *History of the Air Force Reserve Officers Training Corps*, July 1, 1967

to June 30, 1968, Air Force Historical Research Agency, Maxwell Air Force Base, Montgomery, Alabama. Call Number K239.07 K.

12. *History of the AFROTC,* July 1, 1968 to June 30, 1969, AFROTC History Office, Maxwell AFB, Montgomery, Alabama.

13. David Rosenblum, "Today's Next Court Case: ROTC versus 'Democracy,'" *Pitt News,* Oct. 25, 1968, p. 5.

14. Ed Moss, "ROTC: Controversial Comment, Official Facts and Apology," *Pitt News,* Nov. 1 1968, p. 4. Emphasis added.

15. Noel Schutz, "Understanding Student Dissent," *Air University Air Force ROTC Education Bulletin* (Feb. 1969), p. 6.

16. Department of Defense, *Selected Manpower Statistics,* May 1978, p. 109.

17. Andrew Malcom, "New Enrollment in College ROTC Shows Sharp Dip," *New York Times,* Oct. 20, 1969, p. 1, col. 1.

18. "Statement regarding ROTC Programs from National Association of State Universities and Land-Grant Colleges," Mar. 18, 1970, University of Illinois Archives, Chancellor's Office Papers, Series Number 24/1/1, Box 42, Armed Forces Folder.

19. *Summary Report: Status of Reserve Officer Training Corps Programs at AAU Member Institutions* [1969], University of Illinois Archives, National Association of State Universities and Land-Grant Colleges Papers, Series Number 10/3/57, Box 16.

20. M. R. Rose to Joy Klieger, Sept. 19, 1969, University of Pittsburgh Archives, Hillman Library, Classification Number 3/1/1, File Folder 232.

21. "ROTC Enrollments and Number of Commissioned Officers," n.d., University of Illinois Archives, President David Henry Papers, Box 235, ROTC Folder.

22. *Air Force ROTC Bulletin,* Dec. 1970, p. 22.

23. "ROTC under Fire."

24. Robert C. McMath et al., *Engineering the New South: Georgia Tech, 1885–1985* (Athens: University of Georgia Press, 1985), p. 388; Wayne Bridges to President Hansen, May 28, 1970, Georgia Institute of Technology Library and Information Center, 86–05–01, Office of the President Records, 1961–1972, Box 14, Folder 33.

25. Herring, *America's Longest War,* p. 243.

26. Sheehan, *A Bright Shining Lie,* p. 741. Lieutenant General Harold (Hal) Moore, USA (Ret.), was an American field commander at the first large-scale battle between American ground troops and North Vietnamese soldiers. His account of the 1965 battle in the Ia Drang Valley can be found in Harold Moore and Joseph Galloway, *We Were Soldiers Once—And Young: Ia Drang, the Battle That Changed the War in Vietnam* (New York: Random House, 1992).

27. This is, of course, not to deny the brutality of the war before Tet. For more on the nature of the war following Tet, see Ronald Spector, *After Tet: The Bloodiest Year in Vietnam* (New York: Free Press, 1993).

28. For more on the origins and controversies of the lottery system, see George Q. Flynn, *The Draft* (Lawrence: University of Kansas Press, 1993), chap. 9.

29. Robert Goldrich, "The Senior Reserve Officer Training Corps: Recent Trends

and Current Status," Apr. 19, 1974, Library of Congress Congressional Research Service, p. 24.

30. B. B. Cassiday, "Report to the AFROTC Advisory Panel," Sept. 18, 1972, University of Illinois Archives, President John Corbally Papers, Box 33, ROTC—Air Force.

31. *Air Force ROTC Bulletin,* Dec. 1970, p. 23. Only 9 percent said they had joined because of a "desire to make the Air Force a career."

32. Cassiday, "Report to the AFROTC Advisory Panel."

33. Lawrence Baskir and William Strauss, *Chance and Circumstance: The Draft, the War, and the Vietnam Generation* (New York: Alfred A. Knopf, 1978), p. 54.

34. University of Pittsburgh ROTC Departments, recruiting poster, 1969, University of Pittsburgh Archives, Hillman Library, Classification Number 35-A, File Folder 3.

35. "Join the Army and See the World," *The Technique,* Feb. 13 1970, p. 3, col. 1.

36. Arthur Hansen to Joseph Spitler, Dec. 1, 1970, Georgia Institute of Technology Library and Information Center, 86–05–01, Office of the President Records, 1961–1972, Box 14, Folder 33.

37. Goldrich, "The Senior Reserve Officer Training Corps," p. 26.

38. Compare these findings to the responses of AFROTC graduates in 1963. When asked, "What one factor was most influential in causing you to seek an Air Force commission?" the draft appeared fourth, after the opportunity to fly, prestige, and career opportunities. See "Summary of Precommissioning Questionnaire," in *History of the AFROTC,* July 1 to Dec. 31, 1963, Air Force Historical Research Agency. Call Number K239.07 K.

39. Kingman Brewster, President, Yale University, Text of Special Report to Alumni, Feb. 22, 1969, University of Pittsburgh Archives, Hillman Library, Classification Number 3/1/1, File Folder 238.

40. Michael Duto quoted in Peter Karsten, "Anti-ROTC: Response to Vietnam or 'Consciousness III'?" in John Lovell and Philip Kronenberg, eds., *New Civil-Military Relations: The Agonies of Adjustment to Post-Vietnam Realities* (New Brunswick, N.J.: Transaction Books, 1974): 111–127. Quotation from p. 113.

41. Andrew H. Malcom, "New Enrollment in College ROTC Shows Sharp Dip," *New York Times,* Oct. 20, 1969, p. 1, col. 1.

42. Michael Kaufman, "Two Students Challenge ROTC Regulations on Hair," ibid., May 28, 1970, p. 41, col. 1.

43. Quoted in Karsten, "Anti-ROTC," pp. 113–114.

44. "End Credit, Faculty Status for ROTC" (editorial), *Daily Illini,* Feb. 27, 1970.

45. Quoted in "ROTC under Fire."

46. Students for a Democratic Society, "ROTC Marches On" [Oct. 1970], University of Michigan Archives, Bentley Historical Library, President's Papers, Box 23, ROTC Folder.

47. "SDS Ejects United Fruit Rep.," *The Washington Daily,* Feb. 25, 1969, p. 1.

48. Bruce Drake, "The Battle over ROTC," *Johns Hopkins Magazine* (Spring 1969): 3–4.

49. *History of the AFROTC,* July 1, 1968 to June 30, 1969.

50. *History of the Air University,* Fiscal Year 1970, Air Force Historical Research Agency, Maxwell AFB, Montgomery, Alabama. Call Number K239.01.

51. Ibid., "Windows Smashed in Protest," *New York Times,* Feb. 2 1970, p. 10.

52. "Report of the Department of Military Science, Academic Year 1969–70," University of Illinois Army ROTC Historical Files, Military Science Department Library, 0.432.

53. Fleming also believed that at Michigan the student radicals "didn't play into [the decision-making on ROTC] very much." Robben Fleming, interview with the author, Ann Arbor, Mich., Dec. 12, 1995.

54. Paul Stoller, "Students Appeal for Vietnam Negotiations in Referendum," ibid., Jan. 25, 1968, p. 1; "SG Referendum," *Pitt News,* Nov. 20 1968, p. 1. The January referendum attracted 2,422 voters. The November referendum attracted 3,869 voters.

55. Kent State University News Service, Aug. 14, 1970, Kent State University Archives, Charles Kegley May 4th Materials 34.13, Box 102, Folder 44.

56. National Association of State Universities and Land-Grant Colleges, Circular Number 154, June 30, 1970; Kent State University Archives, Charles Kegley May 4th Materials 34.13, Box 102, Folder 42.

57. James Foley and Robert Foley, *The College Scene: Students Tell It Like It Is* (New York: Cowles Books, 1969), p. 126.

58. Ibid., pp. 31 and 130–131.

59. Brigadier General Donald Blake to AFROTC Advisory Panel, Aug. 13, 1969, University of Illinois Archives, President David Henry Papers, Box 235, ROTC—Air Science.

60. National Association of State Universities and Land-Grant Colleges, Circular Number 154.

61. "Notes from the Thirty-First Meeting of the Faculty of Rutgers College," May 18, 1970, Rutgers University Archives, President Gross Papers, Box 28, File ROTC 1969–1971. Emphasis mine.

62. Yale University News Bureau, Feb. 22, 1969, Historical Society of Western Pennsylvania, Robert McConnell Papers, Box 1 Folder 8.

63. Damaine Martin, "ROTC Open Forum: The Good Guys vs. The Bad Guys?" *Pitt News,* Nov. 25, 1968, p. 1.

64. "Statement of M. J. Sinnott before the Academic Affairs Committee" [June 25, 1969], University of Michigan Archives, Bentley Historical Library, Vice-President for Academic Affairs Papers, Box 18, ROTC 1968–69 Folder. Despite the ECPD's oversight, a limited number of engineering schools, such as that at the University of Illinois, allowed ROTC credit to count toward elective credit.

65. James Gindin, Carl Cohen, John LaPrelle and Locke Anderson, "Report from the Curriculum Committee on the Issue of Accreditation for ROTC," Mar. 25, 1969, University of Michigan Navy ROTC Accreditation/Relations File 1969, North Hall.

66. "Student Affairs Committee of the University Senate Recommendation," Apr.

4, 1968, University of Pittsburgh Archives, Hillman Library, Provost Office Files 1965–1970, Classification Number 3/1/1, File Folder 239.

67. Princeton University, "Report of the Ad Hoc Committee on ROTC to the University Faculty," Mar. 3, 1969, Historical Society of Western Pennsylvania, Robert McConnell Papers, Box 1, Folder 8.

68. "Report to [Urbana-Champaign] Senate on ROTC Matters," May 7, 1970, University of Illinois Archives, Chancellor's Office Papers, Series Number 24/1/1, Box 42, Armed Forces Folder.

69. J. W. Briscoe to Colonel Frank Bexfield [Maxwell AFB], Dec. 30, 1968, University of Illinois Archives, President David Henry Papers, Box 213, ROTC—Air Force.

70. Quoted in Dave Kuhns, "ROTC 'Dis-Credited,'" *Pitt News*, Dec. 4, 1968, p. 1.

71. H. Malcolm Macdonald to Theodore Marrs, Oct. 1, 1968, University of Texas President's Office Records, VF 20/A.b, ROTC Air Science 1968–1969 Folder.

72. "Notes from the Thirty-First Meeting of the Faculty of Rutgers College," May 18, 1970, Rutgers University Archives, President Gross Papers, Box 28, ROTC 1969–1971 File.

73. Cornell University, "Report of the Special Faculty Committee on Military Training," Nov. 14, 1969, University of Pittsburgh Archives, Hillman Library, Provost Office Files 1965–1970, Classification Number 3/1/1, File Folder 233.

74. Colonel Arthur Wade to Colonel David Clagett, Feb. 24, 1969, Robert McConnell Papers, Historical Society of Western Pennsylvania, Box 1, Folder 8.

75. "Student Affairs Committee of the University Senate Recommendation"; Princeton University, "Report of the Ad Hoc Committee on ROTC to the University Faculty."

76. "Recommendations of the Advisory Committee on Educational Policies," July 22, 1969, University of Michigan Archives, Bentley Historical Library, Vice-President for Academic Affairs Papers, Box 26, ROTC 1969–70 Folder.

77. "Yale 'Busts' the ROTC," *New York Times*, Feb. 2, 1969, sec. 4, p. 9, col. 2.

78. Princeton University, "Report of the Ad Hoc Committee on ROTC to the University Faculty."

79. Gindin, Cohen, LaPrelle, and Anderson, Report from the Curriculum Committee on the Issue of Accreditation for ROTC.

80. David Smith to David Clagett and Reuben Chandler, Sept. 5, 1968, University of Pittsburgh Archives, Hillman Library, Provost Office Files 1965–1970, Classification Number 3/1/1, File Folder 235.

81. Task Force on ROTC to [Kegley] Commission to Implement a Commitment to Non-Violence, July 23 and 31, 1970, Kent State University Archives, Charles Kegley May 4th Materials 34.13, Box 102, Folder 41. Emphasis in original.

82. Princeton University, "Report of the Ad Hoc Committee on ROTC to the University Faculty"; Norman Parker, Chancellor, University of Illinois at Chicago Circle, to David Henry, Nov. 19, 1970, University of Illinois Archives, President David Henry Papers, Box 255, ROTC—Military Science.

83. "The Battle over ROTC," p. 2.

84. "NASULGC Special Subcommittee on ROTC Policy Report," June 1968, University of Illinois Archives, National Association of State Universities and Land-Grant Colleges Papers, Series Number 10/3/57, Box 15.

85. University of Colorado Minutes of the Faculty Meeting, Apr. 16, 1970, Archives, University of Colorado at Boulder Libraries, Central Administration, Faculty Council General Files, Series IV, Box 4, Folder 16; Dean W. E. Briggs to President Thieme, Oct. 28, 1970, ibid. President's Office, Series I, Box 330, ROTC General Information, 1973–1976 Folder. This faculty vote recommended faculty review of ROTC courses, a restriction of weapons training (although the faculty approved drill without weapons), and more use of substitution.

86. Richard Jessor, telephone interview with the author, Sept. 5, 1997.

87. Arval Morris, "ROTC: A Definitive Policy Statement," *Washington Daily,* Feb. 26, 1969, p. 1.

88. Bruce Chalmers to Robert McConnell, Mar. 12, 1969, Robert McConnell Papers, Historical Society of Western Pennsylvania, Box 1, Folder 8.

89. Archibald MacLeish, editorial, *Shannonigans* 13 (1969): 2, ibid.

90. Robert Williams to Robben Fleming and Allan Smith, Oct. 8, 1969, University of Michigan Archives, Bentley Historical Library, Vice-President for Academic Affairs Papers, Box 26, ROTC 1969–70 Folder.

91. Laird articulated his belief in the importance of personnel issues in his book *People, Not Hardware: The Highest Defense Priority* (Washington, D.C.: American Enterprise Institute, 1980).

92. *Report of the Special Subcommittee on ROTC to the Secretary of Defense* (Washington, D.C.: Government Printing Office, 1969).

93. Ibid., p. 2.

94. Ibid., pp. 25–26

95. Ibid., p. 27.

96. Christian Arnold, ed., "Report of the Senate," *Proceedings of the National Association of State Universities and Land-Grant Colleges Eighty-third Annual Convention,* Chicago, 1969 (n.p.), p. 100.

97. Christian Arnold, ed., "Report of the Senate," *Proceedings of the National Association of State Universities and Land-Grant Colleges Eighty-fourth Annual Convention,* Washington, 1970 (n.p.), p. 73.

98. *Report of the Special Subcommittee on ROTC,* p. 4.

99. Maurice Hartle, "A Comparative Study of the Professional Performance of Selected Naval Educational Programs, 1962–1972," Ph.D diss., 1973, Miami University, Ohio, p. 63.

100. National Security Information Center, "Summary of Activities," June 1969, University of Michigan Archives, Bentley Historical Library, Vice-President for Academic Affairs Papers, Box 40, ROTC—Air Force 1972 Folder.

101. "Army ROTC Establishes Curriculum Review Board," *The Technique,* Oct. 31, 1969, p. 1.

102. A 1971 survey of Annapolis students and ROTC students at Ohio State and

Pittsburgh provided some justification for the fear of an academy elite. One in three of the Annapolis students "could conceive of circumstances in which a takeover of the U.S. government by the military would be justified." To be sure, an alarming one in five ROTC students felt the same say, but the point here is that academy students were significantly more inclined to agree. Similarly, three in four Annapolis students found the adage "my country right or wrong" to be attractive, compared with only 40 percent of ROTC students. For more, see Ed Berger et al., "ROTC, My Lai, and the Volunteer Army," *Foreign Policy* 2 (Spring 1971): 135–160, quotation from p. 142.

103. Ralph K. Huitt, Executive Director NASULGC, to John Bitner, Apr. 29, 1970, University of Illinois Archives, National Association of State Universities and Land-Grant Colleges Papers, Series Number 10/3/57, Box 16.

104. Recall that the universities were responsible for overhead costs and the salaries of secretarial and janitorial services.

105. The University of Illinois, "Report of the Board of Trustees," 1966–1968, p. 182.

106. "Expenditures in Support of ROTC Units at the University of Michigan by the Department of Defense, 1968–69," University of Michigan Archives, Bentley Historical Library, Vice-President for Academic Affairs Papers, Box 18, ROTC 1968–69 Folder.

107. This issue took on renewed importance in 1969, when the House Armed Services Committee considered a bill to ban federal funds to schools that dropped ROTC.

108. Christian Arnold, ed., *Proceedings of the National Association of State Universities and Land-Grant Colleges Seventy-ninth Annual Convention*, Minneapolis, 1965 (n.p.), p. 60.

109. "Statement regarding ROTC Programs from National Association of State Universities and Land-Grant Colleges," Mar. 18, 1970, University of Illinois Archives, Chancellor's Office Papers, Series Number 24/1/1, Box 42, Armed Forces Folder.

110. When Nixon was inaugurated in January 1969, the United States had 540,000 men in Vietnam. That June Nixon instituted a policy of withdrawal of American forces. By December 1969 the United States had 480,000 men in Vietnam. By December 1970 troop levels were down to 280,000. See Stanley Karnow, *Vietnam* (New York: King, 1983), pp. 684–685.

111. George Benson, "Academic World and Military Education," *Air Force ROTC Education Bulletin* (Feb. 1971): 6.

112. The figure cited here is from the Criminal Investigation Division of the DOD. Seymour Hersh, who won a Pulitzer Prize for his exposure of the massacre, put the figure closer to five hundred. See his *My Lai 4: A Report on the Massacre and Its Aftermath* (New York: Random House, 1970).

113. Quoted in Berger et al., "ROTC, My Lai and the Volunteer Army," p. 143.

114. Natalie Meisler, "ASUC Senate Backs Five SMC Demands," *Colorado Daily*, Apr. 3, 1970.

115. Quoted in Christian Appy, *Working-Class War: American Combat Soldiers in Vietnam* (Chapel Hill: University of North Carolina Press, 1993), p. 269.

116. Arnold, ed., "Report of the Senate," *Proceedings of the National Association of State Universities and Land-Grant Colleges Eighty-fourth Annual Convention*, p. 15.

117. Christian Arnold, ed., "Report of the Senate," *Proceedings of the National Association of State Universities and Land-Grant Colleges Eighty-fifth Annual Convention*, New Orleans, 1971 (n.p.), p. 43.

118. Robben Fleming to John Pemberton, Executive Director, American Civil Liberties Union, Mar. 19, 1969, University of Michigan Archives, Bentley Historical Library, President's Papers, Box 10, ROTC Folder.

119. William Deibler, "Posvar Backs Faculty's Right to Nix ROTC," *Pittsburgh Post-Gazette*, Mar. 5, 1969, p. 1.

120. Robben Fleming, personal correspondence to the author, Oct. 26, 1995.

121. William Beecher, "Pentagon Is Willing to Alter ROTC but Not 'Degrade' It," *New York Times*, Apr. 30, 1969, p. 27, col. 1.

122. *Air University Air Force ROTC Education Bulletin* (May 1969), Air University Library, Maxwell AFB, Montgomery, Alabama.

123. In 1968 only 11 percent of AFROTC junior and senior cadets agreed with the statement that "most [freshman and sophomore] cadets look forward to and enjoy participating in military drill periods." Only 40 percent of senior cadets agreed with the statement: "Cadets marching in the Ranks learn discipline, respect for authority, and *esprit-de-corps*." Five percent agreed that "the campus respects and encourages drill." The author of the article concluded that these data argued for a "reconsideration [of AFROTC's] position on drill." See "Drill and Corps Training," *Air Force ROTC Bulletin* (Dec. 1970): 23.

124. William F. Muhlenfeld, "Our Embattled ROTC," *Army* (Feb. 1969): 21.

125. Quoted in David Rosenbaum, "Campus Attacks on ROTC Stir Pentagon," *New York Times*, Apr. 19, 1969, p. 19, col. 3.

126. F. Edward Hébert to Mendel Rivers, Aug. 7, 1969, University of Pittsburgh Archives, Hillman Library, Provost Office Files 1965–1970, Classification Number 3/1/1, File Folder 237.

127. Brigadier General C. P. Hannum, Memo for the File, "ROTC Briefing—Congressman Hébert," Mar. 11, 1970, United States Army Center of Military History, Washington, D.C., HRC 326.6.

128. Robert Williams, Meeting with the Bureau of Naval Personnel, Aug. 21, 1969, University of Michigan Archives, Bentley Historical Library, Vice-President for Academic Affairs Papers, Box 39, Advisory Committee on ROTC Affairs Folder.

129. Dayton Pickett to Joseph Spitler, Dec. 18, 1970, University of Illinois Archives, Chancellor's Office Papers, Series Number 24/1/1, Box 70, Armed Forces Folder.

130. Gerald Perselay and Raymond Grenier, "New Directions in Corps Training," *Air University Air Force ROTC Education Bulletin* (April 1971).

131. "Senior Division Army ROTC Program of Instruction," Aug. 7, 1969, University of Illinois Archives, National Association of State Universities and Land-Grant Colleges Papers, 10/3/57, Box 15.

132. Robert Williams to Robben Fleming, May 23, 1969, University of Michigan Archives, Bentley Historical Library, President's Papers, Box 10, ROTC Folder.

133. Donald Blake to Robben Fleming, Mar. 26, 1969, ibid.

134. Robben Fleming to the Regents, June 9, 1970, University of Michigan Archives, Bentley Historical Library, President's Papers, Box 15, ROTC Folder.

135. "Supplementary Memorandum of Understanding," Nov. 15, 1971, University of Michigan Archives, Bentley Historical Library, Vice-President for Academic Affairs Papers, Box 40, ROTC—Air Force 1971 Folder.

136. "University of Pittsburgh Department of Military Science (Army ROTC): An Overview," Jan. 1969, University of Pittsburgh Archives, Hillman Library, Classification Number 90/6-B.

137. "Subcommittee of the Military Education Council for the Review of the Army ROTC Curriculum," Mar. 29, 1971, University of Illinois Archives, Series Number 27/3/1, Box 1.

138. Liaison Officer for ROTC to PMS, PNS, and PAS, Oct. 14, 1969, University of Texas President's Office Records, AR 80–50, Liaison Officer, ROTC, 1969–1970 Folder. Texas began to require a master's degree for all senior officers and a bachelor's degree and a minimum of four years of military service for junior officers. The university also informed the services that preference would go to junior officers with master's degrees and that it would reject candidates for whom it believed ROTC duty would be a terminal assignment.

139. National Security Information Center, Inc., "Summary Report: 1968–1973," New York University/National Security Information Center, Inc., May 1973.

140. Ibid.

141. National Security Information Center, "Summary Report," appendix A.

142. "AFNIA: Atlanta Forum on National and International Affairs" [Nov. 1971], Georgia Institute of Technology Library and Information Center, 86–05–01, Office of the President Records, 1961–1972, Box 14, Folder 33.

143. "AFNIA: Dean Rusk Speaks Thursday," *The Technique,* Nov. 7, 1972, p. 1, col. 1.

144. "Annual Report," Department of Military Science, Academic Year 1968–69, University of Washington Archives, Allen Library, W. U. Reserve Officers' Training Corps Program, Military Science, 95–289, V.F. 2457.

145. Oral History of Major General Stanley Beck, Dec. 12–14, 1988, United States Air Force Historical Research Agency, Maxwell AFB, Montgomery, Alabama, pp. 88–89.

146. Virginia Joyce, "ROTC Head Watkins Analyzes Role," *Pitt News,* Sept. 4, 1969, p. 3.

147. Robert Williams to Robben Fleming and Allan Smith, Apr. 20, 1971, University of Michigan Archives, Bentley Historical Library, President's Papers, Box 23, ROTC Folder.

148. W. L. Rigot, "Status and Future Prospects of Navy Officer Education Program," University of Michigan, n.d., Navy ROTC Accreditation/Relations File 1973–1974, North Hall.

149. Robert Williams to Colonel M. D. Schiller, Apr. 20, 1971, University of Michigan Archives, Bentley Historical Library, Vice-President for Academic Affairs Papers, Box 40, ROTC—Army, 1971 Folder.

150. *History of the Air University,* Fiscal Year 1970.

151. Freeman Miller to Senator George Kuhn, Oct. 15, 1969, University of Michigan Archives, Bentley Historical Library, Vice-President for Academic Affairs Papers, Box 39, ROTC General, 1969 Folder.

152. Senate Appropriations Committee Hearings, June 10, 1969, ibid., Box 26, ROTC 1969–70 Folder.

153. Ben Cassiday to Wesley Posvar, Oct. 17, 1969, University of Pittsburgh Archives, Hillman Library, Classification Number 3/1/1, FF 232.

154. "Curricular and Other Changes Introduced into ROTC Programs, January 1, 1969, to June 1, 1969," June 1969, University of Michigan Navy ROTC Accreditation/Relations File 1969, North Hall.

155. Supplemental agreements between the schools and the DOD provided a way around the statutory provisions of the Vitalization Act.

156. Dayton Pickett to Barry Munitz, Associate Provost, University of Illinois at Chicago Circle, Sept. 24, 1971, University of Illinois Archives, Chancellor's Office Papers, Series Number 24/1/1, Box 90, Armed Forces Folder.

157. Freeman Miller to Senator George Kuhn.

158. Ben Cassiday, Memorandum for the Record, Apr. 24, 1970, University of Michigan Archives, Bentley Historical Library, Vice-President for Academic Affairs Papers, Box 40, ROTC—Air Force 1970 Folder.

159. "Final Report of the Ad Hoc Committee on ROTC Credit," Sept. 8, 1971, University of Illinois Archives, President John Corbally Papers, Box 15, ROTC.

160. This incident is recounted in Arthur Coumbe and Lee S. Harford, *U.S. Army Cadet Command: The Ten-Year History* (Ft. Monroe, Va.: Office of the Command Historian, U.S. Army Cadet Command, 1996), p. 77.

161. Isadore Shrensky, "Pitt Battle May Be Lost, ROTC Chief Says," *Pittsburgh Press,* Aug. 17, 1969, p. 8.

162. Robert Williams to Robben Fleming, Mar. 16, 1971, University of Michigan Archives, Bentley Historical Library, President's Papers, Box 23, ROTC Folder.

163. Muhlenfeld, "Our Embattled ROTC."

164. Senate Appropriations Committee Hearings, June 10, 1969. University of Pittsburgh Archives, Hillman Library, Provost Office Files 1965–1970, Classification Number 3/1/1, File Folder 238.

165. Peter Karsten, "Statement on ROTC," Nov. 29, 1968, ibid., File Folder 239.

166. Provost Charles Peake to Henry Avery, Group Vice President, USS Chemicals, May 7, 1969, ibid., File Folder 238.

167. Robert Williams, Notes for Visit with Admiral Kinney—May 12, 1970, University of Michigan Archives, Bentley Historical Library, Vice-President for Academic Affairs Papers, Box 40, ROTC—1970 Folder.

168. Robert Williams to Robben Fleming and Allan Smith, Nov. 5, 1970, ibid., President's Papers, Box 23, ROTC Folder.

169. John Corbally to Lieutenant Colonel Edward Crum, Oct. 19, 1971, University of Illinois Archives, President John Corbally Papers, Box 15, ROTC.

170. J. W. Peltason, Chancellor, to Lieutenant Colonel Edward Crum, USAF (ret.), Nov. 3, 1971, ibid.

171. Rear Admiral J. L. Abbot, Director of Educational Development, to Captain

William Rigot, July 22, 1973, University of Michigan Navy ROTC Accreditation/Relations File 1973–1974, North Hall.

172. Robert Williams, Memo to the Files, May 14, 1970, University of Michigan Archives, Bentley Historical Library, President's Papers, Box 15, ROTC Folder.

173. "1819–1969: The 150th Year of Officer Training on the College Campus," United States Army Center of Military History, Washington, D.C., HRC 326.6.

174. Freeman Miller to Robben Fleming, Jan. 28, 1974, University of Michigan Archives, Bentley Historical Library, Vice-President for Academic Affairs Papers, Box 45, Military Officer Education Programs (ROTC) Folder.

175. "AFROTC 1973 Commandant's Annual Report to the AFROTC Advisory Panel," University of Illinois Archives, President John Corbally Papers, Box 33, ROTC.

6. ROTC in the Era of the All-Volunteer Force

1. David R. Segal, *Recruiting for Uncle Sam: Citizenship and Military Manpower Policy* (Lawrence: University of Kansas Press, 1989), p. 35.

2. Of course draft resistance and antidraft sentiment in this country were not new to the Vietnam years. They date back to the American Revolution and also inspired riots in New York City during the Civil War.

3. *The Report of the President's Commission on an All-Volunteer Armed Force* (New York: Collier's, 1970), pp. 5–6. The Gates Commission included economists Milton Friedman and Alan Greenspan as well as Notre Dame president Theodore Hesburgh and NAACP director Roy Wilkins. The commission was formed in March 1969 with former Secretary of Defense Thomas Gates as chairman.

4. See, for example, Larry H. Ingraham, *The Boys in the Barracks: Observations on American Military Life* (Philadelphia: Institute for the Study of Human Issues, 1984), and Sar Levitan and K. C. Alderman, *Warriors at Work: The Volunteer Armed Force* (Beverly Hills, Calif.: Sage Publications, 1977).

5. Quoted in James Pullen, "A Comparative Study of Personality Factors and Certain Other Variables of Army ROTC Cadets Terminating with the Basic Program and Those Electing to Continue in the Advanced Program," Ed.D. thesis, University of South Dakota, 1971.

6. These included gaining weight, losing weight, moving to Canada or Sweden, and noncompliance. For some specific examples and a discussion of draft evasion, see Lawrence Baskir and William Strauss, *Chance and Circumstance: The Draft, the War, and the Vietnam Generation* (New York: Alfred A. Knopf, 1978).

7. Lee Sherman Dreyfus, Chancellor, University of Wisconsin at Stevens Point and Chairman of the ROTC Advisory Panel, to Howard Callaway, Secretary of the Army, Mar. 20, 1974, University of Michigan Archives, Bentley Historical Library, Vice-President for Academic Affairs Papers, Box 55, ROTC 1973–74 Folder.

8. Thomas Woodley to Assistant and Associate Deans, Jan. 28, 1974, University of Illinois Archives 27/3/1 Box 1; "ROTC Enrollments and Commissioned

Officers," University of Texas President's Office Papers AR 80–50, Liaison Officer 1969–1970 and 1973–1974 Folders. Total Illinois ROTC enrollments were 1,518 in 1966 and 270 in 1974; total Texas ROTC enrollments were 877 in 1966 and 295 in 1974.

9. Quoted in "ROTC Marches Back," *Princeton Alumni Weekly* (Feb. 1, 1972).

10. Roger Geiger, *Research and Relevant Knowledge: American Research Universities since World War II* (New York: Oxford University Press, 1993), p. 260.

11. The major issues of concern for the architects of Title 9 were equal pay for female faculty and equal access for women to graduate schools.

12. Geiger, *Research and Relevant Knowledge,* p. 260.

13. Ibid., chap. 8.

14. Floris Wood, ed., *An American Profile: Opinions and Behavior, 1972–1989* (Detroit: Gale Research, 1990), pp. 641 and 652.

15. Ibid., pp. 642 and 654.

16. For one example, see Stephen Hersh, "Students Organize ROTC Protest," *Michigan Daily,* Jan. 30, 1975. Hersh noted that "organizers attempting to muster anti-ROTC sentiment at the University found their stock in short supply: they could only attract 40 students and members of local left groups to their meeting at East Quad last night."

17. "Upward Trend for ROTC," *Army ROTC in Review, 1972–73,* p. 11, University of Pittsburgh Archives, Hillman Library, Classification Number 35/2-B, Folder 1.

18. Quoted in William Treml, "Departing ROTC Chief Optimistic," *Ann Arbor News,* June 29, 1975.

19. *The Report of the President's Commission on an All-Volunteer Armed Force,* p. 74.

20. "ROTC: A Silent Retreat from Campus?" *University Record,* Apr. 1, 1974.

21. These auxiliaries were created in the World War II era with the goal of keeping women administratively and functionally separate from men.

22. Kansas State *Industrialist,* Feb. 16, 1927, Kansas State University Archives, Kansas State University Historical Index, Military Training, 1927.

23. "Angels in Blue Brighten Cadet Corps," *Flight Lines: University of Illinois Cadet AFROTC Newsletter,* May 1964, p. 1.

24. *History of the Air Force Reserve Officers' Training Corps,* Jan. 1 to June 30, 1966, Air Force Historical Research Agency, Maxwell AFB, Montgomery, Alabama.

25. "Military Ball Queen Contestants Plan Tea," *Pitt News,* Feb. 15, 1961, p. 5.

26. *Cadet News* [AFROTC newsletter], Oct. 22, 1959, Archives, University of Colorado at Boulder Libraries, V. C. for Academic Affairs, ROTC Box, Cadet News Folder.

27. Army ROTC, *Quality Is the Answer: The Role of the ROTC in the Supreme Contest of Our Times* [1960], University of Illinois Archives, National Association of State Universities and Land-Grant Colleges Papers, Series Number 10/3/57, Box 14. Emphasis in original.

28. *Cadet News* [AFROTC newsletter], Nov. 5, 1959, University of Colorado at Boulder Library, Archives, V. C. for Academic Affairs, ROTC Box, Cadet News Folder.

29. Vance Mitchell, *Air Force Officers: Personnel Policy Development, 1944–1974* (Washington, D.C.: Air Force History and Museums Program, 1996), p. 314.
30. "Women to Train for the Air Force," *New York Times,* June 24, 1956, p. 40, col. 1.
31. Captain Levy Morrow, USAF to All Professors of Air Science, Apr. 12, 1957, University of Illinois Archives, President David Henry Papers, Box 26, ROTC—Air Science Folder.
32. "Women in AFROTC," *Precommissioning Education Review* (Spring 1980): 3–7.
33. Captain John Sibbald, "A History of the Military Department at the University of Illinois, 1868–1964," history term paper, 1965, University of Illinois Army ROTC Historical Files, Military Science Department Library, 0.432.
34. "Report of the Department of Military Science, Academic Year 1959–60," ibid.
35. "Angels in Blue Brighten Cadet Corps"; *Brigade Review,* University of Texas Army ROTC, 1966, University of Texas Archives, U 428.5 B7532 TXC.
36. Military Science Department to Robert White, Mar. 31, 1967, Kent State University Archives, President Robert White Papers, Box 33, Folder 29, Army ROTC Correspondence, 1966–1967.
37. Quoted in Mary Beth Norton, ed., *Major Problems in American Women's History* (Lexington, Mass.: D. C. Heath Company, 1989), p. 397.
38. Lynda Van Devanter, *Home before Morning: The True Story of an Army Nurse in Vietnam* (New York: Beaufort Books, 1983), p. 21.
39. Quoted in Jeanne Holm, *Women in the Military: An Unfinished Revolution* (Novato, Calif.: Presidio Press, 1992), p. 191.
40. In the WAC in 1966 there were 77 female lieutenant colonels and 237 female majors but, by law, only one female colonel. Thirty-nine of the lieutenant colonels were in the "promotion zone for colonel, but, because they were women, could not even be considered." Holm, *Women in the Military,* p. 193. The female officer hierarchy remained pyramidal, while the male hierarchy was at the same time assuming a diamond shape due to the increased presence of mid-level officers. This process, also to be found in other Western militaries, such as that of France, was the result of the increasing level of technological competence the military professional needed.
41. Ileana Brown, *History of the AFROTC,* July 1, 1967 to June 30, 1968, p. 26.
42. *History of AFROTC,* July 1, 1968 to June 30, 1969, Supporting Document 6, "Report of the Air Force ROTC Advisory Panel, 13 January 1969."
43. Holm, *Women in the Military,* p. 267. Holm, then a major, had been involved in the gender-integration experiment of AFROTC in the 1950s.
44. Quoted in *History of Women in the Air Force,* July 1 to Dec. 31, 1968, Air Force Historical Research Agency, Maxwell AFB, Montgomery, Alabama.
45. The Air Force's OCS program is technically called Officer Training School (OTS). For the sake of convenience, I have taken the liberty of referring to the postgraduation commissioning programs of all three services as OCS.
46. Jon Nordheimer, "Lipstick Is Part of the Uniform," *New York Times,* Dec. 17, 1969, p. 37, col. 1.

47. "Eight Coeds Keep in Step—With 537 Male Cadets," *New York Times*, Apr. 8, 1969, p. 22, col. 5.

48. Nordheimer, "Lipstick Is Part of the Uniform."

49. Harvard researchers did find that women had a warmer "feeling thermometer" toward the military than did men. In 1974, for example, women's feelings for the military registered 72.0, compared with 68.7 among men. Women still felt nearly four "degrees" warmer toward the military in 1976. See Philip Converse, et al., *American Social Attitudes Data Sourcebook, 1947–1978* (Cambridge, Mass.: Harvard University Press, 1980), p. 43.

50. "Navy to Keep Its Academy All-Male," *New York Times*, Feb. 9, 1972, p. 43, col. 5.

51. Robert Goldrich, "The Senior Reserve Officer Training Corps: Recent Trends and Current Status," Apr. 19, 1974, Library of Congress Congressional Research Service.

52. Andrew Malcolm, "Coeds Finding a Welcome in ROTC," *New York Times*, Dec. 4 1972, p. 1, col. 1.

53. "Will You Please Be My Angel?" *The Flying Flak*, Oct. 4 1971, University of Illinois Archives, Series Number 27/2/0/6, Box 1.

54. Michael Farrell, "Women's Army ROTC Program at the University of Hawaii," *Army ROTC Education Commentary*, September–October 1973. The contrast between the initial reactions of the Illinois and Hawaii units lends credence to the "contact hypothesis," which argues that the more integrated a unit, the more successful the minority members of that unit will perform.

55. "ROTC Opens for More Women," ibid.

56. "Recommendations of the Air Force ROTC Advisory Panel and Air Staff Comments," Jan. 22, 1973, University of Illinois Archives, President John Corbally Papers, Box 33, ROTC—Air Force.

57. Air Force ROTC, "Capsule Facts for Advisors," June 3, 1974, University of Pittsburgh Archives, Hillman Library, Classification Number 35-A, File Folder 3.

58. Brigadier General Sinclair Melner to Acting CU President Roland Rautenstraus, Aug. 11, 1975, University of Colorado at Boulder Library, Archives, Central Administration, President's Office, Series I, Box 330, ROTC General Information, 1973–1976 Folder.

59. "Coed Leads ROTC Unit," *New York Times*, Jan. 21, 1971, p. 20, col. 1.

60. "Arnold Activities," *The Flying Flak*, Dec. 8, 1976, University of Illinois Archives 27/2/0/6, Box 1; C. Russell Geigon, "The Woman Soldier," *Daily Texan*, Jan. 14, 1976.

61. University of Illinois at Urbana-Champaign Office of Public Information, Aug. 25, 1978, University of Illinois Archives, President John Corbally Papers, Box 120, ROTC—Military Science.

62. Nordheimer, "Lipstick Is Part of the Uniform."

63. "Women in AFROTC," pp. 3–7.

64. Office of the Assistant Secretary of Defense, Manpower and Reserve Affairs,

Central All-Volunteer Force Task Force: Utilization of Military Women (Washington, D.C.: Government Printing Office, 1972), p. 30. Emphasis added.

65. *Central All-Volunteer Force Task Force*, p. ix. In 1973 the Supreme Court, in *Frontiero v. Richardson* 411 U.S. 677 [1973], ruled that the services had to provide the same benefits to military husbands that they provided to military wives. In the same year, the DOD changed "wife" and "husband" to "spouse" in its directives. In several other cases in the early 1970s, the courts forced the services to modify, then abandon, the automatic dismissal of pregnant women.

66. Quoted in Malcolm, "Coeds Finding a Welcome in ROTC."

67. Department of Defense, *Report on the Reserve Officers Training Corps* (Washington, D.C.: Government Printing Office, 1980).

68. "Women in AFROTC," p. 3.

69. U.S. Department of Commerce, *Statistical Abstracts of the United States* (Washington, D.C.: Government Printing Office, 1980), pp. 417–418.

70. In 1966 more than one in five fatalities in Southeast Asia was an African American. The DOD took active steps to reduce that percentage, but throughout the course of the war a perception existed that African Americans were given the most dangerous military jobs and therefore were more likely to suffer casualties. African Americans comprised 10.3 percent of the American military force in Vietnam, but suffered 13 percent of its fatalities. See Bernard Nalty, *Strength for the Fight: A History of Black Americans in the Military* (New York: Free Press, 1986), 298.

71. Bernard Nalty and Morris MacGregor, eds., *Blacks in the Military: Essential Documents* (Wilmington, Del.: Scholarly Resources, 1981), p. 344.

72. Nalty, *Strength for the Fight*, p. 328.

73. Dana Adams Schmidt, "Navy Opens a Recruiting Drive to Increase Black Enlistments," *New York Times*, Apr. 1, 1971, p. 29, col. 1.

74. Ben Cassiday, "Report to the AFROTC Advisory Panel," Sept. 18, 1972, University of Illinois Archives, President John Corbally Papers, Box 33, ROTC.

75. Alvin Schexnider, "Expectations from the Ranks: Representativeness and Value Systems" *American Behavioral Scientist* 15 (May/June 1976): 523–542.

76. Joseph Lelyveld, "Navy ROTC at Negro School Graduates Its First Thirteen Officers," *New York Times*, May 18, 1970, p. 1, col. 7.

77. Nalty, *Strength for the Fight*, p. 341.

78. Quoted in Christian Appy, *Working-Class War: American Combat Soldiers in Vietnam* (Chapel Hill: University of North Carolina Press, 1993), p. 21.

79. Nalty, *Strength for the Fight*, p. 328.

80. Lelyveld, "Navy ROTC at Negro School Graduates Its First Thirteen Officers."

81. Charles Peake to Wesley Posvar, Apr. 27, 1970, University of Pittsburgh Archives, Hillman Library, Classification Number 3/1/1, File Folder 232.

82. Wavie Sharp, "Record Number of Blacks Attend Knox Basic Camp," *Army ROTC Education Commentary*, September–October 1973.

83. Department of Defense, *A Primer on ROTC* (Washington, D.C.: Government

Printing Office, 1982). The University of Alabama was the only unit with a higher total enrollment.

84. "Fact Sheet," Conference of Presidents/Chancellors, of Historically Black Colleges, Tuskegee Institute, Mar. 4–6 1980, pp. 33–35, William Snyder Papers, in the author's possession.

85. "1971 Grand Military Ball (Program)" 1971 Duquesne University Archives, ROTC Box 1, Military Balls and Awards Folder.

86. Geiger, *Research and Relevant Knowledge*, p. 249.

87. Ibid., p. 262.

88. David Halliday to Alan Anderson, Feb. 27, 1969, University of Pittsburgh Archives, Hillman Library, Classification Number 3/1/1, File Folder 235.

89. Peter Karsten, "Anti-ROTC: Response to Vietnam or 'Consciousness III'?" in John Lovell and Philip Kronenberg, eds., *New Civil-Military Relations: The Agonies of Adjustment to Post-Vietnam Realities* (New Brunswick: Transaction Books, 1974): 111–127, quotation from p. 115.

90. Mitchell, *Air Force Officers*, p. 455 n. 78.

91. William Calhoun, "Bullish on ROTC," *Army* 24 (May 1974): 36–38.

92. *History of the Air University, Fiscal Year 1973*, vol. 1. Air Force Historical Research Agency, Maxwell AFB, Montgomery, Alabama.

93. *Report of the Department of Aerospace Studies, Academic Year 1972–1973*, July 27, 1973, University of Illinois Archives, President John Corbally Papers, Box 33, ROTC—Air Force. In 1967 the AFROTC unit at Illinois produced eighty-three officers. Illinois officials predicted that only twelve officers would be produced in 1974.

94. "College to Get ROTC Unit," *Columbus, (Ga.) Ledger,* Jan. 27, 1972, p. 15.

95. "ROTC Approved for CC," Columbus College *Saber,* Jan. 31, 1972, p. 2.

96. Columbus College also agreed to include a rifle range in the new ROTC building, at a time when weapons bans existed on some established ROTC host campuses. See "College to Get ROTC Unit."

97. William Maloy, "The Education and Training of Naval Officers: An Investment in the Future," *Naval Review* 101 (1975): 134–149.

98. "College to Get ROTC Unit." Compare this statement to one made by Michigan vice president Robert Williams to General Wagstaff in the same year: "Ann Arbor is like Berkeley, an anti-military town and has always been so . . . [I] admit that Ann Arbor is a tough town for any military related activity." Robert Williams, Notes for Meeting with General Wagstaff on July 24, 1972, n.d., University of Michigan Archives, Bentley Historical Library, Vice-President for Academic Affairs Papers, Box 40, ROTC—Army, 1972 Folder.

99. Geiger, *Research and Relevant Knowledge*, p. 192.

100. If, for example, a student desired a navy commission but her school offered only Air Force ROTC, she could commute to a nearby school with an NROTC unit for her training.

101. In 1972 the services authorized military officers to travel to cross-enrolled

schools instead of putting the burden of travel on the student. Mitchell, *Air Force Officers,* p. 268.

102. Marvin Grunzke to Robert Williams, Nov. 14, 1972, University of Michigan Archives, Bentley Historical Library, Vice-President for Academic Affairs Papers, Box 40, ROTC—Air Force 1973–1974 Folder.

103. *Air University Air Force ROTC Bulletin,* May 1, 1975, Air University Library, Maxwell AFB, Montgomery, Alabama.

104. Ibid. Michigan's agreements were with Eastern Michigan, Western Michigan, and the University of Michigan at Dearborn. Pittsburgh's agreements were with Carlow College, Carnegie Mellon, Chatham College, the Community College of Allegheny County, Duquesne University, Point Park College, and Robert Morris College. Enrollment figures are from 1980.

105. Harvard's agreeing to cross-enrollment for its students suggests that the university administration and faculty supported the concept of ROTC and the right of Harvard students to choose a military career. The problem at Harvard and elsewhere was the special privileges that ROTC had acquired, such as academic credit, professorial titles, and so on. Allowing Harvard students to take ROTC at nearby MIT allowed Harvard to remain a part of a system it supported without making distasteful compromises on its own campus. Harvard officials had tried once before to remove military training from the campus while still remaining a part of the ROTC system. In 1954 the army rejected the university's request that it conduct all of its military training at summer camps. See Arthur Coumbe and Lee S. Harford, *U.S. Army Cadet Command: The Ten-Year History.* (Ft. Monroe, Va.: Office of the Command Historian, U.S. Army Cadet Command, 1996), p. 308 n. 43.

106. Karsten, "Anti-ROTC," p. 123.

107. *Statistical Abstracts of the United States* (Washington, D.C.: Government Printing Office, 1985), p. 152.

108. Martin Binkin and John Johnson, *All-Volunteer Armed Forces: Progress, Problems, and Prospects* (Washington, D.C.: Brookings Institute, 1973), p. 24.

109. Quoted in Jim Kentch, "ROTC: Aiming at Freshmen," *Michigan Daily,* July 21, 1972, p. 3.

110. Quoted in Roy McHugh, "ROTC in Step with Career Plans, Pitt Students Find," *Pittsburgh Press,* Sept. 20, 1973, p. 2; Lawrence Walsh, "ROTC Here on March Again; New Approach, Viet Cuts Help," *Pittsburgh Press,* Jan. 16, 1972, p. G-1.

111. Quoted in Walsh, "ROTC Here on March Again."

112. McHugh, "ROTC in Step with Career Plans."

113. Quoted in Richard Berke, "ROTC: New Role, Old Conflicts," *The Michigan Daily,* Feb. 19. 1978, p. 4, col. 1.

114. R. E. Stivers, "The Long and Short," *Navy* 13 (Oct. 1970): 30–34, quotation from p. 30.

115. "Military Academies Changing Their Ways," *U.S. News and World Report* 69 (Nov. 9, 1970): 47.

116. Walsh, "ROTC Here on March Again."

117. Berke, "ROTC: New Role, Old Conflicts"; Colonel Warren Spaulding to All Concerned, Jan. 30, 1974, Archives, University of Colorado at Boulder Libraries, Central Administration, President's Office, Series I, Box 331, ROTC—Army 1940–1977 Folder.

118. Minutes of the LSA Curriculum Committee Meeting, Mar. 27, 1979, University of Michigan Archives, Bentley Historical Library, University of Michigan Vice-President for Academic Affairs, Box 116, ROTC—Military Officer Education Programs Folder.

119. "Summary of Precommissioning Questionnaire," in *History of the AFROTC,* July 1 to Dec. 31, 1963, Call Number K239.07 K.

120. Minutes of the LSA Curriculum Committee Meeting, Mar. 27, 1979.

121. Rick Codina, "Veteran Soldiers Become Educators to Command University Curriculum," *Daily Texan,* Mar. 28, 1971.

122. "Military Academies Changing Their Ways," p. 47.

123. Air Force Academy commandant Brigadier General Robin Olds quoted in ibid., p. 49. In another example of the continued strict discipline, in 1970 the entire Annapolis student body had its weekend leave privileges cut in half when "a few plebes overindulged at beer parties after an academy football game." See ibid., p. 48. West Point superintendent Lieutenant General William Knowlton told a reporter: "We're always going to be leaner, meaner, tougher and more conservative than civilian schools." See "Braced for Reform," *Newsweek* 82 (Sept. 24, 1973): 36.

124. "Military Academies Changing Their Ways," p. 46.

125. "Braced for Reform," p. 36.

126. McHugh, "ROTC in Step with Career Plans."

127. Berke, "ROTC: New Role, Old Conflicts."

128. "Why Would Anybody Take ROTC?," advertisement, *Ebony* 27 (Nov. 1971): 99.

129. "Army ROTC: It's No Big Thing," advertisement, *Ebony* 27 (Sept. 1972): 67. Only one of the ads in this campaign seemed to be aimed specifically at African Americans. That ad showed an African American family standing on the steps of an obviously run-down ghetto apartment building. Above the photo the text read, "Save your family $11,280.00." *Ebony* 27 (Oct. 1972): 47.

130. *ROTC: The Margin of Difference: American Business and Industry Assess the Values of Army ROTC* [1985], Duquesne University Archives, ROTC Box 1, ROTC 1958–65 Folder.

131. "Army ROTC: It's No Big Thing."

132. "Why Would Anybody Take ROTC?"

133. Thomas Hritz, "The New ROTC: You'd Hardly Recognize It," *Pittsburgh Post-Gazette,* Nov. 27, 1979.

134. Minutes of the Committee for Military Officer Education Programs, May 4, 1978, University of Michigan Archives, Bentley Historical Library, Vice-President for Academic Affairs Papers, Box 94, Military Officer Education Programs (ROTC) Folder.

7. A New Academic Program

1. See, for example, Roger Geiger, *Research and Relevant Knowledge: American Research Universities since World War II* (New York: Oxford University Press, 1994), chap. 8.
2. University of Michigan Student Government Council, "ROTC Resolution," May 13, 1974, University of Michigan Navy ROTC Accreditation/Relations File 1973–1974, North Hall.
3. Quoted in "Upward Trend for ROTC," *Army ROTC in Review* (1972–73): 11, University of Pittsburgh Archives, Hillman Library, Classification Number 35/ 2-B, File Folder 1.
4. William Snyder to Commanding General, First U.S. Army, May 24, 1972, William Snyder Papers, Princeton University Folder, in author's possession. The referendum involved 2,176 students. Between June 1971 and June 1972, the Princeton ROTC program existed on paper only; for that year no students were enrolled (a few Princeton students took ROTC training at nearby Rider University), and no military officers were assigned to the campus.
5. William Snyder, personal correspondence, May 18, 1995, in author's possession.
6. See Chapter 6 for a discussion of this issue.
7. "Report of the Council of the Princeton Community Ad Hoc Committee on ROTC," August 1973, William Snyder Papers, Princeton University Folder, in author's possession.
8. "Memorandum for the Record, Meeting with Brigadier General Tackaberry," June 15, 1972, ibid.
9. William Snyder to Jack Bitner, Nov. 30, 1973, ibid.
10. "The ROTC Curriculum at Princeton University," Sept. 5, 1974, ibid.
11. Colonel I. J. Irvin to Geza Grosschmid, Academic Vice President, Aug. 9, 1972, Duquesne University Archives, ROTC Box 1, ROTC 1972–1976 Folder.
12. Freeman Miller to College of Literature, Science, and the Arts (LSA) associate dean Jean Carduner, Sept. 27, 1974, University of Michigan Archives, Bentley Historical Library, President's Papers, Box 52, ROTC Folder.
13. Quoted in Cindy Morgan, "FASC Ponders Re-opening ROTC Credit Issue," *Pitt News*, Jan. 28, 1972, p. 1.
14. Ibid.
15. Headquarters, Department of the Army, Army Training Program, "General Military Science Curriculum for Civilian and Military Colleges," Dec. 22, 1960, Duquesne University Archives, ROTC Box 1, ROTC 1958–1965 Folder.
16. Martin L. Zeigler to J. W. Briscoe, Apr. 18, 1968, University of Illinois Archives, Chancellor's Office Papers, Series Number 24/1/1, Box 113, Armed Forces Folder.
17. Colonel Marvin Grunzke to J. E. Keith Smith, Psychology, Sept. 18, 1972, University of Michigan Navy ROTC Accreditation/Relations File 1973–1974, North Hall.

18. "Tentative Grouping of 1975–1976 ROTC Courses by Subject Matter" [1974], ibid.

19. The undergraduate catalog was excerpted in "A Review of the University of Michigan Departments of Military Science, Naval Science, and Air Science," Sept. 1968, University of Michigan Navy ROTC Accreditation/Relations File, 1968 and earlier.

20. "Tentative Grouping of 1975–1976 ROTC Courses by Subject Matter."

21. [Colonel James Bambery], "Department of Military Science Annual Report," SY 76–77, Aug. 30, 1977, Duquesne University Archives, ROTC Box 1, Annual Report 1973–76 Folder.

22. Freeman Miller to LSA Associate Dean Charles Witke, Feb. 22, 1974, University of Michigan Navy ROTC Accreditation/Relations File 1973–1974, North Hall.

23. "Report of the Subcommittee on Military Officer Education Programs to the LSA Committee on Curriculum," Jan. 14, 1975, ibid.

24. [Colonel I. J. Irvin], "Department of Military Science Annual Report," SY 72–73, Aug. 23, 1973, Duquesne University Archives, ROTC Box 1, Annual Report 1973–74 Folder. In 1980 Colonel Frank Reeder, PAS at Michigan, advised his colleagues that the best way to assure good relations with civilian faculty was to "demonstrate your worthiness to become an integral part of the academic community in which you are a relative and perhaps unwelcome stranger." *Air University Air Force ROTC Education Bulletin,* Academic Year 1979–80, Air University Library, Maxwell AFB, Montgomery, Alabama, p. 18.

25. "Report by the Committee on Courses," Apr. 6, 1976, Archives, University of Colorado at Boulder Libraries, Central Administration, President's Office, Series I, Box 330, ROTC General Information, 1973–1976 Folder.

26. Committee on Curriculum Special Meeting—Credit for ROTC, Jan. 14, 1975, University of Michigan Navy ROTC Accreditation/Relations File 1973–1974, North Hall.

27. The results of this survey can be found in *History of the Air University,* Jan. 1 to Dec. 31, 1978, Call Number K239.01, vol. 22.

28. A similar pattern emerged at the University of Texas, but without the unanimity. Between 1954 and 1970 only seventeen of the eighty-seven ROTC instructors whose level of education could be determined had a master's degree. Between 1970 and 1980, however, fourteen of the eighteen officers assigned had a master's degree.

29. "Report of the Army Advisory Panel on ROTC Affairs Meeting," Washington, D.C., June 27, 1974, University of Michigan Archives, Bentley Historical Library, President's Papers, Box 45, ROTC Folder.

30. Robben Fleming to William Bowen, Mar. 10, 1975, University of Michigan Archives, Bentley Historical Library, President's Papers, Box 52, ROTC Folder.

31. Charles Witke to Executive Committee on Guidelines That May Generate Credit, Jan. 2, 1974, University of Michigan Navy ROTC Accreditation/Relations File 1973–1974, North Hall.

32. Some issues that proved contentious in liberal arts colleges in the 1950s never developed as serious issues in engineering colleges. Professional qualifications for instructors mattered much less to engineering colleges, where as late as the mid-1950s, instructors with Ph.D.s were rare at many schools. At the University of Texas in 1955, for example, only 27 percent of the eighty-eight faculty members in the College of Engineering had a Ph.D. At the same time, 86 percent of the College of Arts and Sciences faculty had a Ph.D. Most of those who did not were concentrated in one department, Home Economics. Like the military, engineering colleges were willing to substitute job experience for formal educational qualifications. Qualifications derived from *The University of Texas College of Arts and Sciences Catalogue,* 1955–1957, and *The University of Texas College of Engineering Catalogue,* 1954–1956.

33. "A Statement to the Board of Regents' Meeting," University of Colorado, Sept. 26, 1973, Presented by the ROTC Commanders, University of Colorado at Boulder Library, Archives, Central Administration Faculty Council General Files, Series IV, Box 4, Folder 16.

34. J. W. Peltason to Brigadier General James Leslie, Apr. 27. 1976, University of Illinois Archives, President John Corbally Papers, Box 86, ROTC—Military Science. Emphasis in original.

35. Robben Fleming, interview with the author, Ann Arbor, Michigan, Dec. 12, 1995.

36. John Capitman, "CAS Cabinet Denies ROTC Credit Review," *Pitt News,* Oct. 30, 1972, p. 1.

37. Sara Rimer, "LSA Committee Approves Amended ROTC Plan," *Michigan Daily,* Jan. 15, 1975.

38. "Report of the Subcommittee on MOEP to the LSA Committee on Curriculum," Jan. 14, 1975, University of Michigan Navy ROTC Accreditation/Relations File 1973–1974, North Hall.

39. Quoted in Rimer, "LSA Committee Approves Amended ROTC Plan."

40. John Sinkevics, "LSA Faculty reopens ROTC credit issue," *Michigan Daily,* March 28, 1979

41. B. E. Frye, Acting LSA Dean, to Freeman Miller, Feb. 5, 1975, University of Michigan Archives, Bentley Historical Library, President's Papers, Box 52, ROTC Folder. Emphasis in original.

42. Minutes of the LSA Curriculum Committee Meeting, Mar. 27, 1979, University of Michigan Archives, Bentley Historical Library, Vice-President for Academic Affairs Papers, Box 116, ROTC—Military Officer Education Programs Folder.

43. John Knott, Associate Dean, LSA, to Vice President Harold Shapiro, May 7, 1979, ibid., Box 106, Military Officer Education Programs (ROTC) Folder.

44. Department of Naval Science, "Annual Report for the Academic Year 1972–1973, Aug. 2, 1973," University of Illinois Archives, President John Corbally Papers, Box 33, ROTC.

45. [Rasin Tek], "Proposal concerning College of Engineering—Military Officer Ed-

ucation Program Policies," Apr. 5, 1978, University of Michigan Archives, Bentley Historical Library, President's Papers, Box 86, ROTC Folder (1); Minutes of the Faculty Meeting of the College of Engineering, Feb. 27, 1979, ibid., Vice-President for Academic Affairs Papers, Box 106, Military Officer Education Programs (ROTC) Folder. Michigan required its engineering students to take twenty-four hours of social sciences and humanities. Under the 1978 guidelines, then, two-thirds of a Michigan engineering student's social sciences and humanities requirement could be fulfilled through ROTC.

46. It is not clear, however, that ROTC had more vocal supporters in engineering colleges. Because of the intensity that characterized debates in liberal arts colleges, some faculty members became just as strident and unwavering in their support of ROTC as others became in their opposition.

47. Captain William L. Rigot to Ralph Banfield, Assistant to Vice President for Academic Affairs, May 21, 1976, University of Michigan Navy ROTC Accreditation/Relations File 1975–1979, North Hall.

48. John Shy to Unit Heads and Executive Committee of the History Department, Apr. 25, 1974, University of Michigan Navy ROTC Accreditation/Relations File 1973–1974, North Hall.

49. "Report of Recent Senate Action," Apr. 14, 1976, University of Illinois Archives, President John Corbally Papers, Box 86, ROTC—Miscellaneous.

50. Department of Defense, *Report on the Reserve Officers Training Corps* (Washington, D.C.: Government Printing Office, 1980).

51. ROTC scholarship winners were selected nationally. Once selected, students could use their scholarship to attend any school that admitted them.

52. Impossible though it seems today, the University of California did not charge tuition for state residents until 1970.

53. *Fore 'n Aft*, Georgia Tech NROTC Newsletter, 1971, Georgia Institute of Technology Library and Information Center, T171.G46 F6X.

54. Kenneth Irish to Freeman Miller, Apr. 11, 1974, University of Michigan Archives, Bentley Historical Library, Vice-President for Academic Affairs Papers, Box 139, Army Correspondence Folder, 1973–1978.

55. W. L. Rigot to Center for Naval Education and Training (CNET), Feb. 27, 1975, University of Michigan Navy ROTC Accreditation/Relations File 1975–1979, North Hall; K. M. Irish to Robben Fleming, May 30, 1974, University of Michigan Archives, Bentley Historical Library, President's Papers, Box 45, ROTC Folder; Freeman Miller to LSA Associate Dean Jean Carduner.

56. Captain William L. Rigot to Ralph Banfield, Assistant to Vice President for Academic Affairs, May 21, 1976, University of Michigan Navy ROTC Accreditation/Relations File 1975–1979, North Hall.

57. I am grateful to Professor Kenneth Hagan of the Naval Academy, Captain Bob Shaw of CNET, and Commander Greg Young of the Air Force Academy for sharing their thoughts with me on this subject.

58. Juan Cameron, "Admiral Rickover's Final Battle," *Fortune* 94 (Nov. 1976): 198.

59. The best critique of the 80-20 plan from a uniformed officer can be found in Edward Bouffard, "NROTC: Quo Vadis?" *U.S. Naval Institute Proceedings* (July 1977): 33–42.

60. Rear Admiral James Holloway, "The Holloway Plan," *U.S. Naval Institute Proceedings* (Nov. 1947): 1299.

61. Chief of Naval Education and Training and Director of Naval Educational Development, "The NROTC Academic Program," Oct. 1973, University of Michigan Navy ROTC Curriculum File, North Hall.

62. Captain D. V. Murray to Ralph Banfield, July 5, 1978, University of Michigan Archives, Bentley Historical Library, Vice-President for Academic Affairs Papers, Box 141, Assoc. of NROTCCU, 1973–1978 Folder; Bouffard, "NROTC: Quo Vadis?" p. 38.

63. NROTC SITREP, Presented to ANROTCCU Nov. 5–7, 1978, University of Michigan Archives, Bentley Historical Library, University of Michigan Vice-President for Academic Affairs, Box 141, Assoc. of NROTCCU, 1973–1978 Folder.

64. Adam Yarmolinsky, review of *School for Soldiers,* by Joseph Ellis and Robert Moore, and *Ivory Fortress,* by Richard C. U'Ren, *Society* (Sept./Oct. 1975): 92.

65. Dr. Ray Bice, telephone interview, Feb. 20 1996. Dr. Bice was president of the ANROTCCU during the 80/20 debates.

66. Robert Etheridge to Members of ANROTCCU, Mar. 23, 1977, University of Michigan Archives, Bentley Historical Library, Vice-President for Academic Affairs Papers, Box 141, Assoc. of NROTCCU, 1973–1978 Folder.

67. Captain D. V. Murray to Ralph Banfield, Aug. 1, 1977, ibid.

68. C. Peter Magrath to CNET, July 14, 1977, ibid.

69. Marvin Grunzke, "Status Report on Air Force Reserve Officers' Training Corps Program at the University of Michigan," n.d., University of Michigan Navy ROTC Accreditation/Relations File 1973–1974, North Hall. Emphasis added.

70. "ROTC Marches Back," *Princeton Alumni Weekly,* Feb. 1, 1972.

Primary Sources

Duquesne University Archives, Pittsburgh
ROTC Papers

Gerald Ford Presidential Library, Ann Arbor, Michigan
Theodore Marrs Files, Box 6

Historical Society of Western Pennsylvania, Pittsburgh
Robert McConnell Papers

Lyndon Baines Johnson Presidential Library, Austin, Texas
Alfred B. Fitt Oral History

Kansas State University Archives, Manhattan
Chester Peters Papers
James A. McCain Papers
Kansas State University Historical Index
President's Papers

Kent State University Archives, Kent, Ohio
Charles Kegley May 4th Materials, Series Number 34.13.42
President Robert White Papers
Series Numbers 4.25.30, 4.25.31, 33.13.1, 33.13.2, 33.13.3

National Archives, Washington, D.C.
Record Group 319

Rutgers University Archives, New Brunswick, New Jersey
Army ROTC Headquarters Library Materials
President William H. Demarest Papers, 1915–1925
President James M. Thomas Papers, 1925–1932
President Robert C. Clothier Papers, 1932–1951
President Lewis W. Jones Papers, 1951–1958
President Mason Gross Papers, 1959–1971
President Edward J. Bloustein Papers, 1971–1980

William Snyder Papers (in author's possession)
    Army Advisory Panel Reports
    Princeton Army ROTC Papers

Suitland Federal Records Center, Suitland, Maryland
    Chief of Army Reserve General Correspondence, 1948–1954, RG 319
    Secretary of the Army General Correspondence, RG 335

United States Air Force Historical Research Agency, Maxwell AFB, Montgomery, Alabama
    Histories of Air University
    Histories of Air Force ROTC
    Histories of Women in the Air Force
    J. C. Shelburne Papers
    Oral History of Major General Stanley Beck, Dec. 12–14, 1988.

United States Air Force ROTC Office, Maxwell AFB, Montgomery, Alabama
    Histories of AFROTC

United States Army Center of Military History, Washington, D.C.
    ROTC Papers HRC 326.6

United States Army Military History Institute, Carlisle, Pennsylvania
    General Donn Starry Papers

University of Colorado at Boulder Library, Archives
    Central Administration, President's Office, Series I, Boxes 133, 330, 331, 332
    CU History (Departments)
    Faculty Council General Files, Series IV, Box 4
    News Media Relations Office, Student Unrest 1951–1972
    Regents Minutes, volumes 35, 36
    Vice-Chancellor for Academic Affairs Papers

University of Illinois Archives, Urbana
    Army ROTC Subject File, Series Number 27/3/1
    Chancellor's Office Papers, Series Number 24/1/1
    Committee on Educational Policy, Series Number 4/2/14
    Military Affairs Committee, Series Number 4/6/26
    National Association of State Universities and Land-Grant Colleges Papers, Series Number 10/3/57
    President David Henry Papers
    President John Corbally Papers
    Student Life Papers
    Vice-President for Academic Affairs Papers, Series Number 5/1/2
    Voluntary ROTC Program Files, Series Number 27/3/5

University of Illinois Department of Military Science Library, Urbana
    Annual Reports
    Recommendations of the PMS

University of Michigan Archives, Bentley Historical Library, Ann Arbor
  Harlan Hatcher Papers
  President's Papers
  Vice President for Academic Affairs Papers

University of Michigan Military Officer Education Program Papers, North Hall, Ann Arbor
  Air Force ROTC History/Accreditation Files
  Army ROTC History/Accreditation Files
  Navy ROTC History/Accreditation Files
  ROTC Curriculum Files

University of Pittsburgh Archives, Hillman Library, Pittsburgh
  Department of Military Science, 90/6-B
  Military Science Papers, 35-A, 35 2/B, 35 2/1
  Minutes of the Meeting of the University Senate, 3/10/3
  University of Pittsburgh Chancellor's Papers 0/3/1, 2/10, 55/1
  University of Pittsburgh Provost Office Files, 3/1/1

University of Texas Center of American History, Austin
  Department of Military Science Papers
  General and Comparative Studies, AR 85-215
  Liaison Officer for ROTC Papers, AR 80-50
  University of Texas President's Office Records, VF 17/C.a, VF 20/A.b, VF 30/A.b

University of Washington, Allen Library, Seattle
  Classification Numbers 71-34, 72-14, 72-35, 82-29, 95-281, 95-288, 95-289
  W. U. Presidents Papers
  W. U. Reserve Officers' Training Program

Index

racial integration. *See* minorities

Radical Whig, opposition to professional military, 3–4, 23

Rangers, 100, 163

Rankin, Alan, 79, 80–81

Reagan, Ronald, 5

recruitment: all-volunteer force (AVF), 179; in Cold War era, 41–42, 61–62. *See also* enrollment in ROTC; incentives to ROTC enrollment

Reserve forces, 23–24, 28. *See also* National Guard

retention rate of ROTC-trained officers in career military, 28; all-volunteer force (AVF), 178–179; in Cold War era, 48, 55, 64–65; in Vietnam War era, 133

Reuben, Julie, 6, 26

Rolling Thunder, 108

Roosevelt, Franklin D., 31

Roosevelt, Theodore, 23

rules and regulations of ROTC cadets, 66–67, 176

Rutgers University, 9, 27, 55, 56, 58, 78, 101, 182; academic reform for ROTC, 125; Vietnam War, 109, 121–123; Vitalization Act and ROTC, 100

Sandhurst, 5

SAT scores of ROTC cadets, 196–197

Savannah State College, 167

scandals, 102–103

Schneewind, Jerome, 188

scholarship programs, 197–199; all-volunteer force (AVF), 176; in Cold War era, 36; Vietnam War, 132–133, 149; Vitalization Act and ROTC, 90, 93, 95, 98, 176

segregation, 62–63, 154. *See also* minorities

Shaw, Robert Gould, 20

Sheehan, Neil, 117

Sherman, William, 20

Sinnott, M. J., 124

Skelton, William, 19

Smith, Adam, 3

social class, 11, 19, 63–64; and draft and conscription, 151

Society of Cincinnatus, 14

Southern Colorado State College, 116

Southern Illinois University, 158

Southern Methodist University, 63

Southern University, 167

Spanish-American War, 23

Special Program in Education, 98

St. Augustine's College, 167

St. Cyr, 5

St. Olaf College, 172

Stahr, Elvis, 77

Standard Operating Procedure for Cadets, 66

Stanford University, 36, 130, 171

State University of New York (SUNY), 121

Student Army Training Corps, 25–26

Student Nonviolent Coordinating Committee (SNCC), 102

Students for a Democratic Society (SDS), 86, 119–120

Suitland Federal Records Center, 10

SUNY–Maritime College, 173

Suzzallo, Henry, 26

Temple University, 161–162

Tennessee State University, 167

Tet offensive, 112–113

Texas A&M University, 58

Thackrey, Russell, 41, 49–51, 56–57, 91

Thomason Act of 1935, 28

Title 9, 154, 161

training: specialized vs. general, 68–75; and weapons technology in Cold War era, 43, 46–47, 65–66

Truman, Harry, 12, 44

Tulane University, 130

Tuskegee Institute, 167

two-year program, 89–93, 98–100

uniform regulations, 176–177

United States Army Center of Military History, 10

United States Air Force Academy, 80

United States Military Academy, 2, 5, 17, 18–20, 28, 33, 57, 80

United States Naval Academy, 2, 5, 19, 28, 33, 80; and women, 162

 ## What other people are saying about *TOTAL Power of ONE in America...*

Total Power of One in America is a book for our times. It belongs in every home, school, church, and public library in America. It is truly a masterpiece.

—Dr. Nino Camardese, president, founder,
Americanism Foundation, Norwalk OH

Total Power of One in America is the book of the decade on self-empowerment for effective citizenship in a free society...timely for the challenges we face as Americans today, and timeless in its application of eternal truths. It will grab you, move you, and just possibly change you forever.

—Colorado State Senator John Andrews,
founder, Independence Institute

Fred Holden knows the truths that helped make America great and he explains those truths in this valuable book. A worthwhile read.

—Governor Bill Owens
State of Colorado

> If the people don't have information to wield power correctly, don't take the power from them; give them the information.
>
> —Thomas Jefferson

...a compendium of wisdom...pointing the way toward the
light of freedom.

—Dr. Hans F. Sennholz, past-president,
Foundation for Economic Education,
Irvin-on-Hudson NY

...the only other book you'll ever need, absolutely
outstanding...best reference book I've ever had.

—Katherine Anderson, past-president,
Colorado Union of Taxpayers

...a bold, no nonsense book which provides the reader with
the "Street Smarts" of America's economic, business and
political systems. Every citizen will profit from its
information, motivation and challenge.

—Tom Trembath, elementary school
principal, Arvada CO

...provides an educational framework for understanding the
essential elements within our society...a practical, pragmatic
roadmap for personal commitment and action.

—Kim Woods, vice president
Morris Massey Associates, Boulder CO

On my "Good Idea Per Page" index, your book should
receive a Gold Medal. Books like these are rare.

—Gerald L. Musgrave, Ph.D., President,
Economics America, Ann Arbor MI

With all my education in medicine and experience in life
I still had many serious gaps and misunderstandings.
Total Power of One in America filled every one of them.

—Dr. John Lanzalotti, Physician, Public Policy Director,
Jeffersonian Public Policy Foundation, Williamsburg VA

...an owner's manual for the American citizen—gives us
hope! A textbook every student should study in a required
American civics course...something our education system
grossly ignores.

—Robert Ley, marketing director, Indianapolis IN

...should be required reading for every citizen in our nation...teachers and students in our schools...every candidate for elected office, not excluding present members of Congress.

—James B. Warner, president
Waterworks Sales Co, Denver CO

...informative, inspirational and easy to read. I recommend it for students of all ages!

—Pat Miller, president
Citizens for Responsible Government, Arvada CO

...has given me strength through knowledge by exposing the truth. ...as thousands read your masterpiece, they will heed the call and make the devotion necessary to give our country a rebirth of freedom to endure the ages.

—Claire Orr, President,
Colorado State Board of Education

...one of a kind...teaches us how to live and prosper in our great Free Enterprise System, how to be a good citizen and, most important, how to hold on to our precious tradition of freedom.

—Hazel Barrett, Arvada CO
letter to *Rocky Mountain News*

A target bound missile is no match for the unerring guidance contained on the pages of this masterpiece...Fred Holden invites you to become a stalwart, one who can stand up and be counted.

—A.R. Patten, Jr., President (retired),
Patten and Company, Arvada CO

The wealth of quotations alone is worth the price of admission.

—Steve Olstad, businessman,
freelance writer, Broomfield CO

...to return America to where she was, we need only the Bible, the U.S. Constitution and *Total Power of One in America*. That is the value of this book!!

—Dennis Zellaha, businessman and
concerned citizen, Milford IA

Your book is awesome. If we could encourage districts to use that as a textbook we could save our country starting in Colorado. I just love it, just love it.

—P.J. Johnson, member
Colorado State Board of Education

I believe every library, public and private, ought to have a copy(s)...This book has enriched my life!

—Jim Shook, manager property taxation,
StorageTek Corporation, Louisville CO

A life guide book, should be mandatory to graduate...an understanding of business, economics, politics, taxes, work, enterprise and government.

—John Hancock, WBT,
talk show host, Charlotte NC

...the one to read to understand how the world works, what to do for success. I highly recommend it.

—Terry L. Brock, president,
Achievements Systems Inc., Norcross GA

The best book I ever read on so many subjects vital to us all.

—Carl Wigglesworth, WOAI
talkshow host, San Antonio TX

I consider myself an educated person. I didn't realize how ignorant I was in politics and economics until I read *Total Power of One in America*...it motivated me to get involved, get others too.

—Patricia Patterson-Greeb, book editor,
MA degree, English & Literature, Denver CO

TOTAL POWER OF ONE IN AMERICA

Discover What You Need to Know, Why and How to Be a More Powerful Person and Citizen

TOTAL POWER OF 1 ONE™

IN AMERICA

**Discover What You Need to Know,
Why and How to Be a
More Powerful Person and Citizen**

Fred Holden

Phoenix Enterprises

P.O. Box 1900 ★ Arvada ,CO 80001 ★ 303/421-7619

  2 3 4 5 6 7 8 9 10

Publisher's Cataloging in Publication
(*Prepared by Quality Books Inc.*)

Holden, Fred, 1937-
    Total power of one in America: discover what you need to know, why and how to be a more powerful person and citizen by Fred Holden. —
    p. cm.
    Includes bibliographical references and index.
    ISBN 0-9621767-2-9

    1. United States-Politics and government. 2. Economics-United States. 3. Business. 4. Citizenship-United States. 5. Finance, Personal. 6. Conduct of life. 7. Self-care, Health. I. Title.

JK271   320.973
                                                                          88-92792

QUICK-SCAN
LIFE POWER TOOLS
THE BOOK-IN-BRIEF 1

Table of Contents

YOU COUNT. YOU MATTER. YOU MAKE A DIFFERENCE.
Life Power Tools turn YOU, Power Of ONE into a TOTAL Power
of ONE! Power-up your life, one Life Power Tool a day, one
chapter a day.

List of Illustrations

Gratitude and Acknowledgments

Special thanks to my wife, Dottie, for believing in this book as much as I have believed, and working twice as hard and courageously to see it complete and available for the future of America. And thanks for this great experiment in Freedom and for the undeserved kindness and abundant blessings of living in America.

Thanks to our Higher Power for our lives, children—Lorilyn, Sherilyn and Tamilyn, and grandchildren—Jake, Ben and Ross, for all of "our kids" and good friends who have blessed our lives. This book is for their better and brighter future.

Thanks to America's older people (you know who you are) who have worked so long and hard and sometimes feel unappreciated for the true contributions you've made to the heart and soul of America.

Thanks to the late-John T. McCarty, my mentor, foreman and friend, for his wisdom, counsel, understanding and support. Thanks to the Adolph Coors Company and to the vision, courage and integrity of the Coors family, their highly valuing hard work, healthy competition, "quality in all we are and all we do," and their unswerving commitment to human freedom and dignity, and the competitive, free market.

Thanks to the Founders of America for their Divinely inspired vision, wisdom and courage, and for the Declaration of Independence and U. S. Constitution, with its incredibly important first ten amendments, the Bill of Rights.

Thanks to America's teachers in whose hands are the destiny of the future—the education of our children of all ages. May they be richly blest to share the message of freedom and abundance.

Thanks to each *TOTAL Power of ONE* who makes and keeps commitments to a greater destiny; and who accepts the assignment and the privilege to get involved and take action, to be different and to make a difference

Thanks to those who gave so much loving care, concern and criticism to make this book the best, most useful and complete as possible. Special thanks to my editors and good friends, Andy Patten, Jim Warner and Patricia Patterson-Greeb, plus Dr. Malcolm Tarkanian, Archer Muncy, Martin Brusse, R.G. Jerry Screws and Bruce Douglas; and book producers Tom and Marilyn Ross and book assembler Cathy Bowman.

Limited space does not permit listing all those who helped in so many ways. I cannot risk the terrible disservice of leaving out someone important who helped in these past eighteen years. You know who you are and how much you have done. And it's just the beginning. Thanks, thanks to all of you whose "hearts, minds and spirits" are so much a part of these pages. Thanks for all you do. Thanks for being you.

We are truly privileged to live here, now, in America.

America—Pass It On!

PREFACE

TOTAL POWER!
What If They've Got It and You Don't?

It used to be "they" had the power and you didn't. What power? The power of knowledge, information and understanding. Now all this information is available to you in this first and only book of its kind. After ten years preparation, seven years research, four years writing, in this New Millennium Edition, you hold the promise of personal power, and the challenge and opportunity to use it to make a positive difference.

This book is full of power—personal power—the power of knowing, the power to get in control of your life and to improve your life. It will empower, enable and ennoble you to make positive, lasting change. It is designed to inform and inspire, to motivate to action, to get you and others involved—to make a difference—to bring America back and keep America free.

Why was this book written?

Was It Because of the Kids?

Was it the young woman saying between sobs, "Why didn't anyone tell me?" standing, crying before a group who'd just seen a marvelous slide program of life in America, its goodness, grandeur, freedom and abundance?

Was it the teenager apparently rejected in a job interview, who jumped 46 stories to his death? Was suicide his solution to a teenage misunderstanding of today's economics?

Was it Debbie with "emotional problems" who said I'd brought sunshine into her life by explaining business, economics and money when I served as a volunteer business consultant in Junior Achievement's 1976 pilot program of "Project Business?"

Was It Because of the Grown-Ups?

Was it for countless adults who lead "lives of quiet desperation," those who no matter how long, hard or smart they work to make ends meet, still lose ground?

Was it the senior citizen who lamented, "Why didn't someone tell me I'd get old, and why didn't someone tell me I should save a lot of money to prepare for my old age?"

Was it for all those hard workers, who through no fault of their own lose their jobs because of recession, "downsizing" or "tough economic times?"

Was It Because of ME and My Personal Naivete?

"Will all the morons in the room please stand up?" said the professor to his new class. After a seemingly long, uncomfortable silence a young man stood up. "Sir," quizzed the professor, "do you consider yourself a moron?" Haltingly the student answered, "Not really—I just hated to see you standing there all by yourself."

In the sense of truly knowing how the world works, and in particular, how America works, had I been that moron? Perhaps I'd been naive—deficient in worldly wisdom or informed judgment. But I've not stood there alone. There are tens, even hundreds of millions of people who really don't understand. Do you, like me, wonder why? Have you ever felt you're the one "standing there all by yourself?"

Two events changed my life. The first was when I said "yes" to John McCarty, and the second was when I published my first book, *The Phoenix Phenomenon*.

While serving on a corporate task force to critique the Adolph Coors Company's Employee Economic Awareness Program, its leader resigned. When the late John T. McCarty, Vice President, Corporate Public Affairs, asked me to take the job as Director of Economic Affairs, I said "Yes!" I had a staff of 10 people whose only job was to teach Coors employees and others real-life economics—a commitment made, accepted and funded by that enlightened management.

There I was, former manager of facilities engineering, chemical engineering degree, with a recent masters in business administration (MBA), all part of 20 years large corporation experience in two companies at four mountain states and eastern plant locations.

I thought I was well educated. I wasn't. I was an economic illiterate. To teach real-life economics I had to learn it. I got the gift of five years to work, read, learn, teach, share, attend seminars and workshops, establish new relationships and grow in an area of knowledge previously unknown and unavailable to me.

My second "life-changer" was my book *The Phoenix Phenomenon,* a study of size and growth of government in America from 1948 to 1982, and its damaging effects on America's standard-of-living, quality-of-life and future. Like so many other people, my mind has been primed with the notion that more government is better. It had never made sense, especially in the context of "free enterprise." My book research better analyzed government growth and disproved the idea that more government is necessarily better. It depends on how big it already is.

What is the problem? Economic illiteracy? Misled public opinion? Ignorance?

Nobel laureate Economist Dr. Milton Friedman said, "Our problem's not ignorance. It's what we know that's not so."

It's also what we don't know. It's all this and much more.

Was It Because of the "Education Triple-Gap?"

Following a school in-service about the American economic system, business and profit, a teacher asked my opinion of education in America. I answered, "It teaches just about everything—mathematics, science, reading, art, music, language and all the rest—except three things:

1. How to make a living,
2. How to live, and
3. How to understand life."

That's the education triple-gap.

Another teacher asked how I'd fill the gap. "Teach economics," I said. "Economics helps things make sense and gives each person an immense importance. It's the glue that holds everything together."

Learning and teaching economics is where it starts, but not where it ends. It's much bigger than that. It is a lifelong experience that begins here, now, with you, in *TOTAL Power of ONE in America.*

The Reality and the Dream

I wish I'd had this book in my teen and early adult years. And I'd like to have given it to each of my three daughters in theirs. The reality is that this information has been virtually unavailable and untaught. It is as scarce as it is valuable and useful.

My dream is for each person to read *TOTAL Power of ONE in America,* review it once a year and use it as a reference book. It explains basic concepts, exposes important issues and provides answers to vital questions of concern for America's 275 million people, 133 million workers,

103 million households and 71 million families and 68 million students. This knowledge, information and understanding tells America's people how America works and puts you back in control.

That's why I wrote it!

Release Your Personal Power!

This is a book to unleash your personal power, to go from the *Power of ONE* to *TOTAL Power of ONE*. You'll find your own good reasons for reading and using the book as you take control of your life and positively shape your future. You'll really like "standing there all by yourself." You'll stand out and you'll be outstanding. And guess what? You won't be alone.

Start now, *Power of ONE,* and soon you'll be a *TOTAL Power of ONE in America.*

TOTAL POWER! What if you've got it and they don't?

The Book-in-Brief
The Gathering of Summaries

"Read" *TOTAL Power* in about an Hour

Life goes too fast and we are too busy. *TOTAL Power of ONE in America* is a big book, a comprehensive book, that "puts between two covers everything you need to know to be a powerful person and citizen." Its design also lends itself to a fast read, quick comprehension and instant application. Personally, by phone and on hundreds of talk shows I have told listeners the quick, easy way to "read" the previous edition is to read "The Book-in-Brief,"—

1. Introduction
2. 26 half-page chapter summaries
3. Last "why?" inspirational chapter, "The Joy has been the Journey, to TOTAL Power of YOU in America."

This speedily gives the content, flavor and flow of the book.

In written, verbal and electronic communications I remind myself,

> "People don't care how much you know
> Till they know how much you care."

I care, a lot. I cared enough to spend five years to research, write and publish this book, and another nine years getting it "out there"; then updating and republishing, to keep it available. Your reason to care is in the information, motivation and inspiration of the "Joy has been the Journey" chapter.

People ask why I do what I do, and why I gave up what I had to, to do it. It is to honor the past and the future. The past includes indelible memories of fighting men and women shooting at enemies of America and freedom, getting shot at, some getting maimed physically and/or emotionally and many dying. We, generally, and I, particularly, owe them and their memory a lot, for what we have and are today. From page 217 of the *2000 World Almanac* the numbers speak for themselves. In this century alone, over 36 million people have served in the defense of this country in World Wars I and II, and "police actions" in Korea, Vietnam, Persian Gulf, and many "peacekeeping missions." With over 1.75 million war casualties, 619,432 died. Each of those individuals, much like a "you" or "me," lost not only their lives but their dreams, possibilities, chance to have a family and just to live. Each had a circle of family and friends who still feel their loss. We owe. We can give back.

America's future not only includes our children and grandchildren but countless numbers of unborn, unrepresented generations of people to come, whom we will never meet. What we do here and now can help make their future better and brighter. Someone carried the torch of freedom for us and we have the opportunity now to carry our torch of freedom for them.

TOTAL Power's new millennium edition, "The Great American Book for the 21st Century," has been updated to conveniently reflect this advice and counsel. This Book-in-Brief is your first cut, allowing you to "read" the book in an hour or so, using the half-page chapter summaries that recap each average 20-page chapter, a 40-to-1 reduction. The chapters are "stand-alone," so for a chapter of interest at the moment, go there.

The main thing is to get the gist of the entire book, then conveniently and aggressively read what is of immediate interest, need or concern, knowing also what else is therein.

One other thing about reading and learning: Read the summary prior to reading the chapter, then read the chapter and summary once again to "set" the learning. It is then easy to do a quick review of the summaries to re-learn, remember and relate, to articulate the details.

Your continuous opportunity is to then share your new knowledge and understanding with others.

Future updates and additions may be found on my website, www.fredholden.com.

This new book organization is for you. Read this Book-in-Brief, then read the book. Following Chapter 25, re-read the up-front "Joy has been the Journey," Chapter 26, to finish it up right. Here we go!

TOTAL Power of ONE In America
A Powerful Premise With a Powerful Promise

You count.
You matter.
You make a difference.

The Magnificent Power of ONE

In America there are over 187 million people from teenage to retirement age whose *Power of ONE is* important, significant and considerable. Know that you make a difference, and you do. This simple act of faith makes you a world changer—at any age!

Your *Power of ONE is* an awesome power that carries with it great possibility, great opportunity and great responsibility. Recognize it. Believe it. Use it wisely and life takes on a whole new meaning.

Acclaimed historical personalities exercised their *Power of ONE.* They heard, as we all do, the naysayers and detractors, but they endured the put-downs and overcame the barrage of discouragement. They also heard that powerful small voice within which says, "You count. You matter. You *can* make a difference. You are right! YOU can do it!" Because they believed, they acted. Because they acted, they achieved and changed the world. Believe, act and you too will make a difference.

What can one person do, you ask? A lot. *A whole lot!* Once you start to get involved and act, you will be astounded at the incredible power you have, believing and living the *"Power of ONE,"* a deceptively simple philosophy and creed:

The Power of ONE
I am ONE.
I am only ONE.
But I will do,
What ONE can do.

A Philosophy for Living, a Power for Life

TOTAL Power of ONE in America is an exploration of an idea called freedom in America. It is an explanation of the *Power of ONE* philosophy of living. You will learn how its application will make a major difference not only in your life but in your family's, as well as your friends' lives and community in which you live.

You are about to embark on an exciting journey to create a more meaningful and rewarding life. You will gain a transforming understanding of what life is, who you are, what you stand for, what you believe, and what you can do; then to apply this new philosophy of living to your life as you use and develop your *Power of ONE*.

You will learn how our society creates and consumes wealth, how our world can be more livable, more generous in material wealth with more efficient use of resources, and potentially more abundant in life's important intangibles of success, happiness, well-being, peace and love.

You will consider not only survival but prosperity, failure and success, risk and reward, power and weakness, and other elusive "lifestuff."

The American people have accepted a blatant lie that says simply, "You don't count. You don't matter. You can't make a difference. You are nothing." That is absolutely false. But if you believe it, and act as though you believe it, you make this treacherous lie true.

What we "know," what we choose to believe and how we act are determined by our past thoughts, actions, education and experience, by who we have known and what we have read, by what we have done and where we have been. What we don't know or what we know incorrectly can truly hurt us, and in ways that far transcend physical injury and pain.

Ignorance sets us back financially, economically, socially, emotionally, even spiritually. We are victors or victims, depending on what we know, what we learn, what decisions we make, how we act and react.

Success in life is very much related to an open mind, a state of knowing, a love of learning and a bent for believing. The invisible but powerful world of knowledge beckons, even demands to be explored.

So if we know, truly know we can make a difference, guess what? We can.

Two Obstacles to Learning

The two obstacles to learning are not to learn and not to be taught. The first is under your control, the second is not. If you choose to learn and seek learning, you will learn. You can't learn what you're not taught, especially if it's not available to learn. *TOTAL Power of ONE in America* contains what you should have been taught in eight, twelve, or sixteen years of education but were not taught.

Take, for instance, the phrase "political spectrum." Its terms are familiar and popular. One can read in the newspaper almost daily about "left-leaning, bleeding-heart liberals" or "right-wing, arch-conservatives." But what does "left" and "right" mean? Are they part of the political spectrum that goes from the political left to the political right? What is all that?

To find out you might go to your library and look up "political spectrum" in a dictionary or encyclopedia. It's not there. This crucial measure of how much government and how it affects life on earth is "unavailable for comment." We have no words or phrases, no books or references. Why?

I checked the four largest, most popular encyclopedias. All four research indexes were over 600 pages, two were nearly 1,000 pages. With some 150 line items per page not one lists "political spectrum." The computerized book locator for half a million books, on the subject "political spectrum" brought up the message, "sorry, nothing is found to satisfy this search."

I was asked to teach part of a basic business course in college, so I previewed the textbook. I was certain that average business profit and rate-of-return on investment would be prominent among the topics therein. I was wrong. They weren't there. It's the same with "productivity."

Why don't we know and why can't we find out? It took four months to research and write chapter 14 on the political spectrum. It took four more months for those chapters on business, profit and free enterprise. Now all this and more are conveniently available to you. But that's not all we don't know. We are in an illiterate slump.

Open Minds and Cultural Literacy

Two of 1987's best-selling nonfiction books were on scholarship, philosophy, relativism, morals and a sense of culture and literacy. One of these unexpected blockbusters [1] was a provocative intellectual spanking by Professor Allan Bloom, *The Closing of the American Mind*. The other [2] was Dr. E. D. Hirsch's *Cultural Literacy*.

---

1. Allan David Bloom, *Closing of the American Mind: How Higher Education has Failed Democracy and Impoverished the Souls of Today's Students*, Simon & Schuster, New York: 1987

2. E.D. Hirsch, Joseph F. Kett, and James S. Trefill, *Cultural Literacy: What Every American Needs to Know*, Houghton-Mifflin, Boston: 1987

These told of the barren education America's college students have been receiving, and how little they know about the cultural underpinnings of America, its history, tradition and society. We will have to declare intellectual, cultural and moral bankruptcy if these knowledge trends and curriculum content aren't improved dramatically.

The book in your hands, *TOTAL Power of ONE in America, is* a new beginning for the opening of the American mind and for gaining cultural literacy.

Educating for Democracy: Develop a Sense of Urgency to DO IT NOW!

"Education for Democracy" was a 23-page pamphlet also published in 1987 by the American Federation of Teachers. It expounded how we have a great deal more teaching to do to survive as a nation. I would have entitled it more precisely *Education for a Democratic Republic* and you will learn why that is important.

With that distinction stated, the booklet described democracy as "the worthiest form of human governance ever conceived [3]." It said that we can't take its survival, spread or perfection for granted, and its "survival depends on transmitting to each new generation the political vision of liberty and equality that unites us as Americans—and a deep loyalty to the political institutions our founders put together to fulfill that vision."

They stressed, "citizens must know the fundamental ideas central to the political vision of the eighteenth-century founders ... how democratic ideas have been turned into institutions ... understand the current condition of the world and how it got that way, and be prepared to act upon the challenges to democracy in our own day," and "To go deeper than the words, and truly to understand the ideas."

In calling for a "decisive improvement of education for democracy," they suggested "a more substantial, engaging, and demanding social studies curriculum," with more emphasis on history and geography, "confronting students with the hard realities that shape so many political, economic, and social decisions."

The report called for "a broader, deeper learning in the humanities, particularly in literature, ideas, and biography, so that students may encounter and comprehend the values upon which democracy depends. Through such study, moral education—not religious education and not neutral values clarification—can be restored to high standing in our schools," concluding:

As citizens of a democratic republic, we are part of the noblest political effort in history. Our children must learn, and we must teach

3. *Education for Democracy: A Statement of Principles*, pp 8, 15, 16, 18, 21, © 1987 by American Federation of Teachers, 555 New Jersey Ave, Washington, DC 20001, quoted with permission

them, the knowledge, values, and habits that will best protect and extend this precious inheritance. Today we ask our schools to make a greater contribution to that effort and we ask all Americans to help them do it.

In the intervening dozen years how has American education been doing in these respects?

TOTAL Power of ONE in America is a text to learn and a tool to teach the much-needed, highly-touted *Education for a Democratic Republic.*

Personal Power: Thoughts, Ideas, Knowledge, Understanding, Information, Action

Here are the reasons and sources of your *Power of ONE:*
Thoughts rule the world.
Ideas have consequences.
Knowledge is power.
Understanding is powerful.
Information powers Action.

Have you ever wondered how it would be to have the *knowledge, information* and *understanding* about how America works and what you can do to make it work better? How to get others involved? How to TAKE ACTION and what action to take?

What are the "Life Power Tools" that put you in control, that put more fun, more joy and greater reward in your life?

Modules of life knowledge are power tools in your tool kit of life. Suppose you add over two dozen new power tools to your Life Tool Kit over the next month at a rate of one a day? How poised, prepared and powerful would you be? You would be a "super power"! What would you do with your new-found powers? What if you:

- Understood business, economics, free enterprise and profits?

- Understood inflation and the three functions of money?

- Knew the roles, risks, responsibilities and rewards in the American enterprise system?

- Combined these with knowledge of the political spectrum and a grasp of political and economic systems?

- Combined history, beliefs and philosophies of America's Founders, with an understanding of the Freedom Documents:
    — The Declaration of Independence, the intent of law,
    — The United States Constitution, the law, and
    — The Bill of Rights, its incredibly important first ten amendments?

- Included the powerful concepts of human freedom, self-governing people and individual responsibility?

- Added to that, information about growth of government and taxes, and their effects on our quality-of-life and future?

- Further included useful and practical information about character, work, truth and ideas?

Then suppose to all this you add health and wealth—personal wellness and lifetime financial planning—for financial security and independence?

Finally, what if you learn what you need to know to be a powerful person, a responsible, informed and influential citizen, to get actively involved and motivated and activate others? Your "action of one" then becomes the action of one more, then many more.

Here's "what if?" when you put it all together, you:

- Become a powerful, persuasive, informed human being who makes a profound, lasting and positive difference.

- Have more fun, experience more joy and live a fuller life.

A Quick Look at a Life Science

To get started here is a brief look at economics, the foundation on which our basic understanding of living in America is built:

A Short, Short-Course in Economics

We either live or die. To live we must consume. To consume we must produce. When we produce a surplus, we can exchange, create a market, buy and sell. Our common enemy is scarcity and our mission is survival. Our goal is abundance. We want the best system of enterprise and government to produce the most wealth distributed to the most people. We are in this together. We must be in balance.

Our economic system consists of enterprise and government. The job of enterprise is to create wealth. Government's job is to create a climate for creating wealth but in so doing is a net consumer of wealth. Wealth is anything that has value, that people are willing to work for and pay for. Wealth is basic economics—creation, production, distribution and consumption of goods and services. It is important to understand and control the balance between enterprise and government.

Over time government grows faster than enterprise through "creep"—slow but sure change. With higher wealth consumption and lower wealth production, we are less rich because expanding government is a net consumer of wealth.

When you know basic economics you know a lot. Combined with the concepts of freedom you know a lot more.

An Idea Bigger than Life: FREEDOM

Freedom is bigger than a person, bigger than a home and family; bigger than a community or country, bigger than a planet called Earth. Freedom is a big, big idea.

TOTAL Power of One in America explores freedom in America, economics in action, the American enterprise system and how it is supposed to work. We'll study risk, business and profits, government and the state, and learn some of the legislation, programs and goals of this nation to see if we perform towards our best, long-term interests. Then we explore the important concepts of politics and political systems, economics and economic systems.

Economics ties together seemingly scattered concepts, philosophies, ideas and bits of truth about life. Economics is not one concept, but four: 1) academic economics, 2) real life economics, 3) everyday economics and 4) free enterprise economics. When you put them all together, it's easy to see why "Economics is a *life science!*"

You will learn "the involvement process" of becoming more aware, interested, informed, concerned, involved and active.

You will learn "the change process," how to prepare yourself and others for change. You'll learn how to acquire and process information, how to think about, analyze and use it.

You'll learn how to have an important impact by getting involved, involving others and using your own *Power of ONE.*

Two Frameworks and Your Second Most Priceless Treasure

In short, you are assembling *a framework for thinking* for *a framework for living*—a basic, no-nonsense way to view the world, know how it works, how it can work better, and how to get more from it by giving more to it.

Resolve to set aside time to read *TOTAL Power of One in America.* What you have allotted is your "second most priceless treasure," your *presence.* That is the most powerful statement you can make. It is your time, your attention, your consciousness, your being! For all you are and can become, make and keep this commitment to yourself.

The Value of Time

Benjamin Franklin said, "Is it that you love life? Then use time wisely, for that is the stuff life is made of." Time, "life stuff," is really all we have, and it is the most equal and universal resource available. From richest to poorest, all have 24 hours a day. Fill Rudyard Kipling's "unforgiving minute with sixty seconds' worth of distance run."

The value of your personal time has been eloquently expressed by Dr. Heartsill Wilson [4]:

A New Day

This is the beginning of a new day.
God has given me this day to use as I will.
I can waste it—or use it for good,
But what I do today is important,
Because I am exchanging a day of my life for it!
When tomorrow comes, this day will be gone forever,
Leaving in its place something that I have traded for it.
I want it to be
Gain, and not loss;
Good, and not evil;
Success, and not failure;
In order that I shall not regret the price
That I have paid for it.

The time you spend gaining the knowledge and applying the principles in the book will be for gain, good, and success; not loss, evil and failure.

What makes time so priceless is that it is irreplaceable. Statisticians describe time and space as "mutually exclusive." If you spend time here you forego it somewhere else; and if you spend it elsewhere, you forego time spent here. The same with space, if you're here, you can't be somewhere else; if you're somewhere else, you can't be here. You are here, now, and in a sense, we are spending these special moments together. Let us savor them. We can choose to make this time beneficial and life changing, well spent and well invested.

Learn-and-Teach, Sources of Information, Who For and Book Approach

You cannot read too much. Develop a love for learning and a passion for reading. Always carry something to read. In those seemingly short moments of delay you can do a lot of reading, learning and preparation for action.

For starters, carry this book. It's a learn-and-teach tool. There is sufficient repetition to learn so well with proven techniques that you will be able to "pass it on," that is, teach others—and you are challenged to do so.

This book is intended to be gender-neutral, yet a favored passage explains verbatim quotes and other exceptions:

4. Reprinted with permission of W. Heartsill Wilson, Sc.D., Professional Guest Lecturer, Denver, CO. "A New Day," copyright 1954 by W. Heartsill Wilson

When God created man, he made him in the likeness of God. Male and female he created them, and he blessed them and named them Man when they were created. —Genesis 5:1-2, RSV

Sources of information are documented immediately and extensively. In the past it has been difficult to learn sources of information. When I didn't know, I was reluctant to use information for fear I'd be challenged as to its accuracy or source. I want you, dear reader, to know not only that information is generously available, but wherefrom, and how to use it. On purpose, sources are cited on the same page they are mentioned. You can "look it up" if you wish, to verify or expand on it.

Lessons from a Personal Visit to Japan

Getting away from America gave me a new appreciation of what it means to be American. It revitalized my awareness of the bounty of her blessings. Even after you think you know a lot you learn so much more by "being there."

I stood at "ground zero." Yes, with my wife, Dottie, youngest daughter, Tami, and oldest daughter, Lori, who taught conversational English in Nishinomiya, Japan, we visited that island nation for a week in July 1989. Our tour of Hiroshima was a profound emotional experience.

We learned that at 8:15 a.m., Monday, August 6, 1945, a normal day had begun. Seconds later the first atomic bomb detonated 580 meters, about six football fields, above the center of the city. Decimation is where ten percent are destroyed. What happened to Hiroshima was annihilation. Instantly a large city and 140,000 people were destroyed. The count has steadily climbed to over 200,000 people killed by that "small" nuclear fireball.

That "Little Boy" bomb was "only" 13 kilotons. Three days later the slightly larger "Fat Man" was dropped on Nagasaki with similar results. Today we speak in terms of megatons, millions of tons of TNT explosive destructive power, and tens of thousands, not atomic, but hydrogen bomb warheads.

We can learn from the Hiroshima Peace Park Memorial. All people who can, especially heads of state, should visit Hiroshima to gain an understanding of this immense capability to destroy and the awesome power that created it—the human mind, heart and spirit.

The importance of knowledge, heritage and learning were burned into my consciousness. *TOTAL Power of ONE in America is* a new beginning, but only a beginning. We have much to do and it will take time, energy and commitment. Life expands to greater meaning and wider horizons, not only in the world of ideas and knowledge, but in knowing other peoples, places and cultures. So we start here.

Each powerful person will have to know not one or two, but *three* languages: English, a foreign language and computers. The foreign language may be

European, Russian, Japanese or others. "Computers" doesn't deal strictly with computer languages but with computer literacy, how to operate and use computers. Get it all together as you progress through and beyond, to building a powerful, total life experience. Your New Beginning is here, now.

Learning Love of Learning from the Japanese

The Japanese have caught on. They have adopted English as their second language, "the international language of business," as they refer to it. They require six years English reading and writing through high school, then two more years in college, but with little listening or interpretive skills and even less conversation. Their next wish is to learn to speak and listen to us Americans. Do you realize the competitive advantage that curiosity and love of learning gives them? Do you realize the disadvantage America suffers if we don't respond in kind?

One United States business executive of a multinational corporation said there are more Japanese in one square mile of Tokyo who speak English than there are Americans in the whole United States who speak Japanese.

They have developed a love of learning and of English, America and Americans. One professor from the island of Kyushu, formerly of Omaha, Nebraska, was conducting an 8-week American tour for 10 Japanese students. He said they were paying from $6,000 to $8,000 each for that experience. Further, he confided he knew of a Japanese entrepreneur's new business that set a goal to bring 20,000 Japanese students a year on tour of America. What can we be doing to inculcate a love of learning, and then appropriate action to nurture that love and make the world better for it?

The Unlucky-Seven Dangerous Illiteracies

Many people believe that our greatest national threat is illiteracy—the inability to read, write, think, analyze and articulate thoughts and ideas. But seven specific illiteracies seriously jeopardize America's present and condemn her future: Economic, political, business, constitutional, governmental, moral and citizenship. We are not taught the fun or the joy of citizenship. We don't know what to do, how to do it or why it is so important. But not any more. This veritable handbook of American government, economics, business and politics, *TOTAL Power of ONE in America*, is right here, right now. This citizen power manual is a virtual encyclopedia of 26 mini-books between two covers, a whole library of what has formerly been missing in American education. Put all you can into it to get all you can out of it.

Knowledge is Power

Consider now this new beginning. You put you back in control. Assemble all the mighty ingredients necessary, the potent recipe to make them work, and live a powerful, productive and fulfilling life. Use this book to start you on this New Life.

You will experience your NEW BEGINNING. Through awareness, knowledge, information and understanding, you are *renewed* through personal freedom, economics-in-action and your new *"Power of ONE"* in free enterprise. You command control of your own destiny and that of your society, country and future. Catch the spirit of Freedom!

30 Days to TOTAL Power:
A Chapter a Day Builds Your Brighter Future

Your first "Power Decision" is an unconditional commitment to read *TOTAL Power of ONE in America* in the next 30 days, paced at a chapter a day. For efficient, effective reading and learning, use the time-proven formula:

> Preview what you are going to read.
> Read what you are reading.
> Review what you have read.

Specifically set aside an hour-a-day to read a chapter-a-day. The first day read the front matter in the book: Table of Contents, Preface and book jacket, the book summary. Second day read the Book-In-Brief. Each day read a chapter. Take notes and jot down ideas. Write in the margins. Underline. Highlight. Be an active, even reactive reader.

Some people will want to read the "Gathering of Summaries" at the beginning of the book. Some will read "Questions for Review" at the end of each chapter. Some will read both before, both again after reading the chapter. Do what works for you.

After reading the chapter again read its Summary to "set" the learning, preparing to put your new knowledge, information and understanding into action. Discuss what you have read with others to share the insights of your newly-acquired Life Power Tools. You will be surprised at the positive difference you begin to make from the start. Go for it, *Power of ONE!* Begin changing your world one person at a time starting with yourself.

> You count. You matter. You make a difference.

You are incredibly important. You are amazingly powerful. You are about to set sail on your new journey of self-discovery and self-dominion to become a *Power of ONE.* Why? Because, in fact:

> You do count!
> You really do matter!
> You really can make a difference!

You are a Power of One in America!

Soon, you will be a TOTAL POWER OF ONE IN AMERICA!

Read on! This is your New Beginning as a New American.

America was built into the greatest country the world has ever known, not through government control, regulation and handouts; but rather through individual imagination and initiative. It has been the individual and not government that built this nation, and it will be the individual that will save it for future generations.

—Robert W. Miller, President, Freedoms Foundation

All who have meditated on the art of governing mankind have been convinced that the fate of empires depends on the education of youth. Educated men are as much superior to uneducated men as the living are to the dead.

—Aristotle

Education is a social process ... Education is growth ... Education is not preparation for life; education is life itself.

—John Dewey

Only the educated are free.

—Epictetus

"A Quick Read"
The Gathering of Summaries

Chapter 1
Life Power Tool: FREEDOM

Freedom
Your First Most Priceless Treasure

Freedom is precious and scarce. Freedom is not free. We Americans are part of the "fortunate five percent" born under freedom. In 1984 the U. S. Olympics celebrated freedom, where Lady Liberty's Torch of Freedom was carried high across the land, posing to all Americans the freedom challenge: "Carry it or bury it." *The Continuum of a Civilization* says societies go from bondage, to spiritual faith, to great courage, to liberty, to abundance, to selfishness, to complacency, to apathy, to dependency, back to bondage, a cycle that lasts about 200 years. Are we near the end of this cycle? Who are we? Americans are free, responsible individuals, created and blessed by a beneficent God. Our first job is to make a living, but our greater job is to preserve freedom, offering our sweat, blood, even our lives if need be. Give regular citizen service to America, "a half-hour a day for the USA," or at least an hour a week. Making right choices depends on education. American education teaches everything except how to make a living, how to live, and how to understand life. What we lack is a study of economics to bring it all together and provide a basis of understanding for America's 68-million school children and 133-million workers. Freedom is being free to be, do, choose, dare, and to become. The only person protecting your freedom is YOU. Pray as though only God can protect your freedom. Work as if it's all up to you. Pray hard and work hard to get the whole job done. President John Kennedy said God's work here on earth must truly be our own. That goes especially for preserving freedom. To be born free is a blessing, to live free is a privilege, to die free is a responsibility. Protect your greatest gift—freedom.

Chapter 2
Life Power Tool: The Power of ONE!

The Power of ONE
A Philosophy for Living

YOU COUNT. YOU MATTER. YOU MAKE A DIFFERENCE. But you must be different. Understand Repetition: Mother of Learning, Father of Boredom, King of Conviction. You, *Power of ONE*, have a destiny, to grow, achieve and contribute. Recognize "excuse thoughts" for what they are, destroyers that keep us from being all we are, doing all we can. Positive "do thoughts" replace "mindbinders" for prompt action. *Power of ONE* goes beyond "meet the standard" to "set the standard," to do what is right because it is right. Draw a bigger circle. Include yourself and others within. Don't just do something right, do the right thing—right. "Each one teach one, then ten," to MULTIPLY, get a lot done faster. There is power and majesty in being "ONE," also finite limits seldom approached. Two qualities are FAITH—"I will try it," and ACTION—"I will do it," because "Whatever you can do, or dream you can, begin it. Boldness has genius, power and magic in it." Stretch and grow. "Reach out, touch perfection." Sacrifice, "build spears," prepare for the future. Invest in yourself. Act as if it were impossible to fail. "If it is to be it is up to me," turns acceptance of personal responsibility into personal power. The Power Dare, Power Challenge and Power Deed program you for achievement, like a business contract: offer, acceptance, performance. Use your Power Deed Creed and *Power of ONE* Commitment. Earn your stars. Read a chapter-a-day. Marshal your considerable resources, *Power of ONE* and do all ONE can do. You are the ONE! Go for it!

Chapter 3
Life Power Tool: RIGHTS!

Power Challenge

Read the Bill of Rights!

A teacher in Maine assigned his students to carry petitions urging repeal of "laws that coddled criminals." Three out of four signed, but only one in eight recognized those laws as the Bill of Rights. By these first 10 Constitutional amendments each citizen is sovereign, bigger than their government which spends over $1.7 trillion dollars a year, $1 billion every 5.1 hours. Big government spends over one-tenth trillion dollars more a year than do all Americans on life's essentials, food, shelter, clothing. The 1999 "magic number" is 273, America's population in millions, which, divided into government big numbers, breaks them into understandable per-person bits: $6,692 federal taxes collected each, $6,234 spent, $1,294 interest on the $5.55 trillion national debt for 1999, $353 billion interest per year ($2,654 for each worker, $50/week). Freedom defined: economically, earn $100 and keep $100 you're 100% free; earn $100, keep $0, 100% slave; in life terms, free to be, do, choose, dare, become; in terms of government, an absence rather than a presence. Washington said government is not reason or eloquence but force, a dangerous servant and a fearful master. Understanding government is made easier with the Freedom Documents. The Declaration of Independence is freedom philosophy, belief and legislative intent to the U.S. Constitution, law of the government; the Bill of Rights protects people from oppressive government. Article I lists five freedoms: Religion, speech, press, assembly, and the right to petition government for redress of grievances. Additional rights are described in the remaining nine Articles. What is number nine, number 10? The Power Challenge is to read the Bill of Rights to appreciate freedom.

Chapter 4
Life Power Tool: YOUTH TALK!

Power Challenge

Talk to Kids!

It is a simple, direct and important assignment: Talk to kids. Many must do it. Why? During a patriotic color slide presentation of America's beauty, magnificence, power and grandeur, a young woman stood up in tears, told of quitting school, giving up, and asked, "Why didn't someone tell me about America?" Young people who think themselves failures, may resort to suicide as a reasonable answer to a teenage problem. One of "our kids" did. Why? Kids spend more time with television than in school, get a distorted view of reality. They see the very best, thinking it's the standard, not knowing what it took to get there. What can be done? Say "yes" to possibilities, opportunities. A stint as Business Consultant for Junior Achievement solidified how and why to "talk to kids." Ten classes plus a Federal Reserve Bank field trip proved the kids, teachers, and school system need us. The teachers never get out of school. We did, so we can help them tell students how it really is. Talk to kids in their terms about their world, then listen. They think deep thoughts. One young man published, "give us a chance to be a future generation." Kindle a dream where no dream exists. List your topics, messages you have to share, you, your life, job, business, career. Contact schools. Go there. Bring students to your place of work. Know you get more than you give, a genuine, personal satisfaction that you have positively impacted young impressionable lives. Teacher-in-space Christa McAuliffe put it, "I touch the future—I teach." Touch the future. Accept the Power Challenge: Talk to Kids!

Chapter 5
Life Power Tool: ECONOMIC SAVVY!
Economics
A Short Course in a Life Science

Economics studies scarcity, deals with choice, behavior and action of individuals and organizations. The four types of economics are academic, consumer, today's, and free enterprise (including roles of personal, economic, political freedoms; competition, risk, saving, business, profit, taxes, government). We don't worry that planet Earth's food supply is only 90 days. Why? Because people work. Economics is creation, production, distribution and consumption of wealth—what has value, that people are willing to work for and pay for, valued goods and services. The best system produces the most wealth with least resource consumption and environmental damage. Success depends on the balance between the wealth-creating enterprise (private) sector and the wealth-consuming government (public) sector, which creates a climate of creating wealth. Not wealth itself, money comes in two forms, cash and credit. It is a medium of exchange, a store of value and a standard of value. Lawful money, defined by the Constitution, is "gold and silver" and "coin." The Federal Reserve, a private, central bank formed by Congress in 1913, issues fiat, unbacked money. Money is either asset-based (gold, limited in supply), or debt-based (fiat money, today's, unlimited). Inflation, the "disease of money" is "too many dollars chasing too few goods." Money is produced by banks; goods, by people. Deficits result when Congress spends more than it taxes. Deficits financed by borrowing turn people investment funds into government consumption outlays, but do not cause inflation. When the Federal Reserve "buys" deficits with debt, it issues new money increasing the money supply, eventually causing inflation. Man's material welfare is limited by natural resources and human energy but is multiplied by tools built from savings. Freedom is the magic ingredient in free enterprise, the economic system that serves America and humankind better.

Chapter 6
Life Power Tool: FREE ENTERPRISE!

Free Enterprise
The Mysterious Magical Misunderstood
System That Works Better!

Free enterprise (freedom of private business to organize and operate for a profit in a competitive system without interference by government beyond regulation necessary to protect public interest and keep the national economy in balance) is based on individual freedom, self-governing people, and limited government. Man's greatest threat to freedom and property has ever been government. Man produces more when free to work, to acquire, dispose of and exchange his property, and receive recognition and reward. *Wealth of Nations,* Adam Smith's 1776 economic doctrine was on self-interest for the social good, and laissez-faire, economic liberalism, non-intervention; freedom to try, buy, sell, fail. The Triangle Model defines free enterprise: freedom to work with risk, in a dynamic system, propelled by invention, innovation, competition. Free enterprise, with main touchstone, Economic Freedom, has six characteristics: Private property, Self-interest motives and incentives, Customer sovereignty, Competition, Free markets, Limited government. Economic freedom underpins all other freedoms—political, religious, intellectual, social, personal. Though we are all consumers, a customer is different, sovereign; he pays for what he gets. Free enterprise pleases people, satisfies customers, serves markets. Competition forces higher product quality, with lower resource use. Government provides "for the common defense and the general [not specific] welfare," that which helps all, hurts none. Redistributionist government discourages when it takes from some to give to others. Taxes are a disincentive to produce. Let us make sure America's experiment in freedom succeeds.

Chapter 7
Life Power Tool: CHARACTER!

The Character Imperative of Free Enterprise

Discipline, Honor, Integrity

America's free enterprise society requires personal, public and private sector character: discipline, honor, honesty, integrity, morals, ethics, principle. You are always on record, visible, accountable, responsible. Control your behavior as if every word is on the nightly news, every action in the morning paper. Character is mental, ethical and individual. Culture is custom, belief, intellectual and moral excellence of human behavior. Benjamin Franklin stated, "Only a virtuous people are capable of freedom." "Public virtue" is human maturity in character. The Golden Rule—treat others as you wish to be treated—is morality identified with Ten Commandments, obedience to our Creator's mandate. America is a "Trinitarian system," economic, political and cultural, the last the most ignored. Democratic capitalism depends on fraternity (cooperation and teamwork), equality (opportunity for all), liberty (freedom to think, act, aspire). Government is another facet. Culture involves personal character and self-transcendence—going beyond oneself. Required by the Founders for American education were religion, morality and knowledge. Consider carefully choices and consequences, and personal life management. Know "the whole truth" about freedom, not just fight for it but live it. Be able to make a promise, keep a commitment, smile often, be polite, courteous, respectful. Practice Positive Practical Personal Politics: Treat others when you don't need them the way you'll wish you had treated them when you do need them. Keep language decent. Avoid the obscene, profane, ethnic. Choose to heal, not hurt with words; lavish praise. Be grateful. We take too much for granted. Say thank you and be thankful. Culture and character, combined with the magic of freedom, the miracle of America and the mystery of free enterprise, assure a better present, brighter future.

Chapter 8
Life Power Tool: BUSINESS SAVVY

The Miracle Magic of ROBIS

Role Of Business In Society!

ROBIS, the role of business in society, is to produce goods and services that customers want and will pay for at a profit. Business creates value that pleases people. Business is PEOPLE, five sets of people, four of whom come together voluntarily to please, serve and satisfy the fifth and most important, KING and QUEEN CUSTOMER. The drama of business is so important that we call the other four: Regal EMPLOYEES, Royal SUPPLIERS, August INVESTORS, and Stately NEIGHBORS. Business must have low prices and production costs; high quality; available, reliable products and services, and use minimum resources; with minimal environmental damage; while rewarding employees and investors; and remain in business by staying profitable. The Three C's of organization are: communication, coordination, cooperation; the Three C's of business are customers, choice, competition. A business' only source of money is the customer. Increased wages, prices or taxes are paid for only by the customer. An employee's "customer" is the supervisor, the boss. When people work hard together, business must do right voluntarily (DRV) in the balanced best interests (BBI) of all. Business policy affects business by levels of wages and benefits, national policy, by regulations and taxes and the expense of defense for America's trading partners. High taxes reduce customers and business discretionary buying power, reducing business success prospects. Foreign competition with lower wages, higher productivity and quality levels, puts American business at a competitive disadvantage. Inflation and government growth must be kept low, productivity high and wages increasing. This is all possible through business: five sets of people working together cooperatively and competitively, in a common quest to please a customer, earn a profit and make a living.

Chapter 9
Power Tool: PROFIT SAVVY

Learn and Teach the Miracle Magic of Profit

The Dwarf That Slays Giants!

Profit makes a free market and competitive economy work, encouraging risk and innovation, creating abundance. Though profit is small it fights scarcity and poverty. Profit is business revenue less expense less income taxes. Misunderstanding about profit unfairly taints business. Thought to be 15, 35, even 50% it is 5% of sales. Profit is doing whatever is necessary to make an exchange worthwhile. The investment required to create a job is over $100,000 for large companies. The four sets of people in business distribute in cents, a customer's dollar to employees, 28; suppliers, 53; investors, 3; neighbors (federal, state and local governments), 16. Beyond the obvious (BTO), after taxes, the real distribution becomes employees, 22; suppliers, 43; investors, 2; neighbors 33. Of gross profit after business expense, labor and materials, taxes take over 93%. BTO, Social Security (and all other costs such as health insurance) is passed through to the customer in the price of goods and services. So is a VAT, value added tax. To serve and survive, a business makes a profit by pleasing customers, keeping costs and prices low and beating competition. Prices are signals that relay economic information. Realizing one-third of business revenue goes to government could help smart governments be rich governments. In reporting profits, business should take care to state accurately what they are, less of "200% over last year," more of "20% under our target of 5%." Profit is a small thing that makes a large country work. We must better understand and articulate profit, the dwarf that slays the giants of scarcity and poverty.

Chapter 10
Life Power Tool: WORK!

Work Is Love Made Visible

Let Your Light Shine!

Work is love made visible. Work is contributing to others and getting back from them using all our personal resources. It is working together to survive.

Three mid-high school work questions are: What do you like to do? What can you do well? What needs to be done? In your first jobs you learn to do and enjoy work. Your senior year gives you three more questions: What do you want to do? What does it take to do it? Will you do it? This involves faith and commitment. As in a specialized doctor, the more talent, work, time and education, the lower the supply, the higher the demand, the higher the pay, and psychic income, prestige, travel, achievement. Vocational training includes computers, airplane mechanics; also small business—print shop, service station, etc.—after saving capital for start up. Get job experience before getting an advanced degree as a means to mid-career change. Finding a job is an exercise in faith and frustration. The job is out there. You are ready. It is right and you will find it. Acting makes it so. "Act as if it were impossible to fail." Job-hunting is a full-time job. Be patient and positive. Search with optimism and faith, through people, publications and contacts. Follow-up with enthusiasm and get interviews. Learn about the business, show your stuff. Remember the search, finding, starting a new job. Take good care of your boss. Run a good company in your job, as CEO, CFO, COO, CTO, CIO. You are the President of You, Inc. The first part of life we take from the world, through our work we give back. Take charge, create a job, create a career, create a future, create a life. Let your life and work shine.

Chapter 11
Life Power Tool: ECONOMIC AWARENESS!

Power Challenge
to Business

Start an Employee
Economic Awareness Program!

Business public image is not good. A Gallup poll placed business 15th between senators and congressmen in reputation for "honesty, integrity and ethical standards." Television portrays business as criminal and corrupt, strange in that TV is a business and business dollars support TV. Television is especially powerful because it is used as an inexpensive, entertaining baby-sitter for children during their formative years when they are developing their values and belief systems. Today's students spend 22,000 hours in front of a TV, twice the time spent in class through high school. Student contact with business is limited. Economic illiteracy makes business an easy target. What people don't understand they fear, and urge government to "do something." Business can create The Premier Benefit, an economic awareness program, to help employees better understand their economic and political system. WIIFM, "What's In It For Me?" gains employee acceptance and support, towards higher output, productivity, quality and profits; lower absenteeism, disciplinary problems, material waste, expense and scrap. The Premier Benefit imparts awareness, knowledge and appreciation of work, pay and benefits. When people yearn for the good old days when business was "satisfied with a 15 to 30 percent profit," you know your business has an image problem. Business can and must act to correct its public image, gather information, support educational organizations, insist on media fairness and accuracy, get economics into schools and students into business. Start your own program. Give them The Premier Benefit!

Chapter 12
Life Power Tool: TRUTH!

Power Challenge
Be a Seeker of Truth, and a Finder Also!

    Truth breaks down barriers, enriches life, makes one free, powerful, in control, secure. Humans have built-in protections from "information overload." Not learning keeps us from having to care, revise our biases or confront our ignorance. A curious, open mind lets in new knowledge, information, insights, truth. Horizons expand, opportunities increase, possibilities multiply. Jonathan Livingston Seagull confronted the elder gulls: "We can lift ourselves out of ignorance ... find ourselves creatures of excellence and intelligence and skill." Better than birds, people can learn, live, discover, pursue, find and use truth. We are creatures of habit. Old habit keeps old notions, questions little, shuts out new information. Break old habits for new truth. Help others' truth quest: give evidence, information. Ask questions. Let the answers be theirs. Use the Involvement Process that others become, in order: Aware, interested, informed, concerned, involved, active. Truth goals: acquire more knowledge, update with new information, love learning, go beyond understanding to wisdom. Re-learn today's forgotten treasure truth, the U.S. Constitution. Truth—knowledge plus information plus understanding—comes from variety: books, magazines, newspapers, radio, television and Internet, and especially, people. Read-and-learn formula: Be selfish, active, goal-oriented, broadly interested, people-centered. Read beyond headlines for hard news, commentary/editorial, letters to the editor, business, sports, weather. Truth is the key to your future. Pursue truth.

Chapter 13
Life Power Tool: IDEAS!

It's a Whole New Ball Game

and We're Not Even On First Base!

It is a new ball game, the Game of Life, and we are not even on first base. We are out in left field. Batter up, a hit and first base, Economic Awareness. Next, second base, Political Awareness. Round third base, Political Involvement and Activity. Then head for home plate, Ism's and Ideologies. It is a battle of ideas and knowledge. If you know, you are a victor; if you don't know, you are a victim. Economic and political awareness are essential. When we get politically involved and stay active, the system operates well as a limited government protecting personal freedoms, with responsible citizen self-government. A "contrived ignorance" of economic and political systems leaves people vulnerable to power and plunder. Recent 1999 government spent well over one-and-a-half trillion dollars, $1,703 billion with a $5.55 trillion national debt, and a resulting one-third plus trillion dollar ($353 billion) interest on the debt per year. Government is big and growing bigger. Each of 273 million Americans, directly and indirectly, paid $6,690 in 1999 federal taxes, and had a national debt burden of $20,522 with annual debt interest $1,294. That's $108 a month paid by each American; $221, each worker. What is a billion? In seconds 31.7 years; minutes 1,902 years; hours 114,000 years. In 1999 government spending a billion is 5 hours, 8 minutes. With relentless government growth, new political systems emerge, "losers" of other times and places: Naziism, fascism, communism, socialism, away from a constitutional republic or democracy. To understand, we "round the bases" for economic and political awareness, political involvement and activity, ism's and ideologies: The big Home Run.

Chapter 14
Life Power Tool: POLITICAL SAVVY!

The Political Spectrum

Power of Political Understanding in America!

"Left," "right" and "center" are nebulous terms that describe the political spectrum and government systems. Their meanings are ambiguous and misleading. The popular and wrong continuum shows communism (with Naziism, socialism) left, fascism right; a variant with socialism on both ends. Another, better, measures amount of freedom by size, control and ownership of government. Total government, 100%, totalitarianism, is far left; no government, 0%, anarchy, far right. Democracy is middle to left of center, Constitutional Republic, right of center. Variations are the circle, or clock, moderates at center, increasing either way to "six o'clock," melding one into the other. The "horseshoe" shows how anarchy breaches the gap to a dictatorship. Economic freedom is quantified as the percentage of earned money kept after taxes; living freedom, as permissiveness to act freely without harming others. The reasons for confusion lie in a need for more accurate descriptions such as the "Percent Government," and Dine's "Political Gamut" spectrum. The two-dimensional, four-quadrant Nolan Chart names and explains people and political spectrum types, plus "centrists" and "crusaders." From the Declaration of Independence, freedom comes from God, who created man, who wrote the Constitution, to create government, to protect freedom. A political spectrum knowledge is essential in order to understand what our system is, how it works compared to other systems, how they work, and how to keep the best system for the best future. We must realize that the Political Spectrum determines what kind of government, freedom and life we enjoy, then wisely and vigorously defend, preserve and strengthen this Constitutional Republic, keeping government small.

Chapter 15
Life Power Tool: POLITICAL ACTION!

Rounding Third Base

Getting Active and Involved in Politics!

Life is political as well as economic. The political system shapes how well the economic system works. Politics is essential, and a two-edged sword. Depending on those involved, politics can be "clean" or "dirty." It is the science or art of government, the complex of relations between people and society. Good politics requires truly informed, knowledgeable, concerned, committed people. Politics is the art of compromise, the art of the possible. We are all involved in politics. Participants define the debate, policy and quality of the political arena. Political involvement grows from inactive to spectator, participant, enthusiast, to activist in these roles: supportive, elective, appointive, directive. All help to make or shape public policy. Groups of individuals organize to impact the public policy process through official contact, formal presentation, and confrontation. Choose your civic concern; learn, support, attend, participate, speak out, influence, act, at the local, state, regional and national levels. People don't care how much you know until they know how much you care. Use the "What Formula" for contacts: what, so what, now what, what next? The political process begins with the biennial neighborhood caucus, leading to the local, then national political party conventions for candidates, issues, policies and platforms. Participate. Vote. But don't "only vote." The vote is the beginning not the end. Continued contact with elected officials is the key to good government between elections. Resolve to devote an hour a week (or more) towards better government and future. If the difference is to be made, you are the one to make it—with positive politics.

Chapter 16
Life Power Tool: CONSTITUTIONAL REPUBLIC!
America: A Republic, Not a Democracy
What's the Difference

The subtle difference between two concepts of government, republic and democracy, is important. A republic upholds laws, property and individual rights, avoids extremes of tyranny, results in statesmanship, liberty, reason, contentment, progress. Democracy is majority rule, sometimes called "mobocracy." A republic is representative democracy with rule by law, a written constitution; hence, a constitutional republic. Repetitive use of "democracy" has given it an incorrect connotation of desirability. Plato's "philosopher-king" governed a society of rulers, guardians and tradesmen. Aristotle grouped governments into monarchy, aristocracy and democracy. Greece's Solon "wrote it down" and the Roman Empire implemented the representative approach to government. America's founders recognized the detriment of strict democracy and its "tyranny of the majority." Republican government assumes responsibilities of people, protection of life, person, rights and property, but not confiscation nor redistribution of wealth. Real democracy is the federal income tax which in 1913 affected 1%, those with incomes over $180,000 in today's money, growing to 103-million returns, average $4,471 taxes per person, 14.9% of adjusted gross income in 1986; in 1996, $7,200, 14.5%, 120-million returns; 126-million returns in 1999. Five political systems boil down to two, oligarchy—arbitrary rule, and a republic—rule by law. Two forms of capitalism—monopolistic and competitive—are determined in part by ownership and control of capital, the factors of production. Knowledge of these principles help more precisely define the "ism's"—communism, socialism, Naziism and fascism. America is a republic, not a democracy. Let's keep it that way.

Chapter 17
Life Power Tool: FREEDOM DOCUMENTS!

Discovering the Freedom Documents
Declaration, Constitution, and Bill of Rights

Only people, not any piece of paper with writing on it, protect freedom. Discover that the Declaration of Independence records America's Founders' intent. Law is where the government tells people what to do. Discover that the Constitution in where "We the People" tell government what to do. Discover that the Bill of Rights tells what government cannot do to people, who are self-governing citizens. The Constitution is the "supreme Law of the Land," the law of the government, not of the people. Separation of powers, checks and balances protect people rights as well as states rights. "No *ex post facto* (after-the-fact) law shall be passed," says Article I, Sections 9 and 10. The people, secure in their persons and papers, are guaranteed unalienable rights to life, liberty, property, and the pursuit of happiness. "God ... created man ... gave man freedom ... man instituted government ... to protect freedom ... granted by God." When "King Kongress" makes laws for others but exempts themselves they violate their oath of office and Art I, Sec 9, "No title of nobility shall be granted by the United States." No class above the rest, including Congress, can be created by government. Rulers are bound to obey their own laws, as are the ruled. People are the master, government the servant. In 1913 three ominous changes occurred: Direct, rather than state election of senators (17th Am.), authorization of the federal income tax (16th Am.) and the Federal Reserve, a private, central bank. Since 1215, the Magna Carta, a freedom beacon, has beamed the Rights of Mankind through time. Unaware or complacent, our "contrived ignorance" of freedom and government keeps us vulnerable and helpless. Discover, learn, know and support your Freedom Documents. Understand, assert, claim, challenge to preserve your precious rights.

Chapter 18
Life Power Tool: POLITICAL IDEAS!

The Home Run

Ism's, Ideologies, and Ideas

Words—symbols of ideas—serve as tools for thought and communication. Words of political ideologies and philosophies confuse, change over time. Conservative means attached to existing views. Liberal is open-minded to progress. Conservatism is the established tried-and-true, history and tradition, admits mankind's capacity for both good and evil. Conservatives are skeptical about what government and politics can accomplish, oppose government regulation of the economy, believe rights must be earned rather than given, performance of duties is the price of rights, equal rights but not equal abilities or wealth, freedom linked with private property. Early liberals distrusted big government, preferred written law, thought only those who owned property should govern. Today's liberalism shifts emphasis from means to ends. Not freedom to be or do, but of opportunity to achieve; uses government as a means to assure desirable outcomes, do social programs to ease human suffering, assure economic security. Using comparative rankings, Conservatives are for: liberty, freedom, peace, justice; Liberals: peace, justice, freedom, liberty. Words can become labels that stifle thinking, squelch interchange of ideas. Republican (conservative) and Democrat (liberal) are more relative to right and left, respectively, of "moderate," moving leftward over time. In the *Communist Manifesto* Karl Marx sought to abolish private property, the family, religion, morality and truth, to build communism, a fascinating concept that cannot and will not work. The real conflict in ideas and political systems is total tyranny versus relative freedom.

Chapter 19
Life Power Tool: SMALL GOVERNMENT!

ROGIA

Role Of Government In America

Freedom is not a presence but an absence—of governmental constraint. We know enterprise creates wealth while government is a net consumer of wealth. Some think government should be small and limited; others, larger is better. Balance is best. The two kinds of government are public and private. Described as "incomplete conquest" government's essential purpose is to maintain conquest through control. One person describes government: People called legislators make rules, attach penalties for violations, send men with guns to round up wrongdoers and impose penalties; further describing taxation as theft. After World War II the Full Employment Act of 1946 authorized government to create jobs and businesses and regulate the economy, which increased taxes. Tax something and you get less of it; subsidize and you get more. We tax work, initiative, ability; subsidize non-work, consumption, welfare, debt. Government size and growth can be measured as relative size compared to output of goods and services, gross domestic product. Government's relative size almost doubled, from 18% GDP in 1948 to 35% in 1988, 0.42% a year, settling to about 30% through 1999. In a process called "creep," slow but sure growth, it grew 0.4% a year, from 23% of personal income to 39%. "Stimulate the economy" worked from 1948 to 1988, to make government grow 35 times, with output up only 18 times. From 1959 to 1999 while it "stimulated the economy" government grew 22 times to grow national output (including government) 18 times, while the wealth-creation enterprise sector grew only 17 times. Government stimulus grows government. Cost of "essentials of life"— food, shelter and clothing increased 14 times from 1959-99 while government increased 22 times. Per-person tax growth outpaces both family income, and inflation-plus-population growth. Economic policy must consider all consequences, the far-and-not-so-obvious as well as the near-and-obvious. There is power of freedom in small government, but ours is large and growing. We must restore balance, and freedom.

Chapter 20
Life Power Tool: SMALLER GOVERNMENT!

Smaller Government
A Goal Worth Adopting

Government grows through creep—slow but sure change, to "solve" societal problems and enforce public policy, but good politics and bad economics produce poor results. With no "bottom line" to control government spending, government is out of control. We need to limit its funds to foster better management and restraint, to maintain the delicate balance between government and enterprise. Government growth began with 1929 depression-spawned Keynesian economics, "demand management," to stimulate economic growth. Only Part One was used, deficit-spend to "prime the pump" in bad times. Parts Two, a government surplus in good times, and Three, a long-run balanced budget, little or no debt, were ignored with these

1999 conditions: Continuing deficits since 1969 have added $5 trillion to public debt, with 1992's highest deficit ever, $290 billion (more accurate, operating fund deficit, $340 billion). Four tax-getters are paycheck tax withholding, hidden taxes, a nation of producers and progressive taxation. Income taxes began in 1913 at 1% of income over $180,000 (1998) for a family of four, affecting 0.4% of the people in 1916. Today's average tax level is 14.5% of income for 130 million filers. A taxpaying family can actually follow all IRS guidelines, end up with too little withheld, pay the tax, penalty, interest and fill out form 2210 for last year, BUT, to April 15th, had hundreds of dollars withheld yet truly *owe no taxes* "this year." An estimate of total taxes actually paid is two times total federal income tax, plus half that total again for state-and-local taxes. 1985's $212 billion deficit and $2.1 trillion debt stole a house and a car from the 1985 graduate in future taxes. Since 1975 more people work harder for less money, less leisure time. Why? Government and taxes grew. So did "married working mothers," anti-social behavior, incidence of property and violent personal crime. Another analysis shows while per-capita federal taxation increased 7 times from 1800-1900; from 1900-1997, it rocketed 49 times! Government has grown to be too much, too large and too powerful. We seek a better balance of smaller government. "Producers": Produce freedom.

Chapter 21
Life Power Tool: BALANCED GOVERNMENT!

Government's Role

A Model for Understanding-Size, Growth, Problems, Promise

Our national mind set is that more government is better. True long ago, before government size was 10% of output (GDP), it is still okay from about 10% to 17%. Above 17% or so it increasingly causes damage. We are at 30%, an encouraging drop from 1990's 33%. In 1900 government was 8% of the economy, the majority, state 5%, with federal 3%. Through Keynesian economics and the Full Employment Act of 1946 government grew to 1950's 23%, then increased to 35% in 1982. "Total Misery" (inflation, unemployment, and interest rates) jumped, "prosperity" (productivity and real output) dropped. "GOAL 25-25: The Two Percent Solution," that limits government spending growth to 2% (federal tax growth to 3%), can in 13 years get all-government back to 25% of the economy, all-taxes to 25% of income, and liquidate 1999's $3,633 billion national debt owned by the public. Taxpayer money going to government directly and indirectly is over two-thirds of median family income. Government cost is 46% of per-capita compensation spent thus: 5% National/International/Internal Security (including national defense), 10% Government Services, 23% Social Services, 8% other. The long-term damage from resulting economic deprivation and/or desperation is fragmented families, higher crime and decaying social structure. A professional politician's diagram of government showed increasing, then decreasing "positive climate" as government grew from zero to 100%. We seek to increase "positive climate," some with less government, thinking it to be the problem, others with more government, thinking it to be the solution. By these analyses our assignment is not to cut or freeze government but in three words, *slow government growth,* e.g., GOAL 25-25: The Two Percent Solution, back to 25% government, 25% taxes. Now that we better understand the role of government, and balance in the American enterprise economy, what will we do with that knowledge?

Chapter 22
Life Power Tool: PERSONAL FINANCIAL CLOUT!

Lifetime Financial Planning

For Personal Security and Financial Independence

"Pay yourself first" is the secret to personal security and financial independence. Taxes take over half of our earnings. That leaves the rest to spend, save and invest. Your first assignment is to preserve the rest, your greater assignment, to reduce the over-half taxes. We are programmed by television to spend and consume. Be different. Save and make your money work hard. Save now. Buy later. Short-range taxes are not controllable. Debt is. Know tax laws. Control debt. Buying is prompted by the AIDA sales formula: Attention, Interest, Desire, Action. Know that. Resist buying. What is the real price of anything? It's negotiable. Negotiate. Buy a new car now and three years later, you are back in debt buying another. Or save for three years, then buy with cash. Since a new car purchase costs out-of-pocket $10 a day ($15 with depreciation), each day you don't buy a new car saves you $10! Compute your loan obligations and savings with your "Bizwhiz" financial calculator: present and future value of money, interest, periods, payments. A 1988 bank advertisement said it cost $232,000 to raise a child, $45,000 for his or her college, plus $415,000 for your retirement; a 1998 study indicated over $1.45 million including almost $1 million foregone wages of a parent. Launch your life's financial security with Lifetime Financial Planning (LFP). Plan your retirement based on your present age and earnings, selected retirement age and income, and actuarial age at death. Prepare for old age and retirement. Three important personal goals: how much to earn, how much to save, how much to end up with. Start now with Bizwhiz and knowledge (four case histories show how). Don't be fooled by the "delusion of affluence" where seemingly large life savings permit reduced savings discipline. Learn your net worth, cash flow; prepare and manage a budget. Perform your Lifetime Financial Plan. Control finances for life for P-e-a-c-e--o-f--M-i-n-d.

Chapter 23
Life Power Tools: PERSONAL WELLNESS!

The Triangle + Approach to Personal Wellness

Diet, Exercise, Relaxation, Plus!

Hardy spirits and tough minds inhabit sound bodies. The triangle of life fitness is diet, exercise and relaxation, plus. Fitness is toughness. Know the uncontrollables: heredity, age, sex, race. Then control the controllables: diet, exercise, relaxation, weight and blood pressure. Don't smoke. A good diet involves common sense nutrition and foods. Control the fat, calories and cholesterol intake to balance your diet. Excess fat can clog arteries, cause myocardial infarction (blockage) and coronary thrombosis (heart attack), of which in half the onsets, the first symptom is death. Strokes block blood from going to the brain causing paralysis and/or loss of faculties. High blood pressure—hypertension, "the silent killer" causes or complicates health problems. If overweight, reduce weight gradually by 3,500 calories (one pound) per week. Heart-rated fitness combines pulse rate and aerobic exercise—rhythmic, repetitive, dynamic motions such as walking, swimming, cycling, 3-4 days a week, 20-30 minutes a day. A low, then higher target pulse rate is adopted through carefully selected exercises of the right frequency, duration, type and intensity. Design and commit to a moderate, lifelong exercise program. Equally important, learn to relax through visualization, self-talk. Show restraint from preventable life dangers such as smoking, chewing tobacco, drugs, alcohol and substance abuse. Love your back and use your seatbelts. Develop a lifelong love of learning (books, recorded tapes, thinking, sharing thoughts and ideas) studying history, philosophy, literature, religion, as well as the Freedom Documents. Establish priorities. Live a rich, robust life through total personal wellness: Diet, exercise, relaxation, plus ... .

Chapter 24
Life Power Tool: POWER OF ONE MORE!

Multiply Your
Power of One

To the Power of ONE More

One person makes a big difference. Involve another person to make a bigger difference. The *Power of ONE* starts with you, spreads to others and multiplies. In a constitutional republic, majority rule under law, by representation, is predicated on an informed, involved electorate. We get more involved, then involve others through MULTIPLICATION with the Involvement Process: Be *aware* (tuned in), interested (curious), *informed* (read, think, discuss) and *concerned* (be human). Our ensuing feelings turn into *involvement,* then *action.* Actions can include: running for public office, joining charitable, service and philanthropic groups, citizen involvement in local government, education, political party activity, voting and interim political dialogue with elected leaders. You can offer "a half hour a day to the USA," or at least an hour a week to citizen activities. You really have only half the job, making others *aware, interested, informed.* It is theirs to get *concerned, involved* and *active.* To stimulate minds do not give opinions or conclusions. Ask questions, present evidence, and create doubt. The motivators for involvement are the GREATs: a great love, hate, fear, anger, ambition, greed, passion, a Big Dream, a Great Vision. Put the GREATs to work. Serve big, please big, give big, share big and you will get back big and grow big. Harness the power of ideas, the power of information. The KIMAX revelation says, "You count. You matter. You make a difference." The KIMAX success formula stands for Knowledge (get it), Information (use it), Motivation, (develop it), Action (take it), excellence (be it). Someone left us a better world. Can we do less for those who follow?

Chapter 25
Life Power Tool: POWER OF MANY MORE!

Multiply Your
Power of One More

To Powers of Many More

Changing the world one person at a time adds people not proportionally but geometrically. The Change Process—"telegraph your punches"— prepares people for change: Tell them what is going on and why, get their good ideas and support; communicate progress regularly, directly. MASO— "Multiply And So On"—gets others involved. Go on your journey of change and take them with you. Use the two greatest tools against tyranny, the computer and the copier, to efficiently share information using the "6 Be's": Be aware, interested, informed, concerned, involved, active. Use mail, email, telephone and fax to get people together—family, friends, neighbors, coworkers, citizens—voters and taxpayers. The citizen fun has just begun. Use the 4-part "What-Formula" for communicating to newspapers and public officials: What? (what's wrong), So What? (why), Now What? (the solution), and What Next? (share with others). Be accurate, brief, courteous and respectful. Give evidence and information, not opinions or conclusions; ask questions. Form your "Great American FAN (Freedom Action Network) Club." Develop an action plan that says what to do and how to do it. Read newspapers, contact officials, state your ideas. We can constitutionally "throw the rascals out" with an election of one-third the Senate and a whole new House of Representatives every two years, President every four years. If Congress misbehaves, V-O-T-I—Vote Out the Incumbents. Adopt, support and boost GOAL 25-25: The Two Percent Solution, to limit federal and state-and-local government spending growth to 2%; to limit federal tax growth to 3%; in 13 years, to achieve 25% each for government size of output and tax size of income, and liquidate national debt held by the public; all in 13 years. Use group change techniques and networks of concerned people to multiply your *Power of ONE* to the Powers of Many. Put your network to work, keep your network working, to build "that which is invincible—The Power of ONE."

Chapter 26
Life Power Tool: TOTAL POWER OF YOU!

The Joy Has Been the Journey

To TOTAL Power of YOU in America!

As "Freedom Builders Building Freedom Builders," we meditate, pray, observe silence and dream big, for power to fight the good fight for freedom. The *Power of ONE* believes and lives the creed: "I am ONE. I am only ONE. But I will do, what ONE can do." New knowledge, information and understanding make you a *TOTAL Power of ONE*. Never again say "impossible" with the magic hero numbers 4-2-48-17 which describe the days, hours, minutes and seconds required for *legless* Bob Wieland to *run* the over-26 miles New York marathon, November, 1986. Finishing last, 19,413th he said, "Success is ... where you finish and I finished ... the joy has been the journey," teaching us that it is possible to start, finish and enjoy the journey of life. Ill-fated Challenger astronaut, teacher-in space Christa McAuliffe, whose motto was, "I touch the future; I teach," claimed "to be nothing more than an ordinary person on an extraordinary mission." Define and describe your America on the screen of life, with slides such as Gettysburg, Iwo Jima, the Statue of Liberty, Space Shuttle, Utah Beach landing, and the pencilled note on the Vietnam War memorial wall that said, "Thank you. You gave the highest gift." We do not have to give our lives or our blood, yet, but can give some sweat to the cause of freedom. Are not ballots infinitely better than bullets? The young man pleads "... give us a chance to be a future generation." You, *Power of ONE* traveled the journey. You have heard the Call to Action, received the Call to Leadership. You have the power. What will you do with it? You count. You matter. You make a difference. You are a *TOTAL Power of ONE* in America.

Chapter 26

THE JOY HAS BEEN THE JOURNEY
To TOTAL Power of YOU in America!

Tiananmen Square, the Berlin Wall and a Student's Visit to Russia

They were almost euphoric with the prospect of freedom. The Chinese in Beijing's Tiananmen Square cheered democratic reform in their new found dream of more freedom and power to the people. The dream turned into a nightmare. Soldiers and tanks moved in, fired on the unarmed, defenseless people, and crushed the celebration of freedom. Totalitarianism's iron fist once again gripped China.

Indelibly etched on the television screen of my mind is the lone Chinese student standing in front of a tank, stopping an armored column of tanks. He made a statement about freedom with his body and his being, climbed up onto the tank to talk to its soldiers, then faded into the dispersing crowds.

The loathsome Berlin wall began to tumble in late-1989 after 28 years of citizen isolation and repression. A city and country divided since World War II began exploring a new era of freedom, power and governance.

Various European countries so long satellites of the Soviet Union are experiencing the benefits and costs of newfound freedom. Learn more of the history and struggles for freedom, of Hungary, Czechoslovakia, Romania, Poland and others.

What will happen as the rest of the world begins to see the many advantages and blessings of freedom, and unleashes the freedom-craving energies of their people? What will happen to America if we continue to worship at the altar of big government, with higher taxes and more erosion and restriction of our freedoms?

Jennifer Eberhardt, a student from Denver's Cherry Creek High School, and her mother, Vicky, were part of the Meistersinger mixed-choir tour of the Iron Curtain countries in 1989. They later described their experiences and impressions to a group of business people in the summer of 1989. The trip into Soviet Russia through her European Satellite countries made some profound impacts about freedom on the young woman and her mother. An emotional high came in the young woman's concluding remarks:

> I used to say "God bless America," but we are already blessed. Having seen these other countries with so little freedom, I now say, "God save America."

Keeping the Batteries of Freedom Charged: Motivation and Inspiration

This one is for you, *Power of ONE*. We near the end of your "new beginning" to become a *TOTAL Power of ONE in America*. You are almost there.

It took awhile to get here and it was worth it. You have developed a new kinship with others, new possibilities and a new alliance for freedom and the future, through knowledge, information and understanding. You have learned a great deal of how to use what you know, and how to share with those who will help and carry on.

We are "Freedom Builders Building Freedom Builders." Working together, we are stronger, smarter, mightier.

Sometimes, though, things look less than positive, less than possible, even discouraging. Is it all worth it? Will it really make a difference? Can I really make a difference? Of course we know the answers are yes, yes, yes. But during those moments, doubt creeps in. Our thoughts fool us, divert our energies from what we are doing and can do, to what "can't be done."

We need special insights and reminders, appropriate inspiration to carry on and keep going. Some put it, "Keep on, keepin' on." Others say, "Keep on a-truckin'." We want to forge ahead, to channel our energy and focus our efforts for continuing positive possibilities.

Or, we are not discouraged. In fact, we are "ready, willing and able." We want a boost. We need a burst of personal power. We seek a "critical mass" of human fusion energy for a burst of freedom fission. The power of freedom permeates the present and the future and we vow now to see that it gets there.

We can cogitate, meditate or observe silence while we recharge. We can pray. We can think larger thoughts, affirm our worth and capabilities and visualize the greatness we can accomplish or become.

We can dream big dreams. We can remind ourselves of the contribution we make to our community and society, and the long-ranging, far-reaching effects of our efforts. We can envision a better world, better because we resolutely knew we could make it so, did so, and do so. We have to have a dream in order to make that dream come true. What is your big dream?

You are really something, *Power of ONE.* You are now a *TOTAL Power of ONE.* Let us share some ideas, quotes and observations that may prove meaningful and inspirational as well. Following those, there is room to add your own thoughts and impressions.

Hero Numbers 4-2-48-17:
No More "It Can't Be Done" or "I Can't Do It"

Whenever you feel you cannot do something or something cannot be done, remember the magic hero numbers of total possibility:

$$4 - 2 - 48 - 17$$

These are, respectively, days, hours, minutes and seconds. For what? For a person who ran the New York Marathon—26 miles, 385 yards—in 4 days, 2 hours, 48 minutes and 17 seconds, ending November 6, 1986[1]. It was the slowest time in New York Marathon history—and probably the most important.

Why, you ask? This race was "run" by a man who *has no legs!* Vietnam veteran Bob Wieland 17 years before had his legs blown off by a land mine. The 40-year-old "ran" in a sitting position using weight-developed arms like crutches to lift his body and swing it forward. He lands on a 15-pound "saddle" and repeats the motion. His clenched fists are covered with pads that he calls "Size-1 running shoes." Wieland was the 19,413th and final finisher, the first to run a marathon with his arms instead of his legs.

He even "walked" that way clear across America. It took Wieland 3 ½ years to "walk" from Los Angeles to Washington DC. He counted the 4,900,016 steps required to cover the 3,000 miles, which he said proved his favorite Bible verse, Luke 1:37, "For with God, nothing shall be impossible."

At the end of the race he said:

> Success is not based on where you start.
> It's where you finish, and I finished.
> The first step was the most difficult.
> After that we were on our way home.
> The joy has been the journey.

There are a few things we TABs (temporarily able-bodied) can get from this.

First, what appears to be impossible, isn't. What would be more impossible than a man with no legs running a marathon? That is why Wieland did it. Though

1. "And on the fifth day, he finished the race," *Rocky Mountain News. 11/7/86.* p 94

it was "impossible," he did it anyway. What is impossible to you, that "4-2-48-17" cannot inspire you to do anyway? Practically nothing at all.

Second, it is important to START. "The first step," he said, "was the most difficult." You will never do or finish anything unless you learn how important it is to start. Start. "Once begun, half is done."

Third, finish what you start. "Success is not based on where you start. It is where you finish, and I finished." So start, then finish.

Fourth, enjoy the whole thing, start, doing and finish. "The joy has been the journey." Life is a journey, not a destination. Enjoy today, now, the present. It is really all you have. Make the most of it. Be conscious of it. Revere it. *LIVE IT!* The here and the now are all we have, all there is, all we are. And it is passing away, perishing, fleeting, vanishing.

I know the magic. I got to meet Bob Weiland. Now you know the magic of doing the impossible: 4 - 2 - 48 - 17.

Note your thoughts, *Power of ONE:* _____

_____

_____

An Ordinary Person on an Extraordinary Mission: Touch the Future

Who can forget the Challenger space shuttle tragedy of Tuesday, January 28, 1986? There were seven astronauts, America's brightest and best: five men, commander Francis "Dick" Scobee, co-pilot Michael J. Smith, Ronald McNair, mission specialist Ellison Onizuka, satellite engineer, Gregory Jarvis; and two women, Judith Resnik and the first citizen, teacher-in-space, Christa McAuliffe, from Concord, New Hampshire.

Robert T. Hohler, journalist for the *Concord Monitor,* reports Christa McAuliffe, "asked to be nothing more than an ordinary person on an extraordinary mission."

An ordinary person on an extraordinary mission? Isn't that what we all are, *Power of ONE? YOU* are an ordinary person on an extraordinary mission, a mission of freedom, of growth, of contribution, of making a powerful, positive, lasting difference, of creating a magnificent life!

McAuliffe's two lesson plans were never taught from space. But they had won her her place in space. "She had planned to talk about the connections among space, science and ordinary life, the importance of being good citizens and the joy of serving," according to Ann McFeatters[2].

Hohler[3] described how McAuliffe became the finalist out of over 11,000 applicants. An American history, law and economics teacher, she worked

2. Ann McFeatters, "Teacher shed tears of joy when chosen for shuttle program," *Rocky Mountain News,* Space Shuttle Extra, 1/28/86.

3. Hohler, Robert T., "I Touch the Future ... ," *Reader's Digest,* June 1987, pp 78-85

hard to make her subjects come alive in the classroom. "She sent her students into the community to interview veterans about World War II and Vietnam and senior citizens about the Great Depression. She had adopted as her motto: 'I Touch the Future; I Teach.'"

While her qualifying interview was videotaped she described her philosophy of living, "Well, it's to get as much out of life as possible ... to enjoy life and certainly to involve other people in that enjoyment, but also to be a participant ... "

Power of ONE, you teach. You touch the future. You share the joy of serving. You help create a better future. You are an ordinary person. But you are a special ordinary person. You are on an extraordinary mission. You will get as much out of life as possible, and a whole lot is possible. You are enjoying life and involving other people as participants as well as spectators.

McAuliffe had a special poem in her possession on Challenger. It was "High Flight" by John Gillespie Magee, Jr., a young volunteer with the Royal Canadian Air Force who had died over Britain in 1941. It began and ended:

> Oh, I have slipped the surly bonds of earth ... And, while with silent, lifting mind I've trod the high, untrespassed sanctity of space, Put out my hand, and touched the face of God.

Power of ONE, slip your surly bonds, lift your mind high, put out your hand ... and touch the face of God.

We are all ordinary human beings on an extraordinary mission. Our joy is our journey, the preservation of freedom in America, and showing that and how one person, a *Power of ONE* person, can make a powerful, positive, lasting difference.

Note your thoughts, *Power of ONE:* _____
_____
_____

The Legend of the Thornbird:
One Superlative Song, Existence the Price

The Thornbirds
There is a legend about a bird which sings just once in its life,
More sweetly than any other creature on the face of the earth.
From the moment it leaves the nest it searches for a thorn tree,
      And does not rest until it has found one.
Then, singing among the savage branches,
      It impales itself upon the longest, sharpest spine.
And dying, it rises above its own agony
      To outcarol the lark and the nightingale.
One superlative song, existence the price.

But the whole world stills to listen,
And God in His heaven smiles.
For the best is only bought at the cost of great pain
Or so says the legend.
—from *The Thornbirds*[4] by Colleen McCullough

How much more are we, *Power of ONE,* than the thornbird? We need not worry about singing just once. We sing the song of life all day every day. We sing it with our mouths, our hearts, our minds, our spirits. We need not search for a thorn tree, but the tree of knowledge and the tree of life. We are here, now, and we have life. Let us use it, all of it, to build a better world by building a better you.

Our symphony of life is a bright, happy song, one filled with harmony and a chorus of cheerful voices. We outcarol the songbirds with a superlative song, but exist to sing it again, day after day. If we do the job we are capable of doing, the whole world will "still to listen;" God will smile in His heaven.

We, humankind, sing more sweetly than any other creature on the face of the earth. We are fashioned by God in the image of God. We can rise above and beyond, to create, to change, to improve, to make better, for now and for the future. We are thornbirds, *Power of ONE,* who can and do make a difference. We understand. We know. We are aware. We are concerned. We become involved. We act. *We make a difference.* And that is why we are different.

Let us dedicate ourselves to the legend of "The Thornbird," and sing our superlative song, share it with others, and help them to join a chorus of music to act, achieve and make a difference.

Note your thoughts, *Power of ONE:* _____
_____
_____

America's Finest, In Uniform: The Ultimate Price

To conclude my speeches on a "high" I emphasize a proposed "Fanfare to the Common Person." I tell each member in my audience what a singularly important individual he or she is. I elaborate it is really not someone who is common, but someone who is very uncommon, one who knows and cares and is willing to get involved, to take a stand, to be active, to be different, to make a difference.

It is you *Powers of ONE* who will make the marvelous difference now and in the future.

Once after giving my speech, "The Power of ONE in Free Enterprise" to my local Arvada, Colorado, Chamber of Commerce, a good friend congratulated me at the podium, suggesting I present a slide program with

4. McCullough, Colleen, *The Thornbirds,* Avon, New York: 1978

the musical ending. I gave that a lot of thought. As a semi-professional photographer I have perhaps 12,000 slides from which to choose. I could pick out my favorites and say "That is America," but it would be my America. It would not be *your* America, or *their* America. That is the America that counts.

I would include the Statue of Liberty, the Golden Gate Bridge and Grand Canyon; the first human walking on the moon, July, 1969, American Neil Armstrong; the Lincoln Memorial and the Empire State Building. I would include the cemeteries of the centuries in America's fight for freedom— Gettysburg, Arlington and the Vietnam black marble memorial. There would be space for the Iwo Jima memorial, with five marines planting the flag atop Mount Surabachi, and at Pearl Harbor, Hawaii, the brave sailors of the battleship *Arizona,* still just under the ocean surface.

One thing I would have to include with distant memories, not slides, would be the Utah Beach Landing in France during the Normandy invasion which was the beginning of the end of World War II. Those young soldiers called "GI's" were nervously waiting in the landing barges for the signal to go ashore. It was given, the entire front end of the LSTs hinged forward and the soldiers ran into the water carrying thirty or forty pounds of weapons, ammunition and personal gear. They knew the odds were against them. Over half of them died face down in the water in a pool of their own blood, never to reach shore, never again to see their homes and families.

Why did they die face down in the water in a pool of their own blood? As Abraham Lincoln said in his Gettysburg Address, "they gave their last full measure of devotion."

They died for freedom and the future of freedom. They died so that you and I might live free. Did they die for nothing? What do we do to protect freedom? What measure of anything, much less than their "last full measure of devotion" have we given, or do we give?

When I feel I have done enough, done all I can do, all that can reasonably be expected of me, *I think again!* What have others done? What did they give? Then I ask, "what more can I do?" The answer is "a lot more." I have only begun to do my part. And so have you.

The Misunderstood, Divisive, Vietnam War: A Tribute to Freedom

Shortly after it was opened to the public I was privileged to visit the Vietnam Memorial in December, 1985 in Washington, DC. I had to think back.

While the Vietnam conflict intensified, as a recently-graduated chemical engineer, I had gotten involved in the research, development and production of the *Minuteman* and *Polaris* missiles. Had I been called, I would have gone, and perhaps been killed. So I have a great deal of respect, awe, even reverence for the half-million who served there, and the over 55,000 who died there.

At the memorial all those years of frustration and wondering came back in an overpowering sweep of emotion. Dread, love, hate, disgust, reverence, fear, pride, anger, all drenched my mind and heart. "Who did I know who died in Vietnam?" came a voice in my mind. It queried back "Terry Hicks?" Terry Hicks was my freshman year counselor at Colorado University's Baker Dormitory. He was a helpful, good-natured part of my dorm activities whom I had later heard was killed in Vietnam. I went to the mail order catalog-sized "fat-book" that contained all the names. There it was, black marble slab 46, line 18. I went to that panel and found the name, Terrin Dinsmore Hicks. My dorm counselor had died for the cause of freedom in a faraway land and confusing war. I was personally touched by that war, and deeply saddened.

Then I began to look around at others. There was a child with a piece of paper over a name, lightly brushing a pencil to bring out the marble impressions on paper, saying sadly, "My Dad." Another man knelt with his finger on a name, sobbing uncontrollably while a woman helplessly held her hand on his shoulder trying to comfort him.

Years later I thought I had forgotten the emotion I had experienced that day, but it all came back. A replica of the Vietnam Memorial visited Loveland, Colorado the same time Dottie and I were taking our daughter Tami back to Colorado State University in Fort Collins. We stopped to visit the traveling model, experiencing the same strong emotions, then with more people, even stronger emotions.

I looked up Terry's name again and re-visited slab 46, line 18. His name and memory were still there. I said to Dottie and Tami, "Before we leave, let's walk the whole wall and be with the people." We began to read the notes placed on the grass at the foot of the wall. One had a can of beer in a plastic bag with the note, "Here's the beer we never got to have."

Another said, "I never really knew you but have heard so much about you I think I do know you. Signed, your son, Bobby."

Another said, "We really gave them hell on that hill, didn't we? Your buddy."

The last note I could bear to read said, "Thank you. You gave the highest gift."

Wow! The miracle of freedom sometimes costs an incalculable price.

That "highest gift" was the gift of life. The light went out in exchange for something as great as the gift of life, freedom. The same thoughts and emotions began again. Then the questions. Am I doing my part? Are we losing it? Did they die in vain? What should I do or what can I be doing to in some way repay them for their sacrifice, to do my share for future others to enjoy freedom?

Note your thoughts, *Power of ONE:* _____

_____

_____

The Pride and the Passion:
Miguel Pleads, the People Respond, Avila Regained.

In the movie, "The Pride and the Passion," the peasant fighter Miguel was determined to regain Avila on the plains of Spain, from the French. Their humble peasant army's only hope was a huge cannon that could tumble the walls of the fortress. In going downhill, the mighty gun got away and was hopelessly mired in a river of mud. Miguel went to the nearest town, to the bullring. The bullfight stopped. A silence fell over the crowd. Miguel went to the middle of the ring.

Miguel explained the plight of the resistance, the sunken cannon and it, the only way to win back the fort of Avila. He pleaded for help: "I don't want your life. I don't even want your blood. I only want your sweat." He got it. They helped. The cannon was rescued from the mud, and Avila, from the French, with much bloodshed and sacrifice, including the life of Miguel who gave much more than blood or sweat to free his people from tyranny.

Power of ONE, who is "the common man," the common person, the uncommon person, the extraordinary person? It is you. You deserve a fanfare every minute of every day for all you do. You know you won't get it, you know why, and know that is not what is important anyway. What is important is to do the right thing because it is right and you are right.

What does your America look like? What slides will you project onto your screen? Will you have freedom represented and will fighting to preserve and strengthen freedom be a part of your presentation?

What heroism can you relate for the struggle for freedom? What is your "Normandy Invasion"?

Fortunately we are not often called on to give even our sweat, much less our blood or our lives for freedom. Or is it *unfortunately?* Should we be more involved and giving, even sacrificing, so that we appreciate even more what was made available to us and the terribly high price that was paid for it?

Shall we never forget so many who "gave the highest gift," and resolve to make available "the second highest gift," ourselves—our time, energy, devotion, talent, resources, even sacrifice for an idea bigger than life called freedom?

Shall we understand that by giving our sweat, sometimes even our blood, we may help prevent ourselves and others having to give up life and liberty for these most precious of gifts? What is it truly worth to keep ourselves and our people free from tyranny and oppression?

Are not ballots infinitely better than bullets?

This is heavy stuff but well worth thinking about and caring about.

Note your thoughts, *Power of ONE:* _____

_____

_____

Something to Believe In:
People, Rights, Responsibility, God, Truth, Love

John D. Rockefeller, Sr. captured the essence of a greater set of beliefs in "I Believe"[5]:

I Believe

I believe in the supreme worth of the individual
   and in his right to life, liberty, and the pursuit of happiness.

I believe that every right implies a responsibility;
   every opportunity, an obligation; every possession, a duty.

I believe that the law was made for man and not man for the law;
   that government is the servant of the people and not their master.

I believe in the dignity of labor, whether with head or hand;
   that the world owes no man a living but that it owes every man
   an opportunity to make a living.

I believe that thrift is essential to well-ordered living,
   that economy is a prime requisite of a sound financial structure,
   whether in government, business, or personal affairs.

I believe that truth and justice are fundamental
   to an enduring social order.

I believe in the sacredness of a promise, that a man's word
   should be as good as his bond; that character—not wealth
   or power or position—is of supreme worth.

I believe that the rendering of useful service is the common duty
   of mankind and that only in the purifying fire of sacrifice
   is the dross of selfishness consumed and the greatness of
   the human soul set free.

I believe in an all-wise and all-loving God, named by whatever
   name, and that the individual's highest fulfillment, greatest
   happiness, and widest usefulness are to be found in living in
   harmony with His will.

I believe that love is the greatest thing in the world;
   that it alone can overcome hate;
   that right can and will triumph over might.
                                        —John D. Rockefeller, Sr.

5. Wallis, Charles L., Editor, *The Treasure Chest,* Harper and Row, New York: 1965, p 76

Note your thoughts, *Power of ONE:* _____

_____

_____

A Creed to be Uncommon, Not Common

My Creed[6]

I do not choose to be a common man.

It is my right to be uncommon—if I can.

I seek opportunity—not security. I do not wish to be a kept citizen,
   humbled and dulled by having the state look after me.

I want to take the calculated risk; to dream and to build,
   to fail and to succeed.

I refuse to barter incentive for a dole. I prefer the challenges
   of life to the guaranteed existence; the thrill of fulfillment
   to the stale calm of utopia.

I will not trade freedom for beneficence nor my dignity for a
   handout. I will never cower before any master
   nor bend to any threat.

It is my heritage to stand erect, proud and unafraid;
   to think and act for myself, enjoy the benefit of my creations
   and to face the world boldly and say, this I have done.

All this is what it means to be an American.

—Dean Alfange

Note your thoughts, *Power of ONE:* _____

_____

_____

A 17-Year-Old Speaks Out: Flourish or Perish

An articulate, concerned young man published his statement under the
title "Flourish or Perish." Thomas F. Klein[7] shared some serious thoughts
from a world that had been pretty good to him, but the future had him
worried. He knew a perfect Earth could not be achieved, at least by one
generation. He presented his case to the powers that be:

6. Herbert V. Prochnow, *New Guide for Toastmasters and Speakers,* Prentice-Hall, New
Jersey, 1956, p 185

7. Klein, Thomas F., 'Flourish or Perish," U.S. *News and World Report, 5/5/86,* p 75

What I do ask of those who run our nation is simply to think of coming generations when you make your decisions. Short-term legislative actions don't cure problems—only alleviate them just long enough so that they will no longer bother the politicians involved.

I ask that you think not only selfishly of the benefits for your generation. Think of me, us, those who will inherit your government, your nation, your world. Respect us as if we were voters of today. Only then will your actions take on the long-term perspective that will meet not only your needs but the needs of future generations. Only in that way will you give us a chance to be a future generation.

It is very serious when young people are thinking in terms of getting a mere "chance to be a future generation." They know what is going on, and it is not good. Or is it?

Note your thoughts, *Power of ONE:* _____
_____
_____

Another 17-Year-Old: A Pupil's Hope

Values, "Law of the Harvest," vision and dreams were keys to America's initial success, according to student William "Scott" Baker[8]:

It was the values of the people that brought this nation into existence and established her on a solid foundation. It was in that atmosphere and with those values that a few God-fearing men worked so diligently to outline the Constitution of the United States. It will be those same values that will enable us to keep on building: to keep on making a stronger country. A Frenchman who was in our country during those early years said this: "America is great, because America is good. When America ceases to be good, America will cease to be great."

With the qualities of honesty, respect, diligence, responsibility, mercy, purity, a desire for peace, and a love and fear of God, we will dream.

With the "Law of the Harvest": "What you plant you grow; what you sow you reap." We must plant our dream of a stronger, better America into the hearts of every individual in this country. And then we must be willing to do something about it. It is then that the United States will flourish like never before

8. Baker William "Scott," "A Pupil's Hope," *Colorado Transcript, 4/22/82,* Winning Speech, 1982 Veterans of Foreign Wars Voice of Democracy National Scholarships Awards Competition

What better example do we have than the signers of the Declaration of Independence? They had a vision—a dream so strong that when it came to great personal risk, they counted the cost and supported it anyway. Dreams will lift this nation. Dreams that come from people of character and integrity. With people who remember the values we started with, we can build America. I believe that.

Power of One, do you believe that?

Note your thoughts, *Power of ONE:* _____

_____

_____

America: I Love You, a Song, a Prayer and a Pledge

Sometimes, someone puts down just the right thoughts on paper. They say what should be said, in the way it should be said. Here is how Barbara Barnes[9] phrased her song without notes:

A Song to America

Because I can freely go to the Church of my choice, I love you.

Because I have free access to your newspapers, I love you.

Because I can freely criticize you, I love you.

Because I can freely gather with my friends, I love you.

Because I can sit in my home surrounded by my family without fear that the police are going to enter my home without a warrant as they did in Germany in the 30s and interrupt my peace, I love you.

Because God made thee mine America, I will cherish you always. I will teach my children of your greatness and will do my share in keeping you great. Thank you for the Constitution which safeguards my freedom. I pray that in this time of social upheaval, balancing the budget, and atomic war fear I will have the courage and strength to do what is required of me, for without you to serve in the spirit of '76 I will become enslaved. I pray that God will keep you safe and give me the strength to serve you. I will remain indebted to you forever for the peace and freedom that you have brought me and will forever serve you in love and mercy. Your flame of liberty lights the fire of my hearth, may it forever guide me in respect of my freedom and that of my brothers. I pledge to you my love, my trust and my cooperation so that you may forever beam in the hearts of men.

9. Barbara Barnes. (Denver, CO) "A Song to America," *Colorado Statesman, 8/30/85.* p 2

That covers the Bill of Rights, mostly the First Amendment, *Power of ONE.* It better personalizes America and living in America. It also covers some of the responsibilities that go hand-in-hand with those rights, "to serve in the spirit of '76," and "forever serve you in love and mercy." It is a personal pledge to Freedom and America by a person who has given it all a great deal of thought and come to some profound conclusions.

Note your thoughts, *Power of ONE:* _____

_____

_____

Another Conclusion: Lincoln at Gettysburg, Then; You in America, Now

President Abraham Lincoln's popular "Gettysburg Address" is a concise, old-yet-new statement upon which to contemplate our own destiny, the destiny of freedom and the future of the United States of America:

Gettysburg Address

Fourscore and seven years ago our fathers brought forth on this continent, a new nation, conceived in Liberty and dedicated to the proposition that all men are created equal.

Now we are engaged in a great civil war, testing whether that nation or any nation so conceived and so dedicated, can long endure. We are met on a great battlefield of that war. We have come to dedicate a portion of that field, as the final resting-place for those who here gave their lives that that nation might live. It is altogether fitting and proper that we should do this.

But, in a larger sense, we cannot dedicate—we cannot consecrate—we cannot hallow—this ground. The brave men, living and dead, who struggled here, have consecrated it, far above our poor power to add or detract. The world will little note, nor long remember what we say here, but it can never forget what they did here. It is for us the living, rather, to be dedicated here to the unfinished work which they who fought here have thus far so nobly advanced. It is rather for us to be here dedicated to the great task remaining before us—that from these honored dead we take increased devotion to that cause for which they gave the last full measure of devotion—that we here highly resolve that these dead shall not have died in vain—that this nation, under God, shall have a new birth of freedom—and that government of the people, by the people, for the people, shall not perish from the earth.

Power of ONE, in a sense, we are a new nation. Much of our country today has been invaded by the idea that people are not responsible or capable, are unwilling or unable to take care of themselves. People need a caretaker to solve their problems, to take responsibility for their lives, to provide them a risk-free life from birth to death. That caretaker is government. No problem is too big or too personal that "Big Brother" cannot do a better job than the people who are the citizens of this country.

Yes, we are all created equal, but some are more equal than others. Some go to Washington, DC, to do good and do very well. By recognizing or creating problems and proposing government solutions funded by public money (taxes), they become rich and famous. They are able to make grandiose promises and seem to fulfill those promises using other people's money, extracted in the form of taxes, through power of government and force of law. With the money they buy votes, in the process enriching themselves while gaining power and prestige.

Through our ignorance and apathy, we allow them to take increasingly more of our money and freedoms, do bad, not good, enrich themselves while they impoverish others, and do great and lasting damage to our society, country and future. Most of these ideas are great ideas except for one thing: they don't work.

We need a new nation, like the old nation the Founding Fathers envisioned, but not in a horse-and-buggy tradition. Things change and times change, but human nature does not change. When power is concentrated in a few people, natural inherent human greed and avarice take over. There is no other way.

Our ideas make our society different. World War I really scared us. Our continent was relatively sheltered from the battles but we knew they were there because we were there. We knew how bad it was because our journalists and media brought back the faraway bad news.

The war was over and we rejoiced with the "roaring twenties" until the dream turned into a nightmare. Black Monday, October 29, 1929, the bottom fell out of the stock market. One out of four was unemployed and could not find a job.

A new economist on the scene, John Maynard Keynes, proposed a new solution, a government solution. Keynesian economics included use of deliberate and forced government spending to "prime the pump" or stimulate the economy, in bad times. These included national emergency (war), and economic hard times (depression). With printing press money "to stimulate demand," the federal government would purchase needed goods and services that had national economic value, such as roads and bridges, dams, reservoirs, etc. Further, tax cuts stimulated demand for new goods, while government ran into debt. In good times, the government was to cut spending, increase taxes and run a surplus, resulting overall in a balanced budget and no federal or public debt.

The first step was easy, the second difficult and the third impossible. We must reverse all this to become Lincoln's "new nation," that in economic terms is the old nation, limited government with self-governing people with more personal responsibility, a smaller, more fiscally responsible government, and a more vital, honest, productive enterprise economy.

A new president with both a national emergency—war, and economic hard times—depression, came on the scene and put it all into practice. It worked so well we are still doing it and still paying for it.

Today we wage "a great civil war," but it is not with guns, but ideas. It is not the blue versus the gray, but the "liberal left" versus the "conservative right" versus the balanced constitutional republican center. We need to pull right to get back to center.

The battlefield is in the minds, hearts and spirits of the people. They need to once again become citizen soldiers, participating in the political battles, holding political leaders accountable for their actions. We must advance from a *nation* back to *a people "so* conceived and so dedicated," to long endure. We do not dedicate a portion of a field, but a portion of our hearts and lives "that that nation might live." Indeed, "it is altogether fitting and proper that we do this."

It is an understatement that we cannot dedicate, consecrate, hallow or otherwise deserve all that we have or all that we are, especially when it comes to freedom. That includes the lower level of freedom we enjoy now rather than the higher level we once had and let slip away while we were "too busy."

A Call to Action

One of the things I hear most often about why people don't get involved in citizen things is "I'm too busy." If anything it has gotten worse over time. Since this book first came out I have been on over 620 radio and television talk shows. On many of them, I concluded the show with this "Call to Action":

> We are truly blessed to live in the United States of America. Our great gratitude and enthusiasm for this privilege brings forth the following positive and hopeful resolve:
>
> • Yes we are busy and have seemingly little time or energy to get involved. Sure we may have to give up a television program, a few hours of sleep a week or a meal (for the time, not the calories). We can and will prevail, and make that all-important difference.
>
> • Our greatest weakness is now our greatest strength. We have done so little for so long that if we do a little it's a lot, and if we do a lot it's a lot more. If we also get others involved we can change the course of history and get America back on track.
>
> • If we do, our children and grandchildren will never forget us. If we don't they will never forgive us.

- If we lose it, if America fails, our children and grandchildren will ask, "What were you doing when freedom died? What was so darned important in your busyness of business?"

What will your answer be?

Freedom Fighters, Freedom Builders and Consecrated Lives

Those brave freedom fighters and freedom builders, living and dead, have struggled and consecrated their lives, and now need my help, our help, your help, all the help we can muster. The world will much note and long remember what you do here and now, for freedom and for the future. We can and must dedicate ourselves to the unfinished work others fought for "and have thus far so nobly advanced." We must match devotions, us the living and here, with those, the dead and gone. Many died, "the honored dead," to give us a portion of "increased devotion" for their giving "their last full measure of devotion"—death on the battlefield. They lost every thing so that we could have something—freedom. We speak of all those who died in the cause of freedom, soldiers and citizens alike.

"We highly resolve that these dead shall not have died in vain."

Power of ONE, by all the powers of good, "this nation, under God, *shall* have a new birth of freedom." We pledge, dedicate and consecrate ourselves to this quest.

If we are to have a government *by* the people and *for* the people, it must be a government *of* the people. We are the people. We recruit others. Working together, *Power of ONE,* this Idea of Freedom—America; this Great Experiment in Freedom—the United States of America, SHALL *NOT* PERISH FROM THE EARTH!

Note your thoughts, *Power of ONE:* _____

_____

_____

A Call to Leadership

One of America's most compelling needs is for leadership. We need leaders, true leaders, that know what is going on and what to do about it, who have the integrity, morals and principle not to compromise, and the persistence, determination and courage to stay everlastingly at it and get it done. We need those with a vision, mission and purpose that they can vocalize, dramatize and actualize, those who bring the good out of everyone, getting one and all to become involved, participate and make a difference. Good leaders mobilize good followers for good causes.

This is your Call to Leadership, especially you, Power of ONE, to use and exert your power for the greater good of this country and its inevitably brighter future. We are talking about setting a new Ship to sail—Your LeaderShip. But it is not just any old leadership. It is a new, special leadership that exemplifies the Power of ONE and Your Power of ONE. It is so important that it has three names:

Championship   Citizenship   Leadership

What America and her future need so desperately is YOU and your Leadership. You can exude Champion Citizenship and Champion Leadership, to be a worthy, outstanding example of Championship Citizenship Leadership. You can be if you want to be and know that you need to be. Not only is it simple and fun, it is easy, CITIZENSHIP made as easy as one-two:

1) To KNOW, and 2) To SHARE

KNOW   1) What is going on, and 2) What to do about it.
SHARE   1) Information,   and 2) Concern

Your caring and sharing, and inspiring and leading others, work very hard for America's brighter future.

Congratulations! You are a TOTAL Power of ONE in America! You Made It!

You have all it takes to make a difference—knowledge, information and understanding—and the know-how to be a powerful person and citizen.

Power of ONE, I "Power of ONE" *DOUBLE DARE you* to accept this freedom assignment as a "Power of ONE" Challenge. Do you accept this Power Dare? Will you incorporate the Power Challenge into your life? Will you accomplish the Power Deed?

You have got it all, *Power of ONE.* The future of freedom and America is up to you. It is in good hands. The power is with you. Go for it. Make it happen! We end where we started:

You count!
You matter!
You make a difference!
You are really something!
You are an American!
* * * You are a TOTAL Power of ONE! * * *
* * * A TOTAL POWER OF ONE IN AMERICA! * * *

God bless America. God save America.

Questions for Review

1. Explain "We are 'Freedom Builders Building Freedom Builders.'"

2. What is the difference between a *Power of ONE* and a *TOTAL Power of ONE?*

3. What are the "magic hero numbers" and what makes them so? Why do they help you never say again "It cannot be done," or "I cannot do it"?

4. What does legless runner Bob Wieland say success is based on? Which step is the most difficult? Is the joy the journey or the destination? Why? What four things can we TABs (temporarily able bodied) get out of the story of 4-2-48-17?

5. Christa McAuliffe, whose motto was "I touch the future; I teach," asked "to be nothing more than an ordinary person on an extraordinary mission." How does that relate to being a *TOTAL Power of ONE?* McAuliffe carried with her in the ill-fated Challenger space shuttle, a copy of "High Flight" by John Gillespie Magee, Jr., about flight. What did it mean, "while with silent, lifting mind I've trod the high, untrespassed sanctity of space, put out my hand, and touched the face of God"?

6. How is a *Power of ONE* like a thornbird? Unlike a thornbird?

7. What color slides would be included in your program to describe your America? What views would you include of America's armed forces and defenders of freedom?

8. Discuss how Miguel's plea, "I don't want your life. I don't even want your blood. I only want your sweat ... " fits in with the *Power of ONE* philosophy for living. Discuss "Are not ballots infinitely better than bullets"?

9. What do our young people have to look forward to in the future of America? What are their dreams? Their fears? How does Abraham Lincoln's "Gettysburg Address" fit the America of today? Where is the battle? It is being fought not with guns and bullets but with what? What is the Power of ONE's Call to Action and Call to Leadership?

10. What is the *Power of ONE?* Who has it in America? What is *TOTAL Power of ONE?* Why does it take "knowledge, information and understanding" to become one? Why must one go beyond thinking and caring to involvement and action to be a *TOTAL Power of ONE?* Are you one?

Yes, we did produce a near perfect Republic. But will they keep it, or will they, in the enjoyment of plenty, lose the memory of freedom? Material abundance without character is the surest way to destruction.

—Thomas Jefferson

I touch the future. I teach. —Christa McAuliffe

> How easy for me to live with You, O Lord!
>   How easy for me to believe in You!
>   When my mind parts in bewilderment
>   or falters,
>   When the most intelligent people see no further
>   than this day's end
>   and do not know what must be done tomorrow,
>   You grant me the serene certitude
>   that You exist and that You will take care
>   that not all the paths of good be closed.
>   Atop the ridge of earthly fame,
>   I look back in wonder at the path
>   which I alone could never have found,
>   a wondrous path through despair to this point
>   from which I, too, could transmit to mankind
>   a reflection of Your rays.
>   And as much as I must still reflect
>   You will give me.
>   But as much as I cannot take up
>   You will have already assigned to others.

—Aleksandr I. Solzhenitsyn

Chapter 1

FREEDOM
Your First Most Priceless Treasure

A New Appreciation, a New Future of Freedom

Let Freedom Ring Throughout the Land! America, your destiny is freedom!

"Proclaim liberty throughout all the land unto all the inhabitants thereof," reads the inscription on America's Liberty Bell at Constitution Hall in Philadelphia. The quote is from Leviticus 25:10.

Freedom! Freedom! Freedom!

The word, the concept and the promise have echoed down through the ages from the dawn of recorded history. Freedom is elusive. Mankind has ever been in bondage, either because of nature, man, or both. He has rarely been free, then only by accident and for short periods of time.

We tout the importance of our *presence* as "our second most priceless treasure." Our "first most priceless treasure" is *freedom*. But freedom is not free.

We Americans have had so much freedom available to us for so long, we barely know freedom, what it is, how much we have, or that we are losing it. We know little about those who have never known freedom. We know less about those who knew freedom and lost it.

People who are born free don't fully appreciate freedom until they lose it; then it's too late.

What is this thing called freedom? We can symbolize it as a torch that lights a pathway to a bright new future. Who lights the Torch of Freedom, and who carries it? What happens if the torch is dropped, ignored or neglected?

The Torch of Freedom: Carry It or Bury It!

Spirits soared and hearts swelled with pride the summer of 1984 when the Olympic Torch traveled across America. Skilled runners under committed sponsorship each carried the torch part of the way to its final journey up the steps of Los Angeles Olympic Stadium to light the flame of the games. The pride of America was once again a lump in our throats, a tear in our eyes, a song in our hearts. It was the song of freedom and it was magnificent!

1986 was the 100th anniversary of Lady Liberty originally given to us by France on July 4, our Independence Day. The Statue of Liberty and her torch symbolize mankind's yearnings for freedom, and striving for equality of rights, justice and opportunity. "Give me your tired, your poor; your huddled masses yearning to breathe free..." reads Emma Lazarus' inspiring inscription.

Thus began a five-year "celebration of freedom," from Independence Day, 1986, the Centennial of the Lady of Liberty, to December 15, 1991, bicentennial anniversary of the adoption of the Bill of Rights.

One special date was September 17, 1987, bicentennial of the signing of the United States Constitution by the Congress of the United States, which went into effect June 21, 1788. Another special date was March 4, 1779, when the first Congress met under the Constitution in New York City. Another was December 15, 1791 when the Congress adopted the Bill of Rights. These are the "Freedom Documents" that formally built a foundation of freedom for the fledgling nation calling itself the United States of America.

Those who came by Lady Liberty's gates as immigrants call themselves "Americans by choice." Their citizenship was no accident of birth or good luck, but a choice, frequently an escape from persecution difficult for us even to imagine. They yearned for, found, earned and got freedom in their American citizenship so they could carry the Torch of Freedom to fulfill their wants, needs and dreams.

Freedom is not only precious and blessed, but perishable. It is easy to ignore, take for granted, use freely and abundantly—and lose. Once lost, it is seldom regained.

Where is America in the Life Cycle of a Country?

America was born of a burning desire for freedom, from the fires of revolution and the restlessness and dissatisfaction of the human spirit, unwilling to suffer injustice and oppression.

In *Continuum of a Civilization[1]*, Dean Russell shows how societies begin and end. Nineteen of the world's greatest civilizations have died, not as a direct result of destruction by an outside enemy, but from internal decay. The average age of these civilizations was about 200 years. Each civilization's lifetime, with few exceptions, passed through this sequence of conditions:

Continuum of a Civilization

From Bondage to Spiritual Faith
From Spiritual Faith to Great Courage

1. Russell, Dean, "A Short History of Liberty: How Far Along the Way is America?" *The FREEMAN,* January, 1955

From Great Courage to Liberty
From Liberty to Abundance
From Abundance to Selfishness
From Selfishness to Complacency
From Complacency to Apathy
From Apathy to Dependency
From Dependency back to Bondage

With America well over 200 years old, where do we stand in that cycle? Where should we stand? What must we do to get there? Am I, an individual citizen, a *Power of One,* willing to carry the Torch of Freedom on part of its journey for a part of my life?

Is That Who We Are?
A Look at America's Heritage and the Human Spirit

Many would have us believe that we are pitiful helpless, hapless beings, dependent upon the state for our survival. But look at our heritage. As pioneers, we had a vision of a frontier to conquer. We settled a country, crossed and climbed mountains, forged streams and settled a hostile wilderness. Then, we reached for the stars and touched the heavens. It took courage, will, creativity, imagination, and determination to do this. We had faith in a better world, a better life and in our Creator. We had freedom, challenge and an opportunity to leave a world better than we found it.

We need to reintroduce ourselves to who we are and our heritage. We are Americans, free, responsible individuals—the most productive, hardworking, generous and charitable people on Earth. We are created and blessed by a beneficent God.

A friend from another country remarked with wonder about Americans. "In Europe, we have two jobs: One, to make our living, the second and more important, to preserve our freedoms. In America, you apparently have only one job, to make a living. I wonder who you think is working to preserve, or perhaps even destroy your freedoms."

Our first assignment is to make a living. Our greater assignment is to preserve our freedom.

Will You Give Your Life, Your Blood or Your Sweat?

In the movie, *The Pride and the Passion*, Miguel, the peasant fighter, was determined to regain Avila on the plains of Spain, from the French. The peasant army's only hope to tumble the fortress walls lay in a huge cannon which got away from them while going down a steep hill and had become mired in a river of mud. Miguel, not willing to give up, went to the bullring in the nearest town. He stopped the bullfight and a silence fell over the crowd.

"I don't want your life. I don't even want your blood. I only want your sweat," Miguel pleaded as he explained the plight of the cannon and its being the only way to win back Avila from the French. He got it as the impassioned crowd rescued the cannon, and Miguel and his followers went on to take back Avila with much bloodshed and sacrifice.

In the past, Americans have given their "last full measure of devotion," their lives, for this country so that others might live to enjoy the beauty and bounty of freedom. Today are we willing to give our blood or our lives for Freedom? Sometimes we don't even give our sweat and allow our precious freedoms to ebb away.

Bill Ellis, co-author of the book *MORE*[2] said each citizen should give an hour a month, or better, an hour a week, to the cause of citizenship and freedom. To reclaim lost freedom new generations may have to do even more, "a half hour a day, for the USA."

Failure to make this commitment enables government and institutions to trample freedom and expropriate our hard-earned wealth. To save freedom, we must be vigilant and influence their decisions and actions. We must exercise, protect and strengthen our Bill of Rights. Article I by itself guarantees us freedom of religion, speech, the press, and the right to assemble and petition for redress of grievances. And there are nine other articles!

It is not enough, for instance, to "only vote" every 2, 4, or 6 years. In-between is when we must get into the action and stay in contact with our elected and appointed officials. Learn their positions, offer opinions, demand action. Get involved. That's how the American system works.

What is your choice for the Torch of Freedom: Carry It? Or Bury It?

Freedom through Education and Economics

What people don't know can hurt them. In fact, when those who are in power wish to stay in power and get even more power, they do what they can to keep people from knowing what is happening, getting involved or taking action. When people don't know what's going on, they can't object. If they can't object, they can't do anything about it. That's why it is so important we not only know how to read, but that we *actually READ*. Think, analyze, care, then do something about your feelings and reactions. Take action.

Lack of knowledge, where deliberately withheld or simply unsought, is a form of weakness that leads to suppression and oppression. Minorities were not allowed to learn to read in the 1800's. This kept them at a disadvantage to deal with those who had economic and political power and who wanted to maintain that advantage. We need to add to our knowledge now.

2. Armington, R.Q., and Ellis, William D., *MORE: The Rediscovery of American Common Sense,* Regnery Gateway, Chicago: 1984

Economic ignorance is a mainstay in other's wielding power. Scarcity is the distinguishing characteristic of economics, and the essence of freedom is choice. Making right choices depends on education. A free society requires an educated people who can make intelligent choices. Thomas Jefferson expressed it so well, and poetically:

If a nation expects to be ignorant and free, in a state of civilization, it expects what never was and never will be.

People have to be knowledgeable to be free. They must continually educate themselves, both formally and informally, to adequately understand the world in which we live. Economics is a doorway to understanding our world.

Education for Life: How to Make a Living, Live, Understand Life

Knowledge is power. Combined with current, accurate and relevant information, knowledge helps people get more in control of their lives, and get more benefit out of their lives. But where has our educational system been in all this?

I made a presentation on how to teach students meaningful economics for a teacher's in-service workshop at Cherry Creek High School in Denver, Colorado. At the end of the presentation, I was asked what I thought of the American public education system.

I answered, "American education teaches our students a lot of what they need to know: mathematics, science, reading, art, music, language and all the rest. It teaches our children almost everything except the three most important things: How to make a living, how to live, and how to understand life."

The next equally challenging question was how I would incorporate such seemingly all-encompassing knowledge in the public schools.

"Teach them economics," I said, "because economics helps things make sense and gives each person an immense importance. It's the glue that holds everything together."

That is not all education is. Education teaches people how to visit the past, comprehend the present and touch the future, to meet the great minds and imaginations of the gifted, through *reading*.

Education is how to think critically and analyze. It is how to learn and how to love learning. Education is exposure to strict discipline. It is developing a craving for knowledge, a thirst for truth, a hunger for wisdom. It's how to grow and keep growing, to live and keep living. Education is the key to success, happiness and fulfillment. And economics is a central subject area that helps tie it all together.

Economics: The Educational Void in America

I reviewed my own education and that of my children. It seems the vital *life* science—economics—had been missing in all our curricula. Was it an accident or on purpose, an omission or commission?

In 1976 I served as a business consultant for Junior Achievement's pilot program of *Project Business* which worked with seventh grade business teachers and students. The then-principal at Manning Junior High School in Golden, Colorado visited one of my classes to learn about the role of money in business. He later asked me to join him for a cup of coffee and expressed how pleased he was that I had volunteered for this important assignment. He said most teachers have never been a part of the business world and don't really understand it. They have never had to meet a payroll, and my being there was as much a benefit for them as for the students.

He told why teachers can't learn or experience economics, at least not in a real world business sense. From 16 years of formal education in school, to a career of teaching in school, they never get out of school!

After a few weeks exposure to a businessperson, and to economics, business and finance concepts I presented, the teacher had increased her awareness and understanding of how business works. That helped not only those present but the numerous students who will come along later through "teaching the teachers." This is one reason it is so important for business people to get involved, really involved in economic and business education, in the schools as well as at their places of work.

Parents never learned economics because they were part of the same school system. So students can't learn, either from parents or teachers.

It is not difficult to sense that something has been missing in the education of the American people. Most countries not only teach but *indoctrinate* their students in their prevailing political and economic system, touting theirs and blasting ours and others. The least we can do is teach our students about the American enterprise system that has made us the wealthiest nation in the world, especially through the subject of economics.

The problem is two-fold. We must 1) help those in school to get more economics and economics-related courses as standard curricula, and 2) help those out of school, who are in the working world, to be able to participate and benefit from such economic knowledge and understanding.

TOTAL Power of ONE in America serves both groups by providing new awareness and knowledge, to help individuals achieve new personal fulfillment, control and prosperity.

There are 68-million Americans in elementary and secondary schools, universities and colleges, public and private. Our society, spends $600-billion dollars a year on education, nearly seven percent of our gross national product (total annual output)[3]!

3. *Statistical Abstract of the United States,* 1999, pp 163, 460

Knowledge and understanding of economics is essential, not only to be effective citizens, but to understand our American enterprise system: business, work, risk, reward, profits, entrepreneurship, money, government, taxes, spending, deficits and debt, as well as job and career opportunities and life fulfillment. This system is not perfect. None ever will be, but this one works and works well. As Winston Churchill put it, "Democracy is the worst political system devised by the wit of man, except for all the others."

There are over 133-million working Americans[4] (1999) who create the wealth of America—products, goods and services—to fulfill peoples' wants and needs. They have a right and obligation to understand the system that helps produce and distribute this wealth, and to know their potential roles, responsibilities and rewards in that system. They can know and appreciate the vital role of freedom that makes the system work so well!

Ye Shall Know the Truth, and Use It

Knowing the truth about economics can help us better understand a larger truth of the world around us, and how it really works. Then responsibility for self becomes properly placed, and people realize their roles, their importance and their worth. Some of the former mysteries of our economic and political/legislative/government environment begin to make sense. Others make no sense at all.

In the Bible, John 8:32 says "And ye shall know the truth and the truth shall make you free."

Finally, our quest in this book is not only for survival on this planet but for purposeful prosperity, how it forges the important link between the harsh realities of economics and blessings of freedom, and how they work together if properly understood and used.

FREEDOM in America—Your Most Priceless Treasure

We previously said that your presence is your second most priceless treasure. What is the first? Freedom is your first most priceless treasure, especially in America. What is freedom anyway?

FREEDOM is: Free to be, to do, to choose, to dare, to become!

Freedom is what makes Americans and America different from other peoples. It is something that we take too much for granted and know too little about. That is why a formal, continuing program is necessary in the home, in school, and at the workplace.

Americans need to understand their own importance as individuals, and the relationship between economics and freedom in America. Through knowledge, information and understanding, they'll have better control over their own well-being in terms of standard-of-living and quality-of-life, not

---

4. *Economic Report of the President,* February, 2000, p 346

only in material abundance, but in family, personal and spiritual possibilities and opportunities.

Jonathan Livingston Seagull, a bird, teaches us about freedom, that freedom is a part of life, and that anything that diminishes freedom diminishes life, that each one of us is "an unlimited idea of freedom."[5]

Who Really Protects Your Freedom?

For most of my life I have wondered, who was protecting my freedom? I didn't do much, it seems, if anything at all. Perhaps I thought it was the government, my parents, big business, labor unions, the army, something or someone else. Wrong! None of the above. The answer is as interesting as it is elusive.

On a business trip to Spartanburg, South Carolina, I was picked up at the airport and enjoying a guided tour of the area on the way to our meeting place. What really caught my attention was a bumper sticker on the top right side of a pickup truck's tailgate, in two distinct parts, a symbol and three words. On the left was an American flag. On the right were the words, "GOD BLESS AMERICA."

God Didn't Do It Alone!

The pick-up truck, tailgate and bumper sticker reminded me of the preacher driving in the country, awestruck by a particularly well kept farm. He noted the freshly painted white house and white barn. The freshly painted wooden fence that surrounded the property impressed him. And he couldn't help but marvel at the corn stalks lined up in neat rows like soldiers standing at attention. Then he noticed the farmer driving a huge tractor tending the carefully farmed landscape.

Having pulled over and parked his car by the fence, the minister got out. With a big wave of his arm, he motioned the farmer to come over. The large tractor turned and headed for the fence and the preacher. The door opened, the farmer got out and headed over to the preacher.

"Mr. Farmer, I couldn't help being most impressed with what God and you have done with this property!" the preacher said, as the farmer approached him. "I was so taken by your white, freshly-painted house and barn, and the neat wooden fence around the field. Even the corn stalks stand like soldiers at attention. I just had to stop, recognize and compliment you on the fine job that God and you are doing with this farm.

"Well, thank you for those kind words, Mr. Preacher. It was nice of you to stop and compliment me on what a fine job God and I are doing with this farm. But," the farmer continued, "you should have seen it when only God was taking care of it!"

5. Richard Bach, *Jonathan Livingston Seagull,* p 103, Avon, New York: 1973

That last line made me think. "GOD BLESS AMERICA!" "You should have seen it when only God was taking care of it." Is that what I thought? God was taking care of my freedom? How dumb! If I think so little of my freedom not to protect it, why should God?

Perhaps most people think God is protecting their freedom! Maybe that is why they don't get involved in protecting their country, because they sure don't do much to preserve and strengthen it themselves.

The One-Name Answer: Me!

"Who is protecting my freedom?" ME! That's who. Whatever has been done, is being done, or will ever be done, will be done by *ME!*

So, who's protecting *your* freedom? You are! Got it?

Who is Protecting Your Freedom?_____
(Print Your Name Here)

Now that you know, you are in control. You are totally and absolutely responsible for protecting your own freedom. Anything that has ever been done, that is being done or that will ever be done will be done by YOU! You have total control over your thoughts, decisions and actions. That is what being a *Power of One is* all about. You are powerful because you are responsible, you are under your own control, and you are a good control to be under!

Prayer is Never Having to Say You Did Nothing

To paraphrase the advertising slogan of a Hollywood love story, "Prayer is never having to say you did nothing." Some people pray long and fervently, acting as if all one must do is pray and the deed will be done. Yet God doesn't work that way. God helps those who help themselves. You must pray hard as if it is all up to God *and* work hard as if it is all up to you.

The prayin's easy. The workin's hard. Do both.

Super Shopper Strikes Again—for Freedom!

I watched a "house spouse," super shopper, at a food store, being especially careful to get the most food for the least money. Name brand beans were priced as 60 cents a can. House brand beans cost 55 cents a can. Even better, "generic" beans were 45 cents a can. Buying five cans, can you imagine super shopper's joy upon arriving home and telling the family about saving 75 cents on five cans of beans?

Super shopper then looks carefully at the latest paycheck stub, the other half of the paycheck that buys the beans. In the upper left hand corner Is "gross," pay for two weeks, and "net," actual pay received, in the lower right hand corner. Have you noticed "Gross gets grosser" (inflation), while "net gets netter" (smaller), and what's left buys less and less? What happened to all that money? What are they called? Yes, *deductions,* mostly for taxes, federal, state and local, plus Social Security and other government required taxes on earned income.

Those are the "Deductions of Freedom," the price we pay for the privilege of living in America to have the freedoms and opportunities we enjoy. We all know freedom is not free. But are we getting our money's worth from the taxes we pay? If super shopper has anything to say about it, we will. We will do what citizens must do to enjoy the blessings of freedom.

Notice how hard we work and how good we feel to shop and save 75 cents on five cans of beans. How much harder will we work to get our money's worth for those precious "deductions of freedom," tens, hundreds, even thousands of dollars per pay period?

That begs the question, to repeat, how hard should we work to protect our precious freedoms to get our money's worth in the "deductions of freedom"? How many hours equivalent of your work are deducted each pay period? (Figure it out—divide your total deductions by your hourly pay to estimate total hour's worth.) What should you do to assure value received for price paid?

Preserve FREEDOM: Make God's Work Truly Our Own

President John Kennedy described the situation well in his inaugural address:

> With good conscience our only sure reward, with history the final judge of our deeds, let's go forth to lead the land we love asking His blessing and His help, but knowing that here on earth God's work must truly be our own.

A member of the Colorado's financial community, the late-Robert Boucher, ended his speeches with this thought-provoking quote about freedom:

> To be born free is a blessing.
> To live free is a privilege.
> To die free is a responsibility.

I believe it and live it, and take that responsibility very seriously. You can too.

Yes, freedom is your "first most priceless treasure." Work for it. Pay for it. Pray for it. Cherish it. Protect it! Keep it, not only for yourself, your family and friends, but for future generations as well.

Someone worked very hard to assure the measure of freedom we had when we were born. We have the same responsibility for our children, grandchildren and theirs.

Treat freedom as the precious, fragile, perishable, "first most priceless treasure" that it is. Once lost, freedom is seldom, if ever, regained. Let's keep freedom while we have it to keep.

Questions for Review

1. What is our "first most priceless treasure?"

2. Why is our choice for the Torch of Freedom either "to carry it or bury it?"

3. What is the difference of "American by choice," and "American by chance?" Which are you?

4. What are the nine characteristics along the "Continuum of a Civilization" starting with "Bondage?"

5. What are our "two jobs" in America?

6. Why isn't it enough to "only vote" every 2, 4, or 6 years? What must we do in-between?

7. Why is education in economics so important? What three things does modern day education not teach? What else should it teach?

8. What two groups need to learn economics?

9. Who really protects your freedom? What two steps help protect freedom?

10. What three characteristics describe being born free, living free and dying free?

Love is a universal, human need. But there is another human need—equally universal. That need is freedom—freedom of conscience, freedom of speech, freedom of press, freedom of trade. All of these aspects of freedom are only parts of a larger whole, for freedom is indivisible. Economic freedom cannot be divorced from political and religious freedom. Nor can freedom be cornered in the market, like wheat. No nation can conserve political and economic freedom to itself while denying them to others. It is trite, perhaps, but it is true:

Freedom is the only thing that we can keep by giving it to others.
—Gardner Cowles

More and more, life is best explained not by religion, not by law, but by economics.   —A. Andrew Hauk, U. S. District Court Justice

Chapter 2

THE Power of ONE
A Philosophy for Living

You count! You matter! You make a difference! Why? Because you are different. You are especially powerful in America, where, protected by the Bill of Rights, you can exert your power, through *Freedom with Responsibility.*

These thoughts embrace your *Power of ONE.* What we need do is to learn, to know and to exert the *Power of ONE,* which is the power to make a difference. The purpose of this book is to teach and inspire you how to do just that.

Repetition: Parents of Learning, King of Conviction

Repetition is essential to learning. It is needed to instill, assimilate, and internalize basic knowledge and information, to turn truth into understanding, knowledge into wisdom.

Repetition in learning has three descriptions, all accurate, all correct:

> Repetition is the *Mother of Learning.*
> Repetition is the *Father of Boredom.*
> Repetition is the *King of Conviction.*

Especially when material to be covered is foreign and information to be learned is complicated and new, repetition helps you learn faster and retain longer.

Repeat a thing often enough and you begin to accept it, adopt it, believe it, act on it, and become it. You become invincible because of it. Look out, World. Here comes a new *Power of ONE,* convinced through repetition of the truth that one person can make a difference.

We have had so much repetition—and in fact the wrong kind—that we are "programmed" by it. As impressionable children we are told "NO" literally thousands of times. Now we tell ourselves "yes" and a lot more by repeating, believing and acting on positive ideas that enrich and enhance our lives.

At first, the *Power of ONE* philosophy seems strange, even contrary to how we have learned to think and be. It is threatening to get outside our self-defined comfort zone into a new area of risk and growth. But it provides entry to new, exciting possibilities and a more fulfilled life.

Complacent, shallow attitudes, decisions and actions—or inaction—do not solve anything. They don't build lives, families, civilizations or futures. They build failure—silent, invisible, irretrievable, lamentable, forgettable and regrettable FAILURE. Nothing gets started. Nothing gets done. Nothing happens! Nothing. No thing.

The Power of ONE: A Larger Look, a Harder Look

The *Power of ONE* posture takes a larger view at life, a more realistic, tougher, harder look. The *Power of ONE is* not content only to survive but TO GROW; not get by, but GET AHEAD; not drift along or muddle through, but TO ACHIEVE. The *Power of ONE* stance is not to be the anchor on your boat of life, but to be its propeller, power plant, drive shaft, and rudder; in fact, it is for you to be the captain of your ship, your being, your life.

The *Power of ONE is* mightily described in William Ernest Henley's famous poem, *Invictus*:[1]

INVICTUS

Out of the night that covers me,
    Black as the Pit from pole to pole
I thank whatever gods may be
    For my unconquerable soul.

In the fell clutch of circumstance
    I have not winced nor cried aloud.
Under the bludgeoning of chance
    My head is bloody, but unbowed.

Beyond this place of wrath and tears
    Looms but the horror of the shade
And yet the menace of the years
    Finds, and shall find me, unafraid.

It matters not how strait the gate,
    How charged with punishments the scroll,
I am the master of my fate:
    I am the captain of my soul.

1. Oscar Williams, Editor, *A Little Treasury of Modern Poetry,* p. 564, Charles Scribner's Sons, New York: 1952

The phrases "my unconquerable soul," "finds me unafraid," "master of my fate," and "I am the captain of my soul," capture the spirit of the *Power of ONE.*

The *Power of ONE* looks squarely at the me-person in my life—the single, solitary and only ONE, totally and completely under my control. To me, it is ME. To you, it is YOU. We know that for some reason we resist taking control. We hold back. Why do we do that?

To become an effective *Power of ONE,* it is helpful to better understand this reluctance to risk, this hesitance to act.

We Create, Then Believe our "Excuse Thoughts"

Before we human beings take any action, we take important factors into account. We know *if we don't take action,* there are advantages and disadvantages. The main advantage is you don't make mistakes. The main disadvantage is that you never accomplish anything. Likewise *if you do take action,* there are advantages and disadvantages. You might "fail" or be embarrassed. Or you may become rich, great, happy and famous. For most of us it is hard to envision ourselves that way, so we do nothing, then make up reasons why doing nothing was a good thing to do.

If we tune in to our mind-thoughts, we can hear ourselves thinking "excuse thoughts," or "mind-binders." We make a great effort to make great excuses. Only by recognizing this can we critically examine whether we will do something and why. Consider some common "excuse thoughts":

Who cares?
I don't have time.
I don't know how.
There is no problem.
I've never done it before.
I don't want to get involved.
No one really cares. I don't either.
I'm too old to learn something new.
Oh, that takes writing and I'm not a writer.
I couldn't ask that. I don't know enough about it.
Why should I bother? There are other people paid to do that.
No one will know the difference anyway. Why bother at all?
I've gotten along very well this long. Why change?
I'm too old (or too young) to do that.
I can't speak in front of people.
It'll look like "brown-nosing."
I have too much to do already.
It's never been done before.
That's someone else's job.
We don't have a problem.
It's not important.
It's not my job.
Why me?

A popular song lamented how we never "fail to fail" because it's so easy. But is it? Is life fraught with failure? Are we destined to lose? Only if we entertain and follow "excuse thoughts."

You have heard them all, and more, besides. There are at least two things wrong with "excuse thoughts." One is that they are rarely, if ever true especially if there's a legitimate need to be served. Two, they lead to more of the same. Excuse thoughts become bad habits that regularly come out of our mouths as the spoken word. They sound more plausible, emphasized, legitimized, even more true if spoken in the presence of others.

If we think such thoughts, we act on them *as though they are true.* If we say them out loud to ourselves or to others, they are reinforced. They gain credence, importance and validity, and become true whether actually so or not. Why do we entertain them in the first place? Because they are an "out." They provide a seemingly valid excuse not to try, begin or risk. And not to risk is not only to give up our right to *be,* but our right to *be free.* Dr. Leo Buscaglia[2] relates risk to freedom:

> To hope is to risk pain. But risk must be taken, because the greatest hazard in life is to risk NOTHING. The person who risks nothing does nothing, has nothing and is nothing. He may avoid suffering and sorrow, but he simply cannot learn, feel, change, grow, live or love. Chained by his certitudes or his addictions, he's a slave. He has forfeited his greatest trait, and that is his individual freedom. Only the person who risks is free.

"Excuse Thoughts" Remove Responsibility!
—Or Do They?

"Excuse thoughts" keep us from risking failure and embarrassment. They prevent us from taking advantage of opportunities to benefit our circumstance, our future and ourselves. They excuse us from accepting challenges that could greatly enhance our stature and station, to know, to go and to grow, to be and to become. In effect we give ourselves permission to fail, to shrink and grow stagnant. If we don't say "yes" to new opportunities, we don't have to risk failure—or success.

New Excuse Thoughts for Old:
Do-Thoughts for Don't-Thoughts

Turn around your excuse thoughts, "don't thoughts," that formerly gave you an excuse NOT TO DO something that should be done. Make them "do thoughts," reasons TO DO what should be done. Make a game out of it. Have

2. Buscaglia, Leo, *Living, Loving & Learning,* p.264, Fawcett Columbine, New York: 1982

some fun while you risk, serve, grow and achieve. Here are some helpful "Do Thoughts":

Why not!

How can I lose?

It's a fun challenge!

I wonder what will happen if...

We can enjoy doing it together.

I wonder how well I can do this.

This is a challenge I can't ignore.

I'll meet some new people doing this.

This is just what I've been waiting for.

Anyone can do this, and that includes me.

I'm about due to try something new and different.

No one can do this better than me. I was born for this.

I've prepared all my life for this. I'm ready for it.

I'll see how much of this challenge I can handle.

I'm too good to pass up this opportunity.

Even if I fail, it'll be fun trying.

I've done similar things before.

Who knows where this'll lead?

Here comes another victory!

Why not give it a try!

It might be fun.

Watch me!

"Do thoughts" open up a willingness to risk, therefore to perform and achieve. As long as you try, you are a winner. You have within you all the resources you need to do about anything you want to do. Unleash your inner powers and resources. Say "yes" to "do thoughts." Let them propel you into action.

Don't Just Meet Standards; SET Standards!

"Everybody litters." "No one ever parks their car in the right spot." "Nobody accomplishes anything attending a city council meeting." "You can't fight city hall." "There's no use my going, even though it affects zoning in my neighborhood." "Why vote? My vote doesn't count." More "excuse thoughts."

How do these things happen? They happen because we accept other people's standards, or what we think their standards are. We should dwell more on what we know is right, not on what "they" would or would not do, as if we could ever know.

Negative returning-in-kind to our fellow human is another natural response that does harm instead of good. "I'll make them pay. I'll treat them the way they treated me, 'an eye for an eye, a tooth for a tooth,' you know. That's biblical."

Biblical too, we perversely hide behind the "Golden Rule:" *Do unto others, as you would have them do unto you.* We so handily interpret adverse actions by others as an excuse to get even. "They asked for it!" we say and believe, then act accordingly.

Another common example occurs while driving a car. Someone cuts in front of us, or we cut in front of them. Horns are honked. Glares and gestures are exchanged. The drivers go along their way more prone to have that next accident because of flared emotions and lost tempers. Is there a better way? Of course:

Set the standard!
Don't meet less than the standard.

How? Smile. Wave. Wish them a good day. Say a prayer for them. Give them the right of way. Smile again.

Treat Others As You Wish Them to Treat You

The Golden Rule is still Golden, but we extend our thinking beyond *who's right,* to *what's right.* We exert our personal power to set the example, to break the ice, to first go more than half way. Why? Not because it is normal, natural, expected, or comfortable but *because it is right!* It's amazing how we really do know, but let our "excuse thoughts" get in the way of doing the right thing.

It all starts with you. You are in control. You set the example. Actions speak louder than words, always. You do the right thing. Others will learn from your example.

"Draw a bigger circle." Sometimes we feel left out of groups or events. The natural tendency is self-pity, withdrawal and ill feelings towards others. But there is a better way to handle it. "Draw a bigger circle," and include yourself in it. You draw the circle. *Include you in it.*

Do what you know is right. Leave a situation better than you found it. Everyone bears a heavy load. Help make it lighter. As William Penn put it:

> I expect to pass through life but once. If therefore, there be any kindness I can show, or any good thing I can do to any fellow being, let me do it now, and not defer or neglect it, as I shall not pass this way again.

Go beyond doing the right thing, to *doing the right thing right.* Do it with style, flair and grace. You can send a thank you card. Or you can send a thank you card with a small bouquet of flowers. One does the job. The other adds a special touch.

Overcome the natural barriers:

SET THE STANDARD! Don't just meet the standard.

How Can You Tell Something Needs to be Done?

There's a wee, small (but pushy and powerful) voice within us that tells us what must be done and most of the time it is right. Sometimes we verbalize the assignment with "Someone ought to..." In the place of "someone" place the word "I," followed by the word "will..." For instance:

Not: "Someone ought to call city hall to get this street repaired."

But: "I will call city hall to get this street repaired." or
       "I will attend the School Board meeting and question budget increases."

or

"I will write my Senator to encourage fiscal responsibility."

or

"I will run for City Council to help better manage my community."

or

"I will contact my state legislator about cutting taxes for economic development."

or

"I will form that neighborhood watch for better safety and security."

Send copies of relevant articles or published letters-to-the-editor to friends, elected or appointed public officials. Get involved and involve others.

"Each one, teach one," educator and professional speaker Dr. Ken McFarland used to say. Your work is so important and so urgent, expand that to "each one teach ten," and you're the one. MULTIPLY. Involve others to extend and expand your effectiveness. Take a friend along to the budget meeting. Encourage others to help support a candidate for public office. Take a neighbor and a petition around for citizen signatures. Put your actions where your beliefs are. Impassion others with the need to get more involved in their communities. That's what makes the *Power of ONE* so powerful.

The Power of ONE: Short but Tough

The *Power of ONE* philosophy is powerful and to the point:

The Power of ONE
I am ONE.
I am only ONE.
But I will do,
What ONE can do.

Read it again. Learn it. Live it. Let it make you ten feet tall.

First, "I am *ONE,*" says the *Power of ONE* philosophy. It means, "I count. I matter. I make a difference. I am a total living person, a whole human being. I have all the attributes, capabilities and potential I need. I not only exist, I live. I love. I care. I am. I shall become. I am part of God's creation, and I'm created in God's image.

Second, "I am *only ONE*" recognizes a powerful limitation. There are limits because I am limited. I am a small part of something much larger— the family of mankind, a community, a society, a global population, a player in the drama of history. There's only so much I can do—but I've never even come close to doing it all.

Finally, "But I will do, What ONE can do," says I can do so much more than I have ever done, be so much more than I've ever been. I will exert the full powers of my "ONE-ness," challenging the limitations of my "only ONE-ness." I have only begun to do what I can do, be what I can be, become what I can become. It is a matter of technique and approach; controlling my thoughts, attitudes, decisions and actions. I *will* do what ONE can do—all that ONE can do!

The Powerful Simplicity Goes On

There are two simple techniques to apply the *Power of ONE.* Any person can adopt them and use them. The first is concerned with attitude; the second, with action. They are:

I will try it!

I will do it!

To try confronts the fear to fail. To do activates the likelihood of success. The magic duo are faith and action.

FAITH: "I will try it!"

Willingness to try is an attitude of openness, an admission of faith, tolerance for risk, and the necessary confidence, anticipation, and resourcefulness to begin. You are in effect saying:

> I'll risk success and failure, reward and punishment, profit and loss. I have tried many new things before and did them well. I learned much from things tried and experience gained, even falling short of total success. I have spent my whole life getting right here, right now. So I focus all my years of preparation, education, and experience to accept this new challenge. I am ready for it. I can do it. I will do it, starting right now.

In this attitude-conditioning process, your whole mind, right brain and left brain, conscious and subconscious, sorts out, analyzes and responds to your new challenge. An infusion of confidence, enthusiasm, information and motivation begin their snowballing avalanche to thrust you into the action phase.

ACTION: "I will do it!"

Begin with confidence, purpose and faith in your immense capabilities. "Once begun, half is done." Momentum builds. You find new enthusiasm and excitement in performance. "Automatic pilot" turns on. You are believing, doing and achieving. When it is all done, you have not only completed the assignment, you've grown in the process. You are a more accomplished person. You exerted and expanded your *Power of ONE.*

Overcome "What If I Fail?"

What seems so simple, isn't so simple. There is still a nagging feeling, "What if I fail?" That thought can paralyze, especially if you have tried and "failed" before. The next attempt becomes more difficult. It is then you acknowledge you have untapped powers and capabilities. Work up your courage to use them, to "stretch" and to grow. Make a commitment, follow through to success.

W. N. Murray, in his 1951 book *The Scottish Himalayan Expedition,* touted the value of commitment:

> Until one is committed there is hesitancy; the chance to draw back, always ineffectiveness. Concerning all acts of initiative (and creation) there is one elementary truth, the ignorance of which kills countless ideas and splendid plans: That the moment one definitely commits oneself, then providence moves too. All sorts of things occur to help one that would otherwise never have occurred. A whole stream of events issues from the decision, raising in one's favor all manner of unforeseen incidents and meetings and material assistance, which no man could have dreamt would have come his way. I have learned a deep respect for one of Goethe's couplets:
> 'Whatever you can do, or dream you can, begin it.
> Boldness has genius, power and magic in it.'

The concept of "stretch" is important, *Power of ONE.* It means going BEYOND what you've already done, where you've already been, where your "comfort zone" ends. "Stretch" is a theme of Richard Bach's imaginative and exciting book *Jonathan Livingston Seagull.*[3] This "super-gull" bird was set on seeking and attaining peak excellence in what he "most loved to do ... ":

> ... the most important thing in living was to reach out and touch perfection in that which they most loved to do, and that was to fly ... to fly as fast as thought, to anywhere that is, you must begin by knowing you have already arrived.

---

3. From *Jonathan Livingston Seagull,* pp 60, 104, 85, by Richard Bach. Copyright (c) 1970 by Richard Bach and Leslie Parrish-Bach. Reprinted with permission of Macmillan Publishing Company.

> Break the chains of your thought, and you break the chains of
> your body, too ...
> The gull sees farthest who flies highest.

"To fly" for Jonathan is "to stretch" for you and me. The more we stretch,
the more we grow, and the more we positively impact the world around us.

An Act of Faith

Exercising your *Power of ONE is* doing what you think, feel and believe
is right. It is trusting that your motives are right, your caring is correct, and
if you take appropriate action, you *WILL make a difference!* It is an act of
faith. Almost everything worthwhile in life is an act of faith—pursuing an
education, getting married, buying a car, raising a family, starting a business,
composing a letter-to-the-editor, writing a public official, or just getting out
of bed in the morning.

Opposite to an act of faith are "excuse thoughts" like, "It won't make a
difference anyway." What a cop out! You just got yourself off the hook. Now
you don't have to do anything. But you also canceled an opportunity,
diminished your life experience and possibly prevented something great
from happening. Is that what you really want? Is that who you want to be?

Remove Your Mind-Forged Manacles!

Author John Gardner[4] used the term "Mind-Forged Manacles" to express
the barriers we create to avoid doing unpleasant, threatening, but essential
tasks. Manacles are like handcuffs—restraints that keep us from acting, or
inhibit our willingness to act. With manacles, we can't do anything, but we
have a "good" excuse.

"Mind-Forged" means we mentally create these manacles ourselves. They
really don't exist. We make up barriers to *provide an excuse* to not act; not
exert any effort and not risk. We avoid the issue and do nothing.

If you feel a reluctance to act, to go beyond where you feel comfortable,
picture yourself bound in manacles made by your mind. Recognize that
these constraints and limitations are *self-imposed* and as such are
self-destructible. Picture yourself removing these shackles. Mentally unlock,
vaporize or destroy these life-paralyzing, mind-numbing traps. Once so
recognized they are gone.

"Fear knocked on the door. Faith answered. No one was there."

Luck: Where Preparation Meets Opportunity

To take on the difficult or seemingly impossible, we must be prepared.
That means to learn in advance, to gather facts necessary to assure success,

4. Gardner, John W., *Excellence,* Harper and Brothers, New York: 1961

and anticipate possible pitfalls. Worthwhile pursuits usually require some present sacrifice of time, talent, energy and resources. It's like "building spears," for a better future:

> A man was stranded on an island. He barely stayed alive by catching one fish a day with his bare hands, and filling the hunger gap with roots and berries. Soon he figured "there must be a better way." He chose to starve for one whole day to build a spear, a tool with which to fish!
>
> The sun came up and he was already hungry. But he ignored his hunger pangs and found a long pole and a piece of flint. He stripped and trimmed the pole, and turned the flint into a sharp symmetrically pointed weapon. He lashed it to the end of the pole, and secured it for just the right feel and balance.
>
> Just as the sun went down, the spear was done. And he was hungry—very hungry. His stomach hurt so badly he barely slept that night. As soon as the sun came up, he grabbed his brand new spear, approached the water, took aim and thrust his new weapon. In a short time he speared not one fish, but two. He ate both, then caught another and found time he never had before. He used his newly found time to fashion a hut, to build a place to store dried fish, and in so doing, greatly enhanced his standard-of-living. One long day of hunger pains turned out to be a great investment, well worth the sacrifice of a day and an aching, hungry stomach.

There are many spears to be built and sacrifices to be made. But better prepared, we benefit from our investment and discipline. One subsequently increases one's standard-of-living and quality-of-life and *takes total responsibility* for your own life. What do you need to do to get prepared? Decide. Then act. Here's how.

Act As If It Were Impossible to Fail

The theme of a great old book *Wake Up and Live!* by Dorothea Brande[5] was simply:

> Act as if it were impossible to fail.

Sometimes that is all it takes to do that small stretch beyond what you have ever done before. Visualize as possible the impossible or the improbable; then do it. Apply psychologist William James' notion that "feeling follows action." When we act as though something is the way we want it, our feelings follow that action. It becomes not only possible to do, but "do-able," and we do it.

---

5. Dorothea Brande, *Wake Up and Live,* Simon & Schuster, 1936

What if you "knew" that no matter what, you could not possibly fail? How would you act? "Act as if it were impossible to fail."

If It Is To Be It Is Up To Me

How to take 20 letters to make ten 2-letter words that say the whole Power of One philosophy? Here's how:

If it is to be it is up to me.

That is what this is all about. It depends on YOU, totally and completely on you. You have the entire responsibility for your life, and to some degree, you influence the lives around you. Whatever happens depends on what you do to make it happen. You are in control.

How Much Can You Change?

It is possible to change not only yourself but the world around you. With today's communications, you can extend your influence to whomever and wherever you can visit, write, publish, fax, email or telephone.

Take a look at those who made a difference: Thomas Edison, Dr. Jonas Salk, Adam Smith, Jesus Christ, Ralph Nader, Dr. Martin Luther King, Sister Teresa, Lech Walesa, Sally Ride, Barney Clark, Candy Lightner, Karl Marx, Madelyn Murray O'Hare, Sandra Day O'Connor, Tony Blair, and so many others. You may or may not agree with their accomplishments, but they exerted their *Powers of ONE* and made a difference.

Remember, each ONE of these people was "only ONE," just like you. Rather than place them on pedestals, we equate ourselves and our possibilities to their accomplishments. A mental and spiritual bond between these Powerful ONES and you, Powerful ONE, is a natural link.

The Incline of Your Mind: Ideas, Events and People

It's been said "Great minds discuss ideas; average minds discuss events; small minds discuss people." By definition, you possess a great mind, *Power of ONE*. This book is about ideas, as well as beliefs and motivations. In order to bring about change you put to the test your new knowledge and understanding of these concepts. In other words, some of this is going to be plain hard work! But fun, too!

For plain hard work, this exciting new "power person" YOU, will need special tools to deal with tough assignments. You will better read, think and understand, and stick to your goals till the job is done. Here are some special tools to help do the job.

The Three Powers that Be: Dare, Challenge and Deed

"Magic methods" incite us to action. They throw down the gauntlet and inflame the will. These special techniques are in three parts: (1) "The *Power Dare*," (2) "The *Power Challenge*," and (3) "The *Power Deed*."

The Power Dare is a call to action. It is directed at yourself or others, because something especially important but probably new, difficult or intimidating must be accomplished.

The Power Challenge accepts that call to action. It is where the dare is accepted with firm resolve it will be accomplished.

The Power Deed is "mission accomplished." The deed is done. Anyone can start something but it takes someone special to persevere and finish the job.

When complete, the Power Dare has been made, the Power Challenge met, and the Power Deed done.

A simple example would be my noticing a water meter cover missing in the street, causing a potentially unsafe condition for drivers or pedestrians. I could assume someone has already called city hall (or will call) to report the situation. Or this *Power of ONE* could say to me, "Fred, I Power Dare me to call city hall (or the police for high hazard) and report this problem." That is the Ultimate Dare to do.

Once dared, I accept it as a Power Challenge. I don't worry about it. I don't think about it. I don't find excuses not to do it. I DO IT! I accept the *Power Challenge.* Now the *Power Deed* will be done.

I go to a telephone, call city hall and report the situation. I expect and get assurance that it will be handled. I have completed the Power Deed, for "the deed is done." Or is it?

Have I really done all I can do? No. As always there is more that can be done. I can check and continue to report the condition until it is fixed.

Perhaps the situation's even more a threat to life, an open manhole cover that a child could fall into, or that could throw a moving automobile out of control. The Power Dare would extend beyond a call to the police to personally assure no accident happens. The Power Dare would be to be on the scene, rig up a warning device or route traffic around the hazard and ask someone to call the police.

The Power Challenge is to overcome your feelings of embarrassment and fear of directing traffic. The Power Deed is done when the police arrive and take control of the situation.

Put forth the *Power Dare,* accept the *Power Challenge,* do the *Power Deed.*

A timely "power struggle" might be reading in a timely fashion each chapter of this book, especially the difficult, new, strange or unfamiliar. Give the Power Dare "teeth" in the form of both a challenge and a time.

Commit to read a chapter a day till you finish the book!

Power Dare yourself for practice, Power Challenge for preparation, Power Deed for performance. In less than a month you have read the whole book and become a *TOTAL Power of ONE in America!*

Adopt the POWER DEED CREED,
Get a Handy Bookmark!

TOTAL Power of ONE in America assembles information widely scattered and not readily available. Such reading can be hard work that is easily postponed or avoided. Resolve to use your *Power of ONE* to overcome such barriers.

At the end of this chapter is the "Power Deed Creed." It is a personal power statement with a duplicate, special, unnumbered page to copy or cut out, fold in half and use as a bookmark.

The "Power Deed Creed" uses the Power Dare, Power Challenge and Power Deed for any important assignment or challenge you choose. Use them, for example, to read the whole book straight through, especially chapters that seem particularly tough.

You will also find the *"Power of ONE"* creed and *"Power of ONE"* Commitment." These serve not only as motivators but also as reminders that you have enormous powers and can use them to help create a better world.

Accept the "Chapter-A-Day-Challenge"

Finally, find the "Chapter a Day" Book Reading Challenge Record. Record the date at the top for the first day you begin reading *TOTAL Power of ONE in America*. Resolve to read a chapter-a-day until the book is complete.

You can use some perhaps long-forgotten motivators, "stars." Each day you complete a chapter place the date completed on the blank beside the chapter number. To show you've read, reviewed and thought about them, check the "S" for the Summary for Review, and the "Q" for the Questions for Review. Any day you read a chapter at your original goal of one-a-day give yourself a star (*). Should you get ahead, more than a chapter-a-day, give yourself a double star (**). Let these stars and double stars be your indicators of promises made, commitments met. Go for the stars.

Some 27 days hence you will have finished the book. Congratulations! You can use the remaining three or four days to review the book and to plan your short and long range goals and activities to use your new *TOTAL Power of ONE* and your Life Power Tools of knowledge, information and understanding. Your new life is just beginning and this is the first day of it. Get organized for a lifetime of power, promise, opportunity, service, fulfillment and achievement. This is just the beginning, *Power of ONE*.

The Power of ONE is the Power of God in Man

Your horizons and vistas for change are virtually unlimited. One poet described his vision of an unhappy God, disappointed and angry enough to destroy the planet and its people. One person told God not to do it, so he didn't. Get and cherish the beauty of poems, in this case, James Stephens' "What Thomas Said in a Pub"[6].

Remember, *Power of ONE, you* have the capabilities and potential to profoundly and positively change the world around you. Remember your *Power of ONE* creed:

The Power of ONE
I am ONE.
I am only ONE.
But I will do,
What ONE can do.

You count. You matter. You make a difference. But to make a difference, you must be different. And you are. You are a *Power of ONE.* You are a distinct, unique, distinguished and very special human being. Use your power! The world needs you desperately!

Questions for Review

1. The whole idea of the *Power of ONE is* that ONE person CAN make a difference. What makes that possible and workable?

2. What choice does ONE person have regarding whether ONE can make a difference?

3. In learning, repetition is Father of, Mother of, and King of something. What are they? Why is repetition necessary and desirable?

4. Is willingness to take a risk or try something new a sign of failure or success? Why?

5. What are "excuse thoughts" and how do they work? Name some. What would be the opposite of these "don't thoughts" be called, with examples? Discuss "mind-forged manacles?"

6. Why does "Draw a bigger circle" include us in, not leave us out? Why is it important?

7. "Each one teach one" is a way to pass it on. How does one "MULTIPLY" to do it ten times faster?

8. State the *Power of ONE* philosophy and explain it. What is the two-step *Power of ONE* technique using FAITH and ACTION? What is the 20-letter, 10-word formula for full responsibility, full personal power?

6. Oscar Williams, Ed., *A Little Treasury of Modern Poetry,* p. 595 Charles Scribner's Sons, New York: 1952

9. "Act as though it were impossible to fail" is the theme of a good old book. How does that thought relate to the *Power of ONE?*

10. Explain the Power Dare, Power Challenge and Power Deed. How are they related to a business contract in terms of offer, acceptance and performance? How can you use them to program both performance and achievement, in yourself and others? How can you use the "Power Deed Creed" to achieve? How can you "earn your stars" as a reward to yourself for reading "a chapter a day?"

I cannot believe that the purpose of life is (merely) to be 'happy.' I think the purpose of life is to be useful, to be responsible, to be honorable, to be compassionate. It is, above all, to matter: to have it make some difference that you lived at all.   —Leo Rosten

I am only one, but still I am one; I cannot do everything, but still I can do something; and because I cannot do everything, I will not refuse to do the something that I can do.   —Edward Everett Hale

You gain strength, courage and confidence by every experience in which you really stop to look fear in the face.... You must do the thing you think you cannot do.   —Eleanor Roosevelt, American first lady, 1884-1962

I would rather be ashes than dust! I would rather that my spark would burn out in a brilliant blaze than it should be stifled by dry rot. I would rather be a superb meteor, every atom of me in magnificent glow, than a sleepy and permanent planet. The proper function of man is to live, not to exist. I shall not waste my days in trying to prolong them. I shall use my time.
—Jack London

Power Deed Creed

I Power Dare me to complete this chapter with excellence. I vow to take the time and make the effort necessary to read this chapter carefully, thoughtfully, completely. To accept this Power Challenge and perform this Power Deed is to do the Tough Stuff This is a "life changer chapter" that will make a momentous change in my life and ability to make a significant, positive difference in the world around me. I make this Power Dare. I accept this Power Challenge. I do this Power Deed.

This is my Power Deed Creed.

The Power of ONE

I am ONE.

I am only ONE.

But I will do,

What ONE can do.

TOTAL Power of ONE: A Commitment

I am a *TOTAL Power of ONE in America.* I count. I matter. I make a difference. I commit to preserve the freedom I inherited. Each generation has left a better world. Can I do less? Through knowledge, information, understanding, concern and action, I pledge to make a positive, lasting difference in the world. Starting here and now ...

I COMMIT MY LIFE TO
ACHIEVEMENT.

I COMMIT MY LIFE TO
EXCELLENCE.

_____
Signed   Date

TOTAL Power of One in America
Copyright (c) 2001 by Fred Holden.

Phoenix Enterprises, PO Box 1900
Arvada, CO 80001   303/421-7619

Book Reading Challenge Record

Big Goal: Read Book in a Month

Goal: Read a Chapter a Day

*Date Begun:*_____

*Date to Complete:*_____

Stars	Chap	Sum( ) Que( )	Date Compl.
___	Intro	S( ) Q( )	_____
___	Chapt. 1	S( ) Q( )	_____
___	Chapt. 2	S( ) Q( )	_____
___	Chapt. 3	S( ) Q( )	_____
___	Chapt. 4	S( ) Q( )	_____
___	Chapt. 5	S( ) Q( )	_____
___	Chapt. 6	S( ) Q( )	_____
___	Chapt. 7	S( ) Q( )	_____
___	Chapt. 8	S( ) Q( )	_____
___	Chapt. 9	S( ) Q( )	_____
___	Chapt. 10	S( ) Q( )	_____
___	Chapt. 11	S( ) Q( )	_____
___	Chapt. 12	S( ) Q( )	_____
___	Chapt. 13	S( ) Q( )	_____
___	Chapt. 14	S( ) Q( )	_____
___	Chapt. 15	S( ) Q( )	_____
___	Chapt. 16	S( ) Q( )	_____
___	Chapt. 17	S( ) Q( )	_____
___	Chapt. 18	S( ) Q( )	_____
___	Chapt. 19	S( ) Q( )	_____
___	Chapt. 20	S( ) Q( )	_____
___	Chapt. 21	S( ) Q( )	_____
___	Chapt. 22	S( ) Q( )	_____
___	Chapt. 23	S( ) Q( )	_____
___	Chapt. 24	S( ) Q( )	_____
___	Chapt. 25	S( ) Q( )	_____
___	Chapt. 26	S( ) Q( )	_____

Review Complete:_____

* Chap. On schedule.

** Chap. ahead of schedule.

TOTAL Power of One in America
Copyright (c) 2001 by Fred Holden.

Phoenix Enterprises, PO Box 1900
Arvada, CO 80001   303/421-7619

Power Deed Creed

I Power Dare me to complete this chapter with excellence. I vow to take the time and make the effort necessary to read this chapter carefully, thoughtfully, completely. To accept this Power Challenge and perform this Power Deed is to do the Tough Stuff This is a "life changer chapter" that will make a momentous change in my life and ability to make a significant, positive difference in the world around me. I make this Power Dare. I accept this Power Challenge. I do this Power Deed.

This is my Power Deed Creed.

The Power of ONE

I am ONE.
I am only ONE.
But I will do,
What ONE can do.

TOTAL Power of ONE: A Commitment

I am a *TOTAL Power of ONE in America.* I count. I matter. I make a difference. I commit to preserve the freedom I inherited. Each generation has left a better world. Can I do less? Through knowledge, information, understanding, concern and action, I pledge to make a positive, lasting difference in the world. Starting here and now ...

I COMMIT MY LIFE TO
ACHIEVEMENT.

I COMMIT MY LIFE TO
EXCELLENCE.

Signed   Date

TOTAL Power of One in America
Copyright (c) 2001 by Fred Holden.

Phoenix Enterprises, PO Box 1900
Arvada, CO 80001   303/421-7619

Book   Reading   Challenge   Record

Big Goal: Read Book in a Month
        Goal: Read a Chapter a Day
*Date Begun:*_____
*Date to Complete:*_____

Stars	Chap	Sum( ) Que( )	Date Compl.
___	Intro	S( ) Q( )	_____
___	Chapt. 1	S( ) Q( )	_____
___	Chapt. 2	S( ) Q( )	_____
___	Chapt. 3	S( ) Q( )	_____
___	Chapt. 4	S( ) Q( )	_____
___	Chapt. 5	S( ) Q( )	_____
___	Chapt. 6	S( ) Q( )	_____
___	Chapt. 7	S( ) Q( )	_____
___	Chapt. 8	S( ) Q( )	_____
___	Chapt. 9	S( ) Q( )	_____
___	Chapt. 10	S( ) Q( )	_____
___	Chapt. 11	S( ) Q( )	_____
___	Chapt. 12	S( ) Q( )	_____
___	Chapt. 13	S( ) Q( )	_____
___	Chapt. 14	S( ) Q( )	_____
___	Chapt. 15	S( ) Q( )	_____
___	Chapt. 16	S( ) Q( )	_____
___	Chapt. 17	S( ) Q( )	_____
___	Chapt. 18	S( ) Q( )	_____
___	Chapt. 19	S( ) Q( )	_____
___	Chapt. 20	S( ) Q( )	_____
___	Chapt. 21	S( ) Q( )	_____
___	Chapt. 22	S( ) Q( )	_____
___	Chapt. 23	S( ) Q( )	_____
___	Chapt. 24	S( ) Q( )	_____
___	Chapt. 25	S( ) Q( )	_____
___	Chapt. 26	S( ) Q( )	_____

Review Complete:_____
        * Chap. On schedule.
        ** Chap. ahead of schedule.

Chapter 3

POWER CHALLENGE
Read the Bill of Rights!

Bill Forstchen, a civics, social studies and U. S. history teacher in Vassalboro, Maine, vowed to teach those subjects in such a way that students would remember them six months later, a challenging assignment.[1] He sent his students to the streets with clipboards and petitions urging repeal of "laws that coddled criminals." They contacted people, good citizens just like you and me, and got plenty of supporters. The petition drive took place in two towns, Waterville and Augusta, Maine.

The results were astounding and alarming. Three out of four people, 74%, signed their names to the petitions. In the two locations, 9 and 29 percent, respectively, signed without even reading the contents!

When the petition signing was complete, only about 8 percent, one out of twelve people, recognized that document of laws that allegedly coddled criminals, for what it was—THE BILL OF RIGHTS!

Forstchen said his students were deeply shocked at the ease with which the public could be persuaded to repeal their fundamental freedoms as outlined in the Bill of Rights. The document was hardly disguised. Only the title was deleted. The text was word-for-word.

America—where have you been? Where are you going?

It is appropriate to consider the Bill of Rights, here, up front, when we contemplate freedom. The Bill of Rights is the single most important document of freedom that makes Americans different from all the other peoples on Earth, past and present. The only thing more important is your knowledge, defense and support of the Bill of Rights. Those guarantees of

---

1."Students find Bill of Rights not popular after all," Associated Press, *Rocky Mountain News,* 11/28/79, p 34

freedom assure the American people that they are sovereign over the government! In America, each citizen is "The Boss."

The Bill of Rights is not merely a wish list of the way things ought to be. It is the law of the land, a listing of "thou shalt nots" of what the government can NOT do to you. In addition, the government is not only empowered, but REQUIRED to enforce and maintain those rights that keep you sovereign over the government. But who is the government? It's the citizens, you and me, and we must assure those rights are enforced, and never abused, diminished or destroyed. That is our job as sovereign citizens.

Sovereign means bigger than; in control of, over or superior to all; supreme in power, rank or authority. It means government is the servant, the citizen is master. Yes, it means you are greater than, or above the government. Do you realize the power in all that?

You, the American Citizen: Bigger Than Big!

You, Power of ONE, are an American citizen, with the rights, freedoms and privileges, along with the obligations and responsibilities guaranteed to you by the Bill of Rights. That makes you big, *really BIG!*

How big is big? The Bill of Rights makes you bigger than the government, the Central Intelligence Agency (CIA), the Federal Bureau of Investigation (FBI), Interstate Commerce Commission (ICC), maybe even bigger than the Internal Revenue Service (IRS) and all the others. Wow!

How big is big? It is bigger than all the money government spends in a year. Now that's big! In fiscal year 1999, ending September 30, the federal government[2] took in $1,827 billion and spent $1,703 billion, incurring a "surplus" of $124 billion! As small as that figure is, it doesn't take into account the increases in Social Security and other trust funds. The true deficit—how much the public debt increased, was $127 billion, a considerably smaller difference than in past years.

But you are bigger.

The national debt at that time was about $5.606 TRILLION, written out $5,606,087,000,000! It cost $353 billion for interest alone, to service the national debt. (And as one of 273 million United States citizens in 1999, you paid $1,294 annual interest; for each of America's 133.49 million employed, $3,648 per worker. Your share of the debt was $20,522.)

As an American citizen, you are bigger even than all that.

Learn the First Magic Number: 273, and Growing

These numbers seem overwhelming, but need not be, especially with our first magic number, 273. In millions, that's the approximate mid-1999

---

2. *Budget of the United States Government, Historical Tables, Fiscal year 2001*, pp 20, 86, 111, U. S. Government Printing Office; *Economic Report of the President, Feb 2000*, pp 345, 346

population of the United States. Take any of those seemingly incomprehensible numbers, divide by the magic number, and you will have a better understanding of what those numbers really mean to *one person, you.*

For future estimates use a population of 285 million people [275 plus (4 x 2½) = 285] in 2000 and increase it 2½ million every year thereafter. For instance in 2004 we'll have about 290 million people [280 plus (4 x 2½) = 290].

What is a Billion?

The late Senator Everett Dirksen from Illinois, when chided for some routine budget cuts retorted, "A billion here and a billion there, and pretty soon you're talking about real money!"

Just what is a billion?

Big numbers such as a billion are difficult to comprehend. Let's think about a billion in a different way, in terms of time. A billion seconds is 31.7 years. Looking back, that's the late-60's, with President Lyndon Johnson and the Viet Nam "police action." A billion minutes is about 1902 years, almost back to the time of Christ. A billion hours is over 114,000 years, 100,000 years before the dawn of recorded human history.

A billion dollars is 5.1 hours in United States federal government spending! That is at its 1999 rate over a TRILLION dollars, $1,703 billion (that's $1,703,040,000,000!). In about half a night's sleep, the government spent over a billion dollars. That's enough to keep you awake all night!

Our shortest common time unit is a second. In one *second* the federal government spends over $54,000! Where does all that money come from, and where does it go? What does it do on the way, being collected, "processed" and spent?

Another way to look at all this is to compare what we, the American people, spend on government to what we spend on the basic necessities of life: food, shelter and clothing. In 1999, we spent $145 billion MORE on government than we spent on these necessities of life! Based on national spending do we value government more than life?

The details are instructive. In 1999 our nation[3] spent *in billions of dollars,* 903 on food, 1,266 on housing and household operation, 306 on clothing and shoes, for a total of $2,475 billion on these "essentials of life."

During that same year, what did we spend on government? Federal government spent $1,703 billion, while state-and-local government spent $917 billion. The total of $2,620 billion spent on all government was $145 billion more than we spent on essentials. Here is the information in chart form:

---

3. *Economic Report of the President, February, 2000,* U. S. Government Printing Office, pp 324, 397, 402

Annual Spending, Essentials of Life and Government (Outlays) for 1999, $ Billion

Essentials of Life		Government (Outlays)		Difference
Food	$ 903	Federal	$1,703	
Shelter	1,266	State/Local	917	
Clothing	306			
Totals	$2,475	Totals	$2,620	$145
Population	273 (millions)		273	
Per person	$9,066		$9,597	$531

Using our magic number, 273, we learn on average, each person paid $531 more for government at $9,597 than the $9,066 paid for life's essentials.

We pay a lot for a lot of government, and we might ask why we need so much. Perhaps we should learn more about where the money, taxes, comes from, since we all pay all of them.

Power of ONE: You are Bigger Than All This Big

The design of the American Republic based on the United States Constitution and its first ten amendments, the Bill of Rights, makes you and each American citizen sovereign, bigger than, and to be protected by, the federal government. Knowing, at least in dollar terms, just how big it is, gives you an idea how big you are.

Another important concept of freedom is in an economic and dollar sense. If you earn $100 and keep $100, you are 100% free. If you earn $100 and keep zero dollars because something or someone takes it away from you, you are 100% slave. Because of the vital functions of government, to be free, we must allocate some part of the fruits of our labors, taken in taxes, to protect our freedoms from foreign nations and sometimes from each other.

As government takes relatively more in taxes, we experience relatively less freedom. Therefore, there is a relationship and a balance between the taxes we pay and the freedoms we enjoy. That's why it is so important to understand the economic dimension of freedom.

For Your Eyelids Only: Only People Pay Taxes!

For starters we learn four very important words:
ONLY PEOPLE PAY TAXES !

Close your eyes and etch those four important words indelibly on the back of your eyelids, both eyelids, in stereo, so that you will never forget them: ONLY PEOPLE PAY TAXES!

Those who say oil companies, car companies, computer companies, airlines, utilities, or any other businesses don't pay enough taxes, are only part right. They don't pay *any* taxes! They only *collect* taxes, from the people, their customers. Why? Because the law requires they do so, and we are a law-abiding society. That's the only way it can work and work so well. Remember, not cottonwoods, nor Martians, nor gophers, nor "businesses" pay taxes. *ONLY PEOPLE PAY TAXES!*

Sometimes taxes are openly and predictably collected, such as the federal income tax, where we have the forms and the rules, complicated and complex as they are, and know how much and why we pay what we pay.

Sometimes taxes are called "contributions" such as with Social Security taxes, but they are still taxes; and we, the people, still pay them, even though they are not deductible. Other names for government revenues include fees, fines, permits, licenses and borrowing. Taxes are now called "investments" and more recently, "user fees." These are imposed without reducing the taxes that formerly were paid for the same thing. That is why they are really "tax increases." Similarly, evaluate the meaning of taxes as "investments." The term is nonsensical, except in the sense to fool people into accepting unwarranted tax increases.

Sometimes taxes are hidden in the price of goods and services, such as corporate income taxes, property and excise taxes and the "employer's share" of Social Security payments. But only people pay them. Businesses, in compliance with the law collect them, and must acquire them in the price of their products and services, from their only source of revenue, customers. (That is us.)

One more time, what are the four words about taxes that we shouldn't forget?

Working the Big Numbers: What's it to Me?

Now, knowing the source of tax revenues, the magnitudes need not be so overwhelming and unintelligible. We can apply the first magic number, 273, and find out an individual citizen's view of our colossal government.

For instance, in outlays, the federal government, in 1999, spent $1,703,000 (million) divided by 273 (million), or about $6,264 for every man, woman and child in America. If you happen to be a member of a family of four, your part of the total expense was 4 times that, $24,936. Federal taxes collected per-capita were $6,694—$1,827,500 divided by 273.

Similarly, for interest on the national debt, that is not some far out number recognized and known only in Washington, DC. We can divide the $353,000 million interest paid on the public debt by our magic number of 273 (million) Americans, and learn that *your share* in 1999 was $1,293.

This interest-only money in the form of taxes had to be collected and paid, and you paid it, either directly or indirectly. If there are more than just you in your taxpaying unit, you all paid it all; for example, $5,172 for a family of four, to pay their combined interest on the national debt. That's a lot of money we work for, earn, but do not have to spend, in order to fund a government debt, isn't it? And it doesn't do any work of government in social programs, environmental protection, national defense, etc.

The Real Taxpayers are the Real Workers

The tax burden is even higher than that because the only real taxpayers are those who *create the real wealth* of America, the entrepreneurs who take the risks, and employees who do the hard work. These total over 133[4] million people out of the total population of 273 million. So if you worked in 1999 you paid taxes for at least one other person (1.05 additional, to be exact, or 2.05 times what you initially calculated!) No wonder you feel over-taxed. You are!

This is a way to judge the size and spending of the federal government. You probably have your own opinion of government size, growth and spending. It is important to know how to appraise government impact on the individual citizen. You, *Power of One,* can evaluate the costs of government versus the benefits of government. Then not only as a citizen, but as a provider and consumer of government services, you can evaluate if you are getting your money's worth. Either way, it is your money. You worked hard for it, and you paid your share, your total share, of the total tax bill.

If I'm so Big, How Come I Feel So Small?

Freedoms, rights and liberties are a lot like muscles. If you don't use them, you lose them. They atrophy. Part of the American void in education is in the area of citizen rights, opportunities and freedoms, along with the responsibilities and obligations that go with them.

Freedoms are not free. The greater the freedom, the greater the responsibility that goes with it. There can be no freedom without its commensurate responsibility. That is why freedom is better described in the three-word phrase, "freedom with responsibility."

Part of that responsibility is the recognition that we enjoy priceless freedoms along with the knowledge that freedoms are not free, that they must be recognized, defended and preserved, or they can be lost and likely will be.

So it is back to the question of who is protecting your freedom? The answer is "YOU!" Anything that has been done, is being done, or ever will be done to protect your freedom is done by you. What are you doing to protect *your freedom?*

An important consideration is that freedoms are too easy to take for granted. In America they have (seemingly) always been here. They have been freely given, freely available and freely taken advantage of, and they seem to be

4. Ibid, p 370

forever. They are not. Freedom is delicate, fragile, vulnerable and perishable. Will you bequeath freedom to your children?

Freedom? What's a Freedom?

The difficult part about freedoms is that they are intangible, invisible and mute. What color are they? How big are they? How much do they weigh? Where are they located? Have you ever seen or heard a freedom? These are questions you might ask about material things. Freedoms are not physical material, but are far more important than a physical good. They are ideas and conditions, part of the environment, almost like the air we breathe. Here is freedom expressed in five "to's":

FREEDOM is -- free to be, to do, to choose, to dare and to become.

William Simon, in his book *A Time for Truth*[5] defined *freedom* as follows:

> Freedom is strangely ephemeral. It is something like breathing; one only becomes acutely aware of its importance when one is choking. Similarly, it is only when one confronts political tyranny that one really grasps the meaning and importance of freedom. Freedom is difficult to understand because it isn't a presence but an absence— an absence of governmental restraint.

Contrast that to George Washington's definition of government:

> Government is not reason; it is not eloquence; it is force! Like fire, it is a dangerous servant and a fearful master.

President Woodrow Wilson contrasted government and freedom thus:

> Liberty has never come from Government. Liberty has always come from the subjects of it. The history of liberty is a history of resistance, of limitations of governmental power, not the increase of it.

Arnold Schwarzenegger, famous body builder-turned-actor, was interviewed regarding the 1987 bi-centennial celebration of the Statue of Liberty. He hadn't forgotten what it was like coming here from Austria in 1969, and the moment he was granted American citizenship in 1983:

> This country is something I will never take for granted, no one should. Many have sacrificed so much to gain and keep our freedom, and it's something we must all work to help preserve.

5. Simon, William E., *A Time for Truth*, p 19, McGraw-Hill, New York: 1978

Turning On to Freedom: The U.S. Constitution

Probably the greatest problem is getting students interested in topics such as the U.S. Constitution and Bill of Rights (the first 10 amendments), government and taxes, legislation and politics, along with freedom, economics, business, risk, entrepreneurship, profits and losses, regulations, etc. At a student's age, it does not seem interesting, pertinent or relevant. Later, when it is more important, there's no way and no time to learn what is needed. There seems not to be much stimulating and thought-provoking literature about those great documents. Or maybe it is because we citizens haven't "turned on" so it is difficult for us to know, learn and teach. Your reading this book will change all that.

A New Challenge; A New Beginning

Power Challenge: Read the Bill of Rights.

Our American citizens' Bill of Rights is a good place to start. Find it and read it. Then re-read it. Study it. It is a list of "thou shalt nots" which tell the government what they cannot and must not do to you. This is the document that truly makes you, an American, different.

In a constitutional republic, we are a self-governing people with limited government under the protection of our central government. It protects "Life, Liberty, and Property, and the Pursuit of Happiness" of the people. While the Constitution itself tells the organization, authority and some limitations of the federal government, *the Bill of Rights protects the individual from government.* The Constitution defines what government can do; the Bill of Rights, what it can't do to citizens.

Consider the larger picture. Read the U.S. Constitution, from its preamble to the last amendment; then re-read that also. See how its first 10 amendments, the Bill of Rights, fit in with the Constitution, and with the ensuing amendments. Then *study* the Constitution. You may want to take a few moments to read the Declaration of Independence for basic philosophy and legislative intent to support the Constitution.

Consider how you feel about the whole Constitution, especially in light of late twentieth century issues, such as the proposed Equal Rights Amendment (ERA) and the balanced budget amendment. At one point many states were calling for a first ever Constitutional convention to help assure they would have more power, especially in budget and tax collection matters. What effect would such a convention have on the states? On you? On your rights? On the Constitution itself? Could it all be scrapped and replaced? It has never been done before!

Next, read and re-read the Declaration of Independence. What were its goals? What were its grievances? Do they exist today? If so, to what extent? Just in case you can't immediately find a copy of the Bill of Rights, here's Article I with five "thou shalt nots" in its concise, profound entirety:

Congress shall make no law respecting an establishment of religion, or prohibiting the free exercise thereof; or abridging the freedom of speech, or of the press; or the right of the people peaceably to assemble, and to petition the Government for a redress of grievances.

WOW! The very first amendment provides five basic rights that protect you and make you 10 feet tall in the eyes of your subservient government!

What's Up Front? Freedom of Religion.

What's first? Freedom of religion. And note the very important second phrase we never hear, as though it doesn't exist, "or prohibiting the free exercise thereof." Perhaps that says that you can pray or not pray, be religious or not religious, any place, any time, and no one, not the government or anyone else, can prevent or prohibit it. The government is required to protect but forbidden to prohibit your freedom of religion. Maybe that condones private prayer not only in schools but in other places. And maybe that phrase carries more authority than the non-Constitutional phrase, "separation of church and state." Study the issue and decide for yourself.

There are four other living, vital freedoms enumerated in that brief passage: Freedom of speech, freedom of the press, freedom to peaceably assemble, and freedom to petition your government for redress of grievances.

Protect Sharing of Ideas, Freedom of Expression

We hear more and more that the Constitution of the United States is old, archaic, ancient, antiquated, not suited to the 20th, much less, the 21st century. Is it out of date? Or like the Bible is it timeless? Have we barely really begun to use, know, and understand it? Are we just beginning to appreciate the wisdom of America's founding fathers who worked so hard and gave so much that we might enjoy as well as preserve this beautiful piece of work?

In my speeches I tell my audiences that we usually exercise three of our first amendment rights guaranteed by the Constitution: freedom of religion (invocation, or prayer), freedom of speech or expression, to share ideas, and freedom of assembly, meeting together and association.

Then I pose a question: "How many of you are fearful there is someone outside the door of this room with a machete, waiting to chop your head off for being in this meeting? Why, or why not? How productive would and could we be if we were in such fear of our lives? When we get home, will there be uniformed guards there to say, 'We know where you've been and what you've been doing. We've already taken your family to jail, and we will probably execute you very soon.'"

No, we don't worry about such things, because we are Americans, and we are protected by our Bill of Rights. We think enough of those special rights that we defend them, and if needed, die for them, and for our God-given freedom. Thank God there is no one that will imprison us or hurt us for thinking, sharing and associating, as is common in so many other countries.

We are able to think and talk, create and write, print and publish, to distribute ideas in newspapers and magazines and on the Internet without being threatened, coerced or controlled by the government. We can communicate ideas through the electronic media on radio and television, and through phones, faxes and email. We can criticize our government, and seek reparation without retribution or punishment. It is our right to seek redress of grievances, and to defend our rights!

Power! Protection! Freedom! And Nine More!

Talk about power, about protection, about freedom. Wow! And that is only the first amendment. There are nine more. What do they say? What do they mean? How do they make your life and mine more protected, secure, predictable and safe? How do they afford us opportunity and challenge? What do they mean to you? What is number 10?

We can conclude that the Declaration of Independence, the United States Constitution and its incredibly important Bill of Rights are either an accident or a miracle. All my evidence says they are divinely-inspired. We are part of a miracle, the Miracle of Freedom and the Miracle of America.

Where to find these documents? They are in almanacs and encyclopedias, in history and social studies books.

There you have it, *Power of ONE.* Your first Power Dare is to read the Bill of Rights, and its accompanying documents. Will you accept this Power Challenge? Reading doesn't really serve the whole purpose. There's a history, philosophy, culture, background and precedent for these special freedom documents. More than just being read, they should be studied and enjoyed. What an interesting and exciting challenge! Make this one a Power Deed, *Power of ONE.*

Power Challenge: Read the Bill of Rights!

Questions for Review

1. What "laws that coddled criminals" were to be repealed by petition as signed by 3 out of 4 citizens of the State of Maine?
2. Is the U.S. Constitution the law of people or of government? Explain.
3. What is the name of the first 10 amendments to the Constitution? What is their purpose?
4. An American citizen is sovereign over, bigger than the government. How big is government as expressed in dollars

spent per year? What is the magic number of population and how can it be used to better understand otherwise very large numbers? Characterize government size in individual terms, a citizen's share of spending, taxes, debt, and interest on the debt.

5. If you know 2000's U. S. population of 275 million people grows about 2½ million people a year, what will the U. S. population be in 2006?

6. The federal government spends a billion dollars in how many hours, about half the time we sleep at night? It is about how many dollars a second? An hour?

7. The "necessities of life" are defined as "food, shelter and clothing." Based on annual spending levels, is federal government more or less necessary than life's necessities? By how much?

8. What four important words remind us who pays taxes? Name and describe hidden taxes. Where are they hidden?

9. William Simon describes freedom as an absence, not a presence, of what? Describe freedom in both economic terms ($100) and life terms—"The Five To's."

10. What are the relationships among and distinctions between the Declaration of Independence, the U.S. Constitution and the Bill of Rights? What five freedoms are in the first amendment?

Most of us take freedom too much for granted and think of it in the abstract—in songs, poems and political speeches. But once lost, and then regained, it becomes the most tangible of luxuries, our most priceless natural resource. If we squander it, as we do our mineral resources, there will soon be little left for our children to enjoy. We can find substitutes for our depleted minerals. But there is no substitute for freedom.   —Lawrence K. Lunt

What we obtain too cheaply we esteem too lightly; it is dearness only that gives everything its value. Heaven knows how to put a proper price upon its goods; and it would be strange indeed if so celestial an article as freedom should not be highly rated.   —Thomas Paine

You can only protect your liberties in this world by protecting the other man's freedom. You can only be free if I am free.   —Clarence Darrow

Chapter 4

POWER CHALLENGE
Talk to Kids!

It seems like such a simple assignment, especially for someone else. I hope "they" are doing their share of talking to kids. Well, I mean, teachers can't do it all alone. We adults and parents can make our presence known and felt, tell them our thoughts and philosophies, our lives, careers, business and background. I'm sure someone is doing it. It sure sounds important. They need it.

"Why Didn't Anyone Tell Me?"

My boss had called to tell me to attend a meeting at the Colorado Association of Realtor building, to hear "Howard Post." I was already busy, but being a keen student of "bossology," I said I would be there.

I approached the doorway and met some other attendees. "Is Howard Post here?" I asked, "I've come to meet Howard Post."

"There is no Howard Post here," I was told. "But there is a Howard Propst. Is that who you're looking for?" I guessed so. I either heard, or was told wrong.

"Propst," I said to myself, "That sounds familiar."

The crowd filled the small meeting room, to a gathering of perhaps 40 people. Mr. Propst approached the podium and explained to us the purpose of this get-together.

Howard and his family had grown up and lived in northeastern Colorado. He had served as a state legislator about the time I was growing up in Sterling, Colorado, during the early 1950's. That is why the name was more than vaguely familiar.

Howard explained he had retired and moved to Florida. He and his family had embarked on a new "discover America" project as a hobby. They had photographed a sizable portion of this magnificent country. They traveled all over America visiting her places and meeting her people.

The Propsts had put together a slide program that they wanted to share with us, and then to seek ideas on what could or should be done with it. They thought all Americans would want to see it.

Time seemed to drag sitting in the dark watching color slides during the hour-long, after-lunch presentation. It did a commendable job, though, of showing the real America, her places, people and prosperity. The show was over and the lights came back on. Then it happened.

A young woman in the front row stood up, trembling with emotion. She was fitfully sobbing, yet trying to speak. Mr. Propst, a little embarrassed for her, said he would wait a few minutes while she composed herself, then get back to her. She persisted.

Seeing the panorama of America before her, and hearing Mr. Propst expound on the majesty of America and our great heritage was just too much for the young woman.

She gathered her fragile composure and said, "Nobody ever told me about America, the abundance, glory, goodness, power and freedom. I am 19 years old and I quit high school before I graduated. I thought it was all so hopeless. There just wasn't a good reason to continue, so I dropped out and got a job instead."

Then her voice broke up uncontrollably. She sobbed before the surprised and concerned gathering. "No," she said, still crying, "I'll continue. I must say what I have to say."

"Why didn't anyone ever tell me what I've witnessed today? Isn't there some way the greatness of this country, its people, freedoms and enterprise can be shared with students? Isn't there some better way to get this story in the schools to help inspire kids, give them a sense of direction and purpose and possibility? Isn't there someone who can help shed light on how to know the past, appreciate the present and shape the future; to know about various careers and how to pursue them, and how to contribute to the betterment of our society? Why didn't anyone ever tell me about such realities and possibilities till right now?"

Her outburst really moved me. I had gone into school systems before on a sporadic basis. But she jogged a sensitivity I'd forgotten about—a cordial and genuine welcome I'd always felt as a businessperson in the schools. But I certainly hadn't done all that much. I'd assumed many others were there also, telling America's story to our kids. "Why didn't anyone ever tell me ...?," echoed in my thinking.

The Tragedy of One of "Our Kids"

A couple years later was to be a turning point in my life. Serving on the church council I had been assigned four students for confirmation teaching and counseling, one of whom was "Robert." I had to help Robert understand

and explain not only why the church should confirm his membership, but why he, as well, should confirm *his* relationship with the church. That assignment allowed our lives to touch for several hours, on two or three occasions.

That same year, my wife, Dottie, and I served as co-directors of our church teenage performing group called "Sonshine." The group traveled all over the State of Colorado sharing a faith, joy and excitement only kids can generate and radiate. We practiced once a week and performed about once a month for almost a year.

Robert was a talented and contributing member of Sonshine. Like so many others of the church youth and our three daughters' friends, Robert was one of "our kids." (And our kids were the very best!) Robert was a good example of all that is good in young teenagers today, bright and talented. We watched him grow, mature and gain confidence.

In March of 1981, I read my daily paper to spot a news item that would forever change my life. A young man, 17, had sought a job in Los Angeles. Apparently rejected and dejected, he went to a nearby hotel and jumped 46 stories to his death.

The young man was Robert, one of our kids. I was shocked and saddened.

"Where have we failed?" I heard myself asking in bewildered grief. I recalled an article written about Clive Cussler, author of the book *Raise the Titanic!* which was entitled "Cussler Overnight Success after only Eighteen years." That's where we failed. We tell our kids all kinds of things about success, but we don't tell them about the long, uphill climb it takes to get there. We don't tell as well, about trying and failure, coming back and trying again. We had not told our young people the economic facts of life: "Where 'economic babies' come from!"

These kids grew up on television. There, every performance is the final, finished product, the best there is. Kids cannot see the years of hard work and training, practice and performance, sweat and sacrifice. They only see it as good as it can be. That turns out to be their standard, without more information and understanding.

We had not told Robert about America, her abundance, glory, goodness, power and freedom. We didn't explain challenge, opportunity, work, wealth, risk and survival. We didn't tell him about preparation and frustration, pressure and stress, application and rejection. Nor did we talk about the pain of trying to win, and losing, of failing and trying again. We didn't say this is the expected, the natural order of things. He wasn't told the only losers are those who don't try and risk and take a chance. He did not know the secret to success was to get up one more time than you fell down, and falling down is okay. He wasn't told Churchill's description of success as "going from failure to failure with enthusiasm!"

We haven't been talking to our kids! We don't properly applaud ALL their efforts, because for kids, the applause is for the effort as well as the result.

We didn't tell them about coming back with determination and resolve, and finally *persevering* to win.

WHY HADN'T WE BEEN TELLING THESE THINGS?

Robert's funeral was a painful and transforming experience for me. I watched his grief-stricken father and family trying to understand, to cope, to recover from this tragic loss. My own grief and frustration turned to determination to do whatever I could, to help prevent EVER a repeat of this tragedy. The *Power of One* philosophy says "I am one. I am only one. But I will do, what one can do." What can I do?

I vowed never to refuse to talk to kids. I would seek and solicit opportunities to talk to them. I would go into the schools, and bring the students into my job, to expose them to the exciting real world of business, to real people who care and work very hard, doing their real jobs and making their real contributions to our society. That's what any adult can do:

Talk to Kids!

Working with Kids: The Agony and the Ecstasy

I have always been reluctant to say "no." I say "yes!" Fate will send something or someone very important my way and I don't want to miss it. Sure, there is uncertainty and sacrifice of time and ego, but there are incalculable rewards that are otherwise unattainable and unimaginable. Always, when you give your time and yourself to others, you get more than you give.

"Please Debbie, Don't Bite My Hand!"

In a short-term public relations job my boss asked if I would help pilot a new program called "Project Business" sponsored by Junior Achievement. Without hesitation, I said "Yes, I would like to. What is it all about?" He said it was to supplement classes in the junior high, seventh grade level particularly in business, civics and social studies. The new title they gave me was "Business Consultant." I hoped I could bring that off with pride.

I went to an orientation meeting and soon met the teacher with whom I'd be working. I would conduct a one-hour class every Wednesday for 10 weeks. She would back me up with discipline and coordination with other classwork during the rest of the week.

As usual, after I said "yes," I wondered "why" briefly, then got on with it. I prepared the best I could for the first day, but I was nervous and apprehensive when it arrived. I visited the teacher early and didn't really need to hear what she told me for my first exposure to seventh graders and "Project Business."

"Mr. Holden, Debbie's not here today, but otherwise, everything's about the way it'll be the rest of the classes," she cautioned. "That's fine," I said, "but who's Debbie?" "Well," she said "we had a guest speaker last week and Debbie bit his hand!" She explained that Debbie had emotional problems, but was usually fairly well behaved. I was glad Debbie wasn't there at my first session with those kids. But when it was over, I was still nervous, and especially anxious about the upcoming week when Debbie would be there.

My fears were unfounded. Debbie turned out to be the highlight of the whole fulfilling semester. She wrote me special notes every couple of weeks, telling me how much she enjoyed my being there and teaching her "so many new things."

On one field trip to the Federal Reserve Bank, I felt special again. As you might predict, the whole class—except Debbie—got into the school bus and headed straight to the back. The teacher sat directly behind the bus driver and I sat opposite her in the right front seat. Debbie sat down next to me and began to tell me how much she was enjoying the class and my being a part of it.

We toured the bank. On the return trip, Debbie put her head on my shoulder and fell asleep. I had become someone really special to Debbie, and I felt special. You can never really tell the impact, short or long term, that you make on kids. Your being with them sends a powerful message about more than you'll ever realize, not just you, but adults, citizens, workers, Americans, and other people who care.

At the last class, Debbie gave me a blue card in a yellow envelope. It read "Mr. Holden, you are the sunshine of my life. I've looked forward to having you in class and have learned so much from you. You are a very smart man, and you brought lots of sunshine into my life. Thank you for being here."

Thank you, Debbie, for being there, and for being you. And I gave thanks to you for letting me be there!

As a footnote to this story, I met Debbie, a grown woman seven or eight years later, shopping with her Mom in a local grocery store. When I recognized her I introduced myself and asked how things were going with her. She said things were fine. Her Mother interrupted excitedly to share that they had given Debbie continuing treatment for her emotional problems and found them not to be "the problem." It turned out she had impaired hearing, and with corrective measures, she had become a very successful student.

Many years later I once again saw Debbie as an adult and parent. She attended a public hearing on a new mass transit government proposal and spoke out to those in authority.

If I hadn't said "yes," I would never have met Debbie, nor received the gift of a very personally rewarding experience, talking to kids.

Say "YES!" to possibilities. Say "YES!" to opportunities.

Why Talk to Kids?

Many of us are parents. We "know" it is in a kid's job description to not listen to adults. Well, that is only partially right. It is not in a kid's job description to listen to PARENTS. They love to listen to adults who aren't parents. They do listen to parents, secretly, but don't always show it.

Not immediately obvious is why it is so important for adults who aren't teachers to go into schools and talk to kids. In fact it is common to say "Let teachers do the teaching. That is what they're there for, isn't it? That's what they're being paid for." No, there is more to it.

It is important enough to repeat the message from that junior high school principal: "We're so pleased you decided to come into the schools, Fred," he said. "We desperately need outside help to really provide a good overall education. We teachers never get out of school. We go to school for 16 years to become a teacher and then stay in school, sometimes for the rest of our lives, to teach. We know little about business and we've never had to meet a payroll. We educators lead a pretty sheltered life. I want you to know how important it is to me, and to all of us, that you are here, teaching with us." There's another reason we must: Talk to Kids!

One More Time: Why Talk to Kids?

Our young people are intensely interested in so many things today. Look at the society in which they're growing up. It is complex and changing fast. It appears that youthful human nature cannot catch up or keep up. They can't learn fast enough, and don't have enough of the human exposure and experience they need. Our accelerating technological society has been described in *The Third Wave, The Third Force, Future Shock, Megatrends* and *Megatrends 2000*[1]. Young people are lambasted with thousands of advertising messages, and often conflicting and confusing information from radio, newspapers, magazines and television. They need real live human beings to help them separate, internalize, interpret, sort out and understand what is going on.

In other words, our young people need YOU!

Another source of information, some incomplete or just plain wrong, is their peers. If all kids know is what they learn from television and then from each other, their worldview is limited and distorted. They resist accepting information and guidance from routine authority figures, so it is even more important such discourse come from you and for you in turn, to emphasize their listening to and thanking their parents and teachers.

Television, "the tube" is their window on the world. They learn more about world events by watching the action live and in color, than we ever dreamed possible only a few decades ago. They see scenes of destruction while it happens where we could once only read or hear about it weeks after it was over. They see sex that once had to be viewed in clandestine photos, magazines and movies. They watch science and technology and take for

---

1. Alvin Toffler, *The Third Wave,* Bantam Hooks' (New York, 1971); Frank G. Goble, *The Third Force*, Pocket Books (New York, 1974); Alvin Toffler, *Future Shock*, Bantam Books (New York, 1981); John Naisbitt, *Megatrends*, Warner Books (New York, 1981), with Patricia Aburdene, *Megatrends 2000*, William Morrow (New York, 1990)

granted what once was only in the minds and writings of science fiction writers.

A week-long television news series was once billed with the teaser "At 18 years of age, 15,000 hours of school, 18,000 hours of television." That's a lot of impressions, values, emotions, situations and information to absorb from television. And how can they relate it all to "my life," and to "me"? It can only be done with and through other human beings. That is why you are so important. And again that's why your Power of One is so important. These kids need someone to talk to them, listen to them and respond to them. You are the one to do it. Do what?

Talk to Kids!

What Do You Say to A Kid?

The shuddering question comes to mind, "What do you say to a kid?" You can say practically anything. "Hi there, young man, or young woman," would be a start, "What's your name?" That breaks an opening so the rest can follow. Tell them a little about yourself. That's easy. Talk about your job and hobbies, your education and growing up. Discuss America and freedom, opportunity and adventure, risk and reward. Explore success and failure, trying again and "coming back," winning and losing. Talk about life. Discuss the news, events and odd happenings, even television programs and cartoons, about drugs, booze and moderation. Discuss reading, responsibility and contributing, serving and helping, and the importance of our fellow man and our common problems and possible solutions, and each person's role in all of this.

LISTEN. As important as talking is, listening is even more vital. When they make bold to ask a question or offer an opinion, LISTEN. You will get clues how to relate your experience and background to their interests, anxieties, fears, dreams and uncertainties. One of our great societal problems is that we have so little time, no time to listen! We must listen, and respond to their true, actual verbalized feelings and emotions as well as their logical, reality-based questions.

More than "Talk to Kids" we must really seek to establish a dialogue (more than a one-way "conversation" or dual monologue) with them. Create lasting relationships. In addition to talking to a youngster, create a new friend, possibly for a lifetime. Talk, listen, question, answer, relate, create rapport. Seek to make something special happen between you and your new friends.

Want to hear about what young people want to know? Read letters-to-the-editor in your local newspaper. I liken that to mining—you have to get rid of a lot of over-burden before you get down to the mother lode. Sometimes you even find that special "gold nugget," such as the following letter from Scott Morrill of Gunnison, Colorado. From the 5/6/80 *Rocky Mountain News*:

Editor. Not only are we (America's youth) turned off and burned out, we are also scared to death because the Great American Dream has become the Great American Nightmare. Rising inflation and unemployment, the threat of war (nuclear, no less) and an energy shortage are not what dreams are made of. The number and magnitude of the problems facing this nation today are enough to turn anybody off. I feel helpless and overwhelmed. But I am not apathetic nor do I believe that most of my peers are. Rather I am confused. Where do we start to get this great country back in shape?

America's youth at this time, does not need derogatory criticism. What we do need is encouragement and a little help. Today's problems are complicated and serious and require a similar solution. It will take time, patience and, most of all cooperation to get this nation back on track.

Scott's letter was touching. Again it proved to me that America's youth are sensitive, caring, concerned—and scared. If they are anything like Scott, and most of them are, we adults have our work (and fun) cut out for us in talking to the Scotts of the world.

You think youngsters don't think and care deeply for what's happening in today's world? Read what 17-year-old Thomas Klein, in "Flourish or Perish," said in the 5/5/86 *U. S. News & World Report:*

I am not asking that today's political leaders sit down and bring an end to all the world's troubles. It would be a selfish and unrealistic plea to ask to inherit a perfect Earth. This is not to say that something close to a perfect Earth cannot be achieved, but rather that it cannot be achieved by one generation.

What I do ask of those who run our nation is simply to think of coming generations when you make your decisions. Short-term legislative actions don't cure problems—only alleviate them just long enough so that they will no longer bother the politicians involved.

I ask that you think not only selfishly of the benefits for your generation. Think of me, us, those who will inherit your government, your nation, your world. Respect us as if we were voters of today. Only then will your actions take on a long-term perspective that will meet not only your needs but the needs of future generations. Only in that way will you give us a chance to be a future generation.

"A chance to be a future generation!" Wow! That's a heavy message something to twinge all our consciences to drive us to longer-term thinking and action!

Dreams are What Life's made of

I said "yes" another time, when asked to make a presentation on economic systems, business and profits to a small group of Comprehensive Employment Training Act (CETA) students. The purpose of the course was to provide them with skills and attitudes that would help them find success in matching their capabilities and interests to available jobs. I thought a basic understanding of economics and business would help.

When I finished talking a young man with flaming red hair said, "You mean someone in America can be and do almost anything they want to?"

I said, "That's true. You could probably become a doctor if you wanted to."

He said, "I don't want to be a doctor. But I really like motorcycles. I can take them apart and fix them and I like to do that. Do you suppose I could start my own motorcycle shop?"

I assured him that if he combined commitment and determination with his skill and interest and did a good job, he could do it, that he would probably make a good living at it.

His whole attitude changed. He lit up with that new possibility. Apparently he never had such a dream before. You have to have a dream to make a dream come true, as the song says.

We need to help our young people imagine their dreams and possibilities, then figure out how to make those dreams come true. It can be done, but they need some help from us older kids.

How to Get Started

You can't and won't buy a product unless you know it exists and is available. You're the new product. Get the word out that you are available to talk to kids!

First give some thought to what you would like to talk about, and how you'd like to present it. Make it easy, and talk about yourself to start. Kids are interested in what you do, why and how you do it, and how you got where you are. They're also interested in your thoughts and feelings about a multitude of topics that become apparent after you've begun to share your "basics."

Over 450, the Miracle of Numbers

Contact either the principal or teachers of business, economics, civics, social studies, etc. at your local schools. Let them know you are available and would like to talk to kids. You can visit the central administration of a large school system. Ask about the courses being taught and how you might offer your topic(s) and yourself as a "living resource." An alternative to going into the classroom would be to bring the students into your business, depending on its convenience, practicability and relevance to their studies, and show them around.

Why talk to kids this way? There are two reasons, 1) You are sharing you with a class of 20, 30 or 40 students, you and they have a new friend and new learning, and 2) The teacher also learns from you. When you have talked to a teacher you are talking to a thousand kids over the years. Suppose one superb outsider like yourself supplemented kids' educational experience each week. That would be 36 outsiders per year, over 450 from kindergarten through 12th grade! That's a lot of outside/additional true-life, real people exposure!

Here is your theme: Success is getting up one more time than you fall down. Then talk about your "falling downs"--overcoming a deformity or illness, drugs or alcohol, a bank foreclosure, personal bankruptcy, auto accident or divorce. Why? Because you are "up." They are looking at you, saying to themselves, "Oh that's what it's like to be an adult. That's how you walk, and talk, and dress and act." You are the message.

Share yourself. Share the topic with which you are most familiar and most comfortable. Have you ever failed or made a mistake? How did you handle it? What education do you have or do you recommend? How did you get into the business or job you're in? What is it like to do it? What does it require from you? What are its rewards? When must you be tough? How do you interact with and serve others? What did you do when your were their age?

Make a list and outline the topics you'd like to present, so you'll feel confident and know you can fill up a given space of time with your message. Kids like variety and action. Anything you can do to involve them, provide a little noise or action, will help to keep their attention and interest. Consult with the teachers for advice to learn of recent questions or perceived needs, and ways to capture and hold their attention. Ask questions.

Expect an answer or response. Use the "long pause" to show you really want to hear their concerns. Avoid the temptation to talk. Stretch the long pause. Listen patiently. Expect questions that get to the heart of their concerns. Students appreciate your willingness to listen carefully and answer candidly.

You, Power of One, are a whole bunch of stories and messages wrapped into one fun package and important person.

One Last Time, Why Talk to Kids? You Get More than You Give!

If you are at all selfish, this little secret will convince you. When you give yourself, life and experiences to kids you get it all back. It's a great investment in time, youth and the future. In fact,

You get back more than you give!

You are On Your Way

Now you know how very important you are to kids and others. Consider how few adults know the need and are similarly involved. Taking that into account, it is even more important that YOU get started and keep going! Get others involved too.

You know why, how, when, where and with whom. You have the knowledge, understanding, experience, education and exposure kids need to have shared. So commit yourself to get involved with kids' education. You are desperately needed.

Invest in America's youth and America's future. It is also an investment in you. The contribution you can make is waiting for you to "work the special magic" only you can.

Teacher-in-space Christa McAuliffe, who was killed in the January 1986, *Challenger* space shuttle explosion put it a special way: "I touch the future—I teach." You too can touch the future, and the lives of students who really need to know and learn from you.

Accept the challenge! Exercise your *Power of One*:

Talk to Kids!

Questions for Review

1. "Why didn't they tell me?" said the young woman about her education. Tell me about what?

2. How can television watching shield youngsters from the harsh reality of life and mislead as to what "success" is and how to get it? How many hours of school and of television watching have teenagers spent by age 18? What kinds of results and effects can you expect?

3. How can teenage suicide seem a reasonable solution to a teenage problem through a lack of understanding? Of what?

4. "You get more than you give" describes a reward for what?

5. "Say 'yes' to possibilities. Say 'yes' to opportunities." What and why?

6. Why should you both visit schools and bring students where you are?

7. What do you say to a kid? What can you talk about? What is even more important than talking?

8. Why is newspaper reading described to be similar to mining. What is the "mother lode?" The "gold nugget?"

9. One young man asked for the chance to be a future generation. What did he mean?

10. Once you decide to "Talk to Kids," how do you get started and keep going?

To give wings to the individual human spirit is the highest form of education; to carelessly repress that spirit is the lowest form of government.

—Shirley Mount Hufstedler

Chapter 5

ECONOMICS
A Short Course in a Life Science

More and more, life is best explained not by religion, not by law, but by economics.
> —A. Andrew Hauk, district court justice,
> upon completion of an intensive economics workshop

Life Science, Goldfish and Creation of Wealth: This is Economics?

The most powerful, most neglected course in modern education is *ECONOMICS,* a true *"life science."* Economics is all about people—their survival, dreams, possibilities, harsh reality, potential prosperity—all of life.

Ignoring the existence of economics is like one goldfish in a bowl asking the other, "What do you think of the water?" The other replies, "What water?" The first explaining that water is everywhere was rebuffed with, "Who cares about water? Let's talk about something important." In fact, both fish are totally dependent on "the water." It is of life and death importance to their existence and survival.

An economic system is to humans what water is to goldfish. We know very little about it, perhaps care even less. Yet, our quality-of-life, our very existence, may depend on the type and functioning of our economic system. Many if not most people are "economic illiterates" who know little about the economic system, and the related workings of the political system in which it functions.

America's hardworking people create the wealth of America and they consume it. They have a right to the knowledge of how our economic system works and what their part is in it. A populace that is more informed and involved can compel our politicians to make better decisions, and help the political system perform more responsibly for the good of the most people. Here are four dimensions of economics:

1. *Academic Economics:* A formal course of study, sometimes described as "dull, boring and depressing."

2. *Consumer Economics:* Get from paycheck to paycheck, pay bills, buy things you want, save a little money, and have some fun along the way.

3. *Contemporary,* or *Today's Economics:* Daily issues of inflation, unemployment, taxes, interest rates, productivity, Social Security, government role, size, budgets, spending, deficits, monetary and fiscal policy, etc.

4. *Free Enterprise Economics—Vitality of a "Life Science," Free enterprise economics* in America begins with the freedom philosophy in the Declaration of Independence. It is underpinned by the U.S. Constitution that carefully defines government organization, functions and limits, plus it protects the individual from a repressive government through the Bill of Rights. Therefore, *Free enterprise economics* encompasses all the attributes of the preceding three but adds the precious dimensions of freedom and life, with such precepts as the following:

    • Individual freedoms are the most precious possessions we have: freedom to *be,* to *do,* to *choose,* to *dare* and to *become.*

    • Economic and political freedoms are inseparable, each dependent upon the other.

    • Competition promotes production of the highest quality goods and services at the lowest cost, with maximum availability and reliability, and continually rising productivity.

    • Nothing can be divided, exchanged, distributed or consumed until it is first produced.

    • Profit is created value. In a free market, voluntary transaction, both parties profit as a result of the exchange.

    • Risk is a basic component of innovation and the creation of new goods and services to satisfy emerging needs and wants.

    • Saving and Investing—withholding a portion of after-tax income from consumption—is necessary to provide capital for funding business expansion, financing new ventures and high-risk enterprise.

    • A profit-fueled, free-market society creates the most wealth—goods and services—for the most people, based on historical experience.

- All Americans have a responsibility and opportunity to preserve, protect and pass on our inherited freedoms—personal, economic, religious, social and political—for the generations who come after us.

- Business is people, five sets of people, four of whom—employees, suppliers, owner and neighbors—come together to please, serve and satisfy the fifth and most important, the customer.

- Individuals who would enjoy the freedoms and benefits of our society must also accept the responsibilities and obligations that go with them.

These characteristics of free enterprise economics are the "life stuff" that makes America great, and Americans the luckiest people on earth, a part of the "fortunate five percent" who through no merit of their own live under freedom.

Formal economics textbooks and courses are generously available, both for *macroeconomics,* the economic "bigger picture," and *microeconomics,* economics of the business firm and individuals. These delve into academic economic theories, concepts and ideas, and how they are analyzed, quantified and applied.

Watch TV news, listen to talk radio, read newspapers, news magazines, business and finance publications to give meaning, depth and adventure to everyday events and experiences. In particular, editorials of business publications can breathe life into these concepts for you, *Power of ONE.* This chapter delves more into a broad *overview of economics* as a "life science."

Economics—a New Life Encounter

What is this new life encounter, economics? A tongue-in-cheek zealot might answer "Economics is not a matter of LIFE and DEATH—it is much more important than that!"

A scholarly person might describe economics as "the study of scarcity, or allocation of scarce resources."

Webster's *New World Dictionary* (1976) defines *economics* as "the science that deals with the production, distribution and consumption of wealth, and with the various related problems of labor, finance, taxation, etc."

Economics is defined in Schaum's outline series:[1]

Economics is a social science that studies individuals and organizations engaged in the production, exchange and consumption of goods and services. Economics seeks to develop principles, theories or models that isolate a few of the most important determinants of

1. Dominick Salvatore and Eugene Diulio, *Principles of Economics*, Schaum Study Series, McGraw-Hill (New York, 1980) p 1

course of economic events. The goal is to develop policies that might prevent or correct such problems as unemployment, inflation and waste in the economy.

Schaum elaborates on *scarcity:*

> Economic resources of labor, capital and land are scarce or in limited supply in every society. Since resources are scarce, the amounts of goods and services that can be produced are also limited. As a result, society must use its scarce resources as efficiently as possible to produce the goods and services most wanted by society. Scarcity is the fundamental or central problem of every society. Without scarcity, there would be no need to study economics. It is because economic resources and goods and services are scarce that they are not free but command a price.

Jerome Smith defines economics[2] in terms of human beings living life:

> *Economics* is the study of *voluntary human action,* choice and behavior and, therefore, necessarily of life. *Life,* intelligent, *valuing* life is a prerequisite to choice and action and therefore to the subject matter of economics. Economics is the study of voluntary human actions aimed at increasing life's satisfactions and decreasing life's dissatisfactions, and of the *appropriate means* by which these life improvements can be most effectively achieved. Well understood, the great economic truth is that what is an *appropriate means* (voluntary, peaceful means) is the same for all individuals whether their interests are viewed singly or collectively.

So, economics is about people, life and survival. Economics is the "glue" that holds everything together, that explains and relates life and makes it all make sense.

An understanding of economics is a greater understanding and appreciation of life!

Since economics is so important, we will develop a framework of thinking about just what economics is and how it relates to our own standard-of-living, well being, quality-of-life, and "connectedness" of the people on planet Earth.

Survival: Wants and Needs, Consumption and Production—Life!

Every second of every day we have a choice: to live or die. We choose to live. In order to live, we must consume, a quality we share with every other

2. Jerome F. Smith, *The Coming Currency Collapse,* p 133, Books in Focus (New York, 1980

living creature, especially every human being. We are consumers. To consume, we must produce. To produce, we work, using mind, muscles, machines and money. When we work and produce, we can consume and live. Producing a surplus allows us to share with others, to sell or exchange our surplus for theirs through a market, through the communications system of signals called prices. Prices help us evaluate what we really need, how much we want, what we are willing to exchange, and what we must give up in the process. Wow! Is that how it all works?

In one word, it is SURVIVAL. We are in a battle for survival to overcome our single greatest problem, scarcity. We are in this battle together. We cooperate and compete, divide labor and specialize, so that we can create the most goods and services possible given the resources available, to fulfill our wants and needs.

That is not too complicated to understand, because it is called "life."

What is survival? Corporate leader Bill Coors, Chairman, Adolph Coors Company, said, "Our first assignment is the survival of our business and our industry. But *our greater assignment is the survival of the American Free Enterprise System.* Without that, nothing else really matters."

We will study that super-special American Free Enterprise system, to better know how survival *and* prosperity can pave a golden highway to the future. How well we preserve our freedoms and the free enterprise economic system today assures not only our own future, opportunities and life quality, but of our children, grandchildren and theirs to come.

Survival: A Question Never Asked, and Why

Survival. Another valuable perspective was a front-page article in the October *3, 1974 Wall Street Journal,* entitled "The Food Crisis: Widespread Shortages May Pit 'Have Nots' Against the 'Haves,'" by Mary Bralove. In that article was the answer to a question that I, a long time citizen of America, the country of freedom and abundance, never even thought to ask:

How much food is there on planet Earth?

The answer at that time, with recession, inflation, unemployment and shortages was shocking: 26 *days!* That meant if no food were produced, the human race would run out in 26 days and we would be extinct in another few months. The light of humanity would go out!

Why don't I worry about that? Why don't you? Because people get up each work day and go to work. It is because we use our minds, muscles, machines and money to keep producing not only food, but all the other things necessary for everyday living.

For those who do worry about the food supply on earth, a more normal and expected world stockpile of food is about 95 days. Doesn't it give much greater dignity and importance to all of us who get up and go to work every day?

I once told a good friend at work I felt so miserable I should have stayed home that day. With humor, wisdom and a bit of admonishment he quoted James Cash Penney:

> Ninety percent of the world's work is done by people who don't feel very good.

Since then, I have said that to my children at the breakfast table so often that when any of us complains about not going to work or school because we don't feel good, we say in unison, "Ninety percent of the world's work is done by people who don't feel very good!" Then we go anyway, do our share and are grateful so many others also work long and hard. Thus we don't have to confront such weighty life problems as the whole world running out of food.

Survival is stark, harsh and frightening. We can live 5 to 10 minutes without air, 5 to 10 days without water. How many days can we live without food?

In the early 1980's, Bobby Sands, a member of Ireland's Irish Republican Army, who starved himself to protest England's refusal to free Ireland from English rule, lived 66 days without food before he died. His friend, Kieran Doherty, in a macabre contest, "won" shortly thereafter. He lived 72 days without food.

Survival! Outrunning Bears,
and in America, the Battle for Prosperity

Survival, on the lighter side, was demonstrated by two hunters setting up camp in the forest. They heard a strange noise. One left the tent for a time, returned, and was putting on his running shoes. The other asked what he found out there that had made the noise.

"It was a big brown bear," he answered, starting to leave the tent in haste.

"You can't outrun a brown bear. What do you think you're doing?"

The fleeing runner answered "I don't have to outrun the bear. I only have to outrun you!"

That is survival!

We are in the battle for survival. Even though we may not like to think of it that way, that's the way it is. Here in America, the battle seems much less demanding than perhaps in other parts of the world. We seem more in a battle for prosperity than a battle for survival, with our freedoms protected by citizen involvement and enforcement of the Bill of Rights. With the productivity freedom unleashed, the battle for survival seems less a battle and more a game. It is the game of life.

BASIC ECONOMICS: WEALTH CREATION AND CONSUMPTION

Figure No. 1

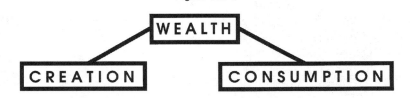

In a nutshell, to survive, we consume. To consume, we produce. If we produce cleverly, there is a surplus we can exchange. Figure No. 1 shows what basic economics is all about—creation and consumption of wealth, the products and services necessary to fill our wants and needs, so that we *live,* not die; *prosper,* not just survive; *flourish,* not flounder.

The Battle of Survival: Creating Wealth

Another way to view our economic job is to realize that we work together to *create wealth.* An economic system may be defined as the system that does the best job possible to create wealth—anything that has value, that people are willing to work for and pay for. Like the common definition of economics, we, as an economic system, are in the dead-earnest business of creating wealth so that we can consume wealth. The better job we do, working together, provides a higher standard-of-living and quality-of-life for all.

We are in this game of life together. There are no time-outs. It is a do-or-die game that must be fought hard and won everyday. Here is a way to picture the workings of an economic system: The material side of life is the creation and consumption of wealth.

With our considerable concern for the environment, the preservation of nature and conserving scarce resources, it is all the more important that we understand the vital ability of applied economics and freedom to accomplish these objectives best. Therefore, we seek the best system, and all parts of the system, which allows us to create the most the fastest with the least. We want to use efficiently and effectively what must be used, and to do it all in the least possible time, since time is another scarce human resource. We seek to waste as little as possible, to conserve resources (energy, minerals, petroleum, air, money and capital) and to preserve the environment (less use of landfill/dumpsites, through less garbage, waste and trash, dumped into our air, water and land).

The ideal economic system, then, encourages creation of wealth: products, goods and services, and promotes their wise use. It is important to understand the interaction between various parts of the economic and political system, how they work better together in balance, or not so well, out of balance.

Staying Private, Going Public. Or are these "Sectors?"

The two main parts of our economic system are the *Private Sector* that creates wealth, and the *Public Sector* on balance that consumes wealth. The private sector called *enterprise* consists of business and individuals. The public sector is called *government*. The two working together form our economic and political system.

I once thought to be common knowledge the meanings and distinctions between the public and private sectors. During early speeches I tested my assuming the differences were generally understood. They weren't.

People thought the public sector was business! They explained, "Oh, you mean out in public, like on Main Street, such as a gas station, barber shop or super market." For the private sector, they'd explain, "Yes I know what the private sector is—those things conducted in secret like the Central Intelligence Agency (CIA), the Federal Bureau of Investigation (FBI), and the National Security Agency (NSA)." In fact, these are public sector, government agencies, while the former are non-governmental, private businesses.

In an economic sense we citizens, workers and employees "create wealth" and are enterprise, contrasted to government which creates a climate for creating wealth, and in so doing, consumes wealth.

The two extremes are *no* government and *all* government.

Consider a system of NO government. It doesn't work. People with no government live a lawless, devastating existence, where plunder and crime run rampant. They live in fear. The strong and ruthless hurt, maim, kill and steal from the weak and helpless, and property is pillaged and destroyed. A healthy economic system cannot exist here.

The other extreme is ALL government. It doesn't work either. When oppression and tyranny prevail, personal freedom, opportunity and abundance cannot exist. The government owns and controls everything. There are no incentives to produce or innovate except fear and survival. The result is a bare-bones existence for the majority of people with the power in the hands of the ruling class who hoard all the wealth.

Walking a Tightrope, Seeking the Optimum Balance

Now consider the best possible balance, a larger enterprise sector to create the wealth, and smaller government sector to create a climate of creating wealth. In balance, government will be large and powerful enough only to provide stability and necessary government services to assure the right environment for producing wealth.

Under the American system of free enterprise, the growth of government up *to a certain size* has provided an ideal environment in which to create wealth. Growth beyond the point of balance, however, starts to infringe upon free enterprise and gets proportionally worse as government continues to expand.

When government gets too large, less wealth is created by a smaller enterprise sector and more wealth is consumed by the larger government sector. This diminishes standard-of-living and quality-of-life. Growing ever larger, government becomes re-distributionist, taking from those who produce, giving to those who don't, discouraging both. The result is fewer producers, more non-producers and less wealth produced.

Somewhere in-between is the happy medium, the smallest government needed to correctly perform all the functions of government, while still being large enough to protect its citizens' life, liberty and property. These functions, which only government can perform legitimately and well, include national defense, law and order, public safety and security, and a legal system to assure adherence to the law.

This is the balance we seek, the optimum size government that protects our individual rights, and assures a positive climate for the creation of wealth and business enterprise, including enforcement of contracts, adherence to laws, with free and competitive, non-restrictive trade. With this optimum size government, the public sector actually stimulates the wealth-producing enterprise sector (business and individuals) to work hard together to flourish.

WEALTH CREATION: PRODUCTION, DISTRIBUTION, & CONSUMPTION

Figure No. 2

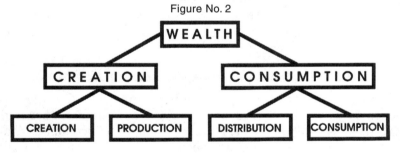

Our Big Job: Creating Wealth and a Model

Consider the creation and consumption of wealth in a more detailed discussion model, Figure No. 2.

We break *Creation* into two components, *Creation* and *Production;* then *Consumption* into *Distribution* and *Consumption.* We create something, organize to produce it, move it to market to make it available to the customer who then buys and consumes it.

Figure No. 3 shows how this all comes about. Briefly the process starts with creation—an idea, production—idea turned real, distribution—product or service available on location, and consumption—utilization. Wealth starts out with a good idea that fills a want or need, creation of something new (science), development of new products (engineering) or improvement of something already in existence (innovation). All are realized by production—manufacturing the goods and performing the services. Still no value is created until the goods and services are physically made available to the customer (transportation), and the customer knows they exist, what they are and where to get theirs (communication).

WEALTH CREATION: IDEAS, TRANSPORTATION & COMMUNICATION

Figure No. 3

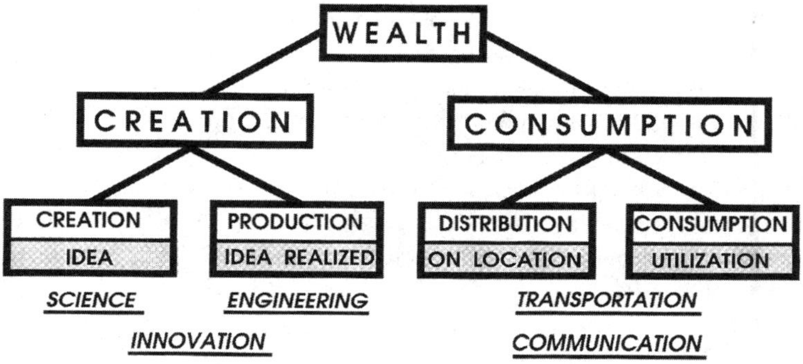

That is not all. We need to define "the creation, production, distribution and consumption"—of what? The answer, of course, is "goods and services" that satisfy human wants and needs, as shown in Figure No. 4. Customer demand gives them value.

Roles and Jobs from the Functions of Economics

With respect to jobs, consider each area, starting with *"Creation."* This function has to do literally with creating goods and services, a better idea, which satisfies human wants and needs. Examples of economic creation would be occupations such as architects, songwriters, inventors, venture capitalists, land developers, artists and entrepreneurs, those who take a risk, seek a profit, and literally create something from a good idea.

"Production" has to do with farming, mining and manufacturing, such as canning of soups, construction of buildings, assembly of automobiles and bicycles, electronics, computers and the like, the idea realized.

"Distribution" has two facets. The most obvious part is the *transportation* of goods from point of manufacture to point of sale, to get them on location where customers can purchase them. The less obvious part is *communications* to make customers aware the products are available and convincing them to buy. This includes marketing, advertising and sales of the products and services; and public relations, publicity and promotion. These are necessary

to *inform and persuade* the customer favorably about all three entities, the products and services as well as the business, for their utilization.

Gaining in importance and popularity are "services" that support those people engaged in material wealth creation activities. Examples include those who repair automobiles, style and cut hair, supply prepared foods, videotapes, and countless similar activities desired by people who produce goods and supply services, to help them work, play and live.

WEALTH IS—GOODS AND SERVICES
Figure No. 4

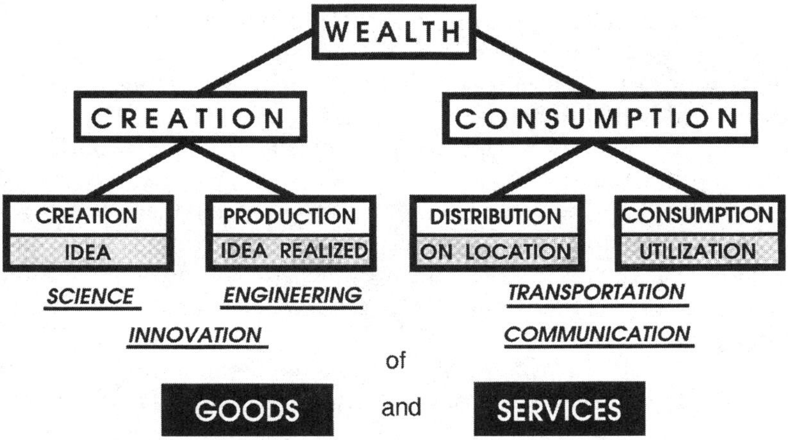

WEALTH

CREATION　　　CONSUMPTION

CREATION	PRODUCTION	DISTRIBUTION	CONSUMPTION
IDEA	IDEA REALIZED	ON LOCATION	UTILIZATION

SCIENCE　　ENGINEERING　　TRANSPORTATION
INNOVATION　　　　　COMMUNICATION
of

GOODS and **SERVICES**

Is Money "Wealth"? Where Does It Fit?

When I ask students to list wealth, and name wants and needs, they mention "money" early on. Everybody wants money. But is money wealth? If it isn't, what is it? Why do we value money? Where does money fit in, and what function does it serve in the economic system?

Money is not wealth. It is an efficient way to exchange wealth. It does represent wealth so that it may seem like wealth.

Money lubricates the gears of commerce. It is so much easier to use money than, for instance, to trade (barter) several dozen eggs for a bushel of wheat, or a bicycle for a chair and seven loaves of bread. Money is a convenience that speeds up our ability to make and record exchanges. Use of a standard unit of money provides valuable information over time in terms of changing prices of goods and services, and the commensurate value of work, time and effort.

Money has magic. It can make dreams come true and buy nice things and influence. But what is money and why does it have value? Money fulfills three basic functions. Here they are:

Three Functions of Money

1) Medium of exchange
2) Store of value
3) Standard of value

As a *medium of exchange,* ideally, money should have intrinsic value, that is, a value all its own. It should be scarce in nature but readily available for commerce, and acceptable by both parties to a transaction. All kinds of things have been used for money including shells, tobacco, salt and metals. Probably the most popular forms of money have been precious metals, mainly gold and silver. Gold, especially, is rare, permanent, has a luster and appeal all its own, and is readily divisible in standard sizes and sub-sizes. Silver is popular too, because, in addition to being a precious metal, it has industrial and metallurgical uses as well.

A certificate in lieu of money has been equally acceptable. Early in this republic, those who stored gold and silver for others issued *certificates* good for redemption back into the metals. They *certified* that there was on hand, the necessary amount of the precious metal for exchange and it could be exchanged. The certificates were much easier to carry and more convenient to exchange, yet maintained customer confidence because they were "as good as gold."

When I ask students what money is and what two kinds of money there are, they know we have "cash" and "credit." Especially if I hold up a credit card and say "plastic money," they can identify credit. It is more difficult that a check is "cash."

I help identify other forms of credit with an example of U. S. Treasury securities, "T-Bills, Notes and ...?" (long pause) They say, "Bonds," and I add that corporations and others also issue bonds.

Holding up a "dollar bill" I ask, "What is this—cash or credit?" When they answer "Cash," I say "Oh?" Then I ask the closest student to read the three words at the top of the bill, "Federal Reserve Note." I conclude by asking "Did you hear what Cindy just told all of us? Cash is not cash. It is credit, too!" They leave a little more informed and a lot more curious about money, what it is and what it isn't, why it works and how to get more.

Lawful Money and its Demise
A Private Central Bank called "Federal"

The U.S. Constitution meticulously defines government's money role in Article I, Section 10, "No state shall ... coin money ... or make any Thing but gold and silver Coin a Tender in Payment of Debts ...," and Art. I, Sec 8, "The Congress shall have power ... To coin Money, regulate the value thereof...'" Notice the word "print" is not used, nor does the Constitution give any but Congress power over money.

A private central bank was formed by Congress in 1913. Though it was and is private, it doesn't sound that way because of its name, Federal Reserve Bank. The creation of this institution separates Congress from the money system, constitutional provisions mentioned above notwithstanding. Though this is alien to our basic understanding of money it is valuable to know that the Federal Reserve is a private central bank and to learn more about it from other sources. Initially this bank honored the basic money practices of the country; that is, it backed printed money with "lawful money," gold and silver.

Look carefully at a $1 Federal Reserve Note on its face to read "This note is legal tender for all debts, public and private." That means it is to be used as money because a private monopoly has the power to say so.

If you take this note to a Federal Reserve Bank and ask for something of value in exchange they will give you another just like it. If you persist they might suggest you go into the marketplace and buy something like a hamburger. The value is in the work someone did to earn the money, but not what the Founders intended, an instrument with the intrinsic value of the "lawful money" itself.

The evolution of money in the United States is interestingly presented by economist Irwin Schiff[3]. He tells how lawful money, "honest" United States currency, was available from 1863-1934 as a U.S. Gold Certificate which had inscribed on it: "Ten Dollars in gold coin payable to the bearer on demand." You could buy goods and services in the private market or exchange it for gold from the government.

The Silver Certificate had inscribed, "One Dollar in silver payable to the bearer on demand" from 1886 to 1963. The concurrent Federal Reserve Notes from 1913-1934 were also redeemable in "gold or lawful money" to the bearer "on demand."

The phase-over came in the Federal Reserve Notes of 1934-1963 when the notes were still "lawful money," but none were backed by gold or silver. During that period, the notes said only "This note is legal tender for all debts public and private and is redeemable in lawful money at the United States Treasury or any Federal Reserve Bank."

This brings us back to the bill from your money supply. Pull one out and read what it says. Think about what it means, with new knowledge.

Central Bank Policy and the Money Supply

The central bank influences "the money supply" by 1) what percent of total lending institution assets must be kept on reserve, and 2) what the going rate of interest is on money loaned. As the required reserves and

---

3. Irwin A. Schiff, *The Biggest Con: How the Government is Fleecing You,* Freedom Books, Box 5303, Hamden, CT 06518: 1977, S7

interest rate are set higher, less money is loaned out and circulating in the economy. Money is "tight."

If the central bank reduces the amount required to be kept on hand by banks, or reduces the rate of interest, more money is "created" by the banks. Money is "loose." All this, however, is limited, controlled by the amount of credit that banks can allow customers based on their cash flow, net worth and credit worthiness.

Money is actually "created" when a loan is made. The bank creates a check based on a customer's creditworthiness and intended use of the money. Deposited into the borrower's account it becomes a part of that bank's reserves, most of which become available for loans. Each loan made similarly makes more money available to loan when deposited, all emanating from the credit worthiness and justified need of the original borrower through the bank loan transaction. Conversely, money is "destroyed" over time as the loan is paid off.

Making Loans on Warehoused Gold

Private gold warehouses stored gold for individuals. They issued warehouse receipts (certificates) for the gold in storage and the receipts circulated and were accepted as money. People knew they could redeem the receipts for gold on demand.

Gold warehouse managers found that all the people never asked for all their precious metals at the same time. These essentially unused deposits permitted them to make loans on which they could charge and earn interest, some of which was paid to the depositors.

Depositors earn interest on their savings while borrowers pay interest on their loans. Financial institutions provide services using a portion of the difference in interest rates paid to savers and those charged to borrowers. In that way financial services are provided, expenses are covered and the bank profits reward bank shareholders for their investments.

Because people never wanted all their money at the same time, lenders found they could loan money they *didn't* have, in the form of the same printed warehouse certificates. This extra money, with no deposit backing, is called *fiat money*. Up to a point there was no danger, especially if the people didn't suspect what the financiers were doing.

Constitutional Money and Fiat Money

As time went on, Constitutional Money (gold certificates) gave way to silver certificates, then to *fiat,* or unbacked money, issued by the *private* central bank, the Federal Reserve, instituted by Congress in 1913, the same year the 16th amendment authorized the federal income tax.

Fiat money is paper decreed by government to be the medium of exchange, the value of which is determined in the marketplace and by the confidence of those using it. *Fiat money* is formally defined as "money or paper currency not convertible into coin or specie of equivalent value." Though it serves the *medium of exchange* function, it also allows the central banking system to issue money far in excess of precious metal reserves, which can lead to abuse of the money needs of the economy.

Once fiat money is introduced, backed by neither a commodity nor precious metal but by the credit of a governmental entity, it is possible to create lots more by just printing it. With checking and electronic transfers it need not even be printed in sheets and bills but merely in numerical entries on a ledger or in a computer memory.

So, money can be asset-based, limited by available assets (gold or silver, etc.), or debt-based—unlimited because debt is unlimited.

Inflation, the Disease of Money

What is inflation? Rising prices? Or falling values of money? To say that inflation causes increasing prices is like saying wet streets cause rain. It is just the opposite. Decreasing value of money drives prices higher. Inflation has been called "the disease of money."

Inflation is literally "too many dollars chasing too few goods." The secret to understanding inflation is understanding who creates the dollars and who creates the goods. Banks create the dollars with printing presses and accounting entries. People create the goods with their hard work.

Congress authorizes public spending supported by many people, and taxes, opposed by most people. It is normal to spend more than they tax so government incurs a deficit. In itself the deficit is not inflationary if it is covered by borrowing to be paid at a future time. Borrowers give up use of their money to the government. The government spends the same money the lender had available to spend. It is the same amount of dollars and purchasing power but by different purchasers.

The U. S. Treasury lends government securities—treasury bills, bonds and notes—to the investing community: corporations, large financial institutions, and individuals. These credit instruments earn interest while the money is spent in the current budget of the government, allowing current spending without current taxation.

There is a finite market for money, that is, only so much is in demand at a given time and interest rate. If government borrowing is excessive, that is, deficits are large but loan demand is limited, there may not be enough demand for all the credit made available by the government's spending. If there is more borrowing than the investment market can absorb, the private, central Federal Reserve Bank, called the Fed, "buys" the government credit instruments. Rather than buying them with money, however, they make entries on a ledger or in a computer, backed up with created debt.

Those entries, created out of thin air like money borrowed at a bank or fiat warehouse receipts, act just like money and expand the amount of dollars in the economy. Even more dollars are created, because they are loaned out a multiple of times ("fractional banking"). In the same time period not as many new goods and services can come into being. With lots more dollars and the same or not many more goods, prices must increase to balance the supply and demand between more money and existing goods. The creation and infusion of newly-created money may take one to two years to work its way into the economy, spreading the higher prices less noticeably over that period of time.

A price increase on a specific product, commodity or service results from true changes in supply and demand. That is not inflation. Price increases over a large or whole group of items is different. It is inflation.

A Little Inflation is Not a Good Thing

In the late 1980's and early 90's we read and heard inflation had moderated to four or five percent, said to be a reasonable, tolerable level. Compared to what? Any inflation "debauches the currency" as classical economists described it. Money becomes worth less until it becomes worthless. Annual inflation of 5% for 10 years requires $163 to buy what $100 formerly bought. The damage it does is a "double whammy." It devalues savings and punishes savers, while increasing income taxes, leaving the people less dollars that buy less. It creates bigger government, poorer people and a less secure future.

One of the most onerous, counter-productive and dangerous economic dirty tricks a government can do is to impose wage and price controls. It seems like the right thing to do. If prices are rising too fast, clamp government controls on them. Except it doesn't work. This "solution" to the problem only makes it worse, and the people suffer economically and financially.

The federal government imposed wage and price controls in August 1971, because inflation was "out of control." Was it? Did it do any good?

First, what conditions precipitated the controls and what happened after? For the years 1965 to 1970 inflation[4] averaged 4.2%, the December-to-December annual percentage increases being respectively, 1.9, 3.5, 3.0, 4.7, 6.2, and 5.6. What levels of inflation now exist and how do public officials view them?

Wage and price controls were phased out through 1974. For the years 1975 to 1980, the average inflation rate *more than doubled* to 8.9% being respectively, 6.9, 4.9, 6.7, 9.0, 13.3, and 12.5!

Wage and price controls didn't solve anything, especially inflation that was at the time termed "out of control." What is important is that inflation should be around zero and could even be negative with high productivity and constrained government.

---

4. *Economic Report of the President,* February, 1999, p 399

If you want to get the students attention regarding inflation tell them that since 1980 the purchasing power of the dollar has been cut in half. Then tear your dollar bill in half. They always watch and gasp in amazement.

Fiscal Responsibility and Vigilant Citizenry

Careful vigilance by the populace is required to help prevent abuse of the money system. Not exercising such control erodes the other two functions of money, *store of value* and *standard of value*. This causes serious reduction in the quality and value of money. As a consequence, great losses over time are incurred by savers or those who are required to use the money as the medium of exchange.

Money's "store of value" quality (money you have saved for emergencies and retirement) is necessary so that people can save some of the fruits of their labors for future needs, retirement and security, and be confident its buying power will be preserved. That saved money is invested in capital, that which produces more for less, providing the source of productivity.

The "regulate the value thereof" provision from the Constitution requires the government to preserve the value of lawful money to protect its purchasing power and stability.

The full character, history and discussion of money are beyond our scope but much information is available in reference books and libraries, and highly recommended for study.

The Complete Economic System: A Model of Life

Putting it all together, then, our model of the total economic system, including the functions of money looks like Figure No. 5.

THE TOTAL ECONOMIC SYSTEM

Figure No. 5

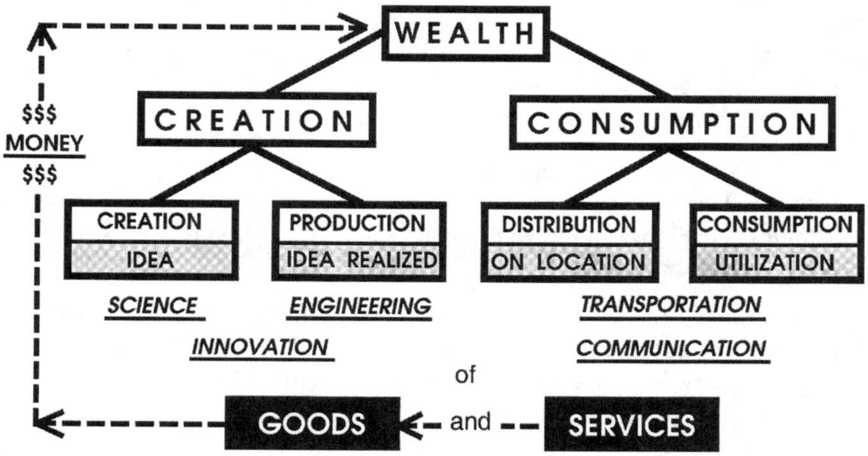

Drawing the very important line from "Goods and Services" through "$$$ Money $$$" back to wealth completes our model of the economy. It defines *"Wealth"* as *"Goods and Services"* which satisfy human wants and needs, and shows that *money is not in itself wealth,* but serves the exchange of wealth, functioning as a medium of exchange—and, as a store of value and a standard of value.

Suffocating in a Closed Vault, and Magic! We are all Millionaires!

To further explore what money is, I tell students to imagine I have a magic power that fills the room we are in with $1,000 bills, wall-to-wall, floor-to-ceiling, with us in the middle. We're millionaires, maybe even billionaires! But wait. Someone just shut the door and the windows are sealed. We grow weaker and breathe shallower. Finally we die for lack of oxygen. We are "rich" but dead.

I have another magic power to make everybody millionaires. In an instant each person has a checking account good for a million dollars. What happens? You drive down to buy a new car. On the way, running low on gasoline you stop for a fill-up. Why are they closed? They don't have to work. They're millionaires. Is the auto dealership open? No, they don't have to work. They're millionaires. You look to see if your milk or newspaper has been delivered. No, again. They're millionaires. It lasts for about a day. Then we realize the first million dollars we each have counts for nothing. We all go back to work to produce goods and services, and give back to our money, value for exchange.

The Equation for Prosperity and Wealth: Man's Material Progress

Why does money have, or seem to have value? The reason is the *directed human effort* behind the money. Hard work by itself doesn't create value. It is the value of directed hard work used to create goods end services that satisfy human wants and needs.

Author Warren Hackett[5] discusses money:

> It is human energy, productively employed, that creates the money supply. The goods, including tools, produced by human energy give money its value. If there were no goods to buy with it money would have no value.

With students I use *mudballs* as an example. I tell them I am going into business to manufacture mudballs, and would they like to invest and work in my company. They usually answer "no" and give the two reasons why:

---

5. Warren Hackett, *It's Your Choice: Freedom and Prosperity or Tyranny and Poverty,* p 42

1) There is no market for mudballs, and 2) If there were a market, nearly anyone could make their own out of dirt and water in their back yards.

"Directed human effort" includes all three, "mind, muscles and machines." Machines are a different kind of wealth where mind and muscles utilize savings (deferred consumption) channeled into them as investment, and in effect, multiply the output of human input. Here it is in equation form[6]:

$$M\,M\,P = N\,R + H\,E \times T$$

MMP stands for Man's Material Progress, the amount of food and goods available to determine people's standard-of-living, NR, Natural Resources (land, minerals, water, air, etc.); HE, Human Energy (physical and mental), and T, Tools.

Natural resources and human energy are limited but tools are not.

Man hasn't changed all that much over the centuries. One of his most primitive tools is the shovel, and with that he can move about the same amount of dirt he always could. Only with new power tools and energy can man move more dirt with less human effort. Man's efforts are multiplied through tools, and tools are available because of deferred consumption (savings) for investment, and creativity and ingenuity of the human mind and passion of the human spirit.

American Enterprise System:
The Exciting Dimension is Freedom

You have just taken a short course through the life science called economics. The exciting dimension is "freedom," and that is what makes living in America different and better. When properly combined, freedom and economics create "free enterprise," a truly mysterious, marvelous and exciting concept that really works to advance peoples' economic well being. To keep it functioning properly, we must assure a balance of enterprise and government that best serves all the people.

The interaction of economics among business, government and people can truly make things better or worse. In her column 7/17/82 *Rocky Mountain News* column, "American migrants," Ellen Goodman tells about a man who lost his job, searched persistently to find another and finally found one over 1000 miles away. He had to uproot his family and move. His wife wrote:

> The economy has become, to me, much more than a word that one finds sprinkled about on the pages ... It's a force that has disrupted my career, torn up my family, put my kids' college plans in jeopardy and taken away my home. What's happening to people because of what's happening in Washington is very real. And the hardest part, I think, is that no one really knows who to blame.

6. Henry Grady Weaver, *The Mainspring of Human Progress,* 1947, p 23

Economics to Share:
A Three Paragraph Short, Short-Course in Economics

Getting down to basics, our continuing choice is to live or die. To live we must consume. To consume we must produce. If we produce a surplus, we can exchange. Our common enemy is scarcity and our common goal is survival. Our higher goal is abundance. We want the best system of enterprise and government, to produce the most wealth and distribute it to the most people. We are in this together. We must be in balance.

Enterprise creates wealth. Government creates a climate for creating wealth. Wealth is anything that has value, that people are willing to work for and pay for. Wealth is basic economics: creation, production, distribution and consumption of goods and services. It is critical to understand, monitor and control the balance between enterprise and government.

We are losing our balance. Government grows relatively faster than enterprise through the invisible, silent, insidious mechanism called CREEP (slow but ever-so-sure change). In 1948, all government was 18% of national output, gross national product (GNP). By 1988, government had doubled to 35% of GNP, growing 4% a year, and stayed at about 30% going into the new millennium. We have relatively less wealth production and more wealth consumption, since government is a net consumer of wealth. If a government were at 24% (as in the 50's), each American would have over $3,000 more in hand. A family of four would have four times that more a year for education, recreation, to save, spend, invest or give away.

Economics best explains how the real world of scarcity works. Freedom, or lack of freedom, determines man's relative victory over scarcity. The two combined, freedom and enterprise, form the concept of "free enterprise," *freedom to work, with risk,* a system that works better than any other.

Free enterprise is a system worth knowing more about. Take time to learn it, understand it, appreciate it, defend it and fight to preserve it.

Questions for Review

1. "Economics is a 'life science.'" Why? What is economics? Define and discuss. Name and describe the four types of economics. Give six "dimensions of freedom and life," that describe "free enterprise economics."

2. Give examples of survival. Why don't we think about that very much? How many days worth of food exist on Planet Earth? Should we worry about that? Why?

3. What does "Creating Wealth" have to do with survival? What is wealth? Is it money? Why? What kind of economic system is best? What must it do?

4. What are the two components of America's Enterprise System? What economic function does each have? What is most important about their relationship?

5. Diagram and explain a model of an economic system with its goals and functions. Name and explain jobs related to each of the functions. What characteristics do all people have in common? Communications are necessary to *inform and persuade* the customer favorably about what three entities?

6. What is money? Constitutional money? Lawful money? Fiat money? What kind do we have? What gives money value? How has American money changed over time? Explain a warehouse receipt, a United States Dollar and a Federal Reserve Note ("Dollar"). Give two illustrations of where money is not wealth.

7. How is money "created" and "destroyed?" How can loans be made on money that belongs to someone else? On money that does not exist? Explain how money borrowed by the government can be non-inflationary or inflationary. Explain when and why government borrows money in terms of government spending and taxing.

8. What is inflation? How does it happen?

9. Illustrate the overall model of an economic system including money in it. What equation relates man's material welfare to human resources, human energy and tools? Explain. What is limited and what is not limited?

10. Give a one-minute "short, short course" description of economics. What is our common enemy, our common goal and our higher goal? What role does freedom play in economics?

If the people don't have enough information to wield power correctly, don't take the power from them. Give them the information.

—Thomas Jefferson

The price we have to pay for money is paid in liberty.

—Robert Louis Stevenson

I have no complex about wealth. I have worked hard for my money, producing things people need. I believe that the able industrial leader who creates wealth and employment is more worthy of historical notice than politicians and soldiers.   —J. Paul Getty

All wealth is the product of labor.   —John Locke

Chapter 6

FREE ENTERPRISE
The Mysterious Magical Misunderstood System That Works Better!

Overview: Survival, Life and Death

We survive or we die. That is life—and death.

To survive, we must consume. To consume, we must produce. To produce, we confront our most critical survival problem, SCARCITY. How we overcome scarcity is Economics. That is why Economics is a "life science." Economics is the allocation of scarce resources. What we need is the best system to overcome scarcity.

We have all heard cows give milk. Cows don't give milk. We have to take it from them! Mother Nature is equally stingy with her vast, abundant resources. We have to work hard to find them, to get them and to keep getting them. But if we use our hearts and spirits to properly exert mind, muscle and machines, Mother Nature will open up her ample resources to allow mankind not only to survive but to *prosper,* for not only subsistence but *abundance!*

Design of a System:
Freedom, Free Enterprise and Government

How does one go about designing a bounteous, productive, generous, prosperous society? What does it take to get people to work hard willingly, loyally, even enthusiastically, to produce a low cost, high quality surplus so that they can exchange and thrive? Those are the kinds of questions America's

Founding Fathers addressed, and it started with government. Why government?

Warren Hackett[1] addressed these questions in "From Freedom to Free Enterprise":

> The new government that resulted was dedicated to protecting the God-given right of *freedom* of each citizen. This new political climate brought into being what we now call the Free Enterprise Economic System, which is the way we produce things we need and want. Under it, in our first one hundred years we became the freest and most prosperous people on earth. It attracted the ancestors of most of us, who were seeking freedom from oppressive, tyrannical governments in the old countries, to settle here.

Hackett discussed the function and role of government in relation to free enterprise:

> Ever since government came into being, whether by seizure of the power to rule, or by consent of the governed, there has been a constant conflict between the governed and government. Politicians, who operate governments, produce none of the food or goods people need and want. The original concept and function of government was a central agency organized to protect people from crime at home and foreign enemies abroad. Nothing more. But, from the beginning of history the greatest threat to man's freedom and property always has been his government.
>
> The governed are the producers. Those who govern take from the producers, with or without their consent, little or much of their production by taxation in order to support the government (and in many cases to enrich the rulers). Historically, the minority which governs always seeks more and more power to control and take more from the governed, who are the majority. Their reason always is, they claim, "for the good of the people."
>
> Any government control, whether legitimate or not, involves some loss of individual freedom.
>
> Governments control people by making laws, which are the rules by which they must abide, or suffer punishment. Laws can be just or unjust. If they protect *each individual's* freedom to act in a constructive manner that harms no one, they are just. If they arbitrarily restrict or deny this freedom, they are unjust. Just or unjust, government alone has the power to punish those who break its laws.

---

1. Hackett, Warren, *It's Your Choice: Freedom and Prosperity or Tyranny and Poverty,* pp 11, 7, 12. Reprinted with permission

Depending upon what kind of government, the type and enforcement of laws, and the extent to which government protects or usurps individual freedom, the nature and workings of a free, or not-so-free enterprise system determines our circumstance and destiny.

Clarence Carson answers the question "What is Free Enterprise?"[2]:

> Free Enterprise is a way of going about meeting our needs and wants by providing them ourselves or by freely entered-into transactions with others. It is free insofar as it does not entail the use or threat of force by any person or organization or deception by either of these. The opposite of free enterprise is hampered, restricted, controlled, or prohibited enterprise. Whether regulations promote or inhibit enterprise depends upon the particular regulations. Enterprise must be conducted according to rules, but if the rules inhibit entry or hamper free activity they become restrictions on free enterprise.

Carson hits on something very important, how we get what we want and need:

> There is every reason to believe that man is naturally inclined to be economic. That is, he is naturally inclined to use as little energy and materials to produce as many goods as he can from them. If this were not the case, it is easy to believe that he would long since have perished from the face of the earth.

Carson tells there are two ways one can get what one wants, provide for oneself or acquire from others. You can get from others in two ways, given as gifts or taken by force:

> It is this latter option that raises hob in determining what is economic. Strictly speaking, robbery could be quite economical for an individual. By stealing, an individual can greatly augment the supply of goods and services available to him with only a very little expenditure of energy and materials. A bank robber may, for example, spend half an hour using a twenty-dollar gun and enrich himself, say, to the extent of $20,000.
>
> That might indeed be economical for an individual, but it is not so for society at large. Economics has to do with the increase of goods not only of individuals but of those that are generally available. The bank robber augments his personal supply at the expense of those from whom he has stolen. Moreover, he may reduce the general

2. Clarence B. Carson, *Free Enterprise: The Road to Prosperity*, 1985, pp 3, 8, 9. Reprinted with permission

supply further by the threat he poses to trade and the loss of incentive people have to produce when they are uncertain that they will be able to keep the rewards of their labor. For these reasons, theft should not be considered economical.

Even so, the example of the bank robber is not frivolous. All redistribution schemes are proposals to use force to take from those who have and give to those who do not have. If governments do such things, it is not at all clear why it is still not theft, albeit, *legal* theft. And its effect on the general supply would reasonably be the same as any other kind of theft.

Magic Ingredients of Free Enterprise: What Makes It Work?

THE question, then, becomes how do we best "use our hearts and spirits to properly exert mind, muscle and machines?" The answer is subtle and profound: Human nature is such that we work hard and produce abundantly for our own very personal and sometimes mysterious reasons. The degree to which we produce determines our material existence and life quality. The degree to which we produce is the degree to which we are free and to which we exercise our freedom with responsibility.

In other words we do well what we like to do. When we do what we like to do, we do more of it and we do it better! It becomes free enterprise when what we do, in the sense of making a living, contributes to our economic system in the creation and exchange of WEALTH.

Hackett explores "the laws of Nature" to which the Founders referred in the Declaration of Independence, whereby people must work and produce if they are to survive, survival being "the first law of Nature":

> The Founders knew that government, which is a man-made-and-operated institution, can give the people nothing that it has not first taken away from them. They also knew that man's nature is such that he works and produces best, and thus lives better when he:
>
> 1. Is *free to work* toward any legitimate goals he personally desires and selects.
>
> 2. Is *free to acquire and dispose* of the rewards of his production as he sees fit.
>
> 3. *Receives recognition and reward* for higher degrees of productive effort and skill.
>
> 4. Is *free to exchange* his product or labor with others, without outside interference or compulsion.

These freedoms are the 'liberty' referred to in the Declaration. Without them history shows that man is a poor or non-producer; there is no incentive to produce more than enough to satisfy one's own needs; one does not strive to excel, and if one is not allowed to own anything he cannot improve his way of life; and then there is no progress.

The Second Great Document of 1776, by Adam Smith

The same year the Declaration of Independence came into being so did a monumental economic work, *Wealth of Nations,* by University of London Political Economy Professor Adam Smith. He was described by Max Lerner as "a mild, Scottish professor of moral philosophy, retiring and absent-minded, a gentle sage with dynamite flowing from his pen."[3] Lerner then describes the book:

> The doctrine he was teaching was a new doctrine—that of economic liberalism and freedom from governmental interference ... The principles are simple. First, Smith assumes that the prime psychological drive in man as an economic being is the drive of self-interest. Secondly, he assumes the existence of a natural order in the universe which makes all the individual strivings for self-interest add up to the social good. Finally, from these postulates, he concludes that the best program is to leave the economic process severely alone— what has come to be known as laissez-faire, economic liberalism, or non-interventionism ... to have fashioned his system of thought in order to blast away the institutional obstructions of the past, and bring a greater degree of economic freedom and therefore a greater total wealth for all the people in a nation.

Free Enterprise: Freedom to Try, Buy, Sell, Fail

Dr. Cleon Skousen highlights Adam Smith's classic work, *Wealth of Nations,* to say that Smith distinguished between gold and silver (money) and *wealth,* the latter being the essentials of life—food, clothes, housing, factories, schools, roads, farms, etc[4]. He said if you wanted to raise the standard-of-living where people truly prosper, goods and services must be abundant and cheap.

3. Adam Smith, *An Inquiry into the Nature and Causes of The WEALTH OF NATIONS,* Introduction by Max Lerner. Modern Library, New York: 1937

4. Dr. W. Cleon Skousen, *"Miracle of America,"* pp. 31, 32, National Center for Constitutional Studies, HC 61, Box 1056, Malta, ID 83342-9704: 1981

This included specialized production, and buying and selling in a free market where supply and demand are served by people "voting" with their money. Incentives are profit or prospect of profit. Such a system results in products being manufactured in higher quantity and quality, at lower expense and prices.

The threat to all this is government interference in fixing prices, wages, controlling production or distribution and subsidizing some production while taxing others. The government, serving only as referee, is to prevent force, fraud, monopoly and perversity.

Skousen summarizes Adam Smith's "tremendously successful formula for prosperity" in the following "natural laws of economic principles" which included four freedoms:

1) Freedom to try
2) Freedom to buy
3) Freedom to sell
4) Freedom to fail

These freedoms work based on people behaving sensibly in the resulting free-market economy at the various levels: individual, family, township, county, state and national. Also, each level of the system had to be self-governing, self-sustaining, and self-repairing.

A Simple Model of Free Enterprise

What is free enterprise and how does it work? The concept of free enterprise is not immediately obvious. First of all, nothing is free. "There is no such thing as a free lunch." Everything costs something because scarce resources must be processed by smart, hard-working, self-sacrificing, other-serving people, to be useful and available. Similarly, there is no such thing as "free" enterprise. To have free enterprise is to have freedom, for which millions have fought and died. We must set up the best economic, political, cultural and governmental system possible to allow the most freedom, and protect and enforce that freedom. Thereby, people flourish.

"Free Enterprise" is a two-word phrase with a third implied. The less-obvious missing ingredient is RISK. Figure No. 6 is "The Triangle of Free Enterprise," a simple model that uses the literal interpretations of the words and adds the missing dimension.

Free Enterprise is *"freedom* to *work* with *risk."* It is freedom with risk; work with risk, freedom to work and take a risk. We have freedom of choice, to work and enjoy the satisfaction, or not to work, and suffer the consequences. When we exercise our freedom to work or create enterprise, we take a risk. If we are smart, we minimize the risk by being better prepared (educated and experienced). We carefully consider what we like and want to do, what needs to be done and how to do it, and what will benefit others and reward us, with profit, with minimal risk of failure.

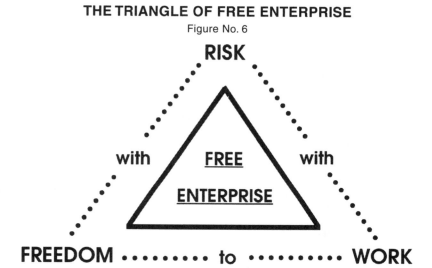

THE TRIANGLE OF FREE ENTERPRISE

Figure No. 6

RISK: Ever-Present Player in the Drama of Life

The part that some business people forget is RISK. In a going business, we are intent on how much profit we make, not on whether we make a profit.

Risk is the disciplinary part with dual possibilities: profit or loss, success or failure, reward or punishment. When we lose sight of both possibilities, we "do what we've always done."

If we keep doing what we've always done, we'll keep getting what we've always gotten! Suppose we keep on making better slide rules or spring-powered, balance wheel watches. What happens, even though we make a better one cheaper? How about buggy whips, wagon wheels and candles? These were once guaranteed to make money. Now they are "losers" because they are obsolete. They have been superseded by something better and cheaper.

In free enterprise, where the creativity of the human mind and spirit is unleashed, progress is fast, change is certain—guaranteed! If we know this and react to it, we always consider RISK in our thinking, and prepare for, and eventually create the future, and not merely react to the whims of fate and fortune!

The free enterprise system is dynamic and constantly changing. Instead of being alarmed to find businesses going out of business, we should understand that the system is working just the way it should and must. If we recognize the dynamic character of free enterprise, we will prosper with it.

What is "the dynamic character of free enterprise"? Let us consider for a moment business formation and failures. In 1997, 798,779 new businesses were formed[5] while 83,384 businesses failed! Ever changing, rearranging free enterprise rewards those who work hard, innovate, keep up with competition, and continue to please customers and make a profit. Dynamic change is *normal.* Though we lament about failed businesses, especially for people who lose their jobs, that is the way the system works. Long-lasting businesses are the exception, not the rule.

If you know the dynamic character and ever-changing demands of free enterprise, you are in a position of power. You can make decisions to take advantage of the system and your knowledge of it to prepare for the future. You can make it work for you, and you get more out of it by putting more into it.

Enterprising individuals who keep abreast of changes react constructively. They complete high school and go beyond, some to trade school, some to business or community colleges, while others enter apprenticeship programs. Some on the "fast track" go to college not for one, but two college degrees or two majors. Or they use one degree in one field to get actual experience, then go back for an advanced degree in the field of their choice. While working they take advantage of seminars, workshops, trade shows, professional and trade associations to upgrade their skills, advance their knowledge and more important, make valuable people contacts. They live more experiential, positive and confident lives.

Learn to recognize the important universal characteristics of enterprise, people, markets and products. Learn the specialties in each area and always have a job. Keep abreast of changes and trends to stay welcome and rewarded by the system. The time and energy we invest today prepare us for the rapidly changing world of tomorrow. Besides that, it is fun!

Many individuals can't plan their careers but slide into a job because Mom or grandfather did it, only to find the job goes away. Many jobs were lost in the 70's and 80's when the trend developed towards smaller automobiles, each using hundreds of pounds less steel. Foreign car competition affected not only the auto industry but the steel industry and mining, as well. The same was true for plastics, aluminum and glass. Another example is energy. For decades when energy was abundant and prices were low, we became wasteful. Then scarcity was imposed by a foreign cartel. We were forced to become frugal, to install conservation measures, to markedly reduce demand while still maintaining our standard-of-living. We applied free enterprise principles then to achieve higher energy self-sufficiency.

These job areas, once so secure, dwindled while others grew. That's the way it is.

---

5. *Economic Report of the President*, February, 2000, p 415

TWII, *The Way It Is!* is our basis of reality. We can know all this, use it and benefit by it, or we can ignore it and suffer. The choice is ours. The real world changes. We, in America, have the most efficient, fairest, though not perfect economic system that recognizes and uses basic human nature to work and produce. It meets our needs through inevitable change. With our needs met we have new abundance to share.

Important Characteristics of Free Enterprise

With ECONOMIC FREEDOM the basic touchstone of free enterprise these basic characteristics make it work:

- PRIVATE PROPERTY
- SELF-INTEREST motives and incentives
- CUSTOMER SOVEREIGNTY
- COMPETITION
- A FREE MARKET
- LIMITED GOVERNMENT

ECONOMIC FREEDOM Provides the Right to Choose, Then Abundance and Surplus

Economic freedom is essential for other freedoms. The less economic freedom one has, the less one has of other freedoms—political, religious, intellectual, social, personal. Freedom is a total package. Restrict one and you reduce all.

PRIVATE PROPERTY:
We Keep What is Ours—or Most of It

We enjoy our right to choose what we do to make a living. But human nature is such that we work harder when we know that what we create and produce is rightfully ours. We can keep it or exchange it, as we judge best. This condition allows us to work as long, hard and smart as we wish, especially if we reap all the rewards for our efforts and sacrifice.

Let us use chairs and the chairmaker, me, as an example.

I am a chairmaker who makes sturdy, comfortable, high-quality chairs. I build and sell chairs, and am unable to keep up with demand.

One day a big, tough character visits me to offer "protection." I explain I don't need protection. My product quality, service and fair dealings have protected me against all the foreseeable hazards of the marketplace. "All but one," he says. "Me!" He crashes one of my finished chairs down upon another, destroying both.

I ask him what he means by "protection," and he explains I must provide him with one chair out of every 20 I produce, or this damage will occur again.

Looking at the two destroyed chairs, it is obviously worth it, so I agree. I have been coerced by threat of force and violence to give up some of my product to protect the rest of it. How long will one chair out of 20 continue my "protection?" How ethical and moral is subscribing to such a "service"? How many others pay for the same "protection"?

A better solution might be to provide the one-chair "tax" to institute a governmental unit funded equally by all producers, to protect themselves and all members of society. We call this a "police force" and designate its function, "to keep the peace, provide for the public safety and security, and to ensure law and order" for all citizens against those who would abuse the freedoms and rights of others.

With the police force in place to protect our freedoms and rights, we have effectively protected all private property. I can again pour all my energies into what I like to do, which serves others as well. That is how government helps "create a climate of creating wealth."

SELF-INTEREST Serves Others Too!

In a free enterprise society it is almost impossible to serve oneself without serving others. That is good. It is equally impossible to enjoy a high standard-of-living without specializing in what you do best, and exchanging with others doing what they do best, to fill your wants and needs.

I think to myself, "Let someone else bake the bread, pick the apples and get them to market. I'll supply the best chairs money can buy."

In this posture I can work as long and as hard as I wish. If I produce more I can enjoy more—leisure time, wealth or peace of mind. I can expand my business and hire others. I can start related businesses. I can go out of business. But whatever I decide to do, I do it for my own reasons. I enjoy the rewards and suffer the consequences. In every case if it doesn't serve others I can't make a living doing it.

I accept full responsibility. I exercise my freedoms prudently and honorably, work hard and flourish in the fruits of my labor. I am in control! I'm happy! How much more incentive and motivation can one person have? Isn't it great to live in a free enterprise society!"

CUSTOMER SOVEREIGNTY:
The Customer Pays the Bill.
The Customer is THE BOSS!

Here is how it works. In a free enterprise economy, for our very own reasons we wish to *enrich ourselves* by *pleasing others*. This works only if others are enriched by what we do. The more good we do, the more others are pleased, and the more successful we are. What others do has value to us as well, and we are willing to pay for it. That's part of the magic of free enterprise. We are in the "people pleasing business."

The customer is the King, the Queen, the Pharoah, *the* Reigning Monarch! In short: The Customer is the Boss!

When you please the boss, good things happen to you. In pleasing The Big Boss, the customer, you please yourself as well and are rewarded, both in satisfaction and money, the return for your risk and hard work.

We began this discussion with one of the harshest facts of life: either we consume or we die. We are all consumers. But we are not all customers. *Customers PAY for what they consume.* For instance while children are consumers, they aren't always customers. Their parents or providers are the customers. They earn the living and pay the bills.

Public education is a good example. Parents work and pay taxes to fund school systems. They are the customers because they pay the bills. Some adults no longer have children in school. They are also customers for education. Many property taxpayers don't have children, or children in school, yet they too are customers for public education. The students are the consumers, beneficiaries or recipients of education.

When we consider who does all the hard work and takes all the risk, it is important to differentiate between consumers and customers, especially assessing the results of government programs, funding and spending, similar to public education. Even in these, the customer, the billpayer and taxpayer, is sovereign.

Understanding the definition of "sovereign" is important to understanding free enterprise. It means superior to or above all others, the chief or greatest, supreme in authority, rank or power, holder of power, ruler.

As sovereign customers, we can feel good about living in the free enterprise economy in America. And the same feeling we have of being "The Boss," we must also grant to each one of our fellow citizens. That is what makes it all work—knowledge, respect, freedom for self, freedom for others, hard work, and pleasing each other to advance our well-being.

How many times do you find such phrases as "serve others," "provide a service," and "here to please and to serve?" In free enterprise when one serves others he serves himself as well. How very important is the customer, and the consumer. Our respect and appreciation for the consumer is because each person is a consumer. We consume to live, and we help each other to live.

"Customer Sovereignty" means the customer is the boss. We serve and please each other, and in so doing exercise our freedoms to fulfill our own destiny, upgrade our own standard-of-living and quality-of-life.

The Customer Pays the Bill.
The Customer is the Boss.

COMPETITION
Great Regulator. Invisible Enforcer. Tough Taskmaster.

Word got around not only about the quality of my chairs, but also my obvious affluence from producing "super chairs." Soon I had to outdo an old friend of mine, an employee, who had helped me make chairs for awhile. He became my COMPETITOR! He was very good at making chairs, and I know why. I taught him everything I know—not just the right materials and methods, but production processes and efficiencies, product finishing and quality control techniques. Not only did he produce a good product, but offered it at a *lower price,* to gain customers and a market. I had to reduce my prices to compete.

I was able to lower my prices because I had invested some of my profits in new machinery and equipment that does a better job at less expense. I can meet or beat his price, and still make a good return even at the lower price. I have noticed when I have a sale, so does he. When he comes out with a new product design, so do I. Who benefits from all this competition? Those same lucky persons: Queen and King Customers. They keep getting more value at less cost.

Competition in the free market is "the policeman," the great regulator. No armed guards need survey my quality or prices, because my customers do that. They insist on high value and settle for nothing less. As long as the market is free and others can get into it quickly and freely, I must produce a better chair and provide increased value, or go out of business. Even if my competitor and I joined forces and jacked up prices, how long would it last? Someone else would realize the opportunities and potential rewards and get into the business. They would love to please my customers!

Being good at making chairs is not enough. I must always get better at it or I perish. That is the "productivity imperative"—doing more and better for less. Competition is the great regulator that keeps me in line. It keeps all of us "lean and mean" and tough. At his lower prices, my competitor's business initially expanded and included his hiring one of my best employees because he paid higher wages. I had to raise my employee wages too, and add training programs and more benefits to obtain, retain and maintain good people as employees.

It sounds almost too good to be true. Competition not only lowers prices and increases value, but boosts jobs, wages, benefits, quality, innovation and design improvements. No outside force required us to do what we set out to do anyway—please a customer. Competition, the invisible enforcer, does it all.

Competition is a tough taskmaster that requires hard work and smart work to maintain the business by pleasing customers in the present, and for an assured future, planning, investment and innovation. Competition creates room for a lot of business enterprises and entrepreneurs too. When the public becomes aware of a good product or service, they want more of it. Those who let down, who don't continue to please their customers, or who skimp and take short cuts soon pay the free enterprise price of mediocrity— they go out of business. Business failure is a serious price to pay, so serious, that it makes people work very hard, to keep customers and survive as a profitable business.

A FREE MARKET is not Free

Important to the idea of competition *is free access to the market*; that is, ease of entry into and exit from the marketplace, by buyers, producers and sellers. If we use government to restrict the market, competition is thwarted, and the benefits of competition become limited or eliminated. With competition controlled, government steps in with laws and regulations, law officers and bureaucrats to assure legal compliance. The courts and legal system become the new regulating mechanism. With such controls come reduced output, higher expense, higher prices and lower availability and quality. Only government can really restrict competition.

Let us use a taxi as an example. With freedom of entry, almost anyone can buy a car, call himself a taxi, and be in business for himself. For self-preservation he would have the integrity to assure safe, economical and dependable transportation. If he didn't, he would soon be driven out of business by competition, because "word gets around."

Suppose the government began to license taxis to assure that the regulations were met, and taxes were paid. Soon, one taxi service would realize that regulation could do them a great deal of good. Suppose "for the public good" only 20 taxis were permitted to exist to "properly service" a community. Free entry and exit of the taxi market has been eliminated through government. So has competition. Only one group would benefit, the original and only taxi company that exists after the legislation was passed. Who do you suppose initiated, sponsored and encouraged the legislation? That company has become a government-protected monopoly. The only kind of monopoly that can really exist is that created by government and controlled by force of law. That is not Free Enterprise!

What happens then? Service deteriorates. Prices go up. Dependability, safety and quality of transportation go down. And with the enforced limit of 20 taxis, no others can enter the market, so that the real regulator of the market, COMPETITION, cannot come into play to keep the game fair, the players honest and the riders happy. If the need expands, prices go up, service deteriorates. All happens supposedly in the "the public interest." Competition and all its benefits are lost. Who loses? The customer, the one who pays the bills and deserves the best in value and service

With a free market, and easy access into and out of it, all the other powerful characteristics of free enterprise can reward the hard worker, the risk-taking investor and producer, as well as customers. It especially punishes those who do not truly serve the public and the public interest.

The market must be accessible and unencumbered to work well. To impose the rigid discipline and to provide the potential rewards there must be freedom in the marketplace!

LIMITED GOVERNMENT: What's the Limit?

The role of government is easy to misunderstand, especially given the restricted historical and operational information we generally have available. The federal government's role is found partly in the Preamble to the Constitution as part of its purpose and goals, and more explicitly in Article I, Section 8, Clause 1: "...provide for the common defense and general welfare of the United States..." Those words were carefully chosen and intended to mesh into the meaning of the first ten amendments, the Bill of Rights.

You will find eighteen specific functions provided to the federal government. Anything not authorized by the Constitution is prohibited per the tenth amendment. Otherwise any dreamed-up government function or program could be put into operation regardless of its cost, need, value or detrimental effect on the citizens. Beyond these provisions we have less "a limited government."

Why Limited Government:
Excessive Taxes Tax Incentive Too

What if the "chair tax" grew to 3, 6, 9, or even 12 chairs out of every 20 manufactured? How much incentive would there be for the entrepreneur and business owner to continue to produce more good chairs with increased value to serve more customers? We might even defend all the good being done by the "chair tax," in that we had even more protection and public services than ever. We can even say we are providing those who can't afford chairs with a higher standard-of-living, etc., but the effect is the same. When limited government becomes not-so-limited, it demotivates all involved, those taken from, the producers, as well as those provided for, the recipients, diminishing everyone's standard-of-living and quality-of-life.

In a brief advertisement entitled "Socialism 101," the Warner-Swazey company described how such a system works.

A group of students took a test, where half received grades of 55% and the other half, 95%. The teacher thought these results unfair and corrected the system simply by dividing the total points and re-distributing them. The teacher took 20 points from the good students and gave 20 points to the failing students. Each student then received 75% on the test. That made it equal and "fair." The good students were asked if they would study as hard for the next test. Their answer was "no." Why? Because they had taken from them points they had worked very hard to earn. The failing students were similarly asked and also said "no." Why? Because they received points without having to work for them. In an academic sense, the *entire level* of effort, pool of knowledge, or "production," was *lowered* in the process. That is the effect that confusing equality of opportunity with equality of results can have.

Government's function is not to meddle or interfere in the marketplace. From the Constitution it is to serve as the guardian for a *climate* of free enterprise—to ensure national security and defense, public safety, "coin money and regulate the value thereof," insure uniformity of weights and measures, and provide a legal system to make and enforce laws and contracts necessary for enterprise to work, to assure equal rights, opportunity and justice for each citizen.

A condition to the founding fathers signing the Declaration of Independence was that the Constitution have incorporated within it a Bill of Rights which guaranteed each individual sovereignty with respect to the central government. The Constitution was complete when the Bill of Rights was added to it December 15, 1791, over four years after the Constitution was signed September 17, 1787. We were without a constitution for over 11 years, and guaranteed no individual rights for another 4 years!

For almost two centuries, these three documents have defined what makes America different. The Bill of Rights is what really guarantees individual liberties, protecting people from government oppression, and helping make the American Free Enterprise System work. That is what makes America different. Without these freedoms, and continuing guarantees of freedom, the power of FREEDOM on the human spirit could not be unleashed.

Standard-of-Living, Quality-of-Life and Entrepreneurship

As we continue to produce, specialize, and choose what we want to do, how and how well we do it, we find our whole life becomes more abundant. As we save and invest, forego present consumption for future security, our capital base of tools, equipment, machinery and technology continues to grow, giving us more goods and services for less expenditure of materials, money, time and labor. Economists call this "the highest and best use of resources."

Our freedom to enter new enterprise and markets triggers that unique risk-taking, challenge-setting, opportunity-seeking characteristic of the human spirit called "Entrepreneurship." We seek to go beyond what we have done and what others have done. We pit ourselves and our faith, ideas and personal resources against the unknown, and pursue a dream. In the process we enrich and are enriched, with a higher standard-of-living, more material goods and convenience.

A higher quality-of-life can flow from the increased standard-of-living. Quality-of-life means we advance as human beings, aspire to become more and better, to know ourselves, our Creator and sources of our strength, to contemplate our reason for living, our purpose for being. What we do with our abundance depends on us, our compassion, care and concern for our fellow man, and on our precepts of the meaning of life.

A higher standard-of-living can be either a blessing or a curse, depending on our personal interpretation, philosophy and higher aspirations. Higher quality-of-life comes more from within ourselves, freed and accelerated by the higher standard-of-living afforded by the most efficient and least judgmental economic system, which depends on character—personal integrity and freedom with responsibility. Freedom and free enterprise work, and work well together!

Back to Basics: Free Enterprise—Two Definitions

We have discussed various aspects and characteristics of free enterprise. We bring it all together by a formal definition. Back to *Webster's New World Dictionary,* 1976:

> free enterprise: the economic doctrine or practice of permitting private industry to operate under freely competitive conditions with a minimum of governmental control

The key words here are "permitting" and "minimum of governmental control." Governments can and do control. If they overcontrol, they do harm.

Here is a more functional definition from *Merriam-Webster's Collegiate Dictionary,* 1994, an outline for a 20-minute speech on free enterprise:

> free enterprise: freedom of private business to organize and operate for a profit in a competitive system without interference by government beyond regulation necessary to protect public interest and keep the national economy in balance.

It works, whether you call it free enterprise, the free market system, the private enterprise system, the individual incentive system, or the competitive enterprise system. And it works better than any other system so far devised by man. It is based on freedom with responsibility, and recognizes the strengths, weaknesses and limitations of its fallible inventors and mortal participants.

America is a great experiment in freedom. But it is only an experiment and experiments can fail. The more we know, understand, defend and support responsible freedom and the system it works best in, the more we can expect from the blessings of freedom and the gift of being alive here, now, as a part of this noble experiment.

Questions for Review

1.   What institution has ever been in power to take from the people and rule over the people? What God-given right of each citizen was protected by the new American government, so necessary in the design of a productive, bounteous economic system?

2.   What original concept and function was government designed for at home and abroad? From the beginning of history what has been the greatest threat to man's freedom and property? Enterprise must be conducted according to rules but rules can restrict free enterprise if they inhibit what and hamper what according to Clarence Carson?

3.   What two ways can an individual augment his supply of goods and services? What two ways by exchange? If we take things from another it is called theft. When government steals what kind of theft is it?

4.   Man's nature is such that he works and produces best and lives better if he is free to acquire and dispose, receive recognition and reward, and exchange. Discuss. What has this to do with the Declaration of Independence?

5.   Adam Smith in *Wealth of Nations* recognized the human drive for self-interest, combined for the social good, and to leave the economic process severely alone. These are teachings of his new doctrine of what two descriptions?

6.   Dr. Cleon Skousen listed four freedoms to illustrate Adam Smith's "tremendously successful formula for prosperity." Name and discuss.

7.   Draw and describe the "Triangle of Free Enterprise" and discuss each concept and its interaction with the others. What is the "ever-present player in life?"

8.   Explain the "dynamic character of free enterprise." Which is really more unusual, businesses that stay the same or those that change? Why is it better to recognize and deal with reality, TWII?

9.   What is the basic touchstone of free enterprise? What are the six characteristics of the free enterprise system? Why are these so important? Discuss and describe each. Relate each to a small business pleasing a customer. Explain the difference between a customer and a consumer.

10.   Give two basic definitions of free enterprise. How can they be
      used to explain free enterprise to others; as an outline of a
      speech?

Freedom is indivisible. Neither individual freedom, nor economic freedom, nor political freedom, nor religious freedom, nor any freedom, can exist separately. They exist as one or they do not exist at all."   —Edwin R Broden

Do not devote all of your energies to building your enterprises, as important as they may seem. Use what seems to be more than your share of time in making certain that your children know the full meaning of freedom.
                                                              —Ervin J. Nutter

People who practice free enterprise must become better at saying why it is the best. Like those who oppose it, they must use every opportunity to expound what they believe in. The essential message is that freedom needs free enterprise.   —Michael Ivens

Chapter 7

THE CHARACTER IMPERATIVE OF FREE ENTERPRISE
Discipline, Honor, Integrity

Concerning colonial America: Never was such a valuable possession so stupidly and recklessly managed than this entire continent by the British Crown; our industry discouraged, our resources pillaged, worst of all, our very character stifled. We've spawned a new race here, rougher, simpler, more violent, more enterprising, less refined. We're a new nationality. We require a new nation. —Benjamin Franklin, "1776"

Better Personal Conduct
Helps Free Enterprise to Work Better

American society and free enterprise require a known, respected and honored code of conduct to function. We are all in this together. We all have dreams and ambitions, wants and needs, problems and frustrations. Keeping emotions under control is essential for this society, or any society to work. We must be sympathetic to others to make allowances for their behaviors, and to make allowances to ourselves for our own peculiarities. How important too, is individual character and group culture to our world, that our society may be more habitable and really livable.

America's free enterprise system and culture cannot work without individual character.

All the ways we act, especially how we treat each other as individuals and deal with others in relationships, shape our impacts and achievements in life. Why we act the way we do comes from our *character.* How we get along with others comes from our culture. How we are able to mold character continually and successfully in tune with our culture is a matter of discipline.

A Power Dare Chapter: Do the Tough Stuff

This is a "Power Dare Chapter," *Power of ONE*. Read your "Power Deed Creed!"

People are Watching.
You, Power of ONE, are a Model for Others!

People are watching you, *Power of ONE*. They don't understand why you are different but they know you are. They can tell by the way you talk and how you act. You are something special. You have a greater sense of destiny, of scope and perspective. You see a larger picture. You fit the smaller features onto a greater canvas, giving everything magnified importance, every person added significance. You see possibilities where others see problems, opportunities where others see difficulties, optimism where others are discouraged. You see promise where they see despair.

You know you are always on record. Because you set the standard, not just meet the standard, you want to know and do the right thing right. That means you know how to act, then do so. You are disciplined, respectful and respected, honorable and honest. You maintain a high level of integrity and moral courage.

We will explore basic concepts in behavior which allow human beings to get along more effectively and harmoniously. We get back to basics with definitions from *Webster's New Collegiate Dictionary*, 1994, to discuss, interpret and apply. Since personal peace, contentment and achievement depend on personal discipline, we begin with discipline.

Discipline: Key to Success, Happiness and Prosperity

Discipline, means "training that corrects, molds, or perfects the mental faculties or moral character, orderly or prescribed conduct or pattern of behavior; SELF-CONTROL; a rule or system of rules governing conduct or activity, to train or develop by instruction and exercise especially in self-control."

"Self-control" appears twice. That is where discipline begins, with self. Discipline means doing the right thing right, because it is right. You can tell it is the right thing because it often seems inconvenient, time-consuming, and a sacrifice of time and energy. You can tell after you have exercised discipline, because you feel good and you have grown by doing what you did and how well you did it.

Discipline is acting as if you are appearing on television when you are not. Discipline is acting as if your parents are watching when they are not. Discipline is acting as if police officers are watching when they are not. Discipline is acting as if the boss were there when he or she is not.

Discipline is acting as if what you say and how you say it will be known by everyone; what you do and how you do it, will be on the front page of tomorrow's newspaper. Discipline is acting as if the short run is important, which it is, because the long run is very important, which it is.

An example of constructive personal discipline is to pay yourself first, saving some money for your peace of mind, security and future, rather than spending your whole paycheck to satisfy immediate desires. Discipline is going on to college from high school, foregoing the pleasures of working, earning money, having earlier personal independence and buying a car. It could be to complete high school or college while holding down a full-time job and fulfilling family responsibilities.

Discipline is to "Say YES" to the right, bright and good things of life: the caring, loving people around you, a good education, work well done at a real job, appreciation of nature, serving your fellow man, foregoing something to give to others.

Discipline is to "Say NO" to drugs, steroids, gambling, pornography, obscenity or promiscuity in favor of your long run personal life quality and well-being.

Lack of discipline is manifested by the "negative self's." These include *self-indulgence*, getting what you want, all you want, when you want it, regardless of the cost, who it deprives or who it hurts—"excessive or unrestrained gratification of one's own appetites, desires or whims." *Self-centered* means thinking first, last and always about your own self before others—"concerned with one's own desires, needs or interests." *Self-satisfied* means feeling you are so totally right, incapable of refining or improvement, then doing nothing to improve—"a smug satisfaction with oneself or one's position or achievements."

Benefits of discipline come from the "positive self's." "*Self-discipline* means being under your own self-control—"correction or regulation of oneself for the sake of improvement." *Self-sacrificing* means doing without now for more or better later, or doing without so that others may have more—"sacrifice of oneself or one's interest for others or for a cause or ideal." *Self-acceptance* means accepting who you are and what you are not, doing what you can to improve, but recognizing human limitation.

Self-assertion means doing the right thing because it is right, regardless of pressure from others, what they say, think or do—"asserting oneself or one's own rights, claims or opinions, self-assured, confident." *Self-sustaining* means to keep going from an inner sense of rightness rather than needing outside reassurance—"maintaining or able to maintain oneself by independent effort."

Finally, there is *self-transcendence*, where you truly go beyond what you thought you could do, or beyond anywhere you ever thought you would be, or be capable of going—"the capacity to transcend oneself."

Once you have discipline and maintain discipline, you are in control. You are free because you have achieved freedom with responsibility.

Character: Who We Really Are, and Moral Excellence

Character has to do with the individual and the group: "One of the attributes or features that make up and distinguish the individual; the aggregate of distinctive qualities characteristic of a breed, strain, or type; the complex of mental and ethical traits marking and often individualizing a person, group, or nation; reputation; moral excellence and firmness."

Here we consider character, who we are, and how having and using high level character, moral excellence, is essential for free enterprise to work.

Culture: How a Plurality of People Get Along

Culture is "the act of developing the intellectual and moral faculties especially by education; enlightenment and excellence of taste acquired by intellectual and aesthetic training; the integrated pattern of human behavior that includes thought, speech and action, transmitting knowledge to succeeding generations." For describing the society in which we live, culture is "the customary beliefs, social forms, and material traits of a racial, religious, or social group," and I would add another.

America has been called "the melting pot of the world." We have varied races, ethnic groups, religions, organizations and associations of people. Such diversity of culture and plurality of opinion and viewpoints make it even more compelling we accord to others their fundamental human dignity and that each one politely observes basic respect for and courtesy with others.

Culture is the expected norm of behavior. In terms of national political organization and government, culture has to do with public service expectations, or "public virtue."

Culture and Freedom Require Virtue and Morality

Dr. Cleon Skousen[1] tells how the issue of American independence "hung precariously on the single, slender thread of whether or not the people were sufficiently 'virtuous and moral' to govern themselves. Self-government was generally referred to as 'republicanism' and it was universally acknowledged that a corrupt and selfish people could never make the

---

1. W. Cleon Skousen, *The Five Thousand Year Leap: 28 Great Ideas that are Changing the World,* pp 49, 50, 54, National Center for Constitutional Studies, NC 61, Box 1056, Malta, ID 83342-9704: 1982, $16 pp. Used with permission

principles of republicanism operate successfully. Benjamin Franklin wrote, 'Only a virtuous people are capable of freedom. As nations become corrupt and vicious, they have more need of masters.'"

Skousen continues, "Morality is identified with the Ten Commandments and obedience to the Creator's mandate for 'right conduct,' but the early Americans identified 'public virtue' as a very special quality of human maturity in character and service closely akin to the Golden Rule."

He illustrated his point with a historian's quote on public virtue:

> In a Republic, however, each man must somehow be persuaded to submerge his personal wants into the greater good of the whole. This willingness of the individual to sacrifice his private interest for the good of the community—such patriotism of love of country—the eighteenth century termed public virtue. . . . The eighteenth century mind was thoroughly convinced that a popularly based government "cannot be supported without virtue." —Gordon S. Wood

Quoting Thomas Jefferson, "Virtue is not hereditary," Skousen elaborates, "'Virtue has to be earned and it has to be learned. Neither is virtue a permanent quality in human nature. It has to be cultivated continually and exercised from hour to hour and from day to day. The Founders looked to the home, the school, and the churches to fuel the fires of virtue from generation to generation."

Our culture-for-free enterprise vocabulary includes *virtue* and *morality*. *Webster's Dictionary* defines *virtue* as "general moral excellence, right action and thinking, goodness or morality, excellence in general, merit, value, and for the work we do, effective power or force." *Morality* is "rightness or wrongness, as of an action, moral quality or character, being in accord with the principles or standards of right conduct, principles of right and wrong in conduct, ethics."

Ethics and *integrity* are closely related to *virtue* and *morality*. *Ethics* is "the study of standards of conduct, moral judgment and moral philosophy." *Ethical* is "conforming to moral standards, or to standards of conduct of a given profession or group."

Integrity is "the quality or state of being of sound moral principle: uprightness, honesty, and sincerity." It is the "quality of being complete, a state of unbroken condition, wholeness, unimpaired, perfect condition."

America—Economic, Political, Cultural: Three Systems in One

The higher virtues of being a human being form the basic criteria for a free enterprise system that works. The more we know about this, the more we seek to establish and maintain a moral, ethical culture. But culture does not stand alone. The American system is three-in-one, a "Trinitarian system," as described by theologian, philosopher and economist, Michael Novak[2]:

> It is three systems in one. It is, at once, an economic system, a political system, and a cultural system. If any one of these is injured, the others are injured, too. If any one is missing, the resulting system falls short of our dreams.

I would add another, fourth dimension, that being government, as distinct from and contrasting to the other three. Government is perpetual. While politics changes, economics is re-interpreted and re-defined, and culture shifts with time, government keeps within it parts of all three, and changes ever so much slower. As pervasive as government is, in power, money and people, it is at least as much a part of the whole as the other three.

Our overall objective is to examine, discuss, and explore in some detail, the economic, political and governmental dimensions. Little discussed but very important is culture, "the ideas, customs, skills, arts, etc. of a given people in a given period; civilization."[3] It is our current society resulting from a historical path or evolution from where we were to where we are. It is who and how we really are, and how we do what we do. How well we understand and preserve culture, determines where and how far we go from here.

American culture is probably the greatest single reason the American brand of free enterprise will not and cannot work as well in other cultures, societies or countries. It is therefore important to consider culture to see how America's traditions and customs operate to best use free enterprise economics in our free enterprise concept of going about the business of America. If we recognize and understand culture, we will be even more effective and powerful *Powers of ONE*.

Democratic Capitalism and the Ideals of Fraternity, Equality and Liberty

"Democratic capitalism depends upon a unique human type," says Novak. "The impact of democratic capitalism upon the sphere of culture is, moreover, the single theme most neglected in the literature. Economists and businessmen worry about the economic aspects of our system, and naively leave the cultural aspects to others."

Novak considers the "ideals of *fraternity, equality* and *liberty*."

2. Michael Novak, *The American Vision, An Essay on the Future of Democratic Capitalism*, pp 1, 10, 19-27, American Enterprise Institute for Public Policy Research, Washington, DC: 1978. Used with permission

3. Webster's *New World Dictionary*, World Publishing, Cleveland: 1994

Fraternity includes a spirit of cooperation and teamwork. Our young people are trained to become both self-starters and good team players, still combining individualism, but "engendering high social skills." We like associational activities. We are "joiners," and have made "forming a committee" a favorite national pastime. We deeply value "the adaptation of self to others, indirect, informal and democratic forms of practicing authority, and prefer leaders who are 'one of us' rather than 'above us,' achieving a high degree of sociality in our citizens.

Equality says "that both elites and those at the economic bottom will circulate, and there is opportunity for all, whatever their starting place, not only to better their positions but also to go as far as imagination, work, and luck will take them. It multiplies occasions for luck and good fortune." Our cultural system is committed to equality in equal rights under the law and opportunity; yet inequality, in outcome. "It recommends hard work and self-improvement, so that when opportunity comes we will not be inadequately prepared to take advantage of it. . . . The marketplace, then does not and cannot reward everyone in a fully rational and appropriate way. The market is a harsh master," but "the first modern societies provided the enormous 'leap forward' that has transformed the face of the planet these last two hundred years."

Liberty promises that each human being will have, by constitutional right, and even by a certain minimal economic opportunity, freedom to think and to act, to aspire, to improve himself and his lot, and to move, go about, and make an almost unlimited series of choices about how to spend his or her life. The system does not promise that each person will, in fact, make out of himself or herself what he or she would like. But it does in fact, give ample room for each person to experiment and to try. . . . In a perfectly free system, a realist would not expect all to succeed equally, nor each to avoid some measure of failure.

Culture is a topical area too often overlooked or underestimated in its importance. Yet, in fulfilling a personal mission and being a benevolent and effective person, cultural recognition and social skills may be the competitive edge that makes the big difference.

Realizing our culture, we see a greater whole and visualize a Bigger Dream. We then make bigger commitments, accomplish more, and achieve greater. The larger view takes into account the human dimension, knowing that an individual may seem limited, but, as President Andrew Jackson said, "One person with courage makes a majority." *The Power of ONE* multiplies itself through other people, and better, through other *Power of ONE* people.

Beyond Economics, Culture and Self to Self-Transcendence

We can go beyond survival to self-transcendence. Economics and culture both start with a single individual, one person--YOU! That magic, motivating force which *freedom* liberates is what we here call *The Power of ONE*. When we set free the human spirit, that spirit soars to whatever heights it sets to conquer or take on as a challenge. The challenge goes beyond survival through what is called a comfortable *standard-of-living* towards a higher *quality-of-life*. We can even transcend that level in the quest for total fulfillment or self-actualization, becoming more what we are and all that we can become. We experience self-transcendence, going even beyond ourselves, farther, higher and faster than we ever thought possible! Wow!

We start with freedom. To live a full, complete life, take on both jobs of living; one, to make a living, the other, to protect your freedom. Life, the good life, begins and ends in freedom.

Freedom: A definition

The characteristics of Free Enterprise begin and end with those of *freedom*. *Webster's New World Dictionary*, 1994, gives us formal criteria of *freedom*, "the state or quality of being free, exemption or liberation from the control of some other person or some arbitrary power; liberty; independence."

A person in bondage acts much differently than one who is free. In bondage of any kind, one is subject to the direction of another; inhibited, controlled, restrained, threatened, coerced; sometimes hurt, deprived or even tortured, in order for a dominant person or power to obtain control, compliance, performance and passivity.

In freedom, people are subject only to themselves and their consciences, so long as they do not violate the freedoms, kin, person or property of others. That is where we confront the idea of "the freeing of the spirit." Mankind is composed of unique beings who have distinct capabilities and each a special destiny. These possibilities can only be met with the freedom required to bring them to fruition. Whether it is creation and invention; aspiration, inspiration and motivation; or just being who we are, and becoming who we can be, *freedom* is the secret, precious, priceless, essential ingredient.

America's Founders: Freedom Basics from the Beginning

Cleon Skousen tells how important the Founders felt the role of religion to be[4]:

---

4. W. Cleon Skousen, *The Making of America: The Substance and Meaning of the Constitution,* pp 676-77, National Center for Constitutional Studies, NC 61, Box 1056, Malta, ID 83342-9704: 1985, $30 pp. Used with permission

In 1787, the very year the constitution was written and approved by Congress, that same body of Congress passed the famous Northwest Ordinance. In it they outlawed slavery in the Northwest Territory. They also enunciated the basic rights of citizens in language similar to that which was later incorporated in the Bill of Rights. And they emphasized the essential need to teach religion and morality in the schools. Here is the way they said it:

"Article 3: Religion, morality, and knowledge, being necessary to good government and the happiness of mankind, schools and the means of education shall forever be encouraged."

Notice that formal education was to include among its teaching responsibilities these three important subjects:

1. *Religion*, which might be defined as "a fundamental system of beliefs concerning man's origin and relationship to the Creator, the cosmic universe, and his relationship with his fellow men."
2. *Morality*, which may be described as "a standard of behavior distinguishing right from wrong."
3. *Knowledge*, which is "an intellectual awareness and understanding of established facts relating to any field of human experience or inquiry, i.e., history, geography, science, etc."

The Founders went even farther, having defined religion as basic to "good government and the happiness of mankind." Skousen tells "the Founders then set about to exclude the creeds and biases or dissensions of individual denominations so as to make the teaching of religion a unifying cultural adhesive rather than a divisive apparatus," that the only religious tenets taught in public schools would be "those which were universally accepted by all faiths and completely fundamental to their premises."

Sometimes misunderstood and misquoted, Benjamin Franklin codified the "fundamental points in all sound religion" in a letter to Ezra Stiles, president of Yale University:

Here is my creed. I believe in one God, the Creator of the universe. That he governs it by his Providence. That he ought to be worshiped. That the most acceptable service we render to him is in doing good to his other children. That the soul of man is immortal, and will be treated with justice in another life respecting its conduct in this. These I take to be fundamental points in all sound religion.

Skousen wrote, "The five points of fundamental religious belief found in all of the principal religions of the world are expressed or implied in Franklin's statement:

1. Recognition and worship of a Creator who made all things.
2. That the Creator has revealed a moral code of behavior for happy living which distinguishes right from wrong.
3. That the Creator holds mankind responsible for the way they treat each other.
4. That all mankind live beyond this life.
5. That in the next life individuals are judged for their conduct in this one.

The Founders knew about oppression and tyranny. They were determined to design a system to free the human spirit and unleash its virtually unlimited potential for accomplishment, growth, development, caring, sharing, compassion and material well-being, providing the most good for the greatest number. They knew that character and morality were essential to a system based on individual freedom and responsibility

Retrieving the Lost Judeo-Christian Ethic

It is an assumption easy to make, easy to ignore, easier to forget. I had forgotten it. The Judeo-Christian ethic is really the ethical, moral and legal basis of the past heritage and modern day workings of American society. It took a sensitive and outspoken journalist to bring it to light.

Colorado Columnist Trisha Flynn, like many of us, had assumed the Ten Commandments "like communism and common denominators, were common knowledge," and found out otherwise. Her son told her he didn't know them because they weren't taught in school, because of the separation of church and state thing, that schools can't teach religion. Her response was crisp and clear, and in all-capitals[5]:

I'M NOT TALKING *RELIGION*, MR. MOUTH, I'M TALKING *EDUCATION*! THIS COUNTRY WAS MOSTLY FOUNDED ON RELIGIOUS FREEDOM! I'M TALKING ENGLISH LITERATURE, WESTERN CIVILIZATION, THE JUDEO-CHRISTIAN TRADITION—I'M TALKING ABOUT CULTURAL LITERACY, THAT HUNK OF INFORMATION EVERY AMERICAN NEEDS TO MAKE SENSE OF WHAT WE HEAR AND READ!

The obvious is too often obscure. This originates from The Bible, the "Judeo"-part from the Old Testament, the "Christian"-part from the New Testament. "The Decalogue" and "The Covenant" are names for these rules.

5. "Commandments Are an Education," *Rocky Mountain News,* 2/18/90, p 3-M

It is interesting they weren't called "The Ten Good Ideas" or "The Ten Suggestions." They are called "The Ten Commandments":

The Ten Commandments

I. I am the Lord your God. You shall have no other gods before me.

II. You shall not make for yourself any graven image and worship it.

III. You shall not take the name of the Lord your God in vain.

IV. Remember the Sabbath day, to keep it holy.

V. Honor your father and your mother.

VI. You shall not kill.

V. You shall not commit adultery.

VIII. You shall not steal.

IX. You shall not bear false witness against your neighbor.

X. You shall not covet your neighbor's house, wife, manservant or maidservant, ox or ass, or anything that is your neighbor's.
—Exodus 20:2-17, RSV

The -Christian part of the Judeo-Christian ethic is wrapped around the Golden Rule, to treat others as you want them to treat you. But there is more to it. Here is how Jesus described it:

> And one of them, a lawyer, asked him a question, to test him. "Teacher, which is the great commandment in the law?" And he said to him, "You shall love the Lord your God with all your heart, and with all your soul, and with all your mind. This is the great and first commandment. And a second is like it, You shall love your neighbor as yourself. On these two commandments depend all the law and the prophets".   —Matthew" 22:35-40, RSV

> So faith, hope, love abide, these three; but the greatest of these is love.
> —1 Corinthians 13:13, RSV

This source has been called "the manufacturer's handbook." It is an apt title for a book that reveals success secrets for an individual, a community or a society to help it work better.

When we put all this together it makes good common sense if one wants to be a part of a successful society and realize the full potential of life, the full opportunity of living and the confident realization of lifelong freedom for our people.

Freedom: "Why Don't You Tell Them the Whole Truth?"

The dangers of freedom may be as important as the blessings of freedom. At a commencement address[6] the speaker talked of the meaning of Independence Day, those who signed the Declaration, how precious is our heritage of freedom and how jealously we should guard it.

"Why don't you tell them the whole truth?" challenged an intense young man with untidy hair and intense angry eyes. "Why don't you tell them that freedom is the most dangerous gift anyone can receive? Why don't you tell them that it's a two-edged sword that will destroy us unless we learn how to use it, and soon? Why don't you make them see that we face a greater challenge than our ancestors ever did? They only had to *fight* for freedom. We have to *live* with it."

The pamphlet goes on to admit that perhaps we do have a blind and misguided concept of liberty. "Ever since our country won its independence, something in us has been deeply suspicious of authority. 'Give us more freedom!' has been our constant cry. . . . freedom from all unpleasantness; from hardship, from discipline, from the stern voice of duty, from the *pain of self-sacrifice.*"

"We want fewer rules," it goes on, "and more elastic ones," plus more leisure and less work, and the freedom to decide moral questions for ourselves: "As a nation, in short, we have clamored for total freedom. Now we have just about got it, and we are facing a bleak and chilling truth: We have flung off one external restraint after another, but in the process we have not learned how to restrain ourselves. . . . A man's worst difficulties begin when he is able to do what he likes."

The pamphlet concludes with the assignment to ask ourselves to what extent this distorted concept of freedom leaves people free to be selfish, lazy, ignoble, and weak:

> If personal freedom of choice is our goal and our ideal as a nation, then our first fundamental choice must be not to abuse that freedom. This is what independence really means: *self-discipline.*

Yet no discussion of freedom can accurately reflect its true meaning without the concept of responsibility. Without responsibility, our freedom allows us to be no more than savages, brandishing force for our own good to the detriment and harm of others.

In a society, freedom without responsibility is anarchy—mayhem, which hurts, maims, kills and destroys. That is why we need government. We need rules and the assurance that all the players understand and play by those rules.

6. "Why Don't You Tell Them the Whole Truth?" Brian Bex Report, Vol. XXIV, No. 7, American Communications Network, Hagerstown, IN 47346

The Odyssey of the Kite

A kite flies across the sky, viewing the world as only a kite can. The wind shifts. The kite veers to a new course. The wind drops and so does the kite. The wind picks up speed and the kite soars to new heights. The kite feels a rush of new power. "If only I didn't have this string to hold me back. Imagine how far I could travel; how much I could see. And this tail, what a drag!" Little does the kite realize, that the string is the tether of responsibility that allows it to soar; the tail is the stabilizer that gives direction and stability. Without the string and the tail, there would be no freedom, only a blinding crash to earth.

People too need freedom. But like the kite they also need the tether of responsibility and the tail of stability to relish and use their freedom without trampling the freedoms of others.

Look for yourself into the meanings of *responsible* and *responsibility*, along with *visibility* and *accountability*. If your words and actions are always considered to be "on the record," you will speak and act more responsibly.

Choices and Consequences:
Looking at Both Sides of Freedom

In America it is obvious we often have freedom beyond all bounds. Coupled to that is pervasive, persuasive television, glamorizing the more lurid aspects of freedom with crime and passion, sometimes quite explicitly. Gratification and indulgence loom much larger than punishment and retribution. While television programs make assaults, robbery and murders of fellow human beings common and popular, less obvious and more subtle is that these are stories made up by people and played out in the safety of sound stages. Mixed with news, weather and sports, they blend into quasi-realism for consumption of impressionable young minds.

A new game in town, in the home and schools might be called "Choices and Consequences." With young people, it would explore freedom with responsibility, that freedom begets choices and choices beget consequences, some good, some not so good and some very bad. It is a people, social, political and economic world we live in and for everything we do or don't do there are payoffs and consequences. There is a price to pay, rewards and punishments to receive.

We would use our most powerful electronic media—television, radio and the Internet—to discuss true, current instances of results of decisions. These would show positively where a person achieves success, fame and fortune, or negatively, failure and infamy, being arrested for a crime, sentenced in court, fined or incarcerated, as aired on the evening news.

We could discuss the obvious consequences, then consider what choices must have been made, and alternatives that could have been taken, both with the likely outcomes. The point is to relate preventable bad outcomes to bad choices and bad decisions.

Consider a convicted juvenile felon standing before a judge, about to be sentenced to a long term in prison. We ask, if he really knew these were to be the inevitable consequences of his decisions and actions, would he have made the same choice? What led to this state of affairs? What were his other options? What would or could have been their consequences?

"Choices and Consequences" can be played in churches and by families at home. It turns freedom of choice into a living, breathing life adventure to dramatize what really happens, how it happens, and what can be done to create desirable outcomes.

"Choices and Consequences" would make an excellent mandatory, one semester high school course, and perhaps be appropriate even at the junior high level. It could include discussions of everyday events, particularly those having to do with drugs, sex, violence, crime and suicide. For dramatic and lasting effect a part could be modeled after the television program "Scared Straight," where prison convicts told juvenile delinquents in very graphic and vulgar terms what it is actually like to live in prison, trying to survive, maintain basic dignity and not be personally, physically attacked, and mentally, emotionally and sexually violated. A recent article entitled, "Scared Straight, 20 Years Later," showed that the program helped almost all of both groups, the convicts who presented and the wayward youth it sought to dissuade.

How many students might stay in school, seek to excel in school, to learn more about the world of work and life, and to contribute to the community if they had wider and more complete knowledge of possible outcomes?

How many better decisions would be made regarding indiscriminate sex, use of drugs and committing crime?

How effectively can freedom be applied to basic economics, that there are choices and consequences of choice, that every action, inaction and reaction has a price and that it can be considered, estimated, evaluated and demonstrated?

Show our youth their choices and consequences. See if they make better decisions.

Basics 101: Personal Life Management

Similarly, another equally needed basic course would be "Personal Life Management." This is where students learn that one day too soon they are in total charge of their own lives. They start out with parents, teachers, clergy and friends telling them what to do, how and why. They hear "don't speak until spoken to," "children are to be seen and not heard," and "don't ask questions." These are all normal and natural for their growth phase, but dead wrong later on.

Up to say, age 18, these are true, then become questionable, then untrue. In becoming an adult they all reverse. With age, education, experience and maturity, they can and must speak, be heard, ask questions and question. They mustn't carry these youthful "thou shalt not's" into adulthood. Being no longer heads down, eyes-to-the-ground, "don't talk backers," they can ask why, question authority and be assertive in righting wrongs.

Most importantly they must be thoroughly taught, realize and act aggressively on the idea that they are the true managers of their lives, their fortunes and future. They take charge to determine what is best for them, do it, and profit by it, or suffer the consequences. They are not victims, blaming everyone and everything about their past for what happens to them. They take charge, accept responsibility and relish the power of the freedom of taking that responsibility. Each Power of ONE is the manager of his or her life.

Freedom Ingredients: Honor. Honesty. Principle.

Making freedom work is no simple task. It depends on how people act, how respectful they are of one another, how well they obey the law, and how they honor ethical and moral codes of conduct. Sometimes an act is not illegal but it is immoral in that it breaks no laws but unfairly takes advantage of another. So carefully woven into the fabric of freedom are our higher codes of honor, honesty and principle which help freedom and free enterprise work a lot better. Learn those important words and meanings too.

Honor is a matter of principle, something we adopt, accept, adhere to, and seek never to deviate from. It too, is a part of everything we are, everything we do. Without honor, does life really have meaning?

Building Character Builds Business and People

After describing a publication on the phone when I was asked the price, I said "$10." While my new customer made out a check I addressed an envelope and placed the product inside. When he asked "Do you realize what just happened?" I said, "No, what?"

"We just made a deal and trusted each other. I said I'd send money and it's on its way; likewise you said you'd send the report. Isn't it amazing how trust in business works?"

What kind of commerce would we have with distrust, lying and dishonor? We would each have to literally get our hands on the goods and the money in a person-to-person exchange, assuring ourselves we would get what we had coming.

Concepts of character and culture may appear out of place or unusual in a discussion of free enterprise. But no economic, political and social system advancing beyond human survival to abundance, especially a system so dependent on personal freedom as free enterprise, can function or endure without them. High level character and culture place mankind above the animals, up there with the angels.

Commitment, Key to Action: A Request and a Promise

Human achievement depends on commitment: to a higher power, to others, to oneself. To commit is to bind as by a promise or pledge. A commitment is a pledge or promise to do something. "Doing something" is taking action, and making a difference.

The whole point is commitment, as Abigail, Founder John Adams' wife, reminded him in the play "1776":

> Have you forgotten what you used to say to me? I haven't. "Commitment, Abby, commitment. There are only two creatures of value on the face of this earth—those with a commitment, and those who require the commitment of others."

A major flaw in our dealings in today's society is our unwillingness to make and/or inability to keep a commitment. Sometimes we lightly accept one, then not keep it. "My word is my bond," was a pledge of honor. A handshake was as good as a signed contract. Don't make promises lightly, but once made, keep them. That is honor, and it is honorable. It is exercising freedom of choice with responsibility. It is the Golden Rule in action, because you are doing to and for others what you expect of and need from them.

A request is stated. A commitment is made. A promise is fulfilled. Freedom of choice is honored responsibly. That is the way it works best.

Courtesy Makes the World a Better Place

Being kind, thoughtful, polite and courteous lubricate the interactions and relationships of human beings. Simple acts as opening a door, reaching out to shake a hand, offering a chair to an older person, and simple phrases as "Please" and "Thank you" smooth the cultural mores of getting things done.

Here is the **"Five-P**'s Must Win/Can't Lose Guaranteed Personal Success Formula":

> **P**ractice **P**ositive **P**ractical **P**ersonal **P**olitics.

That means to treat others when you don't need them the way you'll wish you had treated them when you do need them. It is good human relations and it is worth the effort to be thoughtful in advance. It is worth repeating:

> Treat others when you don't need them the way you'll wish you had treated them when you do need them.

That means be nice to people, all the time, if only for purely selfish reasons.

Thinking about others gets you out of yourself, helps maintain a larger perspective and forms a better pathway to make, preserve and sustain relationships. The total way to get things done begins with you, but continues with and through other people.

Basic Etiquette, a Few Pointers

Basic etiquette makes meeting, greeting and entertaining other people more effective, more fun and less awkward. Here are a few basic actions, based on cultural expectations:

Smile.

Stand for an introduction, or when someone enters a room. Smile.

Shake hands when being introduced. Smile.

Ask for things with "please;" receive them with "thank you." Smile.

When placing a phone call, smile, give your name, affiliation and reason for calling.

When answering calls, especially for others, smile, obtain and give enough information to complete the call.

Offer a sincere compliment. Smile.

When making appointments, be sure to agree on exact details: day, date, time, place, with a "reminder" or "associator" to help complete the appointment. If far in the future, an interim call or reminder may be in order. Then BE THERE, on time and "on Purpose!" Smile.

Be pleasant, positive and complimentary. Smile.

The Power of Right Speaking:
Use the Good, Avoid the Bad and the Ugly

The ethic of "anything goes," is taking over our language. Derogatory, vulgar or ethnic remarks and obscene gestures increase in frequency but not in acceptability. Offensive language serves no useful purpose except to show a paucity of vocabulary, laziness of thought and lack of respect for yourself and others. Offensive language is repulsive, repugnant, obnoxious and disgusting.

Hodding Carter[7] is "continually startled by the open manifestation of what was once considered to be a vice best confined to more private gatherings of the like minded—of actors and stevedores, pimps and reporters."

He says, "Beyond language is the larger problem which is the decline of civility in general. In a deranged perversion of the democratic ideal, the dominant notion in some quarters (not all of them young) is that attire appropriate to the place or occasion is the mark of the snob, the affected or the intellectually constipated."

Carter concludes "The chief blame is not on members of the generations most infected with the dry rot of decency. They either don't know any better, don't care or don't wish to buck their peers' practices. The fault lies elsewhere: with parents and others who didn't bother and still do not bother to demand

---

7. Hodding Carter III, "Our Public Manners, Sir, are Execrable," Wall Street Journal, 6/4/87

a different standard. . . . we created a society in which the lowest common denominator of public behavior has become the norm."

We can help bring the new society back to where the highest common denominator of public behavior is the norm, where our higher thoughts, cares and concerns are manifest in higher forms of actions, words and behaviors.

Take special care that the language you use, especially in the heat of anger, fear or frustration, stays within the bounds of decency, or is not expressed aloud. You diminish considerably your *Power of ONE* with morally offensive words and actions.

Cultivate the Power of Praise

Every time we meet or greet someone, we have an enormous power many do not know exists. It is the power to build or the power to destroy; the power to make feel welcome or unwelcome; the power of grow and live, or shrink and die. It is the power to kill or cure. We can be builders or killers, promoters or destroyers. What a power!

Anyone can criticize, and usually does. It is the easiest thing to do. Criticism seems to elevate the critic up while it puts the victim down. But does it, really? It accomplishes little good. There is no end to things each one of us can't do well or at all. So there is no challenge whatever to criticizing another person. The real challenge is to compliment another person.

We have all heard, "if you can't say something good about someone say nothing at all." A *Power of ONE* goes beyond that to "You can always find something to praise. Find it, and praise it." Look for and find the one thing or several things another person does well, how they look or speak, or how they have made their or your world a little brighter. It is a power all by itself to look for the good, find it and tell the world about it. And don't you think others will seek you out, listen to you and respect your views and wishes?

You are dealing with the power of life and death. Ardis Whitman[8] describes that power, calling it "the profound and painful knowledge that people heal, and people destroy. We help or hinder one another to be and grow, or to surrender and retreat, that we all constantly issue unique and powerful invitations to each other to live or die, to triumph or surrender."

Whitman concludes: "Treasure life in yourself and you give it to others; give it to others and it will come back to you. For life, like love, cannot thrive inside its own threshold but is renewed as it offers itself. Life grows as it is spent."

Power of ONE, you possess The Power of Praise. Use it. Look for the good in people, find it and praise it. People have a high tolerance for praise. One of the greatest characteristics of human beings is that we want to be noticed,

---

8. Ardis Whitman, "The Invitation to Live" *Reader's Digest,* April 1972

acknowledged, praised, complimented and appreciated. That is one of the fun assignments we can accept from here on, in our lives, of building bigger people in a better world.

Look for the good in others. Find it. Shout it to them and to the world. Recognize and use The Power of Praise!

Cultivate An Attitude of Gratitude

We all take too much for granted.
We all take too much for granted.
We all take too much for granted.

It really must be repeated, because, especially in America, we receive so much, and most of the time do so little to earn or deserve it. Make it even more personal: I take too much for granted.

One of the first and repeated cases I make, especially to students, is that we do not say "thank you" (and mean it) nearly enough. I suggest to others to review the many, many blessings that make up our lives, and to consider where they came from, and how they got to us. In most cases, they are from loved ones whom we don't take nearly enough time to thank.

Children, thank your parents for their care and concern, sacrifice, hard work and love.

Students, take a special few moments to thank your teachers, and fellow students for all they do for you.

Thank your friends, relatives, children, fellow employees, clergy, bosses, storekeepers, clerks, mail carriers, and all others who work hard to make the economic system work, and our lives better.

Thank friends for being there when you need them, being trusted and true.

Thank relatives for their support, accessibility and availability.

Thank children for being children and for your being part of their magic world.

Thank fellow employees for all they do and you do together on the job.

Thank your pastor, priest, rabbi or spiritual leader for higher level support.

Thank bosses for guidance and direction, a place to work, and pay to take home.

Thank storekeepers for being there and serving you with America's bounty.

Thank clerks and all workers for their hard work and continuing good job.

Thank newspaper and mail carriers for their day-to-day, reliable deliveries.

Thank all others for all they do, especially that which you don't know about.

Thank *YOU* for all you do!

When someone does something generous or thoughtful, send a thank you note. When someone takes you to lunch or invites you to dinner, they or their family may have gone without a meal to make one available for you. Send them a thank you note. Think how you like to be thanked. Thank others.

Similarly when someone does something notable or worthwhile, send a note of congratulations. Dignify your fellow human beings. Try to catch people doing something right and praise them for it.

The Survival Battle and the Magic, Miracle and Mystery

Life is a battle for survival. Most fight hard to win. Most carry a heavy load, have big dreams and big commitments, big responsibilities and big disappointments. Most want to be liked, loved, respected, or at least noticed.

If we can but do these things unto each other, the Magic of Freedom, the Miracle of America, and the Mystery of Free Enterprise can even more greatly assure our present security and peace of mind, bless our abundance, and enhance our future opportunities and possibilities. The world of business and our success depend on our ability to prepare people and ourselves for the future. Enterprise runs on courtesy, honesty and honor. Build character in yourself and others. Do it starting with yourself, by example. Your "world changing" *Power ot ONE* will amuse and amaze yourself and others, and help create a better world.

Questions for Review

1. "People are watching." What effect does knowing that have on one's behavior and actions? Does one with a larger vision act differently? Why?

2. Why does considerably more relative freedom require a higher level of behavior in a free enterprise society? What is the importance of honesty and honor in conducting business? Personal character can include many such descriptions. Name four, describe, and explain why each is important.

3. Name some "negative self's" and "positive self's" and explain why they are good or bad. How does one go about adopting the positives, resisting the negatives?

4. What is culture? What is the relationship of character to culture? How can a knowledge of both make for a richer more fulfilled, accomplished life?

5. America's Founders created a "success formula" in the Constitution but it depended on a people "sufficiently virtuous and moral" to govern themselves. Ben Franklin related a virtuous people to freedom. What does virtue have to do with self-government?

6.   Cleon Skousen said virtue has to be learned and earned. Who is the teacher? Who is the employer? How does one learn and earn virtue? Discuss related concepts of ethics, morality, integrity, principle.

7.   What are the three parts of the "Trinitarian system," what is a possible fourth, and how do they relate to character and running a free enterprise economic system? How do "the ideals of fraternity, equality and liberty" relate to character? How is freedom related to "responsibility, visibility and accountability?"

8.   Discuss the three requirements "necessary to good government and the happiness of mankind" from Article 3 of the Northwest Ordinance? How did Ben Franklin's creed highlight the "five points of fundamental religious belief." What were they? Why are the Ten Commandments important to the heritage and survival of a free society? Discuss "the whole truth" about freedom? Why is a knowledge of "Choices and Consequences" so important to freedom with responsibility? "Personal Life Management"?

9.   "Beyond survival to self-transcendence" indicates we have potential and capability almost beyond imagination. How is all that related to making a difference? Do we take too much for granted? Discuss.

10. What is so important about making a promise and keeping a commitment? Why be courteous and polite, say "please" and "thank you" and really mean it? Why smile? Is language, especially good or bad language important? Why? How can the power of speech be a matter of life and death?

You give but little when you give of your possessions. It is when you give of yourself that you truly give.   —Kahlil Gibran

> Sow a thought, and you reap an act.
> Sow an act, and you reap a habit.
> Sow a habit, and you reap a character.
> Sow a character, and you reap a destiny.
> —Samuel Smiles

Two kinds of gratitude: The sudden kind we feel for what we take; the larger kind we feel for what we give.   —Edwin Arlington Robinson

Reputation is what men and women think of us; character is what God and the angels know of us.   —Thomas Paine

One can never pay in gratitude; one can only pay 'in kind' somewhere else in life.   —Anne Morrow Lindbergh

> ***Seven Sins in the World:***
> Wealth without work,
> Pleasure without conscience,
> Knowledge without character,
> Commerce without morality,
> Science without humanity,
> Worship without sacrifice,
> Politics without principle.
>
> —Mahatma Gandhi

During my 87 years I have witnessed a whole succession of technological revolutions. But none of them has done away with the need for character in the individual or the ability to think.   —Bernard M. Baruch

If we can implant in our people the Christian virtues which we sum up in the word character, and, at the same time, give them a knowledge of the line which would be drawn between voluntary action and governmental compulsion in a democracy, and of what can be accomplished with the stern laws of economics, we will enable them to retain their freedom, and at the same time, make them worthy to be free.   —Winthrop W. Aldrich

Chapter 8

THE MIRACLE MAGIC OF ROBIS

Role Of Business In Society!

The "Three C's of Organization": Communication, Coordination, Cooperation

Business gets organized to please people. That is how we find the best way to satisfy human wants and needs. That is a big job. It takes a lot of communication, coordination and cooperation to do it. Communication is everyone knowing and being conversant on what the business is all about. Coordination is teamwork in action, everyone doing the right thing in the right way at the right time. Cooperation is working together to resolve problems, celebrate victories, make good things better. To be a more powerful *Power of ONE*, you must be knowledgeable, understanding and conversant in two important questions: 1) What is the *Role Of Business In Society* (ROBIS)? and 2) What is a business? How do we go about getting the business of business accomplished?

This chapter begins your "learn-and-teach adventure." This information is so vital and so needed, particularly by our young people, it is offered in a format you can present in schools and where you live and work. Visualize how you will "talk to kids," and that means kids of all ages, to help explain and create understanding about the American enterprise system.

Your personal power challenge is to learn-and-teach the miracle magic of ROBIS, the role of business in society. Here we go into a classroom mode.

That New "Vette!" How Did They Know?

The title of my special business presentation for students is written:

Wants and Needs and Profits and ???

I begin by writing that title across the top of the classroom chalkboard or white board. Those three last question marks ("???") are very important, and if I forget to mention them, the students are told to be sure to ask. I always forget, and they always remember. And I answer them, later.

For starters, pose an easy question for a teenager to answer: "What do you want?" and repeat it. Sometimes they need encouragement or prodding to get started: "Pretend I'm your parent at graduation and I ask you what you want for a graduation gift, or it is almost your birthday or Christmas and a good friend asks you the big question, 'What do you want?'"

With each answer, I ask the students if it's a "want" or a "need," then I list them beneath the appropriate title word on the chalkboard. This may be the first time they have categorized things into wants and needs. It provides good discussion and gets into why something is a want or a need, both, or "it depends." It is a good way to get into economics, and "scarcity"—where things come from, why they are there, and how they got there. That is the whole point of the discussion, and it works.

Our children are getting smarter in the ways of life. They always mention "money" first, second or third. They mention material things like stereos, cameras, bicycles, video games and especially cars. They get very specific. They want a Mustang, a Probe or BMW.

Cindy Miller informs me she wants a "Vette." "Vette," I say, "What's a Vette'?" Of course Cindy is happy to inform me a "'Vette' is a Corvette, the Chevrolet fiberglass sports car. Then they go "hi-tech." They want a compact disk player, a laser gun hunt down game or DVD (Digital Video Disk) machine.

More often now, they mention less tangible yearnings: peace, love, success, happiness. I create a special column for those kinds of things and explain later they are more internal than external, but still very attainable, especially in America. Apparently they are thinking deeper, more serious thoughts than they did not so long ago.

Whatever they say I list. Sometimes it is best I don't hear some things, and I don't. We eventually list, define and name the "essentials of life," food, shelter and clothing. Here, I digress to tell them how much we, as a nation, spend on these essentials of life, then compare those costs with the cost of government, which is always substantially more. This is their economic introduction to the cost of government, taxes and national priorities. Most understand little about either. Hardly any really understand who pays taxes, and how they are collected and spent.

Students come up mostly with the "fun things of youth," the fads, fashions and foibles of the times. To make the points I wish to make, I list some durable or hard goods, such as those mentioned above. Inevitably we get to the really "fun stuff," most of which are hard to spell extemporaneously, such as Lamborghini, Maserati, Ferrari and Bugatti. Someone will usually mention a "Harley," Firebird, or Camaro.

I pause, then ask, *"How did they know?"* (Longer pause)

The students puzzle over "How did *who* know *what?*" I ask, How did General Motors know that Cindy Miller wanted to buy a new Corvette on exactly month/day/year, from 110 Main St., Hometown, USA, at Johnson Chevrolet Motors just up the street a few blocks? How did they know to build Cindy a candy apple red, four-on-the-floor, air-conditioned ragtop with a high performance, 8-cylinder engine? How *did* they know?

The answer, of course, is that *they didn't know*. They might have thought they knew. They may even have done market research. But they did not know. They made their best guess, invested a lot of money, went ahead and built the car and *took a RISK*. In case we think every new car is an automatic success, remember the Ford Edsel. (You do remember the Ford Edsel, the Packard, Studebaker, Rambler?)

RISK: What You Don't Know Can Help You, and Hurt You

RISK. There's that word again. We don't like that word. It is almost like "freedom" and "survival." We rarely, if ever think about it, and when we do, we get nervous. RISK is one of those words that makes us think, and that makes us uncomfortable. Yet everyday, when each human being, each *Power of ONE* gets out of bed to begin the day's activities, RISK rears its ugly head. RISK is a fact of life—of personal life, family life, business life, national life. The only people who don't take a risk are those who don't do anything. There is probably an even greater risk to doing nothing.

The business of business is accepting a risk, and beating the odds of losing. It is bringing to bear all the resources, intelligence, faith and commitment we have, to anticipate the wants and fulfill the needs of people.

So I ask Cindy Miller, "When you go down to the Chevrolet dealer to find your very special Corvette, is it there?" "Yes," she says, "It's likely to be there." And Cindy's exact model might be there, or can be placed on order.

HOW DID THEY KNOW? *They didn't know. They took a risk.* In this case they were right. Cindy wanted to buy the car. Cindy was "ready, willing and able" to buy it. It was there. She bought it. That is the magic of free enterprise, and business. They took the risk and met Cindy's need. She was able to enjoy the satisfaction of finding, owning and driving her dream. They benefitted from the sale of the "Vette" to Cindy Miller. They took a risk, did a lot of things right, and this time, made a profit.

Sometimes, guess what? It happens the other way. They "know" that people want their "gadget." They do their best to judge the market, design the best, test the prototype and go into production. They place their new product on the market, but surprisingly few people buy it, not enough to make a profit, or even cover expenses. In fact they take a LOSS. They fail! All that investment of time, money and resources was a waste (or was it?). That's the downside of RISK which we hear little about. The investors and producers put their failed enterprise behind them, and start over again.

The difference between business and free enterprise is the relative degree of risk they experience. An established business with much less risk might decide whether to put $15 million or $20 million into advertising and promotion, realizing the difference would make a slight variation in expected profit. A new business might fail with far smaller amounts and greater risk.

This business of business is a tough business. Perhaps we should know more about it. What is business all about? What is the role of business in society?

ROBIS: Role of Business in Society?

The role of business in society (ROBIS)
is to produce goods and services that
customers want and will pay for,
at a profit.

The goods and services we produce must:

- PLEASE PEOPLE! Satisfy human wants and needs.
- Have consistent and predictably high quality.
- Be manufactured at the lowest possible cost.
- Be sold at the lowest possible price.
- Be reliably and widely available.
- Consume minimum resources in their production.
- Exert minimal damaging effects on the environment.
- Adequately reward employees who work hard and produce.
- Make a profit and reward investors and owners.
- Keep us in business, with a continuing stream of profits.

The job of business is to *Please People at a Profit*! That's an important job!

Much has been said about the "social responsibility of business." In its Role Of Business In Society (ROBIS), the business social responsibility is implicit in its mission to satisfy customer needs at a profit. That goal fulfilled, especially on a long term basis, the social benefits stream from the business' existence—creation of jobs and career opportunities, satisfaction of human wants and needs, generation and payment of taxes, and peripheral benefits such as support of the arts and humanities, sponsorship of community charitable organizations and events, student scholarships and the like.

In order to make an exchange—remember we must have a surplus to exchange—to have a surplus, we must produce more than we ourselves need. The key word here is *produce*, which is our way of overcoming scarcity to survive. It all fits together, doesn't it?

To stay competitive, we must produce more and better for less—productivity. That means our hearts and spirits direct our "minds, muscles and machines" to do more and better with less, building into our business this continuing increase in *productivity*. The result: We *beat* the competition, *stay* in business and *improve* our overall standard-of-living and quality-of-life. We remain competitive and improve productivity by better organizing our use of resources including time, labor, materials, money, technology, management and capital.

Business is a means of managing or organizing natural and technological resources to satisfy human wants and needs. It provides products, goods and services to satisfy wants and needs of our fellow human beings. It is worth repeating:

Only when we *please people* do we stay in business.

Size has nothing to do with "business." The various forms of organizing for business tell the size story.

The three most popular forms of business organization are single proprietorship, partnership and corporation.

A *single proprietorship* is a one-person or one-family operation with a singular ownership. An example would be one person and a computer, creating computer software for other businesses.

A *partnership* is a group of people working together under a formal agreement, written or verbal. It can be two or more people, spreading liability, expense, investment and profits towards a business objective. An example might be a restaurant or a bicycle repair shop, owned and operated by two families, close friends or business associates.

Finally, a *corporation*, according to *Webster's* is "a body formed and authorized by law to act as a single person although constituted by one or more persons and legally endowed with various rights and duties including the capacity of succession." It is an "artificial person" whose legal liability is limited to the assets of the corporation, rather than those of the owners or stockholders. A corporation can range from a few persons in ownership or employment, to millions.

There are variations of each of these forms of business, and there are reasons, advantages and disadvantages to select a specific form. Beyond the scope of this work, details are important to the specifics: individual, business purpose, location, and competition.

The most basic question, "What is a business?" prompts another question regarding what all three forms of business organization have in common: How to go about the business of *pleasing people at a profit*?

What is a Business?

What is a business? Students and adults answer this question in terms of things—buildings, machines, land, equipment, vehicles, patents, sometimes even money. They may skirt around what business really is, then get to the vital nerve center answer to "What is a business?"

Business   is   PEOPLE!

One way to help remember the answer to the question "What is a Business?" is to use the "thumb up, wiggling fingers" sign. (While doing so, say, "Business is people, five sets of people, four of whom [wiggling fingers] come together voluntarily to please, serve and satisfy the fifth and most important [thumb up], the CUSTOMER." The "thumb up" is the customer. The four "wiggling fingers" are employees, suppliers, investors and neighbors.)

Splendor and Grandeur:
The Royal Role of Business and the Royal Players

Business is so important to the sustenance and advancement of society, it plays virtually a "Royal Role" in the drama of life. Statesmen, war heroes, sports figures and entertainers are regularly lauded for their victories, accomplishments and good deeds. Similarly, every town in America should have a monument to business in the Town Square. Business quietly, reliably and ably supplies the things we need to do all the things we like to do. In the process, they create jobs for people to make a living and build a life. This whole scheme of things is so important that we decree a Royal Cast of Characters, to give accolades to what we call:

The   Royal   Role   of   Business

We recognize first, King CUSTOMER and Queen CUSTOMER, then the other four Majestic Players in our Royal Drama of Business: Regal EMPLOYEES, Royal SUPPLIERS, August INVESTORS and Stately NEIGHBORS. (We will wiggle a royal digit on our "thumb up, wiggling fingers" hand model for each of these four special groups of people. We'll discuss each as to their functions and relationships to the others, and finally to the customer and society.)

The Reigning Monarch: Long Live KING CUSTOMER!
Long Live QUEEN CUSTOMER!

Our first concern and top priority is our CUSTOMER. It takes the wisdom of Solomon, the cunning of a fox, the patience of Job, a lot of luck, and a whole lot more, to *find, favorably impress, please, serve, sell, satisfy and keep a customer*. When we finally do find one, we work very hard to keep and please the CUSTOMER for now, and from now on.

In the American free enterprise system, a pleased and satisfied CUSTOMER is and must always be *our supreme business objective*: The reigning monarch, the King, the Queen, THE BOSS! Our very existence as a business, any future we have, any hope of continued operation and profit lies in how well we are able to attract, please and retain a customer, especially in a competitive, free market environment.

The CUSTOMER is great example of a *Power of ONE*. The whole world of business revolves around that all-important person whom we strive to "please, serve and satisfy." King CUSTOMER holds the power. Queen CUSTOMER wields the power.

(Hold your "thumb up, wiggling fingers," knowing that the "thumb up" represents the most important person in the world of business, the CUSTOMER, the one who pays all the bills, and must receive all the benefits.)

The Three C's of Business: CUSTOMERS, Choice and Competition

CUSTOMERS, Choice and business Competition force us to be very good and get even better. The CUSTOMER's economic freedom is choice to do business with us, someone else or not at all, with usually a lot of "someone else's." Choice is what another group of people may exercise, and choose to go into business in competition with our business. So the "Three C's of Business," Customers, Choice and Competition, make us good, keep us good and force us to get even better. Excellence is the order of each day, the expectation and right of the CUSTOMER.

That is a gentle reminder that in supplying human wants and needs, there is always a CUSTOMER who MUST BE PLEASED, because the CUSTOMER pays the bill. In short, the CUSTOMER is THE BOSS!

Let's get down to business in free enterprise! Just what is a business?

Business: A Model

A business is PEOPLE. Let us study carefully who are these vital players in the business drama of survival and prosperity; what are their roles and how do they relate?

A business can be any general name you give it, large automaker or small computer software house, national detergent manufacturer or local print shop or gas station. Around where you see "A BUSINESS," in the illustration, pencil in the names of one or several businesses familiar to you, or the one you are in. We will be discussing them and others like them.

In Figure No. 7 note the two EQUAL arrows between the business and the King CUSTOMER or Queen CUSTOMER. Those signify a *voluntary exchange of equal value*. The arrow *from* King CUSTOMER or Queen CUSTOMER is money, the medium of exchange (store of value and standard of value) that helps keep our exchanges as efficient as possible. But what is the arrow from the business *to* the King CUSTOMER or Queen CUSTOMER?

That's it! That is the secret to business success!

It is what King CUSTOMER and Queen CUSTOMER have paid for out of their hard-earned money, to satisfy wants or needs! And it is what they get. But what is "it?"

Many will respond with "goods" or "products" or "services," and they are right. But that is not what the customer really buys. Others will say King CUSTOMER and Queen CUSTOMER seek satisfaction, and therefore quality, availability, quantity, the right size, color or fit. It works, works well and keeps on working. For peace of mind, they want a warranty or a guarantee to protect their purchases.

ROYAL CUSTOMERS EXCHANGE DOLLARS FOR VALUE
Figure No. 7

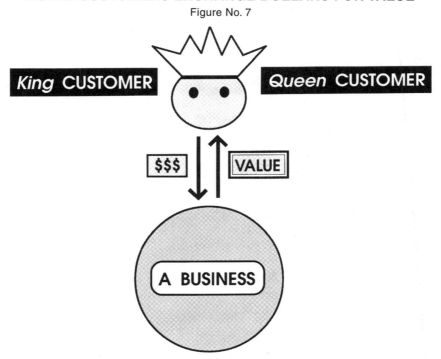

Is "price" what the buyer buys? If so, why does one person want a $12,000 subcompact imported car while another buys a $35,000 domestic 4-door sedan? Or why will one person buy a $25 simple "point and shoot" camera while another insists on an automatic focus, auto-wind, automatic shutter and aperture, 35-200mm macro zoom lens, 35mm camera costing hundreds or thousands of dollars?

What does the customer really buy? V A L U E !

V A L U E is what makes the business world go around!

What does the CUSTOMER seek? Value.
What is the buyer really buying? Value!
What is a supplier really supplying? Value!
What is a business in business to provide? V A L U E !
What is an employee paid to provide? V A L U E !
What is business all about? Creating and producing V A L U E !

That is V A L U E ! Got it?

If the buyer is buying value, that is what business must be making and selling. Value must be a part of every business relationship, every customer transaction. Value must be built into every product, good and service. Value must be reliable, consistent and available. Value provides continuing satisfaction, so that the CUSTOMER will come back for more, and ideally, recommend friends and neighbors do likewise. Not only is Business *People*, but it is a *People Business*! Business supplies people's wants and needs, with products and services, at a fair price, * * V A L U E * *, for a profit.

Please Customers with Goods and Services, or Explanation and Information

We "please people at a profit" with goods and services to fulfill their wants and needs. Sometimes we just cannot do so. The next best thing is to explain why, or provide information how or where else to try. I once requested that my local film processor print on my color slides a date as well as a number. He explained the required machine would cost him over $20,000 and was not cost-justified or affordable. I then had a choice between dates on slides and processing convenience.

Talking Smart: "Quid Pro Quo" is Something for Something!

The equal arrows of exchange are described by the Latin phrase "quid pro quo," which means "something for something," one thing in return for another, something equivalent, or a substitute. It is human nature to seek the best exchange possible, getting the most value for the least expenditure. Exchange of equal value is in the minds of the exchangers. That is why so many businesses can flourish with so many different products and services, to please the preferences of literally millions of customers. This is a totally different concept than another called "something for nothing."

If a business is made of "five sets of people, four of whom voluntarily seek to please, serve and satisfy the fifth and most important, the King CUSTOMER or Queen CUSTOMER," who are these "volunteers," these most important actors in the continuing drama of business?

Regal EMPLOYEES: Hard Workers Who Create Value

The major starring role with which we are most familiar are Regal EMPLOYEES. They are the people who get up and go to work every morning, to assure our continuing survival and prosperity as a people, and as a nation. Most of us have jobs, but how many realize

How vitally, critically important
Our work is in our jobs!

It is sometimes difficult to have the perspective to know how important *my* work, *my* job, *my* output, *my* quality, *my* value added, *my* contribution is, until I understand the greater picture of constantly, continually, always pleasing a customer with VALUE in exchange for VALUE.

What do Regal EMPLOYEES provide to the business? Good and valuable things: full skill, care and effort, hard work and concern. Consider the value of Regal EMPLOYEE's better idea, smile, arriving at work on time, honoring lunch and break rules, working safely and following the direction of a boss to get a job done. In addition, forward-looking employees take appropriate courses, on the job and off, to improve their skills. Some save money in their employer's savings and investment plan, and prepare for the future while performing in the present.

Regal EMPLOYEE's hard work is an input of VALUE to add VALUE to the company's product (See Figure No. 8). The better he or she does, and the more they do, the better the work situation and environment, and *potential* security of their job and future. "Potential" is a key word and concept. "Technological obsolescence" is more than a phrase, but a fact of life. Many would prefer the assurance of a job for an entire lifetime, but the characteristics of progress, technology, management and business are such that there are no guarantees. That's "TWII"—The Way It Is. Knowing really, "TWII," we are even more prepared through continued learning and upgrading of job skills.

What do Regal EMPLOYEES get in return, in this "quid pro quo," equal exchange situation? Money. Buying power. Satisfaction of today's needs. Assurance of fulfilling future needs. Because they are workers in the economic system, they are privileged to be participants in the economic system, to reap the benefits of their hard work, production and customer satisfaction, and share them with others.

When we exchange "quid quo pro" we trade our hard-earned work and investment for that of others, using money to "make it happen."

When we create value as workers and players in the economic drama, we receive money in return, use it also to buy value from others, and achieve satisfaction in our purchases.

Where does the money come from to pay Regal EMPLOYEES? From the CUSTOMER. The CUSTOMER is the single, one-and-only source of revenue the company has, except for initial or additional investment capital.

ROYAL EMPLOYEES DO THE WORK
Figure No. 8

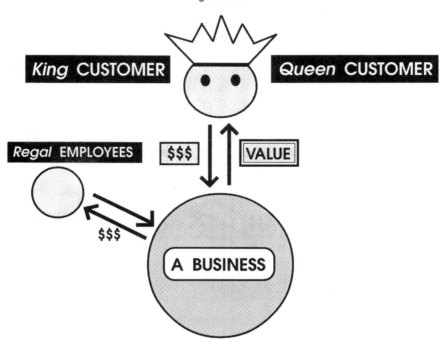

Even the investment capital must be accounted for, and again, the only real source of repayment is the CUSTOMER. Any money the company gets is from a CUSTOMER to satisfy a CUSTOMER want or need, to stay in business to "please people at a profit."

(On our outstretched "thumb up, wiggling fingers" proudly wave the top finger to signal the importance of Regal EMPLOYEES.)

Management's Make-or-Buy:
Royal SUPPLIERS "Fill the Bill" of the Buy

Suppose a Regal EMPLOYEE goes to management with a good idea say, for a forklift truck to handle and transport heavy cartons. Management might say, "Get one from our forklift manufacturing department," only to be reminded, "We don't have a forklift manufacturing department." Right! We are not very good at making forklifts. We make our product, the best there is, anywhere! But we don't manufacture forklifts. We buy forklifts.

Choice and *specialization* are important to business. Each of us chooses what job and what specialty to work, the one we do best, enjoy most, and can make the most money. Our business chooses to supply the needed product or service it does best. This aspect of choice and specialization is vital to people and businesses working together in a free enterprise system, to please CUSTOMERS and satisfy a market. So management makes a management "make-or-buy" decision, in this case, to go outside the company and buy needed items. Who from? Royal SUPPLIERS!

ROYAL SUPPLIERS SERVE THE BUSINESS
Figure No. 9

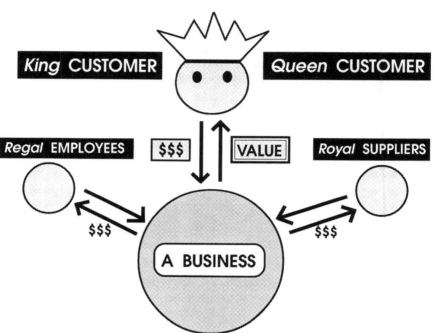

Royal SUPPLIERS are other businesses just like us who help us get our job done better, pleasing CUSTOMERS and providing them value (See Figure No. 9). In turn, we are their King CUSTOMER, to be *pleased* and *provided VALUE.* Sometimes called vendors, Royal SUPPLIERS specialize in what they are good at, producing highest quality consistent with price, availability, delivery and service. We go there for their goods and services, and we go back because they provide continuing value.

Where do we get the money we need to pay Royal SUPPLIERS? From our only source of income, King or Queen CUSTOMER. We will continue to earn and receive it as long as we provide value. We grow by creating more demand by our existent CUSTOMERS and new demand with new CUSTOMERS. But it all comes back to the same simple, vital requirement: Business pleases CUSTOMERS by providing VALUE at a profit.

(Give a "thumbs up" sign and wiggle the second finger to acknowledge the royal importance of Royal SUPPLIERS.)

August INVESTORS:
Entrepreneurs Investing with Faith in a Good Idea

WHERE does a business start? It begins in the heart, mind and spirit of a human being, a *Power of ONE*. WHY does it begin? We all seek our own betterment, which in a business is called *profit*, or *prospect of profit*. HOW does it begin? It starts with a good idea and faith that it will work, often exhibited by a risk-seeking, business-daring person called an *entrepreneur*. It continues with someone who has sacrificed, that is, deferred spending by saving, and having money and faith to invest. It initiates with a decision to put the money *here, now*, in this business, rather than somewhere else. Why? Because in the investor's judgment, the potential for future return is greater here, and the risk is lower. RISK! There's that word again. That is something we ofttimes forget about a business, especially one we are very close to, the one where we work.

Entrepreneurs, especially, take risks. They are willing to raise capital and do the preparation and planning, long and hard work necessary to start a new business enterprise. They work hard and take risks as much for the excitement of business start-up as for mere profit or prospect of profit. Theirs is the "call of the wild," the acceptance of the challenge, the mountain climber's reason to climb, "because it's there."

Risk is ever present. There are no guarantees of continuing business existence. But assurance of existence is enhanced by all working hard and smart in the present, and anticipating and preparing for the future.

Let's get down to business in free enterprise with August INVESTORS, owners, partners, shareholders or stockholders (See Figure No. 10). They have different names, depending on the size and type of business.

The arrows between August INVESTORS and the business are a little misleading. There would first be a LARGE arrow to indicate the initial and usually substantial investment necessary to start a new business. Up front, a business must purchase necessary land, buildings, vehicles and machinery, along with permits, licenses, environmental clearances and the like. Then construction, business set-up, hiring and training employees, setting up a product distribution system, advertising, marketing and sales programs, obtaining insurance and benefits for employees all must be arranged prior to and during start up of the new enterprise. These are already in place in a going business, which we discuss here.

There are various names for those who start up a business, such as *owners, stockholders, share owners*, and *investors*. We group all these under one royal heading of "August INVESTORS."

AUGUST INVESTORS RISK MONEY FOR A RETURN
Figure No. 10

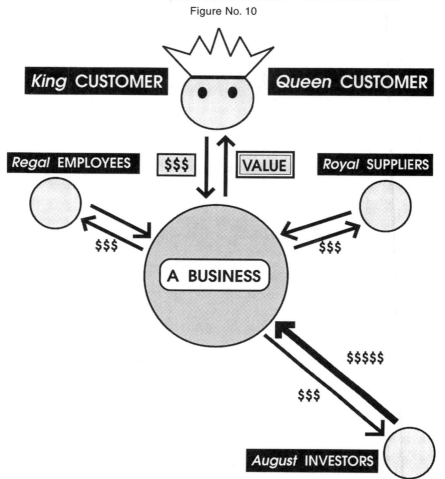

The arrows show a rather different "quid pro quo" for August INVESTORS because of risk and unforeseen circumstance. There is only a return from a business when revenues exceed expenses, usually for an extended period of time. Called PROFITS, they are the "engine of enterprise." Profits are the "harsh discipline of the marketplace" that DEMAND superior "People-Pleasing Performance" from all groups and individuals in a business enterprise. Profits are a by-product, the result of doing a lot of complicated and detailed things well. There are no guarantees. Losses are distinct possibilities. Since we are discussing an ongoing business rather than an entrepreneurial venture, we assume a positive return, or profit.

Profit and Investment Made Simple

Profit is the *positive difference* between revenues and expenses. Put briefly, profits are total sales, less expenses, less taxes. Profits are rarely taken out of a business in total, sometimes not at all. Leaving most of the profits in the business is more to the long-term benefit of the business and investment objectives of its owners and employees, to let, help or make the business grow. People are surprised to learn the relatively small amount of return of *profit on sales* is only 4 or 5 percent. That is for normal manufacturing and service businesses. Others, such as grocery stores, receive only about 1% profits as a percent of sales.

Some ask, "Why would someone invest so much for so little, when they can get much more in banks or bonds with less risk?" Part of the answer is that there is one other important measure. That is *return on investment*, usually somewhat higher, double or triple the 4 or 5 percent *profit on sales*. The answer also goes back to faith in a good idea, pride of ownership, challenge, and the prospect for sizable and growing future returns. As the business gets bigger, profits increase and return on *original investment* multiplies.

Suppose $100,000 is invested, and the business thrives and grows, returning 10%, or $10,000. By reinvesting earnings, the business grows so that the same percentage of profit on sales and return on investment grows bigger from a larger business base. In five years the successful business is worth more because it is making more. The return on the original investment is supplemented by reinvested profits thus making the return on original investment larger. It could get smaller, too, or fail and cease to operate. Keep in mind, always, the sometimes-considerable risk involved, so the *potential* return should also be commensurate with the risk.

August INVESTORS expect to receive a fair return and other benefits from their investment. They want to know the company is profitable, and long term, and part of the profits—dividends—will be distributed to them. That is their motivation to start up and invest in the business.

August INVESTORS want to feel assured of four things:

1) Their initial capital is preserved through wise management and successful operation,
2) Profits are likely, now or soon,
3) Distribution of partial profits or dividends will soon be a regular occurrence, and
4) Possible future sale of the business will be profitable.

Where do we get the profits to pay our investors? From King CUSTOMER or Queen CUSTOMER, our only source of continuing funds.

(August INVESTORS get our "thumbs up" sign, with a third finger wiggle to celebrate the availability of capital and courage to start and continue the business.)

Stately NEIGHBORS:
A Climate of Prosperity and Security

Stately NEIGHBORS are the fourth set of people who help the business please customers at a profit. Neighbors are people like you and me who are employees and do the work of federal, state and local governments.

Government is an absolutely essential part of our society, to protect person and property, preserve law and order and guarantee personal freedom, "to create a climate for creating wealth." Government provides a climate of productivity, an environment of creation, invention, innovation, entrepreneurship, production, protection of private property, and freedom to take risks and receive rewards. Government can give impetus to growth. Government supports the political, economic and cultural systems that provide for the needs, wants and dreams of America's people. These larger systems of communication, transportation, education, protection and law and order are called infrastructure.

Municipal (city) governments provide fire and police protection, roads, bridges and walkways, streets and sewers. Local governments provide county roads and bridges, elementary and high schools, and city-to-city police protection (Sheriff).

State government provides the state system of highways, regulation and coordination of traffic, environment, water, air and ground quality, a system of elementary and higher education, plus a judicial and prison system.

The federal government provides national defense, a court system, enforcement of contracts and settling disputes, plus systems for the "general welfare," that which benefits all the people and neither favors nor hurts any one (such as standard weights and measures, post offices, national highways and bridges, a monetary system, national defense and foreign policy, as defined and described in the U.S. Constitution, Article 1, Section 8.)

The various governments sometimes overlap in the amount, kind and extent of services they provide.

Powers and functions delegated to government are authorized by the United States Constitution and with governmental power over the individual limited by the Bill of Rights to assure the national well-being. Government contributes to a societal framework of our business, cultural economic and political system to form a climate of prosperity and security.

The money provided to Stately NEIGHBORS is called *"taxes"* and like all other revenues generated and spent by a business, is obtained only from King CUSTOMER and Queen CUSTOMER in the price they pay for products, goods and services (See Figure No. 11).

ROYAL NEIGHBORS SUPPLY INFRASTRUCTURE
Figure No. 11

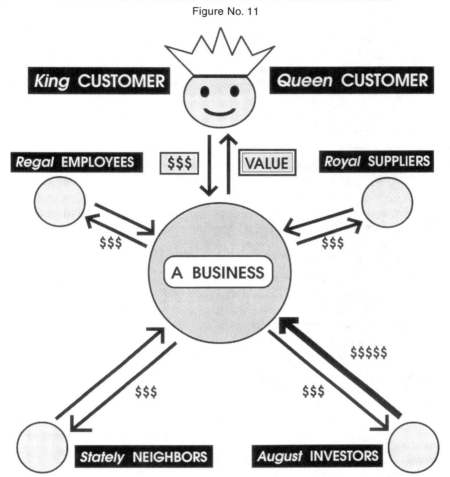

When people claim that businesses don't pay enough taxes, they are only half-right. *Businesses don't pay ANY taxes!* ONLY PEOPLE PAY TAXES! We are law-abiding and it is the law to "tax business," that is, tax the customers of business. As required by law, BUSINESSES COLLECT TAXES in the prices of goods and services, and send them to governments.

It is worth repeating: O N L Y   P E O P L E   P A Y   T A X E S !

(Give a "thumbs up" to King CUSTOMER and Queen CUSTOMER, and for Stately NEIGHBORS, and a lower finger wiggle to acknowledge another important player in the drama of business.)

Who is the "CUSTOMER" of the Employee?

Everyone in business has a boss. The boss of the business is the CUSTOMER. That is who the business must please and to whom the business must provide value, to stay in business. Similarly, each employee has a boss. The boss (or customer) of the employee is the employer. The employee must please, serve and satisfy and provide value to his employer (customer). It is a people-pleasing business world!

The business provides a "happy face" to the CUSTOMER. The employee provides a "happy face" to the employer, the boss. In most cases "the company," "organization," or "business," is, to the employee one person, the supervisor. That one person is "the company" to the employee. Treat your boss like the company treats a CUSTOMER. "Please, serve and satisfy" your direct supervisor, so that your employment is assured by providing satisfaction, quality, quantity, excellence, and everything else that goes into creating and providing VALUE to your customer, the boss.

McDonald's Hamburgers: A Great Business in Action

It is easy to tell what businesses are really doing a great job in a Free Enterprise Society. How? They start. They operate. They keep operating. They are profitable. That means they are pleasing CUSTOMERS, providing value and making a profit.

An excellent example of a well-managed business is that of a tremendously successful hamburger chain. In 1959 while I dated my wife-to-be, Dottie, we went to a new hamburger drive-in called McDonald's, in Boulder, Colorado. They served a hamburger for 15 cents and order of french fried potatoes for 10 cents. With a soft drink at a dime, a date cost less than a dollar! Imagine, a quarter for a hamburger and order of fries!

Why is McDonald's still in business? Recently I saw their famous sign, "Over 99 million hamburgers sold." Is it fulfilling the function of business, providing value, pleasing customers at a profit? Yes it is, and it's doing so everywhere. When you order food at McDonald's, you know what you are going to get, its quality level and price. You also know they employ people and train them, expect and get good performance, provide a wholesome community presence and a clean, responsible and responsive business entity. Their advertising entertains, their promotion is beneficial. They give back to the community in such projects as the Ronald McDonald Halfway House for families of children with terminal cancer.

There are many businesses like McDonald's who provide a customer value at a profit, make a customer "happy face," and keep on doing a day-in/day-out, year-in/year-out good job. Be grateful for their presence in your community, patronize their business, and sometimes say "Thanks," in lieu of that monument that should be erected to all those good, reliable businesses who serve so well, but are so little recognized and appreciated.

A brief but relevant digression, Article I, Section 8, Clause 6 of the U.S. Constitution says one of the responsibilities of the Congress is "to coin Money, regulate the Value thereof." How does the "McDonald's Index" show we are doing? What does a hamburger and order of french fries cost today? Is it the same as or close to the 25 cents in 1959? What is the "McDonald's Index" rate of inflation for a hamburger and order of fries? Divide today's total by 1959's and find out for yourself. How good a job is our government doing with money, "to regulate the value thereof?" Is our money keeping its value? McDonald's is keeping theirs.

Advice to the Actors in the Drama of Business: DRV and BBI

When you consider the overview, "What is a Business?" and it is people working together to survive and prosper, you get a bigger picture. There is no good reason for the four sets of people to fight among themselves especially when they understand their role, importance and relationship to each other in pleasing customers.

A business will continually and critically monitor its operations and practices to assure they Do Right Voluntarily (DRV); that is, do the right thing for all concerned. But it must be done in the Balanced Best Interests (BBI) of all concerned. That means we don't need to get together to conspire against our customers or foreign competition by over-raising wages, benefits or prices. We can carefully consider what is available as a result of our working together, doing what's best for all concerned and taking coordinated, effective and timely action necessary. We cooperate within the business while we compete without.

When prices or taxes get too high, we are at a local and international disadvantage. That places pressure on our competitiveness abroad that can wreak havoc with our balance of trade, one of the more pressing problems of the 1980's, 1990's and in the new millennium.

We all want "MORE" and there is a guaranteed way to get it. That is to work harder and smarter so that we continually produce more valued products and services out of less resources in less time ("increase PRODUCTIVITY"). Productivity is doing more and better for less. We can sell at lower prices, pay higher wages, build investors' return on equity while affording higher quality goods purchased from other businesses.

If we don't innovate, we end up fighting for a larger share of a smaller pie, with squabbling and divisiveness. That means taking from some to give to others. It is difficult, unfair and counter-productive to do so.

When we put more earnings back into our businesses, we "create a bigger pie." We participate in the growth of that pie, and benefit personally, corporately and nationally in our hard work and smart work. We get higher wages, better benefits and create more jobs. The words "Work harder and work smarter" are not a hollow catchphrase, but a way to articulate our dependence on each other for innovation, creativity and productivity. Working together we assure continuing prosperity and future job security.

National Business Success is Affected by National Policy

Inside national boundaries, national policies affect all businesses essentially the same. For instance, all businesses are required to raise and pay Social Security taxes, over 15% of wages and salaries. These uniformly increase the prices of American goods and services to cover the cost.

Outside the country it is a different story. If we are taxed and they aren't, they can sell the same or better products at lower prices. All taxes imposed on business end up in higher prices paid by the customer.

Following World War II there was concern that soldiers coming home seeking jobs would create high unemployment. It didn't happen. There was a great deal of pent-up demand channeled into expanding capital and consumer goods production. We rolled up our sleeves and went back to work.

As the economy grew so did government. Starting at 18% in 1948, government spending as a percent of gross national product (GNP) had grown to 28% by 1965.

About that time foreign imports began to pour into America, providing variety along with lower prices and higher quality. Economic, rational customers bought more imported goods.

By 1983 government had grown to one-third of the economy. We placed a heavier tax burden on American enterprise making it increasingly less competitive in the world marketplace. Compounding the inequity, "world policeman" America spent more for defense, theirs and ours. While we protected their economies they claimed increasingly more of ours. For instance about a third of American car sales went to foreign producers.

We also raised wages higher and faster than our foreign competitors. In the mid-1980's, compensation in America's basic industries, auto manufacture, steel, chemicals, rubber and mining, around $25 per hour, were over twice European and Japanese wage rates at or below $10 an hour. In addition, it took less worker-hours to build a car overseas and the quality of some foreign products was higher, or perceived so by customers.

In the mid-60's and '70's our federal government chose a program approach called "guns and butter." That meant we spent some $2 billion a month on an *undeclared* war half a globe away in Vietnam while we spent $1 billion a month on a *declared* "war on poverty" here at home. We didn't win either war but are still paying for both. In so doing we substantially diminished our present day standard-of-living and quality-of-life in America.

These two national policies were paid for by the taxpayer, directly in the form of income taxes, indirectly in inflation and business taxes (in the price of goods and services) collected by business and paid to governments.

More recently Congress and the administration have declared another "war" on drugs. It has opened up all kinds of potential abuses on personal freedom such as "no-knock" raids on businesses and homes, individual surveillance of personal and business finances, confiscation of property without due process and potential undue and unrestrained police power.

We must carefully assess the impact of such national policies on America's standard-of-living, quality-of-life and national interest, and take appropriate action to preserve our national prosperity, freedoms and free enterprise system.

Another important consideration is the interdependence of businesses, one with another. For instance, in the 1970's, a foreign oil cartel forced crude oil prices up inordinately, from $2 a barrel to over $30. That really helped the foreign oil cartel, the oil business and the energy industry. But it hurt King and Queen CUSTOMER. Having to put more money into oil and energy, they had less money for other durable and consumer goods purchases. That hurt all other businesses in operation and those to be formed that would have benefitted from the purchases not made.

At any point in time, we have only so much money to save or spend. Our basic income is not all ours. It is reduced, even before we get it, by deductions for federal and state income taxes, and for "social insurance."

Income after taxes is called *net disposable income* by economists. Even with that, there are bills that must be paid because of past financial commitments made such as a house mortgage or car loan payments. The money left after these fixed and required payments is called *discretionary income*. That is the relatively small amount left after taxes, major and minor financial obligations are met. Part goes for gasoline to get to work, and part for food, entertainment, recreation and soft goods shopping.

If energy (or any other) prices go up, whether by the market or forced up artificially by government, there is less money for other discretionary consumer purchases. When one part of our society secures a major economic advantage for themselves, either through government or foreign actions, the economic consequences ripple throughout the entire economy, affecting all other businesses and people.

The important point is that all price changes affect the entire economy. Money is as scarce as other resources. When it is used to buy one thing, it is no longer available for another.

The Question of the Question Marks, ???

I always forget to tell the students what the question marks ("???") mean. But they always ask. So what do they stand for? They stand for Y-O-U, the most important part of the business, economic, political, cultural and governmental system called the United States of America. YOU are the direct benefactor of the intent and philosophy of the Declaration of Independence. YOU directly benefit from the government defined, organized, authorized and limited by the United States Constitution. And YOU, especially, are the individual citizen protected against government tyranny by the Bill of Rights, the incredibly important first 10 amendments to the U.S. Constitution, which command the federal government to respect and protect your rights and freedoms as a self-governing United States citizen.

YOU are the most important, the most sovereign, the most royal player in the drama of freedom, of America, of business and government. In this constitutional, republican, free enterprise society, YOU, dear citizen, precious Power of ONE, are the most important of all. Preserve that dignified and important status by knowing and participating in the greatest political, economic and business system in the history of mankind.

One More Time, ROBIS: The Role Of Business In Society

An understanding of the Role of Business In Society (ROBIS) and "What is a Business?" can help us to better structure our economic and political system to meet the varied and conflicting demands on American business.

> The Role Of Business In Society (ROBIS)
> is to produce goods and services
> that customers want and will pay for,
> at a profit.

Business is PEOPLE, five sets of people, four of whom come together voluntarily to please, serve and satisfy the fifth and most important, the CUSTOMER. King CUSTOMER and Queen CUSTOMER are regally courted by the royal players in the drama of business. The other four royal sets of people are Regal EMPLOYEES, Royal SUPPLIERS, August INVESTORS and Stately NEIGHBORS. If Business Does Right Voluntarily (DRV) in the Balanced Best Interests (BBI) of all concerned, business, though risky, can be profitable and fun, and beneficial to the society in which it exists and serves.

Almost anything important has an "ode." Here is an "Ode to Customers"[1]:

Ode to CUSTOMERS

OUR CUSTOMERS are the most important persons in this business—
in person, by mail, by telephone [or by fax or Internet],
OUR CUSTOMERS are not dependent on us. We are dependent
on them.
OUR CUSTOMERS are not an interruption to our work—they
are the purpose of it. We are not doing them a favor by
serving them—they are doing us a favor by giving us the
opportunity to do so.

---

1. Herbert V. Prochnow, *New Guide to Toastmasters and Speakers,* Prentice-Hall, Englewood Cliffs, NJ. 1956, p 166

OUR CUSTOMERS are not outsiders to our business—they are a part of it.

OUR CUSTOMERS are not cold statistics—they are flesh-and-blood humans with feelings and emotions like our own, and with biases and prejudices.

OUR CUSTOMERS are persons who bring us their wants. It is our job to handle them profitably—profitably to both the customer and ourselves.

That is what customers are—in our business or in any business. Some people seem to have forgotten a few of these basic truths in recent years, but it is high time to be remembering them again. Tomorrow may be too late.

—Paul Talbot, The Management Review

Learn, then teach, the Miracle Magic of ROBIS: Role Of Business In Society.

Questions for Review

1.   What are the "Three C's of Organization?" In what two important questions must we be knowledgeable, understanding and conversant? What does ROBIS mean?

2.   How can the concept of wants and needs be used to communicate business concepts to students? How is risk brought into the discussion? Which costs more, the "essentials of life" or government? Why is that important? How does risk differentiate free enterprise from business?

3.   What are nine criteria for the goods and services business produces? What is the single main job of business? What is the social responsibility of a business?

4.   Why is it important for us to produce more and better for less? What is it called? What are the two motivations and what are the three means to do so? What is it called when we produce more for less, increasing our standard-of-living and quality-of-life, one more time? What effect does increasing this important criterion have on our security and future?

5.   What are the three forms of business organization and which is best? Why?

6.   What is a business? Name and describe each of the five sets of people who comprise a business? Why are the players described as "royal?" Draw a diagram of circles to show their relationship to the business. Who is most important? What is the job of

business that is most important? How can a "thumb and wiggling fingers" be used to help describe business to students?

7. What single condition or description does a customer buy and must a business sell at a profit? Is price what the buyer buys? Name and explain the "Three C's of Business?" What is "quid pro quo?" Why is it so important to business success?

8. Where does the money come from, for a business to pay taxes? How or where is it obtained? What four conditions do investors require? Why is it unlikely that investors will remove all profit from the business? What is profit? How big is it as a percent of sales? Explain why "Businesses don't pay enough taxes" is an incorrect statement.

9. Who is the "customer" of an employee in a business? Why? What does the "McDonald's Hamburger Index" indicate about inflation and government's money performance "to regulate the value thereof?" What is DRV and BBI and why are they important?

10. How is national business prosperity affected by national policy? What two "wars" damaged the American business competitive edge in the 70's, 80's and 90's? What is the "third war"? How much did government grow from 1948 to 1983? What was "guns and butter" and what did it cost?

Some see private enterprise as a predatory target to be shot, others as cow to be milked, but few are those who see it as a sturdy horse pulling the wagon.   —Winston Churchill

The business of America is business.   —Calvin Coolidge

Business demands faith, compels earnestness, requires courage, is honestly selfish, is penalized for mistakes, and is the essence of life.
—William Feather

I like business because it is competitive, because it rewards deeds rather than words. I like business because it compels earnestness and does not permit me to neglect today's task while thinking about tomorrow. I like business because it undertakes to please, not reform; because it is honestly selfish, thereby avoiding hypocrisy and sentimentality. I like business because it promptly penalizes mistakes, shiftlessness and inefficiency, while rewarding well those who give it the best they have in them. Lastly, I like business because each day is a fresh adventure.   —R. H. Cabell

The American Republic and American business are Siamese twins; they came out of the same womb at the same time; they are born in the same principles and when American business dies, the American Republic will die, and when the American Republic dies, American business will die.
—Josiah W. Bailey

Chapter 9

LEARN AND TEACH THE MIRACLE MAGIC OF PROFIT
The Dwarf That Slays Giants!

The profit motive is virtually universal in human nature. Yet, compared to what many people think, profit is not a giant, but a dwarf. We need that dwarf to slay the threatening giants that are ever with us: scarcity and poverty.

Every person seeks to make a profit, to exchange something—labor, money, goods or services—for something to him or her of higher value. Each one of us seeks to make a profit in about everything we do. It is manifest in finding a job, or a better job, in buying, investing or working, even giving money to a charity, where how good you feel about yourself is of more value than what you gave away.

Profit is one of the most misunderstood concepts in America. Profit is the galvanizing force that motivates people to energize America's free enterprise economy. Profit provides personal incentive for risk-taking, hard work, invention and innovation. Profit leads to wealth, progress, opportunity, the prospect of getting and keeping a job, of getting and staying rich, and of having a full and abundant, rewarding life.

Profit is small, but mighty, powerful enough to slay the threatening giants of want, poverty, insecurity, fear and stagnation. If profit is so marvelous, so incredible, powerful and desirable, why is it so little appreciated and defended? Lack of understanding and misleading information breed fear of profit.

Scarcity can impoverish us and keep us poor. Profit is the instrument that harnesses freedom and human nature to fight poverty. Profit encourages risk-taking and investment that fuel the creation, production, and distribution of goods and services for consumption by humans. Profit is a helper and a friend. It rewards (sometimes punishes) us for accepting risk, to start businesses and to innovate. It makes us want to work, to produce a surplus and be able to exchange goods and services.

What is profit? How big is it? How is it determined? What makes it work? We will understand profit so well and appreciate profit so much that we will effectively share with others the concept of profit, what it is, how it works and why it is so important to our present abundance and future well-being.

Ignorance about Profits Breeds Contempt for Business

When people do not know or understand the truth, they react to untruths, half-truths or lies. There is much misunderstanding about the level of profits. Business itself is partly to blame for the misunderstanding, first, in the way profits are reported; and second, because business does not do enough economic awareness education either in their communities and schools, nor in the business itself with its own employees. When customers and consumers lack information about the small size, big impact and importance of profits, the business system is vulnerable to damaging legislation, unnecessary and expensive regulation, and mistreatment by a misinformed public.

For instance, survey upon survey shows Americans do not know the average level of profits as a percentage of sales. High school students think profits are around 33%, where college students estimate over 40%. When asked what a "fair after-tax profit" would be, student estimates run from 17% to 26%. Wouldn't business be happy with that!

Advice columnist Ann Landers published a reader's letter in the 8/11/83 *Denver Post* which concluded:

> Wouldn't it be nice if greed, power and dishonesty (how well they go together) could be relegated to obscurity? Remember when business people were satisfied with a 15 to 30 percent profit and labor didn't make demands that closed a lot of plants? Why go on? You've got the picture.

It was a distorted picture, when Ann Lander's 90 million readers learned of the "15 to 30 percent profit" businesses supposedly were satisfied with, at an earlier time, hinting profits are now much higher. "Why go on," indeed! We must go on, to dispel these myths which warp reality, distort truth and foster rancor.

I asked one of my daughter's teachers what she thought profits were as a percentage of sales. She said "About 40%." I asked why she thought that. "I once worked at a department store and they marked up their goods about 40 or 50%," she answered. That means when they were sold at the marked up price, the difference was a 'profit' of 40 or 50%." She didn't realize how much store expense that relatively small gross profit margin, or mark-up of goods had to cover.

That reminded me of a summer job before college when I worked at a service station. Whenever we bought a car air filter from an auto parts supplier, we doubled its cost to price it for the customer. At the time that markup appeared to me to provide the business a 100% "profit." Perhaps the misunderstanding is partly that of *mark-up*, required to cover all other business costs, including my meager wage at the time.

The price of materials, parts and services is a starting point. But unseen, and most times unknown but very real, are all other business costs such as insurance, legal services, taxes, accounting, employee pay and benefits, etc. All must be paid and are, out of "mark-up." Anything left over after all expenses are paid is profit as we will discuss.

Thinking profit to be 40 or 50% (or 100%!), no wonder people feel business takes unfair advantage of customers! The fact is, actual profits, on a continuing annual basis for American business are about 5%, as a percentage of sales! Business profits are actually less than one-third to one-fifth what students would consider a "fair" profit!

The recession in 1982 brought out a lot of truth about business profits. "Profit margins at lowest level in 30 years," 9/8/83 *Rocky Mountain News*, reported a Standard and Poor study which showed profits as a percent of sales of 400 Industrial Companies to be 3.95 cents on the dollar. The survey showed the 3.9 percent return was the lowest return since 1952.

When the actual level of profits is so low, it is strange indeed that people "know" profits are too high. We all need to know "the number five keeps business alive."

Basic Business Text "Forgets" Profit

My middle daughter, Sheri, had signed up to teach a basic business course at a Colorado Mountain college in Aspen. She was unable to teach the second class and asked me to do so for her. I reviewed the text, eager to see what profit level and rate of return on investment the text would reveal. It revealed nothing!

This 500-plus page basic business book mentioned nothing about level of profit or investment return. The only mention in the index or the text had to do with determining the amount of money budgeted for marketing based on planned profit or sales levels. So those basic business students still won't know what you know about profit.

When Profit's at Five, the Dwarf's Alive, the Giants Take A Dive!

The number "5," and the profit concept are so important, that we print it here boldly. Learn and remember it forevermore, and tell others, the size of American profits as a percentage of sales is around 5%.

5% !

We will more thoroughly discuss and provide sources of information about this magic number but let's lay the groundwork for a better understanding of some very important concepts.

Profit Makes Exchange Worthwhile

Profit is commonly thought of in terms of money (dollars) as rate-of-return on sales, investment or assets. We will define profit more generally for our purpose of understanding and appreciating not only the role of business, but the role of government, economics, politics, people, YOU, and other entities and organizations. We will also define it more specifically for business purposes. Both general and specific concepts are important.

Constitutional scholar Cleon Skousen defines profit[1] generally, as "doing whatever is necessary to make an exchange worthwhile." If one person likes another and mows their lawn, repairs a bicycle or bakes a cake to show affection, both profit, or benefit, even though no money is exchanged.

Formal definition from *Webster's* includes specifically "advantage, gain or benefit, excess of returns over expenditures for a series of transactions, and compensation accruing to entrepreneurs for assumption of risk in a business enterprise as distinguished from wages or rent."

Profit in business is simple and straightforward. Expressed in dollars, *PROFIT* is *Sales*, less *Cost of Goods Sold*, less *Expenses*, less *Taxes*. Expressed more in accounting form, here is how to calculate profit:

> Sales
> - Cost of Goods Sold
> Gross Profit
> - Expenses
> Profit before Taxes
> - Taxes
> Profit after Taxes

If Sales, less Cost of Goods Sold and Expenses is negative, that is *loss*, not profit. With a loss, no income taxes are paid, although property, sales and excise taxes are still paid and are included as part of business expense that must be covered by sales to customers.

One might observe quite accurately, that true profit is sales less all expenses including taxes.

---

1. Dr. W. Cleon Skousen, *The Miracle of America*, (National Center for Constitutional Studies, HC 61 Box 1056, Malta, ID 83342-9704, p 32

Profit is, in effect, a "by-product" after all the work is done, the products made and sold, the money taken in and spent. If the difference is positive, we are profitable and we stay in business. If the difference is negative, it is a loss and the business is failing.

The business must be or become profitable, or it goes out of business. The owners lose their investment. Employees lose their jobs. Customers lose a source of products and services. That business is gone. All of this is called RISK, and risk is normal, natural, expected and real.

Sales is the total of number of units sold times price per unit. A business may produce one or many products, but each has a price, is sold and the total is determined for a given time period. During the same period of time, expenses of doing business are being incurred and paid.

Employee Expense includes wages and salaries, but goes well beyond pay to such employee benefits of medical and dental insurance, life insurance, Social Security taxes, accidental death and disability income protection, vacations and holidays, sick pay, retirement and savings plans, tuition reimbursement for continuing education, etc.

Supplier Expense is for purchased goods and services including raw materials and supplies, assembled parts, power and light, rent, advertising, vehicles, stationery supplies, plant equipment and office machines, land and facilities necessary to keep a business operating.

Company Expense includes fire and liability insurance, unemployment taxation, interest expense on inventory, computers for calculating payrolls, keeping track of raw materials and finished inventories, and expenses related to required reporting to stockholders and government authorities.

Gross Profit (or loss) is total income less total expense. This is profit which under our laws, is subject to corporate or business income taxes. These taxes are computed and subtracted from gross profit to arrive at net profit. *Profits* are a mathematical result of subtracting one number, expenses, from another, total sales, gross income or total revenue.

A Simple Subtraction: "Does That Make You Mad?"

You, a prospective customer, visit an automobile dealership to find a sporty new "Whizzer 8, Phoenix" model, fully equipped, with a sticker price of $15,000. You offer the dealer $10,000. He counters with $14,000, and you finally agree on a net price of $12,000. Does that "make you mad?" Probably not. You have negotiated a better price than the dealer's starting price. You know what other brands and models sell for, and this is at least as good or even better deal than others have received. You like it and buy it.

Suppose you get "insider information" about the car dealership, to learn monthly expenses required to operate the business total $100,000. Does that "make you mad?" Probably not. Employee salaries, wages and benefits, and sales commissions must be paid. The dealership's employees are people just like us. They work hard to make a living, and deserve fair pay for their work. We also know that rent, insurance, power and light, advertising, promotion, supplies and materials, a facility with a showroom and service center are required to keep the business serving customers.

Suppose we learn the dealer sold 10 cars during the current month. Does that "make you mad?" Probably not, at least not until you think about it. Wait a minute. Sales is the sum of each unit times price. If 10 cars are sold for $12,000 each, total sales are $120,000. Profit for that month is $120,000 sales less $100,000 expenses, or $20,000. The subtraction has revealed— can we say it out loud—*"PROFIT."*

Did someone get cheated? No, likely not. A voluntary, free-market transaction with competition, profits both parties. The dealer had many cars and needed money to buy inventory and pay expenses, plus risk more capital hoping for profit or more profit. The buyer wanted a special means of transportation and was willing to part with his money to get it. Both parties profited! Does that "make you mad?" It shouldn't.

But there's more. When the "profit" is divided by 10 units sold, you learn the dealer made $2,000 from *your* sale! That's getting closer to home. They made $2,000 off *you*! Does that "make you mad?" You are able to estimate what the dealer made from the sale of one car to one person, YOU. That is close and personal. Does that mean you could have bought the car for less money? Possibly, but probably not. We want the dealer to stay in business to serve us and the next customer, and to provide service and warranty coverage when needed. We want the dealer to *be there*. To do so, he must stay profitable.

Another consideration is that we have calculated 1) only profit *before taxes*, for 2) only one month. Profit *after taxes* will be less, sometimes much less. We are a law-abiding society and obey the law. Taxes are a part of business and must be paid by business. Since all pay taxes, "the playing field is level," and no one, without government favor, is at a competitive disadvantage.

With more "insider information" you learn about last month. Only six cars were sold. Sales revenue was 6 times $12,000, or $72,000. With monthly expenses of $90,000, the dealer LOST $18,000 that month, over $3000 per car sold. If that keeps up, they will be unable to remain in business, and that doesn't serve anyone. Customers could not buy new cars or get service on their previous purchases. Suppliers would have no outlet for their goods and services. Jobs for employees would disappear. No taxes could be paid to help fund necessary community services. An unprofitable business is a detriment to an entire community.

For the two months, then, the auto dealership sold 16 cars for total sales of $192,000, with total expenses of $190,000, yielding a two-month profit of $2,000, or $125 per car. Such a small return jeopardizes the existence of the business. We can only hope the other ten months of the year are more profitable for the dealership.

If they went out of business would that "make you mad?"

PRICE: You Pay Now or You Pay Later, but You Pay

PRICE is a fascinating concept. Prices are information. Economists refer to prices as "signals" sent to all participants in the economic system as to relative value of their time, output, and work, and the relative availability and scarcity of resources, goods and services. Price helps decision-making both for the *producer* on what and how much to produce, and the *customer* on what and how much to buy. Prices are fluid and subject to change. Just watching the price of gasoline change at the local service station is puzzling but fascinating.

What is not so obvious is the impact of foreign conditions, politics, wars, rivalries, even the OPEC cartel (Organization of Petroleum Exporting Countries), fixing a higher price of gasoline. OPEC members may get together and conspire to raise prices by limiting production. To work, all members must abide by the agreements. A single country can make a lot of money by getting others to withhold supply while they increase their own. With the same demand and lower supply, the price will increase. In violating their agreement, they get both the higher price, and higher unit sales. And they almost always get caught. It is a fascinating game to watch, both what they do and how, and what effects it has on the market, visible within blocks at our local gas station.

The Too-High and the Too-Low of Prices

It seems there are two prices in the world, one always too high, the other too low. The price that seems too high is the one *I pay* for goods and services I get. The other price that seems too low is the price *I am paid* for my services! That is the paradox of prices, but they are essential to a free market economy in a free enterprise political system.

Everything you buy, everything you don't do, everything you do and how well you do it, has a price. The price must always be paid—by somebody.

If What "Makes You Mad" is a Business NOT Making a Profit, You are "Right On!"

If there is any one thing in all this that would make a knowledgeable and caring person angry, it is a business or profit-seeking organization that does *not* make a profit. In our American enterprise economy, that's the sign of failure, and those who fail, pay the price of failure. They go out of business. Those who stay in business, stay profitable, and vice-versa. The whole world knows they are doing most things right most of the time. Give them your business and your gratitude. They are helping to make a better world.

Purchasing goods and services from a business shouldn't "make anyone mad." We should be grateful the business is there and freely available. We can shop there or not. But we want service and value when we do. Only profit can provide what guarantee is possible that the business will survive to serve customers another day. To really understand the concept of *profit*, we need more information and a better understanding of where the customer's sales dollar goes in the business.

Distribution of the Sales Dollar: Where from? Where to? What else?

An ideal way to learn "the distribution of the dollar," the sales dollar, from Queen CUSTOMER or King CUSTOMER, is through the "five sets of people" business model. We discuss real business numbers from a real business for 1988, when such numbers were still available.

The business is Adolph Coors Company, comprised of over twenty companies, the largest of which, Coors Brewing Company, has produced Coors products since 1873. The other two major divisions are Coors Ceramics Company and Coors Technology Companies, all of which include business entities in ceramics, energy, food, packaging, graphics, and water, with 35 facilities at various locations.

The source of this information is "Economic Impact of Adolph Coors Company and Subsidiaries on the State of Colorado, 1988" (Adolph Coors Company, Community Affairs Department, Golden Colorado 80401). For simplicity, we first use distribution of a single CUSTOMER dollar, then finish with the "big numbers."

King and Queen CUSTOMER sacrificed one dollar to buy one dollar's worth of VALUE from Coors. Where did the dollar go? Regal EMPLOYEES received 28.5 cents, Royal SUPPLIERS 54.4 cents, Stately NEIGHBORS 14.3 cents, and August INVESTORS 2.8 cents.

With numbers in *cents*, look at our "Business is People" model, Figure No. 12, showing where the CUSTOMER'S sales dollar goes.

Contrary to what we "know," note that August INVESTORS don't get very much of the CUSTOMERS' dollar. Regal EMPLOYEES get over 10 times the investor. But that is not the whole story. Beyond the obvious, BTO, investors are in for the long haul, too, and want to get the most they can for their invested capital. So they do not take all of the profits out of the business. They take out partial profits, called *dividends*, and reinvest the rest called retained earnings.

In this example, they kept only 1.1 cents and put the other 1.7 cents back into the business to build a bigger, better business. They chose to forego present enjoyment of their earnings and instead to reinvest to create more products, services, jobs and profits and "please, serve and satisfy" more CUSTOMERS.

Therefore employees got not 10 times, but 26 times what the investors received, along with the prospect of more jobs, higher pay and better job security!

Also interesting is that Stately NEIGHBORS received 13 times what August INVESTORS received. As a result of the business operating successfully and profitably in the community, governments (Stately NEIGHBORS) receive sizable and continuing benefits.

A good example of reinvested capital was in the mid-1970's when the company allocated $16 million to build a new glass bottle production

DISTRIBUTION OF ROYAL CUSTOMER'S DOLLAR
Figure No. 12

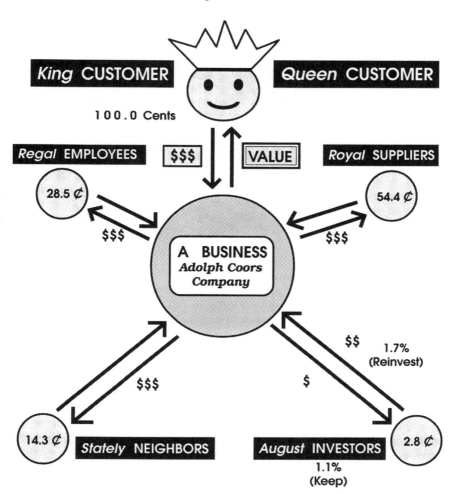

the clock. Had no profit been available, or had management chose instead to spend the profits elsewhere or take them out of the business, those jobs would not have been created. To create more jobs, we have to please more customers better at a profit. This "makes a bigger pie," from which all parties can get a bigger "piece of the pie," share, or "profit!"

Most companies document what money they have invested and reinvested to create the company and the jobs within it. This real live business example, Adolph Coors Company, was founded in 1873 with an initial investment of over $14 million. (That was a *lot* of money in buying power, that long ago.) Since that time $1,042 million, including over $28 million from profits in 1988, were *reinvested* in the company for a total accumulated capital invested of $1,062 million, based on *1988 Coors Annual Report*, (p 23). If we divide the then-10,500 employees in those jobs, that's an average investment of $101,000 invested per job!

August INVESTORS had to reinvest the money to assure the future of the company, its employees and CUSTOMERS. That is how reinvestment works to "create a bigger pie" so that there is more for everyone involved to share. Now we go from "one buck" to "big bucks."

The Big Picture, Big Bucks, Big Expenses, Lots of Hard Work and Happy CUSTOMERS

In addition to dividing up one dollar, we go from those percentages to actual "big numbers" on our diagram to see what kind of dollars customers provided the business and how they were distributed, as shown in Figure No. 13.

"Go BTO": Going Beyond the Obvious to "What Else?"

But what about "what else?" We must Go BTO to see what really happens. Why? Because it is very important, and not very obvious. Our quest is to know and understand:

> Who really pays the bills?
> Who really takes the risks?
> Who really does the hard work?
> Who really gets the benefits?

One of the marks of a *Power of ONE* is the ability and determination to go BTO to figure out the real situation. Then you are better able to understand the bigger picture and solve the real problems.

Going BTO we ask the question "Do employees receive all of the 28.5 cents?" The answer is, of course, "No." Employees must pay taxes to obey the law, and the employer withholds appropriate taxes and deductions to assure adequate funds to pay federal and state income taxes, Social Security and Medicare taxes. Respectively, let us suppose these average about 13%

federal, 3% state, 7.5% Social Security and 1.5% Medicare, total, 25% of earnings. That means in fact, Regal EMPLOYEES receive after taxes 21.4 cents, the deducted 7.1 cents diverted to Stately NEIGHBORS.

DISTRIBUTION OF ROYAL CUSTOMER'S "BIG BUCKS"
Figure No.13

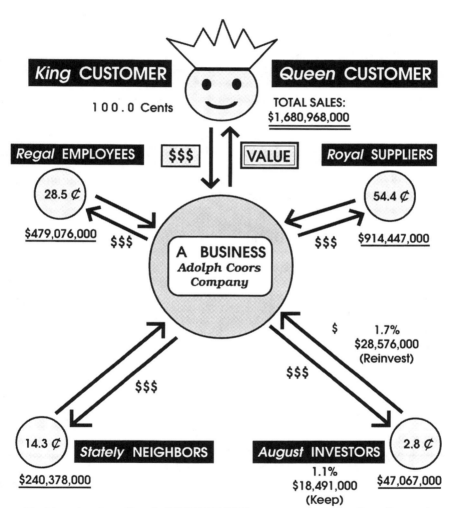

To this point then, Stately NEIGHBORS, governments, don't really receive 14.3 cents of the Queen or King CUSTOMER sales dollar, but 21.4 cents, when the 7.1 cents deducted as taxes from Regal EMPLOYEES are included. Similarly, part of the Royal SUPPLIERS sales dollars from this CUSTOMER, using the same 21.4 per cent, or 11.6 cents, will also be paid to neighbors, federal, state and local governments as taxes, leaving 42.8 cents for the suppliers.

In the same way the earnings distributed to August INVESTORS are also subject to taxes. As investments, they are likely paid at the highest marginal tax rates. Estimating their marginal federal and state income tax rates total at 40%, August INVESTORS receive not 1.1 cents but less than 0.7 cents, multiplying the 60% difference by 1.1. Because of taxes, then, August INVESTORS really keep 0.7 cents, not the 1.2 cents declared by the business as a dividend. Added back to their already once-taxed, reinvested income of 1.7 cents, their total return is 2.4, not 2.8 cents.

Remember, this business effort all happens as a result of the PEOPLE involved in the business, making the investment, taking the risk, doing the work, making the sacrifices, and seeking the rewards for operating the business.

As a result of one year's business operations pleasing Queen and King CUSTOMER by satisfying their wants and needs, the CUSTOMER's dollar is distributed truly quite differently. After taxes it looks more like this: Regal EMPLOYEES, 21.4 cents; Royal SUPPLIERS, 42.8 cents; August INVESTORS, 2.4 cents and Stately NEIGHBORS, 33.4 cents.

Here it is in chart form:

Distribution of King or Queen CUSTOMER's Sales Dollar

	Obvious (Before Taxes)	Beyond the Obvious (After Taxes)	Difference
Regal EMPLOYEES	28.5	21.4	-7.1
Royal SUPPLIERS	54.4	42.8	-11.6
August INVESTORS	2.8 (1.1)	2.4 (0.7)	-0.4
Stately NEIGHBORS	14.3	33.4	+19.1
King, Queen CUSTOMER	100.0	100.0	

We are sometimes led to believe that August INVESTORS really get the major part of the King and Queen CUSTOMER's dollars. Now we know it is just not true. The investor's share is relatively small. Contrasting, we find Stately NEIGHBORS receive a substantial portion of the CUSTOMER's dollar, 33.4 cents, over a third of total company revenue.

The final "After Tax" readings show Regal EMPLOYEES at 21.4 cents, over 30 times that of August INVESTORS 0.7 cents.

Stately NEIGHBORS received 47 times what August INVESTORS got.

Stately NEIGHBORS at 33.4 cents received 1.56 times the 21.4 cents the employees received for their time, talents and hard work. Instead of Regal employees getting twice what Stately NEIGHBORS received, they ended up ultimately with less than two-thirds.

An important point, BTO, is that profits received by owners of the business are taxed twice! They are taxed first as business profits, then taxed a second time as personal income received in the form of dividends.

WHERE ROYAL CUSTOMER'S "BIG BUCKS" REALLY GO

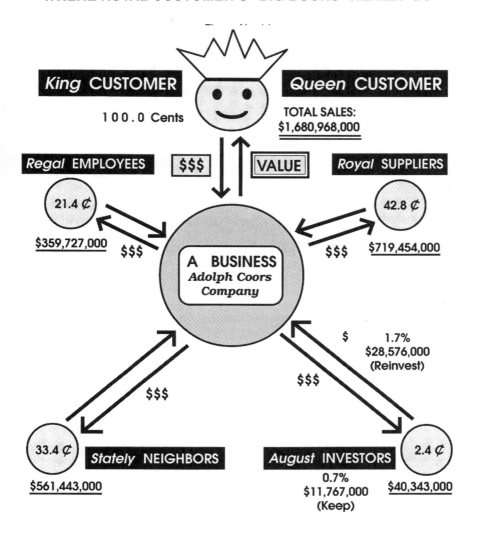

The "Beyond the Obvious, Bottom Line" of Where the Big Bucks Go!

Figure No. 14 shows how our "Big Bucks" business diagram looks going BTO, *after taxes*, the true distribution of the CUSTOMER's sales dollar.

Why Not More and Bigger "Geese" Laying Golden Eggs?

One-third of this total business revenue from customers goes to neighbors—local, state and federal governments. Knowing what we now know, an important question emerges: Why don't governments, Stately NEIGHBORS, do anything and everything possible to encourage formation of business, with tax decreases rather than increases; with more business support and cooperation, less antagonism and regulation?

Business is a generous goose that lays golden eggs for government, while satisfying human wants and needs, supplying jobs and support for other businesses, and paying lots of taxes.

It seems governments would want more businesses and larger businesses, and do everything within their considerable powers to *encourage,* NOT *discourage* the only true economic improvement there is, business formation, development and growth.

Smart governments could be very rich governments using this basic (though not very obvious) understanding of the Role Of Business In Society (ROBIS).

BTO II: What is the Real Tax on Profit?

The diagram shows us how much earned income is really paid as taxes. Gross Income is Revenue less expenses. Expenses are what is paid to suppliers (purchased goods and services), $719,454 and employees (labor), $359,727.

What is left is gross profit before taxes, the total of net profit (after taxes) and taxes. That total is $601,786,000, from profits of $40,343,000 and true ultimate taxes of $561,443,000.

The true tax rate on gross profits is 93.3% (!), ($561,443,000 / $601,786,000).

BTO III: Who Really Pays Social Security?

While we are into this level of understanding, let us look at another not so obvious result of social legislation. We have heard and we "know" that the employer "matches" the Social Security deductions of the employee. It looks that way, but that is not th way it is.

When an employer decides to hire an employee, provisions must be made to be in compliance with all applicable local, state and federal laws. This means that not only will the employee be paid the agreed-upon salary and benefits. By law, in addition to federal unemployment and state workman's compensation, the employer must also pay the additional 7+% Social Security (whatever level law requires) to "match" that paid by the employee, deducted from the paycheck.

Therefore, the money—*all the money* to compensate the employee in pay and benefits, and uphold the law—must be available to hire the employee. If the money did not have to be paid to the government by law, it would be available to pay directly to the employee for work performed. Therefore, the employee, in reality, pays *both* parts of the Social Security deduction!

Whatever amount an employee pays to Social Security, in reality he pays twice that, and it is a considerable amount to have to put into such a pay-as-you-go system. (That is one that simultaneously pays out to beneficiaries what was deducted from workers.) There is no trust fund, *per se*, but essentially, accounting entries for moneys deducted over the years.

Who really pays employee Social Security? King and Queen CUSTOMER.

BTO IV: Who Pays YOUR Social Security?

Another interesting bit of information can be gleaned from available data. The 1988 economic impact statement indicates "Colorado Payroll" to be $323,112,000 for 8,600 Colorado employees. Dividing, we learn the average annual employee pay to be $37,571. Finding it to be well below the then-Social Security base maximum of $45,000, at the 1988 Social Security rate of 7.51% Coors Colorado employees average annual average deduction was $3,380. This is $35.5 million paid to Social Security by all 10,500 Coors employees. Added to the employer's matching amount, Coors withheld some $71.0 million and paid it into the Social Security trust funds.

We know *ONLY PEOPLE PAY TAXES*, and in this case, *ONLY CUSTOMERS PAY TAXES*. Product sales are measured in 31 gallon barrels, each containing 55.11 6-packs. In 1988, Coors sold 16,534,000 barrels. Therefore $4.29 of the price of each barrel was tax paid by the CUSTOMER to fund Coors' employee Social Security. That amounts to 7.78 cents per 6-pack, or 1.30 cents per container. The CUSTOMER pays Coors employee Social Security, and that fee is part of the price of the product! Coors calculates a total tax paid per 6-pack to be about 35.5 cents, or 6 cents a can. The CUSTOMER pays it all. By law the company collects it in the price of the product and sends the money to the government. How is that for going beyond the obvious?

The customer pays for Coors employees' Social Security. But that's all right because Coors employees pay the customer's Social Security when they purchase their company's products, goods and services. We are all in this together, and we all help pay the bills.

Generalizing, consider what happens with a Social Security increase. Looking at our "What is a Business?" diagram, where will the increased deduction come from? With increased Social Security obligations, will Suppliers reduce their prices? No. Will employees accept lower pay to fund higher Social Security? No. Will investors accept lower rates of return? No, not for very long, (They may consider removing their money from the business and placing it elsewhere to get a higher, more safe return.) Will governments take less? No, armed with power of government and force of law to assure collection, they are the ones raising the taxes. That leaves only one person to pay the higher Social Security taxes—the CUSTOMER—the only one who not only pays the taxes, all the taxes, but all the other bills as well.

Who really pays YOUR Social Security?
King and Queen CUSTOMER.

BTO V: Beyond all that to the VAT

We are ready for another issue that comes up every several years and that is called the VAT—Value Added Tax. Why? Governments must tax people to raise funds. Income taxes are already approaching a point at which taxpayers are highly resistant to increases. So a VAT is "the solution."

VAT is an add-on tax at selected points in the manufacturing and distribution process. Every time value is added (costs are incurred), another increment of tax is added. As far as the CUSTOMER is concerned, it is all paid upon final purchase of the product. And guess who pays it? The CUSTOMER.

BTO, *Power of ONE*, we know the tax will have to become a part of the price of goods and services. We will supposedly have more money from paychecks by not raising income taxes, but our dollars after taxes will buy less because the taxes become part of the product prices. We are taxed more indirectly rather than directly, but taxed more nevertheless.

Now we better understand VAT for what it is—another tax, cleverly hidden in the price of goods and services, but still paid by CUSTOMERS. Politicians sometimes say they don't want to raise taxes on people, but instead suggest higher taxes on businesses (easy, they can't vote) such as a Value Added Tax. The *Power of ONE* strikes again, and says "no."

In fact, with taxes at their present levels and government at its present size, *it is unlikely a legitimate case can ever again be made for a tax increase.* Since all taxes are tied to population or inflation, as either or both increase, so do all taxes. In their various forms, income, sales, property and excise taxes, all "growth-driven" and "inflation-driven," automatically increase. Perhaps we should get the words "tax increase" forever out of politicians' vocabularies, and substitute instead, "tax cuts."

Reporting Profits: The Enemy is Us

Earlier, business was mentioned to be one of the main propagators of confusion about profits, in the way they are reported, and for business' lack of economic awareness programs for employees and others.

When businesses report profits as they must by law, they express changes in percentages. For instance, we know that on average, business profits are around 5% on sales. Suppose a business earns a profit of 2.5% compared to the previous year when they earned only 0.5%. As far as mathematics and statistics are concerned, they can legitimately report a "400% increase in profits." Though improving, profits are still at a disappointing half the normally expected successful business profit level of 5%, but seem bigger.

Business should carefully word their news releases to better explain business performance. They can first compute reported results on a target return on sales or historical average, say 5%: "ABC Company reported earnings of $5 million, one-fourth our target rate of $20 million, up from last year's disappointing $1 million." Following this kind of report, more traditional financial information can follow. As the recipient of such information, you have a responsibility to more accurately interpret the reported results in light of new knowledge and understanding.

Sources of Profit Information

The *Wall Street Journal* is an excellent source of the reported earnings of various businesses on a daily basis. *Business Week* magazine and others publish quarterly summaries of business profits information, sales and return on investment, as well as industry averages and overall averages. The famous "Fortune 500" is published annually in *Fortune* magazine to show America's 500 largest businesses in order of sales, profits and assets. Stock brokers and bond dealers are happy to furnish such information.

"Excess Profits" as Imposed Taxes

With more knowledge and understanding, we can tackle another interesting "taxing" situation, that of oil industry profits. They too, are about 5% of sales, so we can guess on a $1.60 gallon of gasoline, there are about 8 cents profit.

On a gallon of gasoline there is actually a total of about 49 cents in taxes, 14 cents federal, 25 cents state, 10 cents "other." When you hear how "Big Oil doesn't pay enough taxes," it is only half right. Big Oil doesn't pay any taxes. Only people pay taxes. Like any other business they collect taxes from customers and send the money to government in compliance with the law. Their profits are about the same low level of other business entities, about 5%.

When such profits are derisively call "excess profits," it is interesting to think them through much like we have done in learning about profits in a business. Suppose oil profits doubled for a year, to ten cents a gallon. Is that "excessive?" Compared to the 49 cents taxes levied by government on gasoline, it still looks reasonably small.

As with other companies, oil companies *don't pay taxes*. Only people pay taxes. People are CUSTOMERS who pay the taxes in the prices of goods and services, oil and gasoline they buy.

Productivity: Getting More for Less;
Working Smarter, And Harder

The concept of PRODUCTIVITY fits well in a discussion of profits, business survival and increasing the "size of the business pie." The overall concept of productivity is to squeeze out more value for less expenditure of human and natural resources, and money. Productivity begins with a good idea that is made marketable to fulfill peoples wants and needs. Two examples come to mind, the ball-point pen and the semi-conductor chip.

Back in the late 1940's a new "wonder pen" was developed and introduced. It wrote for a much longer time, had a very hard point, and was more legible and convenient. The greatest wonder of the ballpoint pen was its price, almost $20, equivalent to over $160 in today's buying power. Back then those dollars bought a lot of other things, making the "wonder pen" affordable only by the very rich. But time, investment and ingenuity placed us where we can buy a dozen or so ball-point pens for today's much cheaper dollar. This is over 1600 times, about $160 to a dime.

We saved and invested money, and used ingenuity to design and build mass production machines to make such inexpensive, miracle "wonder pens" possible.

The semi-conductor chip is where we "turned sand into gold." In a few short decades, we progressed from the vacuum tube to the transistor to tens of thousands, to millions of transistors and other electronic components on a chip of silicon smaller than a fingernail. Similarly, production cost and prices dropped while reliability and value increased. The outputs were the quartz watch, the calculator and the computer.

The quartz watch came out in the late 1970's in a "blinky," Light Emitting Diode (LED), ruby-red digital readout, a "battery-burner" if you ever saw one. Their considerable accuracy was degraded by lack of convenience (you pushed a button to tell the time) and high price, several hundreds of dollars. Soon, the Liquid Crystal Diode (LCD) was developed, and battery life was extended from months to years. Prices dropped to less than a hundred dollars, then to disposable watches for less than $5 including battery. This led to the laptop computer with an LCD color screen.

The pocket calculator was developed. Initially, with scientific functions it cost over $600 in the mid-1970's, and a "four-function" machine was over $200. Mass production, mass marketing and mass use of human ingenuity soon got the prices *under $5 and $20*, respectively! Compare these "Silicon Valley Marvels" with the previous twenty-pound, typewriter-sized electro-mechanical calculators that in 1962 cost $1,200 (with square root, $1,600). In today's money, those would cost over $6,500 and $8,700, respectively. In 1990 you can buy the same capability for $4!

Soon, there was a calculator-watch, a combination of both, for *under $20*! It had all the capability of a computer in mathematical computations, and the time accuracy of the quartz crystal, formerly reserved only for government-funded laboratories. There are now "throwaway" quartz watches available for a dollar, less than the price of a watch battery! Americans wear space-age technology on their wrists for a few dollars and change.

The early 1980's brought what formerly filled several rooms to a typewriter-sized "Personal Computer," for under $2,000, the late '80's, under $1,000, in cheaper dollars, and today even more with 10 times the speed, performance and capability! Ten or 15 years prior, earlier models with similar capabilities cost 50 times that, or twice that *every month* on a lease basis, all in "double size" dollars.

These great strides in technology are attributable to the profit motive, the pursuit of profits, and the American Dream of trying and sometimes succeeding and getting rich. Sacrifice and savings, risk, investment and ingenuity turn the prospect of profits into exciting new ventures of "wonder products" for all mankind to enjoy at mass production prices.

Profit is not only the dwarf that slays giants, but the "magic genie" that provides a cornucopia of abundance, and consequently for us, not only survival, but PROSPERITY.

A Foreigner Views Profits:
How Did Anya Yermolenko Learn About Profit?

Anya Yermolenko, a young Soviet journalist on temporary assignment to a Colorado newspaper, *The Denver Post*, and television station channel 4, KCNC, was doing a story on procrastinating Americans filling out their income tax forms on 1990's tax day, April 16. She commented on the reporting requirements, the nervousness of some American taxpayers and complacency of others, while standing outside the United States Mint in Denver, Colorado.

She told how in Russia there were no forms or deadlines, but instead a direct deduction of 15% from her pay each pay period. Then she signed off, "This is Anya Yermolenko, helping channel 4 make a profit."

How many American employees know their job is to help their employer make a profit?

Another Foreigner Views Profits:
Why Did They Lie to Viktor Belenko?

Viktor Belenko, a Soviet Defector, flew his MiG-25 to Japan and freedom[2]. While in Washington, DC, for debriefing, he needed new clothes. Those escorting him headed for a nearby shopping center. He selected a grocery store to explore and could not believe his eyes at what he saw. Here was a store with literally tons of fresh fruits and vegetables, and yards of counters full of fresh meat and frozen foods. He thought it was a trick. They knew

2. Barron, John, "MIG Pilot: The Final Escape of Lt. Belenko," *Reader's Digest,* 1980. New York

where he would want to stop. They had emptied many other stores to fill one, all to impress this frightened foreigner from another political system.

He thought to himself, "If this were a real store, in less than an hour a woman could buy enough food to feed a whole family for two weeks. But where are the people, the crowds, the lines, the guards? Ah, that proves it. This is not a real store." There were few and short lines. There were no armed guards. Most important of all, there was *food on the shelves*! It was unbelievable. Why did they lie to Viktor Belenko? Well, they didn't.

Lt. Belenko was witness to the fruits of a freedom-based society, the free market, American enterprise system. He saw the power of profit and the profit motive harnessed to provide more goods and services for more people. He found clothes that fit and color television sets *that worked* with clear, true, glowing color! He found America and the results of a system that encourages people to work, produce, innovate and risk, and to supply wants and needs with goods and services. Revealed to Lt. Belenko was the modern market miracle that successfully beat his considerably different system that began in 1917 and had seen over 72 consecutive years of bad weather!

Along with freedom, the thing that makes it all work is PROFIT. Lt. Viktor Belenko learned in an indelible, unforgettable way what harnessing imperfect human nature can do, what miracles people and businesses can perform working together, cooperatively and competitively.

Belenko's observations from a far different viewpoint reveal to us the obvious, taken-for-granted system we have come to use and abuse, but seldom defend or build.

Supermarket Profits: A Midget Dwarf

What is so interesting about supermarket profit is that there is so little of it. Unlike other levels of profit, a chain grocery store makes not 5 cents on the sales dollar, but only about 1 cent, or during a lucky quarter, a little more. Contrast that number with what we pay almost unconsciously in sales taxes, 5, 8, even 10 cents on each dollar spent. Some people get angry about the "outrageous profits" of a grocery store, which we now know to be only 1 or 2 percent. Yet we hardly give a second thought to the much higher sales taxes on grocery store purchases. We may choose to buy different items, even at different stores, take back unsatisfactory purchases, and even complain to the store manager! But no matter what, and with no choice, we pay the sales taxes and all others.

It is worthwhile to contrast different payments we make, the conditions under which we make them, and the value we get for them. We can buy whatever we wish, and have free choice. Yet there is no free choice concerning the taxes on that product. It is mandatory. From the standpoint of a business, even if it makes no profits and pays no income taxes it still pays all other taxes—excises, sales, property and others.

Profit is a very small thing that makes a very large country work very well. Let us be sure our people understand, support and propagate profit, the "dwarf that slays giants." Those giants of poverty and scarcity are the curse of civilizations past that God willing, we may forever relegate to history through hard work, faith and the use of knowledge, development of wisdom and the soaring freedom of an unfettered human spirit. Tell the profit story, *Power of ONE*!

Questions for Review

1. Is seeking to better oneself a form of profit? Is it normal? How widespread is the profit motive? What is profit? How is it determined? How do competition and a free market limit its size? How does ignorance about profit breed contempt for business?

2. What percent of sales do people think businesses earn in profit? What level do they think excessive? Justified? On what do they base perceptions of profit? What is the true level of profit in American business? Is profit always related to money, business, sales, etc.? Express profit in accounting form in terms of sales, gross profit, expenses, profit before taxes and profit after taxes. Discuss these terms.

3. How does "risk" fit into the profit picture? Profit is a mathematical quantity. Discuss each part of the calculation, if it "makes you mad" and how the end product—profit—might "make you mad" if you didn't understand it.

4. What are prices? What does it mean to say prices send signals and convey information? What price is too high? What price is too low?

5. Draw the diagram of "What is a business?" and show where one hundred cents come from and where they go. Do investors make the most money? Describe the relative results of where the money goes. Does it cost money to create a job? How much? Where does the money come from? Why is reinvestment so important? What does all this have to do with a piece of pie?

6. Take your thinking about profit "beyond the obvious." Show where the money eventually goes and how it ends up *after taxes*. How is the money really divided up after it is all done? Who gets the larger share, employees, investors or neighbors? How well do neighbors do compared to employees *and* investors? How are profits taxed twice?

7. In the saga of business how does it all come out? Who pays the bills? Who takes the risks? Who does the hard work? Who gets

the benefits? What is the real tax on profit? How could smart governments become very rich governments?

8. Explain who really pays Social Security. Who pays your Social Security? A VAT purportedly comes from each part of a business that adds value to a product and pays a tax on the added value. Who really pays the tax and how?

9. How is it possible for a business to have a relatively low profit yet report seemingly high profits? How can that hurt a business, or at least its image? What are sources of business profit information? What is the comparison of profit vs. taxes on a gallon of gasoline? Give examples of profits helping develop useful products. How does a ball-point pen show profits actually increase workers standard-of-living by providing more for less? The calculator, quartz watch, computer?

10. How did a Soviet defector illustrate the bounty and abundance of America's free market, profit-motivated, competitive, private enterprise system? It was a supermarket that impressed Lt. Viktor Belenko. What is the profit level of a supermarket compared to most businesses? How does it compare to the sales taxes imposed on supermarket sales by state and local governments? Profit is described as "a very small thing that makes a very large country work very well." How does that evoke the phrase "the dwarf that slays giants"? What are the "giants?"

In business, the earning of profit is something more than an incident of success. It is an essential condition of success. It is an essential condition of success because the continued absence of profit itself spells failure.
—Justice Louis D. Brandeis

If business is going to continue to sell through the decades, it must also promote an understanding of what made those products possible, what is necessary to a free market, and what our free market means to the individual liberty of each of us, to be certain that the freedoms under which this nation was born and brought to this point shall endure in the future. . . . for America is the product of our freedoms.
—E. F. Hutton

There can be no freedom of the individual, no democracy, without the capital system, the profit system, the private enterprise system. These are, in the end inseparable. Those who would destroy freedom have only first to destroy the hope of gain, the profit of enterprise and risk-taking, the hope of accumulating capital, the hope to save something for one's old age and for one's children. For a community of men without property, and without the hope of getting it by honest effort, is a community of slaves of a despotic State.
—Russell C. Leffingwell

Chapter 10

WORK IS LOVE MADE VISIBLE
Let Your Light Shine!

Work is love made visible. —Kahlil Gibran

Welcome to Your World of Work. Make It Work for You.

Work empowers. In life you are either working or looking for work. Both are demanding, exciting and sometimes frustrating. On the job we remind ourselves how important our work is. But the longer we work the more we forget how to effectively seek work. Working and seeking work are both important parts of life.

Work is powerful but misunderstood. Lifework starts out hectic, then flows into a more reasoned, controlled direction—if we direct it. Early on we know little about the world of work and our place in it. With exposure, knowledge and actual experience the world of work opens up. One's choice of work is crucial, to be not only powerful but also productive, personally profitable and fulfilling. Work can be haphazard or planned, fear-directed or faith-directed, life enriching or life draining.

Without background knowledge of economics, politics and business enterprise, the world of work can be a mystery. Little about one's lifework is available in school. Work starts as an after-school activity, as a source of initial capital for school, business or to buy the necessities and niceties of life.

Choice of work and performance at work may be two of the most life-changing, life-supporting activities you will undertake. Knowing all this, it is important to know and understand work, to develop an appreciation for how important work is, and to develop attitudes and skills for finding a job (or building a business) for a rewarding, full life experience.

To be a powerful person and citizen one must have a reliable and continuing source of income. That is possible by working for yourself (start a business) or for someone else ("find a job"). Because of the economics and finances, initial need for income usually requires finding a job as a place to start. That means one must:

1. Find a job.
2. Keep a job.
3. Perform in the job.
4. Grow in the job.
5. Work, save and spend wisely in the job.

At Any Age:
What Do You Want to Be When You Grow Up?

A woman whom I admire once began her speech with "I have 5 children and 9 grandchildren, I am 55 years old and I still don't know what I want to be when I grow up." Most people are like that—doing what they are doing, working, exploring, learning, then stretching their limits, growing and serving, and being rewarded for it. Some know from an early age, "I want to be a doctor" or whatever their early life career decision happens to be. Most start out wondering what is "out there," where they fit in, and seek to find their place.

When they get "out there," what they do and how they do it shape their whole life, its fortunes, opportunities, possibilities and pitfalls. It is worth knowing more about it, thinking it through, and for you, creating and shaping your best future, especially in the world of work, which we here explore.

There are really three questions that give insight into your work goals and directions:

1. What do you want to be when you grow up?
2. How do you want to live your life?
3. What do you want to do with your life?

The latter two can be quite immediate and important. All three are under your control.

The Power of ONE is the Power
to Make a Difference—Through Work

The *Power of ONE* is the power to make a difference. Probably no more powerful or lasting difference can be made than through one's life work. Work is a tapestry we weave, a combination of all the positive and essential efforts we perform. It is also the means through which we earn the money to buy the products and shelter we need in order to live. We work almost a third of our lives. What we do and how we do it have an important impact on our society. Work done well, consistently and reliably, makes a positive and worthwhile contribution.

Just what is work? It is many things to many people. Author Erma Bombeck's father responded to the notion that a whole generation thinks work must be "fun, relevant, and meaningful"[1]:

> The hell it is. It's discipline, competition, and repetition. So the paper route wasn't the religious experience they thought it would be. And the dirt and sweat from the construction job didn't fulfill them? . . . That's because they're confusing work with success. Success is fun, relevant and meaningful. Work is just plain dogging it. So why do we do it? Because those are the ethics that count for something, and if we don't maintain these things, we lose something we desperately need to survive . . . called dignity.

Work is noble. Work is essential. Good work is a treasure. To work well and hard is to LIVE, to experience, to take from and to give back to life.

Work is the means by which we give of ourselves to others, receive from others and in so doing, contribute to building the society in which we live and the future in which our children may flourish and prosper.

Work is life. Philosopher Eric Hoffer tells us about the busy life and the purposeful life[2]:

> The individual's most vital need is to prove his worth, and this usually means an insatiable hunger for action. For it is only the few who can acquire a sense of worth by developing and employing their capacities and talents. The majority proves their worth by keeping busy. A busy life is the nearest thing to a purposeful life. But whether the individual takes the path of self-realization or the easier one of self-justification by action he remains unbalanced and restless. For he has to prove his worth anew each day.

Three Questions to Answer for the World of Work

Entering the world of work is a major decision that influences the entire rest of your life. Going to work usually takes place first on a part-time basis. Three questions are asked and answered:

1) What do you like to do?
2) What do you do well—or can you learn to do well?
3) What needs to be done?

1. Erma Bombeck, *Family—The Ties that Bind . . . and Gag,* p 212, Fawcett Crest, New York: 1987

2. Hoffer, Eric, *The Ordeal of Change,* p 25, Harper and Rowe, New York: 1963

These questions surface early in high school. Answering all three directs your first work efforts.

A simple example is that you like to make hamburgers and you are good at it. You can even learn to do it better and faster! You discover a local fast foods business provides hamburgers to the buying public, and they need "hamburger flippers." All three questions are answered positively and you have a job. It would be the same, for instance, in servicing automobiles, mowing lawns or delivering landscaping supplies and plants.

Early on: 1) you may be able to do a job well, that 2) needs to be done, but 3) you don't think you *like* to work. Two out of three is a good start. All of life is working, sharing and exchanging the fruits of your labors with those of others. Part of the job of those early employment experiences is to learn to appreciate the positive side of working, and to develop tolerance for the rest of the job. A job by its nature is a sacrifice, an inconvenience, a testing of patience, wit and resilience. Perhaps that is in part why you get paid for it!

Too, when we know what work is and how hard it is to do, we more fully appreciate the hard work of others.

Three More Questions, Bigger Impact, Longer Range

During the high school senior year, you confront three new questions regarding your future in the world of work:

> 1) What do you want to do?
> 2) What will it take to do it?
>   and the BIG QUESTION,
> 3) Will you do it?

You may decide to continue doing what you are doing, hoping to advance while you work. You may have incurred financial obligations that must be fulfilled—purchase of a car, television, videocassette recorder, stereo sound system or digital camera. The more such obligations you have, the less free you are to make future commitments to education.

If you decide to continue working, you may preempt another decision, whether or not to go to college. That decision should be made carefully and deliberately. Should you go to college? If so, which one, and what would be your major? That takes us back to the second three questions. Here's an example.

What do I want to do? I want to become a doctor, a family physician.

What does it take? Besides good grades, it takes a sharp mind and good health—mental, physical and emotional. It will take four years of college, in biology, chemistry, nuclear engineering or other major that provides a background in the natural sciences. But that's not all. It will take another four years of demanding advanced education in medicine with long hours of study, classes, little sleep and on-the-job work at a hospital or medical clinic. Should you decide to specialize, say, in brain surgery, you will need another six years for specialization. One of those years would be an internship in general surgery followed by five years neurosurgery residency in order to gain the necessary knowledge and skills. Finally, you will affiliate with other doctors or establish your own medical practice.

Will I do it? Only you know that answer. With a "yes" answer goes all the commitment one person can muster.

The demands, efforts and sacrifices necessary for such a rigorous profession as medicine explain in part why some occupations pay so much more than others. We don't want just anyone to operate on our brains or eyes, or treat our diseases and discomforts. We want someone who knows, *really knows* what they are doing. That kind of reliability takes *total commitment,* energy, money and resources, and the most precious and scarce of life's gifts, time.

There are few people willing to face and meet those challenges. Basic economics indicates the supply is limited, the demand is great and the value is greater. So the price paid, compensation, will be correspondingly higher. It is, especially if four years of college are spent for an undergraduate degree, and even more time, effort and money are spent for a graduate or post-graduate degree. Even within medical specialization, there are differences in compensation. For example, the "higher" paying specialties would include orthopedics, neurosurgery and thoracic surgery; the "lower," family care, pediatrics and general internal medicine.

The more the investment, the more the reward, other things being equal. There is no better investment than in yourself, especially in your formal education and continuing personal and professional growth.

Making and Keeping a Commitment—to Yourself

Answering that second question is a tough assignment, but not nearly as demanding as the third question, *"Will you do it?"* If and when you say "Yes," you have made a most important and demanding long-term commitment, important not only to you, but also to your family and society. This is true whether you decide to become a doctor, aerospace engineer, lawyer, or go into business, political science, marine biology, computer science, liberal arts, or any other technical, business or academic discipline.

America and the world need skilled, intelligent, disciplined, college-trained, committed and capable people. College graduates will be paid well and gladly for their services. The hard work is there to be sure, but so are the rewards. And the rewards are not all money income and benefits. There is also "psychic income," which includes prestige, status, contribution and recognition for professional work well done, as well as the community standing in and organizational contribution to the world around you. There are opportunities for travel, meeting important people and contributing to vital, long-lasting professional achievement.

College Isn't the Only Way to Create Your Future and Prepare for Life

Getting a high school education is essential to your economic future and personal prosperity. College is desirable, but not the only way to make a living and serve your community. One can attend a trade school to get an Air Frame and Power Plant education and license to service jet airplanes, or to learn optometry, auto mechanics, computer operations, barbering or dental assisting. One can take an apprenticeship program to learn a trade, such as carpenter, pipefitter, welder or electrician.

There are "white collar" trades that are beneficial and rewarding, and serve our fellow humans. These include working one's way up in a bank or lending institution, getting into insurance, auto or real estate sales, or commercial property development. With suitable background, experience and sufficient capital, you can go into a business of your own such as a restaurant, print shop, e-business Web sites, lawnmower repair service, barbershop or bookstore. Get information from parents, friends and those in businesses in which you may be interested, to help you pose your questions, develop answers, make decisions and take action.

The first three questions, then the next three, are vital. They are worth a lot of time and contemplation. They are worth exploring not only with your parents, teachers and friends, but also with members of the professions or working communities you are considering for your life work.

Work is important. Work is honorable, ennobling those who do it. Philosopher Eric Hoffer muses about work and fulfillment [3]:

> No one will claim that the majority of people in the Western world, be they workers or managers, find fulfillment in their work. But they do find in it a justification of their existence. The ability to do a day's work and get paid for it gives one a sense of usefulness and worth. The paycheck and the profitable balance sheet are certificates of value. Where the job requires exceptional skill or tests a person's capacities there is an additional sense of exhilaration. But even a job of the sheerest routine yields the individual something besides the wherewithal of a living.

Education and Career Changes: When and How to Change Your Mind

Though the decisions seem awesome, and are, there are propitious decision points available on the way. During the first years in college, a major or school can be changed or an academic year delayed, though it may delay graduation and increase costs. Carefully selecting a major can result in a worthwhile and personally rewarding career. But if it is found to be less than

3. Ibid, p. 28

expected, a career change is possible "down the road" by gaining on-the-job experience, then going back to school to earn an advanced degree in the same or another field.

For instance, an engineer who finds he likes working with organizations, people and business problems, can go back to college to get a Masters Degree in Business Administration (MBA). Depending on the institution, the engineer can select a specific emphasis in a new area of interest, such as production, accounting, human resource administration, finance, marketing, transportation, operations research or computer science.

The beauty to all this is in the options available and the challenges and rewards possible upon dedicated application and successful completion of the selected curriculum. In America, an individual can choose a calling or line of work, then change and try something else more suited to his or her preferences, requirements, responsibilities and rewards. This is not the case in many other societies in the world.

The Job Search: An Exercise in Faith and Frustration.

When we enter the world of work, we are usually young and inexperienced. With limited or no savings, we choose to work for someone else—"get a job." Initially, you take an entry-level job that may pay low wages, be tedious, repetitive and boring. An existing business is a ready-made opportunity with a hidden advantage: You don't have to raise capital! You don't assume much risk, as does your new employer who provides you a job. You don't market or sell. You perform the work for which you are paid. You have a job, get paid for doing it, and in the process, acquire a valuable *liberal education* and actual experience in the world of work and enterprise.

Think about, thank and remember kindly the very first jobs and those first few special people who dared have faith enough in you to give you a chance, train you and get you started in that important job. Then "pass it on" and similarly take a chance with someone else in the future.

You begin to "look for a job." Part of the privilege of working is to exercise your freedom to choose, to look for and find a job, to learn to enjoy it while doing it well and being paid for it. Since so much of our time is spent working, love of work can enhance one's whole life, making each one of us an enthusiastic, optimistic, powerful and contributing *Power of ONE.*

Finding a job is an *exercise in faith.* This is where you exercise your *Power of ONE* oath "I am one. I am only one. But I will do, what one can do." This affirmation will be combined with your not-so-secret success formula:

Act as if it were impossible to fail!

You know somewhere there is or will be a job you can do, and you will find it. It is just a matter of time, with a generous expenditure of effort and faith, a lot of hard work, creativity and cleverness—and a "little bit of luck."

You will *spend*: time and effort making contacts, and money, finding and answering appropriate want ads for employment, from magazines and newspapers. You will read the paper carefully and sensitively, seeking and finding potential employment opportunities in stories about company's improved earnings, expansion or new products and markets. You will visit Web sites and make contacts in person, by letter, fax, email or phone, from referrals solicited and received from family, friends and acquaintances. You will ask for and get leads on the way, and follow up on each one.

You will prepare a resume of "you" and your educational, professional and/or work experience, and send copies with an interesting cover letter to carefully selected potential employers. You will make phone calls, appointments and obtain interviews. You will present your best self to obtain a suitable job offer, with the strategy that you want to be in a position to select, evaluate, decide, obtain a job offer, and either accept or reject the job possibility.

The Job Interview:
Meeting of Minds, Hearts and Possibilities

You approach the job interview with optimism and enthusiasm, with a confident walk, positive carriage, a big, sincere smile and a countenance that says *and means* "I'm glad, really glad, to meet you! I am truly excited about the possibilities!" Isn't this really true about many of life's exciting yet risky situations? "Act as if were impossible to fail" is similar to seeking a loan at a bank. If you can absolutely prove you don't really need the loan, you'll get it! Approach the job situation similarly, positively, confidently and enthusiastically. It will work out better than you could ever imagine, any rejections and disappointments all being an important part of finding that one right job for you.

You not only *tell* your story, but you *sell* your story. *Show* them what you have done, and can do. In keeping the appointment, take into account the other person's valuable time and presence. You are really "there" and on time. You give a firm handshake, flash a genuine smile and a "good word." You express enthusiasm to the person and optimism at the job possibilities, the potential to work, contribute, grow and serve.

You have "done your homework," and found some important information about the company. That helps you know if you want to work in their employ, and you are able to skillfully communicate a knowledge about the organization, to receive an employment offer. You inquire as to a written job description, and ask specific, detailed questions about the job requirements, and even how they judge your doing a good job. Find out about your potential new situation and meet the boss if possible. Ask questions about the company and its management philosophy about people, employees, suppliers, customers and others. Explore answers with your interviewer. And you are asked questions which you graciously, positively and honestly answer.

You may have a "personal portfolio" you have carefully assembled, featuring tangible proof of results and past performance, where possible. The portfolio will include educational assignments as well as professional and work-related proof of achievements, honors and awards received. Some will take the form of written proposals, others, certificates of completion or commendations for a job well done. You skillfully "showcase" your potential and capabilities, based on past jobs, education and specialized courses and experience. You not only *tell* previous job responsibilities and content, but also *sell* results and accomplishments!

This is no time to be bashful or modest. Tell them what you have done and how well you have done it. Illustrate how reliable, creative and hardworking you are with actual stories about previous work. Tell of your awards and honors. Communicate you will be there to work as directed, to work hard, solve problems, accept direction and offer solutions, to follow rules and observe policies. In short, you will want to be perceived as an answer to The BOSS's prayer, not another nightmare in his dreams!

"Work the Numbers," Up the Odds, Boost the Results

During any one specific interview, the odds of a good match between you and clinching a job opportunity are heavily weighted against finding a job. If you are skillful and effective (even lucky), you will find a potential job situation where you like them, they like you. There are three other possibilities: you don't like them, they don't like you, or you don't like each other, and there is no match or fit. The odds against aren't just one out of four, though. In the case you do like each other, requirements of the job must closely match your experience, education, background, interests and ambitions. You must be satisfied you will like the people, organization, services and products, your supervisor, as well as the pay and benefits of the potential job, and that there is not only a present job, but a future career.

The Agony and the Ecstasy of the Job Hunt

Job applicants complain how frustrating and disappointing job hunting and interviews are. They are and must be. With the freedom we have we know the odds are great to find a job we like and want, are qualified for and will grow in, and are adequately compensated in pay and benefits. But odds are also great in finding a very desirable opportunity. That makes the whole job search more exciting and fulfilling, though more exasperating and drawn out. It also gives you time to fully appreciate and perform the job once you find it.

Such likely complications illustrate why it is so important to allow a lot of time for mismatches, rejection and frustration in the job search. It is all an act of faith. You know you will find one because you are that good, because you must, and because you have great faith that it is there. *You will find the job!* You know the odds are against any one individual situation being exactly the right one, so *you work on MANY job possibilities*, any way you can, through newspapers, organizations, relatives, friends and old school mates, plus word-of-mouth and follow-up on tenuous leads. But the freedom to search, the excitement of the search and the search itself are all necessary and well worth the effort.

Looking for work is a full time job, requiring at least 8 hours a day and likely more. Use weekends to review classified advertisements, plan telephone calls and appointments, write letters of follow-up, for initial contacts and prepare for the week ahead. Get up early enough to be ready to make calls and keep appointments and interviews in plenty of time and on schedule.

Know there will be disappointments, discouragement and frustration. Anticipate, even enjoy them! One "positive thinker" told me she just got another rejection and was glad to get it over with. "I know I will receive so many rejections, and I just got one more out of the way! Now I am closer than ever to my new job!" That is a *Power of ONE* in action.

The important thing is not to allow yourself to get discouraged. Put all your emotional energy into your job search. Keep on working very hard at finding a job. Job-hunting is a full time job.

Never Forget the Job Search, and the First Day

Some are lucky. With seemingly little or no effort, they find a job and begin. Others find the job search to be a long, drawn out, frustrating and discouraging experience. It is that way because we have an open and free market labor system. It takes time to find a job because of the dynamic character of the job market and the various work attributes you bring to a job opportunity. The search is inefficient at best, relying on personal contacts, advertisements, word-of-mouth, the telephone "yellow pages" and other lists of companies, and sometimes employment agencies, professional and other work-affiliated organizations. But the job search is the price one pays for *job freedom*. It is worth the price, the hard work and the expense in time, energy, and resources including money.

Never forget your job search. Never forget your first day at work. Those are rare, insightful, enriching experiences that should be burned into your memory. Remember not only the place, people and products, but your emotions—scared, excited, fearing, anticipating, and just plain thankful to have this new opportunity. These feelings will serve you well to recall them at appropriate later times.

An Attitude of Success: Take Care of Your Boss!

In the economic world of work, we are there for only one purpose: to please, serve and satisfy the most important person, The BOSS. If you are in your own business, the customer is The BOSS. If you're in another's business, your supervisor is The BOSS. It is so important it bears repeating.

You are there for only one purpose: *To work very hard to please, serve and satisfy that most important person, The BOSS.* And everyone has a boss.

Some people forget why they have a job and why they are being paid to do that job. Now you know. It is not "to work for the company." It is not just to show up. It is not just to put in the required time. It is to *work for your boss.* It's to do the work of your boss, and to do it well. To you, the boss IS the company, your friend, confidant, coach, counselor, leader, supervisor, sponsor, BOSS. Boss is one of those words that is so important that it might as well have a halo around it.

There are two, half-joking, two-thirds serious "rules" for getting along with a boss: Rule 1, The boss is always right. Rule 2, When you think the boss is wrong, go back to Rule 1.

In any organization, *your boss is your destiny.* Select yours carefully. Then do your very best to "take care of the boss," in your job, always, all ways. Find out exactly what your boss wants you to do, how it is to be done, and do it—plus a little extra. Communicate well and often what you are doing. Find out if it fits your boss' requirements. Work just as hard at knowing your boss' expectations, then meeting or exceeding them. Your progress, remuneration, special benefits and considerations, your future success, will directly or indirectly come from or through your boss. The *Power of ONE* takes care of *The BOSS!*

Job Down Days and Paying More Dues

There will be future days you will wonder if it is all worth it. Should you give your all? Should you show great enthusiasm? Is the expenditure of time and energy all worth it? Is the job worthwhile to your current goals and your lifetime calling? These questions occur and beg an answer. The answer is, and must be *YES!* If it is not yes, get active on your alternatives.

Remember back to when you searched for your job? How did you feel when you found it? Were offered the job? Accepted it? Started it? Learned and grew in it? What were your feelings in your first day on the job?

How would you feel without a job? How would you like to hunt for another job? What about your unemployed friends? How about others unable to find work? Or unable to work? What about those losing their jobs and ill-prepared to compete in the ever-changing job market, demanding new skills and capabilities? How does their situation stack up with yours?

These questions, and your answers to them, can give insight, inspiration and perspective on how fortunate you are in your job.

Beware the cop-out feeling, "I've paid my dues." "They owe me something and I haven't received it. I'm going to hold back until I get treated more fairly." It is also illogical and unfair to your own future.

YOU NEVER PAY YOUR DUES! As long as you are receiving a paycheck from a business organization, you owe them total performance, total output, total loyalty, total quality on the job and total commitment to the job.

For instance, if you work for a tire factory, it is part of your job to buy and use the tires your company manufactures. If you don't, you send a very "loud and clear" message that your company and its products are no good. Another equally powerful message goes out about you. You appear disloyal, shallow, lacking basic honesty, integrity and respect.

Actions, always, speak louder than words! Never forget it.

It is common and disappointing, even regrettable, to view disgruntled employees who somehow forget the blessings and abundance of a good job. They act, perhaps sincerely feel, that they are owed something for just showing up and being there. They forget that a forthcoming paycheck allows them to meet their financial commitments and obligations, furnishes them with special benefits, material blessings, abundance to share, plus security and peace of mind. Accepting that remuneration without really doing the job well, during all the hours paid for, is accepting money under false pretenses. Though it is less obvious than a shoplifter taking goods, it is stealing just the same. Do not steal from your employer or anyone else—ever!

When the inevitable "down times" come, remember your job search and those wonderful "new job feelings" of your first day, week, month and year. Those memories help provide valuable stability in times of stress.

Consider someone may want YOUR job, want it in the worst way, and perhaps be able to do it better than you. To be motivated to grow, to do more and better, imagine your invisible but ever-present competitor, your possible job replacements. Who might they be? What are their skills, education, experience, and ambition? What must you do to meet and beat them?

If your pulse is pounding and your breathing is rapid, you are visualizing that possible replacement and fighting hard and well to keep them out of your job and you in it. Use the adrenaline that flows from the fear, respect and energy of competition to give the biggest, best, grandest job performance possible. You always have your competition to out-perform even if you cannot readily know who, what or where they are.

A Love of Your Job is a Love of Life

LOVE YOUR JOB! It puts you in touch with life, with who you are! Keep in mind "man" means "human" in the following verbatim quote:

> A man's job is his best friend. It clothes and feeds his wife and children, pays the rent, and supplies the wherewithal to develop and become cultivated. The least a man can do in return is to love his job. ... If you ask any successful man the reason for his making good, he will tell you that first and foremost it is because he likes his work; indeed, he is wrapped up in it. He walks his work; he talks his work; he is entirely inseparable from his work, and that is the way every man worth his salt ought to be if he wants to make of his work what it should be, and make of himself what he wants to be.
> —Arthur Capper

Loyalty: The Secret Ingredient of Success

Loyalty comes in giving your job all you can give while accepting the paycheck and benefits from the employer providing the job. It means supporting totally the products and community presence of your employer. Don't "bad mouth" your company, job, boss or company products and services.

> If you work for a man, in heavens name work for him. . . . if he pays you wages which supply you bread and butter, work for him; speak well of him; stand by him and stand by the institution he represents. . . . if put to a pinch, an ounce of loyalty is worth a pound of cleverness. . . .   —Elbert Hubbard

If all this seems unacceptable, you are probably in the wrong job, with the wrong boss or wrong organization. If so take appropriate action to make it right.

Company YOU:
You are the CEO, CFO, COO, CTO, CIO,
the President, The BOSS!

You are your own *Chief EXECUTIVE Officer*, or CEO. Once you are in the work force, no matter what your job or role, you are the chief executive of you. You must consider, marshal, oversee and sustain all the resources necessary for you, not only to survive, but prosper in your life work. You know how important it is to have and maintain sufficient skills and proper attitudes for job qualification and performance. That means you not only work hard today, but also prepare for tomorrow. Your continuing application and continual preparation assures the future of your life. Once you know and accept this challenge, you are in control and destined for greatness.

You are your *Chief FINANCIAL Officer*, CFO, carefully monitoring the income, expenditures and budget of your job and of your personal life. You assure you have the proper resources to do your job and do it right. You know what is available and you make it work for you, and for your job and company. With your paycheck you pay you first.

You are your *Chief OPERATING Officer*, or COO, assuring you do the right job right at the right time, making and honoring commitments, touching base with the necessary organizational departments and people, cultivating them to make your total job a total success. You know, honor and comply with company policies, follow procedures and assure adherence to safety and security regulations designed to protect you, your fellow workers and company assets.

You are your own *Chief TRAINING Officer*, or CTO. First, you want to do your job right and well, all day, every day. Second, you want to grow in your job, to be able to do more and better with less, and then take on even more. You want to sharpen old skills and acquire new skills. You want to keep up in working relationships and keep professional politics and personal ethics on course. Third, you may want to take on and learn a whole new area of expertise to supplement your present job, prepare you for a new job. Fourth, you recognize that there is ever present, demanding competition in the job market.

You are the *Chief INFORMATION Officer*, CIO. You know what is going on. It is your job to stay current in your job, company, career, field of expertise, town, society and nation. You subscribe to and read daily newspapers and weekly magazines, listen to radio for hints and watch television for clues as to what is going on that directly or indirectly affects you. You join appropriate professional, service, charitable and philanthropic organizations to contribute to your community, to make and cultivate contacts. You know your elected and appointed public officials and they know you. You have got the knowledge and understanding. You get the information to stay on top and up to date. You know what's going on and use it.

You are not just doing a job. You are creating a career towards living a full, productive and rewarding life. Get in control of your job and you are in control of your life.

Mr. President: Hail to the Chief!

You are the *PRESIDENT* of "You, Incorporated," with full and complete authority, and total responsibility for everything that you do and every thing that happens as a result of it. You are in charge. Take charge, create a job, create a career, create a life.

You want to prepare for and create your future. As you work and grow, achieve and contribute, you learn a great deal about yourself. You find what you like to do and what you are good at. You learn things you can do you thought you couldn't do. How much more important is trying, accepting and working, over doing only the tried-and-true. Accepting risk and meeting challenge and adversity, create opportunity and build for the future.

You are the *Big BOSS!* Look the part. Act the part. Dress the part. Be the part. You are totally in charge of your performance on your job. Perform with pride and feel good about what you do, all you do, and how well you do. Remember, to an employee, the boss *is* the company.

Hey, Mr. President of "You, Inc." Hail to the Chief!

From What to Do, to What to Get Done

The nature of your level of responsibility has to do with being told *what to do* or *what to get done*. Entry level jobs are usually well established, with a precise method of operation or operating procedure. You perform specific tasks in a prescribed sequence, satisfying predetermined conditions of acceptance. You get done *exactly* what is required and specified, nothing more, nothing less. As a carpenter, you might take two 10-penny nails, drive them in two 2 x 4's at a right angle, insert a corner bracket and place the assembly at the next workstation.

Higher skill jobs require more conceptualization such as designing the bracket, creating a marketing plan, or researching and writing a quality assurance procedure, or what to get done in a similar functional work area.

As you grow in your job, you find yourself accepting more responsibility. You build up more trust between you and your boss at performing the required functions and tasks. You reflect that at first you waited to be told exactly what to do, you did it, then waited to be told what to do next.

Next, you knew what to do, suggested to your boss that it be done, obtained approval or authorization, then did it. Later on you know what to do and do it; then let the boss know it was done. You know and honor the fact that *a boss doesn't like surprises*. Let the boss know what is going on, especially if it is negative or could be damaging or embarrassing.

Finally, you reach a level where you perform what has to be done and occasionally inform your boss what you are doing and its results, plus what's next. You go from implementing other people's solutions to problems and situations, to identifying and solving them yourself.

You grow in your job and performance, your quality and reliability, and in your relationship with your boss and your place in the organization. You are on your way, *Power of ONE*. Go for it!

Promotions: Moving up the Ladder of Success

How to get a promotion, a raise, a bonus, a better opportunity? You go beyond doing what is expected, to *doing more than expected*. You take on extra assignments—join a task force, volunteer for a committee, or do a special project for your boss or department. Your first eight hours a day are to do your job and earn your money. The next several hours are to earn a promotion and build your career.

You join professional or related groups to represent your specialty, function or profession, your company and industry. You not only join but get involved; not only attend, but participate. You are not only a spectator but a participant. You not only show up but are committed and active.

You learn management and teamwork by doing. You learn and grow in an unthreatening environment, letting the benefits gained flow into your work and your job performance. The more you do, the better you do it, and the more you grow and reap the rewards of growth. You are an asset to an outside group as well as your company, and you go farther and grow faster.

Take on an educational goal, not only getting the boss' approval and blessing, but backing and understanding. Bring new skills and concepts to your job to make it easier, better and more fun, while your department and boss look better. When the boss is away, seek to become acting boss, make decisions, accept responsibility, take actions, and learn by doing.

When a new department is formed or an opening becomes available, you are the likely candidate to be considered for it, and you get it. You have worked for, earned and received a new opportunity. It is not uncommon for the increased pay to follow the new opportunity by several months or even a half-year. That's a safety valve to allow you to prove yourself, or find yourself unprepared without the embarrassment of a demotion or termination.

Be patient. Do and continue to do a good job. Grow in your job. Serve your boss. Protect your boss. Communicate with your boss. You will turn your world of work into a world of fun, challenge and achievement, and a continually increasing opportunity to contribute to your society, and be rewarded generously by it. You will turn it into a world of gold, remuneration, as well as fun and accomplishment.

Building a Life

In a nutshell, here is what happens:

> You start out by *seeking a job*, then *finding a job*. You begin *working a job*, then *building a job*. Soon you are *building a career*. Finally, you are *building a life* through your life work. You are helping create a better world by contributing to it in concert with others who work, create, build and grow. You are in control. You are valuable. You are generously compensated and rewarded.

In the first part of life you take from the world. Later, you are "giving back" much more than you are taking. You are in fact contributing to building a better world. This is where your work allows you to do what others did for you. You are able to contribute and build for the future of those you will never meet so that they can do the same. What a wonderful opportunity to pay back what you owe, then more to build to a better future.

A passionately concerned observer of the human condition, businessman Andy Patten, put this all together:

> "Giving back more than you take has got to be the magic key to mankind's progress over the ages. In fact this single idea has put things in more proper perspective for me." He cheers the idea "that careers are the result of past achievements, each building on the preceding one. There are no overnight successes. Daily, monthly, yearly advancement toward a goal is success. Success is not a thing, it is a PROCESS. It is a recognition that one's living is contributing to the advancement of mankind. What a powerful thought!"

What a *Power of ONE*!

You are a *Power of ONE* where you are, inspiring others to become *Powers of ONE*. Your influence extends by example and action, improving the community and world around you. Your hard work and good works form the light you shed on your fellow human beings.

> Let your light so shine before men, that they may see your
> good works. . . .   —Matt 5:16

Congratulations! Your good works shine before others. Your work is love made visible. Your light shines to make a brighter future. As you build a better life, you build a better world.

You count. You matter. You make a difference. You are a *Power of ONE* hard at work.

Questions for Review

1. Why is the power to work the power to live? Is work all taking or all giving? Explain. What is work?

2. What three questions about the world of work are important to starting to work in life? At what age? Year in school? Under what circumstance?

3. What are the next three questions, when and why do they occur? Why is the answer to the third yes-or-no question so important? How does it involve faith and commitment?

4. Why isn't college the only way to make it in the world? Name and explain others. What is their purpose? Why is it important to space advanced education with on-the-job experience?

5. Looking for a job is frustrating but beneficial. Why? What good is it? How does one act in seeking a job? How should you approach a job interview, mentally, emotionally, physically, in appearance and attitude? Explain "the odds" of job hunting.

6. Why is job hunting a full time, 8-hour-a-day job? How do you go about it? Where do you find jobs and job opportunities? Why is it especially important later on to remember seeking, finding, working hard to get, and starting a new job?

7. Why does an attitude of success include developing a good relationship with and taking good care of your boss? What good does it do to develop a fondness for your job, work and employer? Why is it possibly detrimental to have the attitude, "I've paid my dues?" Why is it incorrect? What is the secret ingredient of success?

8. You are the President of You, Incorporated, and hold the job titles and functions of CEO, CFO, COO, CTO, CIO and President. What are they and why are they so important?

9. What is the progression of a person on the job with increasing experience, confidence and responsibility? What does it take to get raises, promotions and bonuses?

10. Discuss "Work is your opportunity to give back." How can your work be looked at as "building a career, building a life?"

The privilege of doing useful, necessary work would be recognized as one of the great satisfactions of living. Being needed—the knowledge that you are doing something useful and necessary—is an essential ingredient in human happiness. Work—done well and to the best of your abilities—is one of the most satisfying of human experiences. What a pity more people don't recognize this!

Why do we lose sight of this fact? Because most of us *have* to work in order to live. And it rarely occurs to us that something we *have* to do could actually be *enjoyable*. The job hasn't been invented yet which is all peaches and cream. But even if a job is sometimes difficult or boring, we can still get a great deal of satisfaction by doing it well.

That's the only way we can enjoy any job; by doing it well. Anyone who's never had the experience is missing something. The half-hearted worker will never know or understand this pleasure. The only joy he'd ever get from a lifetime of labor is stopping at the end of each day. The contentment we find in our work spreads to everything else we do. "Find happiness in your work," a wise man once said, "or you may never find it anywhere else."

—Bits and Pieces, May, 1975.

To be idle is to become a stranger unto the seasons, and to step out of life's procession, that marches in majesty and proud submission towards the infinite . . . when you work you fulfill a part of earth's furthest dream, assigned to you when that dream was born, and in keeping yourself with labour you are in truth loving life, and to love life through labor is to be intimate with life's inmost secret.   —Kahlil Gibran, *The Prophet*

Chapter 11

POWER CHALLENGE TO BUSINESS
Start an Employee Economic Awareness Program!

The Image of Business:
The Not-So-Good, the Bad, and the Ugly

Business has been and is the Big Bad Villain on television. On steamy "Dallas," when asked by a harried competitor how he could even live with himself, famed TV business bad guy, J. R. Ewing, replied, "It's easy. Once you give up integrity the rest is a piece of cake."

The way business is portrayed on television forms the public image of business. And it is all bad. Business men and women become convenient, vulnerable and defenseless victims of a continuing negative public relations campaign.

A TV documentary[1] on business as villain was aired March 25, 1987. Benjamin Stein, writer and TV producer, explored reasons for businessman as villain. Business(usually)men "Heavies" are shown commonly and popularly as lawbreakers who lie, steal, cheat, blackmail and even resort to murder, with such rhetoric as "I'm making you a final offer: Sell or die."

---

1. Pack, Michael, & Polin, Daniel B., Producers, *Hollywood's Favorite Heavy: Businessmen on Prime Time TV*, Great Projects Film Co., Inc., 6584 9th Ave., NY, NY 10036, Copyright 1987 by Manifold Productions, Inc., Used with Permission

"Producers may say they're reflecting reality and to a small degree that's true," says Stein, "but you never see a green mailer or a corporate looter on TV. What you see are businessmen and murderers; and a very few heads of publicly-held companies are murderers."

Predictably, a *Reader's Digest* article, "Waste 'em," had revealed underworld criminals as the perpetrators of dumping toxic wastes into municipal waste treatment systems, endangering whole populations. When the TV writers developed the idea, instead of "the mob," they used big business as villain, explaining television management did not want to mention the mob. Besides, business is a more logical, vulnerable and less defensible villain, confirming all the public suspects of those who ask customers to pay their bills or do their jobs.

A group discussion of writers from several quite popular TV programs identified the businessperson as an easy target, personifying power, especially to impressionable, uninformed, unaware viewers. The result? A majority of the crimes on prime time TV are committed by business. A majority of heads of corporations break the law. By age 18 on TV, a youngster has seen business people commit or attempt 10,000 murders.

Was the writer group correct in its unanimous judgment that these misleading portrayals of business had little or no lasting affect on the perceptions and attitudes of our children? That it amounted to no more than fiction, fantasy, a story, entertainment? No! They were proved wrong!

Herb London, program director and dean of New York University, explored the effects with 15 high school students in Brooklyn. Initially they said they were unaffected by TV in their perceptions and attitudes of business. The actors were definitely not real people. Ensuing discussion brought out their true feelings. Business wields power. Business people are never satisfied. They can corrupt people. They get what they want. They do whatever they must do to get it.

London asked, "If you knew you wouldn't get caught, would you" and then posed several scenarios regarding pollution, cheating, stealing and embezzlement. At first the students said they wouldn't commit the crimes. Then, if it were the only way to save the business, they would do it, but only if it didn't hurt members of their own families. Finally, *unanimously,* they would break the law if necessary, to save the business, even if members of their families were adversely affected.

Eli Wallach, narrator, concluded: "People get many of their values from entertainment, especially young people. TV may not be the only force that shapes their ideas, but it has become an increasingly powerful one. . . . With TV as their guide, today's young people will become more and more confused about their economic system. The real story of business has heroes and villains, and a complex mixture of good and evil, and people facing many difficult moral dilemmas. Wouldn't that make for better television?"

Ignorance May Be Bliss,
But It is Costing Business a Fortune

Lack of enlightenment in the American public is a serious threat to American enterprise. So few really understand the basics of society, specially creation of wealth, free enterprise, risk, choice, investing, job creation, working and the work place, pleasing a customer, economics, business and profit. Even fewer people understand taxes to fund government, their uses and sources: people, directly and through business, indirectly.

When people do not understand something, they fear it. When people fear, they inevitably turn to government for protection. When government protects it costs everybody including business, a lot of money, and not surprisingly the results still are elusive. So we pay more but get less.

If you think education costs money, what is the price of ignorance?

Five Selfish Reasons Business Should Have
an Economic Awareness Program

You in business, exercise your glorious best skills to make a multiplied personal difference. Your *Power of ONE* extends to a greater power, and that is to positively influence employees and other businesses, as well as the community.

Over 133 million people are employed in America. Most have not been sufficiently exposed to economic or business concepts to truly understand and be able to fully participate in our society. Basic economics and business can be presented to the work force as a great and continuing benefit, not only to the business, but to the community and society in which the business operates. This "Premier Benefit" will help many businesses and employees to work together to make dramatic, continuing positive change for business' present, and America's future and freedoms.

America's workers create the wealth of America and they consume it. They have a right to the knowledge of how our American system works and what their part is in it. A more informed populace can help our leaders and politicians make better decisions for better long-term political system performance. Business can fight back.

Include an employee economic awareness program routinely in normal, everyday operations of your business for five good reasons, three business, one human, one societal:

1. When people, as *customers,* understand economics and business, they are more patient, tolerant, understanding, less demanding and critical of business, less moved to say, "There ought to be a law. . . ." and sometimes end up with another law, or lawsuit.

2. When people, as *employees,* truly understand economics and business, they can become more sincerely and completely involved in the short and long run success of the business. They better understand the demands of schedules, quantity of output and product quality, the desirability of being on time and taking correct work breaks and eating periods, and the importance of safety for their fellow workers, facilities and company. They better accept the work place, its appearance and utility, and are more tolerant of change, foibles of supervisors, and some of the "silliness" that is part of the ever-changing workday and work place. With such resilience comes higher productivity and quality through adherence to rules, procedures and standard practices, and often valuable and creative "better ideas" or suggestions on how to do the work more efficiently.

3. An *employee economic awareness program* is a business' long term competitive edge, providing employees "The Premier Benefit." That is an understanding and appreciation of ALL benefits, not just money, vacations and holidays, but the non-monetary or less monetary compensation provided employees. That brings with it more involvement in the vision, mission and goals of the business, and a stronger appreciation of the goods and services businesses provide, plus getting and staying competitive by being better.

4. *Major personal problems* often exist among valued employees because of bungled personal finances, over-extended credit, small savings and lack of security and peace of mind that goes with them. Most marital and family problems are caused by lack of understanding of and control over money, budgeting, saving and investing, and the larger picture of building an estate, thereby providing for heirs and enjoying a comfortable and rewarding retirement.

5. *Societally*, when people put together all they know, not only about business and economics, but finance, government, taxes, freedom, the U.S. Constitution and the Bill of Rights, they become more knowledgeably involved. They are more effective, active citizens.

Working hard together, we enjoy a more enlightened, effective and enduring society, with a government that better protects the individual and preserves freedom, opportunity and security for our children and those to follow.

The Premier Benefit:
Two Bogus Reasons Why NOT Provided

Business leaders offer two unacceptable reasons for not having an employee economic awareness program—time and money. Either business is too good and there is no time. Or business is not good and there is no money.

Either way, your commitment can and must blast through these pseudo-obstacles. Offer the program anyway.

American business has taken great strides to improve working conditions through increasing employee wages and salaries, benefits and improved work place environment, both physical and atmospheric. Successful business managers have learned there needs to be an atmosphere of affection and respect in the work place. When these conditions are present employees will pay you back in performance, productivity, quality and loyalty.

Employees who truly understand the business and the workplace will participate in the battle of staying in business. If they realize that ultimately their jobs, security, prosperity and future are on the line, they will help fight the business battle. Because they know it is their battle, too.

Survival Weapons: Employee Economic Understanding and Business Appreciation

Most Americans do not understand the workplace. Nor do they understand work, business, free enterprise, productivity, production, entrepreneurship, risk, money, economics, taxes and the like. Most Americans are economic illiterates! Their schools and teachers never taught them economics and their parents never learned economics either. As a result young people do not learn economics—either at school or at home, and people in the work place today, 133 million strong, are ignorant of "the economic facts of life."

A nation of economic illiterates is a handicap to our freedom. If we do not understand how our economic system works, we cannot effectively participate in it and reap the benefits from it. Our people need to understand the blessings and responsibilities of freedom, and how they affect our standard-of-living and quality-of-life.

While our public education does not teach economics and free enterprise, other countries not only teach their economic system, but also indoctrinate their students in the political systems and ideologies of their countries. Students know what their governments want them to know about these "life sciences." Americans haven't yet caught on to the importance of the need for our people to know, and to have our citizens involved in the American economic and political system, to preserve and strengthen our American way of life.

We are all engaged in an everyday battle for survival. Even beyond survival, we have unlimited wants still fettered by limited means and resources.

We all learned that cows give milk. Cows don't *give* milk! You have to take it from them! Mother Nature is stingy. She forces us to work very hard and very smart, cooperatively and cleverly to fill our needs from her vast but difficult storehouses. And we do a pretty good job. But think how much better a job we could do if we corporately and individually understood our system of enterprise better. And what a profound impact each one of us can have on the system and on our own place within it.

The Need for Employee Economic Awareness: A Few More Reasons and "Two-Fisted Selling"

WIIFM is the name of the game. WIIFM stands for What's In It For Me? That question answered is the secret to why people do something new or different. Who is "Me?" Let's start with business itself.

WIIFM, *business*? When employees learn and understand what business is all about, why it is so demanding, why a customer must be pleased, they do a better job. Employees then are motivated to be more supportive, tolerant, resilient and patient. They perceive common goals and common survival and job security. They better accept direction, follow rules and work practices, ensure higher quality, productivity and output, and a safer operation. This leads to *higher* output, productivity, quality; and *lower* employee absenteeism, tardiness, disciplinary action and turnover, material waste and scrap. In turn, costs are reduced, profits enhanced, resulting in increased sales by offering higher quality products and services at lower prices.

All this is possible because employees develop understanding about business and economics. Part of this process is better communications with employees and a more effective partnership in getting the job of business done and done well.

WIIFM, *employees*? All employees—labor and management—can profit from a better understanding not only of business, but of applying good economics to personal situations, company, community and country issues. Individuals will have higher confidence in themselves, their industry, company and job. They can achieve higher financial independence, more security, safety, and control over their own lives. Through awareness, knowledge and understanding, this new existence offers more personal power and freedom.

WIIFM, *America*? The United States of America also benefits. A more complete knowledge and understanding of economics leads to better decisions and direction in government and politics. This assures a more secure, abundant, and freer future for all citizens.

Another WIIFM, *business,* to sell your product or service, *and* America? The late Dr. Kenneth McFarland, freedom speaker and sales motivator, put it this way:

This is *leadership* and *salesmanship* of the highest form. It's the thing that has got to be done in America. And you have a magnificent opportunity with the enormous aura of influence that you have, contacting people constantly. The enormous opportunity you have, for selling not only your own great product, but selling the Great

American System. That makes magnificent companies and magnificent successes like yours possible.

This is the job. This is what I commend you on. It's the greatest opportunity for leadership and salesmanship that we have ever had. I congratulate you on the medium you have of service. You can serve other people *better* than the competition. And when you do that, *you succeed!* This is fundamental Americanism. So I say this to you. Congratulations, for being with this great company in such a great time. I say to you, let me give you this challenge:

Go out there and *Sell Them AMERICA* with your right hand, while you're selling your own products and your own services with your left hand. And if you'll do that, I'll promise you something. *You will sell more with your left hand than you ever sold with both hands before!* That's called *two-fisted selling!"*

—Dr. Kenneth McFarland

Awareness, knowledge, information, decisions and action are *POWER!* Multiplied by the many employees in a firm, and their influences within a community, you are building a solid work force, a network of support, and a mighty future, not just for your business and community, but for your country!

So we all win—when business is smart enough, selfish and enlightened enough, caring and concerned enough to provide its employees with The Premier Benefit, an employee economic awareness program for working, living and life.

The Premier Benefit: To Life, and a Better Life!

What is The Premier Benefit? The Premier Benefit is:

- The employee's and citizen's understanding of economics and appreciation of the free enterprise system in America.

- The person's awareness and understanding of the value of employee benefits.

- An intimate knowledge of the value, dignity, honor and integrity of work, and the contribution it makes not only to the worker, but also to the company, community and country.

- A knowledge and appreciation of what the nature of business is, including free enterprise, profits, wealth, money, scarcity, freedom, supply and demand, and our constitutional republican form of government. It is an answer to the question, what are the roles, powers, responsibilities and potential rewards to the individual?

• A measure of happiness and peace of mind that comes from knowledge, information and understanding that can be applied to personal decisions and action taken for the betterment of one's present well-being and future prospects.

Thomas Jefferson said, "If people don't have the information to wield power correctly, don't take the power from them. Give them the information." Give them The Premier Benefit!

A Better Image for Business

Public relations has been defined as doing good and getting credit for it. Note you first must do good, then get credit for it. It starts with doing the right thing right. Then good public relations and publicity build the reality into a positive image perceived by the public.

Image isn't everything in business. It is the only thing. Perception and image are much more important than fact or reality. What is the public's picture of business? Here are three examples:

First, two men lay on the beach in Florida, enjoying the fresh air and sunshine. One breaks the silence with, "What brings you to the sunny beaches of Florida?"

The second explains, "I'm in business, and mine burnt to the ground. I got a half million dollars insurance settlement and came down here to rest up to go back and rebuild my business. How about you?"

The first answered, "I too am a small businessman. My business was wiped out by a flood. I got $750,000 insurance and I'm getting rested up to go back and start all over again."

The second man queried, "Flood? How do you start a flood?"

Second, a cartoon shows a young college man, wearing a "Western State School of Business" sweatshirt, leaning against a wall talking on a payphone, saying, "You can be proud of me, Dad. Today I conned my first sucker."

Third, another cartoon shows a secretary asking her high-up boss if his friend was giving a lecture at the local business school. He replied "Yeah, weird, isn't it?"

She responded, "I wonder what he's talking on?"

The boss answered "Welcome to 'Loot and Plunder 101.'"

Business has received a bum rap from time immemorial and it is their own fault. They act as if their maligning were justified instead of "The Big Lie." Today the image of business is an even bigger problem than in the past, and in more subtle ways. When people don't know and understand, they are easily misled and malevolently influenced. Why? TV. Television? Yes, television—and our ignorance of its power, effect and lack of positive reaction to television.

Three Bogus Business Bad Boys: Are These You?

The Media Institute (307 M St., Washington, DC 20007), did a study of 200 prime time TV entertainment episodes from the 1979-80 season. They found that two of every three business people were portrayed as foolish, greedy or criminal. More than half of the characters identified as heads of big businesses were portrayed as engaging in criminal acts ranging from fraud to murder. People in small business were shown primarily as know-nothings or social climbers who serve as the butt of sit-com jokes, the study found. The study also confirmed the strong anti-business bias in TV entertainment.

The name of this study: *Crooks, Conmen and Clowns.*

Is that who we are? I personally take offense to this title, statement and implication. After being in business over four decades, I have found surprisingly little dishonor, and much care and concern—even high level dignity, love and respect in the work place. The ploys and plots portrayed on television just wouldn't work in the real world, anyway not very long for a business to reach and maintain profitability. People are too sensitive and too smart to be so mistreated and so involved in scandalous illegal dealings and operations. Always, where there are humans, there are human weaknesses and failings, but not to the extent shown on pervasive and impressive television.

There is a small minority of business, big and small, that are criminal. They are out to make a fast buck, rip off an unsuspecting public, and feel no qualms about being illegal, unethical and immoral. These businesses should be brought to justice by the law and condemned and exposed by legitimate business. As in television and the arts, there are bad actors as well as good actors, but the bad ones are a small minority. They should be dealt with justly but severely. The rest of business must continue do our best to please customers with value while earning a profit.

Business People and TV: Prime Time Crime

The same Media Institute came out with a later version with more interesting facts, emphasizing that television viewers are getting a picture seriously at odds with real life. Not only is murder the most common crime on television but it is 200 times more frequent than in real life. TV criminals are usually affluent males over age 30. In fact, most real life criminals are young and not well off. Businessmen continue to be responsible for more TV crime than any group other than professional criminals. Leonard Thebarge, president of the institute, commented that scriptwriters "send out distorted messages about the reality of crime and law enforcement in America. Over time, these subtle messages may affect the way the public thinks about the issue." Perhaps he much understates TV's mind-bending image power.

Two strange facts in these tales of deception and destruction are 1) TV is itself a business, and 2) Business pays for these death-dealing, image-damaging weekly episodes. Question: Why does business do this to itself, aiding in its own deprecation and debasement, even destruction? The answer may be shortsighted greed for money, or just plain ignorance.

Why are business people cast as villains? Dr. William H. Peterson, Lundy Chair at Campbell University, once told how those who produce our TV dramas and sit-coms have a low opinion of business and the American way of life if Ben Stein's book, *The View from Sunset Boulevard,* is right. For example, a former producer of "The Rockford Files" saw businessmen as part of "a dangerous concentration of power." A former producer of "The Mary Tyler Moore Show" gave his impression of business people, "They're all sons of bitches. They're all cannibals. I think of them as eating their own, like in the GE price-fixing scandal" (of the late 1950's).

Peterson, then professor at the University of Tennessee, elaborated[2]:

> So the dark image of business grows. Business is productive, it works, it puts bread and butter on the table better than any government could ever hope to do. But the widespread acknowledgment that American business is an efficient economic institution is not enough. No one is really satisfied with efficiency as an exclusive justification for a private enterprise system.
>
> Economics is just one leg of a three-legged stool. . . . business needs three legs to stand up to the slings and arrows of the media. If economics is the first leg, then the second is ethical: business is moral. Why? Because it practices the Golden Rule, and does so voluntarily, in contrast to the coercion of socialism. Business says let me give you what you want and you give me what I want. Let me help you so that you will help me. In other words, business is giving. You must give in order to receive in commerce. Moreover, you must give today for a return that you may or may not get tomorrow.
>
> The third leg is that business is also a *political institution.* Economics founding fathers—Adam Smith, David Ricardo, John Stuart Mill, and so on—didn't call economics economics. They called it political economy, two words, *laissez faire,* freely translated meaning *hands off.* If you don't want adverse repercussions like a failing economy, don't tamper with business by imposing tariffs, quotas, licenses, subsidies, regulations, controls, inflationary measures, onerous taxes, and so on. . . .
>
> Consumer sovereignty, in short, is economic democracy. It is also the *sine qua non* of a free society. Business and freedom are but

2. "Pathfinder," Texas A & M, Center for Education and Research in Free Enterprise, Apr/ May, 1980, p 4, Reprinted with permission

two sides of the same coin: A free people without free enterprise is a contradiction in terms. One cannot exist without the other.

The Two Problems of the TV Image of Business

In his 4/1/83 *Wall Street Journal* article "The Video Generation Gives Business Low Ratings," Benjamin Stein reinforces one problem, then highlights another. He says years of study in direct contact with students at four high schools in Los Angeles confirmed his "suspicion that youngsters do uncritically absorb business's overwhelmingly negative TV image."

He first asked their career plans, only to find fewer than 5% (2 out of 50) planned a career in business. When asked what words came to their minds about business as a career, many answered with "shaky," "cutthroat," "dishonest," "hard to survive," and "very intelligent but only looking out for themselves."

When asked what contacts they'd had with business, they were confined to the level of small shop proprietors. They had not read any articles or books about business people. Most couldn't recall a news story about business but almost all could recall episodes of weekly television business programs "Dallas," "Dynasty," or "Falcon Crest," within the preceding month.

Their comparison of images showed they thought "the businessman on TV was more dishonest, more selfish, more likely to commit crimes than his real world counterparts," and concluded nonetheless they were "highly persuaded by TV input they knew to be false," showing the extraordinary selling power of television.

An experiment in condemning business included his hypothetical cases of whether an oil company would kill Indians to get their oil, or whether an automaker would proceed to sell a car with an untraceable but lethal design flaw. Almost all students thought they would commit murder and sell the "profitable deathtrap."

Only one of the fifty knew any officers of an auto company; none knew any oil company officials. Are people in business too busy with "busy-ness" to really attend to business—the whole business, past, present and future?

Two points are clear: 1) Business' image is negative, powerful and compelling, and is received mainly from television; and 2) Students have very limited or NO CONTACT with real, live, warm, human business people. That provides two assignments:

1. Do what you can, where you are, to provide employees and others the truth about business, and about YOU. This is a personal indictment! It requires personal action, by YOU.

2. Assign yourself to regularly get out in the schools and among students, and to get them to your business. Tell them the business

story, *your* business and *your* story, so they have the benefit of a role model worth knowing and emulating: *YOU*! Again, for emphasis,

Talk to kids!

TV: The Powerful Instrument that Blurs Image and Reality

How does television have such a profound effect on our people? Because it is a "window on the world," and the image it portrays is exceedingly powerful, especially in prolonged and repeated doses.

Dr. Morris Massey[3], who has studied "generational programming" and the effects of events on people says a child's values and belief systems are programmed during the first 10 years of life, "imprinting" the first five or six years, "modeling" the next six or seven years, followed by "socialization" up to about age 20.

During these critical years television is used as an inexpensive and entertaining baby sitter. Recall the facts on youngster's media habits: The *U. S. News & World Report* 10/28/85 article "What Entertainers are Doing to Your Kids," offered some astounding statistics:

> Studies show that teenagers listen to an estimated 10,500 hours of rock music between the seventh and 12th grades alone—just 500 hours less than the total time they spend in school over 12 years. . . . Televised violence is so pervasive that the average high school student by graduation day has seen 18,000 murders in 22,000 hours of television viewing—that's twice as many hours as are spent in the classroom.

Students spend 22,000 hours in front of a TV, often without benefit of adult interpretation, explanation or conversation, in their most impressionable, formative years! That is twice the time they spend in school classrooms! Powerful stuff!

Knowing the negative business bias on TV, one understands and appreciates the tremendous impact of "mainlining" big bad business image over the years. Couple that with the educational void about business, economics and finance, and it is clear how important it is to survival and profit, that business combat these half truths and deceptions with a continuing program on the economic and business "facts of life."

Business must work hard on its public image, proved by the 1982 Gallup poll of 24 professions ranked in order for honesty, integrity and ethical standards. It showed business executives 15th, sandwiched between

3. Morris Massey, *The People Puzzle: Understanding Yourself and Others*, pp 9-22, Prentice Hall, Reston, VA: 1979

stockbrokers and senators on the high side, and building contractors and congressmen on the low side.

Another distortion of business was published in a popular advice column where a disgruntled reader complained about business profits "Wouldn't it be nice if greed, power and dishonesty (how well they together) could be relegated to obscurity? Remember when business people were satisfied with a 15 to 30 percent profit? . . ." Inflated and unrepresentative business profits were conveyed to 90 million readers.

The Business Power of ONE
Takes Seven Powerful Actions!

The evidence is in. The verdict is obvious. We are *guilty*—of being a nation of economic illiterates, and this condition is undermining our present prosperity and threatening our future survival as a free people.

Start where you are with what you have, and make it a better world. What an exciting challenge in an exciting time! Here is what YOU can do:

1. Read newspapers, listen to radio and watch television, and then REACT! Take appropriate action to assure that business reporting is objective, balanced, unbiased and fair. Don't let a thing go by. Respond. Keep the media honest. They have freedom of speech and of the press. These are great freedoms, and with every great freedom is a great responsibility.

2. Start a personal economic and political education program, along with a meaningful, dynamic and continuing employee economic awareness program in your own business. Involve your employees in the program, and encourage other businesses to do likewise. It is easier than you may think and the rewards are greater than you may realize, both for the short and long terms.

3. Organize a community public education effort that will include a one or two semester course in Free Enterprise to be added to the high school curriculum. Work to get the formal, established free enterprise education efforts (listed in two above) active in your school system. Work actively to support and encourage Junior Achievement and your (State) Council on Economic Education to work with teachers and students to teach free enterprise and economics.

4. Contact local schools and offer to tell your business story to appropriate classes. Offer as well, to bring students into your business to explain the business "facts of life" as they really are, where you are. Remember, when you talk to a teacher you talk to a thousand kids.

5. Start your own student economic and free enterprise program in your community, perhaps with your chamber of commerce or service organization. Involve other enlightened, concerned and caring business people you know in a program to explain business and economics to the community.

6. Support service organizations doing something positive and necessary to combat economic illiteracy. They are many and good, including Future Business Leaders of America (FBLA), Phi Beta Lambda (FBLA college group), Students in Free Enterprise (SIFE), Junior Achievement companies and their "Project Business," Hugh O'Brian Youth Foundation (HOBY), various state Chambers of Commerce-sponsored "Business Week," and Distributive Education Clubs of America (DECA). Each state has a (State) Council on Economic Education, and "Boys State" and "Girls State." Some cities have an "Adopt-a-School" program. Youth economic, free enterprise, business and freedom programs are sponsored by various service organizations such as Rotary, Kiwanis, Optimists, Lions, American Legion, Veterans of Foreign Wars (VFW), etc. They do a remarkable job helping supplement student perceptions and knowledge of the American economic, business and political system.

7. Find and support organizations that purposely pursue media objectivity and fairness such as Accuracy in Media (AIM) and Foundation for American Communications (FACS).

So, don't just sit there. Do something valuable and important for people, business, your community, your country and yourself.

Questions for Review

1. One TV business bad guy said, "Once you give up integrity the rest is a piece of cake." What kind of image does television project for business? Is the frequency of crime committed by business on television typical with that of real life? Why is business cast in such roles with such frequency?

2. Business is an easy target for television. Why? Are viewers able to adequately separate the story from the reality? Are viewers adversely influenced by television portrayal of business? What two conditions make it self-defeating for television to disparage business?

3. Lack of enlightenment in the American public is a serious threat to American enterprise. What kind(s) of enlightenment? What don't Americans understand or appreciate, that makes them particularly easy to so persuade? How many hours do students spend watching television compared to hours in school? With what effect?

4. What two groups are particularly vulnerable to television's unreal portrayal of business? What is an employee economic awareness program, who and how will it help? Who must do it? What two reasons are given for not doing it? Are they valid? Why?

5. An employee economic awareness program is a business' long term competitive edge. Why is it called "The Premier Benefit?" What is "The Premier Benefit?" Give five good reasons—three business, one human and one societal—why such programs are a good idea?

6. Business sits on a three-legged stool. What are the legs and why are they important? There is a love relationship in the work place between employees and their employer. What does that mean? How can it be developed to help the business be more competitive?

7. How does a nation of economic illiterates adversely affect business? Why can't American education alone do the economic education job?

8. What's In It For Me (WIIFM) is an important ingredient of a program. Describe WIIFM for business, employees, America. How can "selling the Great American System" sell your goods and services as well? How is it possible that "two-fisted selling"—selling America with your right hand while selling your products and services with your left—allows your left hand to sell more than otherwise using both hands?

9. If people don't have information to wield power, why should they be given the information, not denied the power? Who supplies the information? What is public relations and why is it important? What does image have to do with anything? Where does business fit in people's perceptions of "honesty, integrity and ethical standards?" What percent profit do people think business makes?

10. What seven powerful actions can those in business take to use basic knowledge and truth to improve the public's image of business?

Do not devote all of your energies to building your enterprises, as important as they may seem. Use what seems to be more than your share of time in making certain that your children know the full meaning of freedom.
—Ervin J. Nutter

People who practice free enterprise must become better at saying why it is the best. Like those who oppose it, they must use every opportunity to expound what they believe in. The essential message is that freedom needs free enterprise.   —Michael Ivens

If a nation expects to be ignorant and free, in a state of civilization it expects what never was and never will be. . . . No other sure foundation can be devised for the preservation of freedom and happiness. . . . Preach . . . a crusade against ignorance; establish and improve the law for educating the common people. Let our countrymen know that the people alone can protect us against these evils (of misgovernment).   —Thomas Jefferson

The six big challenges to business in the next decade—political turbulence, slow economic growth, expensive capital, weakening of industrial discipline, increasing governmental regulation, the attack on profit making—all boil down to a single problem: How to create public understanding of the American incentive system and a conviction that it is the best economic system for our society. Businessmen will have to help solve this problem, the sooner the better.   —Neil H. Jacoby, Professor UCLA

Chapter 12

POWER CHALLENGE
Be a Seeker of Truth,
and a Finder Also!

We have a tremendous advantage. We live in a country with a flood of free-flowing information protected by the First Amendment of the Bill of Rights. It is a society worthy of each person's protection to perpetuate and preserve it, and in so doing, seek and find Truth. Here, an active *Power of One* can not only exist and survive, but thrive, prosper, grow and LIVE! Truth breaks down barriers, makes you freer and more powerful.

Lower the Barriers. Let Truth In.

We humans have a natural built-in defense that protects us from what we fear, do not know or do not want to know. We have an innate mind set, a comfortable set of biases. We keep *in* the comfortable notions and the old. We keep *out* the threat of change, and the new. It is a way to survive and to cope. But these same barriers keep out what we desperately need—new knowledge, information, insights and thoughts, change and truth. Open up. Adopt an attitude of letting in fresh information, new concepts and stimulating ideas.

Aggressively seek Truth! Once gained and evaluated, it can always be rearranged or even rejected. Initially, let truth in. Your horizons expand, possibilities multiply and opportunities increase. Freedom comes from options and choices. Truth provides more possibilities, more freedom, potentially higher material abundance and life quality. Truth is the key to your future.

Wisdom Floweth from the Beak of a Bird,
a Special Bird-JLS

A book well worth reading and re-reading, is Richard Bach's *Jonathan Livingston Seagull*. This marvelous bird is the epitome of the Search for Truth: life, growth, daring and adventure. Jonathan does not listen to his contemporaries who "know" what a bird is supposed to know. Jonathan listens to that powerful "wee small voice within" to explore, find, test and extend limits.

Jonathan exudes life, living and loving freedom. A Council Flock member chastised him saying, "Life is the unknown and the unknowable except that we are put into this world to eat, to stay alive as long as we possibly can.[1]" Jonathan explores whether a truly responsible gull adopts a higher calling in life:

> For a thousand years we have scrabbled after fish heads. But now we have a reason to live, to learn, to discover, to be free!
> ... there's a reason for life! We can lift ourselves out of ignorance. We can find ourselves creatures of excellence and intelligence and skill.

The symbol of the seagull is best expressed by Judy Granger on the record album jacket cover[2]:

> Jonathan Livingston Seagull is a soaring symbol of man's unquenchable yearning to go as far as the reaches of his daring and imagination will take him; to discover the limits of himself and in doing so discover himself. Jonathan is not just a bird: he is a teacher, prophet, Messiah, if you will. He dares outfly, outreach the flock, he dares death and disgrace for the sake of something so powerful in him that it must be given expression.

We have it within ourselves to "find ourselves creatures of excellence and intelligence and skill." We can "go as far as the reaches of our daring and imaginations will take us." We can "dare death and disgrace for the sake of something so powerful in us that it must be given expression." That expression is the song of our lives in making the difference we can and must make to help mold a better society, world and future. In short, we can live and learn

---

1. From *Jonathan Livingston Seagull* by Richard Bach, pp 39, 30, Copyright © 1970 by Richard Bach and Leslie Parrish-Bach. Reprinted with permission of Macmillan Publishing Company

2. Granger, Judy, *Jonathan Livingston Seagull,* Pickwick International, Inc., 1974

and discover. We can pursue and find TRUTH, and know better ourselves and our inestimable limits.

John 8:32 makes the point:

And ye shall know the truth and the truth shall make you free.

The pursuit of TRUTH and knowledge can open wide doors that serve us and our community well for our whole lives. They can fuel our ambitions and spark our dreams. Henry David Thoreau tells how dreams mold success:

If one advances confidently in the direction of his dreams, and endeavors to live the life which he has imagined, he will meet with a success unexpected in common hours.

With a new dream we create a new destiny:

Destiny is not a matter of chance, it's a matter of choice. It's not a thing to be waited, it's a thing to be achieved.
                                        —William Jennings Bryan

Drop the Barriers, Creatures of Habit

We are creatures of habit. We have carefully developed our ability to unconsciously screen out new knowledge and information. This precludes thought and analysis, concealing or not revealing truth. We do so because we are bombarded with messages and advertisements.

We tune out the "noise" to prevent "information overload." It is a natural mental defense mechanism to help us cope. Part is because we have our private thoughts and concerns. Part is because we don't know what to do if we allow ourselves to "turn on," so we "turn off" and "tune out."

We can turn back on and tune back in. Break the "tune out" habit. Creatures of habit? Yes we are. Professional speaker Dr. James Melton[3] offers three exercises to illustrate how we have become creatures of habit. Once we are so aware, we can lift our mental barriers to let in new light, knowledge and information, better leading to TRUTH. We become true Seekers of TRUTH.

1. Cross your arms. Fold them in front of you as you do when standing— becoming tired of waiting, you cross your arms in resignation to an interminable wait. Note carefully which arm is outward and "on top." Consciously and slowly cross your arms the opposite way, with the other arm on top. How does that feel? Quite different, I imagine.

2. Fold your hands. Intertwine your fingers of one hand in-between those of the other hand. Note which thumb is on top. Now change them all to place

---

3. Dr. James Melton, PO Box 2030, Palm Springs, CA 92263

the other thumb on top. That is probably a different handclasp than you are used to. It feels different because it is something you have no reason to consciously think about.

We are creatures of habit and this is one habit that doesn't make all that much difference. But that is why it is so powerful, to illustrate what happens when we become aware that we are comfortable creatures of habit. We stop thinking, experiencing and growing, being and becoming. Now your mind is opening up, better to pursue and perceive TRUTH.

Doing this exercise with an audience, Dr. Melton commented casually, "If your right thumb is on top, you're sexy. If your left thumb is on top you think you're sexy." One man replied, "Can we do it again?"

3. Clap. Clap your hands and notice their relative positions and which one impacts the other. Reverse the procedure. Whose hands are those? It not only feels different. It even sounds different. (Now, thank yourself for giving you a "sitting ovation!")

You are a creature of habit. It seems a lot easier to do things the same old way. "If you do things the way you've always done them, you'll get what you've always got." Is that what you want? To become a Seeker of Truth, you must open your mind. Free your natural innate curiosity. Drop the barriers and be open to TRUTH. You will get it and grow by it.

TRUTH: the Elusive, the Essential, the Challenging, the Powerful

Truth is elusive. Seeking truth is essential. Finding truth is challenging. Seeking and finding truth is powerful. The search for truth is a lifelong and continuing pursuit. It takes a special mind set of curiosity, open-mindedness, courage and an attitude of trust. It is an impartial, impersonal, receptive and faithful search for what is known, what is still to be known, what is missing and how it all fits together.

One must be inquisitive, anxious to learn, stretching beyond, to know, *really know*! The search for truth is as fun as it is frustrating, as rewarding as it is provoking. Armed with truth, and more importantly, being a continuing seeker of truth, you are building a new arsenal not just for survival, but prosperity, in a lifelong pursuit of personal growth. Your quest is to become an ever more powerful *Power of ONE*. Go for it, truth-seeker!

You think more critically and accurately. You are more interested and more interesting. Your efforts, activities and relationships are more productive and profitable.

Thinking and *thought* in themselves can be threatening. Recognize the threat, confront it, conquer it. Bertrand Russell said it well:

> Men fear thought as they fear nothing else on earth—more than ruin, more even than death. Thought . . . is merciless to privileged,

established institutions, and comfortable habits; the well-tried wisdom of the age. Thought looks into the pit of hell and is not afraid.

An early caution—to recognize that others have not so embarked on the journey to knowledge, information, understanding and wisdom. They are not as far along as you. Be as patient with them as you are impatient with yourself. Be as understanding with them as you are often misunderstood. Be as communicative and respectful to them as you want others to be with you in your quest for truth.

How do you help others to learn, know and understand? Part is not to give them your opinion or conclusion. Help them develop their own. Make them aware. Impart knowledge. Provide information. In other words, offer your *evidence* and sources, especially those outside yourself that are credible, acceptable and recognizable. They will likely reach the same conclusions as you, but instead of absorbing or mouthing your opinion, they will have formed their own, and defend it vigorously.

Don't give answers. Isn't it more effective to ask questions? Aren't we programmed to answer questions? If we're not given answers don't we find our own? Don't the questions remain so we answer them over and over with new information? Doesn't this help our minds open up, being offered questions rather than answers? It works doesn't it?

Bring people along the same pathway to enlightenment in their quest for truth. Travel together and make the trip even better. The joy is the journey.

The INVOLVEMENT PROCESS Really Works!

Your reading and applying the concepts of *TOTAL Power of One in America* are important steps towards learning the incredible impact one person, you, can have on the world around you. But with more knowledge, information and subsequent TRUTH, comes even more personal power. Knowledge is power. Information is power. The more you know and understand, the faster and greater an impact you have. When TRUTH strikes, power strikes with it!

How does one become interested in what appears to be unrelated, irrelevant, perhaps just plain dull to others? Change can be threatening, so is often unconsciously avoided. Change is necessary not only to survive, but to prosper, especially in a fast-changing world. Fortunately, there is an almost magical formula not only to accept but seek change. Called the INVOLVEMENT PROCESS, it first helps you change by getting you involved with issues and events. It works equally well with others.

The involvement process involves the "Six Be's": *Be aware, be interested, be informed, be concerned, be involved, be active.* This sequence, in order, can change the world, your world and that of others. It is a natural, common, human thing. It gets you directly and intimately involved in change.

The involvement process works whether one seeks to find a job, purchase a car or computer, pursue a college education or to woo and win a mate.

Whatever sizable change you undergo, you become more aware, interested, informed, concerned, involved and active. Realize there is something to be learned, develop an interest in learning more, and become informed.

What happens next is magic. With acquired knowledge and new information, you don't dispassionately file it away for future retrieval. You analyze it, process it, react to it. Become emotional. Demand things be made better. Make the right decision. Take the necessary action. Becoming aware, interested and informed becomes a Great Awakening. That naturally develops concern, which turns into becoming involved and active.

An Example: Seeking Truth about the Constitution

Where does one begin to study, for example, to learn the basic truths of the Constitution of the United States? Where can it lead? How can you go beyond what you already know to new information that really contributes to your knowledge? How does all this help to enhance your life experience, impact, enjoyment and achievement? Such questions are difficult to answer, but legitimate.

The main answers are the goals of education and seeking truth:

1) Acquire additional knowledge.
2) Continually update information.
3) Develop a lifelong love-of-learning.

Learn not only facts and figures but times and places, people and experience, history and philosophy. Develop a thirst for knowledge, a hunger for information, a craving for wisdom.

Turn knowledge and information into understanding. Put understanding with experience, intuition and vision to gain wisdom. Combined together you make decisions and take actions that enhance and enrich your life.

The Constitution: Getting Back to Basics

My personal love affair with the Constitution of the United States came through some strange turns of events. I had begun receiving a weekly newspaper, *Human Events* (One Massachusetts Avenue, N.W., Washington, D. C. 20001). Therein was an advertisement for a "Freedom Kit" that was to better explain (author Irwin Schiff used the term "expose") the United States federal income tax system. I ordered the kit of five cassette tapes and documentation of a federal income tax seminar Schiff originated.

The information therein went far beyond anything to which I had been exposed. I was predictably suspicious. Lecturer and author Schiff explained how the federal government had been going outside the letter and intent of the Constitution, then explained the presumed voluntary, rather than mandatory, nature of federal income taxes. He also referred to various court cases to back up his allegations and conclusions.

Schiff referred to "lawful money" and the "Fifth Amendment" of the Constitution, and related them to tax law, procedures and audits. He touted individual rights in the Declaration of Independence, specific functions and responsibilities of the federal government as defined by the U.S. Constitution, and personal freedoms guaranteed by the Bill of Rights.

What did all this have to do with the income tax?

Schiff referred to *The Biggest Con*[4], his readable, fascinating and anger-provoking book. One man to whom I loaned it told me he could only read it for 10 minutes at a time. I asked him, "Why, was it that boring?" He answered, "Heck no! It just makes me so darned mad I can't read any more in one sitting!"

Schiff later published two scholarly, highly documented books with comprehensive interpretations of income tax law, *How Anyone Can Stop Paying Income Taxes* and *The Great Income Tax Hoax*[5]. These refer specifically to the Internal Revenue code. Schiff magically transformed a distant, dull reference into a vital, exciting, timely and living document. He applied the Constitution directly to the economic and political events of our times, and more personally, its first 10 amendments, the Bill of Rights, to the application and collection of federal income taxes. This kicked off many other applications, exposing new, related and interesting issues.

These stimulating ideas and "different" thoughts shook my sensitivities and got me interested in the United States Constitution, a document I had either forgotten about, or ignored. I could no longer ignore it because it came alive. It hit me "where I live" and will probably shake your sensibilities in the same way.

Gold and Silver, Silent Prayer, Roger Sherman and Those Monumental 17 Words

Another "happenstance" turned out to be F. Tupper Saussy's book *Miracle on Main Street*[6]. Saussy says, "Let's have 60 seconds of silent prayer for the good deed of Roger Sherman." Sherman authored "those monumental 17 words" which became Article I Section 10:

No state shall make any Thing but gold and silver coin a Tender in Payment of Debts.

4. Irwin Schiff *The Biggest Con: How the Government is Fleecing* You, Freedom Books, 544 East Sahara Ave., Las Vegas, NV 89104: 1977, $10 pp

5. Same publisher information, $15, $20, respectively. (Incidentally, Schiff, a courageous and principled seeker of truth, has spent time in jail for his communications and actions.)

6. Saussy, F. Tupper, *The Miracle on Main Street,* pp 31, 33, 74, Spencer Judd, Sewanee, TN: 1980

Saussy explores the constitutionally-defined functions of government and how they apply to our currency. This further piqued my curiosity about money, and the relevance and modern day application of our precious and phenomenal more than two-centuries-old Constitution.

Because of our Independence Day holiday, we know the Declaration of Independence was signed July 4, 1776, but fewer know the U.S. Constitution was approved and adopted by Congress over 11 years later, on September 17, 1787. The Bill of Rights was approved by the states four years later, effective December 15, 1791. We were a country without a constitution for over a decade, without formally-defined individual rights over 15 years! The rest, as they say, is history. But there is so much more. Each American can make it all a proud part of one's citizenship and heritage.

The Search for Truth, A Seeker of Truth

I attended an all day "Miracle of America" seminar in 1980, following my newfound fascination with the Constitution. I had to "stretch" to get myself to go to it, because it was so different, so foreign to what I had experienced before. Overcoming my reluctance I found more truth. The audience reaction went beyond interest to intense fascination and grim seriousness. They perceived a need for a profoundly basic understanding of that unfamiliar basic document. The seminar was conducted by the National Center for Constitutional Studies (NCCS), based at HC 61, Box 1056, Malta, ID 83342-9704, 1/800/388-4512.

The NCCS founder is Dr. W. Cleon Skousen. In the FBI for 16 years, Dr. Skousen served 4 years as Chief of Police in Salt Lake City, Utah, and 13 years as a university professor. He searched all over America to find a definitive and enlightening book about the United States Constitution and the founding fathers.

As Dr. Skousen tells it, one day, in asking another about locating such a book, he was told "If there is to be such a book, you will have to write it." So he did, creating *The Miracle of America,* a 12-cassette tape series and study guide[7].

Like every other *Power of ONE,* Dr. Skousen was a Seeker of Truth in search of truth. In this case, truth had to be researched and published. That is how *The Miracle of America* came about.

With renewed vision and purpose, Dr. Skousen extensively researched his subject and accumulated enough constitutional knowledge to produce the most comprehensive book[8] available today about the history, meaning and

---

7. W. Cleon Skousen, *Miracle of America,* NCCS: 1981, National Center for Constitutional Studies, HC 61, Box 1056, Malta, ID 83342-9704, 1/800/388-9702, "Seminar"—7 VHS tapes, study guide, $145; or 12 audiotapes and Study guide, $66 pp

8. Skousen, Dr. Cleon, *The Making of America: The Substance and Meaning of the Constitution,* NCCS, $30, Study Guide, $8 pp

interpretation of the Constitution, entitled *The Making of America*. In it he describes the Constitution:

> ... the Founding Fathers' inspired vision of the possibilities for human achievement in a new age that produced this remarkable charter of liberty. It created an entirely new political and economic climate that made it possible for Americans to organize themselves into a free nation and attain the three great desires of all humanity: freedom, prosperity, and peace.

I highly recommend this book, with its attendant study guide. You will learn the history, culture and principles of the Constitution, the trials and tribulations of the Founders. You will learn the earlier "ruler's law" which gave birth to a new idea of freedom, "people's law" and what Dr. Skousen calls "The Success Formula of the Founders."

The Making of America explores the background and philosophy of the founding fathers and how they sought to put together the ideal government. It was to be small yet powerful enough to protect but not stifle or trample the freedoms of the individual, but large enough to "provide for the common defense and the general welfare." This "success formula" reveals the history, heritage and patriotism of America's beginnings.

The book covers the making of the Constitution, its background and history, and the individual characters each of the Founding Fathers. Skousen tells the need for a miracle and "the Miracle of Philadelphia." He relates their bold "New System of Political Science" with "Prosperity Economics."

Dr. Skousen discusses in detail 286 phrases from the Constitution. He explores and explains the Legislative, Executive, and Judicial Branches and other provisions, then the Bill of Rights and remaining Amendments. The book's concluding chapter is "Striving for a Higher Level of Civilization." It is a mighty adventure in history, and all relevant to what is happening right here, right now!

His follow on volume was *The Majesty of God's Law*[9] in 1996. He tells how the American Founding Fathers "recognized that the Constitution was the indispensable foundation for such an inspired system of prosperity, justice and peace." He said they knew that eventually the Constitution would become unraveled and would have to be restored "in all its pristine power by some future generation."

A Different Source of Truth: An Atheist

Truth—difficult and elusive—comes from surprising sources. While driving to work I listened to a radio talk show with featured guest, famed atheist, Madalyn Murray O'Hare. At work, I phoned the station to ask, "Mrs. O'Hare, I've heard so many times the phrase 'separation of church and

9. Skousen, Dr. W. Cleon, *The Majesty of God's Law*, NCCS, $27

state.' I have read the Constitution a number of times, but am unable to locate that phrase. Could you tell me where to find it?"

She replied, "You couldn't find that phrase in the Constitution because it's not there. It was articulated by Thomas Jefferson in a letter to the Danbury Baptists in 1802." She then gave me the phone number of the local Atheist Society to obtain a copy of the quote. I called, listened to a two-minute recording berating the Congress for setting aside 1983 as "The Year of the Bible," then left a note of what I wanted and my mailing address, on the impersonal answering machine. I soon had a copy of the document quoted here from Appendix C of the book, *The Separation of Church and Government* by Frank Swancara, as Jefferson's reply to the Danbury Baptists:

> Believing with you that religion is a matter which lies solely between man and his God, that he owes account to none other for his faith or his worship, that the legislative powers of government reach actions only, and not opinions, I contemplate with sovereign reverence that act of the whole American people which declared that their legislature should 'make no law respecting an establishment of religion, or prohibiting the free exercise thereof,' thus building a wall of separation between church and State. Adhering to this expression of the supreme will of the nation in behalf of the rights of conscience, I shall see with sincere satisfaction the progress of those sentiments which tend to restore to man all his natural rights, convinced he has no natural right in opposition to his social duties.
>
> I reciprocate your kind prayers for the protection and blessing of the common Father and Creator of man, and tender you for yourselves and your religious association, assurances of my high respect and esteem.

So the truth is, that "separation of church and state" is not the law of the land. What is? The First Amendment to the Constitution, in the Bill of Rights:

Congress shall make no law respecting an establishment of religion, or prohibiting the free exercise thereof. . . .

Truth, Like Gold, Is Where You Find It

Once you are a seeker of truth, you learn quickly you never know where you will find it, or where it will come from. The preceding story of finding religious and constitutional truth from Atheists makes the case.

In a more humorous way, here is the story of the lost keys. An obviously inebriated gentleman on his hands and knees was searching desperately under a streetlight when a policeman came along. "Have you lost something?" he asked.

"Yes, I've lost my keys, officer."
"Where do you think you lost them? Maybe I can help find them."
"I think I lost them up there in the middle of the block,"
"Then why are you looking for them here at the corner?"
"Because the light's better!"

We must seek truth where it is, not where it is convenient, where we would like it to be or where we think it should be. We cannot expect to find it "where the light's better." There has been so much made of being "comfortable" in the past decade. We hear, "Are you comfortable with this, or does that make you uncomfortable?" Have you ever been really "comfortable" about anything in your whole life? What is this "comfortable" stuff? Truth is often very uncomfortable!

There were those who called President Truman "Give 'em hell Harry." Harry Truman said, "I never give them hell. I just tell the truth and they think it's hell." If hearing the truth is hell, then learning the truth must be heaven!

Back to Basics: Knowledge and Information

Get the knowledge. Update it. If you can acquire the basic knowledge about a subject, then update it with current information, you have an unbeatable combination for making good decisions and taking propitious action. The questions before us are where to get basic knowledge concerning economics and freedom, and where and how to get a continuing stream of current information.

Knowledge is gained from conversation, reading, study and analysis. It can be acquired formally in the classroom, or informally at the library, the local bookstore and at home. The point is to gather resource materials from which to glean the necessary knowledge, "starter books," to get you on your way in your quest for truth.

Truth is a Many-Splendored Thing

Truth has an elusive character. And truth changes. With new knowledge and information what is true now may turn out not to be true later. An example is the denunciation of Galileo by the Roman Catholic church[10].

In 1633, at the age of 69, the noted Italian scientist was judged by the Inquisition to have violated a church edict against espousing the controversial Copernican view that the sun, not the earth, was at the center of the universe. For the last nine years of his life, Galileo was under house arrest.

As early as the 13th century, the likes of Thomas Aquinas warned against too literal an interpretation of the Bible. Having invented the telescope, Galileo, literally, got a different view of the moons of Jupiter, phases of Venus, and mountains of Earth's moon. His new truths, couched in arrogance

---

10. Golden, Frederic, "Rehabilitating Galileo's Image," *Time,* 3/12/84, p 72

and flamboyance, made more difficult the acceptance of his new findings and new truth.

Ptolemy had formulated the theory that the earth was the center of the universe. That was the "truth of the day." It coincided with the precepts and interpretations of the Bible. With new evidence, Galileo espoused the views of Copernicus who said the Sun was the center of the universe[10], the "new version of truth." Today's latest and greatest version of truth shows that not only is the sun not the center of the universe. There is no "center of the universe!" Everything is relative to everything else and it is all in motion. We are a mere speck in the Milky Way Galaxy, an insignificant part of billions of known galaxies, in an unknown inky black expanse of space, in an infinitely large universe with no known boundaries.

Truth is truth, but with new knowledge it is subject to change! The outgrowth of Galileo's newly discovered truths was that the Bible may not be interpreted as literally scientific, speaking accurately but metaphorically about creation and movement of the stars. Truth is an elusive, moving target.

Mine for Meaning. Search for Significance. Find Fulfillment.

A search for truth is much like working a mine. You process tons of overburden or waste material, irrelevant thoughts, words and phrases. Occasionally you discover the "Mother Lode" and rarely, but surely find a "gold nugget." That makes the search exciting. There is a virtual guarantee you will unearth new nuggets of wisdom and in looking for them, grow and become. Mining for meaning can be satisfying, even profitable.

> If the public really want to get at the truth, they can read a variety of publications whose owners and writers have different points of view and in so doing they will be able to decide where they themselves stand.
>
> —Eleanor Roosevelt

The key point is a "variety of publications." That doesn't mean only the printed word. It also includes our most powerful electronic medium, television, its sound equivalent, radio, and the new vast expanse of exploring the Internet. It also includes books, magazines, newspapers, newsletters, and reports from acknowledged "think tanks" that do issues reporting and public policy analysis. Seek also information not of your point of view to broaden your thinking.

Books are great for receiving thoroughly documented knowledge, well-thought-out and analyzed ideas, recording of historical background and precedent. Books explain and focus attention on the fine points of broad subjects to force scrutiny and intense exposure of sometimes-complex concepts. As such, they lend themselves well to formal academic courses taught in schools and institutions of higher learning.

Magazines provide more current information with a continuing exposition and analysis in light of new information. A variety of topics, issues and trends are what give perspective and insight to emerging issues and trends. The point Eleanor Roosevelt makes is that in order to develop perspectives, viewpoints and opinions, many sources of information, especially those that do not agree with your views, are necessary in order to find "The Truth." With emerging knowledge we can only guess what truth will turn out to be, if we ever know it. But the necessary variety of information makes essential the commitment of time, attention and diversity of information resources.

What to do? Start simple. Read a newspaper a day, a magazine a week, a book every month. Eventually build up to where you read two or three newspapers a day, including your local paper and several others, some national as well. Read three or more magazines, bulletins and newsletters a week. Read two or three books a month.

A Seeker of Truth Secret: How to Read a Newspaper

A newspaper is an excellent place to conduct your Search of Truth. It is a common and reliable publication. It has much variety, and by its nature, being put out quickly, presents much information on an evolving basis.

Columnist and television personality Andy Rooney, in his "Newspapers let us do it our way" *(Rocky Mountain News, 5/20/86)* put it:

> Considering how much time I've spent reading newspapers in my life, it's amazing how little thought I've given to how a newspaper should be read. There's nothing I do so much of that I do so badly . . . . I wish I were more disciplined about the way I read the newspaper. . . . For all the information we have available, most of us are stupid and uninformed. And it isn't our newspaper's fault, it's our own. It might be a good idea if schools had courses in how to read a newspaper, although I don't know who is qualified to teach it. Not me.

For you, Seeker of Truth, here is *How to Read a Newspaper.*

How to Read a Newspaper for Fun and Profit

> Along with responsible newspapers we must have responsible readers. No matter how conscientiously the publisher and his associates perform their work, they can do only half the job. Readers must do the rest. —Arthur Hays Sulzberger

The American newspaper is a daily miracle. Four, forty, even hundreds of pages of valuable information and advertising are purchased for a dollar or less. You will find human triumph and tragedy, natural calamity and disaster, humor, advice, entertainment and expert opinion. New ideas, challenges and opportunities daily find their way into print. How do you get your money's worth?

BE SELFISH. Know how to read your newspaper. Invest reading time wisely.

BE ACTIVE. When passive you turn pages almost unconsciously, wave at or talk to others nearby, or think about something else. Go beyond mentally *active* to mentally *reactive*, where you think "Oh yeah?" or "Prove it." Sometimes get physically active. Respond with a letter, visit or phone call.

SET YOUR GOAL. What do you seek? Look for it. Find it.

GET A BROAD OVERVIEW. Survey each page for stories of value to you, or of interest to your friends. For example, perhaps you are not a "sports nut," but your friends are. Glance at several pages in the sports section. (For whatever reason, that is where auto parts and lucrative sales jobs are advertised.)

CHECK THE MAGIC OF ADVERTISING. When you don't want or need something, it is seemingly not there. When you do need something, almost magically, it is advertised and you find it. The money you save "newspaper shopping" will likely pay for the paper, with a bonus of extra time and reduced travel expense.

WHAT TO LOOK FOR? Sensitize or program your mental "information filter" to find your special interest topics.

UP WITH PEOPLE! Find stories about your friends or acquaintances. Seek stories that laud their accomplishments. Use the opportunity to send a short note and an appropriate clipping to your friend or a "new friend," (someone you don't know but admire). Reach out. Draw a bigger circle and include yourself in it.

CONSIDER YOUR PERSONAL TOPICAL INTERESTS. Look for articles that enrich your life, buying, selling and investing, education, books, politics, economics, personalities, hobbies, business and other human interest. Seek the unusual, the element of surprise, that "something special" that makes life special.

READ BEYOND HEADLINES. They attract your attention, but don't always accurately convey the story. The more important points are first, followed by supporting information. The further you read, the more detail you get.

FIVE MAIN TOPICAL AREAS are hard news, human interest, business, sports and weather. Hard news includes current events—local, state, regional, national and international. Also included are syndicated columnists, opinion leaders and storytellers. Human interest includes hobbies, advice, entertainment and comics.

THE FRONT SECTION has the "hard news" already prioritized for you. The front page and those following are the most important current news. "Hard news" seeks to avoid bias, report facts and a balance of differing viewpoints and observations. Here is the reporter's "who, what, where, when, why, how and how much" of the news.

COMMENTARY AND EDITORIAL SECTIONS convey individual and usually expert opinion about the more complicated issues. The newspaper provides its own opinion of the news in its editorial section. Facts may be used, but they are selected to support the chosen viewpoint. Here, you can read, analyze, then formulate your own considered opinion.

LETTERS TO THE EDITOR are of special importance. These are concerned citizens who share their opinions. You can be one of them. Responsible, responsive public leaders, business policy makers and others are sensitive to such published public opinion. For each letter printed, they know there are hundreds, perhaps thousands of others with the same viewpoint.

BUSINESS, SPORTS and WEATHER round out your broader appreciation of today's world.

Each page is a potential adventure. Read it, experience it, use it. Challenge yourself. What does this mean to me? How can I benefit from it? How can I profit by it?

Clip and save special articles in personal information files for future reference. Do your research in advance. Learn about new products and services. Shop sales for your purchases. *Make your newspaper work for you,* to make your life better and save you money!

YOU WILL BE ABLE TO MAKE A DIFFERENCE as you become more aware, interested, informed, concerned, involved and active. If you are AWARE of the issues and events, you'll be more INTERESTED (and more interesting). As you become more INFORMED about the details, you develop genuine CONCERN. Then you become INVOLVED and TAKE ACTION. That is how ordinary people perform extra-ordinary deeds to improve the world in which we live.

The "daily miracle," the newspaper, is a valuable tool to make life more meaningful. Learning how to read it is worth your time and effort.

Read your newspaper for fun and profit.

> The basis of our government being the opinion of the people, the very first object should be to keep that right; and were it left to me to decide whether we should have a government without newspapers, or newspapers without a government, I should not hesitate a moment to prefer the latter. But I should mean that every man should receive those papers, and be capable of reading them.—Thomas Jefferson

The Mother Lode: Getting Started in Economics

People frequently ask how to get started in economics. The first part of the answer is that they have already started. We are all economists. We all confront scarcity. We must all help to create wealth—to work, to produce— in order to obtain or exchange wealth. We learn everyday of our life how to do that, and hopefully to do it better and make it more personally rewarding for ourselves. We are already on our way.

We also make choices and most are economic choices. Should I keep this job or look for a better one? Do I need a computer to do the work in my new job? Should I buy one good suit or two cheap suits? Shall I go to college or get a job now? Making good decisions means having basic knowledge and current information available.

One way to get more knowledge faster, is to take a formal economics course, or to find a textbook, read it and study it. But there are many sources that can be found at a local or college library, magazine and newspaper store, book store and Internet. Seek and find organizations, "think tanks" and newsletters that study, analyze and report public policy issues. Go after all of these and more, find them, read them and relish in the joy that you are seeking and finding truth, growing and going in life. You are becoming an even more powerful *Power of ONE*. Use your power wisely.

Go for the Gold! Capture the Truth!

Go for the gold! Get the truth, as much of the truth as you can, and have an exciting, fulfilling and profitable life, all your life.

Questions for Review

1. Lower the barriers. Aggressively seek truth. Discuss. Where do you find truth?

2. Are we, like Jonathan Livingston Seagull, "put into this world to eat, to stay alive as long as we possibly can." Why? What else is there? What kind of creatures can we find ourselves to be?

3. How is seeking, finding and using truth related to personal freedom? How can we "creatures of habit" go beyond ourselves to find truth?

4. Why won't people simply understand the truth you tell them and accept it? How is it possible to impart truth? Why is it important to "present the evidence" and take the risk to let others form their own opinions based on their own experience and the evidence? Why is it better to ask questions than give answers?

5. What is the involvement process and how does it work? Why does it work?

6. List the three goals of education and seeking truth. What "love" and what "thirst" are important and why? Why is the U.S. Constitution a good place to start, in seeking truth? How can something so old be interesting? Why can't one find the phrase "separation of church and state" in the Constitution?

7. If truth is truth how can it change? Give an example. How can the search for truth be compared to mining for precious metals?

8. What kind of reading habits are fruitful in the search for truth? What should be read daily, weekly, monthly, continually, occasionally? Why is it important to read so much?

9. Reading a newspaper is a life investment. Why? How can it save time and money? Enrich life? List nine important points in an effective, systematic approach to "read a newspaper for fun and profit." What are the five main topical areas in a newspaper and why should you read them all? What is different about reading a paper passively, actively, reactively? What can be done with valuable newspaper information? What are the "Six Be's" How do they relate to reading a newspaper?

10. How does one "get started in economics?" Freedom, money, information, politics and statistics? What five (5) nonfiction books in order of importance will you resolve to read within the next 3 or 4 months in your search for truth? What reference books do you need? What organizations are you going to learn more about? What will you do with all this truth?

The people have a right to the truth as they have a right to life, liberty and the pursuit of happiness.   —Frank Norris

It is a common heresy and its graves are to be found all over the earth. It is the heresy that says you can kill an idea by killing a man, defeat a principle by defeating a person, bury truth by burying its vehicle. Man may burn his brother at the stake, but he cannot reduce truth to ashes; he may murder his fellow man with a shot in the back, but he does not murder justice; he may slay armies of men, but as it is written, 'truth beareth off the victory.'   —Adlai Stevenson

Truth is the greatest of all national possessions. A state, a people, a system which suppresses the truth or fears to publish it, deserves to collapse.   —Kurt Eisner

Truth is such a rare thing, it is delightful to tell it.   —Emily Dickinson

There is nothing so powerful as the truth, and nothing so strange.
—Daniel Webster

Winston Churchill's Commentary on Man: Man will occasionally stumble over the truth, but most of the time he will pick himself up and continue on.

Headline on a Vera Cruz, Mexico editorial, echoing nostalgia for the boom that gave Mexico 8 percent annual growth from 1978 to 1981: "Enough of Reality. We Want Promises."

Interview with Andy Rooney, Columnist and Television Personality: *Question.* What bugs you the most? *Answer.* Oh, the American public's or mankind's great preference for not knowing the truth. *Q.* Preference for it? *A.* They have a preference for not knowing the truth, yes. They prefer to fool themselves constantly. I think there is no doubt it's sort of a lovable characteristic too, considering I hate it as much as I do. I think that the average person feels that if all the facts . . . about everything are known by everyone, and that his or her future depends on what action he takes in light of all the intelligence he has gathered . . . it is much better, in his view, if his future depends upon luck or praying or hoping or legend or rumor or something like that.

Knowledge will forever govern ignorance and a people who mean to be their own governors must arm themselves with the power which knowledge gives.   —James Madison

Thomas Jefferson, on the University of Virginia: This institution will be based on the illimitable freedom of the mind. For here we are not afraid to follow the truth wherever it may lead, nor to tolerate error so long as reason is free to combat it.

Chapter 13

IT'S A WHOLE NEW BALL GAME
and We're Not Even On First Base!

We are in a battle of ideas. Ideas have consequences. If we are using the right ideas, the consequences are rewards and prosperity. If we are using the wrong ideas, or if we are being used by the wrong ideas, the consequences are punishment and austerity. You are either a victor or a victim. If you know what is going on you are a victor. You win. If you are unaware or uninformed you are a victim. You lose. Whether or not you are informed is up to you. You are in control.

We all play The Big Game called *LIFE*. We are in it whether we know it or not; whether we like it or not. It is the game of survival. There are no time outs, no instant replays. The game goes on, and whether you win or lose depends on what you know and what you do. We liken this big game to the Great American Pastime, Baseball.

Where are we as a society?

We are in a whole new ball game and we are not even on first base. We are way out in left field, wandering around, as shown in Figure No 15.

We may have even bigger troubles than we think, because we *think* we know. That is why a mind open to truth is so important.

> Beware of false knowledge; it is more dangerous than ignorance.
> —George Bernard Shaw

Out in left field? The term "left" is not a play on words. Its connotation in a political spectrum context is leaning more towards big and powerful

WAY OUT IN LEFT FIELD IN THE BALLGAME

Figure No. 15

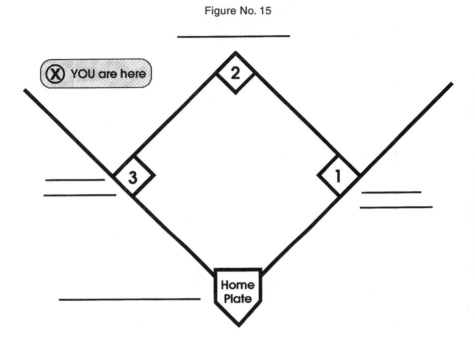

government systems, away from powerful, sovereign, freedom loving, self-governing people. "To the left," we consequently get diminished personal freedom, authority, responsibility, and political liberty. What are these abstract concepts of governmental systems and the political spectrum, both quite important to the quality of our lives and the security of our future?

We do not carefully study these concepts in American public education; thus cannot fathom their importance to our society or their impacts on our lives. They extend to the future of our children and the destiny of an Idea of Freedom called America. The more we know and understand these concepts, the more we can positively impact our society and political system, each person knowledgeable, informed, concerned, active and effective.

To be consummate world changers, we must better understand the world in which we live. We are all part of The Big Team. How can we be better players in the game of life? What do we need to know to get up to bat, to make The Big Difference?

Let us explore, get into and *win* The Big Game! It is the game of life, expressed in ideas. Ideas have consequences. What ideas must we know, understand, and be able to articulate to others, to assure better consequences for us now, and for our progeny in the future?

Take Me to the Ball Game. Take Me to the Crowd

There is a ball game. There is no crowd. The ball game is the game of enlightenment, in economic awareness, knowledge and understanding, and in political acuity. The object of the game is not only personal survival but survival of freedom, with responsibility, through personal involvement and action.

The ball game, likened to baseball, requires of us the same as baseball players. You win by making The Home Run. To make The Home Run, you must touch each base, in order. Running to first base requires you make a hit, or at least get a "walk." To get that chance, you must pick up your bat and step up to the plate, see Figure No. 16. Are you ready to face the pitcher's mound? Batter up!

Why is there no crowd? People are denied knowledge about The Big Game, what it is, and that it even exists. The Big Game overshadows the many small games we play to survive on a personal and individual level. Why does The Big Game concern the survival of the American free enterprise system and the freedoms on which it is based?

There exists what might have been called a "contrived ignorance" about economics, politics and political systems. When I first heard the term "contrived ignorance," I thought it to be overstated. If true, it would mean someone or something contrived it, and having decided to do so, did so. Is the situation understated? Does there exist a "contrived ignorance" about economics, politics and political systems?

We will go back a few years and see what has been happening.

The One Penny Concept Makes One Person a Millionaire, One Government a Trillionaire

During childhood, finding out there are over 100 million people in America, we mused, "If I got just one penny from each person, I am a millionaire." Just a little bit from many is a lot.

Multiply that small thought and number not by pennies, but by thousands of dollars, in fact by $6,895. That is the *average* of the 1999 federal revenues (taxes) $1,827,454,000,000, paid by *each* of America's then-273.1 million citizens and taxpayers[1], not including state and local taxes.

Yet government spent slightly less, $1,703.04 billion, a "surplus" of $124.4 billion, fortunately increasing from a peak deficit of $290 billion in 1992, the largest in history! The deficit is how much more the government spends than it collects in taxes. Money for that deficit portion

---

1. *Economic Report of the President,* February 2000, pp. 245, 400

STEPPING UP TO THE PLATE

Figure No. 16

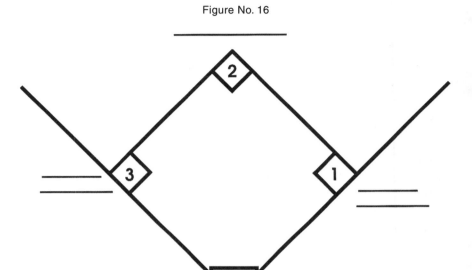

of federal government spending had to be borrowed from the future—from our children, each of whom on average, will pay over $10,000 additional taxes during their lifetimes, just to "service" interest on that one-year 1992 deficit, according to the National Taxpayers Union.

Ironically, this result was a trust violated, a law broken. Here's why. Back in 1985 the deficit was $212 billion and climbing. The deterioration in fiscal responsibility and control was so bad that in late 1985, Congress passed the Gramm-Rudman-Hollings Balanced Budget Act , a law that mandated the 1986 deficit be no more than $172 billion. That act, and Congress' resolve to honor it were so good that while the Senate voted for a balanced budget amendment to the Constitution, the House of Representatives voted against it—no need. How did it all come out? Not good. Instead of the 1986 deficit being $40 billion *lower* than the previous year, it was $8 billion *HIGHER,* and $48 billion higher than required by their new law! But there is more.

If you scrutinize the "surplus or deficit" data, you find the true federal funds deficit for 1986 was much higher, $283 billion. The difference includes off-budget receipts and interfund transactions, plus the $45.1 billion surplus contributed by the trust funds (Social Security, highways,

A SINGLE TO FIRST AND ECONOMIC AWARENESS

Figure No. 17

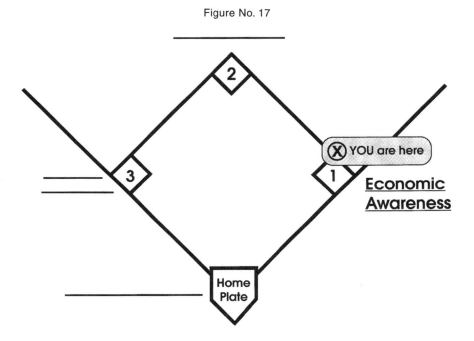

airports, etc.). Combining these budgets allows a massive, irresponsible budget deficit to appear as a somewhat less massive, irresponsible deficit. And where before the 1980's, a deficit of double-digit billions was cause for alarm, the string of *triple-digit billion dollar deficits* went on for fifteen years into the nineties with little more than a yawn from the Congress.

For the record, the Bretton Woods Agreements Act (Public Law 95-435) approved by Congress October 10, 1978, states, "Beginning with fiscal year 1981, the total budget outlays of the Federal Government shall not exceed its receipts." This section was amended in 1980 (P. L. 96-389) to read, "The Congress reaffirms commitment that beginning with Fiscal Year 1981, the total budget outlays of the federal government shall not exceed its receipts."

Since this was the law and Congress did not uphold it, were members of the Congress lawbreakers? Are they exempt from lawmaking and laws that bind taxpayers and citizens?

Can a "contrived ignorance" of a country's population help increase such a transfer of wealth from individuals to a government power structure? This situation brings up some national life-or-death questions.

Do we need this much government? Can we afford this much government and this continued growth of government? What are the limits to the size of government in a freedom-based economy? Do we really accomplish our goals when we spend these large and growing sums of money for and by government? What are the limits to growth, both of the economy and the government?

We now have the data and expertise to know, with certainty, at what level of government is more spending better, the same, or worse for our economy and future.

Is this massive transfer of wealth from the people to the central governing authority consistent with the design of America, and the Constitutional "Success Formula" of the Founding Fathers? What would the peoples' wishes be after their trip "around the bases?" Let's go for *The Home Run* and see.

Batter Up, and a Solid Hit to First Base. Safe! For the Moment.

First Base is Economic Awareness. We have touched and passed first base (See Figure No. 17), with our understanding that the purpose of society is to create wealth by people working hard together, and smart—saving and investing, creating tools as capital, and producing more and better with less—productivity. Our standard-of-living increases and our quality-of-life improves. We fulfill our wants and needs by producing a surplus and exchanging freely through competitive markets.

Producing more goods and services from fewer resources we are better able to help those truly in need from both the private (enterprise) and public (government) sectors. As a more productive society, we have more to share with potentially more caring, sharing and compassion.

We have set out to accomplish economic awareness, but also interest in, knowledge of, and information about economics. We have achieved economic awareness. We are passed first base, heading for second.

Second Base: New Vistas of Knowledge in Government, Politics, Freedom

Second Base is Political Awareness. It is an understanding of government and politics, and an appreciation of how freedom with responsibility helps it all to work better. Are politics better left to others? "Politics is dirty and I don't want to get involved," we hear people say. Perhaps politics is dirty because you are not in it, to make it clean and keep it right. Like it or not, we are all involved in politics. We don't have a choice. Politics is as positive as it is negative. There is no organization or group of people in which politics doesn't play a major part in human

ROUNDING SECOND, GAINING POLITICAL AWARENESS

Figure No. 18

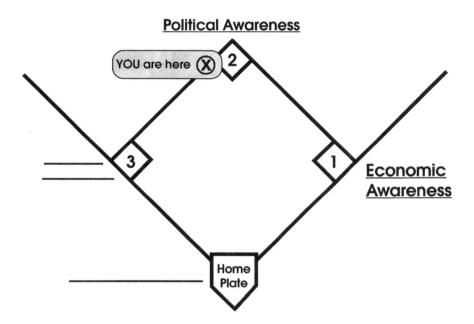

activities and achievement. Like love, politics makes the world go around. Knowledgeable, dedicated, concerned people make politics positive, especially if they are self-transcendent, that is, going above and beyond their immediate self-interests.

Politics is only a small part of the political awareness of second base (See Figure No 18). There is also an awareness and understanding of government systems and the political spectrum, of which there is "right" and "left" and "center." There is the Constitution and Bill of Rights, and their relationship to the Declaration of Independence. There is also the comparison of these specific American attributes and history to other forms of government and political systems. Until we know these subjects and understand their interrelationships, we are at a disadvantage, a great handicap in the game of life.

We want to know and understand politics, governments and political systems, and their important relationships to freedom and prosperity, tyranny and poverty. To third base!

Third Base: Political Involvement and Activity

Third Base is Political Involvement and Activity. Here is where you exert your power to make a positive difference (See Figure No. 19). When you understand the necessity, pervasiveness, and power of politics, you get really *involved* and *active!* You push for positive change! Here's why.

George Santayana said, "Those who cannot remember the past are condemned to repeat it."

History is important. Where have we been? Where are we now? Where can we go?

From 1986 to 1999, while inflation grew 52% and population grew 13.5% to 273.2 million[2], total 65.5%, government grew more in those thirteen years. Federal government spending increased 72% to $1,703 billion ($6,234 per-person), with revenues (taxes) of $1,827.5 billion ($6,690 per-person) and a $124.5 billion net deficit[3]. The national debt swelled to $5,606 billion ($20,522 per-capita), with interest of $353 billion ($1,294 each, or $2,648 for each of 133 million workers). That is $108 a month average paid by each citizen, $221 per-month for each of America's then-133 million workers.

These are enormous amounts of money, a lot of government power, much debt, much interest payment on the debt and a lot of government control. Is it too much?

Thomas Jefferson said it was immoral for one generation to pass on the results of its extravagance in the form of debts to the next generation. He wrote:

> . . . we shall all consider ourselves unauthorized to saddle posterity with our debts, and morally bound to pay them ourselves; and consequently within what may be deemed the period of a generation, or the life (expectancy) of the majority.

"Compared to what?" you might ask and should. Good question. We don't have to go very far back to when federal government spending exceeded $100 billion a year, specifically $107 billion in 1962. Seventeen years later federal spending passed half a trillion dollars in 1979, $503 billion. Nine years later federal spending passed a trillion dollars, $1,064 billion in 1988; $1,516 billion in 1995 in seven years, and to $1,703 billion in 1999.

To complete the picture, estimated total government revenues (taxes) for 1999 are $2,783.1 billion. For 273.1 million people that's a $10,190 per citizen cost of government. That's nuts.

2. Ibid, pp 345, 373, 397

3. *Budget of the United States Government, Fiscal Year 2001, Historical Tables,* pp 62, 111

ROUNDING THIRD BASE, POLITICAL INVOLVEMENT

Figure No. 19

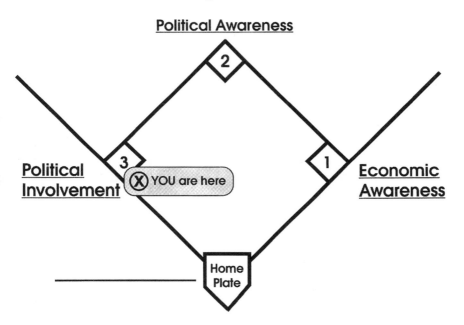

Recall "What is a billion?" A billion seconds is 31.7 years. A billion minutes is 1,902 years, almost back to the time of Christ. A billion hours is over 114,000 years, 100,000 years before the dawn of recorded human history. During 1986, a billion dollars was spent by the United States government in only 8 hours and 21 minutes; in 1999, 5 hours, 8 minutes. Should we look *Beyond The Obvious* (BTO) to analyze what is really happening?

Can the American people, with limited economic awareness and political understanding really look BTO to determine if government has grown too big, too fast? If they knew a larger picture, might they want otherwise? Do the people truly understand the impact of increasing taxes and government size and power?

> The trouble with people isn't ignorance. It's what they know that's not so.   —Dr. Milton Friedman

With a broader basic understanding of how the world works, can we act more intelligently and get better results? Can we better understand time frames and events and be more sensitive to judge whether what we are doing works to achieve our goals? In The Big Baseball Game are we ready to "Shoot for Home?"

The Home Run: Into "Ism's" and Ideologies

The Home Run is an understanding of "ism's" and ideologies (See Figure No. 20). We have accomplished economic and political awareness and gotten politically involved. Our perspective has widened from a provincial view to a worldview of history, trends, issues and events. We better know how things fit together and how they work. With our understanding of economics and politics, government and freedom, can we work together to assure a better, more prosperous world for our children and theirs? Can we leave a better world than we got? We begin "where we live," where we think and believe.

We like to think ourselves to be independent thinkers. To a certain extent we are. But ideas influence our every thought and move. Beliefs of unknown origin set our course and steer our direction.

John Maynard Keynes, the guru of depression economics put it all into context[4]:

> The ideas of economists and political philosophers, both when they are right and when they are wrong, are more powerful than is commonly understood. Indeed, the world is ruled by little else. Practical men, who believe themselves to be quite exempt from any intellectual influences, are usually the slaves of some defunct economist. Madmen in authority, who hear voices in the air, are distilling their frenzy from some academic scribbler of a few years back. I am sure that the power of vested interests is vastly exaggerated compared with the gradual encroachment of ideas. But sooner or later, it is ideas, not vested interests, which are dangerous for good or evil.

"The gradual encroachment of ideas" is a critical concept. The world runs on ideas. How you value freedom or peace, security or political liberty determines your worldview of how things are or ought to be. Whether you seek society's solutions in government, in law, in individual or group action; at the local, state, national or international levels, all influence not just your view but your inaction, actions and reactions.

Is it not important to know the difference between a constitutional republic, which America was designed to be, and a democracy, which it is becoming? Is it important to know the difference between political "left" and "right;" liberal and conservative; capitalism and communism; anarchy and totalitarianism; oligarchy and monarchy; oppression and

4. Keynes, John Maynard, *The General Theory of Employment, Interest and Money,* Harcourt, Brace & Co., 1936

HOME RUN OF "ISM'S" AND IDEOLOGIES

Figure No. 20

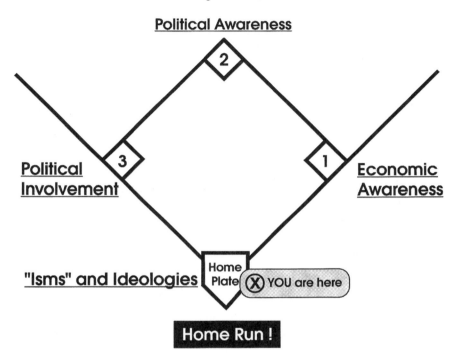

tyranny; socialism, fascism and Naziism; monopoly and competitive systems?

What are the roles and restraints of freedom in the various systems? Who owns property, exercises control over property, controls people? Are we better off to know, understand and support the system that best serves the most people with the least restraints on their personal lives, consistent with law and order? Shouldn't we strive for equality, and what kind? Which are better: Equal rights, equal opportunities and equality under the law, or equal incomes, properties, outcomes and results? Which work?

Samuel Adams said the founders did everything possible to make the ideas of socialism and communism *unconstitutional*. Dr. Cleon Skousen records Adam's thoughts:

> The Utopian schemes of leveling (redistribution of the wealth) and a community of goods (central ownership of the means of production and distribution), are as visionary and impractical as

those which vest all property in the Crown. (These ideas) are arbitrary, despotic, and, in our government, unconstitutional.

The Founding Fathers knew the damage of ignorance and the blessings of liberty, of awareness and education. Skousen[5] tells how Thomas Jefferson hammered home the necessity for an educated electorate:

If a nation expects to be ignorant and free, in a state of civilization, it expects what never was and never will be. . . . No other sure foundation can be devised for the preservation of freedom and happiness. . . . Preach . . . a crusade against ignorance; establish and improve the law for educating the common people. Let our countrymen know that the people alone can protect us against these evils (of misgovernment).

Benjamin Franklin stressed the point not only of education but of the common good ("the public weal"):

. . . I think with you, that nothing is of more importance for the public weal, than to form and train up youth in wisdom and virtue. Wise and good men are, in my opinion, the strength of the state; more so than riches or arms. . . . I think also, that general virtue is more probably to be expected and obtained from the education of youth, than from the exhortations of adult persons; bad habits and vices of the mind being, like diseases cured (in adults). I think, moreover, that talents for the education of youth are the gift of God; and that he on whom they are bestowed, whenever a way is opened for the use of them, is as strongly called as if he heard a voice from heaven. . . .

Early Americans touted the "Public Virtue" as a very special quality of human maturity in character and service, as interpreted by historian Gordon S. Wood:

In a Republic, however, each man must somehow be persuaded to submerge his personal wants into the greater good of the whole. This willingness of the individual to sacrifice his private interest for the good of the community—such as patriotism or love of country—the eighteenth century termed public virtue. . . . The eighteenth century mind was thoroughly convinced that a popularly based government "cannot be supported without virtue."

Our search for truth in a knowledge of history, and especially about the interrelationships between economics, politics and freedom, continues

5. Quotes, respectively, from Skousen, W. Cleon, *The Five Thousand Year Leap: The 28 Great Ideas That Are Changing the World,* pp 30, 31, 55, 50; National Center for Constitutional Studies: 1981, HC 61, Box 1056, Malta, ID 83342-9704, 1/800/388-4512. Used with permission

for life. Things change and world events affect the present and shape the future. We look for more depth in ideologies and Ism's, what political and economic systems exist, how they have worked, what is good and what is bad about them.

The *Power of ONE* is a lifelong search for truth. We find new ideas. We expand our horizons by regular, effective learning, and a continuing search for new knowledge and information. We aim for a meaningful trip around the bases and head for The Home Run in the Big Game of Life.

We have rounded first base in *Economic Awareness*.

We streak towards second base for *Political Awareness*.

We anticipate the third base of *Political Involvement and Activity*.

Then we relish our trip around the bases to home plate in our *Home Run* of learning, studying and mastering *Ism's and Ideologies*.

You are well on your way, world-changer!

Play ball!

Questions for Review

1. What is the Big Game we are in called? What determines whether we win or lose? How can we describe that game as a baseball game? Where are we in it? Why is that location on the ball diamond more than just a position on a field? Why is it really a state of mind, knowledge or awareness? Why is it very serious if this is in fact a "contrived ignorance?"

2. How big is federal government in terms of 1999 spending, taxation, debt and interest on the debt? What is it called when government spends more than it takes in?

3. What is first base and why are we already past it, headed for second? Why is this awareness the heart and soul of a preliminary basic understanding of what life is all about, at least on a material level?

4. What is second base? Why does this awareness clarify and reinforce first base? How are they related? Why are politics not better left to others? Why is the statement "Politics is dirty," not a good reason for not getting involved? Why is it a cop-out and how can one person make a positive difference?

5. What is third base? Why should citizens become more involved with and in their government? What is the per-person cost of federal government only updated to 1999? What is total government cost if state-and-local government cost half again more? What are various ways of expressing those costs? What is a billion? How large is the national debt, where does it come from and how fast

does it grow? How much is annual interest on the debt? Per person? Per worker?

6. What is The Home Run? Are we really "independent thinkers?" What is the "gradual encroachment of ideas" and how does it relate to our country, government and state of being?

7. Why is it important to know the difference between a democracy and a republic? A constitutional republic? Which works best? Why? What is America designed to be? What is it becoming?

8. Name three "ism's" and three non-"ism's." Why might it be important how we define who owns property and who controls property? What does equality seek to make equal? What cannot be made equal? What do Sam Adams' "Utopian schemes of leveling" and "a community of goods" stand for in modern terms?

9. How are the "damage of ignorance" and the "blessings of liberty" related to "awareness and education?" How did Thomas Jefferson state the difference? Who was most important to "form and train" in "wisdom and virtue." What was Benjamin Franklin's "public weal?"

10. Why must the bases be run *in order* for the Big Win? How does this analogy serve as a guide to where we are, and a compass pointing to where we are going?

The greatest dangers to liberty lurk in insidious encroachment by men of zeal, well-meaning, but without understanding.
—Justice Louis D. Brandeis

Men become free only as they achieve self-government. I take it that a man governs himself to the degree that he acts upon his own judgment. Freedom thus presupposes first that people are capable of judging for themselves, and second, that they are permitted to do so.
—Everett Dean Martin

If you make people think they're thinking, they'll love you; but if you really make them think, they'll hate you.   —Don Marquis

It is the tragedy of the world that no one knows what he doesn't know—and the less a man knows, the more sure he is that he knows everything.   —Joyce Cary

Human knowledge had become unmanageably vast; . . . Perspective was lost. 'Facts' replaced understanding; and knowledge, split into a thousand isolated fragments, no longer generated wisdom. —Will Durant

Chapter 14

THE POLITICAL SPECTRUM

Power of Political Understanding in America!

Second Base, The Political Spectrum:
What's Left? What's Right? What's Wrong?

We have heard the terms "liberal left" this and "right wing" that. They confuse more than enlighten, yet they seem not a part of any formal education we have experienced before. What is left? What's right? What's wrong? What do these terms really mean?

A Power Dare Chapter: Do the Tough Stuff

This is a *"Power Dare* Chapter," *Power of ONE.* Read and heed your "Power Deed Creed!"

Freedom to Work, to Earn, to Keep, to Be.
Freedom to LIVE

It is helpful to describe the dimensions of freedom in economic terms: If you make $100 and keep $100, you are 100 percent free. If you make $100 and keep $0 (that's zero dollars) because something or someone takes it away from you, you are 100% slave. We are somewhere in between. But where?

The five-word headline leaped off the page at me: "Tax Bite Approaches 60 Percent." I have defended, even convinced others taxes amount to 30, 40, even 50 percent. But 60 percent? Not even a 50-50 deal, why would people work to keep less than half their pay?

The author, economist Dale Sommer at *Industry Week* magazine explained in his October 3, 1983 article that total wages and salaries were over 59% percent of money spent on all government (taxes). That included 39 percent to the federal government and 20 percent to state and local governments, leaving workers only 41 percent of their earnings.

Economically speaking, then, we are 41% free and 59% slave!

Freedom to LIVE!

I had also described human freedom for one person as

FREEDOM: Free to *be,* to *do,* to *choose,* to *dare,* to *become*

In other words, free to *exist, Be, LIVE!*

This dimension of personal freedom might be called social freedom or civil liberty—human choice and action that are not easily measured in units such as dollars. These choices include: what you do for a living, who you date or marry, how many children you have. Also whether you go to church or get a college education and what kind, where you shop, whether you wear a seatbelt or not, what books you read, foods you eat, how you invest.

The more measurable dimension of freedom is what portion of the fruits of your labors do you get to keep. This relates solely to the relative size and power of government, in its respective political system. In America we have heard that system variously called:

Capitalism	Free Enterprise System
Americanism	Private Enterprise System
Freedomism	Personal Incentive System
Free Market System	American Enterprise System

Which is the correct way to measure freedom—economically, through personal rights, or something else?

An Unusual Newspaper Discourse
About an Unusual Word: "Fascism."

A newspaper repartee developed about some confusing political spectrum concepts. An assistant professor started it all with a published letter to the editor saying the word "fascist" was a term we need to better understand and use. He said "Fascism means governmental action of a right-wing type. . . ." He described fascist and semi-fascist governments in the world "including Nazi Germany, Mussolini's Italy, Salazar's Portugal, and Franco's Spain," adding that investigative reporting at all levels stood "between however much democracy we have and fascist acts."

Fascism? Right Wing? Democracy? What are these words?

Far Left, Far Right, Far Out!

Two weeks later two letters were published in response. A woman was fascinated by the professor's new definition of fascism, writing, "Back in the '50's I was taught that fascism was a *left-wing* ideology,' citing her *Random House* dictionary definition, "a governmental system led by a dictator having complete power... regimenting all industry, commerce, etc. ...." She continued, "The political spectrum is not circular, but goes from the far right of *no* government (anarchy) through increasing government to the far left of *total* government.... I have wondered why many young people and the media have a tendency to refer erroneously to fascism and Naziism as right-wing, as well as using the mutually exclusive (or oxymoron) phrase 'right-wing dictator'," concluding, "Evidently they are being taught this in college and have never checked it for themselves."

"Political spectrum." What is that?

The other letter, mine, was titled "Keep terms straight." I referred to *Webster's Collegiate Dictionary* definition of fascism, "a political philosophy, movement or regime that exalts nation and race above the individual and that stands for a centralized autocratic government headed by a dictatorial leader, severe economic and social regimentation, and forcible suppression of opposition," in other words, a totalitarian government. The differences are in *control* and *ownership* of capital—accumulated goods devoted to the production of other goods, or the means of production.

I continued, "Far right is anarchy and chaos. Far left is totalitarianism or authoritarianism, including communism, socialism, Naziism (Germany's 'National Socialism') and fascism. In all four of these political systems, capital is *controlled* by the state. In communism, the state owns all capital; in socialism, it owns most capital; in Naziism, some capital; and in fascism, the government owns no capital. That puts fascism on the far left of the political spectrum."

I concluded, "America is a Constitutional Republic, not a democracy. The important and profound distinction is that a republic is ruled by law with diffused power; a democracy by majority with concentrated power. A Republic is center right, pulled left, while a democracy is center left, gravitating leftward to more centralized and concentrated government control. Go farther left and you are 'fascist.' America began as a Republic. Let's keep it a Republic."

Two More Letters Add to the Diversity of Opinion

Six days later two more letters were published. One man said there are no absolute answers to what is left and right, that these labels originated in the French Revolution: "On the right of the speaker in the National Assembly sat the Monarchists. Most of them supported the concept of a noble class of people, superior to the common people. The 'right wingers' favored a strong pervasive government. It was the folks called 'Liberal' or 'Republican' who were the original 'left-wingers' of history."

He said, "If we applied that spectrum to the Nazi Party of 1933-45, it would be difficult to label it 'left' or 'right.' The title 'Third Reich' was chosen to link Nazi rule to two predecessor Reichs considered more virile. In this sense it seems more like the 'right wing' of the French Revolution. Of course, the Nazis were advocating change, a 'revolution' of a kind, and we usually use 'left wing' for those who advocate revolution."

The letter cited historian Crane Brinton, who wrote in his 1950 book *Ideas and Men* about "totalitarian movements of the right as well as those of the left." Brinton used this historic Nazi belief in a strong authoritarian government as his base line of 'right wing.' Others, perhaps more simplistically, see the anti-communist party line of Hitler as evidence that Nazis were at least further 'right' than the Communists.

The widespread void of meaning regarding political spectrum terms leaves them up in the air, subject to making them say what an author means, rather than any precise meaning of their own. Thus the major problem becomes misunderstanding, misinterpretation and misapplication of these terms and concepts.

The other letter seconded the confusion criticizing the "twisted definitions attempting to show that anarchy is a right-wing philosophy, with fascism belonging to the far left," maintaining these contentions to be false. "A conservative is 'disposed to preserve existing institutions,' which obviously cannot include an anarchist, defined as 'a person who excites revolt against any established rule, law or custom.' Liberalism is 'a political or social philosophy advocating the freedom of the individual,' a label that hardly applies to a government that exterminated 12 million individuals."

"Dictatorships can initially be either left or right-wing, but with the passage of time must become conservative to survive. The first priority of a dictator is to remain in power; the second priority, to institutionalize and maintain the conditions established by the regime—goals that fall on the right-wing side of the political spectrum."

Last Letter: A Fascism Named Gangsterism

The last published response a week later said "The term 'National Socialistic Party' was coined to make the German people feel there was an alternative to communism. At that time, 1919 to 1933, there was a real danger of Germany going communist because of the terrible inflation and economic depression following World War I."

The author said the quickest ticket to a concentration camp after 1934 was to let the Gestapo even think you had leftist leanings. "Communism is a system where the state owns everything; private enterprise and ownership do not exist. People are reduced to numbers. Fortunately, no nation has achieved true communism. God forbid they ever do."

"Fascism is directly opposite. It is based on private enterprise and ownership, but with an all-powerful central government that makes all the decisions: Who lives, who dies; who advances, who is reduced to slavery, etc. Fascism is best described as gangsterism—but not left wing," concluding "In our genuine concern over the spread of left-wing totalitarianism, and our struggle against it, we must never forget that the far right came the closest to enslaving the world."

Ambiguity Confuses Thought and Communication

Consider the importance of these concepts and the implications of their meanings—"concentration camps," "all-powerful central government," "enslaving the world," "left-wing totalitarianism," "leftist leanings," and "reduced to slavery." What kind of talk is that in America, "land of the free and the home of the brave"?

Consider the ambiguity that results from these unfamiliar terms and concepts. How important are they to fashion our thinking about past world civilizations, their victories and defeats, successes and failures and their relationship to our society? Perhaps a great responsibility and advantage for you is to gain a basic political spectrum knowledge and understanding, then work towards a better society with new insight and resolve.

Information about the political spectrum is not widely available. In our search for truth, remember "Truth, like gold, is where you find it." It is found in unfamiliar, strange and sometimes fascinating places. We find indeed, the political spectrum to be at once evasive, essential, stimulating, even "life-stuff" itself!

The Spectrum of Socialism: Are We All Socialists Now?

I first saw the "spectrum of socialism" in a small 1971 pass-along paperback, *None Dare Call It Conspiracy*[1]. A 1985 update and revision by co-author Larry Abraham[2] early on explains the fallacious continuum of political systems. (See Figure No. 21).

Abraham discusses the perversion of terms used in describing the political spectrum. "On the far Left of the political spectrum we find Communism, which is admittedly dictatorial. But we are also told that equally to be feared is the opposite of the far Left, i.e. the far Right, which is labeled Fascism. We are constantly told that we should all try

---

1. Gary Allen, with Larry Abraham, *None Dare Call It Conspiracy*, Concord Press, Rossmoor, CA: 1971

2. Abraham, Larry, *Call It Conspiracy*, pp 30, 31, Double A Publications: 1985, PO Box 609, Wauna, WA 98395, Used with permission

to stay in the middle of the road, which is termed democracy, but . . . means Fabian (or creeping) socialism. (The fact that the middle of the road has been moving inexorably leftward for forty years is ignored.)"

THE POLITICAL SPECTRUM OF SOCIALISM

Figure No. 21

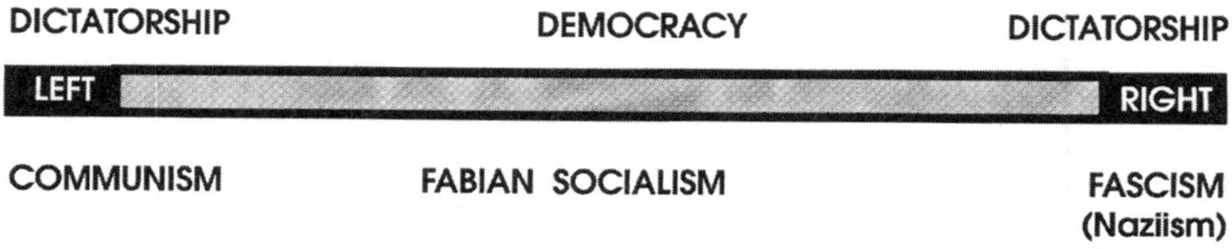

DICTATORSHIP	DEMOCRACY	DICTATORSHIP
LEFT		RIGHT
COMMUNISM	FABIAN SOCIALISM	FASCISM (Naziism)

"Here is an excellent example of the use of false alternatives," says Abraham. "We are given the choice between Communism *(international* socialism) on one end of the spectrum, Naziism *(national* socialism) on the other end, or Fabian socialism in the middle. The whole spectrum is socialist! This is absurd." He questions, "Where would you put an anarchist on this spectrum? Where do you put a person who believes in a Constitutional Republic and the free enterprise system? He is not represented here, yet this spectrum is used for political definitions by probably ninety percent of the people of the nation."

He says there is an accurate political spectrum. "Communism is, by definition, total government. If you have total government it makes little difference whether you call it Communism, Fascism, Socialism, Caesarism, or Pharaohism. It's all pretty much the same from the standpoint of the people who must live and suffer under it. If total government (by any of its pseudonyms) stands on the far Left, then by logic the far Right should represent anarchy, or no government." (See Figure No. 22).

"Our Founding Fathers revolted against the near-total government of the English Monarchy. But they knew that having no government at all would lead to chaos. So they set up a Constitutional Republic with very limited government. They knew that men prospered in freedom. Although the free enterprise system is not mentioned specifically in the Constitution, it is the only one which can exist under a Constitutional Republic."

POLITICAL SPECTRUM OF ALL-GOVERNMENT TO NONE

Figure No. 22

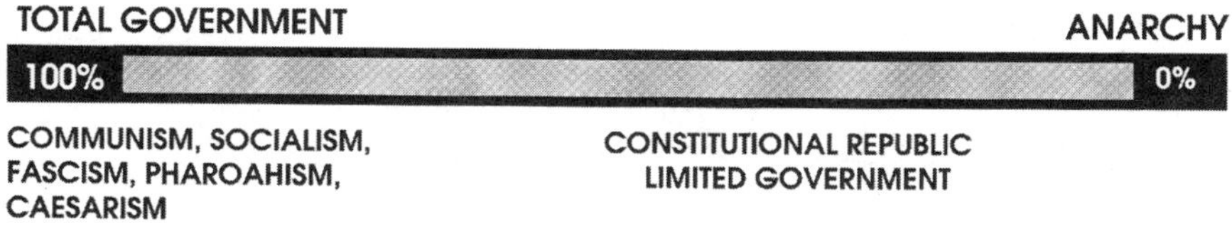

TOTAL GOVERNMENT　　　　　　　　　　　　　　　　ANARCHY

100%		0%

COMMUNISM, SOCIALISM,　　　　CONSTITUTIONAL REPUBLIC
FASCISM, PHAROAHISM,　　　　　LIMITED GOVERNMENT
CAESARISM

Abraham concludes:

All collectivist systems require power in government which the Constitution did not grant. Our Founding Fathers had no intention of allowing the government to become an instrument to steal the fruit of one man's labor and give it to another who had not earned it. Our government was to be one of severely limited powers. Thomas Jefferson said: 'In questions of power let no more be heard of confidence in man, but bind him down from mischief by the chains of the Constitution.' Jefferson knew that if the government were not enslaved, people soon would be. His view was that government governs best which governs least. . . . Times change, technology changes, but principles are eternal. Primarily, government was to provide for national defense and to establish a court system.

A similar description of the socialist political spectrum laid the groundwork in a breakthrough concept, "The Nolan Chart." Marshall Fritz[3] says, "People are trying to make sense of libertarians on the scale they know best, the standard left-right political spectrum. There may be an advantage for politicians, academics, and journalists to use such a simplistic model, but it confuses the libertarian perspective. If there is no room for an idea on their map, it gets ignored." (See Figure No. 23)

POLITICAL SPECTRUM:
EUROPEAN SOCIALIST LEFT & RIGHT

Figure No. 23

Mitterrand　　　　　　　　　　　　　Thatcher

Left		Right

3. Fritz, Marshall, "The Nolan Chart: A True Political Spectrum," Advocates for Self-Government, PO Box 5039, Fresno, CA 93755, from the Spring, 1986 issue, "Libertarian Party News." Used with permission

Fritz uses France's President Francois Mitterrand for the more socialist left, and England's Prime Minister Margaret Thatcher for the less socialist, more conservative right side of the political scale. The whole scale remains socialist.

The Fabian Socialists: Wolves in Sheeps Clothing

The Fabian Socialists are worth exploring in the political spectrum world of ideas. In *The Miracle of America* Cleon Skousen discusses various political systems studied by the Founders to fashion their "Success Formula." He gives "the classical definition of Socialism which describes the ultimate objectives of this system regardless of what name it may assume: 'Government ownership or control of all the means of production (farms, factories, mines and natural resources), and all of the means of distribution (transportation, communications and the instruments of commerce).' It virtually takes over the entire economic system[4]."

He explains, *"Democratic Socialism* seeks to achieve its goals by peaceful means . . . by appealing to individual economic groups" such as farmers, industrial workers and business owners and operators. That is contrasted to Communism, "international revolutionary Socialism," which uses the tactics of "terrorism, violence, subversion and propaganda against other nations as though it were at war with them."

Skousen explores *Fabian Socialism* as a "deliberately deceptive method of getting Socialist control over the people and their property while pretending to be merely helping the unfortunate." The approach is to use every crisis or emergency to greatly increase taxes, emphasize the people should look more to government to solve the problems of the poor, sick, unemployed, elderly, under-privileged, etc., with a continuing transfer of power from the people to the government, called "gradualism." Fabian Socialism was named for a Roman general named Fabius, famous for his ability to win wars by whittling away the forces of his enemies a little at a time. Interestingly, the Fabian Society's cynical sense of humor was shown in their coat-of-arms emblem, a wolf in sheep's clothing!

The "How Much Government" Spectrum

Skousen intensively analyzes and explains his amount-of-government spectrum. The Founders, he says, began with the basics, the individual, and the core unit of society, the family. The whole search was to design a system of government that was not and could not become oppressive, bucking a sordid past of political structures, systems and outcomes. The

4. Cleon Skousen, *The Miracle of America*, p 4, National Center of Constitutional Studies: 1981, HC61, Box 1056, Malta, ID 83342-9704, 1/800/388-9702. Used with permission

legal power, or sovereign authority to govern, rests with the people. All laws and selection of leaders was by the approval of the majority.

POLITICAL SPECTRUM: TYRANNY TO ANARCHY

Figure No. 24

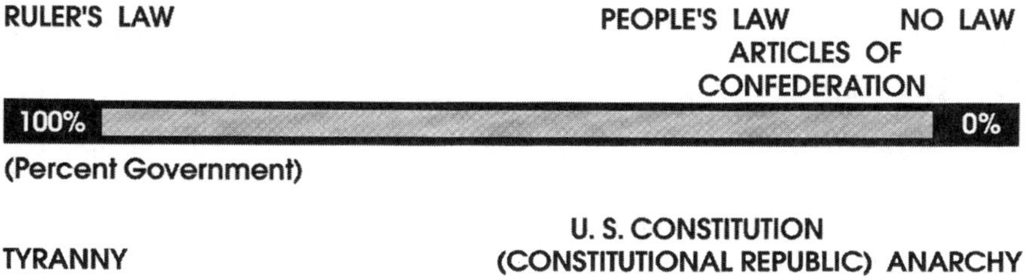

RULER'S LAW	PEOPLE'S LAW NO LAW
	ARTICLES OF
	CONFEDERATION

| 100% | | 0% |

(Percent Government)

| | U. S. CONSTITUTION |
| TYRANNY | (CONSTITUTIONAL REPUBLIC) ANARCHY |

Government officials were looked upon as servants of the people. The thrust of government was from the people upward, not from the government downward. People's basic rights were considered endowed by the Creator and therefore, inalienable; that is, rights cannot be abused or taken away without coming under the judgment of God.

On Skousen's political spectrum (See Figure No. 24) zero government to the far right ("No Law") was anarchy, with 100% government, tyranny, to the far left ("Ruler's Law"). Toward the center was what he called "People's Law," which was gleaned from past societies and philosophies, including those from the Bible and of Moses as described in Exodus. People's law relies heavily on individual and personal responsibility—self-government.

Skousen explained that the Articles of Confederation didn't work because they were deficient in government; that is, they were too far right and too close to anarchy. They provided for no executive branch, no judiciary, no taxing powers and no enforcement powers.

On the position of "People's Law" Skousen symbolized a three-headed eagle (three branches of government, separation of powers) saying "The American eagle finally came to rest in the balanced center of the spectrum."

The Socialist Spectrum: Where from and When?

More revealing insights on the political spectrum come from J. H. Ingraham's discussion[5] regarding the impossibility of a "right wing despot." Ingraham quoted President Reagan—"We are opposed to both

5. Ingraham, J. H., "Right Wing Despot: Impossible!" *The New American*, Appleton, WI 54913, 7/14/86, p 49. Used with permission

left-wing and right-wing dictatorships," FBI Director William Webster—
"This neo-Nazi network, based on racial and religious hatred, is a menace
of the extreme," and feminist author Shirley Radl—"The American New
Right shares with the Nazi party the goal of overthrowing our democratic
government." Ingraham described all three quotes as "an absurd
conception—the widely accepted idea that authoritarianism and Naziism
and Fascism occupy a position in the political spectrum on the right."

He traced these illogical ideas to Frankfurt Institute social scientists
Theodor W. Adorno and Max Horkheimer, who arrived as refugees from
Hitler's Germany to start the New School of Social Research in New
York City. To these political left leaning academics, it seemed reasonable
to classify Naziism as the hated opponent on the Right—their opposite.
They deduced "since Naziism and conservatism were both on the right,
the thought processes and attitudes of each must be similar. And anyone
holding conservative views about patriotism, religion, defense, politics,
or culture could, by nature of these views, be accurately adjudged racist
and anti-semitic," said Ingraham.

These views were published in *The Authoritarian Personality*[6], seeking
to prove authoritarianism as "purely a 'rightist' characteristic with which
everyone on the right is afflicted to some degree. How did they determine
this degree? Simple—they provided a 'Fascist Scale' that individuals
could be measured on as well as on the basis of certain beliefs, held
guilty of harboring racist or anti-Semitic prejudices they never expressed."
These concepts were widely disseminated via the media and academia,
propagating the false notion of the "Fascist Scale" or political spectrum.

The Great Circle Political Spectrum

Further, the spectrum had been described as "the circular conception
of political philosophies that the liberals derived from Adorno. For over
30 years teachers in our high schools and colleges have taught this
liberal concept of the political spectrum as a circle, like the face of a
clock."

"At 12 o'clock they placed the 'middle of the roaders,' the 'fence
straddlers,' those without much conviction. On the near left are liberal
Republicans and Southern Democrats; further to the left are liberal
Democrats and British Conservatives. Still further left are Socialists,
British Laborites, and American Progressives. At the extreme left and all
the way to six o'clock are the Communist parties." "To the right of center
the liberals placed the conservatives along with the Ku Klux Klan, South
African Nationalists, . . . phased into Fascists and Nazis on the extreme
right at six o'clock."

6. Adorno, Theodor, W., et al, *The Authoritarian Personality*, Harper & Row, 1950

Ingraham corrects this argument saying, "The political spectrum cannot be visualized correctly as a circle. Like other spectrums it must be measured from one extreme to another," going into the single line, from 100% government on the left to 0% government on the right. "Totalitarian systems include Fascism, Naziism, Socialism, and Communism. Liberalism is also a system of the left, philosophically related to the totalitarian belief in state monopoly."

From Line to Circle to Line to Horseshoe

Ingraham endorsed an even more imaginative interpretation of the political spectrum as horseshoe, described by John F. McManus[7]:

> Because the jump from no government on the extreme right to total government on the extreme left is such an easy jump, I have begun to think the political spectrum could best be portrayed as a horseshoe, that the extremes are close together and the system of limited self-government is furthest from both (See Figure No. 25).

THE GREAT HORSESHOE POLITICAL SPECTRUM

Figure No. 25

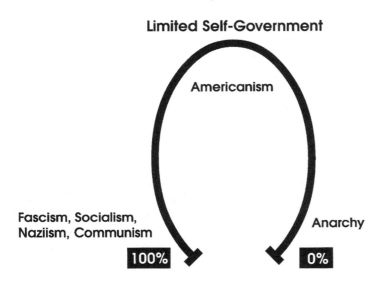

7. John F. McManus, *An Overview of Our World,* 1971, The John Birch Society, Appleton, WI 54913. Used with permission

In other words, when you have anarchy, its consequences are so disastrous, the people, unable to tolerate total lawlessness, prefer instead the "quick fix" of a dictatorship.

Ingraham concludes "In either case, line or horseshoe, the conservative position of limited government, a free market and private property bears no relationship to the systems of the left . . . 'conservatives,' far from being associated with authoritarian beliefs, are the advocates of limiting government to its proper functions, keeping government out of the economy, decreasing government spending and taxation, and doing away with regulations. They believe in *limited* government, and they are striving to keep America free."

Government Size: Not Only How Big but How Oppressive

To freshen our thinking about these things, we mustn't get caught up only in the size, however measured. It is far better to have a government controlling and spending, say, 25% of the national output, redistributing or returning some of that back to the populace, than taking only 15 or 20% of the output but putting it all into a secretive, oppressive George Orwellian *1984* type police state. Still, relative size, or amount of government, is a handy tool to conceptualize and understand political systems, their relative pluses and minuses, for the people they serve or who serve them. We are better able to understand the exquisite beauty, and appreciate the magnificent design of the Founders' Constitutional Republic, with its naturally occurring American System of Free Enterprise.

A More Detailed, more Defined View of the Political Spectrum

Andrew Melechinsky, head of Constitutional Revival[8], teaches and touts the basics of the U.S. Constitution and how to use it in everyday life. He has distributed a more in-depth political spectrum which also shows his interpretation as to the political position and understanding of the press. We have discussed the components sufficiently, so only his chart is shown. Note "ochlocracy" is defined as "government of the mob; mob rule." (See Figure No. 26) This contrasts the bogus "Media Spectrum" with the "Real Life Spectrum."

8. Constitutional Revival, 29 Fairfield Road, Enfield, CT 06082. Used with permission

MEDIA VS. REAL LIFE POLITICAL SPECTRUM

Figure No. 26

THE MEDIA SPECTRUM

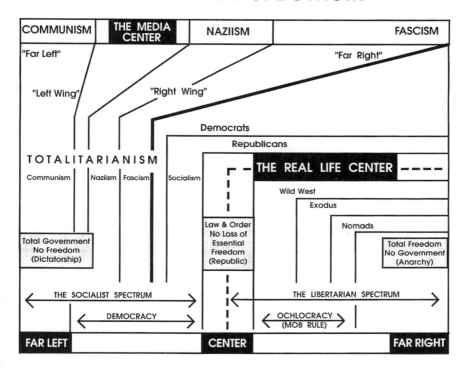

THE REAL LIFE SPECTRUM

The Political Job of the Power of ONE—
to Shift the Political Spectrum

James Evans in *America's Choice*[9] uses his own political spectrum version to explain where we are, where we are heading, where we must go and how to get there. He calls 100% or all government, "regimentation," and 0% or no government, "freedom;" and incorporates a concept of the popular political parties into the spectrum. Here's how he puts it:

Although most people regard political action as the final answer to our problems (and who would deny the importance of elected

9. James R. Evans, *America's Choice: Twilight's Last Gleaming or Dawn's Early Light*, p 118, The Fisher Institute: 1981, 7041 Regalview Cir, Dallas, TX 75240. Used with permission

officials of quality and integrity?), I'm convinced that *we,* in fact, *do* provide the key.

"If we regard the far left of the political spectrum as *Regimented,* i.e., Communist or Fascist (although nominally one regards these as opposites on the spectrum, both obviously represent regimentation and should be cast into the same bag) and the far right as *Free,* i.e. *Free Market* with the resulting personal freedom, we are then able to establish a center-line. 'If dotted line 'A' (left of center) represents what the political establishment thinks is the position of public opinion (it may or may not be an accurate assessment), historical evidence demonstrates that the two major political parties will embrace those centrist views. The result is choices of insignificant difference, both tentatively dedicated to 'regimentation by degree.' In short, two unacceptable alternatives or no alternative. Conversely, if the political perception of public attitudes arrives at dotted line 'B.' the same scenario repeats and we find ourselves with choices relatively committed to a free economy, both acceptable to those who favor personal liberty. Although the above theorem may not describe the nominally understood political workings of the system, I'm convinced that it represents reality. My conclusions? Political realities being what they are, a tremendous effort is essential to educate the public in the principles of liberty" (See Figure No. 27).

REGIMENTATION, FREEDOM & RELATIVITY SPECTRUM

Figure No. 27

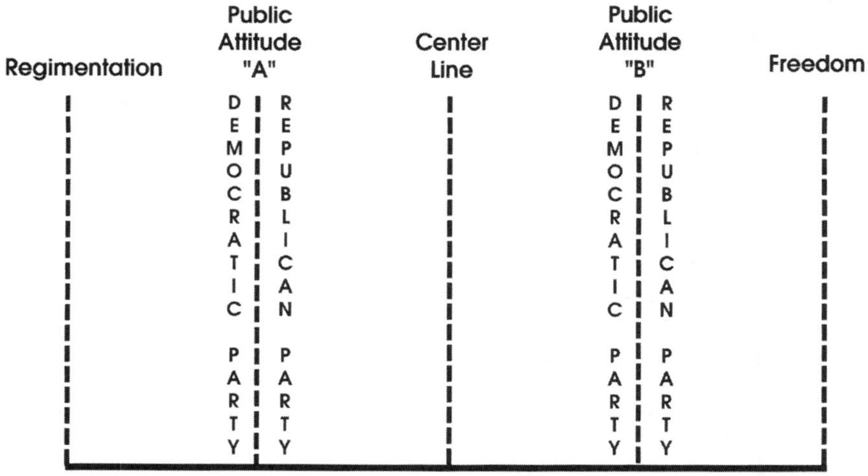

"The Political Gamut of the 20th Century" is another single line continuum political spectrum that may clarify the concept[10]. (See Figure No. 28).

DINE'S "POLITICAL GAMUT OF THE TWENTIETH CENTURY"

Figure No. 28

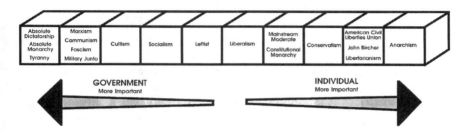

The missing piece to the political spectrum puzzle may be all of the above plus two more pieces of information. First, the late 1770's French government had what may be the original "Left Wing" and "Right Wing." The left wing was simply and coincidentally several groups, the *Jacobin* clubs, the *Cordeliers* and *the Gironde,* groups of men who dominated *the Mountain,* because their seats were in the highest part of the hall on the speaker's left. Members of *the Plain,* more conservative members, sat to the speaker's right.

Second, according to the *Dines Letter,* "While it shocked the world in August 1939, it should have been unsurprising that Adolph Hitler and Josef Stalin signed a peace pact. These two far-left wolves, and supposed opposites, actually concluded an agreement on how best to divide Poland between them! Stalin achieved quite a coup when he placed himself to the left and Hitler to the antipodal right of the political spectrum, thereby engendering an imaginary division that still deludes political innocents today. Looking back, we view it as a diabolically clever Stalinist ploy so that he could set himself up as an *alternative* to fascism, thereby garnering nearly all the anti-Hitlerites as his natural allies. No wonder political neophytes are confused by most terminology!"

---

10. Dines, James, *The Dines Letter*, " What Do 'Left' and 'Right' Mean in Politics?", January 20, 1989, James Dines & Co., PO Box 22, Belvedere, CA 94920. Used with permission

The Best Way to Describe Freedom:
Economics? Personal Rights? Both?

The best way to describe freedom may not be on a one-line scale after all. The Nolan Chart mentioned previously was conceived by a Denver, Colorado, advertising executive David Nolan, and was published in the January, 1971 *Individualist,* "Classifying and Analyzing Politico-Economic Systems." Two professors at the University of Central Florida, William Maddox and Stuart Lilie, extended the research in their book, *Beyond Liberal and Conservative*[11]. They suggested a matrix approach with four quadrants (See Figure No. 29).

In effect, the single-dimension political spectrum line turns into a two-dimensional figure having two axes and four quadrants. The origin, "0" is at the lower left. The horizontal axis is "Economic Freedom" from 0 to 100%. The vertical axis is "Social Freedom" from 0 to 100%. Horizontal and vertical lines at the halfway (50%) points form four quadrants that are labeled liberal, conservative, populist and libertarian. Within the four categories, there is room for diversity and variation of views. Fritz uses "Interventionist" instead of "Populist," or even "Totalitarian," to better explain the concepts without being noxious or "evoking defensiveness."

NOLAN CHART: POLITICO-ECONOMIC
SYSTEMS MATRIX

Figure No. 29

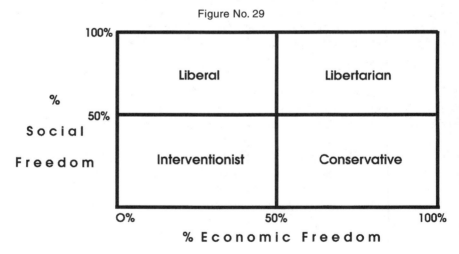

11. Maddox, William, and Lilie, Stuart, *Beyond Liberal and Conservative*, Cato Institute, 1984

Fritz explains the quadrants, first with how much economic freedom conservatives want:

Most conservatives aren't too sure they can run other people's economic lives, and they sure don't want other people bossing them around, so they like quite a bit of economic freedom. If you ask them 20 questions about economic intervention versus allowing individuals to make their own choices, conservatives will answer 50 to 90 percent in favor of individual choice. Imagine the response of liberals to these same 20 questions. Oops! We see a different attitude. They would allow individual choice much less often, usually 20 percent to 50 percent. They want the collective to be intervening in people's economic decisions, and they plan to be running the collective.

The vertical scale, what Nolan calls 'social freedom,' is often called 'civil liberties.' Here we are measuring the percent of freedom (from government intervention) in those human actions which are not measured in dollars—the way you worship God, or don't (compulsory church attendance); how much attention you pay to safety (compulsory seatbelts), etc. Imagine asking conservatives 20 questions about who should make decisions in such matters of personal morality. Now it is the conservatives who want to run other people's lives; in this case, to stamp out sin. Indeed, while some civil liberties can be very important to conservatives (e.g., the 2nd amendment right to keep and bear arms), they typically score only 20 percent to 50 percent in favor of the social freedoms. They want 'community standards,' and they plan to be running the community. Liberals, while they have strong desires to regulate other people's economic behavior, are more easy-going in social liberties. They usually score 50 percent to 90 percent on the vertical scale.

The lower left, interventionists, want to intervene in all parts of society—to go overboard and be in total control. The libertarians are strong defenders of civil rights that people deserve to make their own decisions in matters of personal behavior as long as they are not trampling on the rights of someone else. Like conservatives, they hold deep convictions in favor of free enterprise.

Fritz brings author Richard Maybury's further interpretation: "Liberals generally advocate economic encroachment and civil liberty. Conservatives generally advocate economic liberty and civil encroachment. Interventionists advocate both economic and civil encroachment. Libertarians advocate both economic and civil liberty."

Relabeling the two axes "tolerance of economic diversity" and "tolerance of behavioral diversity," here are Maybury's definitions:

"Liberals tolerate behavioral diversity but compel economic conformity. Conservatives tolerate economic diversity but compel behavioral conformity. Totalitarians compel both behavioral and economic conformity. Libertarians tolerate both economic and behavioral diversity."

Nolan Chart Fallout: Centrists and Crusaders

A fascinating concept developed from the Nolan Chart, was published in the June 1984 *Time for Liberty* by Philip Mitchell. The original chart differentiated people by *what* they believed—the substance of their political ideas. Another way is *how* people approach political issues, not *what* the issues are, which can help us more deeply understand political diversity.

Fritz reports, "For the purpose of making his (Mitchell's) point, people near the center are labeled 'centrist' and the people outside the center area, no matter what quadrant, are called 'crusaders.' The center area represents people who look at political issues with primary concern for *how* things are done, *how* things appear, and the *intentions* behind a person's political actions. Each of the corner areas represents people with clear distinctions in ideology. These differences in *what* they believe are key to their attitudes. They are deeply committed to *what* they believe . . . they're 'crusaders.'" (See Figure No. 30).

SOCIAL, ECONOMIC FREEDOM VS. CENTRISTS & CRUSADERS

Figure No. 30

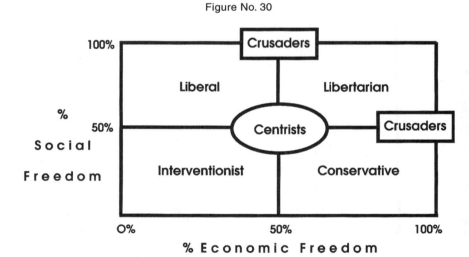

"Centrists and crusaders view each other with hostility. Crusaders divide people according to how 'pure' their beliefs are. They see centrists as 'unprincipled, wishy-washy cattle' who are 'pawns' of another corner. Centrists divide people by how they put their beliefs into action. They see crusaders, even those with similar ideology, as unreasonable radicals whose very methods will prevent reaching their shared goals. . . . By themselves, neither side of the how-what split can make a significant change. Both have something to offer: The crusaders provide the 'fire, drive, and sense of direction.' The centrists have sheer numbers and a 'sense of how to present things' so they will be accepted."

Unfreedom: The Holden Extension of the Nolan Chart

The preceding interpretations and presentations of the political spectrum have portrayed 100% government (all government) on the left, and 0% government (no government) on the right. In order to be consistent with previous concepts, the Nolan chart is re-presented in the same terms but in varying degrees of "Unfreedom," expressing the x-axis (abscissa) as 'Government, % of Economic *Un*freedom,' and the y-axis (ordinate) as 'Government, % of Social *Un*freedom.' The chart looks like this, with 100% government (0% freedom, 100% unfreedom) on the left, or bottom; and 0% government (100% freedom, 0% unfreedom) on the right, or top (See Figure No. 31).

HOLDEN EXTENSION: FREEDOM & UNFREEDOM

Figure No. 31

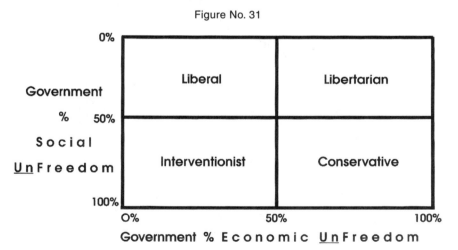

So perhaps the better of ways to describe the political spectrum must involve more than one dimension of economic freedom or social freedom. At least in exploring these concepts, we have more and better tools to consider the political and economic system in which we live, those around us, and the various choices and directions we have as alternatives.

MARSHALL FRITZ' "WORLD'S SMALLEST POLITICAL QUIZ"

Figure No. 32

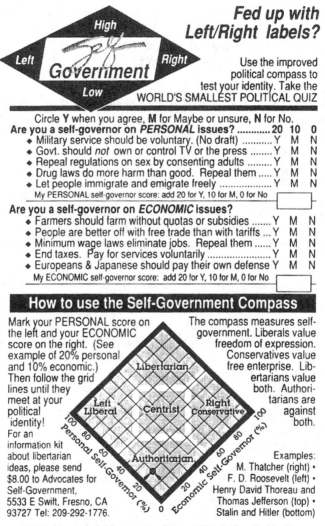

Fed up with Left/Right labels?

Use the improved political compass to test your identity. Take the WORLD'S SMALLEST POLITICAL QUIZ

Circle **Y** when you agree, **M** for Maybe or unsure, **N** for No.

Are you a self-governor on *PERSONAL* issues? 20 10 0
- ◆ Military service should be voluntary. (No draft) .... Y   M   N
- ◆ Govt. should *not* own or control TV or the press .... Y   M   N
- ◆ Repeal regulations on sex by consenting adults .... Y   M   N
- ◆ Drug laws do more harm than good. Repeal them ..... Y   M   N
- ◆ Let people immigrate and emigrate freely .... Y   M   N

My PERSONAL self-governor score: add 20 for Y, 10 for M, 0 for No ☐

Are you a self-governor on *ECONOMIC* issues?
- ◆ Farmers should farm without quotas or subsidies .... Y   M   N
- ◆ People are better off with free trade than with tariffs ... Y   M   N
- ◆ Minimum wage laws eliminate jobs. Repeal them ...... Y   M   N
- ◆ End taxes. Pay for services voluntarily .... Y   M   N
- ◆ Europeans & Japanese should pay their own defense Y   M   N

My ECONOMIC self-governor score: add 20 for Y, 10 for M, 0 for No ☐

How to use the Self-Government Compass

Mark your PERSONAL score on the left and your ECONOMIC score on the right. (See example of 20% personal and 10% economic.) Then follow the grid lines until they meet at your political identity! For an information kit about libertarian ideas, please send $8.00 to Advocates for Self-Government, 5533 E Swift, Fresno, CA 93727 Tel: 209-292-1776.

The compass measures self-government. Liberals value freedom of expression. Conservatives value free enterprise. Libertarians value both. Authoritarians are against both.

Examples: M. Thatcher (right) • F. D. Roosevelt (left) • Henry David Thoreau and Thomas Jefferson (top) • Stalin and Hitler (bottom)

World's Smallest Political Quiz is "Self-Government Compass."

Marshall Fritz gives permission to print his "World's Smallest Political Quiz," to help illuminate various political positions in a self-test format. It is short and simple but may help clarify political labels and ideas. Fritz stands the square on edge to give the "Diamond Chart." In terms of self-government, it is high at the top, low at the bottom, and the more familiar left-right spectrum is operative across the middle. Conversely, big government is at the bottom, small government at the top. Take the quiz. (See Figure No. 32).

Freedom and Government on a Small Planet

It finally dawns on our consciousness. There is a relationship between the amount of freedom we have, and the amount and kind of government we have. The future of freedom is foretold government growth. We begin to understand the important topic of freedom and government on this small planet Earth.

Freedom is not government. Government is not freedom. Judicious government protects and preserves freedom. Excessive government weakens and destroys freedom. Big government becomes "unfreedom."

Where does freedom come from? The government? A monarch? A piece of paper? The military? Somewhere else?

The essence of the source of freedom is articulated in the *Declaration of Independence:*

> We hold these truths to be self-evident, that all men are created equal, that they are endowed by their Creator with certain unalienable Rights, that among these are Life, Liberty and the pursuit of Happiness.

That is preceded by the introduction to the *Declaration:*

> When in the Course of human events, it becomes necessary for one people to dissolve the political bands which have connected them with another, and to assume among the powers of the earth, the separate and equal station to which the Laws of Nature and of Nature's God entitles them . . .

Freedom comes from man's Creator, from "Nature's God."

> That to secure these rights, Governments are instituted among Men, deriving their just powers from the consent of the governed.

Government, then, is created, empowered, then commanded "to secure these rights," that is, to protect human freedom. The *Declaration of Independence* was a 1776 statement-of-intent leading 11 years later to the

1787 U.S. Constitution, which defines the framework and function for government.

Putting them together:

God created man
God gave man freedom ("free will")
Man wrote the *Constitution,*
to form government,
to protect man's freedom,
granted by God.

Too small or weak, government is unable to protect freedom. Too large or powerful, government does not protect, but diminishes freedom. So a carefully defined balance-of-power was established and must be maintained to protect freedom.

What on Earth Is Freedom?

So close and so much for so long blurs the existence of something so precious. Spoiled Americans are like that with freedom.

Recall in an economic freedom sense, that government is about 30% of our national output. In terms of wages and salaries, government is over 66%. In terms of "the essentials of life," Americans spend 145 billion dollars more on government than on food, shelter and clothing combined.

In a human sense, freedom is free to *be,* to *do,* to *choose,* to *dare,* and to *become.* In short, freedom to *LIVE.*

On Earth, Freedom is America

What in the World is Government?

For a civilized society, government is absolutely necessary for national defense, to preserve law and order, promote a climate of productivity and guarantee personal freedom. Such freedom permeates an environment of invention, innovation, entrepreneurship, production and productivity to provide for the needs, wants and dreams of Americans.

Properly constituted government protects freedom. Article I, Section 8, Clause 1, broadly defines yet specifically limits the functions of the federal government ". . . to provide for the common defense and the general welfare" (not the *specific* welfare).

These same thoughts are also expressed in the Preamble to the *U.S. Constitution*:

> We the People of the United States, in Order to form a more perfect Union, establish Justice, insure domestic Tranquility, provide for the common defense, promote the general Welfare, and secure the Blessings of Liberty to ourselves and our Posterity, do ordain and establish this Constitution for the United States of America.

What is the "general welfare?" The general welfare is that which helps everyone and hurts no one. It is a court system to preserve law and order, and assure sanctity of contracts. It is the assurance of public safety. It is standard weights and measures, a postal system and coinage of money. For the federal government it is the 18 defined functions of Article I, Section 8.

An example of the "general welfare" is where a woman in California buys a hair dryer manufactured in Kentucky, flies to Maine, plugs it in and it works! The prongs are the right size and distance apart, the voltage and frequency of alternating current matches its design. It hurts no one, helps everyone.

Rather than a Constitutional Republic or a Democracy (the less desirable of the two), most countries have oligarchies or dictatorships. They use the more arbitrary and brutal "Ruler's Law" rather than constitutionally-defined "People's Law" to govern. Marxist, socialist or communist political philosophies rule most of the nations of the world, with governments that are repressive and despotic.

In the World, government is tyranny

When does Freedom become "UnFreedom?"

An economic system can support only so much government at a given level of national output. Different levels of government have varying effects on the standard-of-living, quality-of-life and freedoms of the people.

With no government we have no security. From zero government, more government provides greater security. More freedom exists to about 10 percent government, where government fulfills its defined and intended functions.

Based on my book *The Phoenix Phenomenon* and ensuing studies, empirical analyses of what has already happened in the past half century, relative levels of government have various effects on freedom. Government can function marvelously up to 17% of GNP (about half that of 1999); federal, 13%, state, 4%. So there is small difference from 10 to 17 percent.

Above 17%, more government becomes destructive, redistributionist, taking from those who produce, giving to those who don't, demotivating both. The more above 17%, the more threat government becomes to freedom. Bigger government becomes "unfreedom."

As government grows larger, standard-of-living drops, quality-of-life decays and freedom shrinks. Government helps some but hurts or deprives others. Above 17% more government is less freedom.

No government is the enemy of freedom.

Big government is the enemy of freedom.

Big and growing government is the death of freedom.

That is freedom and government on a small planet, Earth, especially in America.

What's Wrong?

What has been wrong is that we have had little knowledge or information available to conceptualize political and economic systems, specifically, the political spectrum, and the role and size of government. The available "conventional wisdom" model was flawed and confusing. A more descriptive and logical model aids immeasurably in our quest to find truth about freedom and government, and the various options and continuum available within the political spectrum for those options. The better we understand freedom and how it is lost, and the role government plays and each individual citizen must play in maintaining, strengthening and preserving freedom, the more assured we are to preserve it.

In America we have more freedom, and it is built into a system that has the capability to protect and strengthen freedom—as well as destroy it. The question is, will we use this knowledge to improve our future, the destiny of America, and an Idea called freedom?

The answer obviously is *YES WE WILL!* We will use all our tools, resources of heart, muscle, mind and spirit, and a commitment to a greater cause of life, to changes that can, will and MUST be made, with care, concern, love, courage, compassion and dedication that make a true long-term difference worth making—to save freedom in America.

Go for it, *Power of ONE!*

What is the Political Spectrum—a Definition?

Stated before, a definition or explanation of the term political spectrum is unavailable from orthodox reference resources, whether it be dictionary, encyclopedia or subject reference in a library computer system. Having been on over 620 talk shows with this book I have so-defined "Political Spectrum" for show hosts, callers and listening audience:

The Political Spectrum is the single, most important concept to our standard-of-living and quality-of-life on Planet Earth for every human being. It is how much and what kind of government we have, which determines how much and what kind of freedom we have, which determines how much and what kind of life we have.

With that kind of far-reaching, all-encompassing importance it is about time that we know, understand and act upon our concepts of what kind of society we want to live in, especially with respect to that of the Political Spectrum. We had better know a lot about various types and sizes of government, especially our own, then wisely and vigorously defend, preserve and strengthen this Constitutional Republic, constantly sensitive to government's propensity to grow bigger.

Questions for Review

1. Describe freedom in terms of dollars. Are we more slave than free? How can you tell? What levels of wages and salary taxation go to federal, state and local governments?

2. Describe freedom in terms of life, "Free to be, to . . .?" Explain what freedom is, how it works, how you know you have it. What is another dimension to explain freedom in addition to economic freedom?

3. What are the political left, right, and center? What is the political spectrum? How is it related to government systems?

4. What is fascism? Is it "right" or "left"? Why does a right-wing dictator or left-wing anarchist make no sense? How can government and private, control and ownership of property and the means of production be used to differentiate various especially left-wing political systems?

5. "Far right is anarchy and chaos. Far left is totalitarianism or authoritarianism." Explain. What common characteristic of capital do all four political systems—communism, socialism, Naziism and fascism, have in common? What is capital?

6. "America is a Constitutional Republic, not a democracy." What is the difference? What is preferable? Why? What two countries really mixed up this "perversion of terms" and used the meaning of the political left and right to their wartime advantage?

7. Describe two political spectra where "we are all socialists now." What is a "choice between false alternatives?" What are Fabian Socialists? What is democratic socialism? What is a better political spectrum of the various governments? Describe Dr. Skousen's. Why is a straight line inadequate?

8. Describe the circle or clock analogy. The horseshoe. Andrew Melechinsky's "Media Spectrum" vs "Real Life Spectrum." James Evans concepts. James Dine's "Political Gamut." What is "the missing piece of the puzzle?"

9. Why was it necessary to have two axes and four quadrants in the Nolan Chart? Explain social and economic freedom, encroachment and liberty, tolerance of economic and behavioral diversity, centrists and crusaders, "unfreedom" and government.

10. Where does freedom come from? How can rights be "unalienable?" Why is "big government the enemy of freedom, growing

government, the death of freedom"? Give a definition of "Political Spectrum."

Freedom is government divided into small fragments.
>   —Thomas Hobbes

Liberty has never come from government. Liberty has always come from the subjects of it. The history of liberty is a history of resistance, of limitations of governmental power, not the increase of it.
>   —Woodrow Wilson

Liberty lies in the hearts of men and women; when it dies there, no Constitution, no law, no court can save it.   —Judge Learned Hand

Government is not reason; it is not eloquence; it is force! Like fire, it is a dangerous servant and a fearful master. —George Washington

The world has never had a good definition of the word 'liberty.' With some the word may mean for each man to do as he pleases with himself and the fruits of his labor; with others the same word may mean for some men to do as they please with other men and the product of other men's labor. Here are two different, incompatible things called by the same name—liberty. And it follows that each is, by the respective parties, called by two different and incompatible names—liberty and tyranny.
>   —Abraham Lincoln

The dangers to liberty lurk in insidious encroachment by men of zeal, well meaning, but without understanding.—Justice Louis D. Brandeis

If men were angels, no government would be necessary. If angels were to govern men, neither external nor internal controls on government would be necessary.   —James Madison

Chapter 15

ROUNDING THIRD BASE
Getting Active and Involved in Politics!

A Home Run in the Making:
Beyond Economic and Political Awareness to Activity

We are gathering momentum in our quest to score the "home run" in the Big Ballgame of Life. We have been "safe on first" (economic awareness) and proceeded beyond toward second. We are aware, even super-sensitized to the "economic facts of life." All life is economic, and our existence is dependent upon our understanding and application of economics, as individuals and as a society.

We have streaked beyond second base (political awareness) to political understanding and its crucial impact on economic awareness. Political systems encourage or discourage good economics and the resultant impact on goods and services, capital investment in machines, technology and innovation for the future, determine the direction and condition of our survival, perhaps even our prosperity.

Politics, through government, is a manipulative tool that redistributes wealth, almost always increases taxes, and provides enabling or disabling legislation for business to create wealth, produce jobs, goods and services. Politics works to get business to collect taxes for the government from working employees through payroll deductions, and from customers through higher prices. Misused or abused, politics becomes less a tool working for the good of all. It becomes more a weapon against some, a shield for others, and for some, a means of legalized theft, taking from some to enrich others. Along the way it can buy votes and engender power.

Politics doesn't just happen. People make politics happen. Politics can be a blessing or a curse. There are good politics and bad politics. Politics exists wherever people live, work and aspire, in small groups, large organizations, communities or nations. To deny politics is to deny life. So the *Power of ONE* accepts politics and resolves to learn, use, participate and propagate "positive politics." Know that politics can help you, to contribute greatly, grow and achieve.

Basic definitions explain politics to be an art or science of government, the art or science concerned with guiding or influencing governmental policy, and with winning and holding control over a government. It is political affairs or business, power and leadership in a government or any other group, and the political opinions or sympathies of a person.

Wrapped up in one phrase, politics is the total complex of relations between people and society. Wow! That is too much to ignore.

We must go beyond being politically aware to being politically astute. Then we become politically active and effective in order to wield influence on our own lives and the direction of our country and future.

Politics: the Art of the Possible; the Art of Compromise

In his editorial, John Podhoretz[1] explores the "excuse" of politics:

> Politics is the art of the possible. That bromide has been the excuse for every leader whose policies failed to live up to his ideological limitations. For there is no definition of the term "possible" in that sentence; if Machiavelli was right when he said that the mark of a great leader is his ability to aim and redirect the river of destiny, then what is possible is a matter of choice and action, not submission to the whim of fate and the difficulty of getting one's ideas expressed and adopted.

In other words, *politics* necessarily exists and changes things. We therefore acknowledge that politics can be used to direct the destiny of the family, organizations, political systems and nations. Politics must be recognized, understood and used.

A key thought is "what is possible is a matter of choice and action." In a large and complex society, choices and actions are directed by people through politics and the political process. If we are to be more than casual observers (or oblivious bystanders), we become more informed and accept the challenge of "getting one's ideas expressed and adopted."

Politics as "the art of compromise" sometimes gives us second best. A person or group in a political system can come up with the great idea,

1. Podhoertz, John, "Success Needs No Bipartisan Basis," *Insight,* 5/26/86, p.72

the perfect solution in an absolute sense, and wish to reduce it to practice through legislation. It is the job of "the loyal opposition" to loyally oppose it, and place their mark upon it; therefore, to change it and in this case degrade it. If by definition, we already had the very best proposal possible, any changes will make it less than the best.

The process usually works in the forum of a political body. People offer varied viewpoints and opinions regarding a proposal. Bringing many people and ideas about an issue to a legislative body drums up support to assure its eventual success. All involved work together to "make it work." The political process can be a blessing as well as a curse, depending on the course it takes, and that may depend in part on you.

Is Politics "Dirty," and if so, Why?

"Why is politics so dirty? I don't want to get involved," is a common lament. That question might be responded to with, "If you know the answer, why do you ask the question?" If politics does not provide the right actions, programs or results, perhaps it is because more good people are not personally involved, people like you.

We are all involved in politics, whether we like it or not. We pay enormous amounts of money for the programs of politicians and governments. Involved or not we pay the political price in the form of "taxes." They are big bills, will be paid, and require our money that we cannot spend as we wish.

The means and mechanisms are available to compel all to pay, through power of government and force of law. If you don't pay your taxes, bad things happen to you. That's called *force*. The authorities can take your home, break up your family and send you to jail. So we must work very hard to assure the bills and expenses of government are for legitimate purposes, and are well spent. That is the closest we can get to "the bottom line."

It is as true for business as for individuals and families, perhaps even moreso. Business had better get into politics because politics is certainly into business. It is easy to impose regulations and taxes on businesses. They can't vote. Businesses are "artificial beings" created by the state. Their only alternative is to lobby a lawmaking body, plus inform the people, along with the business and social community, and to seek to achieve the best results for all concerned.

Whether involved politically or not, businesses and individuals pay the taxes, support the services, obey the laws and reap the consequences.

It is quite clear that however relatively dirty or clean politics is, depends upon the participants. You can choose whether or not to be involved. There is a price to pay whether you are involved or not. But the results can be better or worse, the price higher or lower, depending on whether and how much you are involved. So what is your choice? It is to *get involved in politics* if you want to keep your freedoms! If you are the kind of person a *TOTAL Power of ONE* is, politics will be cleaner and the world will be better because you are involved.

Edmund Burke said, "The only thing necessary for the triumph of evil is for good men to do nothing."

Conversely, the thing necessary for the triumph of good is for good people like you to do something. That means get active, get involved, attend, participate and contribute.

So we are rounding third base together, on an exciting journey to winning The Big Game that is not only worth training for and playing in, but fighting and dying for, in the context of human freedom and the brightness of the future of man.

The nature of politics is the nature of people. We realize our getting involved won't solve all the problems. But just by getting involved in whatever role, we make a genuine and positive contribution, not only our own activity, but to influence others by word and deed. We shape the political process by our standards and our being there.

Political Involvement:
Spectator, Participant, Enthusiast, Activist

Politics and citizen involvement can be a lot of fun, as well as do a lot of good. Know or learn what is going on, and how it happens. Starting perhaps as inactive, proceed to become at least a *spectator.* Start easily by "tuning in" more to the political environment.

Watch television more critically to know what politicians are doing and saying. Listen to radio to learn the issues of the day, especially the statements, activities and actions of government officials, legislative and deliberative bodies. Read newspapers to learn background and information about the issues and personalities. Read magazines for a more in-depth analysis. Then discuss issues, ideas and trends with friends and neighbors. Get their thoughts and opinions. Do this for a week or two and you are a *spectator* watching from the sidelines, and preparing.

After learning about issues discussed, legislation in motion, proposed tax increases, and the people and organizations behind them, something happens. You become more aware, then interested and informed. Your mind internalizes the data. You discern potential or actual results that will affect you or people you know. You begin to *care.* You develop *concern.* You *care more.* Then you get *involved,* that is, you advance from *spectator* to *participant.*

As a *participant*, you work to advance a political party, an organization, or a cause. It may be as simple as phoning people to go to the polls and vote on Election Day. You may walk neighborhoods, handing out political literature for a candidate or issue you support. You attend a city council, County Commission or Board of Education meeting. Because you are there, involved and participating, things are getting better. You are informed and becoming more influential, helping set the agenda and changing the thrust of issues and direction of action.

Once really into the swirl of activities, events and personalities, you begin to "glow." It is exciting and you are loving it. You have now advanced from *participant* to *enthusiast*.

Finally you are a *political enthusiast*. You are very happy, really enthusiastic, sincerely angry, terribly excited, or all four and more. Something is very wrong or could be so much better. You get involved, help others, debate, arrange speaking engagements or get-togethers for interested people to obtain information. You assist with an initiative or a referendum by obtaining signatures on a petition. You help select candidates or shape the policy of a political party. Whatever needs to be done is fair game for you to do. You are into the activity and swirl of things.

Then it happens. No one is more informed, more enthusiastic and committed to make a positive difference. No more sidelines, it is center stage for you-know-who. No one, no other single person, could possibly do the job or improve the situation more than you. You run for office. You tell your friends. You are a candidate. You offer yourself for public service. You're an *activist*. You are involved in politics and are making it a positive power for good, because you are good.

Activities for the Activist:
Supportive, Elective, Appointive, Directive

When you reach the activist level of politics there are several routes to follow to become a functioning, contributing part of the system—supportive, elective, appointive and directive.

You are *supportive* when you perform activities that support a candidate, organization or issue. This includes finding supporters and volunteers, assigning districts to volunteers, obtaining funds, researching issues, setting up office facilities and phone banks for campaign activities.

You are *elective* when you actually run for office or for a position requiring election. This can be the City Council, Board of Education or state treasurer. It can be for mayor, governor, state or national senator or representative.

You are *appointive* when you apply to serve on a legislative or municipal board, planning commission, liquor control commission, zoning etc., and do so.

You are *directive* when you follow carefully what is going on and attempt to influence elected, selected or appointed officials or governing boards. You attend and speak out at public meetings. You write letters to the editor of appropriate newspapers. You contact public officials by letter, phone, fax, email or in person to influence their decisions and actions. In other words, you *get and stay informed, and get and stay involved* in the process and with the people, and *make more and better things happen.*

There is public policy shaping and public policy making. Policy shaping is offering analysis and opinion and getting others to do likewise. Policy-making is where programs, projects and directions are created, funded and implemented. There are deliberations, decisions to be made and actions to be taken! There are evaluations and investigations needed as to whether intent was accomplished on policies and programs set into motion.

There is that tendency to hold back, that "wee, small voice" that discourages your doing anything new. Recognize it as contrary to your *Power of ONE* philosophy: I am one. I am only one. But I will do what one can do. And I will do it now!

One person can make a difference, and always does when he believes he can and acts as he believes. The power is with you because of what and who you are, what you believe and what you do.

Do what you can, with what you have, where you are.
                                                    —Theodore Roosevelt

Influencing Government at the Local, State and National Levels

A republic is a representative democracy of laws. It is composed of citizens who insist on citizen obedience to laws, and government obedience to the Constitution, all of which govern they the rulers as well as we the ruled.

Office holders are selected by people and parties, and elected by a vote of the citizens to represent their best interests and those of the community and nation. It is the citizens' job to communicate their views and expectations to their representatives. It is the job of the representatives to carry out those wishes and to serve the citizens in other ways, with full time energy, intelligence and integrity. Communications is the tool to inform and to influence.

Individuals and groups mobilize for communications and civic action. Letters, phone calls, and personal contacts serve well. Phone calls and personal faxes and emails are good ways to communicate effectively and efficiently. When one writes down thoughts, more consideration is given to details and background information as well as the formulation of opinions, ideas and suggested solutions. Phone calls are more personal, but instantly time demanding, so they can be more hurried, less effective.

Letters, faxes and emails, followed by calls or visits not only multiply frequency of contact and "power-up" personal relations, but increase the chance of acceptance and implementation. Appointments made and kept are very effective. There is nothing like a personal face-to-face conversation to get answers to questions, resolution to problems, action and results.

When in formal session in legislative chambers, special protocol is observed to maintain order and allow discussion of many viewpoints. Observe what is done and how it is done. Sometimes printed rules of order are available to explain what is expected and how a meeting is conducted. Being prepared, especially in tight time frames, can help immeasurably to get a lot done in a short period of time. Be organized to support or oppose local and national matters to make the difference in the outcome you desire. The pressure felt by elected officials in a room packed with interested voters is formidable.

Illinois Senator Everett Dirksen once said, "When I feel the heat, I see the light."

A How-To, What-To Guide to Getting Politically Involved

"Don't get mad, get even" doesn't work. "Don't get angry, get involved!" does work. There are so many opportunities for individual involvement. There are many "targets" for human concern and action. The biggest challenge is to carefully select one or two involvements or causes from the many; then concentrate all your energies and resources on them. It is like the focusing power of a magnifying glass, able to start a fire by concentrating the rays of the sun on a small dot of paper.

One can't do everything. But one can do something. Pick your civic concern and adopt it. Learn it. Support it. Attend, participate, mediate, conciliate, negotiate, speak up, influence, act.

If your chief public policy concern is, for example, your child's education, join a parent-teacher association or advisory committee. Attend school board meetings regularly. Make it a point to know personally on a first name basis, the members of the board of education, the presiding officer or school district superintendent and others in the administrative hierarchy. Research, learn, know and understand the issues. Inject your considered judgments into discussions to help influence a "better way" of educational direction and administration. Bring others with you. Just your presence helps influence. Your voiced or written opinions and suggestions are powerful, solicited and needed!

At the local government level, similarly, attend town council meetings regularly. Keep your elected officials honest by voicing concerns, asking questions, expecting straight answers and wise action. A city government sometimes has planning boards, citizen advisory committees, boards of adjustment and inquiry. Select your area of interest and concern and get involved. Put your awareness, knowledge, intellect and concern to work for good in local government and the betterment of community quality-of-life.

Public utilities provide another opportunity for personal impact. You may wish to attend public utility hearings for rate increases and get to know the officers or commissioners personally. See that their findings of fact are thorough and accurate, that their decisions are fair to all involved. Again, ask the tough questions. Expect accurate answers and decisions based on complete and correct information.

Attend town meetings or gatherings called by public representatives and civil servants. Ask questions. Listen. Give opinions. Your input will be sought and appreciated.

Special groups can be formed for special interest situations. An example would be forming a homeowner's association in your neighborhood to block a major zoning change that would adversely affect the character of your neighborhood or quality-of-life in your community.

Don't be afraid or intimidated. You are a citizen with all the rights of citizenship and they are considerable. Most of those in elective and appointive office began where you are.

Trial Balloons: Ready. Aim. Fire! Shoot' em Down!

Watch for the tried-and-true trial balloon. It is a handy political tool. A media release turns into a newspaper article or television story that says something new will happen. A real-life Colorado example was headlined, "Romer runs $1 billion tax on services up the flagpole." The first three sentences of the *Denver Post,* 10/14/87, article said:

> Governor Roy Romer suggested Tuesday that Colorado taxpayers cough up nearly $1 billion more than they do now for schools, colleges, prisons and highways. One way to do it Romer said, is to subject services like auto repairs, legal advice, dry cleaning and consulting work to the state's 3 percent sales tax. Services are now exempt from taxation.

At that time Colorado spent about $5.3 billion a year, with $811 million collected from the sales tax. This trial balloon suggested a whopping 123% sales tax increase, a regressive tax that hits hardest those least able to afford it. It also assumes the present tax burden inadequate, and the tax and tax growth of the state insufficient, all wrong, bordering on irresponsible.

Do you salute this flag or shoot down this trial balloon? Realizing such a precipitous action would probably sink a state's economy the latter is probably the most desirable action. Your bullets to shoot down such a ridiculous proposal are political fireworks—letters to the editor, calls, contacts and similar expressions of opinion and preference fired from a human Uzi, AK-47 or Mac-10, a big gun called a *Power of ONE!*

More How-To, What-To, Getting Politically Active: People Don't Care How Much You Know Until ...

A key point about being effective in things political is in a short saying:

> People don't care how much you know,
> Until they know how much you care.

The thing that really sells ideas and sways audiences comes from those who have done their homework, know the issues and care, really care, and let that care be known. People can tell. Don't just spout off all you know about a subject. Tell them up front that you care, why you care, then present your case.

Human beings as individuals and in groups make things happen. They explore the problems, determine and evaluate alternatives, make decisions and take action to implement them. With intense involvement, they usually do the best job possible.

Feel comfortable making your concerns known. That is how America works, with a plurality of opinions, ideas and purpose. There are many ways to be active, to represent yourself and others.

Write letters to the editor of local newspapers. Publicly share your opinions and concerns. Help to influence others to think, care and respond.

Write letters to your senators, congressional representative and president. They vitally need citizen input to guide their decisions and actions, programs and policies. Such letters are important. They are read, evaluated and often answered. The public servant is in office at your pleasure. If he or she doesn't do the job, that person can be voted out of office, "fired" by those not served, or served unsatisfactorily.

Are there guidelines to follow in writing a public representative? Yes. Let common sense, clarity and courtesy prevail. Personal, rather than form letters are best. Be brief. Usually one issue per letter is best. Give your reasons for writing. Be accurate, reasonable and polite but firm, determined and insistent—and brief. Include your return address and phone number. If possible, identify any legislation by number, or name the issue. Enclose supporting information, if available and brief. Sign your letter legibly.

Send them your "three-by-three" letter—three paragraphs, three sentences each. Most Americans can string nine sentences together. Include 1) the problem, issue or situation as you see it, 2) relevant, supporting information and 3) your question or recommended course of action with reasons why. Or make it a longer "four-by-four." You may also request a return response regarding the representative's position, opinion or intended action. Thank your representative for the job being done in your behalf.

All this and your own good ideas and action help to establish your credibility. That further opens the door for your credible contacts with elective and appointed officials.

Use the "What Formula": Three Steps-Plus-One

A guide to letter writing is the three-step (plus one) formula. The three steps are "What?", "So What?", "Now What?"—and—"What Next?" the "plus one" step.

What: State what's wrong. What is the issue, the complaint, the plaudit? Why are you writing the letter?

So What: Say why. What is your information? What difference will it make? What are the consequences short term and long term? What could go wrong? What are your reservations? What has been overlooked or forgotten?

Now What: Tell what should be done. What are your good ideas? What do you suggest? What is a better alternative? Why should it be done? Ask a question.

What Next: Get others to respond also. Make copies of your letter and share them with others. Tell them your concerns and actual, personal experiences. Tell how they are affected and why they should get involved. Get another *Power of ONE* in motion in the arena of public policy and involved citizenship.

Shortcuts to letter Writing, and Other Approaches

A letter is not necessarily the best or only way to communicate. You can send a two- or three-line postcard with a question and your return address. You can copy a news clipping on an 8 ½ x 11 sheet of paper and with a bold red or black marker, pose a question, "How do you feel about this issue?" or "Please vote *for* (or *against*) this proposal," or "I agree," or "What are you doing to help solve this problem?" One need not be prolific or fancy, or a historian, accountant or government financial wizard. Have good questions, valid concerns, timely, legitimate issues. Anyone is allowed to ask questions, get information, seek answers.

Congressman Thomas N. Kindness of Ohio said, "Letters from our constituents are extremely important. They sometimes provide us a spark that triggers a new thought with respect to a particular piece of legislation. This can result in direct input by a citizen into the make-up of a new law."

A letter has the greatest impact on legislation while the bill is still in committee, not after it is out on the floor for vote, or voted. Also, verbal communication is often the best of all, face-to-face or by phone, especially before or after a letter is sent.

One politician gave the three rules of politics: 1) Get elected. 2) Get re-elected. 3) Never get mad, get even. Our representatives are as security bound as are all of us. Their all-the-time question to each other is, "What do you hear?" They will listen because they want to and because they have to. What we need do is let them know that we think, care and expect their very best.

Remember, there is so much going on at one time, particularly with complex issues, that one person's input may be vitally, even critically needed. The importance of a person, business or organization's input cannot be over-emphasized. It is a fact: You count. You matter. You make a difference.

Influencing Candidates and Platforms
at the Local, State and National Levels

"I have no say in who runs for office. I just see who's running, then usually vote for the lesser of two evils," is a common remark. It need not be that way. Each citizen can have a bearing on who runs for office and who gets elected, especially if you are the one who runs for office and gets elected.

The formal national political cycle starts at the "neighborhood caucus" which usually takes place the first Monday of April or May in even numbered years. It is organized by both major political parties. Meetings are held in homes, schools or municipal buildings designated by politically defined boundaries called precincts. Each precinct contains approximately the same amount of registered voters—those eligible to participate. Just showing up can get you "put to work," and into a new position of status and influence.

Nomination and election of those present fill official neighborhood committee positions. Issues are discussed and delegates are selected to attend various political assemblies which in fact determine who run for various offices. People from these caucuses formulate the official party structures and platforms, so your attendance at these meetings should receive your high priority. Determine and reserve these dates ahead of time, preempting vacations and other delayable or avoidable schedule commitments.

As a delegate, you can be an effective supporter of the good candidates and a formidable foe of bad ones. You will be wooed and hopefully won by candidates for high public office, those who desperately need your understanding, support and vote. They will talk to you, answer your questions, seek your advice and solicit your opinions on issues. They will want you to sway others to vote for them too. You are a VIP, a very important person, especially to those who seek local and national elective office.

Investigate the record and credentials of incumbents, those already in office. Then study opposing candidate positions. Talk to them. Make a personal contact. Attend "meet the candidate" public meetings. Examine their qualifications, education, and past experience. Learn their attitudes and approaches, and determine if they have basic honesty, sincerity, integrity, judgment and concern, and if you think they will communicate well with constituents. Determine their suitability for the office being sought.

You will come in contact with the "kingmakers" and opinion leaders of the political parties, earn a say in what goes on and how it happens. As a concerned citizen no greater service can be offered than participation in the biennial political neighborhood caucuses and ensuing political assemblies to select candidates for office. Besides that it is fun, and you meet some nice people just like you.

Register to Vote; then Vote; Vote Every Chance to Vote

Military service personnel and others have fought in defense of the American economic and political system and died to preserve our freedoms. One of the most precious of these is the privilege and power of the VOTE. It, and you, are parts of the selection process of leaders in our elected and representative republic. It is a mystery how otherwise solid citizens and good people refuse to register or fail to vote. But there is an unspoken, unwritten, but understood tradition that seems to be operative about the vote. It is the wrongful notion, "Only vote." This whole concept is so important, it is worth showing a "don't just only-vote" symbol, and enclosing the VOTE page within an appropriate border (See Figure No. 33).

Your Super Power of ONE Vote Multiplied

Some people say they don't vote because it won't make any difference anyway. They have no clout. There are any number of stories of how one vote changed the course of an election, even of history. Let us look at some numbers to learn the power of your one vote based on 1996 presidential election year data.

Incumbent William Clinton got back into office with a popular vote of 47,402,000, 49.2% of the 96,278,00 votes cast for the two major parties, according to the 1999 Statistical Abstract of the United States (p 283). Bob Dole got 39,199,000 (40.7%). A few more numbers complete the picture. Taking the USA population of 265,463,000 (p 8) and subtracting out those who can't vote, underage, 68,947,000 (p 8), those incarcerated, 1,139,000 (p 231) and others, leaves 193,651,000 potential registered voters (p 301). Of 127,616,000 actual registered voters only 104,959,000 voted (8.7 million for other than the two major parties).

Summarizing, of 193.7 million potential registered voters in 1996, 127.6 million were registered, 105.0 million voted, 96.3 million for the major parties, 47.4 million for president. For the entire population your vote had the clout of 5.6 votes (265.46 million/47.4 million); for all potential registered voters, 4.1. For registered voters your vote had a clout of 2.7.

Next time you are tempted to say your vote doesn't count, remember, at a minimum it counts for almost three votes, and for the entire U. S. population, over 5 votes. That's why it is not only important to vote but vote knowledgeably. You, Power of ONE, have a lot of clout in the voting booth. And that doesn't even count the influence you wield among your friends as an opinion leader and community and political activist.

Is a Drowning Man Interested in Water?

A "Dear Abby" column summarized the importance of voting, 2/24/80:

CONFIDENTIAL TO YOU: The number of people in our country who do not bother to vote is a national scandal. If you aren't registered, call the headquarters of the political party of your choice and find out where to register so you will be eligible to vote. And come Election Day, vote! The person who says he isn't interested in politics is like a drowning man who says he isn't interested in water!

For More Information, Go to the Source or to the Library

We are not self-sufficient and sometimes not self-sustaining, especially when we attempt something new. To become politically involved and active,

DON'T "ONLY-VOTE"
Figure No. 33

"Don't Only-Vote" Go Beyond, Way Beyond

VOTE ★★★ VOTE ★★★ VOTE ★★★ VOTE ★★★ VOTE

"Vote" has the connotation to register to vote, vote, and it is done. That is misleading, incomplete and wrong. You have the opportunity to vote only every two, four, or six years. In-between is when new laws are made, past mistakes set right, and new visions and programs promoted. When you hear the word "Vote," *don't* hear "ONLY VOTE." Your vote is the beginning, not the end. It is really where it all starts, but your continued involvement is the key ingredient to promote a more responsive, effective government, and a better society, especially on an individual basis.

Vote at *every* opportunity. All elections are important! To some people it seems as if only the national elections are vital, to select national leadership. They are, but local elections are vital also.

Determine here and now that *you will vote in every election at every opportunity for the rest of your life,* from the largest national election to the smallest tax district or school board election. Every vote you cast will cost or save you precious, hard-earned money. Assure it is money well spent. Don't allow it to be squandered or wasted. These voting decisions go on for the rest of your life and beyond. Taxes are forever.

Register to vote. Vote. Keep voting. Get others to vote. Encourage them to know the candidates and issues. Get politically involved and stay involved. Make your concerns known. Make your voice heard. Get others knowledgeably active in the political system. Never give up. Never let up. There is no greater service for the long run good of this country and political system than your vote. Vote, then continually and regularly stay in touch with elected representatives, appointed and employed public officials. Don't "Only-Vote."

VOTE ★★★ VOTE ★★★ VOTE ★★★ VOTE ★★★ VOTE

do so with others who are politically involved, those with whom you would like to serve. If it is a political party, contact party headquarters for work sessions and assignments. Express your concerns and interests and what you think you might like to do to help. Ask what there is to do and how to do it. Ask questions along the way to be sure you are on track.

More information, either for initial enlightenment or professional opinion and depth, is available at your local library. You will find newspapers, books and magazine articles that can be immensely helpful to provide ideas, guidance and organization for your efforts and goals.

An example of a "one book treasury" of ideas[2] is *How You Can Influence Congress*. In it you learn how your senators and representatives work and about their working day, why and how to write letters, organizing for influence, maintaining an organization, communication, legislative campaign tactics, and building long-term influence, among many other pertinent topics and ideas. Similar books can give you answers you need, strategies that work and missing pieces to the puzzle of effective political involvement, activity and influence.

Get Started, Get Going, Keep Going, Get Others Going

The main idea is to know how important, how *very important* it is that you get involved in the political sphere of things, no matter how small or limited the involvement. If each person would do only one activity a day, a week, or even a month, this citizen involvement would keep our public servants more on the people's agenda and less on their own. They will better support the long-term interests of good economics, good politics and a more effective political system. Your doing so will encourage, empower and inspire others, and the total effort will make a sizable difference that must be made.

Resolve to devote an hour a month, a week, or even more, as Bill Ellis says it so well[3]:

> Give an hour a week for the U. S. A. One-hour per week by each of us would be revolutionary and reclaim our democracy. Isn't that worth as much time as bowling?

America, freedom and the future well being of our children and theirs, and the destiny of mankind are worth this kind of commitment and involvement. Besides that, it is fun and fulfilling too.

Go for it. If the difference is to be made, you are the one to make it—with *positive politics!* Become politically involved and active, and you are flying by third base! Now lead off third base for the home run!

2. Alderson, George, and Sentman, Everett, *How You Can Influence Congress, The Complete Handbook for the Citizen Lobbyist,* 1979, E. P. Dutton: New York

3. R.Q. Armington and William D. Ellis *More: The Rediscovery of American Common Sense,* p 184, Regnery Gateway, Chicago: 1984

Questions for Review

1. How can politics, through government, be a "manipulative tool?" What does politics do, or for what is it used? Discuss the definition of politics. Politics is "the total complex of relations between men and society." What does that mean, knowing that "men" means people— men and women?

2. With politics "the art of the possible," why is what is possible a "matter of choice and action, not submission to the whim of fate?" How does participation eradicate "the difficulty of getting one's ideas expressed and adopted?"

3. When we agree "Politics is the art of compromise," why does that limit the quality of policy to a level less than the best, especially considering the ever-present obligation of "the loyal opposition?"

4. Is politics dirty? Why? Must it be? How can politics be elevated to a high level activity and calling? John Adams said, "The science of government is my duty to study, more than all other sciences; the arts of legislation and administration and negotiation ought to take place of, indeed to exclude, in a manner, all other arts." Discuss. Do you think Adams meant every citizen, or only those formally in public service?

5. Each person has the choice whether or not to be politically involved. What happens with involvement? Without involvement? We have a choice to get active, involved, to attend, participate, contribute. Why should we? Who cares? Does it make a difference? What?

6. What are the four levels of political involvement, beginning with the letters SPEA? Discuss each. What are the four involvement opportunities of those who go beyond enthusiast to political activist? When you are directive what three activities do you perform? What effects do these have on public policy? To which do citizens contribute more directly? To which do officials contribute more directly? How do citizens go about helping shape public policy?

7. Why is it important that citizens not only obey laws but also see to it that their rulers obey the same laws? What is that kind of political system called?

8. How can individuals and groups "mobilize for communications and civic action?" How can an individual get politically involved? How can one person get politically active? Can one person politically make a difference? How? What are some guidelines for contacting elected and appointed officials?

9. What is the "What Formula?" Why is it "three-steps plus one?" Why is it wrong to say one has no say in who runs for office, only the option

of voting for the lesser of two evils? Why is it dangerous to interpret "Vote" to mean, "Only vote?" What else does it mean? Where does the formal national political cycle start? How often does it happen? Who can attend?

10. What kind of information is desirable for politics, issues, policies and candidates? Where do you find such information? Why is it important not only to get started, get going and keep going, but also to get others going too? Why is making a time commitment to being an active citizen important? Will it make a difference? How do you know? Discuss "Give a half hour a day to the U. S. A."

The greatest dangers to liberty lurk in insidious encroachment by men of zeal, well-meaning but without understanding.   —Louis D. Brandeis

The credit belongs to the person who is actually in the arena—whose face is marred by dust and sweat and blood—a leader who knows the great enthusiasms, the great devotions and spends himself in a worthy cause—who, at best if he wins knows the thrill of high achievement—and if he fails, fails while daring greatly—so that his place shall never be with those cold and timid souls who know neither victory nor defeat.   —Theodore Roosevelt

Be doers of the word, and not hearers only, deceiving yourselves . . . But he who looks into the perfect law, the law of liberty, and perseveres, being no hearer that forgets but a doer that acts, he shall be blessed in his doing.
—THB James 1:22,25

Of course we look to the past for inspiration, but inspiration is not enough. We must have action. Action can only come from ourselves; society, government, the state, call it what you will, cannot act; our only strength, our only security, lies in the individual. American institutions are built on that foundation. That is the meaning of self-government, the worth and the responsibility of the individual. In that America has put all her trust. If that fail, democracy fails, freedom is a delusion, and slavery must prevail.
—Calvin Coolidge

The science of government is my duty to study, more than all other sciences; the arts of legislation and administration and negotiation ought to take place of, indeed to exclude, in a manner, all other arts. I must study politics and war, that my sons may have liberty to study mathematics and philosophy. My sons ought to study mathematics and philosophy, geography, natural history and naval architecture, navigation, commerce and agriculture, in order to give their children a right to study painting, poetry, music, architecture, statuary, tapestry, and porcelain.   —John Adams

Chapter 16

AMERICA: A REPUBLIC, NOT A DEMOCRACY
What's the Difference?

Leading off third base, we gather more knowledge and information, to anticipate heading for home plate to score a home run. We explore in depth two words and two concepts, "republic" and "democracy." Our understanding and interpretations of government organization may mean life or death for freedom in America. This includes individual rights and elected representative rule by majority, with protection, appreciation and respect for the minority.

Going past third base will take two tries before we make it. Our knowledge, awareness and background are so barren we will first explore the difference between a republic and the less desirable democracy, then the Freedom Documents: Declaration of Independence, U.S. Constitution and its incredibly important Bill of Rights. Finally, in the Big Ball Game of Life, we score the Home Run: political ideas, ism's and ideologies, including a brief visit to Karl Marx and his *Communist Manifesto*.

A Power Dare Chapter: Do the Tough Stuff

This is a *"Power Dare* Chapter," *Power of ONE*. Read and heed your "Power Deed Creed."

Take the Pledge: The Pledge of Allegiance!

THE PLEDGE OF ALLEGIANCE

I pledge allegiance
To the Flag
Of the United States of America
And to the D E M O C R A C Y
For Which It Stands
One Nation Under God, Indivisible,
With Liberty and Justice for all.

Something is wrong here. This is the Pledge of Allegiance to the American Flag, the "Stars and Stripes," "Old Glory," the symbol of our freedoms and heritage, our precious "Land of the Free and Home of the Brave." Why do we always say, "And to the *Republic* for which it stands," and not, as above, "to the *D E M O C R A C Y* for which stands?" Is there a difference? Yes! There is a big difference, with quite a story behind it.

The difference between a republic and a democracy is subtle, especially if we leave out one very important word, "constitutional."

Checking word meanings for *democracy* and *republic* makes them sound nearly the same. Both are majority rule of and by the people, the latter with representation. When we add rules, the Constitution, we have majority rule, with representation, by law; hence, a Constitutional Republic.

In the introduction to his book, James Evans[1] poses the case for understanding the fabric of freedom, and the related details and nuances of various economic and political systems:

> There is overwhelming evidence that American Freedom is declining and soon will be only a memory. Almost no one will state that he is against individual liberty, but a substantial majority of Americans simultaneously propose, support, or at least fail to reject scheme after scheme that limits their liberty, raises their taxes, grants the state powers over their lives, or trades security for government control.

To be a renaissance *Power of ONE,* a cosmopolitan citizen of the world and of history, one needs a fundamental background in the history and philosophy of various political and economic systems. Without this knowledge and understanding we are trapped into decisions and laws that deteriorate our quality-of-life and condemn our future.

---

1. James R. Evans, *America's Choice: Twilight's Last Gleaming or Dawn's Early Light* p ix, Fisher Institute, Dallas: 1981

We need to cherish individual freedom and protect it by understanding the language of politics, "total tyranny against relative freedom,[2]" and the link between personal freedom and governmental power:

> Though we cannot foresee the values and spiritual climate of post-economic man, certain conjectures are permissible. While the majority of Europeans are still hypnotized by the anachronistic battlecries of Left and Right, Capitalism and Socialism, history has moved on to a new alternative, a new conflict which cuts across the old lines of division. The real content of this conflict can be summed up in one phrase: total tyranny against relative freedom. —Arthur Koestler, "An Outgrown Dilemma" (1950) in *The Trail of the Dinosaur* (1955).

A Democracy as a Republic: Total Tyranny against Relative Freedom

What if "democracy" is not what we think it is or should be? What if a republic is really what we want to be? What if democracy is a flawed political system that degenerates into a form far worse? What if a republic were the grand design of the Founding Fathers and they did all in their power to prevent a democracy or worse?

What if these words are not synonyms with similar meaning, but antonyms, with opposite meaning? What if one is tyranny creeping towards socialism and slavery, while the other protects personal freedom, and commands the full power of government to uphold individual rights and strengthen personal freedoms?

What if we are careless with our words, thoughts, ideas and understanding, so much so, that we jeopardize the very conditions we seek to enjoy, preserve and propagate?

Why Study and Know Political and Economic Systems?

John Marshall, Chief Justice of the Supreme Court in the early 1800's said, "Between a balanced republic and a democracy, the difference is like that between order and chaos." Perhaps there is more we ought to know about the indepth meaning of these two words.

"Make the World Safe for Democracy." We first heard those words extolling "democracy" from President Woodrow Wilson in 1917, defending America's entry into World War I. If the true and total concepts of the word "democracy" were known and understood, that rallying cry might better have said to "Make the World Safe *from* Democracy," when we know more about that emancipatory political system called a republic.

2. Bryan Magee, "The Language of Politics," *Encounter,* p 23, May 1986

History repeats itself. With the prospect of another world war, another U. S. President, Franklin Delano Roosevelt, told us we must gear up to defeat the enemies of freedom by making America "the arsenal of Democracy." Another war, another slogan. Another injection of a supposedly favorable, even desirable social, economic and political system called democracy. It must be good. Everybody's talking about it. They are all in favor of it. What is it?

Democracy as Republic:
Changing Definitions Lead to "Fuzzy" Understanding

In 1928, the *U. S. Army Training Manual*[3] quite accurately defined democracy:

Democracy

- A government of the masses. Authority derived through mass meeting or any form of "direct" expression. Results in mobocracy.

- Attitude toward property is communistic—negating property rights.

- Attitude toward law is that the will of the majority shall regulate, whether it be based upon deliberation or governed by passion, prejudice, and impulse, without restraint or regard to consequences.

- Results in demagogism, license, agitation, discontent, anarchy.

The manual then gave the characteristics of a *republic,* which the Founders had vigorously and knowledgeably supported over a pure democracy or any other form of government:

Republic

- Authority is derived through the election by the people of public officials best fitted to represent them.

- Attitude toward property is respect for laws and individual rights, and a sensible economic procedure.

- Attitude toward law is the administration of justice in accord with fixed principles and established evidence, with a strict regard for consequences.

- A greater number of citizens and extent of territory may be brought within its compass.

- Avoids the dangerous extreme of either tyranny or mobocracy.

3. W. Cleon Skousen *The Five Thousand Year Leap: TwentyEight Ideas That Changed the World,* 1981, p. 157, National Center for Constitutional Studies, HC 61, Box 1056, Malta, ID 83342-9704 Reprinted with permission

- Results in statesmanship, liberty, reason, justice, contentment, and progress.

Then something changed. The 1952 *Soldiers Guide* stated:

- Meaning of democracy.

- Because the United States is a democracy, the majority of the people decide how our government will be organized and run,

- And that includes the Army, Navy, and Air Force.

- The people do this by electing representatives, and these men and women then carry out the wishes of the people.

Democracy Not Mentioned in the "Freedom Documents"

Wheedling its way into our thinking, our vocabulary, even our approbation, was so abhorrent a word and concept that the Founders of America never once placed "democracy" into the Declaration of Independence, U.S. Constitution, or Bill of Rights.

The power of a word is the power of an idea, which is ultimately the power to shape destiny. More directly, to be responsible we pledge ourselves to know old words, learn new words and look up and understand exact definitions and usages of unfamiliar words. Words are the tools of our thoughts, ideals and motivations.

To know words is to adopt new powers of knowledge, understanding and analysis, and subsequently, new powers of communication and persuasion. Keep a dictionary and encyclopedia handy. Use them! Be "picky" about the words you use and how you use them. Be equally particular about words others use and how they use them. If you have a question, ask, challenge, learn. Keep your thinking and communications tools—words—sharp and accurate.

The definition of *democracy is* "government by the people; especially: rule of the majority; a government in which supreme power is vested in the people and exercised by them directly or indirectly through a system of representation usually involving periodically held free elections" *(Webster's New Collegiate Dictionary,* 1994).

Contrasting, a *republic* is "a government in which supreme power resides in a body of citizens entitled to vote and is exercised by elected officers and representatives responsible to them and governing them according to law."

The important distinction is that a *republic is* rule "according to law." A *democra*cy is "rule of the majority." The concept of a republic, then, places the governors—the "rulers"—under the same law as the governed—the "ruled."

America was carefully designed to be a republic, not a democracy. It is a nation of law, called People's Law, where the rulers as well as the ruled obey the law. A *democracy* is where a majority of the people rule, prone to distort, possibly ignore or "creatively interpret" the law for self-serving purposes. As it becomes increasingly more powerful and oppressive of the rights of the minority and the individual, it becomes "mobocracy," defined less precisely as a "tyranny of the majority."

The Word Democracy: Used and Heard, Over and Over

We cannot be tricked into adopting something that if we knew it was potentially or actually harmful, we would reject out of hand and fight. Or would we?

Former Governor Lehman of New York in his first inaugural message in 1933, did not once use the word democracy. Two years later he used it twice. In 1939 it was used 25 times and a year later it was invoked 33 times.

When we like the sound of something, especially our favorable perception of it, we can really have a love affair with it.

America's Founding Fathers studied these concepts with depth and concern.

The Father of the Constitution, James Madison, offered a concise definition of a republic[4]:

> We may define a republic to be ... a government which derives all its powers directly or indirectly from the great body of the people, and is administered by persons holding their offices during pleasure for a limited period, or during good behavior. It is *essential* to such government that it be derived from the great body of the society, not from an inconsiderable portion or a favored class of it; otherwise a handful of tyrannical nobles, exercising their oppressions by a delegation of their power, might aspire to the rank of republicans and claim for their government the honorable title of republic.

Of democracy Madison said[5]:

> Democracies have ever been spectacles of turbulence and contention; have ever been found incompatible with personal security, or the rights of property; and have in general been as short in their lives as they have been violent in their deaths ... A republic, by which I mean a government in which the scheme of representation takes place, opens a different prospect and promises the cure for which we are seeking.

4. Ibid, p. 154

5. Concepts and quotes for this section come from the 1961 article, "Republics and Democracies: Without the proper foundation Liberty will crumble!" by Robert Welch, *The New American,* p 27-34, Appleton, Wisconsin, June 30, 1987. Reprinted with permission

Alexander Hamilton said: "It had been observed that a pure democracy if it were practicable would be the most perfect government. Experience has proved that no position is more false than this. The ancient democracies in which the people themselves deliberated never possessed one good feature of government. Their very character was tyranny; their figure deformity."

Samuel Adams warned:

Remember, Democracy never lasts long. It soon wastes, exhausts and murders itself! There never was a democracy that 'did not commit suicide.'

Hamilton said,

We are a Republican Government. Real liberty is never found in despotism or in the extremes of Democracy.

Other world thinkers of history had their own thoughts about all this. Herbert Spencer, English philosopher, wrote in an article on *The Americans*:

The Republican form of government is the highest form of government; but because of this it requires the highest type of human nature—a type nowhere at present existing.

Thomas Babington Macaulay said,

I have long been convinced that institutions purely democratic must, sooner or later, destroy liberty or civilization, or both.

Ludwig Lewisohn observed,

Democracy, which began by liberating men politically, has developed a dangerous tendency to enslave him through the tyranny of majorities and the deadly power of their opinion.

G. K. Chesterton, almost echoing prophecy for an unknown future, said:

You can never have a revolution in order to establish a democracy. You must have a democracy in order to have revolution.

Alexis de Tocqueville warned,

If ever the free institutions of America are destroyed, that event will arise from the unlimited tyranny of the majority.

Get a Horse, a Posse and a Rope. Find a Tree. We are having a Hanging!

Two illustrations clarify the difference between a pure democracy and a republic. The first involves The Old West and "prairie justice." The horse stealer has been caught, the ranchers band together to hang the thief. At voting time it is 12 for hanging, 1 (the accused) against. It is pure democracy. The total vote is taken. The man is hanged.

A republic, the "system of laws, not men," is exercised. In the same scenario the horse thief is apprehended and about to suffer vigilante justice. But stop! The marshal rides up, says the man is innocent until proven guilty. The accused is taken into town for a trial, with evidence and testimony offered to a jury of his peers in front of a judge. Upon reaching a verdict, the law is carried out, the appropriate sentence made and justice served.

A second example is more contemporary, but illustrative. A college fraternal group consists of ten upperclassmen, five freshmen. At a meeting a motion is made and seconded that all five new members have their heads shaved. The vote, not surprisingly, is ten "for," five "against.' The "frosh," subject to the will of the majority in this minidemocracy, get their heads shaved. Very "democratic."

But this is a republic. The rights of the minority are respected, and their persons are protected by the Bill of Rights, Article IV, "The right of the people to be secure in their persons, houses, papers, and effects against unreasonable searches and seizures, shall not be violated. . . . " The law protects all equally, even the minority from the whims of the majority.

The Pathway to the Magic of the Miracle of the Republic

George Santayana said, "Those who cannot remember the past are doomed to repeat it." When the Founding Fathers were forging their new nation, they were determined to consider the experience and mistakes of the past, combined with the wisdom of the political philosophers. They recognized their opportunity to fashion the best, freest, fairest, most just and durable, government and society possible. They took into account the foibles of frail, imperfect man and the unlimited potential for evil of unbridled power and potentially uncontrolled and unconscionable government.

The extremes of government have already been mentioned. Zero, or no government, is *anarchism* or anarchy. That is a fatal form of government because all the evils of humankind run rampant, and destroy the fiber and fabric of society.

The other extreme is total government, *totalitarianism*. There are no individual rights or freedoms, and all effort and allegiance is subordinate, from the individual, the family and the people, to the state, and to the ruler(s).

Somewhere in between is the best way and the best balance of government that provides the most protection and the most freedom for the most people. For the Founders, the best guide available was a look back through history to examine the wisdom of the political philosophers.

Plato's Political Community: Guardians, Soldiers, Artisans

Plato[6] offered to posterity the gift of a vision of a better world in his famous work, *The Republic*. There he divided the community into three basic elements: the *rulers*, or guardians; the *soldiers,* or auxiliary; and the *artisans,* or tradesmen.

People were best suited to fill one of these three roles. It would be unusual that a person born into one could emerge into another. He said what distinguished rulers was wisdom, "a form of knowledge." The guardians had courage, while temperance was possessed in common by all three classes and consists of "a unanimity or harmonious agreement between the naturally superior and inferior elements on the question which of the two should govern."

In today's context, these would be a nation of willing people, those willing to work, and those willing to let them. Those "willing to work," who create the necessary goods and services for society to survive, are the artisans. Those "willing to let them" are the rulers and soldiers—the governing class—who in this context are the elite, the enlightened intelligentsia, destined to enact punitive laws to tell others how to live their lives. But the concept was predicated on enlightened, compassionate leadership.

Enter Stage Right, Plato's Philosopher-King

Plato coined the term and concept of the "philosopher-king," a kindly, wise and all-knowing ruler that would create the best government and living conditions for the most people. He said, "Unless either philosophers become kings in their countries or those who are now called kings and rulers come to be sufficiently inspired with a genuine desire for wisdom . . . there can be no rest from troubles for states . . . nor can this commonwealth we have imagined ever till then see the light of day and grow to its full stature." In other words, the perfect government envisioned by Plato had to be staffed by perfect people, few available, difficult to create and hard to come by.

The stringent and demanding criteria for a philosopher-king as defined by Plato included the following:

- a constant passion for any knowledge that will reveal to them something of that reality which endures forever;
- a love of truth and a hatred of falsehood that will not tolerate untruth in any form;

6. F. R. Duplantier, "Wise Men Bearing Gifts," *The New American*, 12/22/86, pp 31-36, Appleton, Wisconsin. Reprinted with permission

- the renunciation of those pleasures of which the body is the instrument;
- freedom from the love of money, meanness, pretentiousness, and cowardice;
- fairmindedness, gentleness, and sociability;
- a quick mind, a good memory; and
- a sense of proportion.

In short, the king who is a philosopher will be "quick to learn and to remember, magnanimous and gracious, the friend and kinsmen of truth, justice, courage, temperance."

Looking back from what we know today, those who worked hard to create the wealth in Plato's society of course were the tradesmen, or workers. The rulers and soldiers lived off the fruits of the tradesmen's labor, offering in return, peace and harmony and a desirable climate in which to live and work. In other words, much like today, they espoused "a nation of willing people, those willing to work, and those willing to let them."

Aristotle's Government: Monarchy, Aristocracy, Polity

Aristotle, the father of political science, said all governments belong to one of three main groups: 1) *monarchy,* rule by one person, 2) *aristocracy,* rule by a few persons, and 3) *democracy* or *polity,* rule by many persons. He further described monarchy and aristocracy as government by men of superior character and intelligence. Democracy was described as government by and of the people—and also for the good of all.

A government that ruled only for the rulers was termed *corrupt.* A corrupt monarchy was a *tyranny;* a corrupt aristocracy was an *oligarchy*; and a corrupt democracy was a *tyranny of the majority.*

A tyrant ruled to satisfy his personal need for power. An oligarchy ruled to enrich the ruling few. A tyranny of the majority was the rule by the crowds, or "mobocracy." None of these three is directed to advantage of the whole body of citizens.

Groupthink, Life, Liberty, Property, Happiness, and Lessening of Freedom

A government "directed to the advantage of the whole body citizens" is difficult to come by in a pure democracy. Such a government of the majority, immersed in "groupthink" and trying to be all things to all people, can lead to abuses.

The Founding Fathers envisioned a government that was to protect "Life, Liberty and *pursuit* of Happiness" (Declaration of Independence) as "the self-evident truths endowed by their Creator . . . the unalienable Rights." The government was to provide protection to assure citizens not be "deprived of life, liberty, or property, without due process of law," per Article V of the Bill of Rights (U.S. Constitution).

Government Can Assume Only Responsibilities of People to Protect People

Another way to interpret these actions was that government was a servant of the people and could only perform such duties as delegated by the people, *which the people themselves could do,* such as self-protection and self-preservation. Government can protect people if authorized by the people, because people can protect people.

Protection of property, or protection from being victimized by stealing, is another legitimate function of government. Stealing itself, is *not* a legitimate function of government, even if it is "legal theft." Stealing was and is against the law, and every citizen has a right to expect government protection from such invasion, intrusion or loss—especially from the government. Government can protect people's property if authorized by the people because people can protect their own property.

Government Legalized Theft in a Democracy: Cut the Subtleties

What happens in a pure democracy? The majority can vote to invade the rights of the minority, and seemingly grant government the power to do what the citizen cannot do as a citizen; or if done, would be punished by imprisonment, fine or both.

I can look to my neighbor on the left and see two cars in the driveway, and to the right, see none, and think, "that's not fair." But should I go beyond thinking to acting, to take one car from the left and give it to the neighbor on the right, the sheriff will rightfully be there to arrest me for stealing. We can do the same thing more subtly using government as the "middleman," and money as the means. We overtax one person, expropriate money legitimately earned, useful to buy food and other goods and services; then "the government" supplies food to another. Because it is done indirectly and invisibly, with government as an intermediary, it seems acceptable.

It is not acceptable in a constitutional republic. It is theft, perhaps legalized theft, which is against the meaning and intent of the constitution.

Another way to look at it is to change things just a little. Instead of this commonly-accepted transfer of earned wealth, do it another, less subtle way.

A representative from the government tells you they have determined that you had a bad year compared to your neighbors. Five of them each earn $31,000; you earn only $25,000. The government determines that's not fair and authorizes you to demand payment from each, of $1,000. All you need do is go door-to-door, show them your government authorization and collect the money, $1,000 from each neighbor.

How would you like that assignment? How different is that in principle from a graduated income tax to take relatively more from some, government the taker, to give to others, government the giver. Who gets power and money, who loses power and money? What does this do to incentive to work?

This works well with those who receive—specific groups such a farmers, business, cultural arts enthusiasts, even lately, sports and sport complexes financed with government dollars (read that "taxpayer dollars").

Without the government as go-between, what is really going on is more apparent, less tolerable. It is theft, with an intermediary with clout— power of government and force of law. If it can be done to one citizen, it can be done to all citizens, but should be done to no citizens.

Pure democracy encourages strange things in the name of good, but which are not, as Aristotle wished them to be, "directed to the advantage of the whole body of citizens." Some are helped, but others are injured in the process, definitely not "all men are created equal," nor "the general welfare" which hurts no one, helps everyone.

Horatio Bunce: Not Yours to Give
Congressman Davy Crockett told "I Won't Vote for You"

In the early 1800's Congress was voting to appropriate $10,000 public money for a widow of a distinguished naval officer[7]. Davy Crockett said, "We have the right, as individuals, to give away as much of our own money as we please in charity; but as members of Congress we have no right so to appropriate a dollar of the public money. . . . We cannot, without the grossest corruption, appropriate this money as the payment of a debt. We have not the semblance of authority to appropriate it as charity." He then said how relatively poor he was but would be willing to give one weeks pay, and should all the members do so, even more money would have lawfully been raised.

Congressman Crockett learned this lesson from constituent Horatio Bunce who said bluntly, "I voted for you the last time . . . I shall not vote for you again." When asked why, Bunce said he knew of Crockett voting to appropriate $10,000 "to some sufferers by a fire in Georgetown." Crockett said he had voted for it and wondered why the concern. A learned and principled Constitutionalist, Bunce's answer was instructive:

7. Stedman, W. David, and Lewis, LaVaughn G., Eds., *Our Ageless Constitution,* pp 211-213, Americanism Foundation, 48 N. Linwood Ave., Norwalk, OH 44857. Reprinted with permission

The power of collecting and disbursing money at pleasure is the most dangerous power than can be intrusted to man . . . for there is not a man in the United States who can ever guess how much he pays to the government. So you see, that while you are contributing to relieve one, you are drawing it from thousands who are even worse off than he. . . . If you have the right to give to one, you have the right to give to all; and, as the Constitution neither defines charity nor stipulates the amount, you are at liberty to give to any and every thing which you may believe, or profess to believe, is a charity, and to any amount you may think proper. You will very easily perceive what a wide door this would open for fraud and corruption and favoritism, on the one hand, and for robbing the people on the other. No, Colonel, Congress has no right to give charity. Individual members may give as much of their own money as they please, but they have no right to touch a dollar of the public money for that purpose . . . and the people about Washington, no doubt, applauded you for relieving them from the necessity of giving by giving what was not yours to give. . . . The people have delegated to Congress, by the Constitution, the power to do certain things. To do these, it is authorized to collect and pay moneys, and for nothing else. Everything beyond this is usurpation, and a violation of the Constitution.

Think about, ". . . by giving what was not yours to give . . ." Congressman Crockett gave the "surprise ending":

You remember that I proposed to give a week's pay. There are in that House many very wealthy men—men who think nothing of spending a week's pay, or a dozen of them, for a dinner or a wine party when they have something to accomplish by it. Some of those same men made beautiful speeches upon the great debt of gratitude which the country owed the deceased—a debt which could not be paid by money—and the insignificance a sum as $10,000, when weighed against the honor of the nation. Yet not one of them responded to my proposition. Money with them is nothing but trash when it is to come out of the people. But it is the one great thing for which most of them are striving and many of them sacrifice honor, integrity, and justice, to obtain it.

Here contrast a constitutional republic, a nation governed by law, versus democracy, by the majority, in violation of the law of the land.

'Education' and Dissipation for Reverence for Law

Author F. R. Duplantier comments on gradual change:

The decline in American leadership has corresponded to the gradual transformation of our country from a republic into a democracy, accompanied by the dissipation of that reverence for law that is the basis of a republic and the concurrent rise of the factionalism that is typical of democracy. Education is at the root of this problem. Our education system not only fails to produce philosopher-kings, or any distant approximation of such ideal beings, but it also inculcates in the mass of people a dissatisfaction with their lot in life that in turn leads to presumption and contentiousness. It is in large measure due to our 'education' that we have come to regard our true callings as somehow ignoble and that, with our ambitions enlarged beyond the limits of our aptitude, we aspire to occupations for which we are unfit. Furthermore, we have developed an unwillingness to submit to authority and an inability to recognize our superiors, with the result that we are reduced to selecting for leaders men who are no more qualified than we are. We have become an intemperate people.

Democracy, Progressive Income Tax, and the Middle Class, a Goose being Plucked

Aristotle gave great thought to the workings of a democracy, particularly to "the tyranny of Equality":

> In democracies, justice is considered to mean equality. It does mean equality—but equality for those who are equal, and not for all.

Despite the weakness of democracy, it can be a relatively more stable form of government than an oligarchy because of the number and character in the middle class. In a democracy with no middle class, there are only slaves and masters, those powerless and those empowered to rule. Thus, delaying the inevitable, one saving grace of the America Republic becoming more a democracy on its way leftward to socialism is buoyed up still by the large middle class.

Adoption of the sixteenth amendment and imposition of the progressive income tax in 1913, set in motion a mechanism to tax at much higher amounts *and* rates, on those who worked harder, created more wealth and made more money. The initial premise which helped sell the idea of the progressive income tax was to "soak the rich," along with the envy, jealousy and anger that were propagated by those in power, towards those with more, by those with less.

At that time, in equivalent terms, only about 1% of the population was taxed, and they at relative levels of 1 to 7%, above incomes over $180,000 in today's dollars[8]. According to Goode, "The 1913 act was expected to

8. Richard Goode, *The Individual Income Tax,* p 3, Brookings Institution: 1976; Irwin Schiff *The Great Income Tax Hoax,* p 179, Freedom Books, PO Box 5303, Hamden, CN 0651E 1985, $18

apply to only about 1 percent of the population, including taxpayers and their independents, and the actual number was smaller. As recently as 1939, only 5 percent . . . were subject to the income tax. In 1970, 81 percent were covered." For 1998, 126-million 1040 forms were filled out and signed under penalty of perjury by individuals and families, afflicting virtually the entire population.

Helped by inflation, "the disease of money," which requires more dollars to buy the same or less goods and services, most taxpayers are progressively placed in much higher tax brackets and taxed as though rich. Though taxpayers with inflation-driven incomes do not gain more buying power, the government acquires more taxing power with a net purchasing power loss to the individual or family, even while "making more money." In 1986 over 103 million returns were filed with average tax liability of $4,471, a 14.9% tax on adjusted gross income.[9] In 1996 the average tax grew to $7,200, 14.5% of adjusted gross income for 120-million returns.[10]

As population grows and more of the ruled have to work longer and harder, representative democracy, sometimes termed a republic, begins to better serve the purposes of government, not the people. The "consent of the governed" became a guidepost of modern representative government, those words the third sentence of the Declaration of Independence. The governed were cajoled or lulled into consenting to practically anything.

The Evolution of the Constitution

Constitutional government came into the picture.[11] Its first requirement was "write it down"; that is, put in writing what constitutes the government we wish to design, implement, operate and support, a "Constitution." That is what Solon did in Greece about 594 BC. Elected as Archon of Athens, Solon took a whole new approach to government, but he went only half way with his principle of "government by written and permanent law." The result was that the people obeyed the rulers, and both the people and the rulers obeyed the laws. "Write it down" worked because all the people knew the law, knew each other knew the law, and all were expected to abide by the law.

Solon canceled all debts, virtually freeing the slaves. He set up qualifications for public office based on wealth; then reorganized and published the laws of Athens.

The Romans completed the work of Solon by establishing a framework or organization for carrying out the laws. The Roman Senate sent a

9. *Statistical Abstract of the United States, 1989* pp 314, 315

10. *Statistical Abstract of the United States, 1999*, p 359

11. Continuing from Robert Welch's "Republics and Democracies"

commission to Greece to study and report on the work of Solon. The Roman Assembly chose ten men, the *Decemviri,* to rule with supreme power while formulating a new code of laws for Rome. The Romans quickly picked up on the essentials of a stable, lasting and beneficial government. They incorporated into their new republic checks and balances of power, and the diffusion of power (rather than historic concentration of power).

So intent were the Romans on protecting the people from government oppression, Tribunes were set up around 350 B. C. with the express purpose and duty to protect the people of Rome against their own government. (This was much similar to some cautious signers of our Constitution, who refused to sign until they were assured, even guaranteed an individual Bill of Rights, to protect individuals from government oppression.) Proposed and adopted were *The Twelve Tables* of the Roman Republic, which according to historian Will Durant, remained intact for 900 years as their written constitution, the basic law of Rome.

Powers Beyond Angels and Binding Man-Government in Chains

The Founders[12] took note of all this—the frailties of man, his ambitious nature to aspire to power, and the natural proclivities of government to grow and control. George Washington knew government could protect or destroy freedom: " is not reason, it is not eloquence—it is force! Like fire, it is a dangerous servant and a fearful master."

Thomas Jefferson explored the propensity of misplaced confidence in man:

It would be a dangerous delusion were a confidence in the men of our choice to silence our fears for the safety of our right; that confidence is everywhere the parent of despotism; free government is founded in jealousy, and not in confidence; it is jealousy, and not confidence, which prescribes limited constitutions to bind down those whom we are obliged to trust with power; that our Constitution has accordingly fixed the limits to which, and no farther, our confidence may go. . . . In questions of power, then, let no more be said of confidence in man, *but bind him down from mischief by the chains of the constitution.* [emphasis added]

James Madison recognized human frailties to govern:

It may be a reflection on human nature that such devices (as Constitutional chains) should be necessary to control the abuses of government. But what is government itself but the greatest of all reflections on human nature? . . . If angels were to govern men,

12. Skousen, pp 164, 165

neither external nor internal controls on government would be necessary. (But lacking these,) framing a government which is to be administered by men over men, the great difficulty lies in this: You *must first enable the government to control the governed; and in the next place oblige it to control itself.* [emphasis added]

Thus the case for written law and the defined organization of a written constitution, a framework for government, was made to assure a republic of representative government and laws, rather than a democracy and the foibles and follies of mankind in search of power through government over his fellow citizens. More understanding of government and political systems may further clarify the enormous responsibility and near-magic outcome of the Founders' efforts.

Five Political Systems Boil Down to Two

John McManus[13] explains, "Americanism starts off with belief in God, who is the source of unalienable rights. It proceeds to the limitation of government as the essence of freedom and to freely accepted moral restraints as the guide to individuals." He extolls America's heritage:

> It took close to six thousand years of recorded history for the truths embodied in the Declaration of Independence to be incorporated as the foundation of a nation. We, who have enjoyed more freedom than any men who have ever walked this earth, owe it to ourselves to preserve, to protect, and to strengthen Americanism. We also owe it to our children and to generations yet unborn.

Democracy, he explains, is from two Greek words, *demos,* people, and *kratein,* to rule, meaning "the people to rule." Republic is from two Latin words, *Res* meaning thing, and *Publica,* meaning public, or "the public thing," the law. He says "A true Republic is one that has a law which recognizes the rights of individuals and, therefore, the limitation in the law is not upon individuals but upon the government." Putting these concepts together, he says, "The essence of freedom is the limitation of government."

Shifting to government's role in freedom, he says the most important feature of a government is not the form but the amount. "There is only so much freedom or power available. If the government has all of it, the people have none and are slaves. If the government is limited, and has little power, then freedom resides with the individual."

Government, says McManus, seems to be present in five forms but they really come down to just two. The initial five are *Monarchy*

13. John F. McManus *An Overview of Our World,* p 3, 1971, The John Birch Society, Appleton, Wisconsin 54913. Reprinted with permission

TOTAL Power of ONE in America

Dictatorship, rule by one; *Oligarchy*, rule by a few, an elite; *Democracy*, rule by majority; *Republic*, rule by law; and *Anarchy*, rule by no one (See Figure No. 34).

McManus crosses out *Monarchy Dictatorship* right away because it rarely if ever exists. Every king, or reigning monarch has a cabinet, round table or council, so it is in fact, rule by a few—the elite. It is really an *Oligarchy*, the most popular form of government in the world, probably even in history. *Anarchy* too is ruled out as so unstable the people panic and insist on any other form of government, even a dictatorship. With *anarchy*, we have total freedom, but no law and order; with a *dictatorship* we have total law and order, but no freedom.

POLITICAL SYSTEMS FROM MONARCHY TO ANARCHY

Figure No. 34

Monarchy Dictatorship	Oligarchy	Democracy	Republic	Anarchy
Rule by ONE	Rule by ELITE	Rule by MAJORITY	Rule by LAW	Rule by NONE

So besides *Oligarchy*, we are left with a *Democracy* and a *Republic*. McManus further analyzes that because of its nature even the democracy is an unstable form of government. It can only change in one of two directions, to an oligarchy, or to a republic. As he puts it "You may for a time live in Democracy, but not for long. Democracy *must* lead to mobocracy and thence to tyranny. It cannot go any other way."

Historian, Professor Alexander Tytler described Democracy:

A Democracy cannot exist as a permanent form of government. It can only exist until a majority of the voters discover they can vote themselves largesse from the public treasury. From that moment on the majority always votes for the (political) candidates promising the most benefits from the public treasury with the result, that a Democracy always collapses over loose fiscal policy, always followed by a dictatorship.

Therefore, there are really only two forms of government: a *Republic*, a government of law which limits the government and protects the individual; or an *Oligarchy*, with rule by man, where the rulers have unlimited power, while the individual is vulnerable and powerless.

Capitalism: Two Forms, Competitive and Monopolistic

Capital is that which can be used to produce—it is the means of production. It is not only machines and facilities that can manufacture or produce goods and products. Capital is also money, and in addition to machinery and facilities, it includes technology, management, patents and innovation, all parts of the "factors of production," land, labor and capital.

We can see that all economic and political systems must have capital for their survival and sustenance.

Ownership and control of capital are what differentiate the various systems. And even these can be broken down basically to two, *competitive capitalism* and *monopolistic capitalism.*

Ownership is who owns something, has purchased and holds title to it. Control is who actually uses it and decides how, where and when it is used. For example, a parent owns a car. The teenager drives it. The parent who paid for it and keeps it in safe operating condition, obviously maintains the joy (and expense) of ownership. The student who really enjoys its use in driving and transportation is in control, at least most of the time. As McManus puts it, complete ownership allows you to "keep it, sell it, trade it, or give it away; in short, to do whatever you want with it as long as you don't infringe on the rights of others."

Back to political systems, in the competitive system, capital is both owned and controlled privately, recognizing a citizen's inherent right to own property. In the monopolistic system, capital is owned either privately or by the state, but is controlled by the state. The state denies the citizen the right to hold private property.

Some very predictable things happen to prices and quality of production in either system. In the competitive system, the customer has a choice of competing products, so prices are low, quality is high, and must be so for the business to survive in the free marketplace. In the monopolistic system, it is just the opposite. With no competition, prices are high and quality is low. Why should it be otherwise? You have no choice but to buy the one thing that is available, or not to buy.

Preferring the competitive system are individual workers who want high prices for their own quality, productive labor, and customers who want low prices and high quality for goods and services.

Only those who want power over others prefer the monopoly system in its various forms. This is especially true if you are the ruler who controls the state monopoly in its various forms:

Communism: *All* capital owned and controlled by the state
Socialism: *Most* capital owned and controlled by the state
Naziism: *Some* capital owned and controlled by the state
Fascism: *No* capital owned, but *all* capital controlled by the state.

Capital is fairly simple to understand. A child sells lemonade using as capital a table, pitcher of lemonade, glasses and sugar, to provide exchange of goods and services for money.

The important factor of who owns and controls capital tells the freedom story. The best system for the most people is the free enterprise system where individuals own, control, use and dispose of property. "Freedom and private property go hand in hand and always have," emphasizes McManus.

Republics that Aren't

A convolution of words and contradiction in terms are found in names of countries who choose to improperly use words to confound. Just because it is in the name do not think to be republics those such as the People's Republic of China and the former-Union of Soviet Socialist Republics. A communist regime by any name is still communism, not a republic.

America: Let's Keep This Republic a Republic!

We have explored the difference between a democracy and a republic The republic has more features, a better design, and a better outcome and future for all of us. We can say that:

- America is a republic and was designed to be so.

- A republic is democracy with the added feature of *representation* and critical distinction of *rule by law,* for both rulers and ruled.

- America is a republic that works by the democratic process of the will of the majority, with full protection of the minority.

- America was designed as a Constitutional Republic where laws are written down for all to know and follow. The Constitution provides a framework for organization and direction, telling the government what it can and must do, and what it cannot and must not do.

- Protection of the individual citizen is spelled out by the first ten amendments to the Constitution, the Bill of Rights, which serve as a list of "thou shalt nots" of what federal and state governments cannot do to people. In addition, the government is empowered, even *commanded* to protect those rights with all the DEFINED powers of the government. The fourteenth amendment extends the Bill of Rights to "the several states."

- The difference between a republic and a democracy is subtle. We must know the difference and expend time, effort, resources and courage to preserve that difference for our posterity—those who

come after us, much as those in the past did for us, and sometimes
didn't.

• America is a republic, not a democracy. Let's keep it that way!

After the constitutional convention, Ben Franklin was asked "What kind
of government have you given us?" He replied, "A republic, ma'am; equality,
if you can keep it."

Thank God, *Power of ONE,* that we have been given a Republic called
the United States of America. Let us pledge. Let us say it right and mean it:

THE PLEDGE OF ALLEGIANCE

I pledge allegiance
To the Flag
Of the United States of America
And to the R E P U B L I C (!)
For Which It Stands
One Nation Under God, Indivisible,
With Liberty and Justice for all.

America is a republic, not a democracy. Let's keep it that way.

Questions for Review

1. Why does the "Pledge of Allegiance" sound strange to say ". . .
   And to the DEMOCRACY ? . . ." What is the subtle but important
   difference between a democracy and a republic? Why is even a
   republic lacking without one more important word? What is that
   word? How is it possible that "American Freedom is declining and
   soon will be only a memory?"

2. Why is it important to have "fundamentals, historic knowledge
   and philosophical background of the various political and economic
   systems?" Discuss how it is possible that "democracy" is the
   opposite of the political system that we need and want for a long
   run society of freedom and prosperity?

3. Give two 20th century U. S. Presidents' statements, with time and
   occasion in history, when "democracy" was touted, giving enhanced
   but undeserved desirability to the word and concept. What
   fundamental changes took place in the U. S. Army manual's
   description of democracy between 1928 and 1952? How important
   is the power of a word or the power of an idea? Why? What is the
   "important and profound distinction" between a democracy and
   constitutional republic?

4. Did America's Founding Fathers have any knowledge of past democracies when they set out to design the United States of America? Did they have strong feelings about a democracy? How many times is "democracy" mentioned in the Freedom Documents—the Declaration of Independence, U.S. Constitution and it incredibly important Bill of Rights?

5. Give an example of pure democracy in action. A republic. Why is it best always to learn what has gone on before, then to proceed forward?

6. What three roles were in "Plato's Community?" Whose were the government? The workers and producers? Were they equal classes? What is the likelihood of finding or creating Plato's kindly and wise "Philosopher-King?" What were the "qualities of the true philosopher and leader?"

7. What three main groups did Aristotle say governments belonged to? What was a government ruled only for the rulers termed? What were the three types of flawed government and the terms used to describe them?

8. Discuss how a government can only assume responsibilities held by its citizens? Can it protect people? Protect property? Assure performance of contracts? Confiscate property from some to give to others? Tell Representative Davy Crockett's story, "Not Yours to Give." Why is Horatio Bunce a Power of ONE hero? How did the progressive income tax begin? How is it now?

9. What did Solon, Greek Archon of Athens, do that began more stable governments? How did the Romans (Decemviri, Tribunes) carry on and add to Solon's work. Why is a defined and restrained government needed? What five political systems boil down to what two? Name and describe the two forms of capitalism. How do ownership and control differentiate different governments, particularly the four despotic "ism's"? What is capital?

10. What is a Constitutional Republic and why is it a more preferable form of government?

My premise is that the destiny of man is to emerge or to evolve toward an advancing potential, and that individual liberty is essential to such progress.   —Leonard Read

The history of mankind teaches the immutable lesson that whenever men have placed their destiny in the man-made political force of all-powerful government in order to attain social progress, they doom themselves and their posterity to personal regimentation and economic mediocrity.   —James R. Evans

What do we mean when we say that first of all we seek liberty? I often wonder whether we do not rest our hopes too much upon Constitutions, upon laws, and upon courts. These are false hopes; believe me these are false hopes. Liberty lies in the hearts of men and women; when it dies there, no constitution, no law, no court can do much to save it.
—Judge Learned Hand

All, too, will bear in mind this sacred principle, that though the will of the majority is in all cases to prevail, that will to be rightful must be reasonable; that the minority possess their equal rights, which equal laws must protect, and to violate would be oppression.
—Thomas Jefferson

What experience and history teach is this: that people and government have never learned anything from history.
—Georg Wilhelm Friedrich Hegel

To know things as they are is better than to believe things as they seem.
—Tom Wicker

The death of democracy is not likely to be an assassination by ambush. It will be a slow extinction from apathy, indifference and under-nourishment.
—Robert M. Hutchins

It is of great importance in a republic, not only to guard the society against the oppression of its rulers; but to guard one part of the society against the injustices of the other part.
—James Madison

Caretakers of Freedom
Having elected leaders doesn't relieve us of the responsibility of being the caretakers of freedom. In America, We the People have the final responsibility and authority to see that our government stays within the bounds of God's purpose for it. Every employee of government is answerable to an appointed official. Every appointed official is answerable to an elected official. Every elected official is answerable to We the People. Within this constitutional republic, We the People are the highest human authority. We cannot shrink from our awesome responsibility as stewards of this freedom.
—Dr. Sterling Lacy

Chapter 17

DISCOVERING THE FREEDOM DOCUMENTS
Declaration, Constitution, and Bill of Rights

Liberty has never come from Government. Liberty has always come from the subjects of it. The history of liberty is a history of resistance, of limitations of governmental power, not the increase of it.   —President Woodrow Wilson

Back to the Basics of Freedom Documents

Be very clear that no piece of paper with writing on it protects rights or freedoms, no good idea enforces obligation, and no good intention compels responsibility. Ink on paper provides a record, and a means to communicate and preserve that record. The force behind it is *the people* who understand, resolve, and "solemnly publish and declare" that certain things are so and will remain so. Freedoms are maintained solely by "We the People."

That is you, *Power of ONE.* It is up to you, me and the rest of us to cherish and nourish freedom. We assure strong government to preserve, protect and strengthen freedom; yet not get so bullying it tramples, nor so big it destroys freedom. That is our assignment. To carry it out we become thoroughly familiar with the freedom documents. Then we share that knowledge and understanding with others, lots of others, so that all of "We the People" know our freedom documents and so fortify our freedoms.

A Power Dare Chapter: Do the Tough Stuff

This is a *"Power Dare* Chapter," *Power of ONE*. Read and heed your "Power Deed Creed."

The Freedom Documents: An Overview

The *Declaration of Independence* gives the values, beliefs and philosophies of the Founders. The *Constitution* is where the people authorize the government to exist, organizes, empowers and limits it, and tells it what to do. The *Bill of Rights* tells the government what it cannot do to the people. None of these tell the people what to do. We are a self-governing people.

Discovering the Declaration of Independence

The Declaration of Independence is the intent of Law. It puts into words what the Founding Fathers of the English Continental Colonies knew, thought and felt about the new country, America, and her deteriorating relationship with the Mother Country, England. Things were not as they should be and were quickly getting worse.

The Declaration was an affirmation of the source of freedom, God, as a statement of beliefs, values, ideals, and philosophies about how a country should be governed and how a people should be treated by their government. Signed by 54 representatives of the Colonies on July 4, 1776, it consisted of a preamble (probably the most important statement for freedom in the world), a declaration of rights, a bill of indictment against The Crown of England, then a statement of independence. It ended with,

> "And for the support of this Declaration, with a firm reliance on the protection of Divine Providence, we mutually pledge to each other our Lives, our Fortunes, and our sacred Honor."

This was not a mere formal signing of a document. It was "the fatal pledge." They signed this freedom document with their own blood. To the Crown they were committing high treason against England. These men knew the punishment for high treason[1]:

> To be hanged by the head until unconscious.
> Then cut down and revived.
> Then disemboweled and beheaded.
> Then cut into quarters.
> Each quarter to be boiled in oil.

The remnants were scattered abroad so the last resting-place of the offender would remain forever unnamed, unhonored and unknown.

That was their big commitment to freedom and the future!

1. Skousen, W. Cleon, *The Making of America,* p 31, National Center for Constitutional Studies, HC 61, Box 1056, Malta, ID 83342-9704 1/800/388-4512, Salt Lake City, UT: 1985

To truly appreciate, understand and enjoy the drama, spirit and personalities of the signing of the Declaration of Independence, see the play "1776," or get the videotape version. I need my "1776 fix" at least three times a year.

Discovering the Constitution

The United States Constitution specifies the structure, organization and functions of the central government, and defines its authority and responsibilities. Signed September 17, 1787, it lists the aims and methods of government, establishes the division of powers in three branches—legislative, executive and judicial, and their respective officials and assignments. It defines exactly what the federal government can and must do, what it cannot do, and what the states cannot do.

Though the Constitution is, by definition, the "supreme Law of the Land" (Article VI, Clause 2), it is *not* the law of the people, but of the government. There is nothing in the Constitution that tells people what to do or not do; only what government is, what powers it has and does not have, and how it is organized.

The Founders could have established either a national government or a federation of states. They ended up with a combination of both, to provide more flexibility, more freedom and a more effective government:

> The powers delegated by the proposed Constitution to the Federal Government are few and defined. Those which are to remain in the State Governments are numerous and indefinite. . . . The powers reserved to the States will extend to all the objects which, in the ordinary course of affairs, concern the lives, liberties, and properties of the people, and the internal order, improvement, and prosperity of the State. —James Madison, *The Federalist Papers,* No. 45

Here is *Webster's New World Dictionary* definition of *federal*:

> of or formed by a compact; specifically, designating or of a union of states, groups, etc. in which each member agrees to subordinate its governmental power to that of the central authority in certain specified common affairs.

Discovering the Bill of Rights

The Bill of Rights was added four years after the ratification of the Constitution, to protect the individual citizen from a potentially large and powerful government. Ratified December 15, 1791, the Bill of Rights is the first 10 amendments to the Constitution. Of 189 amendments proposed, 12 were voted upon and 10 were accepted. One, The Madison Amendment to control Congressional Salaries, though initiated back then, was ratified by the states in 1992. It is the 27th amendment, "No law varying the compensation for the services of the Senators and Representatives shall take effect until an election of Representatives shall have intervened."

Some thought the Bill of Rights unnecessary because essential protections were built into this limited federal government by the Constitution. The federation of states would never allow it to get powerful enough to abuse the people. Others thought a constitution useless without a bill of rights to protect people from government growth, power, taxation and abuse. In retrospect, who was right?

The Declaration is a statement of philosophy, principle and intent. The Constitution defines the central, federal government and tells it what to do and how. The Bill of Rights lists "thou shalt nots" to prohibit government abuse of citizens.

Rather than study these freedom documents in detail, we will become familiar with them in a way that is meaningful and contemporary. We will experience them in a "today" sense, rather than treat them as dead documents of the distant past.

The Freedom Documents are HERE, NOW!

Break the Law, Pay the Price

You are driving along in traffic, listening to the radio or talking with a friend. Why that uneasy feeling? You notice something unusual and unpleasant in your rear view mirror, a flashing set of red, yellow and blue lights. "Someone's in trouble," you say to yourself as you pull over to let "them" by. But "they" don't go by. "They" pull up behind you and stop. Someone gets out and approaches your car.

"Driver's license and car registration, please. Remove them from your billfold."

"What seems to be the matter, officer?" you query in your most innocent voice. She answers, "You were doing 50 miles an hour in a 25 mile school zone. I clocked you for two blocks. The fine for speeding 25 over a school zone speed limit is $75. You can mail in the fine or testify on your own behalf in court, date of which is set for two weeks from Friday on November 10th."

The law is clear or made very clear. You are presumed to know the law, and expected to follow it, and if you break the law, to be punished by it, with a fine, jail sentence, court appearance, etc. In case you have forgotten, you are reminded. The police officer performed her job by telling you the law and reading you your rights. You have a new problem—paying the fine, appearing in court, or both.

The Law is Where the Government Tells People What to Do

Governments make laws that tell people what to do. Through the elective process and majority rule, our representative government enacts laws for that which is considered best for society, and then include punishments for those who violate the laws. If you break the law, you pay the penalty.

Government lawmaking is only part of the process of governance.

The Constitution is Where "We the People" Tell the Government What to Do

"We the People" created a Constitution that tells government what to do. Think about that. The first three important words of the United States Constitution are: *We the People.*

"We the People" is where government begins. It starts with you and me, and all of us citizens. President Abraham Lincoln concluded his Gettysburg Address with, "that government of the people, by the people, for the people, shall not perish from the earth." He did not say "people of the government, by the government and for the government."

The people are the master. Government is their servant. This servant's purpose is to serve the master by preserving "life, liberty and property" (Bill of Rights, Amendment V and Amendment XIV), and to assure "certain unalienable Rights, that among these are Life, Liberty and the pursuit of Happiness" (Declaration of Independence).

Government exists to serve people, not the opposite. Through the Constitution, "We the People" establish, define, direct, empower and limit government. That is people's law, where *all* the people obey the law, the rulers as well as the ruled. Here is the Preamble with its purpose in six objectives:

> *We the People* of the United States, in Order to form a more perfect Union, establish Justice, insure domestic Tranquility, provide for the common defense, promote the general Welfare, and secure the Blessings of Liberty to ourselves and our Posterity, do ordain and establish this Constitution for the United States of America.

With knowledge and understanding of our Constitution, *we police the government.* Each of us is the citizen officer who "pulls them over" if they transgress beyond Constitutional boundaries. To enforce "Peoples' Law" on government, *we must KNOW that law, the U.S. Constitution,* as adequately as law enforcement authorities know "Government's Law" to impose it on the people.

We empower government to enforce laws for our own good. We must *so impress and empower ourselves to enforce Constitutional law on the government* to keep it within bounds. We monitor and maintain, sometimes constrain or restrain government. How can we do that unless we KNOW our United States Constitution and our own state's constitution, the philosophy behind them in the Declaration, and the freedoms, rights and responsibilities afforded us by the Bill of Rights?

Just as the police officer stopped us, reminded us of the law, that our activity violated the law and there was a price to be paid, we will know our constitutional law. It is all we have between us and tyranny. We must know, care for and safeguard our Constitution. If we don't who will? "We" means each one of us, each family of us—not someone else.

Is the Constitution merely words on a piece of paper? Yes it is, without the understanding and fervent support of the people whose life, liberty, property and pursuit of happiness it safeguards.

The law literally, is in our hands. Let us learn our law to enforce it.

A Contrived Ignorance: Will What We Don't Know Hurt Us?

Does it seem as if we do not know much about the Constitution? Has it been portrayed as a dreary, long-forgotten, faraway, archaic, useless parchment? Why would that be? If we don't know our law, how powerfully can we enforce it? If we do not enforce it, what is to assure we keep it? Nothing. In fact, if anything, there are ever-present and powerful forces that seek to strip away the protections set out in the Constitution. Without vigilance we will lose those protections.

Is it overstated to call America's lack of awareness and understanding of vital topics "a contrived ignorance?" If true it is downright frightening. To be a "contrived ignorance," it is "contrived" by something or someone; even worse, it is accomplished.

It may more likely be *understated* to call it a "contrived ignorance." It is our job to "un-contrive" this ignorance by fighting and overcoming it, starting with "me," then with "thee," then "we."

It is first up to you: Learn the freedom documents. Teach them. Then enforce them. Constitutional education is barely touched upon in the schools. The people are left vulnerable and helpless without such Constitutional knowledge and understanding, bordering on wisdom and patriotic fervor. Get the "freedom fervor!"

We won't go into the freedom documents word-by-word, clause-by-clause, page-by-page. That has already been done sufficiently and brilliantly by other people. You will study concepts now and learn the details in good time. See the end of the chapter for excellent recommended reading and study.

We are going to have some fun with a few brief examples to show the Constitution to be a vital, contemporary, living document, directly appropriate and applicable to everyday situations.

We Declare Ourselves to Be a New Nation

Read the words. Don't listen to what others say they say. Know what they say, and what they mean.

". . . equal station to which the laws of Nature and of Nature's God entitle them, . . ." "We hold these truths to be self-evident, that all men are created equal, that they are endowed by their Creator with certain unalienable Rights, that among these are Life, Liberty and the pursuit of Happiness. That to secure these rights, Governments are instituted among Men, deriving their just powers from the consent of the governed . . ."

These statements identify a Supreme Being in various words and phrases, "Nature's God," "their Creator," and at the end, "with a firm reliance on Divine Providence, . . ."

Freedom, in the form of "unalienable Rights, that among [not limited to] these are Life, Liberty and the pursuit of Happiness," is real and defined, granted by God to man, "endowed by their Creator." This is profound. If only God gives freedom, neither man, nor government, nor anyone or anything else can take freedom away. That's a far different explanation than had previously been interpreted or experienced by man.

> God . . .
>> created man . . .
>>> gave man freedom . . .
>>>> man instituted government . . .
>>>>> through the Constitution . . .
>>>>>> to protect freedom . . .
>>>>>>> granted by God.

Man wrote the Constitution to create government, defined and empowered, yet controlled, to protect man's freedom. This puts man above government and man's freedom above the angels.

The Living Constitution:
Ex Post Facto, Title of Nobility and Rights

Let the Constitution come alive. It is not long ago and far away. It is here and now. Many of its provision have to do with the formalities of government, functions and responsibilities, departments and qualifications. We go beyond them to some important specific concepts, *Ex post facto* laws and *title of nobility*.

There are everyday happenings, laws and enforcement of laws that cry out for constitutional interpretation and appropriate action. *Ex post facto* laws are a good example. *Ex post facto* means "after the fact." It was fashionable in days of old, that when a King or ranking official did not like someone, he could fabricate an ordinance making illegal a condition already existing or an act already committed; then punish or do away with the person, expropriate his worldly belongings and destroy his family and property.

Thus, the so-called "grandfather clause" became law. You hear a lot about "that's been 'grandfathered'" or similar phrases that make the governing bureaucracy seem compassionate, reasonable and generous. They would rather be thought so than for you to know it is the law and they must abide by it. If everyone knew about absolute prohibition and illegality of *ex post facto* laws, much power would be lost. Knowing it gives you power, reduces theirs.

The *ex post facto* provision of the U.S. Constitution is so important, it is there not once, but twice. It is boldly stated for the federal government in

Article I, Section 9, Clause 3, "No bill of attainder or *ex post facto* law shall be passed," then for the states in Art I, Sec 10, Cl 1, "No State shall . . . pass any bill of attainder, *ex post facto* law, or law impairing the obligation of contracts, . . ." For clarification a bill of attainder is an act passed by the legislature to punish a person without trial.

The government has provably followed the *ex post facto* law. It is easy to tell if you know what to look for. Take mail boxes for instance. Mine is on my house; two blocks away theirs is on the street, and in a new development there are multi-boxes on the street. My house was built before 1964. Theirs was built after 1964 when Congress made effective a law that required street mail delivery to houses built after 1964. Even though Congress changed requirements to street side locations, those already there were not affected. Why? Because of the *ex post facto* provisions of the Constitution.

Better than hypothetical or theoretical discussion, we will explore four true instances in the 1980's: Davie's Chuck Wagon Diner in Lakewood near Denver, Mt. Lindo Cross in Jefferson County, Colorado, tinted car windows, and federal reserve-mandated banking laws that violated people's property rights in savings institutions.

Take Down the Cowboy and the Horse. They Violate the Sign Code.

The city of Lakewood, Colorado might just as well have said, "Kill the cowboy and shoot the horse." These revered landmarks were "nonconforming." Here is how it developed:

> The mean-spirited Lakewood Board of Adjustment initiated the ugly ambush years ago by ordering the removal of the landmarks. The cowboy sign was erected in 1957, but the code prohibiting abnormal-sized signs wasn't established until 1983. It isn't fair to force Davies' Chuck Wagon Diner to comply with the new code.
> —Woody Paige, columnist, *Denver Post 12/22/87,* "Sign of times: '57 diner malled"

It is also unconstitutional.

This action violates the *ex post facto* provision of the Constitution. Not only was the 36-foot-high cowboy erected much earlier in 1957, and the horse added in 1962, both were prior to the 1983 establishment of the non-conforming sign code. They were in place much before Lakewood even became a city (in 1969)!

A governing body can make laws it deems necessary, and has the obligation to enforce those laws. But it can not make laws effective for the past, only for what is to follow after the law goes into effect. That means, in this case, the city of Lakewood can ASK, TELL or even DEMAND the sign be taken down, but they can't force the owner to take it down. And if it is not taken down the owner can't be punished. Why? Because as a U. S. citizen, he is protected by the United States Constitution, if he knows it.

The city didn't "grandfather-in" existing signs. Instead they gave five years for existing structures to come into compliance. Question: Do citizens' rights described in the Bill of Rights have a 5-year shelf life or expiration period? Answer: Of course not! Unless through ignorance, misunderstanding or lack of courage you allow it to happen. To keep your rights you must know your rights, protect and insist on your rights.

What is critical? To know the content, meaning and application of the Constitution, and more importantly, know, voice and demand observance of your rights. There is no amendment to the Constitution that repeals or rescinds the *ex post facto* law that is very clear: No *ex post facto* law shall be passed. Period. Any body that tries to pass one is in violation of the Constitution and of their oath of office to abide by and enforce the Constitution.

Remove That Cross from the Mountain! It Destroys My Sobriety.

A second attempt was made to violate the *ex post facto* provision on the same sign law, and side-stepped. An atheist insisted the law be observed, that a lighted cross be removed from the side of a mountain in Lakewood.

"I'm very pleased they've chosen to apply the law equally to all of us," he said in a letter to the editor. "I have only asked that religious signs and icons (same things) comply with the codes and laws with which the rest of us are forced to comply."

Newspaper accounts showed the person to say the sign not only made him sick but argued the cross threatened his sobriety and therefore his life. Such a storm of controversy ensued that various groups formed to get petitions signed to protect existence of the cross.

The lighted cross was placed on Mt. Lindo in 1964 before there were sign codes. It is 393 feet tall and 285 feet wide. The county sign code adopted in 1981 permits signs no larger than 40 square feet, so the cross was certainly not in compliance with the codes.

In this case the codes are not in compliance with the Constitution. The codes are legitimate as long as they are enforced on structures and signs built *after* the codes are in force. But enforcing the 7-year old code against a 24 year-old sign is unconstitutional. Offering a grandfather clause requiring non-conforming signs be removed by Jan. 1, 1989 didn't make it right, but violated the "granddaddy" of the grandfather clauses, Art I, Sec's 9 and 10 of the Constitution.

Luxuriating in the joy of impending victory, the atheist began to consider even more and better targets of enforced sign codes, all religious. Next was the 22-foot-high statue of Jesus Christ, built in 1954, at the Mother Cabrini shrine West of Denver. Targeted, too, were two crosses, one on the chapel of the Federal Correction Center in rural Jefferson County and another atop Hosanna Lutheran Church in Littleton, Colorado. The same man was asked to make seminar and workshop presentations on this new approach to eliminating God and religion at various atheist conventions in Minnesota and Illinois.

He got his wish and the laws were applied equally to everybody. Perhaps even the elected and appointed officials were unaware of the *ex post facto* provisions of the Constitution, because the signs were finally designated historic landmarks putting them outside the sign codes and presumably beyond Constitutional purvey. However, in doing that, the important Constitutional provisions were not exposed to the people.

Several questions can be asked about the provision: Is it vague, confusing, ambiguous? Does the Bill of Rights have a limited expiration, a five-year "shelf life"? Has there been a constitutional amendment repealing the *ex post facto* provision? Has a municipal or state government the power and authority to supersede the Constitution?

The answer to all these questions is simply, "NO."

Tinted Car Windows:
Pay Out $300, Risk a Fine, or Exercise Your Rights

Explained the secretary of the Tinters Association[2],

" Vehicle owners with a passion for privacy could find themselves paying double to have windows stripped and retinted. "A Customer who spent $150 to get his car tinted may need to spend $300 to remove it and have it re-treated."

The law went into effect January 1, 1989. It placed standards of tint density on the various windows of a car. According to the newspaper account a man "recently paid $144 to have the car's windows stripped and retinted to comply with the law. He had the car tinted last January . . ." He was protected by the *ex post facto* provision for almost a year!

Must a police officer, another public servant sworn to uphold the Constitution that forbids passage of *ex post facto* laws, accept your receipt as proof your windows were tinted before the law went in effect? Are you in conformance with both the law *and* the "supreme Law of the Land?" Which takes precedence?

Can you save this $144, or $300, knowing "people's law?"

Why is "No Title of Nobility" Important?

It is matter-of-fact and near unknown in the Constitution, Art I, Sec C1 S:

"No Title of Nobility shall be granted by the United States."

Yet so important it is included a second time for the states, Art I, Sec 10, C1 1:

"No state shall . . . grant any Title of Nobility"

2. Michael Cote, "Dark side of car windows addressed under new law," *Rocky Mountain News*, 1/8/89

What does this mean? Why is it important?

In *The Federalist Papers*[3], James Madison says:

Could any further proof be required of the republican complexion of this system, the most decisive one might be found in its absolute prohibition of titles of nobility, both under the federal and the State governments; and in its express guaranty of the republican form to each of the latter.

The last phrase is from Art IV, Sec 4, "The United States shall guarantee to every State in this Union a Republican form of government, and shall protect each of them against invasion;"

In No. 44, Madison elaborates:

The sober people of America are weary of the fluctuating policy which has directed the public councils. They have seen with regret and indignation that sudden changes and legislative interferences, in cases affecting personal rights, become jobs in the hands of enterprising and influential speculators, and snares to the more industrious and less informed part of the community. . . . They very rightly infer, therefore, that some thorough public measures, inspire a general prudence and industry, and give a regular course to the business of society. The prohibition with respect to titles of nobility is copied from the Articles of Confederation and needs no comment.

Alexander Hamilton, in No. 84, said:

Nothing need be said to illustrate the importance of the prohibition of titles of nobility. This may truly be denominated the cornerstone of republican government; for so long as they are excluded there can never be serious danger that the government will be any other than that of the people.

No. 85 similarly refers to "the absolute and universal exclusion of titles of nobility," as an "additional security to republican government, to liberty, and to property . . ."

David Hutchison[4] describes the debate in Congress, May 11, 1789:

Madison said he opposed titles because they were not reconcilable with the nature of American government, or the genius of the American people. They diminished the true dignity and importance of a republic instead of increasing it. Samuel Adams said that the framers "probably foresaw that such titles, vain and insignificant

3. *The Federalist Papers,* No. 39, by "Publius" —Alexander Hamilton, James Madison and John Jay, Mentor Books, New York: 1961

4. David Hutchison *The Foundations of the Constitution,* p 149, University Books, Secaucus, New Jersey: 1975

in themselves," might in time lead to the absurd and unnatural claims in America of exclusive and hereditary privileges. These things have no place in a republic "based upon equality of rights." Several of the state constitutions make a similar statement as to the cause of inserting the provision, namely, the government ought to be instituted for the common benefit, protection, and security of the people, and not for the particular emolument, or advantage of any single man, family, or set of men.

Emolument is a "gain from employment or position." The Founders wanted to assure that though government had considerable power it was illegal to use that power to enhance the power of favored constituents or enrich those already in power.

The crucial importance of the concept and clause twice in the Constitution, is belied by the matter-of-fact tone of Floyd Cullop's explanation,[5] "No title of nobility (mark of rank raising a person above other citizens and in some cases above the law) can be given by the United States. . . ."

Titles and Privilege Repugnant to Republican, Constitutional Government

The "no title of nobility" clause went beyond a literal title to creation of a class above the rest, a privileged group or aristocracy. Government is so powerful it can (and does, illegally) create a "title of nobility" in several ways; "government" being the Congress, and "title of nobility" conferred by and to the Congress. It manifests in such areas as tax policy, ethics, pay and privilege.

Dictionary definitions may shed some light. *Title is* "an appellation of dignity, distinction or preeminence, given to persons or families, as titles of office, nobility, distinction, degree, etc."
Nobility is "high station or rank, especially distinction of rank. . . . "

Aristocracy is "government by a privileged minority or upper class usually of inherited wealth or social position. . . . those who rise above the rest are considered the best in some way, as in knowledge, character, etc. A titled ruling class or nobility of a country."

Here is what *Black's Law Dictionary*[6], says of nobility:

> In English law, a division of the people, comprehending dukes, marquieses, earls, viscounts, and barons. These had anciently duties annexed to their respective honors. They are created either by writ, i.e., by royal summons to attend the house of peers, or by letters patent, i.e., by royal grant of any dignity and degree of

5. Floyd G. Cullop *The Constitution of the United States,* p 44, Mentor, New York: 1983

6. *Black's Law Dictionary,* p 944, West Publishing, St. Paul: 1979

peerage; and they enjoy many privileges, exclusive of their senatorial capacity.

These concepts are repugnant to the republican form of government the Founders desired and designed into the fabric of the Constitution.

King Kongress:
Can It Grant a "Title of Nobility"—to Anyone?

Lord Acton said, "Power corrupts and absolute power corrupts absolutely." He may have had Congress in mind. Those who serve there usually begin by wanting to create a better, more equitable world. But something happens. They lose touch with reality and people, and get caught up in the whirl of raw, central, big government power and politics. It is easier and more natural to append that power to themselves first.

The answer to where a 7-foot, 500-pound gorilla sits is "anywhere it wants to." If King Kong can do it, so can King Kongress, and they do, especially if we sit idly by and watch, or worse, let it happen. Some specific instances are illustrative.

The Unkindest Cut of All,
Congress Cuts Its Taxes but Not Ours

In January 1982, the Congress tried to slip something by on the coattails of the Black Lung Benefits Bill, something else considered more worthy. It was the old "rider-attached-to-a-bill trick," and most members claimed they didn't know it was in the bill. "It" was a carefully designed congressional loophole in the tax code which according to one senator, in effect virtually "exempted legislators from paying taxes." The legislation, combined with liberal Internal Revenue Service guidelines, would have made lawmakers virtually tax-exempt on their (then) annual salaries of $60,662.50.

Members of Congress voted themselves three options: 1) Deduct $75 a day for the 165 days in session, which with careful planning, could be stretched into 256 eligible days, about $19,200 additional tax exempt; 2) Deduct $50 a day plus all interest and property taxes, or 3) All property deductions as before. All three would preempt the old upper deduction limit of $13,000. While they were at it, they elected also to break the *ex post facto* provision and made the new law *retroactive* not even to January 1, 1982, earlier that year, but to the *previous* year, January 1, 1981!

Congress' creating of themselves a privileged class exempt from their own tax laws clearly violated the "no title of nobility" clause and their oath of office.

We once complained bitterly about "taxation without representation." Here we didn't even have "taxation *with* representation." Instead we had "representation without taxation"!

The press reported it and an angry electorate responded with 34,000 letters that the Internal Revenue Service (IRS) dumped on the floor of Congress. Poetic justice reigned when a contrite "we got caught" Congress attached a rider which rescinded the generous tax break to a $5.4 billion bill which averted furlough of thousands of federal workers. Each one of those 34,000 *Powers of ONE* made the difference.

An Awesome "Backdoor" Congressional Pay Raise

Front page headlines blurted "50% fed pay hike urged," in the 12/14/88 *Rocky Mountain News*. The Congress-created "Commission on Executive, Legislative and Judicial Salaries" which reviews federal pay levels every four years recommended a 50% Congressional pay increase from (1988) $89,500 to $135,000 a year.

It was shrewd. Such recommendations go directly to the President to approve Congress automatically getting the raise. The only way Congress *can't* get the raise is to convene, so move, second and vote against it in both the House and the Senate. Fat chance.

With the proposed salary over four times the then-$31,000 median family income, (already earning nearly three times that amount), they create for themselves a "title of nobility." The public hue-and-cry forced them to vote it down. But it didn't stay down.

A half-year later contrary to the public's expressed wishes Congress enacted a generous pay raise into law. As reported on page 3219 of the 11/25/89 *Congressional Quarterly,* the House' salary went to $96,600 along with $26,850 allowed for honoraria (speaking fees), then going to $124,400 in 1991, with no honoraria and "outside income" limited to $18,660. In February 1990, the Congress raised the Senator's salary $98,400 allowing $26,568 honoraria, with that staying the same and the salary rising to $101,400 in January, 1991. Title of Nobility?

Interestingly, as this New Millennium Edition is being updated, members of Congress are attempting to get a 13.5 percent tax-free increase of about $18,000 a year to add to their 1999 salary of $136,700, according to "Congress' pay raise criticized," (*Denver Rocky Mountain News, 3/21/99, p 61A*). They want to change House rules to allow them a tax-free per diem of $125 to $150 to offset the costs of maintaining houses in Washington and their home districts.

Congress Exempt from Civil Rights and Labor Laws. Another Title of Nobility?

Editorial, "Above the Law," appearing in the March 4, 1988, *Wall Street Journal*, told how Congress had excluded itself over the years from federal laws which included the Civil Rights Act, Equal Employment Opportunity Act, Equal Pay Act, Fair Labor Standards Act, National Labor Relations Act, Occupational Safety and Health Act, Freedom of Information Act and Privacy Act:

Congress routinely excludes itself from all the regulatory laws it passes. Indeed, back in 1984 the House defeated an amendment to extend the civil-rights laws to Congress by a vote of 277—125. . . . Members defend such exemptions by arguing that Congress has the right to manage its internal affairs and that they must be given complete freedom in hiring and firing employees. . . . But why should voters have to accept the blanket hypocrisy of a legislative body saddling private citizens and businesses with burdensome regulations it itself is exempted from?

They don't need another law. They already have two—"no title of nobility" in the Constitution, and their oath of office to uphold it.

Perhaps they become above their laws only because we let them. If we do not know peoples' law, the Constitution, we therefore cannot enforce it. Yet it works, as proved by the 34,000 letters of protest sent to the IRS.

Raising Revenue in the Senate? Unconstitutional.

Another example: In August, 1982, then-Senate Majority Leader Robert Dole desperately wanted a new revenue bill to raise taxes. Under his direction the Senate wrote a bill for a $98.5 billion tax increase. This was clearly a violation of the expressed and implied intent of the Constitution. Art I, Sec 7, Cl 1 is explicit:

All bills for raising revenue shall originate in the House of Representatives; but the Senate may propose or concur with amendments as on other bills.

It was just the opposite. The Senate originated, the House concurred.

It may seem minor but it isn't. It was a serious breach of the supreme Law of the Land which they are sworn to uphold. We must be ever vigilant to assure the law is inviolate to protect us, our families, society, freedoms and future.

Substantial Penalty for Early Withdrawal: Legalized Theft, Savings Death

You dutifully place in savings what is left of your hard-earned money after taxes, paying your bills and doing without. You sign a private contract between you and a savings institution whereby if you leave the money there for a year they will pay you 8% interest. Upon maturity you have 7 days to withdraw or it goes back into contract status a minimum of 6 months. The "penalty for early withdrawal" is that you forfeit your interest.

It sounds straightforward, and is. Well, it was. But we had "tough economic times," requiring new laws and powers. That is what happened when the private central banking system, the Federal Reserve, initiated *"substantial penalty for early withdrawal,"* for "any certificate account issued, extended or renewed after June 1, 1980."

The Depository Institutions Deregulation Committee required *forfeiture* of six months' interest on certificates over a year, *whether earned or not!* This meant if you withdrew your own money, say, a month after placing it on deposit you would lose 6 months interest. Suppose you had invested $10,000 at 8% interest for a year but it had to be withdrawn after a month. You earned $67 but forfeited $407. By that arbitrary and illegally imposed regulation you lost $340 of your principal, *your property!*

There is more. You had already placed your money for a year and were not notified of its renewal and legal encumbrance by the lending institution's arbitrary rule. If you did not take it out within 7 days, you could not get it without being obligated under the new "substantial penalty for early withdrawal" provisions. You legally signed one contract but were bound by another to which you did not agree, had no say in, nor were apprised of. What went wrong? Your constitutional rights were violated.

Government can't interfere with private contracts, "No state shall . . . pass any . . . law impairing the obligation of contracts," U.S. Constitution, Art I, Sec 10, Cl 1.

According to then-executive vice president of the Savings and Loan League of Colorado, the rule "is intended to reduce movement of money market cash, stabilizing money available for mortgage lending" and applied to "federally insured savings and loans, commercial banks as mutual savings banks."

These Bill of Rights violations could have been invoked:

Article IV provides for the right of the people to be "secure in their persons, houses, papers, and effects, against unreasonable searches and seizures."

Articles V and XIV say no citizen shall "be deprived of life, liberty property, without due process of law; nor shall private property be taken for public use, without just compensation." Did the individual saver have "due process of law?" Was that private property—principal—"taken" without just compensation?

Article VIII protects citizens from "cruel and unusual punishment." Is it cruel and unusual to confiscate personal property, principal, for "early withdrawal" of your own money on which taxes had already been paid?

Article IX says rights enumerated by the Constitution "shall not be construed to deny or disparage others retained by the people;" that is, those not mentioned aren't denied for that reason.

Article X says any other rights "not delegated to the United States by the Constitution, nor prohibited by it to the States, are reserved to the States respectively, or to the people;" that is, all rights not mentioned are still held by the people. Were the rights to their own money maintained by savers and citizens?

Art XIII: "Neither slavery nor involuntary servitude, except as punishment for crime whereof the party shall have been duly convicted shall exist within the United States." Involuntary servitude is where you are forced work for a master—government—with no compensation. Was this the case? Was there a "crime," and was someone "duly convicted?"

David Hutchison (p 158) explained the importance of these Constitutional provisions in terms of the "terrible distress" in the collection of private debts following the war of independence. He cites Chief Justice John Marshall's explanation why these Art I, Sec 10, Cl 1 "state prohibitions" were included in the Constitution:

> These measures were subversive of private contracts and public faith, and called out this clause prohibiting the states from enacting any law impairing the obligation of contracts. The intention or purpose of the Convention was not only to prevent a repetition of such evils, but also to establish the great principle that contracts should be forever inviolable against legislative interference. The state governments are not to have even the power to interfere with private contracts, such as that between debtor and creditor.

Read the past several paragraphs and Articles with reference to what has grown to be America's complicated and confiscatory tax system that takes over half a family's income. Is it in compliance with the letter and intent of the "supreme Law of the Land?"

Consider the 1986 tax code allowing interest to be deducted from no more than two residences. Why is that? Could it be that those who make tax law reside in two homes? Is that some form of "nobility" or just a "tax loophole" designated for some special interest? Suppose the Congress makes interest on the second home once again not deductible, yet you purchased a house taking into account its deductibility. After the fact if they say it is no longer deductible, is it still deductible for you, under the *"ex post facto"* provisions of the Constitution?

During "tough economic times" (aren't they always?)—war or international police action, we get "temporary emergency" regulations that become permanent. One prominent past example is income tax withholding where tax moneys are deducted and sent to the government even before you take possession. That was a "temporary emergency wartime measure" begun in 1942 as a part of the "V for Victory" World War II campaign.

Withholding is even more punitive. You will pay a "substantial penalty"—not only the tax, but also penalties and interest, if you haven't prepaid at least 90% of what is due for taxes. Is this constitutionally wrong since as of the income tax deadline, April 15, for the current year you have had substantial withholding with essentially no tax liability?

Think about it. If you quit working tomorrow how much tax would you owe? How much has been withheld?

Another example is the post-World War II "Marshall Plan," military protection and foreign aid provided to rebuild the economies destroyed by the war. Today we still provide that protection even though those economies, Japan, France and Germany combined, are 11% greater than America's $7.8 trillion output, GDP, gross domestic product in 1997, and that protection began over 53 years ago[7].

"Throw the Rascals Out," Shakespeare and Art I, Sec 2, Cl 1

In 1986, over 98% of incumbent congressional candidates we returned to office. In 1988 it was 99%. We have created a perpetual, virtually unchangeable set of representatives not contemplated by the Founding Fathers. Further, they were thought to remain more as citizens than politicians, but in fact reside at the seat of government, virtually non-resident in their home districts.

Suppose we judge the tragic consequences from flawed policy legislation and congressional ethics. The Founders left a way out, that of voting them out. Article II, Cl 1 allows for electing a president every four years. Art I, Sec 2, Cl 1 provides for re-election of Representatives every two years. We can have a complete, constitutional change of representatives every two years if we wish. Likewise Sec 3 provides for re-election every two years of one-third of all Senators, each with six-year terms. Are these the "legal revolution" clauses?

Whenever the natives get restless to challenge old laws or institute new ones through the referendum or initiative, those in power disparage the idea. Citizen initiatives are met with, "This is representative government. Vote them in. If they don't perform properly, 'throw the rascals out.'" Sure. That would work fine if you could also throw out their bad legislation, big and growing government and steadily increasing taxes. But you can't.

William Shakespeare put it well in *Julius Caesar,* Act III, Scene 1:

> The evil that men do lives after them;
> The good is oft interred with their bones.

We must do our best to put the best people in office, those you know who love liberty, understand and support the United States Constitution. Then we must be everlastingly in contact with them to keep them "the best people." Finally, when needed, we must be skillful, sensitive, tactful and courageous enough to "throw the rascals out."

---

7. *Statistical Abstract of the United States, 1999,* p 841; *2000 + World Almanac,* p 528

A Living, Perpetual Freedom Document

Why do you think we Americans as a people know so little about our heritage and history, freedoms and freedom documents? Is it because people who don't know such things are easy to fleece and fool? What if we not only knew how important all this is, but could become fascinated and captivated, even motivated and inspired by it? What if we took on as a lifetime assignment the learning, personal adoption and enforcement, then teaching of the Freedom Documents? What if we continue with a few more notes of interest concerning the Freedom Documents?

How many times is the word "education" mentioned in the Constitution? None. "Democracy?" Not once.

Where is the phrase "separation of church and state" in the Constitution? Nowhere.

What three major events took place in 1913, and now negatively influence our present day quality-of-life? The 16th and 17th amendments and legislation creating the *private* central banking system.

The Federal Reserve System is authorized to use debt as backing for what we now know is fiat or paper currency having no intrinsic value, contrary to the U.S. Constitution (Art I, Sec 8, Cl 4 and Art 10, Cl 1). The value of this "money" is what it buys from the goods produced only through the hard work, output and productivity of the people.

When declared ratified (notice careful wording) the 16th amendment authorized the federal income tax that today removes almost one-fourth our earnings before we see them.

The 17th amendment is little known and even less understood. In creating the separation of powers, the Founders went beyond the separation of powers—legislative, executive and judicial. They further divided the legislative, law-making body in two. The House of Representatives directly representing the people had to return for a vote every two years to get re-validated by the people. The Senate directly represented the States.

The Founders were supercautious against increasing central government power and subsequent usurpation of States' powers and rights. Federal senators were selected and elected by the State legislatures. (Perhaps the state government should even have paid them.) But in 1913 the Constitution was amended to direct election of Senators by popular vote of the people. Was that better?

Government and the People: Top, Middle and Bottom

Good freedom friend, Marj Nickum from Denver, Colorado illustrated the relationship of the people to their various governments. She explains:

The Sons and Daughters of Liberty joined to erect four (4) fences around their government—fences that cannot get out of hand or out of bounds—the executive, legislative, judicial AND the individual. The final fence, the Individual (the PEOPLE), is the most powerful check of all! No despot, no tyrant, not even a majority mob can separate us from our unalienable rights. In the individual's hand is the power to bring government to heel! After the Supreme Being, the individual comes first. Only by our consent can government govern, protect life, liberty, property and pursuit of happiness. All people have equal opportunity. When an individual denies or is unaware of these rights, government prevails. The individual can become a slave to government—as opposed to being in charge of all functions of the government. Are we masters or slaves? YOU have the power and the right to decide.

UNITED STATES — CHAIN OF COMMAND
"of the people, by the People, and for the People."
Figure No. 35

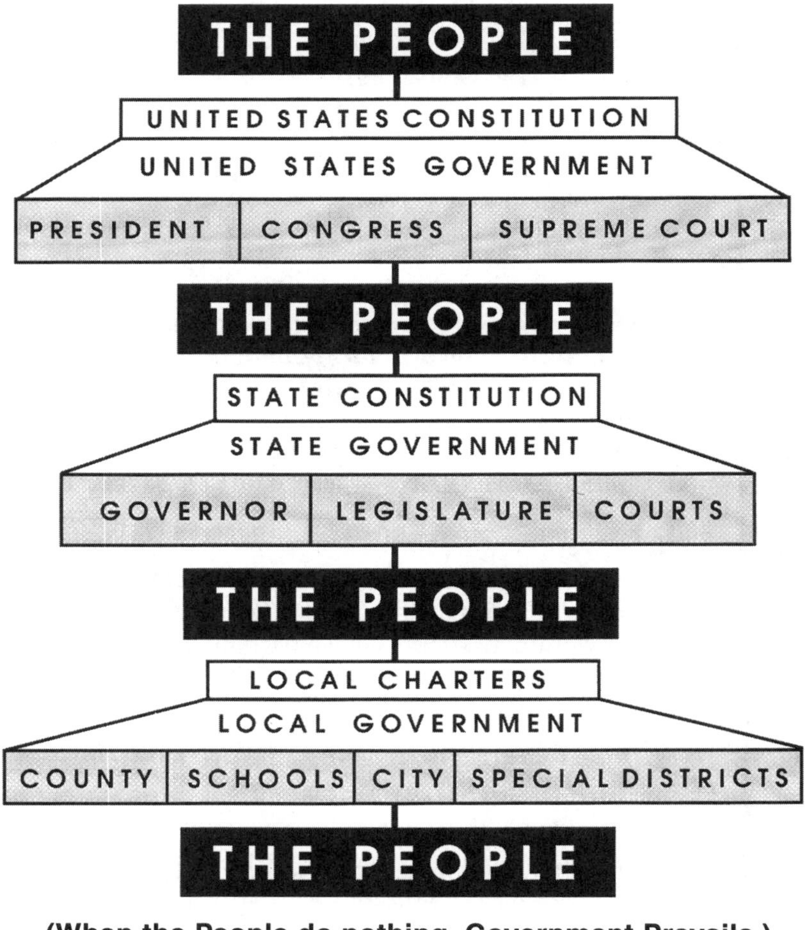

THE PEOPLE

| UNITED STATES CONSTITUTION |
| UNITED STATES GOVERNMENT |

| PRESIDENT | CONGRESS | SUPREME COURT |

THE PEOPLE

| STATE CONSTITUTION |
| STATE GOVERNMENT |

| GOVERNOR | LEGISLATURE | COURTS |

THE PEOPLE

| LOCAL CHARTERS |
| LOCAL GOVERNMENT |

| COUNTY | SCHOOLS | CITY | SPECIAL DISTRICTS |

THE PEOPLE

(When the People do nothing, Government Prevails.)

Ponder Nickum's diagram, Figure No. 35, and explanation. I would add that "We the People" have the freedom and the obligation to be on top of and in the middle of our governments. The people will always be on the bottom. If they abdicate their roles in the middle and on top, the people will be crushed by governments.

The Magna Carta: A Document, a Symbol and a Beacon

In 1215, England's King John literally had a sword at his throat to grant rights to the people, initially, only those of the ruling aristocracy, not common folk. The Magna Carta, "Great Charter," later became a model to provide individual liberties to all people. Basic principles were involved. *Ex post facto* laws had been used to abuse the people and dispose of their property at the king's whim. They were recognized as destructive and declared unconstitutional.

The Magna Carta is a symbol of freedom for citizens, to empower government to protect their rights. Human beings, societies and governments are not perfect, but they can continually improve. Enduring principles of justice aid to keep mankind on an upward quest.

In much the same way, bad laws cannot produce a good society. Between the intent of the Magna Carta and the Seventh Amendment, trial by jury of one's peers or neighbors, implies not only careful evaluation and judgment of the facts, but of the law as well.

A judge instructs members of a jury to consider only the facts and the law. But what if it is intrinsically a bad law, or a bad law for a specific person or situation? It is up to the jury to determine justice that includes the law as well as the facts presented; in other words, the whole situation, time and place. If such a law is "struck down" it is called "jury nullification." The people have rightfully nullified what they consider an onerous, inappropriate or bad law.

"We the People" are especially in charge when serving on a jury. Once sworn in, the juror becomes judge, and the judge becomes referee. The juror-judge citizen judges both the law and the facts of the law. Roy Hookanson articulated such principles in: "What if a juror voted 'not guilty'?" from the *National Educator,* June 1988, p 16:

American jurors' duty and absolute power to nullify bad law helps guard the God-given rights of every individual to life, liberty, property and the pursuit of happiness. Our jury power is secured by the Supreme law and our Bill of Rights. . . . All Americans need to understand that when they are on jury duty, their jury vote is the most direct and powerful vote they can ever cast—to help preserve equality of true justice and freedom for every fellow American.

The Magna Carta serves as a freedom beacon regarding the Rights of Mankind. History has shown human rights to be rare and precious, won but easily lost, delicate and fragile, but unspeakably valuable.

Protect Your Constitutional Rights!
Challenge, Assert, Claim.

You know your Constitution, People's Law, Citizen's Law, *YOUR* Law, and if it is being trampled or violated. What do you do then? Suppose you are with your elected representative and you are confident that what is at issue is unconstitutional. Here is how you "pull 'em over" and "read 'em *your* rights," their responsibility to the law:

> The U.S. Constitution is the "supreme Law of the Land," because it says so. You have taken your oath of office to support it because it says so and you said so. If you take this action, clearly unconstitutional, you violate your oath of office and break the law of the land, by definition committing a criminal act. If I let, or help you, I become an accessory to your crime. This should not be necessary, should it? If you persist in this illegal act you blatantly and willfully break the law. By the equality provisions of the Declaration of Independence—the intent of law, and the U.S. Constitution—the law, by your actions you give license and authority to all citizens to break the same laws. Is that what you want? Here is what you are doing and why it is wrong. (Or, *ask pointed questions of the action and the law.*) Please think through what you are doing and be sure it is within the letter, spirit and intent of the Law, the supreme Law of the land, the United States Constitution, which you are sworn to uphold.

You are challenging the authorities, invoking the law, addressing the issue squarely, and more importantly, creating doubt. Next, you can publicize it in the many ways you know how. You may wish to take it up with newspapers, citizen watchdog groups or other concerned citizens. Never let an opportunity such as this go by.

Know all you can about your rights and their incumbent responsibilities. Especially gain a thorough knowledge and understanding of the Freedom Documents. Through them you can preserve freedom for yourself and those to come.

Questions for Review

1. Government comes from "We the People" spelled out in the Constitution. Why won't that document, even including the Declaration of Independence and the Bill of Rights preserve your freedom? What or who will? How?

2. What is the Declaration of Independence? What does it do? What was the "fatal pledge" of the Founding Fathers? What would likely happen to them if executed for treason by the English Crown?

3. The U.S. Constitution is the "supreme Law of the Land" because it says so. Is it the law of the government? Of the people? Why? Who is bound by it? How? What is the difference between a national government and a federal government? Which did we end up with?

4. Was the Bill of Rights a part of the original Constitution? If not how long did it take them to become so? What does the Bill of Rights do?

5. Law is where the government tells people what to do. What is the Constitution? Explain how people are apprised of the law and controlled by it. What is the people's tool to control the government? How? What is "sovereign" and who is sovereign? Between people and government, who is the master and who is the servant? What "unalienable rights" do the people have? How are they spelled out in two places, slightly differently, and where? What is the difference between People's Law and Ruler's Law? Which is the Constitution?

6. What are two reasons a "contrived ignorance" regarding the Free Documents is ominous? What is the "freedom fervor" that provides "knowledge and understanding bordering on wisdom and patriotic fervor?"

7. Explain the source of freedom from the first few paragraphs of the Declaration. Is the Constitution "long ago and far away" or "here and now"? Are governments compassionate when they "grandfather" people into not having to comply with a new law? What is another name for that, where does it come from and how twice? How does postal delivery illustrate government adherence to *ex post facto* laws? How do zoning and sign code laws relate to *ex post facto* provisions? Other examples?

8. What is a "title of nobility," where is it found and why is it important? Is Congress exempt from the *ex post facto* and "title of nobility" provisions? Since they have taken an oath to uphold the Law of the Land, if they ignore these provisions what are they? What must be done? Give examples of past specific legislation they have exempted themselves from the law.

9. What specific constitutional provisions are abridged by excessive taxation? Discuss withholding. Can government interfere in private contracts? What is "jury nullification?"

10. How did the Founders not only make it possible but legal to have a "revolution" where power is transferred to a new set of rulers? Why doesn't "throw the rascals out" solve the problem? What

events profoundly changed the nature of America in 1913? What is important about the Magna Carta? What action(s) can you take when you perceive a public servant has violated the Constitution?

A nation of well informed men who have been taught to know and prize the rights which God has given them cannot be enslaved. It is in the region of ignorance that tyranny begins.   —Benjamin Franklin

There is no good government but what is republican. That the only valuable part of the British constitution is so; because the very definition of a republic is "an empire of laws, and not of men." That, as a republic is the best of governments, so that particular arrangement of the power of society, or, in other words, that form of government which is best contrived to secure an impartial and exact execution of the laws, is best of republics.   —John Adams

Having elected leaders doesn't relieve us of the responsibility of being the caretakers of freedom. In America, We the People have the final responsibility and authority to see that our government stays within the bounds of God's purpose for it. Every employee of government is answerable to an appointed official. Every appointed official is answerable to an elected official. Every elected official is answerable to We the People. Within this constitutional republic, We the People are the highest human authority. We cannot shrink from our awesome responsibility as stewards of this freedom.   —Dr. Sterling Lacy

The Freedom Documents: Highly Recommended Reading

The Five Thousand Year Leap: The 28 Great Ideas that are Changing the World, by W. Cleon Skousen, $13.95 + $2.00 (paperback) 1981, National Center for Constitutional Studies, HC 61, Box 1056, Malta, ID 83342-9704 1/800/388-4512

The Making of America: The Substance and Meaning of the Constitution, by W. Cleon Skousen, $26.95 + $2.50 (hardback) (Study Guide, $4.95), NCCS: 1985

Our Ageless Constitution by W. David Stedman and LaVaughn G. Lewis, A timeless, inspirational classic, $14.95 + $2.50 (paperback) Americanism Foundation, 48 Linwood Ave., Norwalk, OH 44857 1987

The Federalist Papers, by "Publius": Alexander Hamilton, James Madison and John Jay, Mentor Books, New York: 1961

Chapter 18

THE HOME RUN
Ism's, Ideologies, and Ideas

The U.S. Constitution recognizes the importance of a republic and commands the federal government to protect it. Article IV, Section 4, says, "The United States shall guarantee to every State in this Union a Republican Form of Government. . . . " Nowhere in the U.S. Constitution is the word "democracy" used, for good reason. We headed for Home Base as we concluded "America is a Republic, not a Democracy. . . . Let's Keep It That Way!"

Now we complete the home run. After first base (economic awareness), second base (political awareness and understanding), and third base (political involvement), we "head for home," the ism's, ideologies and ideas.

We need to know and understand still more words to think clearly, decide rationally and act wisely in the political arena. We will explore *conservative* and *liberal, republican* and *democrat,* and how they mesh in today's popular political systems. Then we "get ideological" in a brief review of Karl Marx's popular 1848 book, *The Communist Manifesto.* We will not only learn more new concepts but prepare for future new horizons and ideas.

A Power Dare Chapter: Do the Tough Stuff

This is a *"Power Dare* Chapter," *Power of ONE.* Read and heed your "Power Deed Creed!"

Precision Learning: Get Back to Basics
with The Dictionary and Encyclopedia

Words are symbols, tools for thought and communication. Words related to political ideologies and philosophies are probably the most confusing of all. Good examples of confusing terms are "conservative" and "liberal."

It is best in unfamiliar territory to "get back to basics," and use the dictionary and encyclopedia to learn and understand unfamiliar, ambiguous or confusing terms.

First, from *Webster's New Collegiate Dictionary (1994):*

> conservative: tending or disposed to maintain existing views, conditions, or institutions; traditional; moderate; cautious

> liberal: one who is open-minded or not strict in the observance of orthodox, traditional or established forms or ways

> conservativism: disposition in politics to preserve what is established; a political philosophy based on tradition and social stability, stressing established institutions, and preferring gradual development to abrupt change

> liberalism: a theory in economics emphasizing individual freedom from restraint and usually based on free competition, the self-regulating market, and the gold standard; a political philosophy based on belief in progress, the essential goodness of the human race, and the autonomy of the individual and standing for the protection of political and civil liberties

Continuing this fundamental approach to learning, we explore these terms with the *World Book Encyclopedia.*

Liberal and Conservative: Gradually Changing Meanings

Meanings and shades of meaning of political words change over time. Where liberalism once meant a small, passive role for government two centuries ago it now embraces a larger, more active government role. We begin with liberalism[1] and its change over time:

> *Liberalism* is a political and economic philosophy that emphasizes freedom, equality, and opportunity. The philosophy called *conservatism,* on the other hand, emphasizes order, tradition, and ownership of private property. Liberals have generally favored more rapid social change than have conservatives. But liberalism

1. *The World Book Encyclopedia,* Volume 12. pages 227-228. Copyright (c) 1990 World Book, Inc., Chicago. Used with permission

is a confusing term, because its meaning and emphasis have changed considerably over the years.

The earlier form of liberalism permitted, even encouraged rebellion against a government restrictive of individual freedom. Such ideas inspired the 1776 American Revolution, the near-century earlier English revolution and the French revolution 13 years later. These movements brought back people's rule and consent to be ruled by their government, with written lists of freedoms and rights for all to know, observe and enforce. These included those in America's first amendment—freedom of religion, speech, press, assembly and right to petition government for redress of grievances. They were clearly articulated in the Declaration of Independence by Thomas Jefferson who in turn was influenced towards freedom by John Locke, an English philosopher.

Early liberals didn't trust democracy but liked a government by constitution. They thought only those who owned property should govern. As the middle class became larger and more affluent, they participated more fully in the political process, but in so doing, leaned more towards a broad-based democracy.

Early liberals were probably more conservative than today's conservatives. They believed the economy left alone was self-adjusting, powered by the best interests of the participants, that larger government interfered with the process of economic self-fulfillment and self-determination.

Today's liberalism has shifted its emphasis from means to ends. Rather than freedom to do or be, it became more freedom of opportunity to achieve results. Consequently government may be a means to help assure more desirable outcomes and aid people to go farther faster with government assistance or encouragement.

World Book describes modern liberals:

> Today, liberals favor active role government regulation of the economy in the public interest. They support government programs to provide economic security and ease human suffering. Such programs include unemployment insurance, minimum wage laws, old-age pensions, health insurance, civil rights legislation, and various antipoverty measures. Modern liberals believe in the primary importance of individual freedom. But they maintain that government must actively remove obstacles to the enjoyment of that freedom. Persons who support the earlier ideas of economic liberalism are now frequently called *conservatives* or *reactionaries*. A number of former liberals often called *neoliberals* have favored less government regulation of the economy. Neoliberals also express a sense of limits about government activity in general.

No wonder words fail us. Sometimes in word evolution, they turn out later with nearly the direct opposite meaning they had earlier. Now for more basics on "conservatism."

Conservativism: Another Evolving-Meaning Word

Conservatism in a political context leans heavily on culture, history and tradition. The tried and true should be preserved. Progress was sought but kept in line with accepted values. As with *liberal* the meaning of *conservative* varies with time and circumstance.

Conservatives are skeptical of what government and politics can accomplish. While government should help create an environment of good living, politics is not an effective way to do so. Conservatives acknowledge man's capacity for evil as well as good, explaining their insistence on a "government of laws, not men."

Conservatives believe in personal responsibility and hard work[2]:

Conservatives emphasize the performance of duties as the price of rights. They also believe in the desirability of maintaining social classes. Conservatives believe that all people have equal protection under the law, but they deny that all are born with equal advantages and influence in society. Conservatives maintain that only a few are natural leaders, and that the leadership provided by these few is essential to social order. For these reasons, conservatives consider political and economic leveling foolish and bound to fail.

Conservatives see a connection between freedom and private ownership of factories and other means of economic production. They maintain that abolishing such private ownership would destroy individual liberty. Therefore many conservatives consider that socialism and communism are the greatest threats to modern society.

A true conservative should also be distinguished from a *reactionary.* Reactionaries want to revolutionize existing society according to a model in past history. True conservatives are never revolutionary. They want to preserve the best in the past and continue it into the future.

The word *conservative* as used in the United States today is often confusing. Many Americans who call themselves conservatives advocate a return to the principles and theories of liberalism of the 1800's. They oppose almost all government regulation of the economy, and are economic liberals in the tradition of Adam Smith. Traditionally, however, conservatives have

---

2. *The World Book Encyclopedia,* Volume 4, pages 991-992. Copyright (c) 1990 World Book, Inc., Chicago. Used with permission

opposed both economic liberalism and socialism. They have tried to steer a middle course between the extremes of individualism and collective ownership, and have generally favored a strong central government.

Some authors have the gift to combine humor and wisdom to shed light on such ambiguous concepts. Conservative columnist Michael Rosen[3] caustically clarifies:

I'll avoid the temptation to use some of the more derisive treatments of contemporary liberalism such as "A liberal is one who would give you the shirt off of somebody else's back," and quoting Leonard Peikoff, "Liberalism is a cry from one heart to another, bypassing any intermediary, such as the brain." My own description of today's liberal is one who honestly believes that behind every problem lies a government solution; that individuals must be compelled by the state (in its highest form, of course, managed by enlightened liberals) to make personal sacrifices for the common good (as defined by liberals); that private enterprise is, at best, a necessary evil, but that it should and will evolve into an increasingly nationalized status over time.

Rosen explains the term "liberal" was been expropriated from conservatives known as "classical liberals," John Locke, David Hume, Edmund Burke and Adam Smith, who believed much as conservatives do today. "They believed that the individual took precedence over the state; that freedom of choice and voluntarism were essential, not only for the most efficient society, but also for the most just; that basic human rights are not something awarded to the individual by the state, but reside from birth in the individual, having been endowed by his creator."

"A liberal," Rosen says, "envisions a government program in terms of the seemingly nice results it can produce in the short run. The conservative is sensitive to the longer-term effects of a chain reaction. . . . Liberals are long on promises and short on results." He concludes, "Having no faith that an individual will behave morally in a business environment, they somehow expect virtue from those of the same species who are selected to patrol the bureaucratic hallways of Washington."

Liberal as Conservative: A Lesson in Priorities

Another way to categorize differences in worldview and order of values between liberals and conservatives is through ranking their priorities. In another article Rosen explores "the fundamental differences

3. Michael Rosen, "A 'conservative' defines 'liberals,'" *Denver Post,* 6/6/84. Used with permission

. . . that are simply irreconcilable." Rosen[4] draws from James Burnham's 1964 book *Suicide of the West,* first defining *liberty* in the sense of "national independence and self-government, sovereignty"; *freedom,* "in the sense of freedom, or liberties, of the individual," *justice,* "distributive justice of a social welfare sort . . . more toward equality of result than merely equality of opportunity;" and *peace,* "the absence of large-scale warfare among major powers." His rankings followed, including the priorities of the Libertarian for comparison:

Liberal: 1. Peace   2. Justice   3. Freedom   4. Liberty
Conservative: 1. Liberty   2. Freedom   3. Peace   4. Justice
Libertarian: 1. Freedom   2. Peace   3. Liberty   4. Justice

Their worldviews differ greatly. "Today's liberals have elevated pacifism to a principal value," says Rosen. "They remain committed to the welfare state; and they increasingly oppose nationalism in favor of internationalism. To liberals, tradition is an obstacle. Their philosophy is utopian: Human nature can be changed; man is perfectible; disarmament is achievable; war can be eliminated."

Contrasting, Rosen says, "The conservative's order of values reflects a traditional view of human nature and society. It recognizes that the world is often a harsh and competitive place, populated by imperfect—and imperfectible—human beings; that there are limitations to what public or private institutions can do to ameliorate this condition. Conservatives believe that the American experiment in democratic capitalism has produced the greatest measure of political freedom and economic achievement the world has ever known, and that it is threatened by serious adversaries both within and without."

Is a Conservative a Conservative, or What is a "Neo"?

Even within names we think we know, there are new interpretations. Dr. Edwin J. Feulner, president of the Heritage Foundation, defined several variations of conservative in a Sydney, Australia speech[5]:

Traditional conservatism stresses the primacy of individual freedom, the economic merits of free enterprise, the importance of limited government and the need for a strong national defense. Neoconservatives are generally individuals formerly associated with the political left. . . . tend to stress the importance of tradition,

4. Michael Rosen, "The fundamental differences between liberals and conservatives," *Denver Post,* 8/6/86. Used with permission

5. Gene Amole, "Conservative face has different look," 1/22/87, *Rocky Mountain News.* From the *Glimpse* newsletter. (Amole concludes "A liberal is someone who tries to tell a conservative how to spend his money.")

institutional stability and the rule of law. They are staunchly anti-Communist but their views of free enterprise range from mildly supportive to overly hostile. New Right conservatism identifies itself as a morally-based conservatism and concerns itself mainly, but not entirely, with social issues—option in education ("vouchers"), voluntary school prayer, busing, pornography, abortion and job quotas.

So even when you think you know, it is still difficult to know exactly what these terms mean. And when you do, they change. The "neo" or new liberals and conservatives mix in new ingredients to old recipes that seem never to be just right after they are cooked.

Terms can become labels. Labels stifle thinking and squelch interchange of ideas. If we ask, "Are you a liberal or a conservative?" and get an answer, we may think we know all there is to know about a person's political persuasion, beliefs and convictions. In almost all cases, these interpretations are wrong or incomplete. Not discussing viewpoints and sharing differences is probably even more detrimental in the sense of learning from ideas and growing in relationships.

The Confusion of Political Party Labels: Republican and Democrat

These problems spill over in the meanings of the words "Republican" and "Democrat." We can almost use the same basic meanings, respectively, as those previously discussed, for "conservative" and for "liberal." "Almost" is "not quite." More realistically, "Republican" and "Democrat" lean close to the society's political center of whatever is the current meaning of "moderate." The Republican persuasion is a bit more conservative ("to the right of center"). The Democratic persuasion is a bit more liberal ("to the left of center").

The relative location of the center is the more important consideration.

Concluding a speech, I was approached by a frustrated listener who blurted out, "I can't tell if you are a Republican or a Democrat." I was pleased that no apparent party label showed. Labels inhibit discussion and thinking. I said, "Actions speak louder than words, always, and though Republicans and Democrats talk differently, they act the same. Our big government, growing taxes, spending and national debt aren't Republican or Democrat. They are both, "bipartisan," and that is when both parties gang up on the taxpayers and citizens."

Over the past century, society has been drifting ever more leftward, pulling the "moderate" label also leftward. We sometimes hear Democrats say they must change parties and become Republicans. It is not because they have changed, but that the parties have shifted. It is not an unexpected shift, following the gyrations the United States government, economy and polity went through during and after the Great Depression of 1929.

We got more and bigger government, seeking to solve economic
doldrums, smooth out boom-and-bust business cycles, and supposedly
better control the economy through government. Government became
more powerful, and at times, appeared to fulfill these objectives. As it
turns out the more we solved problems with more government, the worse
the problems got over time, and the bigger government got.

Regardless, we were determined. As a nation, over the years, we
sincerely sought to use government to solve our national problems, to
fabricate a more fair, equitable and just society. We not only wanted to
eradicate disease but to eliminate hunger and conquer poverty.
Government was to be all things to all people, the great arbiter of taking
from those who have and giving to those who have not, in the name of
fairness. It seemed a good idea. We spent a lot of money on it. We gave
these good ideas of using government to right wrongs a good try. The
only thing wrong after it was all over was:

It didn't work.

A Sink or Swim Case Study:
The Partisan Issue of Taxes and "Fairness"

The *Wall Street Journal* editorial[6] called the battle for a capital gains
tax, ". . . a rare opportunity to understand the two ideologies now
competing for their assent":

> As a substitute for the Republican plan for a tax cut that
> would raise federal revenues, House Democrats are now officially
> offering a plan for a tax increase. Revenues aside, they just prefer
> higher taxes.

In that issue lay a contemporary view of the philosophical differences
between Republicans and Democrats, the age-old struggle between lower
taxes and higher taxes. The Republicans in Congress push for much
reduced capital gains taxes, time-proven to bring in more revenues to the
treasury and create more businesses, opportunities, wealth and jobs. The
Democrats back a tax increase with the politics of envy. Why should
stockbrokers get a tax break a plumber or steelworker can't get? *WSJ*
explained:

> So the House Democratic leadership has proposed to stop the
> capital gains tax cut and instead increase the top rate on the highest
> personal incomes from 28% to 33%. Since this change would
> affect only the very top tier of income, it wouldn't raise much
> money, but this is not the object. Rather House Democrats have
> been convinced that high taxes are good politics.

6. "A Clear Choice," *Wall Street Journal*, 9/22/89, p A 10

Opposing views were aired[7]. In "Measure encourages investment," Colorado Congressman Hank Brown told how "In 1987 the United States ranked last among major industrialized nations with investments representing 16.7% of gross national product while Japan invested 32.8%," Canada, Italy, France and West Germany all invested over 20%, and some capital gains are illusory taking inflation into account. In "Tax cut neither fair nor efficient" Professor Alan S. Blinder, chairman of Princeton's economics department, argued that good investments are "already munificently rewarded by our capitalist system," that capital gains are tax-advantaged because the investor chooses the time to claim them. He failed to mention the many not-so-good investments that cost a lot, gain little or lose greatly. That is called risk.

Brown concludes, "The proper tax rate on the sale of capital assets is one that maximizes government revenue yet increases savings and investment. A lower tax rate on capital gains can do that. Our goal should be to expand economic opportunity for all."

Blinder ends, "This discussion leads to the conclusion that we should index capital gains and then tax them as ordinary income. That approach is fair, efficient and will not lose much revenue."

An opinion page debate[8] between columnists Jesse Jackson and Patrick Buchanan further highlights the differences.

Entitled "Capital gains tax cut: 20 bucks for average families, bonanza for rich," Jackson says the Bush administration,

> . . . wants to use the tax system to throw another lavish party for the rich at the expense of America's working people. He [Bush] proposes excluding from taxation 30 percent of the profit from the sale of an asset in order to 'encourage investment.' But what cutting the capital gains tax will do in reality is make the rich richer and rob tens of billions of dollars from the federal treasury over the next 10 years.

Jackson refers to the "welfare-for-the-wealthy tax scheme" and advocates taking a strong stand against "Robin-Hood-in-reverse economics," that "the congressional representatives who believe in invest-in-America economics should be separated from those who believe in born-again, trickle-down 'voodoo' economics. . . . "

In "Whining left misrepresents results of a needed capital gains tax cut," Buchanan offers three examples of investing Americans who "cash in," pay 19.6 percent of their gains in taxes and enjoy the benefits of their work, investing, sacrifice and risk. He counters that with previous, higher

7. "Point/Counterpoint: Should Congress Grant a Capital Gains Tax Cut?, *Denver Post,* 9/25/89, p C2

8. *Denver Post.* 9/24/89, p 3H

capital gains rates the rich paid less of the taxes, the poor more. "In 1979, the top 10 percent of taxpayers paid 49.5 percent of the income tax load; by 1987, their share had risen to 55.4%," and "In 1979, the bottom 50 percent paid 6.8 percent of total income taxes; that fell to 5.9 percent. . . ." He concluded,

> . . . the income tax burden shifted toward the upper class and the rich; for the working class it was reduced; for the poor, it was eliminated. Yet, you can put burning coals under the fingernails of liberals, and they will not concede what statistics plainly show. Why? Because socialism, the Democratic ideology that dare not speak its name, is a religious belief, impervious to evidence, the hidden agenda of which is the constant transfer of power from producers to politicians.

The *Wall Street Journal* said the higher capital gains rate "is to punish success, and thereby garner the votes of the unsuccessful. Voters are presumed to be too dimwitted to recognize that the 33% proposal is the camel's nose under the tent, to be followed by higher taxes for the rich, the near-rich, the not-so-rich and everyone else."

In this real-life political, economic and ideological debate the *Journal's* editorial covers the territory, "The House Democrats have decided conclusively that the party's identity will sink or swim on the issue of taxes. They want *more*. The Democrats believe that the government is the most important institution in the nation's life, that the government exists to create programs and raise whatever taxes are necessary to fund those programs."

The *Journal* commended President Reagan's "support for tax cuts and his opposition to increased federal spending were based on his belief, stated at every opportunity, that the federal government and its great panoply of programs were smothering private initiative in the United States. He sought to reverse the Democrats' idea that America's growth and greatness depend on government initiatives and that the government is entitled to the taxes necessary to sustain and expand its responsibilities. It depends instead on letting *all* workers keep most of the country's newly produced wealth and letting them decide, individually, how best to spend and invest the wealth their work has created."

Concluding this case study, the *Journal* aptly summed it up reporting Connecticut's freshman Democratic Senator Joseph Lieberman's eloquent plea to his party:

> The argument of some Democrats against a cut in the capital gains tax—that the rich will benefit more than the rest of us misses the point and is politically divisive. Lower- and middle-income people won't realize most of the tax savings for the obvious reason that they have less capital, but they could get something better: a

job, if they have none, or a better job, if they are underemployed. After all, the whole idea of a capital gains tax cut is to induce people who have capital to move it into new investments that will make America more productive and competitive and benefit all of us with greater economic opportunity and security.

Communism: A Great, Inevitable Idea That Won't and Can't Work

Another important concept is that of socialism and communism. The theory originally advanced but losing sway is that capitalism, or free enterprise, will inevitably evolve first into socialism, then into communism. Proponents say the first part can be done peaceably through democratic socialism, the second part forcibly, through violent revolution. The latter is known as Leninist Marxism, following Marxist interpretations made by Vladimir Ilyich Lenin.

Most of the thinking along the idealistic lines of the classless communist society began with publication by Karl Marx of the influential *Communist Manifesto,* where he and Friedrich Engels recorded the ideas of George Wilhelm Friedrich Hegel, as well as their own, in this 11,000 word pamphlet of 28 pages[9].

The Communist Manifesto is required reading by students in communist countries. It is read by few in the American educational system, those studying economics, political science, Western Civilization and European history, and those at the college level.

Only if one knows ideas can one understand, interpret and defend ideas. It behooves the American people not only to know capitalism (free enterprise economic and business system), but competing economic and political systems as well, especially socialism and communism.

The Communist Manifesto: If It is Sacred, Get Rid of It!

Marx's *Communist Manifesto* has some key thoughts and ideas worth mentioning, though the book should be read and studied thoughtfully. So much of the world's political ideology is predicated on this book that one can't truly understand or evaluate contemporary political happenings or institutions without a passing familiarity with the book.

Probably the most startling realization is that the book recommends abolition of much of what we consider sacred: property, family, and religion. Here is a brief book review to learn the substance and flavor of its propositions.

Marx published *The Communist Manifesto* in 1848 when he was 30 years old, with its opening sentence (p 35), "A specter is haunting Europe—the specter of communism."

9. Karl Marx and Friedrich Engels, *Selected Works,* (800 pp) "The Manifesto of Communism." pp 35-63. International Publishers, New York: 1980. Used with permission

Marx divided the human population (p 35) into "two great classes directly facing each other, the bourgeois and the proletariat:

> . . . By bourgeois is meant the people in the class of modern capitalists, owners of the means of social production and employers of wage labor. By proletarians, the people in the class of modern wage laborers who, having no means of production of their own, are reduced to selling their labor power in order to live.

Disregarding the nationalist bent of the times and of a century to come, Marx and Hegel romantically ignored all that to emphasize an upcoming clash or "class struggle" whereby the proletariat would overthrow the bourgeois, set up a temporary "dictatorship of the proletariat" to evolve into a peaceful, classless society where there are no social or political distinctions, and all citizens are equal and free.

The wording of Chapter II (of IV) really makes Marx's communist case (p 46):

> The immediate aim of the Communists is the same as that of all the other proletarian parties: formation of the proletariat into a class, overthrow of the bourgeois supremacy, conquest of political power by the proletariat. . . . The distinguishing feature of communism is not the abolition of property generally, but the abolition of bourgeois property. . . . the theory of the Communists may be summed up in the single phrase: Abolition of private property. Defending that goal, Marx adds, "Communism deprives no man of the power to appropriate the products of society; all that it does is to deprive him of the power to subjugate the labor of others by means of such appropriation."

Marx' second communist goal (p 49) was:

> Abolition of the family! Even the most radical flare up at this infamous proposal of the Communists. On what foundation is the present family, the bourgeois family, based? On capital, on private gain. In its completely developed form this family exists only among the bourgeoisie. But this state of things finds its complement in the practical absence of the family among the proletarians, and in public prostitution. The bourgeois family will vanish as a matter of course when its complement vanishes, and both will vanish with the vanishing of capital.

His broadside at the family was succinct (p 50):

> The bourgeois clap-trap about the family and education, about the hallowed co-relation of parent and child, becomes all the more disgusting; the more, by the action of modern industry, all family

ties among the proletarians are torn asunder, and their children transformed into simple articles of commerce and instruments of labor.

His continuing comments about free love, the wife as "a mere instrument of production" and the bourgeois having available "common prostitutes, take supreme delight in seducing each other's wives," suggest "an openly legalized system of free love." Here is some real social engineering upon which to base a revolution.

His third revelation (p 52) is equally startling:

> Undoubtedly, it will be said, religious, moral, philosophical, and juridical ideas have been modified in the course of historical development. But religion, morality, philosophy, political science, and law constantly survived this change. There are, besides, eternal truths, such as Freedom, Justice, etc., that are common to all states of society. But communism abolishes eternal truths, it abolishes all religion, and all morality, instead of constituting them on a new basis; it therefore acts in contradiction to all past historical experience.

Therein are found the three tenets of communism: abolition of 1) private property, 2) the family and 3) religion, morality and truth.

Marx ends the chapter with his famous ten points (p 52), preceded by ". . . the first step in the revolution by the working class is to raise the proletariat to the position of ruling class to win the battle of democracy."

He introduces the ten points with:

> Of course, in the beginning, this cannot be effected except by means of despotic inroads on the rights of property, and on the conditions of bourgeois production; by means of measures, therefore, which appear economically insufficient and untenable, but which, in the course of the movement, outstrip themselves, necessitate further inroads upon the old social order, and are unavoidable as a means of entirely revolutionizing the mode of production.

Here are the ten points:

1. Abolition of property in land and application of all rents of land to public purposes.
2. A heavy progressive or graduated income tax.
3. Abolition of all right of inheritance.
4. Confiscation of the property of all emigrants and rebels.
5. Centralization of credit in the hands of the state, by means of a national bank with state capital and an exclusive monopoly.

6. Centralization of the means of communication and transport in the hands of the state.

7. Extension of factories and instruments of production owned by the state; the bringing into cultivation of wastelands, and the improvement of the soil generally in accordance with a common plan.

8. Equal liability of all to labor. Establishment of industrial armies, especially for agriculture.

9. Combination of agriculture with manufacturing industries; gradual abolition of the distinction between town and country, by a more equable distribution of the population over the country.

10. Free education for all children in public schools. Abolition of children's factory labor in its present form. Combination of education with industrial production, etc., etc.

Utopia in Evolution: Marx's Miracle

Marx then explains how it all comes together (p 53):

> When, in the course of development, class distinctions have disappeared, and all production has been concentrated in the hands of a vast association of the whole nation, the public power will lose its political character. Political power, properly so called, is merely the organized power of one class for oppressing another. If the proletariat during its contest with the bourgeoisie is compelled, by the force of circumstances, to organize itself as a class, if, by means of a revolution, it makes itself the ruling class, and, as such, sweeps away by force the old conditions of production, then it will, along with these conditions, have swept away the conditions for the existence of class antagonisms and of classes generally, and will thereby have abolished its own supremacy as a class. In place of the old bourgeois society, with its classes and class antagonisms, we shall have an association in which the free development of each is the condition for the free development of all.

Marx concludes the book (p 63):

> In short, the Communists everywhere support every revolutionary movement against the existing social and political order of things. . . . The Communists disdain to conceal their views and aims. They openly declare that their ends can be attained only by the forcible overthrow of all existing social conditions. Let the ruling classes tremble at a Communistic revolution. The proletarians have nothing to lose but their chains. They have a world to win. WORKINGMEN OF ALL COUNTRIES, UNITE!

You, Power of ONE: The "Home-Run King!

After the constitutional convention, a citizen stopped elder statesman Ben Franklin with the question, "What kind of government have you given us?"

"A republic, madam, if you can keep it," he replied.

We have a republic. We can keep it, preserve and strengthen it.

We previously quoted Arthur Koestler[10] regarding "a new conflict which cuts across the old lines of division (between Left and Right, Capitalism and Socialism). The real content of this conflict can be summed up in one phrase: total tyranny against relative freedom." He extends this thought:

> Sometimes I have a feeling in my bones that the terrible pressure which this conflict exerts on all humanity might perhaps represent a challenge, a biological stimulus as it were, which will release the new mutation of human consciousness; and that its content might be a new spiritual awareness, born of anguish and suffering, of the full meaning of freedom. And I don't mean by that, freedom from want, freedom from fear and the rest. Since the dawn of civilization people have fought under that slogan of freedom; but it was always freedom from some particularly irksome oppression, freedom in a restricted, negative sense. I mean freedom in a much deeper and fuller sense than any we can conceive today, or see realized anywhere in organic nature. If that is the case, then we are indeed living in an interesting time, and the answer which we shall give to destiny's challenge is not without import for the future of our species.

Power of ONE, you are no longer "way out in left field." You have gone around the bases, touched them all and crossed home plate. You made a home run as a knowledgeable citizen of America and of the world, conversant in some very esoteric and important political, economic, cultural and ideological topics and ideas. You have the power of knowledge and understanding, and with them, the privilege and responsibility to "pass it on." All Americans need this information, to better understand the political and economic system in which we live, what other systems are "out there," and why America's is better and worth "passing it on." It is a big assignment. But you are a powerful and important person. *Power of ONE,* you are now even more ready to be a "world-changer." Go for it!

America—Pass It On!

---

10. Koestler, Arthur, "An Outgrown Dilemma" (1950), in The Trail of the Dinosaur (1955), quoted in "The Language of Politics," by Bryan Magee, *Encounter,* p 23, May, 1986

Questions for Review

1. Where in the U.S. Constitution is the word "democracy" used? How many times?

2. What are the "bases" and why must they be "run" in order? What politically descriptive words are familiar but confusing? What happens to words over time to make them communicate less precisely? Give an example. Why is it important to know not only many words but their exact meanings and usages?

3. Discuss definitions and meanings of the following: conservative, liberal, conservatism, liberalism.

4. What is the difference or evolution of the meaning of early liberalism and today's liberalism? What contributed to the shift in meaning? What is the difference in the perception of the role of government? The nature of human nature?

5. Repeat No. 4's questions substituting "conservatism" for "liberalism."

6. Liberals have a different set of priorities than conservatives and even those called Libertarians, concerning ranking of freedom, justice, peace and liberty. Discuss the meanings of these words and their rankings. In what order do you rank them?

7. What are labels and why are they undesirable? How are they useful or helpful? The precise meanings of Republican and Democrat are elusive, especially when compared to "moderate." Why? What does it mean to say "society has been drifting ever more leftward, pulling the moderate label to the left?"

8. What is "the great inevitable idea that will not and cannot work?" Why? What three things did Karl Marx seek to abolish? Discuss what each one means to you personally.

9. Read and discuss individually the ten points cited by Karl Marx that are necessary to form a communist society. How does each one relate to modern America? Socialism has been explained as "the government owning and controlling the factors of production." Knowing that the factors of production are land, labor and capital, discussing each alone, what does this mean to you, especially "labor" being owned and controlled by government.

10. Discuss Arthur Kessler's comments regarding the conflict between "total tyranny against relative freedom." "Full meaning of freedom?" Contrast "freedom from want, freedom from fear and the rest," and "freedom from some particularly irksome oppression,

freedom in a restricted, negative sense," with "freedom in a much deeper and fuller sense than any we can conceive today, or see realized anywhere in organic nature."

Liberalism is a force truly of the spirit proceeding from the deep realization that economic freedom cannot be sacrificed if political freedom is to be preserved.   —Herbert Clark Hoover

If you limit the search for truth and forbid men anywhere, in any way, to seek knowledge, you paralyze the vital force of truth itself. In the best sense of the word, Jesus was a radical. His religion has been so long identified with conservatism—often with conservatism of the obstinate and unyielding sort—that it is almost startling for us sometimes to remember that all of the conservatism of his own times was against him; that it was the young, free, restless, sanguine, progressive part of the people who flocked to him.   —Phillips Brooks

The system of party responsibility in America requires that one of its parties be the liberal party and the other the conservative party. This has been the division by which the major parties in American history have identified themselves whenever crises have developed which required definite choice of direction.   —Franklin D. Roosevelt

Criticism also comes from our native Communists who want to overturn the system. And from the fuzzy-minded totalitarian liberals who believe that their creeping collectivism can be adopted without destroying personal liberty and representative government.
                    —Herbert Clark Hoover

Mankind can pass directly from capitalism into Socialism, i.e., into social ownership of the means of production and the distribution of products according to the work of the individual. Our party looks further ahead than that: Socialism is bound sooner or later to ripen into Communism, whose banner bears the motto: "From each according to his ability, to each according to his needs."   —V. I. Lenin

Communism is based on the belief that man is so weak and inadequate that he is unable to govern himself, and therefore requires the rule of strong masters. Democracy is based on the conviction that man has the moral and intellectual capacity, as well as the inalienable right, to govern himself with reason and justice.   —Harry Truman

Chapter 19

ROGIA
Role Of Government In America

Freedom is strangely ephemeral. It is something like breathing; one only becomes acutely aware of its importance when one is choking. Similarly, it is only when one confronts political tyranny that one really grasps the meaning and importance of freedom. Freedom is difficult to understand because it isn't a presence but an absence—an absence of governmental constraint.

—William Simon

Is Government the Opposite of Freedom?

To paraphrase, "Government is difficult to understand because it isn't an absence but a presence, the presence of force, coercion, control and constraint." If there were ever a living, breathing definition of the words *ubiquitous* and *perpetuity,* it would be GOVERNMENT, seemingly everywhere at once, lasting forever.

ROGIA: What is the Role Of Government In America?

Government is a presence, a major presence. We feel it everywhere we go, in everything we do. It permeates our thinking, decisions and actions. Government makes law and enforces law. Government law is to protect us from fear, force and fraud. How much law is necessary, effective, enforceable? How much government is essential?

Opinions differ. Some think government should be small and limited. Their view is that people are responsible, self-governing; that government, especially in excess, is force and coercion, an infringement on, rather than a protection of, their rights to "life, liberty and pursuit of happiness," a barrier to rather than a booster of freedom.

Others think government should be large and powerful. Their view is that people are not responsible but rather need guidance and help. Well-meaning programs are designed to help those less advantaged, taxing those more advantaged and smoothing things out all around. All it takes is a few tax dollars from everyone to gather large amounts of money to do good deeds and amass power to enforce the doing.

Here is a reminder of how our economic system works: Our common enemy is scarcity. Our mission is survival. Our goal is prosperity. To live we consume. To consume we must produce. We want the best system of enterprise and government, economic and political, to produce the most goods and services for the most people. Enterprise creates wealth. Government, a net consumer of wealth, creates a climate of creating wealth. When government grows bigger, enterprise shrinks. More wealth is consumed, less wealth is produced. Material well being and quality-of-life drop. That is why balance is critical.

The Riddle of Government: What is it?

Winston Churchill once described Russia as "a riddle wrapped in a mystery inside an enigma." The same words could be used to describe the "puzzlements" of government. Government also is "a riddle wrapped in a mystery inside an enigma."

Groups of people need government. Whether it is a small social unit or a large political division, government is needed to preserve order and assure a climate of productivity and well being. Government is a means of making and enforcing decisions that affect the behavior of a whole group of people[1]:

> Every group of people—from a family to a nation—has rules of conduct to *govern* the lives of its members. . . . The rules made by a group are really decisions about matters that affect the group as a whole. The decisions are designed to encourage or require certain kinds of behavior, or to discourage or forbid other kinds of behavior by individual members. . . . Those who have the power to control behavior by making and enforcing the rules of a group are often called a *power structure.*

Related matters include the source of governmental power, *sovereignty*, which in democratic societies emanates from the people; the concept of *legitimacy*, acceptance by the people; and *jurisdiction*, the right and scope to make and enforce laws. *Socialization* is where the people are encultured through an educational learning process to accept and support government, its laws and standards.

1. *The World Book Encyclopedia,* Volume 8, pages 282-283. Copyright (c) 1990 World Book, Inc., Chicago. Used with permission

When we speak of *government* as the process within a group for making and enforcing decisions that affect human behavior, it does not matter whether the decisions are conscious or unconscious, or enforced by persuasion or by punishment.

A further distinction is made between a *public government* and a *private government*—the family, a company, business, church or private organization. Private government rules are enforceable only within the confines of the group. Public government has jurisdiction within its political boundaries, i.e., a city, county, state or country.

The private government's jurisdiction and rules are closer and more personal, such as limiting membership to people over 65 years of age, or requiring an initiation fee and annual dues. A public government's rules govern national behavior, public safety and health, immigration, transportation and communications, licensing of various businesses and occupations, law enforcement and taxation.

A private government may fine or even expel a disobedient member. But only a public government can legally imprison or execute a person.

Government:
The Incomplete Conquest We Want Not to Complete

Government is the "institutionalization of conquest," according to Dr. Theodore J. Lowi[2], defining *conquest* as "the action gained by force of arms; acquisition by war; subjugation of a country . . . by vanquishing; gaining of victory." He says conquest, bringing a territory and its population under control, is not government, but precedes government; that government is inconceivable without conquest. He then defines government as "the institutionalization of conquest." He explains:

> The essential purpose of government is to maintain conquest. Conquest never ends; it only changes form. It becomes *control.* The United States has been politically so stable that its government has often been viewed implicitly as a source of benefits and services and of occasional controls imposed on wrongdoing. In actuality, there are controls behind every benefit, and there is conquest behind all control.

It is instructive that Lowi organized the five parts of his book over that spectrum, from Conquest, to Constitution, to Consent, to Command, finally to Control.

Lowi concludes his book, "If the government is to maintain its stability, unthreatened by revolution, it must justify its control at every level.

2. Lowi, Theodore J., *Incomplete Conquest: Governing America,* pp 7, 468, Holt, Rinehart and Winston, New York: 1981

Citizens, in turn, must make sure each justification is given. They must be sure the forms government takes continue to deal with the contradiction inherent in incomplete conquest."

"Taxation as Theft": A Libertarian Viewpoint

The Libertarian perspective is a world of little government where each individual is self-governing and personally responsible. One does what one wishes as long as it does not infringe on the life, liberty, property or finances of other persons.

David Bergland, one time Libertarian Party Candidate for President, repeats several times for emphasis[3], "The essence of government action is this. Some people, called legislators, make rules of conduct, and attach penalties for violation of the rules. When the rules are broken, they send men with guns (policemen) out to round up the wrongdoers and impose the penalty."

Describing "Taxation as Theft," Bergland quotes Franz Oppenheimer's book, *The State*:

> . . . the development of the state as an institution is based on tribal conquests and the exaction of tribute by the conquerors from the conquered people. Invariably one tribe or group would conquer another and require the conquered peoples to pay in crops, labor, or other property on a continuing basis. In return, the conquerors would typically protect the conquered people from other marauding tribes. The protection money paid by the conquered peoples came to be called taxation.

Bergland continues, "Libertarians are willing to call taxation by its accurate name: 'theft.' Taxation is simply some people using the force at their disposal to steal the earnings or property of other people. The taxpayer-victim is threatened with fines or jail if he refuses to pay. If the taxpayer resists the government force, the tax enforcing officials have the power (not the moral right) to crush the resistance with whatever force is necessary, including lethal force."

The enterprise sector of an economic system creates wealth. Part of this wealth, in the form of taxes, is channeled into government to fund the legitimate functions of government. To a certain size and activity, benefits of government justify the payment of taxes. Beyond this point taxation becomes confiscation, less justified, serving more as a penalty and a punishment for working and producing.

When people keep only a portion of what they work for, they don't work as hard. But the negative effects of taxation are minimized if the people perceive positive, cost-justified benefits that accrue from taxation.

3. Bergland. David, *Libertarianism in One Lesson*. pp 1, 12, (1984) Orpheus Publications, 1773 Bahama Place, Cost Mesa, CA 92626. $5

Promotion for Congressman Jack Kemp's book[4], *An American Renaissance* put it this way:

If you tax something, you get less of it. If you subsidize something, you get more of it. In America we tax work, growth, investment, employment, savings, productivity, initiative and ability, while subsidizing non-work, consumption, welfare and debt. Isn't it time to allow our people to probe, test, prove their character and sensibilities, to be inspired to growth and initiative?

It is perhaps not so obvious that the "you" and "we" to whom Kemp refers, is government.

As government grows relatively larger, it becomes a bureaucracy. Rather than accomplishing a purpose, its mission becomes "to survive" (even grow), its job becomes "to follow a procedure." Its mission becomes more self-serving, not to truly solve a problem but to survive and grow as a separate, living organism, likely worsening the problem it was created to solve.

The government sector is quite different than business, the private or enterprise sector. Enterprise accepts and faces risk, takes a chance and must, *must, MUST please a customer at a profit* to survive.

Some say government should be run like a business. It can't. Government has essentially no risk and must please no one. Instead, it has power of government and force of law. If you do not do what they say, they can do bad things to you. You must pay your taxes. If you don't you can be punished—fined, imprisoned, or both, your family broken up, your house seized for taxes, and your property confiscated and sold.

The role and size of government must be understood, carefully monitored, controlled and kept in balance lest it become the master rather than the servant.

America's constitutional form of representative government is designed to function in a free enterprise, free-market, private incentive economy. The important question is how much has government's relative size increased? "Relative size" indicates since government is part of a two-part system, the other, enterprise, is the remainder. Hence, as government gets bigger, enterprise gets smaller.

Government is essential. An economy with little or no government would be very *un*productive. People would spend much of their waking time protecting themselves, with little time to work, or energy or incentive to produce. As government grows somewhat larger, functional public safety and security that protects the populace combines with a court system to

4. Kemp, Jack, *An American Renaissance: A Strategy for the 1980's,* Harper and Row, New York: 1979

assure law and order, sanctity of contracts and adherence to fair and reasonable business practices. The enterprise sector responds with division of labor and specialization increasing productivity, output, quality and quantity of goods and services and an increase in standard-of-living. As confidence grows so do entrepreneurship, invention, innovation and other forms of primary wealth creation.

As government grows relatively bigger, government begins to do things formerly done by the enterprise sector. We could have government fire protection, rather than private or volunteer. We might have government trash removal. We could even have government-supplied public transportation, electrical power, water and waste treatment, paid from taxes, rather than to private or quasi-government entities through user-related billings.

As government grows much larger it becomes re-distributionist, taking from those who produce while providing more to those who do not or cannot produce, for whatever reason. These shifts are legislative decisions made through the political process. They begin with seemingly good reasons, but the programs and costs inevitably grow large, cumbersome, wasteful and expensive, often not accomplishing but actually defeating the purposes for which they were created. Too, such distributions use public money to buy politicians, elected and appointed public officials votes and power from various constituencies.

Redistributionist schemes inevitably fail. While they seem good ideas with the highest intentions and motivations, because of human nature and "government nature," costs escalate while results deteriorate.

Government GROWTH: Almost Half Percent a Year, 1948-1988!

Government growth is relentless. We can study it over a significant but relatively stable period for analysis. World War II ended in 1945. Congress began to support "full employment" in 1946. If we study government growth beginning 1948 it allows a sufficient transition period from the war economy into implementation of this far-reaching new national policy.

Our good intentions were formalized in this "full employment" legislation. The declaration of policy of the *Employment Act of 1946* defined our government's new mission:

> The Congress declares that it is the continuing policy and responsibility of the Federal Government to use all practicable means consistent with its needs and obligations and other essential considerations of national policy, with the assistance and cooperation of industry, agriculture, labor, and State and local governments, to coordinate and utilize all its plans, functions, and resources for the purpose of creating and maintaining, in a manner calculated to foster and promote free competitive enterprise and the general welfare, conditions under which there will be afforded useful employment

opportunities, including self employment, for those able, willing and seeking to work, and to promote maximum employment, production and purchasing power.

The federal government is required to do all within its considerable power to "promote maximum employment." This assumes government understands wealth creation where enterprise pleases a customer at a continuing profit by creating and producing wealth—goods and services, thus creating real jobs and a positive source of taxes. It also has come to mean that employment can be favorably "stimulated" if government "does something."

That single statement of policy (in one very long sentence) is in large part why government grows. We have assigned to government the nearly impossible function of providing "maximum employment," whatever that is. What if *in fact,* such government action virtually guarantees *less* than full employment? A vicious circle is created where the more government "does" the worse the problem becomes.

The more government "does," the more government grows. The more government grows, the more taxes taken, the less enterprise gets to keep to put into its main mission of investing *to create wealth,* with resultant diminishing prosperity and abundance.

Grow it does. Government grows slow but sure, a process called *creep,* slow change over time. Like a person's age it takes a long period of time, but it takes its toll and does its inevitable damage. In terms of national output government grew almost half a percent a year, from 18% of GNP in 1948 to 35% in 1988! Total government growth was 0.42% per year.

Here is the data[5] in table form:

Comparative Growth Rates: PERSONAL INCOME vs Government and Gross National Product, 1948-1988, 40 Years, $ Billions

	1948	%GNP	1988	%GNP	Change	Growth/Yr
Gross Nat'l Prod	$ 262		$ 4,881		+18.6x	7.59%
Personal Incom	209		4,065		+19.5x	7.70%
Fed Gov't Spending	30		1,064		+35.5x	9.33%
% GNP		11.5%		21.8%		0.26%
St/Lc Gov't Spnd' g	18		652		+36.2x	9.39%
% GNP		6.9%		13.4%		0.16%
Tot Gov't Spending	$ 48		$1,716		+35.8x	9.35%
Total % GNP		18.4%		35.2%		0.42%
Gov't as % of Pers Inc	23.0%	———	42.2%	———	+ 83%	———

5.*Economic Report of the President, February,* 1990, pp 294, 322, 383, 390

Note that output—GNP, and Personal Income grew at annual rates of 7.2% and 7.7% while all government grew significantly more at 9.3% per year. Why should government grow faster than the economy or our ability and willingness to pay? Also notice what happens when the size and growth of government are compared as percent of personal income. That is all the money all the people earn in wages and salaries, interest, dividends, profits from business and rents, etc. What it does not include is government spending, which gross domestic product, GDP (national output) by definition does include.

In 1948, 23% of personal income was required to pay for government. Growing 0.48% a year, it took over 42% of all personal income in 1988 to fund government. In this sense we work nearly half a year each year to support government at its present size, in direct and hidden taxes. As a nation we spent over 40% of our hard-earned money for government!

As wealth-consuming government is allowed, even "stimulated," to grow ever larger, wealth-creating enterprise shrinks, greatly reducing the economy's ability to provide its full potential of production.

You cannot distribute, or re-distribute, what you do not produce.

Government Got Big and Stayed Big, Then to 1999

Government growth has stabilized since 1988. From the February, 2000 *Economic Report of the President*, all in $billions, with 1999 gross domestic product at $9,248 (p 306) and personal income $7,791 (p 338), we find federal government spending at $1,703 (p 397), state-and-local at $1,089 (p 404) with total government at $2,792. That puts 1999 government size at 30.2% of GDP and 35.8% of personal income.

All three levels of government as well as all taxes must be taken into account in our search for the most desirable size of government and its balance with the enterprise sector.

Only people pay taxes. All the people pay all the taxes—federal, state, local, special district; sales, income, property, excises, fees, licenses, fines and all the others.

More and more there are costs not called taxes but which act the same way, money over which we have no control in our spending. On each new automobile, for example, the combined cost of government-mandated safety and pollution control equipment runs in the thousands of dollars per vehicle.

If your state requires an exhaust emission or safety inspection of your car, though it is not called a tax it acts just like one. It is the same for car registration or a driver's license. When those costs are increased it is no different than a tax increase. You have less money to spend, called discretionary income.

Here is how a "user fee" is just another name for tax increase. A city council member told how they were going to impose user fees. I asked, "Since we are already all paying taxes to support those activities will there be a commensurate reduction in taxes upon imposition of the user fee?" She answered, "We have never been asked that question." What is that predictable outcome? Right. New fees, same taxes—a tax increase.

When a government authority requires a business to meet a specific law such as minimum wage or a regulated health benefit such as annual mammograms for women or prostate exam for men, each is a cost that seems not a tax. It is a regulation a business is required to enforce or comply with. It costs the business (read that "the customer"), not the government. Politicians enact the legislation and get the political benefit. Business pays for it. That means YOU pay for it.

Further, filling out forms and hiring people to comply with government regulations are also costs not called taxes but act just like them. We here evaluate only those assessments measured and reported as taxes directly attributable to government. True "total taxes" have an even greater impact than those herein presented, adding perhaps half again or more the cost of the taxes we can measure directly in dollars.

When Government "Stimulates the Economy," What Grows?

When government is used to "stimulate the economy," they spend money they don't have—borrow, while holding or reducing taxes. It is all done to force-feed the economy to grow. The economy does grow but gets more out-of-balance.

Trying to determine "balance" in wealth creation of the enterprise sector and "creating a climate of creating wealth" of the government sector we study these numbers a little differently. By simple subtraction, we reveal the growth of "enterprise national product," the private sector, compared to growth of national output, GDP and government.

Comparative Growth Rates: BUSINESS ENTERPRISE vs Goverment and Gross Domestic Product, 1959-1999, 40 Years, $ Billions

	1959	% Size	1999	%Size	Increase
National Output, GDP	$ 507		$ 9,248		+ 18.2 times
Total Gov't Spending	-$ 127	25.1%	-$ 2,792	30.2%	+ 21.9 times
Enterprise Nat'l Prod. (Difference)	$ 380	74.9%	$ 6,456.4	69.8%	+ 17.0 times
Wealth Creation Ratio	2.99:1		2.31:1		

With highly-touted "government stimulus" what grew was government, by 22 times. That boosted national output 18 times with enterprise, the wealth-creating sector growing only 17 times, and that is the one we supposedly were trying to use government to grow. Government itself a part of GDP grew at almost twice the rate of enterprise. When wealth-consuming government is used to "stimulate the economy" what we get is more government.

A "wealth creation ratio" reveals the direction and power of the economy to create wealth. The one decision we have as an economy is how large government will be. As that net-wealth-consuming sector gets larger, by definition the wealth-creation sector gets smaller. The wealth creation ratio has shrunk from 2.99 to 2.31 from 1959 to 1999. Too far out of balance can diminish citizen standard-of- living and quality-of-life.

Another way to look at size and growth of government is to compare it to the "essentials of life"—food, shelter (housing, household operation, furniture and equipment) and clothing[6]. From 1959 to 1999 cost of government grew 22 times, essentials 15 times. In 1959 government cost $127 billion, 67% of essentials $189 billion. In 1999 government cost $2,792 billion, 101% of, $27 billion *more* than essentials of life. In terms of our national priorities we value government more than essentials of life! Check the chart.

Comparative Growth Rates, 1959-1999:
ESSENTIALS of LIFE vs All-Government, $ billion

	1959	1999	Increase
Food	$ 81	$ 903	+ 11.2 times
Shelter	82	1,556	+ 19.0 times
Clothing	26	306	+ 11.6 times
Essentials Total	$ 189	$ 2,765	+ 14.6 times
All-Government	$ 127	$ 2,792	+ 21.9 times
Difference	$ 62	($ 27)	
Gov't, % of Essentials	67%	101%	

The Illusion: The Near-and-Obvious vs
The Far-and-Not-So-Obvious

Because of its nature, every time government "does something," it appears something beneficial and desirable happens. However, in the longer term there is little real progress or few or disappointing results for the community and society as a whole. Good intentions almost always

6. *Economic Report of the President*, February, 2000 edition, pp 324, 397, 404

exceed results. It is kind of like, "we've got to do something even if it is wrong." We do, and it is.

It is so easy to show—and mislead—on television. Here is the big new public works project, low income housing, a second airport or "upgraded" hockey stadium, built with tax dollars. The interviewer shows a worker asking, "What do you think of the new project?" He answers, "I was unemployed so I'm excited to have a job." Then they show his wife and daughter in a supermarket buying groceries. What is not possible to show are the jobs or businesses not created, jobs lost and businesses failed because of the higher taxes required to finance the "obvious" public works project. That is how we get the illusion of government "job creation." We must look at the whole picture so as not to be fooled by it.

Another example is using taxes to tear down buildings, to be replaced by tax-financed apartments quite visible in their new existence and the obvious good they do. The not-so-near and not-so-obvious are the businesses and jobs NOT CREATED, and those business bankruptcies or job layoffs farther away and scattered, as a result of the money taxpayers DON'T HAVE TO SPEND. What are the effects of such money not available in the enterprise sector?

Economist Henry Hazlitt says, "The art of economics consists in looking not merely at the immediate but at the longer effects of any act or policy; it consists in tracing the consequences of that policy not merely for one group but for all groups[7]."

Hazlitt's message prompts us to carefully consider not only the short term but the long term, and not only those directly and obviously affected, but those indirectly and not-so-obviously affected. We call this going "beyond the obvious": BTO.

The Most Important Look at Cost and Growth of Taxes, One Person: YOU!

This discussion has centered around "macro" or very large national numbers. A more understandable discussion may be to personalize taxes, to discuss them in terms of *one person*. The cost and growth of taxes are considerable, especially since they have been high for decades. We can break them down into per-capita (not per-family) state, local, sub-total, federal and total per-capita taxes. It is helpful then to compare with growth in median family income ("ability to pay") and inflation-plus-population to get a better assessment of the cost and growth of government on a one-person, or per-capita basis. Yes, you can take this personally. This represents closely an American's average tax burden and especially its growth for the 11 years, 1985 to 1996.

7. Hazlitt, Henry, *Economics in One Lesson*, p. 17, Arlington House, Westport, Connecticut: 1979

1985 to 1996 Per-Capita Tax Burden and Growth Compared to Growth in Median Family Income, and Inflation-plus-Population

----

		Per-Capita Taxes			
		1985	1996	Change	%/yr (comp)
State	1)	$904	$1,577	+74%	5.2%
Local	1)	558	1,020	+83%	5.6%
Subtotal		$1,462	$2,597	+78%	5.4%
Federal	2)	3,078	5,473	+78%	5.4%
Total		$4,540	$8,070	+78%	5.4%<<===

Median Family Inc. 3)	$23,618	$35,492	+50%	3.8%<<===
Total, Inflation-plus-Population			+57%	4.5%<<===
Inflation (CPI—U) 4)	107.6	156.9	+46%	3.5%
Population, million 5)	238.5	265.5	+11%	1.0%

Sources: 1) Dept of the Census, "Colo State & Local gov't Finances by Level of Gov't 1995-96," and *How Colorado Compares, State and Local Taxes,* 1985-1995 editions, Colorado Public Expenditure Council, and U. S. Dept of Commerce, Bureau of the Census, *Government Finances in* 1987-88 (GF-87-5), pp 44-96; *2) Economic Report of the President,* February, 2000, pp 397, 345; 3) *Statistical Abstract of the U.S.,* 1999, p 474; 4) Ref 2, p 373; 5) Ref 2, p345.

Taxes (and government) in the past have increased significantly faster than median family income, or inflation-plus-population. Over the 11 years, 1985 to 1996, while family income increased 50%, and inflation-plus-population increased 57% (46+11), per-capita (not per-family) taxes went up 78%. Compound annual growth rates show taxes up 1.6% per year more than family income, 0.9% more than the inflation-plus-population.

These average taxes include federal, state-and-local, direct and indirect. They are the average total taxes each person pays through the labyrinth of taxes—federal and state income, property, excise and others, many assessed on each other. It is the important total that has a marked effect on the ability of individuals and families to survive economically.

Note that these figures are only taxes called "taxes." They do not include other government revenues such as licenses, permits, fines, fees and borrowing.

What is not immediately apparent is that over the period 1985-1996 average family size dropped from 3.23 to 3.19 people. In two-parent families more married mothers worked, increasing from 53.4% to 62.7%

for those with children under 6, and from 67.8% to 76.2% for those with children 6 to 17. Those numbers back in 1948 were 11% and 26%, respectively[8].

Simple arithmetic shows in 1996 the American family paid $25,743 in taxes (3.19 x $8,070) on income of $35,492, paying 72% of income in taxes. That is why two members of a family must work, one to support the family, the other to pay taxes, to support government.

Does this have a bearing on the breakup of the family? Parents are less at home to raise the children. To age six kids acquire values and belief systems, self-esteem and a sense of self-worth. From Mom and Dad they learn the two behaviorial basics, "keep your hands to yourself" and "respect other people's property." Too soon they are "latchkey kids" who come home to an empty house, some of whom resort to sex, crime, drugs, gang violence and teenage suicide as solutions to teenage problems.

Taxes continue to grow with a profound impact on our families, freedoms and future.

Big Government: The Riddle, the Mystery, the Enigma

As time flies, government grows. The *riddle* is, why does it grow? The *mystery* is, is government growth beneficial and desirable? The *enigma* is, can it get too big, and if so, what to do about it? As we better understand the role of government, we learn how big government is and how big it should be, how to achieve a more ideal size and what to expect as a result of achieving a better balance between enterprise and government.

It is obvious there is power of freedom in a small government. Too bad we do not have one. We have a large government and it is growing larger. Yet there is a lot one person can do to help achieve a better balance between enterprise and government. Most is involved with learning more, understanding what you know, getting more and better information, communicating what you know to others, then taking effective action to make a difference. You are on your way, *Power of ONE!*

Questions for Review

1. "Freedom is difficult to understand because it isn't a presence but an absence. . . . " of what? Explain, discuss. What is the parallel of freedom to government?

2. What does government law protect us from? Who from? What protects the people from government and government law? Why is government absolutely essential?

8. *Statistical Abstract of the United States, 1999*, pp 60, 417; *Historical Statistics of the United States, 1975*, p 134

3. What is the Role Of Government In America (ROGIA)? Explain it in terms of wealth creation, enterprise and "balance." Explain "Enterprise is a net producer of wealth." Explain "Government is a net consumer of wealth." If the wealth-creating sector shrinks while the wealth-consuming sector grows, what must happen to material well-being and quality-of-life?

4. Defend "Government should be small and limited." Defend "Government should be large to do a lot more good for a lot more people." Defend "What we really seek is a balance."

5. Explain why wherever people work and live together they need government. Discuss two kinds of government, public and private. Where are they the same? Different? Which can legally execute or imprison a person? Explain "Government is the institutionalization of conquest." Why must citizens "be sure the forms government takes continue to deal with the contradiction inherent in incomplete conquest?" Discuss the sequence of government impact "from conquest, to constitution, to consent, to command, finally to control."

6. Discuss, where each individual is self-governing and personally responsible, taxation is theft. What is the Libertarian's explanation of "the essence of government action?"

7. How does one measure government over time? How do taxes affect human being's motivation to work hard, innovate and take a risk? What two affects describe the effect of taxes on people, to serve as a _____ and a _____ . Describe the opposite effects of taxing and subsidizing. What do we tax and what do we subsidize?

8. What does enterprise accept and face that government doesn't? Why is it impossible to "run government like a business?" Discuss the declaration of policy of the *Employment Act of 1946*. How can government serve those purposes? How has it served those purposes? Did it work?

9. Describe and discuss government size and growth in terms of percent of gross domestic product, total output of goods and services, and of percent of personal income. In terms of the "essentials of life," food, shelter and clothing. In terms of non-tax "hidden costs." In terms of per-person taxes and their growth. What is "creep" and how does it do its inevitable "dirty deeds?" Give an example of creep. Compare growth over time of total output, government and "enterprise national product."

10. What is "the art of economics?" Why is it important to look not only at the near and obvious, but the distant and not-so-obvious? What are the two central economic fallacies and why are they

important? Why is it important to consider jobs not created, businesses not formed, businesses gone bankrupt and taxes not collected and paid as a result of governmental policies and action?

All government without the consent of the governed, is the very definition of slavery.   —Jonathan Swift

Government is a contrivance of human wisdom to provide for human wants.   —Edmund Burke

The divine right of kings may have been a plea for feeble tyrants, but the divine right of government is the keystone of human progress, and without it government sinks into police and a nation into a mob.
                                                      —Benjamin Disraeli

The legitimate object of government is to do for a community of people whatever they need to have done, but cannot do at all in their separate and individual capacities.   —Abraham Lincoln

Government is too big and important to be left to the politicians.
                                                      —Chester Bowles

We stand in the presence of a revolution—not a bloody revolution; America is not given to the spilling of blood—but a silent revolution, whereby America will insist upon recovering in practice those ideals which she has always professed, upon securing a government devoted to the general interest and not the special interests.   —Woodrow Wilson

Chapter 20

SMALLER GOVERNMENT
A Goal Worth Adopting

Parkinson's Law:
Government Grows because Government Grows

"Work expands so as to fill the time available for its completion," begins the book *Parkinson's Law.* Observing and studying British government gave substance and wisdom to a whole new way of viewing a government as a set of bureaus, a "bureaucracy."

Parkinson explains[1]:

> Politicians and taxpayers have assumed (with occasional phases of doubt) that a rising total in the number of civil servants must reflect a growing volume of work to be done. . . .The fact is that the number of the officials and quantity of work are not related to each other at all. The rise in the total of those employed is governed by Parkinson's law and would be much the same whether the volume of the work were to increase, diminish, or even disappear.

He describes two motive forces of growth: "(1) An official wants to multiply subordinates, not rivals, and (2) Officials make work for each other."

This gives three realizations about government:

---

1. Parkinson, C. Northcote, *Parkinson's Law.* pp 15, 17, 21, Ballantine. New York: 1957

1. Government bureaus are CREATED to recognize, identify and quantify public sector problems, real, imagined or fabricated, based on emerging trends, developing issues and political realities.
2. Bureaucracy EXISTS to administer the problem, but not necessarily to solve it. If life's first motivation is survival, then solving the problem is antithetical to preserving a job, occupation or employment condition of the *status quo*.
3. The bureaucracy GROWS for its own sake.

Parkinson used the British navy as an actual example. "The strength of the Navy in 1914 could be shown as 146,000 officers and men, 3,249 dockyard officials and clerks, and 57,000 dockyard workmen. By 1928 there were only 100,000 officers and men and 62,439 workmen, but the dockyard officials and clerks by then numbered 4,558. As for warships, the strength in 1928 was a mere fraction of what it had been in 1914— fewer than 20 capital ships in commission as compared with 62."

Results? "While capital ships decreased 68% and naval personnel dropped 32%, dockyard officials and clerks increased over 40%; admiralty officials, up 78%, giving what they described as 'a magnificent navy on land.'"

Bureaucracies and governments grow because they grow. The only hindrance to growth may be funding, which for government, is taxes in all forms, for all reasons, direct and indirect, obvious and hidden, and they rarely if ever decrease.

Governments, like other social institutions, are operated by people, with their strengths and weaknesses, failings and foibles, dreams and vision. The complicating factor is the use of the democratic majority vote of elected representatives and the capability to grant favors at government ("taxpayer") expense to gain votes and reward constituencies.

The resulting legislation is usually for genuinely or pseudo-compas-sionate and politically expedient good causes, often however, with disastrous economic and long-term human consequences. When the *specific* welfare is rewarded through the political and legislative process, some citizens are helped, but others are hurt. That violates the equality provisions and intent of America's freedom documents. Specific instances of poverty and butter may be helpful.

Fighting the War on Poverty: Poverty Won.

An example of "good politics" with bad economic results is the "War on Poverty" declared in the mid-1960's. The question is, "Did it work?" The answer is "No," but it cost taxpayers and hard-working Americans a lot of money to find that out. Then, when we found out, what did we do with what we learned? Nothing.

In 1965, there were 25 million defined "poor" people[2]. Between 1965 and 1975, the government spent over $1.46 trillion to combat poverty. When tallied up in 1975, the government counted 25 million poor people. Little changed, it seemed, except the expenditure of an enormous amount of tax money.

We tried again, more, harder and differently. From 1975 through 1983, over $4 trillion more was spent. During that time, the defined poor did not decrease, but increased, to 35 million, from 12% of the American people to 14.9%!

That's $5 1/2 trillion spent on the War on Poverty. Poverty won! The war is still on, and poverty is still winning. Had the money been given directly to the poor, it would have averaged over $35,000 tax-free every year for a family of four. On a taxed-income basis, it was worth nearly $50,000 a year! Where did most of it go? To bureaucrats and others to administer the government programs. Perhaps that is why it is called "the poverty industry"!

Governmental control always goes with government funding and that control costs money. Much of the money goes to the bureaucrats, consultants, social and case workers, and the "beltway bandits," so-named because these consultants and professionals "do business"—present studies, analyses and recommendations—within the beltway around the nation's capitol, in Washington, DC.

Greasing the Poverty Skids with Butter

Another example of superb politics and flawed economics is that of price supports for farm products. Dairy farmers lobbied (influenced) elected government officials to provide them *price supports,* that is, guaranteed prices for their products. They wished to achieve "parity," a government program policy set up whereby the farmer received the top prices for farm products, those existent between 1910 and 1920. In order to help accomplish this in 1980, the government purchased dairy products off the open market and placed them in refrigerated storage in mammoth limestone caves in Kansas City, KS and Independence, MO.

Did it solve the problem? No.

When the government bought butter off the market, with supply diminished and demand the same, prices went up—exactly what the program was to accomplish. With a guaranteed market and the government buying the surplus, what happened to production? It went up too, forcing the government to buy even more supplies of the dairy products. Who paid for all these surplus dairy products to be placed in storage? YOU. The American taxpayer.

2. Ulrich, William J., Editor *Capital Gains,* "The Inflation Wave and Beyond," p 5,6, August, 1986, 700 Shelard Plaza North, Minneapolis, MN 55426

In 1982 the government had about 2 billion pounds of surplus dairy products in storage. The butter was purchased for $1.45 a pound, with a total $2.4 billion spent for inventory. By year's end, it had grown to almost 2 1/2 billion pounds in storage. As more storage was needed, the government contemplated giving away surplus to those in need.

To reduce stockpiles by some 220 million pounds of butter, the U. S. Department of Agriculture suggested selling it to the Soviet Union (our declared enemy in an undeclared cold war) for $1.05 a pound. The State Department countered U. S. butter shouldn't go on Russian bread, so it was eventually sold to New Zealand for 70 cents a pound[3]. (Perhaps New Zealand sold the butter to Russia for a profit of 35 cents a pound!) So butter that taxpayer dollars bought from American dairy farmers at $1.45 a pound was sold to a foreign country at less than half price[4].

That was not all the expenses incurred with this program. In addition to the $1.45 per pound the government spent for the butter, there were additional expenses for handling, storage, refrigeration and interest that amounted to over a million dollars a day more in tax dollars, "annual storage cost at $383 million.[5]"

When butter stocks got so high as to require additional storage, they decided instead to distribute to the elderly and the needy, costing another $1 million a day.

A by-product of the distribution policies of free foodstuffs of cheese, butter and milk was a noticeable drop in the demand for those foods[6], requiring the government to buy even more surplus stocks. What else could have been predicted with the distribution policy? It is plain and simple economics. Giving away butter, milk and cheese reduced the open market demand for butter, milk and cheese. We are all economists now!

The Quad-Punch Taxpayer Bash—and the Cows Didn't Cooperate Either!

So taxpayers paid for:

1) Initial government purchase of butter,

2) Handling, storage, refrigeration and interest expense,

3) Distribution of surplus supplies, including selling it to foreign powers at less than half price, while having to buy ever more

3. "Let Them Each Cheese," *Newsweek,* 2/1/82, p 21

4. "Embarrassment of riches," editorial, *Denver Post,* 12/24/81. p 2B

5. "Surplus Cup Runneth Over," *Parade,* 6/26/83, p 8

6. "U.S. cuts cheese giveaway in half after sales drop," *Rocky Mountain News,* 6/10/83, p 74

stocks because distribution further decreased market demand, and

4)   Contrived, higher prices for the consumer.

When a taxpayer went to the store to buy butter for home use, did it cost the same $1.45 a pound paid by the government, or the 70 cents a pound paid by New Zealand? No. It cost over $2.00 a pound, with the normal wholesaler, retailer and tax collector markups on the product.

Even the dairy farmers didn't cooperate. They added 72,000 cows to the dairy herds in 1980[7], and an additional 100,000 cows in 1981! Government purchases had so increased demand that dairy farmers placed more cows into milk production to make more milk products needed to satisfy that demand! The more we solved the problem the worse it got.

Finally, the cows didn't cooperate either! The annual output of milk jumped 258 pounds from the 12,147 pounds per cow in 1981 to 12,405 pounds in 1982[8]. More farmers produced more cows that produced more milk that caused overflows in storage. Those supplies were given away, reducing demand, requiring more storage for the growing quantities of dairy products being produced from more cows giving more milk!

That is good politics producing bad economic results, and Mother Nature joining in the fun to make it even more complicated—and expensive.

Programs that Cost More, Accomplish Less, Waste Lots

The paradox that unites these two examples was outlined in a mid-1983 story, that while the dairy surplus continued to rise to record levels, the U. S. Conference of Mayors declared that hunger had become "the most prevalent and most insidious" problem facing the nation's cities[9]. In 1987, the government was emptying the caves of surplus dairy products through donations to the needy, creating a shortage of commodities to give away. Neither problem was solved but a powerful special interest was protected and enriched by this political, legislative and government process, wasting taxpayer money and resources.

These "War on Poverty" and "Dairy Subsidies" stories vividly and accurately portray what happens when so-called "good politics" collides with bad economics in the real world, resulting in predictably bad results.

These kinds of policies cost more than taxpayers were thought to be willing to pay, so taxes weren't raised. Not only was raising taxes bad

---

7. "Buttering Up the Farmers," *Time*, 7/6/81, p 53

8. "Plugging up milk gusher," *Rocky Mountain News,* 3/10/82, p 60

9. U.S. Paradox: Dairy Surplus, Hunger Rise," *Denver Post,* 7/24/83

politics, it was bad economics too. Doing so would have severely weakened the economy as a disincentive for people to work and produce.

The alternative was for the government to borrow ever-larger amounts of money, which increased the magnitude of government money spent over that collected in taxes. The result was a staggering increase in the annual deficit. Each year these deficits are added to the national debt, which itself began to climb to dangerously higher levels, increasing the amounts of money paid to service the debt in annual interest payments.

The situation proved to unexpectedly accelerate government growth. Government spending went out of control, beyond what the output of the economy could support, and what the people were willing to pay.

Checking the Ballooning Budget Binge Facts

We "get the facts" about these seemingly uncontrollable expenditures by referring to the annually-published *United States Budget in Brief,* 1984, (p 74) and 1989 (p 111) editions.

In 1983, Farm Income Stabilization, as it was called, was projected to be $7.9 billion for 1986. That year it actually turned out to be $29.6 billion, almost four times the 1983 prediction. Such out-of-control expenditures contribute greatly to the meteoric rise in the national debt, which grew from $780 billion in 1978 to almost $2.6 trillion in 1988, more than tripling in 10 years, this in peacetime. The interest on the debt increased from $49 billion to $214 billion, more than quadrupling over the same period.

These ballooning budget binges expand government. Their lack of control or predictability puts enormous pressures on money and debt markets, with long term negative effects on other important aspects of the United States economy, not the least of which are the future and freedoms of America's citizens and taxpayers.

Why Expenditures Zoom,
Taxes Increase and Debt Mounts

The nature of government, once it gets into a redistribution mode, is much like a cancer. It becomes a terminal, uncontrolled carcinoma that guarantees society's doom and accelerates its demise. Government naturally begets more employees who make more money, create more programs to do more good deeds and to spend more taxpayer money to do them. One characteristic of government, whether it does what is supposed to, "needed" or how well, is that *GOVERNMENT GROWS!*

The only way to contain government growth is to limit its funds. As a popular business newspaper once put it, the bottom line of what's wrong with government is there is no bottom line. Therefore the only way to assure good management—establish priorities and make effective decisions—is to limit its money and force it to control spending.

Therefore, priorities must be carefully set, then combined with the industrial engineers' time-proven formula "combine, simplify, eliminate, postpone, phase out."

There is not enough money in the universe to fund all the good governments want to do. The first problem is that for every dollar government uses to "do good," a dollar is not available to the person who earned it to "do" his or her own personal good. The greater problem is, there is a limit on the amount of goods and services a population can create and produce, and only so much that can be allocated to government. When these limits are surpassed the result is a diminished quality-of-life, then eventual economic catastrophe and financial collapse.

Society's first job is to create wealth by maintaining the critical *balance* between government and enterprise. Annual production is limited, as is the money we use to fuel it, to represent and trade the wealth produced. We acknowledge that only a certain amount of resources and money can be put into government functions and programs. We must assure these moneys are carefully prioritized and administered, and recognize there are limits on these resources. The balance comes in the amount of hard work and taxes that the populace is willing to support, or tolerate, and staying below those limits, as well as determining the need and effectiveness of money spent on government to do its job.

"Priming the Pump" Supposedly Gets Things Going, Keeps Things Growing

Back in 1929 a terrible thing happened. We had an economic catastrophe called "The Great Depression." About one-fourth of America's people were unemployed and unable to find work. A concerned British economist, Dr. John Maynard Keynes, carefully considered the situation and concocted an economic theory called "demand management." The government would "prime the pump"—spend money it didn't have (deficit spending) to stimulate demand, thus creating a need for products, goods and services, bringing about jobs which then would lead the country out of the economic dislocation being fought.

"Deficit spend" was Part One of Lord Keynes three-part theory. First, government was to spend money it did not have by borrowing heavily, cutting taxes, and loosening monetary policy, that is, putting increasing amounts of money into the economy.

Part Two, in times of prosperity and business boom, government spending was to be curtailed, taxes increased, money policy tightened, with the resulting government surplus used to pay off the previously created deficits and debt.

Part Three, and finally, there was to be in the long run, a balanced budget and little or no public debt.

Part I worked. The politicians had fun "stimulating the economy," spending money the government didn't have. They bought votes, prestige and influence, but with taxpayers' money, not their own. As the 1981 Economic Recovery Tax Act began to take effect, then-House Speaker Tip O'Neill, D-Mass, said on January 3,1983, "It is time to stop waiting for an economic theory to work and instead to do what we have done before—stimulate the economy." That meant spend more money faster and incur additional deficits, debt and debt interest. And they did.

Politicians do not heed Keynes' Part Two and Part Three. It is easier to spend money they don't have to spend, "to stimulate the economy," even when it doesn't need stimulating. By doing so, they can't balance a budget, nor can they do anything but increase the public debt with a never-ending string of annual budget deficits.

No. 542. Federal Budget—Summary: 1945 to 1999

(in millions of dollars)

Year	Receipts	Outlays	Surplus or deficit(-)	Outlays as percent of GDP [1]	Gross Federal debt [2] Total	Federal gov't account	Held by the public Total	Federal Reserve System	As percent of GDP [1]
1945	45,159	92,712	-47,553	41.9	260,123	24,941	235,182	21,792	117.5
1950	39,443	42,562	-3,119	15.6	256,853	37,830	219,023	18,331	93.9
1955	65,451	68,444	-2,993	17.3	274,366	47,751	226,616	23,607	69.4
1960	92,492	92,191	301	17.8	290,525	53,686	236,840	26,523	56.1
1965	116,817	118,228	-1,411	17.2	322,318	61,540	260,778	39,100	46.9
1970	192,807	195,649	-2,842	19.4	380,921	97,723	283,198	57,714	37.8
1975	279,090	332,332	-53,242	21.4	541,925	147,225	394,700	84,993	34.9
1980	517,112	590,947	-73,835	21.7	909,050	199,212	709,838	120,846	33.4
1981	599,272	678,249	-78,976	22.2	994,845	209,507	785,338	124,466	32.6
1982	617,766	745,755	-127,989	23.2	1,137,345	217,560	919,785	134,497	35.4
1983	600,562	808,380	-207,818	23.6	1,371,710	240,114	1,131,596	155,527	40.1
1984	666,486	851,874	-185,388	22.3	1,564,657	264,159	1,300,498	155,122	41.0
1985	734,088	946,423	-212,334	23.1	1,817,521	317,612	1,499,908	169,806	44.3
1986	769,215	990,460	-221,245	22.6	2,120,629	383,919	1,736,709	190,855	48.5
1987	854,353	1,004,122	-149,769	21.8	2,346,125	457,444	1,888,680	212,040	50.9
1988	909,303	1,064,489	-155,187	21.5	2,601,307	550,507	2,050,799	229,218	52.5
1989	991,190	1,143,671	-152,481	21.4	2,868,039	678,157	2,189,882	220,088	53.6
1990	1,031,969	1,253,163	-221,194	22.0	3,206,564	795,841	2,410,722	234,410	56.4
1991	1,055,041	1,324,400	-269,359	22.6	3,598,498	910,362	2,688,137	258,591	61.4
1992	1,091,279	1,381,681	-290,402	22.5	4,002,136	1,003,307	2,998,834	296,397	65.1
1993	1,154,401	1,409,414	-255,013	21.8	4,351,416	1,103,945	3,247,471	325,653	67.2
1994	1,258,627	1,461,731	-203,104	21.4	4,643,705	1,211,588	3,432,117	355,150	67.8
1995	1,351,830	1,515,729	-163,899	21.1	4,921,018	1,317,645	3,603,373	374,114	68.4
1996	1,453,062	1,560,512	-107,450	20.7	5,181,934	1,448,967	3,732,968	390,924	68.6
1997	1,579,292	1,601,232	-21,940	20.0	5,369,707	1,598,559	3,771,148	424,507	67.2
1998	1,721,798	1,652,552	69,246	19.7	5,478,724	1,758,846	3,719,878	458,131	65.2
1999, est	1,806,334	1,727,071	79,263	19.7	5,614,934	1,945,197	3,669,737	(NA)	64.2

Source: U.S. Office of Management and Budget, *Historical Tables*, annual.

How have we done? It is easier to see it all on one chart, *No. 542* Federal Budget—Summary: 1945 to 1999 (in millions of dollars), page 348 from the *1999 Statistical Abstract of the United States*, reproduced here for reference. It shows Receipts (taxes), Outlays (spending) and Deficits, Outlays, percent of output, GDP (gross domestic product), then Gross Federal Debt in total, "held by" and also as percent of GDP. Until 1998 there was only one year, 1969, of surplus (not on chart) in 36 years. A new era began in 1998 with continuing surpluses. The government has projected a 10-year, 2001-2010 surplus of $4.19 trillion[10]. This is

10. "As Surplus Surges, Clinton-GOP Deals look more likely," *Wall Street Journal*, p A32, 6/27/00

truly good and big news depending on how it is managed. That, Power of ONE, depends on you.

Since that surplus budget of 1969, to 1998 through a continuous string of deficits we have added over $5 *trillion* in public debt, averaging $178 billion annually. The highest "deficit" was 1992's $290 billion which belies the more accurate $340 billion operating fund deficit, masked by surplus trust fund collections. These are enormous failures in government fiscal policy, and a terrible disservice to the hardworking taxpayers. The latest two years, 1998-99 had surpluses over $190 billion, still ironically, as the public debt continued to increase.

The *Budget of the U.S. Government, Fiscal Year 2001*, p 420, projects a string of "surpluses" from 2001-2010 totaling $2,518 billion that should by definition cut the debt that much. In fact it *grows* by $853 billion, and now projected for an additional $1.6 trillion, a major and positive reversal. Yet how can there be sizable surpluses and increasing public debt? Talk about "smoke-and-mirrors" accounting! In the private sector people would go to jail for such as this.

Keep in mind this discussion is for federal government only. State-and-local government taxes and spending run at about half the federal levels. They are big and growing too but with far less debt—and the people pay them all.

Note that federal spending right after World War II in 1950 was only 15.6% of GDP, growing to as high as 23.5% in 1983 and dropping back to 18.7% in 1999. All this while federal receipts were stable at about 18% (not on chart).

The public debt burgeoned from less than a trillion dollars in 1981 to over $5.6 trillion in 1999. Not shown is the interest on the debt that went from $75 billion on 1977's $909 billion debt, to $353 trillion on 1999's $5.61 trillion debt. That billion dollars a day interest costs each citizen on average over $100 a month, each worker, over $200 a month.

For a recent overview three reference tables are included from the 1999 *Statistical Abstract of the United States*, for more details on Federal Receipts, Trust Funds and Outlays. "No 544. Federal Receipts, by Source: 1980 to 1999" shows overall government income. "No. 545. Federal Trust Fund Receipts, Outlays and Balances: 1996 to 1998" shows their income, growth and balances of the various funds. "No. 548. Federal Outlays, by Detailed Function: 1990 to 1999" gives a great one-page overview of where and how much the federal government spends.

See also the breakdown at the bottom of the page of "Net interest, total," contrasting to interest on the public debt. Politicians like to quote net interest because it is a much smaller number, but the nation's fiscal debt position is the total debt, total interest which is $1 billion a day in round numbers. That amounts to over $1,300 per citizen in 1999, and almost $2,800 per worker—on average, the first $50 each worker earns every week, withheld not even to buy any government services other than interest on its debt.

No. 539. Federal Receipts, by Source: 1980 to 1999

(in millions of dollars)

Source	1980	1985	1990	1995	1997	1998	1999, est.
Total receipts [1]	517,112	734,088	1,031,969	1,351,830	1,579,292	1,721,798	1,806,334
Individual income taxes	244,069	334,531	466,884	590,244	737,466	828,586	868,945
Corporation income taxes	64,600	61,331	93,507	157,004	182,293	188,677	182,210
Social insurance and retirement receipts	157,803	265,163	380,047	484,473	539,371	571,831	608,824
Excise taxes	24,329	35,992	35,345	57,484	56,924	57,673	68,075
Social insurance and retirement receipts [1]	157,803	265,163	380,048	484,473	539,371	571,831	608,824
Employment and general retirement	138,748	234,646	353,891	451,045	506,751	540,014	575,740
Old-age and survivors insurance: Trust funds (off-budget)	96,581	169,822	255,031	284,091	336,729	358,784	383,176
Disability insurance (off-budget)	16,628	16,348	26,625	66,988	55,261	57,015	60,860
Hospital insurance	23,217	44,871	68,556	96,024	110,710	119,863	127,363
Railroad retirement/pension fund: Trust funds	2,323	2,213	2,292	2,424	2,440	2,583	2,656
Railroad social security equivalent account	(NA)	1,391	1,387	1,518	1,611	1,769	1,685
Unemployment insurance	15,336	25,758	21,635	28,878	28,202	27,484	28,765
Trust funds	15,336	25,758	21,635	28,878	28,202	27,484	28,765
Total excise taxes [1]	24,329	35,992	35,345	57,484	56,924	57,673	68,075
Federal funds	15,563	19,097	15,591	26,941	27,831	21,665	17,592
Alcohol	5,601	5,562	5,695	7,216	7,257	7,215	7,240
Tobacco	2,443	4,779	4,081	5,878	5,873	5,657	5,213
Crude oil windfall profit	6,934	6,348	(NA)	(NA)	(NA)	(NA)	(NA)
Telephone	(NA)	2,147	2,995	3,794	4,543	4,910	5,213
Ozone depleting chemicals/ products	(NA)	(NA)	360	616	130	98	52
Transportation fuels	(NA)	(NA)	(NA)	8,491	7,107	589	811
Trust funds	8,766	16,894	19,754	30,543	29,093	36,008	50,483
Highway	6,620	13,015	13,867	22,611	23,867	26,628	38,464
Airport and airway	1,874	2,851	3,700	5,534	4,007	8,111	10,397
Black lung disability	272	581	665	608	614	636	638
Inland waterway	(NA)	40	63	103	96	91	102
Hazardous substance superfund	(NA)	273	818	867	71	(NA)	147
Post-closure liability (hazardous waste)	(NA)	7	-1	(NA)	(NA)	(NA)	(NA)
Oil spill liability	(NA)	(NA)	143	211	1	(NA)	35
Aquatic resources	(NA)	126	218	306	316	290	376
Leaking underground storage tank	(NA)	(NA)	122	165	-2	136	212
Vaccine injury compensation	(NA)	(NA)	159	138	123	116	112

Source: U.S. Office of Management and Budget, *Historical Tables*, annual.

No. 540. Federal Trust Fund Receipts, Outlays, and Balances: 1996 to 1998

(in millions of dollars)

Description	Income			Outlays			Balances [1]		
	1996	1997	1998	1996	1997	1998	1996	1997	1998
Total [2]	835	878	932	720	752	771	1,391	1,515	1,669
Airport and airway trust fund	3	5	9	7	6	6	8	6	9
Federal employees health benefits fund	16	16	17	16	17	17	7	7	6
Federal civilian employees retirement fund	68	71	73	40	42	44	402	431	461
Federal old-age, survivors and disability insurance trust funds	418	449	481	352	367	382	550	631	730
Foreign military sales trust fund	15	15	14	14	15	14	6	-	-
Highway trust fund	(NA)	25	29	(NA)	25	25	(NA)	22	18
Health insurance trust funds: Medicare: Federal hospital insurance	124	129	138	128	138	137	125	116	117
Federal supplemental medical insurance	82	81	83	69	73	77	27	35	41
Military retirement fund	33	38	38	29	30	31	131	139	146
Railroad retirement trust funds	9	9	10	8	8	8	14	15	17
Unemployment trust funds	32	33	32	26	24	24	54	62	71
Veterans life insurance trust funds	2	2	2	2	2	2	14	14	14
Other trust funds [3]	10	10	10	9	9	9	31	31	33

Source: U.S. Office of Management and Budget, *Analytical Perspectives*, annual.

No. 543. Federal Outlays, by Detailed Function: 1990 to 1999

(in millions of dollars)

Superfunction and function	1990	1995	1996	1997	1998	1999, est.
Total outlays	1,253,163	1,515,729	1,560,512	1,601,232	1,652,552	1,727,071
National defense, total	299,331	272,066	265,753	270,505	268,456	276,730
Department of Defense—Military [1]	289,755	259,442	253,187	258,311	256,122	263,556
Military personnel	75,622	70,809	66,669	69,724	68,976	71,957
Operation and maintenance	88,340	91,078	88,759	92,461	93,473	96,839
Procurement	80,972	54,982	48,913	47,690	48,206	48,422
Research, develop., test, and evaluation	37,458	34,594	36,494	37,015	37,420	36,758
Military construction	5,080	6,823	6,683	6,187	6,044	5,287
Family housing	3,501	3,571	3,828	4,003	3,871	3,894
Atomic energy defense activities	8,988	11,777	11,644	11,275	11,268	12,012
Defense-related activities	587	847	922	919	1,066	1,162
International affairs, total	13,764	16,434	13,496	15,228	13,109	15,474
International develop. & humanitarian assist.	5,498	7,599	6,160	6,054	5,446	5,714
International security assistance	8,652	5,252	4,565	4,632	5,135	5,737
Conduct of foreign affairs	3,050	4,192	3,761	3,919	3,262	4,617
Foreign info. and exchange activities	1,103	1,417	1,187	1,173	1,159	1,216
International financial programs	-4,539	-2,026	-2,177	-550	-1,893	-1,810
General science, space & technology, total	14,444	16,724	16,709	17,174	18,219	18,529
General science and basic research	2,835	4,131	4,016	4,118	5,353	5,738
Space flight, research, and supporting activities	11,609	12,593	12,693	13,056	12,866	12,791
Energy, total	3,341	4,936	2,839	1,475	1,270	49
Energy supply	1,976	3,584	1,649	626	181	-894
Energy conservation	365	671	624	572	621	560
Emergency energy preparedness	442	223	141	23	233	182
Energy information, policy, & regulation	559	458	425	254	235	201
Natural resources & environment, total [1]	17,080	22,078	21,614	21,369	22,396	24,261
Water resources	4,401	4,791	4,617	4,536	4,721	5,454
Conservation and land management	3,553	5,318	5,396	5,067	5,475	5,074
Recreational resources	1,876	2,801	2,673	2,785	2,984	3,952
Pollution control and abatement	5,170	6,513	6,182	6,292	6,422	6,855
Agriculture, total	11,958	9,778	9,159	9,032	12,206	21,449
Farm income stabilization	9,761	7,020	6,477	6,272	9,297	18,405
Agricultural research and services	2,197	2,758	2,682	2,760	2,909	3,044
Commerce and housing credit, total [1]	67,600	-17,808	-10,472	-14,624	1,014	452
Mortgage credit	3,845	-1,038	-5,025	-4,006	-2,934	-1,112
Postal Service	2,116	-1,839	-58	77	303	964
Deposit insurance	57,891	-17,827	-8,394	-14,384	-4,371	-5,047
Transportation, total [1]	29,485	39,350	39,565	40,767	40,332	42,640
Ground transportation	18,954	25,297	25,650	26,795	26,004	28,333
Air transportation	7,234	10,020	10,135	10,138	10,622	10,559
Water transportation	3,151	3,732	3,460	3,554	3,507	3,502
Community & regional development, total	8,498	10,641	10,685	11,005	9,720	10,428
Community development	3,530	4,744	4,860	4,962	5,118	5,437
Area and regional development	2,868	2,615	2,667	2,691	2,456	2,570
Disaster relief and insurance	2,100	3,282	3,158	3,352	2,146	2,421
Education, training, employ., & social serv.	38,755	54,263	52,001	53,008	54,919	60,065
Elementary, secondary, & vocational education	9,918	14,694	14,871	15,073	16,571	16,989
Higher education	11,107	14,172	12,191	12,298	12,070	14,047
Research and general education aids	1,577	2,120	2,215	2,136	2,271	2,448
Training and employment	5,619	7,430	7,030	6,681	6,636	7,941
Social services	9,723	14,882	14,769	15,811	16,335	17,532
Health, total	57,716	115,418	119,378	123,843	131,440	143,095
Health care services	47,642	101,931	106,622	109,973	116,336	126,190
Health research and training	8,611	11,569	10,827	11,847	13,073	14,681
Consumer & occupational health & safety	1,462	1,918	1,929	2,023	2,031	2,224
Medicare	98,102	159,855	174,225	190,016	192,822	204,982
Income security, total [1]	147,076	220,493	225,967	230,899	233,202	243,130
General retirement & disability insurance [2]	5,118	5,106	5,234	4,721	4,632	2,437
Federal employee retirement & disability	52,037	65,882	68,071	71,539	73,485	76,262
Unemployment compensation	18,889	23,638	24,898	22,888	22,070	25,178
Housing assistance	15,891	27,520	26,754	27,798	28,741	28,376
Food and nutrition assistance	23,964	37,594	37,933	36,061	33,585	35,271
Social security	248,623	335,846	349,676	365,257	379,225	392,608
Veterans benefits and services, total [1]	29,058	37,890	36,985	39,313	41,781	43,526
Income security for veterans	15,241	18,966	18,201	20,407	21,322	22,640
Veterans educ., training & rehab	278	1,124	1,114	1,156	1,102	1,337
Hospital & medical care for veterans	12,134	16,428	16,586	17,093	17,545	17,933
Veterans housing	517	329	66	-342	837	468
Administration of justice, total	9,993	16,216	17,548	20,173	22,832	24,467
General government, total	10,734	13,835	11,914	12,749	13,444	14,852
Net interest, total	184,221	232,169	241,090	244,016	243,359	227,244
Interest on the public debt	264,724	332,414	343,955	355,796	363,793	353,429
Interest received by on-budget trust funds	-46,321	-59,871	-60,869	-63,776	-67,208	-67,233
Interest received by off-budget trust funds	-15,991	-33,305	-36,507	-41,214	-46,630	-51,869
Allowances, total	(X)	(X)	(X)	(X)	(X)	3,118
Undistributed offsetting receipts, total	-36,615	-44,455	-37,620	-49,973	-47,194	-40,028

Source: U.S. Office of Management and Budget, *Historical Tables*, annual.

If I Were the Government, How I'd Collect Taxes: Where Taxes Come From

Where does all the tax money come from? Taxpayers. Citizens. Voters. Workers. From fathers and mothers. From teenaged baby sitters and hamburger flippers. From professionals and blue-collar workers. From pink and white-collar workers. From those who can't afford collars. From PEOPLE. All the people. From you.

Four magic, true, never-to-be-forgotten words:

ONLY PEOPLE PAY TAXES!

The art of taxation consists in so plucking the goose as to obtain the largest amount of feathers with the least possible amount of hissing. —attributed to J. B. Colbert

Congress biggest job is how to get the money from the taxpayer without disturbing the voter.   —Anon.

The question is not WHERE to get the money, but HOW? The answer is to make it as painless as possible and hide most of it from careful scrutiny and obvious view. In other words, minimize the open and direct taxes; maximize the hidden and indirect taxes. If I were the government, here is my Secret Success System of Tax Collection:

1) Have *tax withholding.*
2) Have *indirect* or *hidden taxes.*
3) Have a nation of *producers.*
4) Have *progressive taxation:* "Soak the rich!"

Have Tax Withholding

The income tax was created and authorized when the 16th amendment to the U.S. Constitution was declared to be ratified in 1913[11]. The personal exemption was $3,000 ($45,000 in 1999 dollars) and the income tax rate was 1% up to $20,000 ($300,000). Under these conditions, today's family of four could earn $180,000 before having to pay taxes. No wonder the electorate voted for it. "They won't get anything from me but those rich people will sure take a hit"—the politics of envy. The graduated tax rate for between $20,000 ($300,000) and $50,000 ($750,000) was 2%, increasing to the top rate of 7% over $500,000 ($7,500,000).

At its inception few paid the tax. In 1916 only 362,970 Americans out of the population of 102 million, less than four-tenths of one percent, paid taxes. In 1996, 120 million tax returns (mostly joint returns, meaning virtually the entire 127 million working population) filed to pay an

11. Schiff, Irwin, *The Great Income Tax Hoax,* pp 179, 180, $20, Freedom Books, PO Box 5303, Hamden, CN 06518

average tax of $7,200 each[12]. The 1996 average tax rate was 14.5% of adjusted gross income. Tax returns for 1999 totaled over 130 million.

To gain support for imposing a tax on income, high incomes were made progressively more taxable to exploit what is called "the politics of envy." (Those rich people have a lot of money. We have far less because they have so much more. We, the majority, will use government to take away some of their money and make them more like us. We will "soak the rich" with an income tax.) So the rich began to pay income tax. Now who else pays—we all pay, a lot? Does that mean we are all rich? Are you?

It was once suggested to a member of Congress, that the income tax might get as high as 10%. He laughed at how ridiculous such a thought was, saying there would be a taxpayer rebellion well before any 10% level were reached!

Review the preceding several paragraphs with your more current knowledge of deductions, exemptions, tax rates and levels of income taxed.

Initially income taxes were assessed and paid once a year by those being taxed, beginning with "self-assessment and voluntary compliance" taxation. As is commonly done during a national emergency, in this case World War II, a "temporary, emergency, wartime 'Victory Tax'" was imposed, as well as an added feature, "voluntary withholding." That temporary expedient—voluntary withholding—is still with us today. And it is not voluntary, it is mandatory. Without withholding, today's near confiscatory levels of taxation on income would be very difficult to enforce, leading to potential taxpayer and citizen rebellion.

Without withholding, we wouldn't hear on or around April 15, the national income tax return deadline, some really dumb comments: "Harry, we only have to pay $240," or "Marcia, we're going to get back $470." These are the *differences* in taxes we pay. You, *Power of ONE* take into account *ALL the taxes,* the *TOTAL you* pay. That is all the hard-earned money you did without, to comply with our country's income tax laws.

Without that kind of attention to how things really are, we might imagine Nancy saying to President Ronald Reagan in 1982, "Ronnie, we're getting back a $14 refund in our taxes."

What she would actually have said was "Ronnie, we paid $165,291 income taxes on our adjusted gross income of $412,730[13]. Because we over-withheld by $14, we'll get that back. But *we did pay $165,291 federal income* tax, Ronnie, er, Mr. President, I mean!"

Creep—slow but sure change, has crept even into withholding. As Congress continues to increase spending faster than it chooses to tax,

12. *Statistical Abstract of the United States, 1999,* p 359, 411

13. Based on "What the President Told the IRS," *U.S. News & World Report,* 4/26/82, p 5

less obvious, more stringent tax collection policies are instituted. Mid-1980's tax law required withholding 80% minimum tax due. That was boosted to 90% in 1987, with penalty, interest and filling out the detailed form 2210 the price. This turned out to have some strange effects, especially going beyond the obvious.

Strange things happen when a desperate government needs money: A 1999 family of four has two jobs, breadwinner, $30,000, spouse, $15,000, earning $45,000 annually. Breadwinner claims four deductions, and per the tables has $191 withheld monthly; spouse claims no deductions and has $108 withheld; for a yearly total of $3,588 being withheld[14].

At tax time, with a $7,200 standard deduction and $11,000 in exemptions, their taxable income is $26,800, and the tax obligation is $4,157. 90% of that amount is $3,741. They not only owe the $569 difference, but are $153 short of the 90% withholding requirement. They have to pay the $569 in taxes due, but also a penalty for underwithholding and interest thereon, and they lose a couple hours filling out complicated form 2210, "Under Payment of Esimated Taxes."

Two Strange Tax Quirks

There are two things strange about all this. First, they have worked 3 1/2 months into the new year to April 15, having regularly withheld from their paychecks a total of $1,047 on earnings of $13,125. If they quit working that day what would their tax liability be? Zero! In fact, they will not owe their first dollar of federal income tax for over another month. They have already paid an additional $1,047 *not due*, but must pay all the penalties for insufficient withholding the previous year—and the IRS has the money!

Second, the taxes are not recognized as collected until the actual date due. In the case of January of the preceding year, the first money withheld was 15 months ago. From the special agents tax handbook here is how the interpretation is stated under the heading "IRC 6513. Time Return Deemed Filed and Tax Considered Paid"[15]:

(a) *Early Return or Advance Payment of* Tax.—For purposes of section 6511, any return filed before the last day prescribed for the filing thereof shall be considered as filed on such last day. For purposes of section 6511(b)(2) and (c) and section 6512, payment of any portion of the tax made before the last day prescribed for the payment of the tax shall be considered made on such last day.

---

14. Thanks to Rodney Johnson, CPA, of Wheat Ridge, Colorado, May, 1989, updated May, 1999

15. IRM 9781, *Handbook for Special Agents*, 8/17/82, p 9781-20, Sec 242

(b) *Prepaid Income Tax.—For* purposes of section 6511 or 6512, any tax actually deducted and withheld at the source during any calendar year under chapter 24 shall, in respect of the recipient of the income, be deemed to have been paid by him on the 15th day of the fourth month following the close of his taxable year.

So no matter when it is withheld or how much is deducted it is considered by the authorities all to be paid on the single date due. That you could keep and pay the money on that date. If it is defined as due, payable, paid and received that day, indeed, there can be no interest payable on it.

If I were the government, I would certainly have *withholding.*

Have Indirect or Hidden Taxes

Indirect taxes are hidden taxes, assessed on and collected by business in compliance with the law, obtained through higher prices on goods and services. An example is the corporate income tax; another, Social Security taxes ("Social Insurance Receipts"). The employer deducts them from the employee wages, "matching" them with deductions from the corporation. Where does "the corporation" get them? From customers. These are legitimate "pass through" business expenses recovered in the price of goods and services.

Hidden taxes are a handy way to collect taxes. When prices are raised, business takes the heat, not the government. Business is an easy target because it must obey the law and has no vote. For instance, take state and federal excise taxes on a gallon of gasoline as an example of hidden taxes. They are collected in the purchase price at the pump. To show their impact, the mid-1989 wholesale prices (on 5/4/89) for a gallon of unleaded gasoline, $0.7225, regular $0.7375. (Yes, unleaded cost *less* because no tetraethyl lead was added. Then-legal leaded gasoline cost more because it had anti-knock tetraethyl lead added. Unleaded didn't, and doesn't. But because clean air regulation requires unleaded gas, its legal requirement distorted the pricing structure). Add to the wholesale cost seven or eight cents mark-up to cover retailing expenses. With the price the customer pays at $1.05 a gallon, the 25 cents difference is federal and state excise taxes, a 31% add-on (2000, it is over 40 cents per gallon).

Another illustration of hidden taxes is found in the *Budget of the United States Government, Fiscal Year 2001,* which is here reproduced. "The Federal Government Dollar Fiscal Year 2001 Estimates" shows, in pie charts, where government money comes from and where it goes. "Individuals" pay 48 cents of each dollar in income taxes (same for years 1999 and 2000), paid directly based on the income tax laws of the land. What about the remainder of the taxes described as corporation income taxes, excise taxes, and all the rest? They also come from YOU and other

customers when you buy those companies' products and services!
Remember our magic four words: ONLY PEOPLE PAY TAXES!

The Federal Government Dollar
Fiscal Year 2001 Estimates

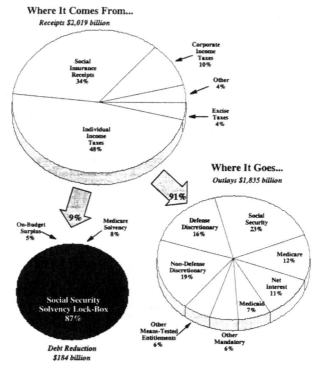

All the people pay all the taxes; 100% of the people pay 100% of the
taxes. It becomes a simple mathematical exercise to calculate how much
tax you *really* pay. Here is a "magic number" that makes things easier
to understand. Divide 100% by 48% (Year 2001 "Individual Income
Taxes") to get a multiplier of 2.08. Multiply your direct personal federal
income taxes paid by 2.08 to know the TOTAL federal taxes you *really*
paid, direct *and* hidden. For instance, if you calculate $1000 federal
income taxes paid in 1999, the TOTAL federal taxes you paid are $2,080.
That makes the difference of $1,080 the amount of indirect taxes you
paid, those hidden in the price of goods and services you bought.

There is a shift toward more direct taxation at the federal level.
Compared to the 48% for 2001, for 1990 it was 41%, for 1988 it was
38%, and that "magic number" was 2.63 (100/38).

Understanding indirect taxes gives you the power to find out how the
income tax system affects you. Get out a recent tax form and examine
it carefully. Multiply your federal income taxes *total* (not what you got

back or paid extra) by 2.08 to get TOTAL federal taxes paid. For an estimate of state-and-local taxes, calculate half your TOTAL federal taxes. Add the federal and state taxes to get your "total-total" estimated tax burden. If you divide that by your total earnings you estimate your real over-all tax rate. It may surprise, perhaps even shock you.

Here's an example: Suppose husband and wife's adjusted gross income for two jobs in 1998 is $65,000. They subtract $7,200 standard deduction plus $11,000 for four exemptions, to get taxable income of $46,800 and federal income tax liability of $7,501 (per IRS Instructions, page 62). Multiply by 2.08, for TOTAL estimated federal taxes paid of $15,602. State and local per-capita taxes, about half federal, are $7,801, indicating an estimated total family tax burden of $23,400. By these estimates this family's total tax burden, direct and indirect, is 36% ($23,400/$65,000).

You can roughly estimate your comprehensive total tax burden (all taxes, direct and indirect) by multiplying total federal taxes by three; from above, $7,501 x 3 = $22,503, fairly close to $23,400.

This is why two people must work, one to support the family, the other to pay taxes!

If I were the government, I would certainly have *hidden taxes!*

Have a Nation of Producers

I love producers! (Remember, I'm "government," seeking effective ways to find, increase and collect taxes) Yes, I love producers. Why? Because all they want to do is produce, produce, produce, produce . . . *PRODUCE!* They *love* to produce—everything but one thing: Freedom. Let me explain.

Some people ask me why I wear two watches, especially during my speeches. I go back to 1962 to explain. In the aerospace industry, working for Hercules Incorporated on *Minuteman* and *Polaris* missiles, a major status symbol was the Friden brand calculator. This electromechanical wonder, measuring 14 by 18 inches by 10 inches high, weighed about 65 pounds, and cost about $1,200. (Machines with square root capability cost $1,600, justified only for statisticians with their esoteric statistical functions of least squares regression analysis, confidence levels, etc.)

Based on the consumer price index in mid-1990, today a similar machine would cost $6,500. But something strange and wonderful happened:

The Producers Struck!

You, yes, you, *the producers* did what you always do: You used your God-given talents and creativity, freedom and willingness to take a risk. You producers literally *turned sand into gold,* silicon into circuits! You created "THE CHIP!"

With that came the computer, all kinds of miracle electronics, and the quartz watch. I love watches, I love calculators (and I love computers).

So today, I wear two watches, the insides of which you producers created, THE CHIP. Each watch is phenomenally accurate, with a monitored quartz crystal vibrating over 31,000 times a second. In the one watch are two time zones, a count-down timer, and a four-phase alarm, a "beep-beep" plus three others, "Oh My Darling, Clementine," "Dixie" and "Oh Tannenbaum." There is even a chronometer that measures time down to the one-one hundredth of a second. I've never yet found anything I have to time to one-one hundredth of a second, but when I do, I'm ready!

The other watch is my electronic marvel. It has all that, a chronometer, alarm, second time zone, even world time zones and ten telephone numbers. But in addition to all that,

It has a CALCULATOR, complete with 4-function memory!

That calculator watch didn't cost $6,500 inflation-adjusted to today's economy. It didn't even cost $65! It cost less than half that. There are now "throw away" calculator watches for under $10. Why? Because of you producers!

You produce, produce, produce! You produce almost every darn thing except one—Freedom. You are so very busy producing what you love to produce that you don't get involved in your economic, political, legislative and governmental systems. You leave all that to those professionals out there, to do what they do best, tax people who work, and spend government money on programs and bureaucracies that don't.

Listen carefully and you can almost hear them say, "You keep making it and we'll keep taking it." Then you wonder, "Why do people work so hard to make money and do so little to keep it?"

If I were the government, I would certainly have you—*Producers.* (And you don't even know you're being had!)

Have Progressive Taxation: "Soak the Rich!"

Finally, if I were the government, I would have a progressive income tax. I would want the political support and tax revenues that come from a progressive income tax. That would placate the lower and middle-income people, a majority, allowing a relatively burdensome tax load by them, and get progressively more from those who make even more.

Never mind the well off can spend just so much of their money, that they must invest it in enterprise that confronts risk, creates wealth and in the process, produces jobs and more taxes. Instead, tax it away for all the wrong and negative reasons. Look at where it goes and what it does. It gets consumed, neither creating jobs or wealth. Even with a more fair flat (income!) tax, those who make more pay more, but not progressively more. (But the fairest, most decent tax of all is the proportional, not progressive or regressive, national retail sales tax.)

We have made strides though. In the 1970's the top marginal tax rate was 90%. It dropped to 70% in the early 1980's, and later to 50%. The late-1980's tax legislation reduced rates to two, 15% and 28%, still with a 5% "surcharge" for top income earners. But "flat (income) taxers note. Since then the tax brackets have gone from the original two in 1986, 15% and 25%, back up to five, 15% to 39.5% with 28%, 31% and 36% in between. The strange-but-true economic facts of life are that when these rates are dropped, those who pay them actually pay more dollars in taxes!

If I were the government, for political reasons, I would certainly have *progressive taxes.*

If I Were a Rich Man—Or Would Like to Try to Be Rich

If I were a citizen who aspires to have more and be more, willing to work harder and longer, and hope for better, and I do, I would take good care of those who are rich. Here's why:

1) They likely worked hard to get that way.

2) They pleased a lot of customers and clients, and helped to enrich a lot of suppliers and others to do so.

3) They created enterprise, business, jobs, products, goods and services—and taxes, by getting and staying rich.

4) And besides, don't most people, including yourself, *Power of ONE,* want the door always to be open to get rich if you do all the right things right, please enough people by creating enough value and wealth, and have just a little bit of luck?

5) Can you get a job from a poor person?

Who Cares about the Deficit and Public Debt? We All Care! We All Pay!

For most of the last half of the twentieth century we have had huge deficits. They resulted in a 5 ½ trillion public debt and over $300 billion a year interest on the debt. Hopefully, since 1998 we have hit a turning point, to growing surpluses. Now is when to be a very wary, carefully cautious—to assure our elected officials don't go on a spending binge. What to do? *Cut government growth.* Formulate and execute significant tax cuts, and liquidate the public debt.

Most Americans know that despite claims of a surplus, in fact the public debt increases. Most know that our Congress spends lots more than it takes in taxes, and they must borrow to cover the difference. Most know that despite claims of "cuts" or "budget cuts," through Congress' "smoke and mirrors" accounting, government always continues to grow, even larger than any rational person can justify. There seems to be an attitude of "So what?" or "Who cares?" Once we know and understand what all this means to ourselves and our future, everyone cares, or should.

Our 1985 deficit of $212 billion is easy to remember as "the boiling water deficit." The 1985 national debt was $2.1 trillion. Without paying off one cent of the principal, the National Taxpayers Union estimated that in 40 to 45 working years a 1986 high school graduate will pay $10,000 in taxes just for interest on that deficit. THAT'S A CAR! In the same working lifetime that high school graduate will pay $100,000 in taxes for interest on the federal debt. THAT'S A HOUSE! (The working lifetime cost is about $47,000 for each trillion of public debt.)

We have stolen from our children a house and a car! We are having a party and they get the bill. And they aren't even invited! That is unconscionable, dishonest and immoral. No one did that to us. What right did we have to hedonistically participate in such governmental excess and pass it on to future generations to pay—those who had little or no say in its funding, spending and benefits if any?

What does Posterity have to do with Anything?

There is a very important but subtle lesson here. The U.S. Constitution begins with the Preamble which includes, " ... and secure the Blessings of Liberty to ourselves and our Posterity, ..." Some people did a lot, others did little to get us where we are today. Some even did bad things and we live with and are paying for them. Looking ahead, Power of ONE, we are the torch-bearers of a brighter future for others. What we do here and now, and with a great sense of urgency, will have profound effects on unborn, unrepresented generations of people we will never meet. Yet they are totally dependent upon what we do here and now. See how big and important it all is when you put it in perspective?

What Other Effects are There of Big and Growing Government?

This is not all that happens with big and growing government. Too much government has a negative effect on our quality of life. We have all heard the saying

"Work hard, save and get ahead."

Did it work?

In 1970 (1982 inflation-adjusted dollars) the average weekly salary was $298. In 1980 it was $275[16], 1990 - $259, 1999 - $268[17]. What happened over time? We worked hard. We saved. Did we get ahead? No.

16. 1993 *Statistical Abstract of the United States*, p 424

17. 1999 *Statistical Abstract of the United States*, p 443

The way it is supposed to work is that we work and earn money, spending most, but saving some. Savings result in capital investment, higher productivity, research and development and "high tech," in the short run. In the long run it is our personal peace of mind, a good job, a new car every so often, putting a child through college and having a well-earned decent retirement. It also means over time we ought to work less for more, have more leisure time, and a better, less demanding life.

Did it work? No.

By 1998, 28 years later, in inflation-adjusted purchasing power, our earnings had dropped to $268 but were rising. We had lost $30 a week buying power. How can that happen?

Do we have more leisure time? No. The Harris Poll has asked people for years how much time they have available for leisure. In 1973, we enjoyed 24.0 hours a week. By 1985, 12 years later, our leisure time dropped to 18.1 hours, and by 1987 to 16.6 hours a week and dropping[18].

Are fewer of us working? No again. From 1970 to 1999, while population increased 33%, 70% MORE of us went to work, 46% more men and 109% more women! Is this "liberation from leisure"? During that 28 years America's workforce increased from 60.4% to 67.1% of the population[19].

More of us work for less money to have less leisure time. Shouldn't it be just the opposite?

We worked hard and saved, but who got ahead?

Government.

From Whence Cometh Crime, and Does Big Government Fostoreth Big Crime?

Here is a short digression on the causes of crime.

Why *aren't* crimes committed? For two reasons: First, our Judeo-Christian work ethic and behavior ethic, added to our selfish, sympathetic humanity, tell us it is wrong to commit crime. We reason, if it is all right to attack or plunder others, we thereby grant permission for them to do likewise to us. Second, we don't have the economic necessity to commit crime.

Why *are* crimes committed? For the opposite two reasons; first, some haven't learned to believe, basically value and live their lives as if crime is wrong; and second, as a nation, we may be more economically desperate or deprived. Both reasons provide circumstance and motivation to commit crime.

18. "Decrease in Leisure Time," *Newsweek*, 3/28/88, p 69; "Labor and leisure have lost balance," *Rocky Mountain News,* editorial, 9/5/88

19. *Economic Report of the President, January, 1998,* pp 367, 370, 374

From birth to age ten is when Dr. Morris Massey[20] describes as "imprinting," when children establish their values and belief systems, get their self-esteem and sense of self-importance from constant, loving parenting. Through repetition and discipline they learn the two behavioral basics, "keep your hands to yourself" and "respect other people's property," which if not learned can turn into personal and property crime, respectively. The learning continues through "modeling" to age 17, then to "socialization" to about age 20.

More Government, Less Enterprise: Human Economic Deprivation and Desperation

When all the hard work people do gets preempted through higher taxes, by a big and growing government, bad things happen. As government enlarges, enterprise—wealth creation, and people freedoms diminish. We are allowed to keep less and less of the hard-earned fruits of our labor. People become more economically deprived and/or desperate, psychologically and emotionally-traumatized.

Economic *deprivation* makes more people work longer and harder. Economic *desperation* encourages those who can't make it to give up and resort to less socially-acceptable forms of behavior to satisfy human wants and needs, turning to alcohol and drugs, sex, crime, gangs, violence and suicide.

Federal Bureau of Investigation agent, William Tafoya, in sharing a range of dire predictions[21] made by 15 experts said, "There is a greater link between economic deprivation and the incidence of crime than we previously thought." The message of the conference was that "By the year 2005, the gap between 'haves' and 'have-nots' will be identified as the major factor causing traditional crime." The solution is as complicated as the problem. Tafoya said, "There's still an awful lot of people who are habitually unemployed. Given the . . . kind of frustration that exists for people like that, more stringent enforcement of the law may in fact not serve society well. It may be the trigger mechanism for that urban unrest."

Where's Mom? Where's Dad? In raising a child there is no substitute for a parent's love, time, attention, presence and care. As government grew, taking relatively more of the national wealth, with consequently less wealth being created, family finances became strained, forcing more and more (especially) mothers (see prior employment growth statistics) who otherwise would not have done so, to go to work. Expressed as they are in the *Statistical Abstract*, in 1948 11% of married mothers with

---

20. Morris Massey, *The People Puzzle: Understanding Yourself and Others*, pp 9-22, Prentice-Hall, Reston, VA: 1979.

21. "Crime experts forecast dismal future" by Rebecca Cantwell, *Rocky Mountain News*, 7/7/87, p 4

children under 6 worked. That figure jumped almost six times to 64% in 1997[22]. From birth to about age 10 is when children form their values, belief systems and self-image. Without a doting parent there, children are less likely to develop healthy emotional, psychological and spiritual weapons to cope with the difficulties, failures and successes of life.

The numbers are available but not self-explanatory. There are family and societal effects that can be obtained, to further show what is happening to our society. As government gets relatively larger, with more of the national wealth going to government in direct and hidden taxes, other things happen. From the following chart we glean what has happened in the family and home as government doubled in size from 1948 to 1997, 49 years, with crime figures from 1957 to 1996, 39 years).

Since 1948, the 26% of married mothers with children aged 6-17 who worked, tripled to 78% in 1997. These are the "latchkey kids," those who come home from school to an empty house. This is where later the adults are too busy and tired to adequately share experiences and give guidance as needed. This is the time period when children search for direction and meaning in their lives. If they don't find it, they are more likely to find escape in alcohol and drugs, crime, alcohol, sex, gangs, vandalism, juvenile delinquency and suicide. Higher percentages of unsupervised children can turn into higher percentages in crime statistics.

Government Size vs Working Mothers and Incidence of Crime, 1948 to 1997

Year	% Married Working Mothers w/Children Under 6	6-17		Government Size, as Percent, GDP Fed	S/L	Total		Crime, Incidence per 100,000 Violent Personal	Property	Total	
1948	10.8	26.0	1)	11.5	6.9	18.4	5)	('57) 117	719	836	2)
1997	63.6	77.6	3)	19.7	13.5	33.2	6)	('96) 634	4,445	5,079	4)
	+492%	+198%		+71%	+95%	+80%		+442%	+518%	+507%	
	+5.9x	+3.0x		+1.7x	+2.0x	+1.8x		+5.4x	+6.2x	+6.1x	

Sources: 1) Ref 1, *Historical Statistics of the US*, 1975, p 134: 2) Ref 1, p 413 (earliest available); 3) Ref 2, *Statistical Abstract of the US*, 1999, p 417; 4) Ref 2, p 214; 5) *Economic Report of the President*, Jan '89, pp 308, 397, 401; 6) Ref 5, Feb 2000, pp 306, 397, 404.

22. 1999 *Statistical Abstract of the United States*, p 417

GOVERNMENT GROWTH VS. WORKING MOTHERS

Figure No. 36

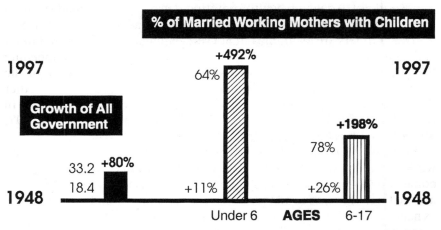

% of Married Working Mothers with Children

1997   +492%   1997
                                  64%

Growth of All
Government   +198%

                                                      78%

         33.2 +80%

         18.4   +11%   +26%
1948 _____ 1948
                 Under 6   AGES   6-17

Repetitive, caring teaching instills positive socially acceptable behavior. How many times do parents drill into their children "keep your hands to yourself," and "respect other peoples' property?" How many times should a child hear such as these to reinforce them? What is the predictable outcome when it happens less often rather than more often?

None of this information or analysis is to take away from men and women who wish to work or pursue a career. It concerns those who prefer to stay home to raise families but are unable to do so because of insufficient after-tax buying power to pay bills and live life.

Crime statistics follow as rational analysis would predict. As government has grown markedly larger and families are more adversely impacted by both parents working longer and harder, there is a higher probability of dysfunction and crime. As time goes on, we have had less teaching and preaching of morals, and less modeling, practicing and showing by example of accepted and ethical behavior. The basics of "how to act" have been diminished. Consequently more people act less civilized.

Inside and outside the family, as people have a more difficult time economically and financially, the incentive to turn to crime as an alternative to working a normal job becomes more pronounced, especially if they are unable to find a job. So theory would predict crime statistics would increase. But would they do so at such alarming rates?

Crime statistics are not available for the entire period of 1948-97. The earliest data are from 1957. However these show a marked increase in the rate of crime during that period, at least partially attributable to diminished parent-child relationships and positive family influence. What do today's conditions and trends portend for the future?

For 39 years, 1957 to 1996, violent personal crime rates (per 100,000 population) jumped over five times, property crimes over six times, with an overall crime increase of 507%, over six times. One might say "of course there is more crime, there are more people." True, but crime frequency is population-based.

The overall youth suicide rate per 100,000 population nearly tripled[23] from 0.6 to 1.7 for the period 1970 to 1993, for children, ages 10-14. For children aged 15-19, the suicide rate increased from 5.9 to 10.9, and for the 20-24 group, it rose from 12.2 to 15.8.

Are people bad and getting worse, or are they more economically deprived and desperate, resorting more to anti-social behavior to survive in an increasingly confiscatory society?

GOVERNMENT GROWTH VS. INCIDENCE OF CRIME/100,000

Figure No. 37

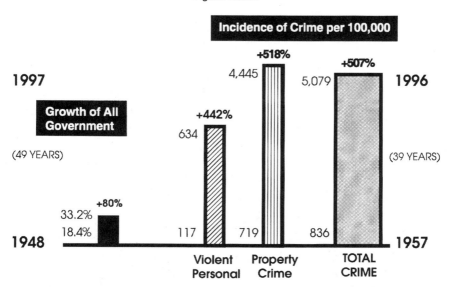

We hear an incessant chorus of calls for more taxes to build more prisons. Perhaps one of the underlying reasons we are having to build more prisons is because of past assessments and continually increasing taxes. If so, as we continue to tax more, our society will get increasingly more violent, unsafe and threatening, placing our homes and lives more in jeopardy. As government grows larger to protect what is supposed to be a self-governing people, it seems the solution compounds the problem!

23. *1993 Statistical Abstract of the United States,* p 99; 1996 *Statistical Abstract of the United States,* p 102

Thomas Jefferson must have sensed these possibilities:

We must make our election between 'economy and liberty' or 'profusion and servitude.' If we run into such debts as that we must be taxed in our meat and drink, in our necessaries and our comforts, in our labors and our amusements, for our callings and our creeds, as the people of England are, our people, like them, must come to labor 16 hours in the 24, give their earnings of 15 of these to the government for their debts and expenses; and have no time to think, no time to call our mismanagers to account.

Big Government? Compared to What?
Itself and Its Growth!

In this last evaluation of big expanding government we take a historical look at United States population growth, federal government spending growth, and resultant per-capita figures, inflation-adjusted, for nearly two centuries, beginning in 1800:

Year	Population, Millions	Multi-plier	Gov't Exp's $ millions	Multi-plier	$ Per-Capita	Multi-plier
1800	5.3 (1)		10.8 (2)		$2.04	
		x 14.3		x 48.2		x 3.4
			Adjusted for Inflation (0.49)			x 6.9<---
1900-------- 76.0		(1)--------------------- 520.9		(3) ------------------ 6.85 -----------------		x 873
		x 3.5		x 3,074		x 873
1997	267.9 (4)		1,601,200 (5)		$5,977	
			Adjusted for Inflation (17.81)			x 49.0<-

Sources: (1) Ref 1, *Historical Statistics of the United States*, 1975, p 8: (2) Ref 1, p 1115; (3) Ref 1, p 1114; (4) Ref 2, *Economic Report of the President*, Feb '98, p 367; (5) Ref 2, p 419; Inflation data, Ref 1, p 210, Ref 2, p395, ERP Feb'90, p 359.

For the century 1800-1900, per-capita federal government spending increased only 3.4 times while population increased 14.3 times. Adjusting for inflation of 0.49, government grew by a factor of 6.9 times for that century.

For the near-century 1900 to 1997, per-capita government spending increased 873 times, while population increased 3.5 times, in 97 years! While population tripled, adjusting for inflation growth of 17.8 times, government spending increased 49 times for the nearly-20th century!

Perhaps in Thomas Jefferson's words, it is time to "call our mismanagers to account." By any measure government has grown very large in terms of both power and money. In so doing it has diminished the people who produce the bounty of this Republic. It is fitting and proper to survey this information, take it to heart and do something about it. In so doing, you will contribute to a more prosperous, free and abundant future.

There is greater personal freedom and power in your future, with the better balance of smaller government.

Here is an assignment for "Producers": Produce Freedom! Produce freedom in the way only you can. Spend "a half hour a day for the U. S. A." and produce freedom.

Questions for Review

1. What is "Parkinson's Law" and how does it apply to a bureaucracy, particularly government? How does Parkinson use the British navy as an example? Discuss "Bureaucracies and governments grow because they grow." As a society what is our first job to achieve between wealth-creating enterprise and net-wealth-consuming government? How is "balance" determined?

2. How do good causes, "good politics" and bad economics result in government growth, such as the "War on Poverty?" What always comes with government funding? Use surplus butter to illustrate "good politics and bad economics." How can such public policy seriously and adversely disrupt supply and demand? How far out of control did Farm Income Stabilization get comparing 1983 predictions and actual 1986 funding? What happens to the federal deficit, debt and debt interest with such fluctuations?

3. How can unwarranted government growth in a society be compared to cancer in a human being? Discuss "The bottom line of what's wrong with government is there is no bottom line." What is a sure prediction about government and what silent, invisible factor explains it? What is the only way to contain government growth? Is there enough money in the universe to fund all that government could do? Why?

4. What are the three parts of Lord John Maynard Keynes "Demand Management?" Why is Part One very popular, but Parts Two and Three are relatively unknown and untried? Give an example or illustration from the U. S. Budget. Why do politicians have more fun "stimulating the economy?"

5. What kind of "track record" have we on government surpluses and deficits? How have federal receipts (taxes) and outlays (spending) varied as a percent of GDP from 1973 through 1988? What caused the differences? Where does tax money come from?

6. If you, acting as government, were to devise a Secret Success System to get as much tax as possible from people, what four approaches could you use? Describe the 1916 federal income tax three years after it was enacted into law. Compare it to today in terms of numbers of people taxed, average tax dollars paid, levels of taxation, and marginal tax rates. What does "marginal tax rate" mean?

7. Our tax system relies on "self-assessment and voluntary compliance." What does that mean? What is the name of the "temporary, emergency wartime measure" begun during World War II that is still with us today, over a half century later? Describe, discuss and explain. What is the really dumb comment one hears around April 15 and why is it dumb? What is overlooked? How has withholding changed and what interesting situations occur from it?

8. Why are hidden taxes a handy dandy way to collect taxes? How are the taxes assessed and collected? Use federal revenues to illustrate direct and hidden taxes. What is the "magic number" multiplier for 2001? How do you use it? Look at a recent federal tax return, preferably your own and calculate what percentage of taxes you really paid, including the hidden taxes. How do "producers" contribute to the tax problem? What is the one product they don't produce? Why is the progressive income tax so desirable for political reasons? What is the "politics of envy"? What five reasons might someone give to defend "the rich"?

9. Why should a deficit be of interest to you personally? Discuss "Work hard, save and get ahead" in terms of weekly pay, leisure time, the numbers and percentages of people working. Discuss "More of us work for less money, to have less leisure time." Why should it be just the opposite? How much does the 1985 $212 billion "boiling water" deficit and the then-$2.1 trillion national debt cost a high school graduate in taxes just for interest alone?

10. Discuss why crimes aren't committed and why they are. What are the causes and effects of "economic deprivation and desperation"? What is the significance of change in the number of married mothers working, government size, and how it relates to the incidence of personal and property crime? What are the two "behavioral basics? Illustrate government growth by comparing changes in per-capita federal taxes for the century 1800-1900 and the present near-century 1900-1997. What is a "freedom assignment" for producers and for *Powers of ONE*?

Liberty lies in the hearts of men and women; when it dies there, no Constitution, no law, no court can save it.   —Judge Learned Hand

Beware of false knowledge; it is more dangerous than ignorance.
                                                    —George Bernard Shaw

Men become free only as they achieve self-government. I take it that a man governs himself to the degree that he acts upon his own judgment. Freedom thus presupposes first that people are capable of judging for themselves, and second, they are permitted to do so.   —Everett Dean

That government is best which governs the least, because its people discipline themselves.   —Thomas Jefferson

The political machine triumphs because it is a united minority acting against a divided majority.   —Will Durant

More often than not, the government grants something today by deciding not to take it away. Your money is yours if the government decides not to take it away—or keep it, as the case may be. Our economy is being regimented by regulation and our incentives to invest in the free enterprise market are being stifled by taxation.   —Donald Kendall

The whole structure of government is directed towards the redistribution rather than the creation of wealth. The impulse to reduce everyone to a common level, to assure not equality of opportunity but equality of results—no matter how poor the results—is in many places the prevailing philosophy.   —Reginald Jones

Chapter 21

GOVERNMENT'S ROLE
A Model for Understanding—Size, Growth, Problems, Promise.

ROGIS? WIPS? NOQ!

What is the *Role Of* Government *In* Society (ROGIS)? *What Is* the Preferred *Size* (WIPS)? *Not Over* a *Quarter* (NOQ)! What does all this mean?

Our national mindset has been that more government is better, or at worst, more government is okay. What did we get? More government. Now we know that more government is not necessarily better. It depends on how much government we already have, and what kind. To a point, more government is good, beneficial, productive. To a higher point it is neutral, nonproductive, a trade-off between the government (public) and enterprise (private) sectors. Above the second point, it is bad, counter-productive, even destructive. We are well beyond that point.

What are these "points?" How are they determined? What is their significance? How can such information be used to help create a better future for the American people, our country and freedom? We will answer these questions and more, and provide a framework for thinking about government—its size, growth and functions—which sometimes get lost in our government do-good gusto.

A Power Dare Chapter: Do the Tough Stuff!

This is a *"Power Dare* Chapter," *Power of ONE.* Read and heed your "Power Deed Creed!"

The Constitutional Imperative: Common Defense and the General (NOT Specific) Welfare

The mission and purposes are spelled out in the Preamble to the U.S. Constitution, the role and functions of the federal government, in Article I, Section 8, Clause 1: "To provide for the *common defense* and the *general welfare.*" The common defense means a safe people in a secure nation, protected from both external and internal threats to its security and safety. The general welfare is that which aids *all* citizens and hurts none, such as coinage of money, standardization of weights and measures and Post Offices. It does *not* mean the *specific welfare* that benefits one segment at the expense of others. All of this serves to limit government size.

The Constitution was designed with this one purpose in mind: to protect individual rights. It is to define and empower a *limited government* that protects life and property, promotes individual well being, fosters productivity and guarantees personal freedom. We have explored how we in America have ignored that fact and have let government grow markedly, and now pay for it in many aspects of our lives.

The Declaration of Independence, in spelling out the *intent* of law, assures *equality* of some very special kinds—rights and opportunities, and equality under the law. It means an equal place to start on a level playing field. It does not mean equal results or equal material goods or income for each citizen, nor equal skills, abilities, intelligence, good looks or experience. It means an equal chance to succeed—or fail.

The Agony and the Ecstasy, or The Misery and the Prosperity?

My book, *The Phoenix Phenomenon*[1], was an analysis of government growth over a period of 35 consecutive, relatively stable years following World War II, 1948 to 1982. Using seven, five-year averages, the resulting fiscal and monetary swings of political cycles were melded out of the analysis. The next few pages are a summary for background and understanding.

Government size was measured based on government spending as a percent of national output—gross national product, GNP (today referred to as "gross domestic product"). That percentage mathematically described government size and growth over time. It is important to realize that government spending, though not all truly "creation of wealth," is by definition a part of GNP or GDP. A substantial part of our defined national output is "government."

1. Fred Holden, *The Phoenix Phenomenon* Phoenix Enterprises, Box 1900, Arvada, CO 80001: 1984

"Misery" and "prosperity" were the bad and good outcomes studied. In the late 1970's economist Arthur Okun coined the term "misery index" to describe the relative effect of the economy on individuals, by adding the rate of inflation to the rate of unemployment. The higher either value, especially both, the worse off we are, that is, the more "misery" we experience. However, not only are inflation and unemployment measures of relative misery, so too is level of interest rates as part of the "misery" one experienced, economically speaking. How many or few, particularly large items can be purchased on credit indicate relative economic wellness. So by adding interest rates to inflation and unemployment, the "Total Misery Index," another measure to describe "economic badness" was established.

These 5-year averages of misery were then calculated and plotted against government size. It became apparent that as government grew, misery grew too. In 1950 (five years inclusive, 1948-52) total government size averaged 22% GNP, federal 15%, state-and-local, 7%. The Misery Index was 7, Total Misery Index, 10.

Average total government size nearly doubled to 35% in 1980 (1978-82), with federal at 22%, state-and-local, 13%. The Misery Index grew to 17, Total Misery Index to 28.

Put another way, while government almost doubled, misery more than doubled from 7 to 17 and total misery nearly tripled, from 10 to 28.

How could "prosperity" be similarly defined and measured? Two means were selected and analyzed—annual productivity and real GDP growth (inflation-adjusted). "Prosperity" dropped drastically. As total government grew from 22% to 35%, average annual productivity dropped from 4.14% to 0.24%, real GNP growth dropped from 5.06% to 1.50% percent a year. These two numbers foretell the future, how our standard-of-living is going to change, what material abundance and leisure we can expect to enjoy. The forecast is down in both cases as government grows bigger.

The next step was to analyze the data in pairs, size of government versus results of government, rather than the previous chronological analysis. Correlating size of government with result more closely describes cause-and-effect, where a stimulus gives a response and when consistent, predictability. The paired data showed convincingly that as government got larger, misery increased, prosperity shrunk. Big and growing government resulted in more misery, less prosperity.

It made sense that the wealth creation process would be stifled by a burgeoning government in the American economic and political system. It is custom-designed for limited government, self-governing people, and personal incentives including a system of private property where producers keep most of the fruits of their labor. If people work hard, smart, and with some luck, they can earn and keep more. A growing wealth-consuming government sector and a shrinking wealth-creating enterprise sector are a combination for sure economic doldrums.

WIPS: What Is the Preferred Size?

The available data allowed what statisticians call a least-squares regression analysis. It is a way to give related data mathematical predictability. By backing the data to an ideal (but admittedly unachievable) state of zero inflation, unemployment and interest rates, the *experienced-based,* minimum government size could be calculated based on the paired data. This utopian approach indicated government size could drop as low as 17%—13% federal and 4% state-and-local. Based on the way the economy operated over those 35 years—its demonstrated performance—that is the smallest and best it could get. Because of political considerations, the public's misunderstanding of the role and function of government, and the nature and size of it, the limit can only be theoretical. We could never get close to that value as long as people are people, politicians are politicians, power is power, and government is government.

What CAN we do? We can define values we experienced before, that were considered acceptable and desirable, and find out where that puts us. They were 1% inflation (You have heard "a little inflation is good." It isn't, but 1% is much preferable to 3% or more), 4% unemployment (some economists have declared this is the absolute least it can be) and 4% interest rates (about 3 points above inflation, a nominal rate-of-return for saving and deferred spending). To get these values the Phoenix Analysis dictates getting government total size back to 24%: 16% federal and 8% state-and-local. Can it be done? Yes, because we have been there before, in the early 1950's. So it can be done. Should we do it again? And if so, why?

NOQ: Not Over a Quarter!

The results are to target total government size at 24%. Rounded, the size of our government should be:

NOQ! Not Over a Quarter! The Target Number: 25%.

In considering the audience and purpose of the report, just saying things were bad and worsening was not how it ended up. I asked my vice president, the late-John T. McCarty, "To whom should I direct the report?" He answered, "Prepare it to be presented by the President of the United States to the Congress and the American People."

That put a whole new light on it. It added to a technical, economic and statistical analysis, a part two, Project Phoenix. That was to create a means to utilize the knowledge and information from the Phoenix Report, and a program to communicate it to the American people. Project Phoenix used the data to set up a national commitment to gradually reduce government size back to 24% or "NOQ," Not Over a Quarter of GDP—a doable 25% (more later).

The main challenge clearly was to communicate the study, explain the reasons for a new direction, then gradually, slowly but surely, reduce America's relative size of government from over 35%, back to a nominal 25%, 16% or so federal and 8% or so state-and-local.

What was a near economic miracle, the answer to a politician's dream, was it required *no spending cuts* and *no tax increases!* The rigorous mathematical analysis required only that government growth be limited to 2.4% per year. Rounding up for simplicity and practicality brought about *"THE 3% SOLUTION": Limit government spending GROWTH to 3% a year.*

At the federal level for example, limit federal spending growth to $36 billion on 1990's estimated spending of $1,197 billion[2]. Anticipated RESULTS for the 1984 study?

> In 5 years (1990) the budget will be balanced. In 15 years (2000) the national debt will be paid off. Then, what formerly went to pay interest on the debt is available to do functions, projects and programs truly for which government was created and taxes paid. Without a tax increase or spending cut, inflation will return to 1%, unemployment and interest rates back *down* to 4%. Productivity and real GNP growth will get back up to 4%. There will be more prosperity, less misery, and hope that once again upcoming generations will enjoy a better life and promise for a brighter future.

How can all of this be put to work? This was the first of two important 25% values.

Astounding National Maximum Tax Consensus for All-Government: 25%

Another validation of 25% as a target comes from a 1995 *Reader's Digest* national survey, "How Fair Are Our Taxes?" published in the *Wall Street Journal*, 1/10/96. It was probably the most consistent survey ever performed. The 1,015 people polled were asked, "What is the highest percentage you think would be fair for a family making $200,000 a year to pay when you add all their taxes together?" Their answer was a near flat out "25%."

---

2. *Budget of the U. S. Government, Fiscal Year 1991*, p A-281

More surprising, to the question, "What is the highest percentage that you think would be fair for any family to pay in all their taxes combined, no matter how high their income?" they answered, "20%." Amazingly there were no significant differences by group—male or female, black or white, rich or poor, earning less than $30,000 or more than $75,000, etc. Everett Ladd, professor of political science and director of the Roper Center for Public Opinion Research said, "This consensus is the single most extraordinary finding in the history of domestic-policy polling in the United States."

Governments (federal, state-and-local *combined*) that tax at 25% of income must over the long haul spend at about that same level, not 38%, allowing overall tax cuts for the difference!

3% Solution No Longer Works, ### *GOAL 25-25: The Two Percent Solution Will*

Alas, Congress acted, but in the opposite direction, accelerating and increasing 1983's $1.39 trillion public debt drastically to $5.5 trillion in 1999. With increasing, rather than decreasing public debt the 3% solution would no longer work. There is plainly too much debt to liquidate. However, there is still time, need and and capability for a different approach, Goal 25-25: The Two Percent Solution. The founders had put together such a strong free enterprise economy that even shackled with considerably excess government it can recover, requiring only lower government growth, not cuts.

But first, for those who love big government there may be anxiety that government has not grown big enough, fast enough, that we cannot or should not limit its growth. Here is some handy statistical and financial background on government growth.

Twenty Years of Government Growth ### *Excessive by 1.55% per Year—a Whole Lot!*

One can make the case that government must grow for two reasons—to keep up with inflation and population growth. If inflation increases 4%, to have the same purchasing power government spending would grow 4%. If population increases 3%, theoretically government would need to grow 3% to service the 3% more (however one of my past analyses showed it need grow only two-thirds that amount, but we here go with the full amount.).

Assume at some condition and point in time government adequately performs its functions. Such a time would be following an expensive war effort when both spending and taxation are high. Here is a 20-year analysis to determine excess government growth from 1975 when the Vietnam conflict ("police action," not war per the Constitution) was winding down, and we presumably had all the government we needed with cessation of hostilities. How did it grow and how could we have predicted it should grow, based on government receipts (taxes) and outlays (spending), compared to population and inflation growth?

Comparison of Growth of Federal Government, 1975-1995 Receipts and Outlays vs Population-plus-Inflation

Year	Federal Finances, $ billions Receipts (Taxes)		Outlays (Spending)		Population (000)	Inflation CPI-U
1975	$279.1	**$279.1**	$332.3	**$332.3**	215,973	53.8
1980	517.1		590.9		227,726	82.4
1985	734.1	**(With**	946.4	**(With**	238,466	107.6
1990	1,032.0	**Yearly Growth**	1,253.2	**Yearly Growth**	249,949	130.7
1995	$1,351.8	**@ 6.33% =**	$1,515.7	**@ 6.33% =**	263,039	152.4
		$952.5 billion)		**$1,134.1 billion)**		
20 yr	$15,719.2	**$12,316.0**	$18,914.2	**$14,664.0**		
Totals	===>	**$3,403.2**	*excess over P+I*	**$4,250.2** <===		

Period Growth	Receipts Growth	Spending Growth	Pop'n +Infl'n Total	Period Growth Population	Inflation
1975 to 1985	163.0%	185%	110%	10.4%	100.0%
1985 to 1995	99.5%	112%	68%	9.8%	58.6%
1975 to 1995	384.3%	**356%**	**205%**	21.8%	183.3%

Compound Annual Growth					
1975 to 1985	10.15%	11.03%	8.17%	1.00%	7.18%
1985 to 1995	6.30%	4.82%	4.53%	0.99%	3.54%
1975 to 1995	8.21% <===	**7.88%**	**6.33%** <===	0.99%	5.34%

(Revenue difference = 1.88%) <<======>> (**Outlay difference = 1.55%**) <<====

Sources: *Economic Report of the President*, February 1999
Government Finances p 419, Population p 367, Inflation p 395

The key discovery and conclusion is that for those 20 years government spending grew 1.55% faster per-year than what population-plus-inflation growth could justify. Incoming revenues grew even faster, 1.88% per year. The excess government growth is shown in bold print by subtracting the somewhat defensible 6.33% growth in population and inflation from the unjustifiable 7.88% growth of government spending. We extend the analysis back to the top of the chart to compare how it was and how it could have been over the 20-year period. Had both revenues (taxes) and outlays (spending) grown at the 6.33% annual rate on a year-by-year basis, taxpayers would have kept $4,400 billion more of their own money in taxes paid ($17,900 per-capita), and government would have spent $5,800 billion less ($23,600 per-capita).

Money is Power,
Government Growth is People Power Lost

The important message here is that money is power, and this excess and unjustified growth of government was an enormous shift of power from the people to government.

Sadly, the benefits as always go more to the politicians, elected and appointed public officials and bureaucrats. They buy votes and influence with "their" goodies handed out, funded by the rest of us working hard, who had much taken from us in taxes to pay these bills. Perhaps some good was accomplished but how much, how well and at what price?

Obviously government has grown considerably faster than any rationale of logic, economics, mathematics or finance. It has grown not only because "government grows" but more importantly because our politicians have forced its growth, and *we let them*. Government need not be anywhere near this large. And being this big exacts a high price that is invisible and mute in economic bondage, that is, in making, perhaps forcing more of us citizens to work longer and harder, and to have less true life to live at our option. That is not the purpose of government.

Realizing excess government growth has been the rule rather than the exception makes it possible for even those who think government growth is a good thing, to support slowing it. *The Phoenix Phenomenon* fostered the Three Percent Solution which put Congress and the government on a budget that could not grow more than three percent. With four times the public debt to liquidate now, an easier slowing to 2% government growth can still be done with "GOAL 25-25: The Two Percent Solution." Understanding as we do that politicians, elected and appointed public officials are in a "Stop me before I spend again" mode, they will not and cannot do it by themselves. Therefore the people must initiate "GOAL 25-25," and enforce it with continuing constituent congressional contact, and at the ballot box.

GOAL 25-25 Limits Government Growth
with No Cuts or Freeze,
Gets both Tax Burden and Government Size to 25%

All day, every day we common citizens face economic and financial limits. Our personal and family money in and obligations out allow us to do only so much. When we decide to do one thing we forego another, a vacation or new car. We do not have the luxury of power-of-government and force-of-law to exact more money from a third party, the taxpayer. Unlike politicians who borrow for their better today from unborn, unrepresented generations for their worse tomorrow, we must make-do with what we have. It is no longer acceptable for us to have a party, not invite them but give them the bill.

Productivity is doing more and better for less. In our jobs, careers and businesses if we do not perform this "productivity imperative," we stand to lose our jobs, careers and businesses. We know the only way to get productivity from government is to limit its taxing and spending.

We already know that government is too big by a quarter at 32% based on government spending as a percent of national output; that it should be relatively smaller, at "NOQ, not over a quarter," 25%. We already know in that truly incredible, once-in-a century poll, that our people agree harmoniously that all-taxation to pay for all-government should not exceed 25%.

That brings us then, to GOAL 25-25. So simple, desirable and doable, it places slow phase-in and reasonable growth limits on all governments— federal, state and local. The analysis is so persuasive and the argument so compelling that the thing can and must be done. We the People impose the limits, but do not tell elected officials what laws to pass or where to spend the money, with this message: From now on you may not tax or spend more than GOAL 25-25 allows and it is not negotiable. These are your new marching orders.

GOAL 25-25: The Two Percent Solution can be met in 13 years. Limiting federal, state-and-local tax and spending growth to no more than two percent gets all-government size to 25% from 1999's 31.8% of output (gross domestic product, GDP). There are no drastic or slight cuts, or even a freeze; only small *growth limits* to federal, state-and-local government taxing and spending.

Federal revenue (tax) growth, particularly, is held to 3 percent a year. Dropping from its past six-year 7.94% compound annual growth, a sizable near-five percent revenue reduction (tax cut) is possible. The 1% difference between federal revenue and spending produces a growing budget surplus starting with 1999's $123 billion. It gradually increases to complete payoff of 1999's $3,633 billion national debt held by the public in 13 years. This is all done with no cuts or freeze and reasonable, doable, desirable government tax and spending restraint.

Over a period of five years federal spending growth will be phased in from its six-year (1993 to 1999) annual *growth rate* of 3.2% to 2.0%; similarly state-and-local government growth will drop from 5.4%, also to 2%; same for all taxes as a percent of personal income. See the diagram on the next page for the numbers in chart form.

Federal Debt: Wasteful, Immoral, Unproductive?

Why is it important to reduce the federal debt? Because it is wasteful, immoral and unproductive. Debt should be incurred for dire emergencies like war, or to truly invest, with a likely and identifiable return. This debt

GOAL 25-25: The Two Percent Solution

With No Cuts, No Freeze, only Contained Government Growth, in 13 Years: Get All-U.S. Government Size to a Level of 25% of Output, GDP (from 31.8%); Get All-Tax Level to 25% of Personal Income (from 37.9%); by holding Federal Revenue Growth to 3%; Government Spending Growth—Federal to 2%, State-and-Local to 2%; and Liquidate 1999's $3,633 Billion Public Debt held by Public.

(figures in $billions)

Target Growth—> Year	(ref)* (5.74%) 5.00% GDP	(ref)* (5.63%) 6.00% Prsnl Inc	(ref)* (7.94%) 3.00% Fed Revs	(ref)* (3.20%) 2.00% (Fd Spg)	(Federal) (Surplus)	(ref)* (5.44%) 2.00% St/Lc Rev	All-Gv Rev	Tax Rate Pl,%All-gv	Gov Size %GDP	1999 debt, held by public: $3,633 billion Fed Cum Surplus
1999act	$9,284	$7,791	$1,826	$1,703	$123	$1,131	$2,957	37.9%	31.8%	$123
2000	9,749	8,259	1,880	1,754	126	1,182	3,062	37.1%	31.4%	249
2001	10,236	8,754	1,937	1,803	134	1,229	3,166	36.2%	30.9%	383
2002	10,748	9,279	1,995	1,850	145	1,272	3,267	35.2%	30.4%	528
2003	11,285	9,836	2,055	1,894	160	1,310	3,365	34.2%	29.8%	688
2004	11,850	10,426	2,116	1,936	180	1,343	3,460	33.2%	29.2%	867
2005	12,442	11,052	2,180	1,975	205	1,370	3,550	32.1%	28.5%	1,073
2006	13,064	11,715	2,245	2,014	231	1,397	3,643	31.1%	27.9%	1,304
2007	13,717	12,418	2,313	2,055	258	1,425	3,738	30.1%	27.3%	1,562
2008	14,403	13,163	2,382	2,096	286	1,454	3,836	29.1%	26.6%	1,849
2009	15,123	13,953	2,454	2,138	316	1,483	3,936	28.2%	26.0%	2,165
2010	15,879	14,790	2,527	2,180	347	1,513	4,040	27.3%	25.4%	2,511
2011	16,673	15,677	2,603	2,224	379	1,543	4,146	26.4%	24.9%	2,890
2012	17,507	16,618	2,681	2,269	413	1,574	4,255	25.6%	24.3%	3,303
2013	$18,382	$17,615	$2,762	$2,314	$448	$1,605	$4,367	24.8%	23.8%	$3,751

Data Sources: Economic Report of the President, Feb, 2000: GDP-p306, Pers Inc-338, Federal Revs-397, State/Local Revs-404; Budget of the U.S. Gov't, Fiscal 2001, publicly-held public debt-420. (ref)*: Compound average values for six previous years of respective data, 1993-1999.

Analyzed by: Fred Holden, 303-421-7619, email: FredHolden@aol.com, July 7, 2000; Phoenix Enterprises, PO Box 1900, Arvada, CO 80001, Rev. 0

was incurred only to satisfy Congress' uncontrolled urgings and political expediency to spend more money on fabricated programs that did not and could not accomplish significant quantifiable results. In many cases such as the "War on Poverty," perhaps even the "War on Drugs," instead of alleviating, they exacerbated the problems.

Public debt is wasteful because it squanders valuable and precious taxpayer resources paid to provide government services which instead "service" government debt (pay interest and financing costs). Instead of "doing government," it enriches investors because of Congress past unwillingness to control spending or raise taxes.

It is immoral because the money finances today's perceived, imagined or fabricated political needs, but will be paid by tomorrow's yet-to-be-born taxpayers and today's non-voting children. They had no voice, no vote, get no benefits but have to pay the bills. Frankly, ever-increasing taxes are used by politicians to buy goodwill and votes for the upcoming election. In the process they expropriate more money and power from the people and future people.

Good economics dictates borrowing only to invest for a greater return or higher productivity. Government spending growth did neither. It should have been greatly curtailed during what was called "longest peacetime expansion in the nation's history," beginning in 1983, then the next, all-time record breaker beginning in 1991. These were to be the times to build a surplus to reduce or eliminate the public debt and debt interest for an overall long-term balanced budget, according to Keynesian theory guidelines.

We did not have the political will or courage to do so. Instead we had a string of triple-digit billion (read that "12-digit") dollar deficits[3] totaling $1,564 billion with a resulting $2,039 billion increase in the public debt from 1979 through 1989. Keep in mind a surplus of $10 billion should reduce, a deficit of $10 billion should increase the public debt, without Congress on-budget, off-budget, "smoke and mirrors," accounting methods where they can "tell the truth" while distorting and disinforming. From 1990 through 1999 their reported cumulative $1,477 billion deficits increased the public debt by $2,738 billion.

In those 20 years, the total debt increase of $4,777 billion is over five times the 1980 public debt of $909 billion accumulated over the preceding two-plus centuries since the birth of this republic in 1776! Since 1900 that supported America in World War I, World War II, the Great Depression in the 1930's, Korean and Vietnam conflicts, plus fighting communism and the Cold War.

The 1999 debt interest of $339 billion[4], almost a billion dollars a day, was enough to fund the entire federal government as recently as 1975. Debt interest cost each American citizen $1,253 on average in 1999; for each of the 133 million employed, $2,539. That is the first $49 earned each week and withheld to buy government services, but buying none, instead paying for interest only on the public debt.

1980's Prosperity: The Exception Proves the Rule

The decade of the 1980's may seem to have been contrary to the findings of the *Phoenix Phenomenon*. While government grew slightly, all three rates declined—inflation, unemployment and interest. Three things contributed to this situation.

First, gargantuan classic Keynesian stimulus was applied, the largest, most relentless and irresponsible in history. Government went on a spending binge rampage. Federal deficits were the largest ever recorded, and even larger than reported. With the combined budgets, federal spending and the trust funds, the highest-ever (to then) 1986 deficit of

3. Budget of the United States Government, Fiscal Year 2001, Historical Tables, pp 20, 110-111.

4. Ibid, p 130, Economic Report of the President, Feb, 2000, p 345

$221 billion was in fact an operating deficit of $283 billion, without the surplus provided by the trust funds. Barely below that was the 1989 total operating deficit of $276 billion[5], with the 1989 net reported deficit of $152 billion.

Second, the 1981 Economic Recovery Tax Act cut tax rates, "stimulating the economy."

Third, when this fiscal stimulus was combined with the likable, patriotic, "Great Communicator" President Reagan, they buoyed up and prolonged an extended business expansion. The people felt good about themselves and their country, and worked hard to produce a lot of wealth.

Related to all this was Congress' own attempt to discipline itself into fiscal responsibility and accountability. The 1985 "boiling water" deficit of $212 billion was so abhorrent they enacted the Gramm-Rudman-Hollings Deficit Reduction Act of 1985. That was so good even though the Republican-controlled Senate supported a balanced budget amendment to the U.S. Constitution by the necessary two-thirds vote in 1986, the Democrat-controlled House of Representatives didn't.

The result? For starters, the 1986 deficit that by law was to *drop* to $171.9 billion, *increased* to $221.2 billion. In 1987 Congress amended the law to excuse their own unwillingness and inability to get the federal budget under control, this during good times! The accompanying tell-tale table[6] summarizes this lack of political will, courage and statesmanship.

You can no longer fill in the blanks for upcoming years. It is over. The whole sham was scrapped because Congress could no longer obey, so conveniently amended its own laws.

Be sensitive to when Congress similarly acts to reduce—or increase— the public debt.

Notice the use of the word "law." Is Congress immune from its own legislation? Yes. While the people must obey the law, Congress had exempted itself from the following Acts: Civil Rights, Equal Employment Opportunity, Equal Pay, Fair Labor Standards, National Labor Relations, Occupational Safety and Health, and Freedom of Information and Privacy[7]. (Following the 1994 turnover in Congressional leadership, House and Senate, the newly-in-power Republicans instituted legislation that would attenuate such favoritism though the past was left untouched.)

Here, Congress again legislated what is good for the country then broke the law with impunity. The one act that binds only themselves is broken annually by themselves and with no consequences. They are re-elected at a high 90's percent rate for those who choose to re-run.

5. *Economic Report of the President, February, 1990*, p 383

6. "Fiscal Follies: Ever-Growing Deficits Establish the Failure of Gramm-Rudman," *Wall Street Journal*, 10/30/89, p A1

7. "Above the Law," *Wall Street Journal*, 4/4/88, lead editorial

Take a look at the two promises and the miserable performance, especially with continually and substantially increasing revenues. No wonder you hear, "Stop me before I spend again." They have been truly out of control.

Gramm-Rudman Deficit Targets

(In billions of dollars)

Fiscal Year	Incoming Rev's, $bil	Original 1985 Law	1987 Revision	Reported Deficit	Operating Deficit
1983	$ 600.6 1)			$ 207.8	$ 208.0 1)
1984	666.5	(Pre-Gramm-Rudman		185.4	185.7
1985	734.1	Reference Data)		212.3	221.7
1986	769.2	$ 171.9	Gramm-Rudman	$ 221.2	238.0
1987	854.4	144.0	Targets	149.8	169.3
1988	909.3	108	$ 144	155.2	194.0
1989	991.2	72	136	152.5	205.2
1990	1,032.0	36	100	221.2	277.8
1991	1,055.0	0	64	269.4	321.6
1992	1,091.3	—	28	290.4	340.5
1993	1,154.4 1)	—	0	255.0	300.5 1)

Sources: 1) *Budget of U. S. Government, Fiscal Year 2001*, Historical Tables, p 20

So much for Congress Gramm-Rudman targets versus their actual budget performance in upholding their own law and controlling their penchant for spending. The only way to describe their abysmal performance is "out-of-control." But they are no worse than the Executive Branch.

As recently as 1995 President William Clinton had ignored congressional conversations to balance the budget in 10 years, or 5 years, or by 2001, or by 2005. His budgets showed an always far-in-the-future budget balancing, always after he was well out of office and beyond responsibility and accountability. But the economy, the American spirit and genius, and a thing called "the chip" in computers, cell phones, faxes, the Internet and email caught up with and passed him. He ended up taking credit for the $69.2 billion "surplus" that first and unexpectedly appeared in 1998. (The public debt still increased $109 billion, a $178 billion disparity.) His Fiscal 2001 budget shows a string of "surpluses" from 2001 to 2010 adding up to $2,518 billion, with the public debt incredibly *growing* $844 billion from $5,658 billion to $6,502 billion, a total contradiction in definition. With surpluses should not the debt drop, not grow? New estimates show the 10-year surplus to be not $2,518 billion, but $4,190 billion[8].

Not surprising, the "smaller-government-lower-taxes-are-better" Republicans seek ways to break the budget gaps earlier imposed in part by defining some $15 billion additional spending as "emergency." Meanwhile President Clinton is looking to greatly increase tobacco taxes to have more money to spend without exceeding the budget caps. The whole pressure, the whole impetus is bigger and more government, more intrusive, invasive and abusive of individual liberties. When will the people learn what is going on, what to be doing about it and then doing it? Or will they wait until it is too late?

How Time, Circumstance and Creep Killed Keynesian Economics

Nothing is static. Things change. Sometimes change is hard to detect because of what is called creep—slow but sure change over long periods of time. A good example is that of government size and growth and the applicability and impact of Keynesian "prime the pump" economics.

Lord John Maynard Keynes, duly concerned about the way economics was working during the Great Depression in the 1930's, carefully crafted his "demand management" theories. There were three elements to our economic society: customers, business and government. Customers purchased goods and services. Business invested in capital to serve customers. Government performed government services and bought things, in doing so, being "the customer of last resort."

Economist Keynes knew that in "bad economic times" both customers and businesses were strapped in buying power. He reasoned only government had the power to borrow and spend money it did not have, to prompt good times, then have surpluses pay off the borrowed spending money. He published it in his timely and important *General Theory*[9].

The phenomenal change that resulted from applying Keyne's theories is the undoing of their application in the big-government society we have today. Keyne's ideas and theories justified, legitimized and created big government. The Employment Act of 1946 both energized and institutionalized the theories. After World War II government took off and began its new era of growth. With government over one-third the economy, Keyne's ideas are of lesser or little value because we have saturated big government to its limits.

Here is how it all has changed:

8. "As Surplus Surges, Clinton-GOP Deals Look More Likely," *Wall Street Journal*, p A32, 6/27/00.

9. John Maynard Keynes, *The General Theory of Employment, Interest and Money*, Harcourt, Brace and Co., 1936

Growth, Shift of Government over Time, Spending as % of GDP, 1900-1999 in $ billion

Year	Output GDP	Federal Government	%	State/Local Government	%	Ratio Fed/StL	Total Gov %
1900	$ 18.7 1)	$ 0.52 2)	2.8	$ 0.9 3)	4.8	37/63	7.6
1910	35.3	0.69	2.0	2.0	5.7	26/74	7.6
1920	91.5	6.36	7.0	5.4	5.9	54/46	12.9
1930	90.4	3.32	3.7	8.0	8.8	29/71	12.5
1940	100.4 4)	9.50 4)	9.5	11.2	11.2	46/54	20.6
1950	288.3	42.6 5)	14.8	22.5 4)	7.8	65/35	22.6
1960	527.4 5)	92.2	17.5	38.1 5)	7.2	71/29	24.7
1970	1,039.7	195.6	18.8	107.5	10.3	65/35	29.2
1980	2,795.6	590.9	21.1	307.8	11.0	66/34	32.1
1990	5,803.2	1,253.2	21.6	660.8	11.4	65/35	33.0
1995	7,400.5	1,515.8	20.5	902.5	12.2	63/37	32.7
1999	$9,248.4	$1,703.0	18.4	$1,089.0	11.8	61/39	30.2

Sources: 1) Ref 1, *Historical Statistics of the United States, U. S.* Dept. of Commerce, 1970, pp 224-228, 2) Ref 1, p 1104; 3) Ref 1, p 1127; 4) Ref 2, *Economic Report of the President*, Feb, 1990, pp 294, 383, 390; 5) Ref 2, *ERP*, Feb, 2000, pp 306, 397, 404.

A ray of hope, government has already receded from its 33% level in 1990. Government took a great leap to fight World War I, nearly doubling from 1910 to 1920. Not inconsequential were the 1913 births of the federal income tax, 16th amendment and the *private*, central bank, the Federal Reserve. With the Great Depression onset in 1929 continuing into the late 1930's, note the growth of government in these turbulent times and dire economic emergencies.

Total government grew relentlessly, decade-by-decade, from 8% in 1900 to 33% in 1990, then slightly dropping in the 1990's. There was a pause in the 1920's while we pondered the Great Depression. Was the near double jump from 12% in 1930 to 20% in 1940 mere coincidence with the 1936 publication of Keynes' *General Theory*? Also with World War II over in 1945, did the ensuing stimulation and legitimization of the Employment Act of 1946 contribute to the ensuing decade-by-decade leaps in government growth to one-third of the economy?

Note not only the shift from small to big government, but from state to federal government. America's Founders designed the "several states" to have power in concert with the federal government, not subservient to it, which remained so early in the 20th century. There was relatively little government and what there was, was predominantly state-and-local. In 1900 they were 37/63, 2-to-1 over federal spending. They became about equal in the 1940's, prior to World War II, then both grew rapidly. State-and-local government more than doubled and federal government increased six-fold since the beginning of the century into 1999 where it has reversed to federal government spending nearly twice that of state government, 61/39. (For your own information, graph percent government and ratio of federal-to-state government versus year from 1900 to 1999.)

With government a third of the economy from 1970-on, there is no more room for Keynesian or any other artificial stimulus. More government growth can only do more damage and is no longer legitimized by any economic theory.

Keynesianism is dead.

What might have been "good medicine" for the economy with a considerably smaller government, at 8%, 18%, or even 23% of GDP, may now be "bad poison" at government size of 30%.

In fact our new "survival imperative" is such that we must do whatever we can do to gradually and relentlessly reduce the *relative* size of government, hence the immense importance of the GOAL 25-25: The Two Percent Solution.

The Family: A Super-Motivator to Adopt GOAL 25-25: The Two Percent Solution

There are many ways to show size and long-term growth of government and their effects. Three are government dollars spent in terms of 1) percent of GDP (above), 2) percent of personal income, and 3) comparison to cost of the "essentials of life," food, shelter and clothing, on a macroeconomic, national basis. All show government to be big, growing and detrimental.

The family is another way to make the point, to show the economic and social effects of government growth on this backbone of America. This core unit of society can be used to compare and evaluate such economic concepts as size of government or level of taxes. Are taxes too high or too low?

We begin with a basic notion that what you work for is yours. You prepare, learn and earn, work hard and produce, and expect to keep a reasonable portion of what you are paid. So it is wise to ask, "compared to what?" We make allowances to pay for legitimate functions of government, to protect our people from fear, force and fraud. We support a reasonable "safety net" to care for the truly disadvantaged, unemployed, elderly and handicapped. And with more limited government the people have more to take care of their own, in their private lives, philanthropic, charitable and service organizations, and churches.

We certainly cannot keep every penny we earn, but a balance between what we earn and what we keep is important. The more service we get out of our tax dollars and the more we keep of what we earn, the more we can take care of ourselves and our own. Also there is more incentive for us to work hard and produce. What is reasonable is really what is reasonable to you.

Keep in mind your first responsibility is to yourself and your family, to provide for the present and future, the "plannables" and the "unpredictables" of life. Providing for your living includes paying your bills and saving for your future. You earn and spend for week-to-week food, shelter, clothing, transportation, recreation, and save for emergencies (such as a medical, dead car battery or dying refrigerator) and retirement. You handle life's necessities and niceties.

How Much of Your Earnings are Taxes And for What Government Expenditures?

This short but revealing exercise will help you better know your "unthought thoughts" about taxes using 1996 (most recent) data. The question explored is, "What percentage of my income or my family's income goes to government to do government things?" You begin with a "thought starter" set of figures, then determine figures you think they *are,* then what you think they *ought to be.* In a few pages you learn what they really áre.

Spending by all governments—three levels in two groups, federal, and state-and-local—is classified for convenience into four functional spending areas: Internal security/national/international, government services, social services, and other.

National/International/Internal Security has to do with national defense, domestic security, foreign affairs, police and fire protection.

Government Services include the administration of justice and prisons, post offices, housing, highways, parks, treasury, natural resources and environmental protection, energy, sanitation and sewerage, public transportation, agriculture, veterans affairs, science, space and technology.

Social Services include public welfare, health and hospitals, income security, Social Security, public education, training and employment, unemployment, aid to families and dependent children, and aging.

Other includes interest on the public debt, financial administration including tax collection, and general government administration and control.

Check the "thought starter" numbers in Column 1, which are hypothetical percentages of personal or family income going to each category of government spending.

Consider government spending in each category, *what you think it is.* Start with column 1 and ask yourself, is this value too high, too low or about right? Then fill in your considered judgment for each Column 2 blank, what percentage of your income or family income belongs in the blank. Don't dwell on the values. Give them fleeting thought, then fill them in.

Determining Personal Perception of
Percent Earnings to Government

Government Spending Category	Column 1 Thought Starter	Column 2 What I think It Is	Column 3 What I think it Ought to Be
National/International Internal Security	5%	_____	_____
Government Services	5%	_____	_____
Social Services	10%	_____	_____
Other	5%	_____	_____
Total Percent Government	25%	_____	_____

Fill in each blank of Column 3 for what percentage of your income or family income you think government spending in that category *ought to be.*

Add up and compare each column for total *estimated percentages* of government spending: Column 1, "thought starter" total of 25%, Column 2 estimate and total of what you think it is, and your Column 3 estimate and total of what it ought to be.

You therefore concede _____ % (Column 3 total) of your family income in taxes to provide what you feel is a fair *contribution* (actually mandatory taxes required by law) for the services, benefits and advantages government provides you, your community and nation. Finishing up, here is what you consider fair *to keep* from the fruits of your labors for your well-being and your family's care, by subtracting taxes from 100%: _____ %.

In a few pages you will see the actual 1996 amounts and distribution of family income to these four broad categories of government spending.

Taxus Terminus: How Does Big and Growing Government Harm the Family?

We have discovered the family has not been doing all that well economically in recent years. The foregoing analysis shows the 1998 tax burden was over 70% on the average American family, over two-thirds its earnings! By using the 1998 median family income of $46,767, direct and indirect calculated taxes amounted to $32,762, for after-tax earnings of $14,005 or about $1,167 per month real money buying power. The average 1998 family size was 3.18 people for 70.9 million families, out of 270,561,000 population.

Federal "total receipts" (taxes) for 1998 were $1,722 billion, or $6,354 per-capita. State-and-local total taxes were $1,070 billion, or $3,948 per-capita. Total per-capita taxation is $10,303, multiplied by average family size 3.18, to calculate $32,767 family tax burden. Divided by median family income of $46,767 it is a family tax burden over 70%.

Percent Median Family Income to Taxes for Years 1950 to 1998

Year	Pop'n mil.	Federal Rec'ts $bil.	Federal Per-Capita	State/Local Rec'ts $bil.	State/Local Per-Capita	Total /Cap Taxes	Avg. Fam. Size	Family Tax Burden	Median Family Income	% Fam Tax Burden
	1)	1)		1) 2)			3)		4) 5)	
1998	271	1,722	$6,354	1,070	$3,948	10,303	3.18	$32,762	$46,767	70.1%
1990	250	1,032	4,128	663	2,652	6,780	3.17	21,493	35,353	60.8%
1980	228	517	2,268	317	1,390	3,658	3.20	11,705	21,023	55.7%
1970	205	193	941	105	512	1,453	3.58	5,202	9,867	52.7%
1960	181	93	514	42	232	746	3.67	2,737	5,620	48.7%
1950	152	39	257	21	138	395	3.54	1,397	3,319	42.1%

Sources: 1) *Economic Report of the President*, Feb 2000, pp 345, 397, 404; 2) ERP1990, p 390; 3) Family Size Data: Statistical Abstract of the United States, 1999, pp 478, 1950, '60 data, SAUS 1986, p 39; 4) Median Family Income Data: SAUS1999, pp 478, 1950, '60 data, SAUS 1986, p 450; 5) ERP2000, p 344.

From 42.1% in 1950 to 70.1% in 1998 the shrinking family's tax burden increased 28.0%, an average per-year increase of 0.58%. Since 1980, going from 55.7% to 70.1%, the family tax burden grew 14.4%, *annual growth average of 0.80% a year*! Government keeps growing more and faster, drastically impacting the family's ability to pay its bills, forcing more members of the family out into the work force.

The process of TAX CREEP, slow but ever-so-sure tax increases over time, places near-impossible financial burdens on the family. A new tax here, small increases there, and "closing of loopholes" all add to higher total taxes.

This increasing economic burden becomes a "family killer." More mothers and fathers must work to make ends meet, depriving children of their parent's presence.

Working married mothers with children under age six increased over 5 times, from 11.9% in 1950 to 63.6% in 1997[10]. Up to age 6 is when children bond with their parents and learn to form long-lasting love and trust relationships, to form their value and belief systems and develop a positive self-image and high self-esteem. By repetition and emphasis they learn the two behavioral basics from their parents, "keep your hands to yourself" and "respect other people's property." Not learned, these turn into personal and property crime, respectively.

Over those same 47 years, working married mothers with children 6-17 almost tripled, from 28.3% to 77.6%. These are the adolescent

10. *Historical Statistics of the US*, 1975, p 134; *Statistical Abstract of the US, 1999*, p 417.

"latchkey kids" who come home to an empty house. Without the security of parent-child bonding, children don't learn to love and form deep, healthy, lasting relationships. These growth years are when more teens turn to drugs, gangs, violence, sex and suicide as teenage solutions to teenage problems.

Do these conditions contribute to growing social problems such as increasing rates of divorce, domestic violence, crime, teenage mothers (and cowardly unidentified fathers), child abuse, and the impoverished and the homeless? We are beginning to see results of the first generation of institutionally, and latchkey-raised children.

Crime statistics[11] are revealing, possibly shocking. The incidence of personal and violent crime increased over six times in 30 years, from 836 per 100,000 in 1957 to 5,079 in 1997. Are more people more violent? Why? Is it because they are more economically desperate and deprived, and must resort to crime to survive? When we increase taxes to build prisons, must crime increase? If so, the more we "solve" the problem, the worse it gets.

Getting back to basics and the U.S. Constitution, does Article IV of the Bill of Rights protect families against such "unreasonable searches and seizures?" Does Article V, " . . . nor be deprived of life, liberty, or property, without due process of law . . . " protect people's sustenance from the tax collector? Does Article VIII protect the family from this insidious and destructive kind of "cruel and unusual punishment?" Is Article XIII, "Neither slavery nor involuntary servitude, except as a punishment for crime ... ," violated by taxation so outrageous the family keeps less than half of what they work hard for and earn?

Historian Will Durant said, "The only real revolution is in the enlightenment of the mind and the improvement of character, the only real emancipation is individual, and the only real revolutionists are philosophers and saints.[12]"

Who will join "the real revolution" back to the principles on which this country was founded: 1) self-governing, independent and responsible people, 2) limited government defined and empowered to prevent fraud, fear and force, and 3) abiding faith in our Creator and God-given abilities to care for ourselves and each other without the confiscation and control of a burgeoning, wasteful government?

The old Jack Benny hold-up joke was "Your money or your life!"

(Long pause)

"Answer me!"

"I'm thinking! I'm thinking!"

---

11. *Historical Statistics of the US*, 1975, p 413; *Statistical Abstract of the US, 1999*, p 214.

12. Durant, Will and Ariel, *The Lessons of History. p 72,* Simon and Schuster, New York: 1968

It is your money *and* your life. With ever-increasing taxes, will assault on the American family, *Taxus Terminus,* become the *demise* of the American family, and of freedom in America? Is excessive taxation the economic AIDS going into a new millennium?

If the family is the backbone of America, the growth of government and its attendant tax burden are breaking America's back!

What Percentage of Family or Personal Income Does Government REALLY Spend?

We here attempt to quantify how much of our income for all Americans—households, families, broken families, singles, young, old, rich, middle income and poor—we are willing to forego to get the benefits and services of government. Fill in this blank from a few pages previous the amount you determined was right for you as a percent of your earnings: _____%. Subtracting from 100% gives what percentage you think is your fair share to keep after taxes: _____%.

Here are the results for this specific 1996 data:

What government takes: 46.2%. What taxpayers get to keep: 53.8%.

Here are the details:

The cost of all government, $2,968 billion, as a percentage of total compensation of individuals for 1996, $6,425 billion (most recent available) was 46.2%. *Total Compensation* included pay for America's workers of $3,631 billion, other labor income - $387 billion, proprietor's income - $527 billion; renter income of persons - $150 billion: personal dividend income - $248, personal interest income - $719 and transfer payments to persons - $1,068.

Here's the 1996 categorized government spending, state-and-local, federal[13], tallied and totaled, expressed as a percent of total compensation of all Americans:

Percent Citizen Remuneration Paid by Category for Government Spending, 1996

Based on 1996 Personal Income of $6,425.2 billion, Government Spending $2,968.1 billion:

Government Spending Category	Column 1 State/Local Spending	%	Column 2 Federal Spending	%	Column 3 Total Gov't Spending	Column 4 Percent of Earnings
National/Int'l/ Internal Security	$ 62.4	1.0%	$ 279.3	4.3%	$ 341.7	5.3%
Govenment Services	472.9	____	154.5	____	627.4	9.8%
Social Services	550.3	____	921.3	____	1,471.6	22.9%
Other	312.0	____	215.4	____	527.4	8.2%
Totals	$1,397.6	____	$1,570.5	____	$2,968.1	46.2%

13. *Statistical Abstract of the U. S.,* 1999, State-and-Local Government Expenditures by function, p 317, Federal Government Expenditures by function, p 351; total compensation of employees, p 466.

If you are curious to determine the percentages for each category of state/local and federal, blanks are provided. The National/International line would include 1.0% (62.4/6,425.2) for state-and-local spending, 4.3% (279.3/6,425.2) for federal, for the first total, 5.3%.

A Quick Look Back:
Is Government Too Big? Compared to What?

Look again at the two tables to see what is happening to percentages of total compensation income paid in taxes and to how much of your family income goes in total and in parts, to pay for government services. How do you feel about this? Compared to what? Look back a few pages to see how you objectively view today's level of taxation and amount of government spending, visible and hidden, direct and indirect.

Government's Role: A Model for Understanding

A special part of my life has been spent as a professional speaker presenting freedom, economics, government, taxes, business, free enterprise (they are not the same), profits and citizenship to small and large groups. Feedback is essential to develop approaches and means to communicate unfamiliar concepts and necessarily abstract thinking to others. At the conclusion of one speech a listener commented, "You really are anti-government, aren't you?"

"No, I'm not at all anti-government," I said. "Either I said the thing wrong or I said the wrong thing, but I am not anti-government. Government is absolutely essential for our modern existence," within the confines of the U.S. Constitution.

The size and type of government are important. The more we know about government the better government we will have. Without government we would die horrible deaths as individuals and as a society. With too much government we lose our rights, freedoms and individuality. Government is essential but balance is necessary.

All that started me thinking. How could I analyze and communicate better? Something has been missing. We have been drilled with and tacitly accepted the notion that more government is better. So what did we get? More government. Is more government better? It depends. Here is how I found out through a review of my previous book, *The Phoenix Phenomenon*, and a third party, Nobel laureate economist, Dr. Milton Friedman.

The Phoenix Phenomenon showed from the end of World War II to 1982 government grew from about 18% to 35% of output, nearly doubling in 35 years. Our economic and political system could work down as low as 17% GDP, 13% federal, 4% state-and-local, and more realistically at 24%—16% and 8%, respectively, based on the empirical analysis. My boss, the late John T. McCarty, had sent a copy of *Phoenix to* his friend,

Dr. Friedman, for review and comment. His analysis was constructive and insightful. In his March 14, 1984 critique, Dr. Friedman wrote:

> When I am asked the question of what the appropriate size of government is, I always reply by saying that history provides considerable evidence. When Britain was at the height of its power at Queen Victoria's Jubilee at the end of the nineteenth century, total government spending in Britain—central and local—amounted to about 10 percent of the national income. In the period from our Revolution to 1929, total government spending in the United states, if we exclude the periods of active war, also averaged about 10 percent of the national income. The Bible has a tithe. I take these to indicate that 10 percent is about the right number for both federal and state and local. We are very far indeed from that, and certainly the levels of 16 percent for federal and 8 percent for state and local would be far better.

The Deity itself defines government at 10% in the Bible. Samuel, the judge, told God the people wanted a king, "that we may be like all the nations, and that our king may govern us and go out before us and fight our battles" (I Samuel 8:1-20). God said he would be their king. But the people told Samuel, "Now appoint for us a king to govern us like all the nations." God then told Samuel to "solemnly warn them, and show them the ways of the king who shall reign over them." Samuel relayed God's warning to the people:

> These will be the ways of the king who will reign over you: he will take your sons and appoint them to his chariots and to be his horsemen, and to run before his chariots; and he will appoint for himself commanders of thousands and commanders of fifties, and some to plow his ground and to reap his harvest, and to make his implements of war and the equipment of his chariots. He will take your daughters to be perfumers and cooks and bakers. He will take the best of your fields and vineyards and olive orchards and give them to his servants. He will take the tenth of your grain and of your vineyards and give it to his officers and to his servants. He will take your menservants and maidservants, and the best of your cattle and your asses, and put them to his work. He will take the tenth of your flocks, and you shall be his slaves.

Three things intrigued me: 1) Government taking the first and best 10%, 2) the 10% must have been a minimum rather than a maximum, and 3) the next, Verse 18 was ominous:

And in that day you will cry out because of your king, whom you have chosen for yourselves; but the Lord will not answer you in that day!

Putting this all together provides the answers we seek. It is a continuum from no government to much government. A short review of the government and economic system brings the puzzle into focus.

Government is absolutely necessary for any society to preserve law and order, guarantee personal freedom and promote a climate of safety, security and productivity. Such protection and freedom provides an environment of creation, innovation, invention, risks and possible rewards, entrepreneurship and productive output, to provide for the needs, wants and dreams of its citizens.

"No government" is anarchy. "Total government" is tyranny. Somewhere in-between is the best size that does the most good for the most people, that is, truly provides for the common defense and the general welfare. That means the welfare of ALL the people, not just a selected or elected few. "Government" is all government, federal, state and local.

A Politician's View of Effect of Government Size

A professional politician's point of view is insightful, from a Capitol visit to a Colorado State legislator. In 1988, Representative Jim Dyer, Democrat from Durango, Colorado, shared some thoughts having to do with government size and growth in two diagrams. (See Figure No. 38.) He drew two circles to represent an individual, an inner circle "core person," and three quadrants of an outer circle, "areas of influence" on the individual. For both years 1908 and 1988, Dyer said, the inner circle was essentially the same, that is, human beings are basically the same in their core makeup. The outer circle changed a lot in 80 (now 90) years. In 1908, the influence of government was perhaps a ninth of the circle, with the two remaining parts of about equal size, four-ninths each, "family" and "society." The representation for 1988 (and 1998 for that matter) had the same geometry, but "family" and "government" were interchanged, showing the far greater influence of government on the individual compared to the family. Here are his two diagrams:

In Figure No. 39, Representative Dyer showed a spectrum of no government, anarchy, to total government, totalitarianism, on the horizontal scale, with "positive climate" increasing upwards on the vertical scale. Coincidentally, he drew a rising, then falling curve indicating from anarchy, as government grew gradually larger, positive climate got higher, but peaking out in the middle. As government continued to get larger, "positive climate" got smaller until it was back to zero with "total government."

INFLUENCES ON INDIVIDUAL, 1908 TO 1998:

Figure No. 38

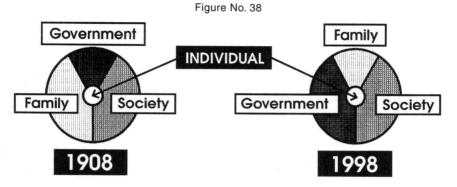

In Figure No. 39, Representative Dyer explained that we seek to maximize "positive climate," and do so based on our individual perceptions of where we are on the curve. Those more liberally inclined who look to government for solutions believe we are on the near side, at "x," so more government can improve society. Those who perceive government already too large, at "y," think reducing government size will improve quality-of-life. Dyer pointed out that both points of view seek to get the curve higher and higher as we go through time. As politicians deliberate to implement political solutions to society's problems, where they are on the curve dictates their judgments and decisions.

MAXIMIZED "POSITIVE CLIMATE" VS. PERCEPTION:

Figure No. 39

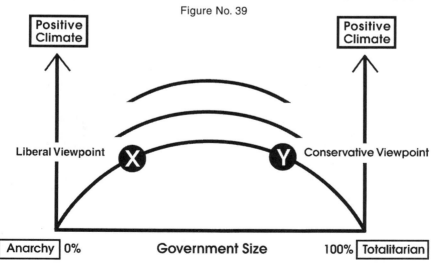

From the Phoenix: Putting Numbers on the Curves

Figure No. 40, going from no government (zero percent GDP) to a certain absolute minimum size of government, more government is better. From that size to a larger size, there is no apparent difference, but merely an exchange of services from the private (business or enterprise) sector to the public (government) sector. Above that value more government does more damage than good.

Zero government is anarchy. At no government, a society would essentially self-destruct and many people, families and communities would be severely hurt or destroyed. From the foregoing we can put numbers on these values.

Growth of government is productive and beneficial from zero to about 10%, the first level of government; that is, *more government is better.*

From that level to a second point, about 17%, it does not make much difference. It is a trade-off whether the public sector (government) or the private sector (enterprise, or business) provides the service.

Above the second value, *more government is worse.* As it grows larger it phases through non-productive to counter-productive to destructive. Over 30% it is too large, and highly questionable it could survive above 42%.

The government target size of 24% was determined by statistical analysis at these more tolerable levels: Inflation down to 1%, unemployment and interest rates down to 4%; and annual productivity

QUALITY-OF-LIFE VS. SIZE OF GOVERNMENT:

Figure No. 40

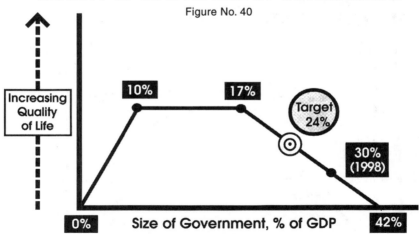

HOW TO GET TO 24%?
THE CITIZEN TWO PERCENT SOLUTION:
HOLD GOVERNMENT GROWTH TO 2%.

and real GDP growth back up to 4%. Even more doable and no less desirable, America has done it before, as recently as the early 1950's.

It is of interest to note here that if government were reduced from 30% to 25% of GDP, it would leave a family of four with over $7,000 more after-tax dollars a year to spend, save or invest.

HOW? GOAL 25-25: The Two Percent Solution
HOLD GOVERNMENT GROWTH TO TWO PERCENT

Our assignment can be stated in three simple words: *Slow government growth!* We do this by implementing "GOAL 25-25: The Two Percent Solution" and carefully controlling the growth of government spending, *all government,* to 2% a year.

It is presently politically impossible to even freeze government growth, much less truly cut the size of government. The American people are stuck with the mindset that more government is better, which if once true, is no longer. About the best we can hope to achieve is to reduce its growth rate enough to allow the growth of the economy to reduce government's relative size. This is considerably different than what has been happening the past half century.

With ever-growing government, we have been on our way to uncertain decline for the past half century. We have a choice and that is to stop or strictly control the growth of government relative to the size of the economy *to get it back in balance.* If we do not, we will lose the Constitutional form of government we enjoy, and with it, our possibilities, potential, freedoms and future.

The destiny of freedom is in our hands. If we do not seize this opportunity and promote rapid and constructive change towards less government, we will never again have for our children and theirs, the freedoms and opportunities that were provided for us.

How will we answer their question, "Where were you and what were you doing while freedom died?"

We now have the gift of understanding the role of government and its proper balance in the American enterprise economy. How will we use it, *Power of ONE?*

Questions for Review

1. How did our national mindset become "more government is better?" Explain, "Size of government is a continuum or spectrum. Up to one point more government is better, to a second point there is no difference, and beyond that point it makes a significant and not positive difference." What are the "points"? What is the "significant difference"?

2. What is "ROGIS?" Why does it make the "Constitutional Imperative" so important? Where are the purposes and mission of the federal government found? Role and functions? Explain the difference between the "general welfare" and the "specific welfare." What are the two defensible reasons for government growth? How much more and for how long were those reasons exceeded? By how much?

3. As time went on from 1950's to the 1980's what happened to government, misery and prosperity? What is the "preferred size" of government? Why? How big a spending cut and/or tax increase are necessary to get there? Explain "The 3% Solution." Why will "The 3% Solution" no longer work? What is "GOAL 25-25: The Two Percent Solution"? What are its effects on government size vs output, tax size of personal income, government spending and debt? Why "Citizen"? By limiting federal spending growth to 2% how long does it take to get to 25% government, 25% taxes and pay off the national debt owned by the public?

4. For what two reasons does "good economics" justify borrowing? Why liquidate the federal debt? How fast did the public debt grow? How much does it cost annually per person? Per worker? How does the exception prove the rule in the 1980's prosperity? What happened in Congress when the "boiling water deficit" of 1985 reached $212 billion? What is "Gramm-Rudman" and how well did it work? Does Congress obey its own laws? Give examples.

5. What 1946 law was combined with Keynesian economics to legitimize and accelerate government growth? Describe government's growth since 1900. Discuss the size and importance of the shift from state-and-local to federal government. Discuss "we have saturated big government to its limits." Why can Keynesian "stimulus of the economy" no longer be effective?

6. Four categories of government spending are defined. What are they and what is included in each? Considering all personal income in America, what level of taxation expressed as a percentage of personal income did you think you were paying? What level did you think you should be paying? What 1996 level was actually spent in each category? What was the total percentage? What is left for the wage earner and taxpayer? Are these tax levels too high or too low? Why?

7. What percent of 1998 median family income was taken in taxes? How was that determined? How has it grown over the years? What is the process called that operates so slowly but ever so surely to increase taxes and size of government? What possible family and societal effects result? How do you explain the evidence?

8. What is Will Durant's "real revolution" and who are the "real revolutionists?" How do such economic studies as these help to know what directions are appropriate and what changes are necessary?

9. What size government has Dr. Milton Friedman's research indicated to be possible and desirable? Explain. What additional backup is there for that view? Explain the "continuum from no government to much government" that evolved. What is the significance of 0, 10, 17, 24, 32? What three words simply state our assignment?

10. How has there become a "far greater influence of government on the individual compared to that of the family?" Discuss two opposing points of view about the role of government to improve quality-of life. What is your philosophy of the "positive climate" approach to size of government? How can we use "the gift of understanding the role of government in the American enterprise economy"? Why isn't it America's *free* enterprise economy"?

The marvel of history is the patience with which men and women submit to burdens unnecessarily laid upon them by their governments.
—William E. Borah

No government can long be secure without a formidable opposition.
—Benjamin Disraeli

The less government we have the better—the fewer laws, and the less confided power. The antidote to this abuse of formal government is the influence of private character, the growth of the individual; the appearance of the principal to supersede the proxy; the appearance of the wise man; of whom the existing government is, it must be owned, but a shabby imitation.

—Ralph Waldo Emerson

Some have said that it is not the business of private men to meddle with government—a bold and dishonest saying, which is fit to come from no mouth but that of a tyrant or a slave. To say that private men have nothing to do with government is to say that private men have nothing to do with their own happiness or misery; that people ought not to concern themselves whether they be naked or clothed, fed or starved, deceived or instructed, protected or destroyed.

—Marcus Portius Cato

A politician thinks of the next election; a statesman of the next generation. A politician looks for the success of his party; a statesman for that of his country. The statesman wishes to steer, while the politician is satisfied to drift.

—James F. Clarke, 19th Century clergyman

The great difference between the real statesman and the pretender is, that the one sees into the future, while the other regards only the present; the one lives by the day, and acts on expediency; the other acts on enduring principles and for immortality.

—Edmund Burke, 18th century historian

In Germany,
The Nazis first came for the communists,
And I didn't speak up because I wasn't a communist.
Then they came for the Jews,
And I didn't speak up because I wasn't a Jew.
Then they came for the trade unionists,
And I didn't speak up because I wasn't a trade unionist.
Then they came for the Catholics,
And I didn't speak up because I was a Protestant.
Then they came for me,
And by that time there was no one left to speak up for me.

—Rev. Martin Niemoeller

Chapter 22

LIFETIME FINANCIAL PLANNING
For Personal Security and Financial Independence

It is natural to want to be "healthy, wealthy and wise." To be personally powerful we must be all three. Twenty-four chapters of this book are devoted to "wise" because it is so important. But equally important are the topics of personal wealth, health, wellness and wholeness. We here extend and strengthen our *Power of ONE* with personal financial power.

The First Rule of Saving: Pay Yourself FIRST!

Pay yourself first. It is the primary, fundamental "secret" to personal security, financial independence and a bright future. We are programmed otherwise and the results prove it. The 1999 personal savings rate as a percent of personal income was 2.4%, the lowest in forty years[1], hitting as high as 10.9% in 1982, averaging 9.1% in the 1980's, and dropping to 5.9% in the 1990's. 1999 was the first year in four decades where Americans slipped into a negative savings rate, spending more than they earned.

We work hard. We get our money—what is left after taxes, deductions and inflation—and we spend it. We seek the good life. We want it all. We want it NOW. When we get it now, we pay for it now, and later, in many ways.

"Pay yourself first!" is the important first rule of lifetime financial planning (LFP).

1.*Economic Report of the President,* February. 2000, p 340

The Day Freedom Dies,
and Working Your Money as Hard as You Work

An *Industry Week* magazine article[2] showed taxes as a percent of wages and salaries were high and rising, hitting 59.3% for 1982, 39.0% federal and 20.3% state-and-local.

Dr. Steven Shwiff, Corporate Economist, worked his economic and statistical magic to determine more about this. He plugged his computer into the Data Resource Institute data banks to go back as far as he could, using the necessary information and methodology. He found that taxes (government) expressed as part of "people earnings" were 45% in 1946, 50% in 1959. By 1982, taxes had grown to 59.3%. Dr. Shwiff said that statistically, it was a perfectly straight line, which theoretically gave perfect predictability. (For math buffs his analysis showed the resultant curve to have a slope of 0.0053875 and intercept, 0.4331.) That seemingly innocuous slope number means taxes and government grew relentlessly one-half percent a year since 1946. By 1998 it[3] had climbed to 66.7%, still growing 0.43% per year from 1982 to 1998.

Here is a flashback of the economic freedom concept: If you earn $100 and keep $100 you are 100% free. If you earn $100 and keep $0, because something or someone takes them away from you, you are 100% slave. By this analysis we were 59% slave in 1982, and in 1998, one-third free, two-third's slave, and getting more so at half percent a year. When the curve reaches 100% is symbolically "the day freedom dies." Beginning January 1, 1946, here is the prediction of the exact day, date and time that freedom dies:

Saturday, March 18, 2051, at 5:49 p.m.

Will those alive then offer the dismal greeting, "Happy Deathday, Freedom?"

This is noteworthy not so much literally, as for two important freedom lessons: 1) Freedom is not free, and 2) Freedom is not forever.

Freedom is not just a matter of life and death. It is much more important than that! Yet we lose our economic freedom to taxes at the rate of a half percent a year.

The analysis brought up several questions. Those who believe in religion and God know of tithing, giving 10% of your income to the work of God. Question: If God only asks 10%, why does government want and take 66%? If government takes that much it leaves only 34% for the person earning the money—not even a 50/50 deal.

2. Dale W. Sommer, "The tax bite approaches 60%," *Industry Week,* 10/3/83, p 61

3. *Economic Report of the President, Feb, 2000*, pp 338, 397, 404.

Question: Why do people continue to work? Answers: 1) People do not know, realize or even suspect how much taxes are plundering the fruits of their labors, and 2) People must work to survive.

Little do people realize, with limited knowledge, understanding and information available, that so much earned wealth inevitably finds its way to government. It happens through the insidious, ubiquitous and over-lapping tax system of sales taxes, property taxes, state and federal income taxes, excise taxes, head taxes and others, plus borrowing, licenses, permits, fines and fees used to control business and finance government!

One other profound bit of wisdom emerges. By this analysis, realize you keep only about one-third of what you earn!

How very important it is then, that you carefully spend, save and invest, that you force your money to work for your best interests. You work hard for it and keep pitifully little of it. Make sure your money works as hard for you as you work for your money.

Your First Assignment and a Greater Assignment

Your *first assignment,* short term, is to manage carefully your shrinking earned income you get to keep, and over which you have some control.

Your *greater assignment,* long term, is to work very hard to reduce the majority that now goes to government; then to assure that what remains with and for government is well spent on legitimate government pursuits, and wisely used for the freedoms and future of America.

Those are big assignments, *Power of ONE,* uniquely suited to your vast capabilities and powers. Let us get to the first assignment.

The Journey to Financial Awareness, Knowledge and Power: Wisely use "What's Left"

We will explore financial approaches to saving ("pay yourself first"), evaluating economic alternatives, "buy-or-wait" decisions, using the 5-function financial calculator, "Bizwhiz," plus broad concepts to make your entire life financially more fruitful, satisfying and secure. We will determine a planned retirement at a level that is adequate and secure.

One cannot be powerful without a powerful financial condition. How to get, keep and assure financial power and security is our quest. It begins with a paying job leading to higher pay and a better job, then working hard and smart, spending and saving, while enjoying life along the way.

Easy Credit, Easy Buying, Expensive Paying, Enriching Bankers

We must own everything NOW, mustn't we? Credit is readily available, easy and convenient—till the bill arrives. Then you discover you have bought a lot of something invisible but expensive called "interest." Payments are made, more purchases charged, increasing the unpaid balance with more interest due on the larger total. This buys a lot of purchases sooner. For that convenience you benefit bankers and enrich savers more disciplined than yourself.

The Short Range Uncontrollable and Controllable

The short range uncontrollable is the tax environment and regulations. They are in place. Do all you can to learn the tax system. The reason? It is your money, you work hard for it and must pay only those taxes you legitimately owe. No one cares more than you about your money. A tax accountant, certified public accountant (CPA) or tax preparer mostly help you record history, after the fact. What is immediately important throughout the tax year is that you base financial decisions on timing and tax consequences to minimize required taxes, before it is all history, that is, before December 31.

The short range controllable is the money you owe. Minimize or eliminate personal debt where possible. We are programmed perhaps 20 or more times each television viewing half-hour to buy, consume, spend, borrow. Get and stay in control. Curb buying impulses that place immense current financial burdens and potential hardship later.

It is most important to establish and maintain credit that is above reproach. Pay bills, especially credit cards, in full, on time. Assure you have adequate credit available to meet financial needs.

There are smart ways and dumb ways to buy. For instance, you can buy on credit card, treat it as cash, and pay it all off when due, with no interest charges. That is smart. You use other people's money (OPM), get the convenience of credit and not carry lots of cash. You pay no interest, while your money earns interest, either in savings or an interest-bearing checking account. Of course you know that those who honor credit cards must get the fees they pay for that service in the prices of their goods and services you buy.

Conversely, using your credit card for unnecessary or unwarranted debt can be dumb, especially with long-term payments with double-digit interest, commonly over 15%.

Delayed borrowing can be smart. By postponing purchase, you "pay yourself first," earn interest, then purchase later with no payments. With available cash you are in financial control, with piece of mind and more secure finances. Outside forces seeking to control you would wish otherwise.

Always being in debt, especially burdensome, excessive debt, disempowers you. When you owe you are not in control. You become in effect, an economic slave. Look around. It happens a lot. Take control of your finances and life and you will be more powerful.

Television Advertising and AIDA:
Not an Opera but a Formula for Sure Sales

American television sets are on over seven hours a day. We practically raise families on television. "Free" television is paid for with generous advertising budgets of large corporations. They make their products and services immensely appealing, so much so, you gladly part with your hard-earned money to buy them. Their secret is the "AIDA" sales formula: Get the buyer's *Attention,* stimulate *Interest* in the product, arouse *Desire* for the product, then direct *Action* that results in sale of the product.

You can think of many commercials with a variety of appeals. All tell their benefits to get you to buy. Enter the heroic product, exit the problem and your money. You can diminish the power of these potent suggestions during commercials by occasionally saying "cancel, cancel," believing you "deprogram" the mighty influence of television advertising on your mind and buying behavior.

Take control. Plan purchases by what you truly need, by what is best for you, not for reasons outside yourself. Your financial present and future are solely and completely your responsibility. Keep purchases and personal debt under control. You have the power of make your life much better by your knowledge, information, decisions and actions. Get in control and stay in control.

Buy Now or Later? Evaluate and Save a Bundle.

It is natural to identify with the advertisements and to wish to respond to them, now or soon. HOW and WHEN you respond can be very good for your finances, or not so good. Evaluate carefully and thoughtfully.

The time value of money is important. Today's money is much more valuable than next year's money, assuming inflation remains reasonably under control. Suppose you invest $1,000 (the "principal") in a financial institution at 5% interest. In a year it has grown to $1,050, having earned $50 interest. If you leave it in savings, both the principal and interest work to earn more interest, compounding your savings. Regular saving, adequate time and compound interest turn into large savings, financial security and personal independence for you. That makes you even more a *TOTAL Power of ONE.*

Regular saving is your "money power multiplier." Make a commitment to yourself to save a set amount on a regular basis such as $100 a month. Because life is unpredictable you may wish to save an additional $100 a month to assure that emergencies or unforeseen events do not interrupt your $100 a month savings program. Plan for both—regular savings and emergencies.

How does a person make a commitment to financial preparation for financial independence and personal security? It is part of life. You can do it if you understand how it works. Look at how it sometimes happens when buying that first new dream car.

You are Worth It, You Dreamer. Buy That New Car!

You have worked your job faithfully over a year, paying off a few bills on the way and taking on some new ones. Your raise is sizable, even after taxes. Your dedication to your job, employer and customers paid off. What next?

You think about buying a new car.

You talk about buying a new car.

You dream about buying "your" new car.

Finding and Buying Your Dream: A New Car

Your present car runs well but you see a convincing advertisement for a new one. With enough dissatisfaction, you might even buy it. You have had a recent offer of $4,000 for your car. You are persuaded to visit a car dealer.

Your new "dream machine" is a candy-apple red, $15,000, Neatcar V6 convertible with a white top. It has everything you ever wanted, style and color, air conditioning, built-in stereo system, automatic transmission and enough power to move out in style.

You resolve to look, not to buy, but sales associate Randall shows you "your" car with a surprise. He offers an unexpected price cut of $1,500. The dealer's inventory is overloaded, he says, because too many cars were shipped to the dealership. When he brags that with only two days left in their sales contest he is in first place, you know there is opportunity to negotiate. There always is.

Price in the American Enterprise Economy?
It's Negotiable!

What is the real price of something? "It's negotiable." Always. The first secret of negotiating is: It's negotiable. Nothing is really set. Before immediately accepting any price offered, determine if it can be bought for less, counter-offer, stall, suggest, pause, explore, all in your favor. They will do the same. Negotiate and save money. It is normal, natural, expected. Negotiate.

You tell salesman Randall you would never consider spending more than $11,000 on a car, not even a "Neatcar" V6 convertible. He says he has already offered you $1,500 off and cannot go lower. After a long pause he allows another $500 off to win the sales contest. You say, "Too high, but I might consider $11,500." Long silence. He excuses himself to go see the sales manager (don't they always?). Back again he relays $12,500 is the lowest the dealership will go. That is their "lowest and best offer."

Thinking deep buying thoughts you look around the sales floor. You call your spouse, your bank, your insurance agent. "What about other cars?" you ask. Then heading towards the door you tell Randall you are really not ready to buy but you will think about it. He says, "Wait a moment. Let me see if there is anything more I can do." He heads for the sales manager's office. Back again he says he is authorized to lower the price to $12,250. You say still too much, but you'd look seriously at $12,000. Randall is about to lose a sale. He thinks about sales points in the sales contest and disappears again. He comes back, willing to give up some of his sales commission to get you to buy the car. At $12,000 he says, "Sold," and so do you.

You have bought a $15,000 car at $3,000 under the original price, proving what? It's negotiable! Selling or trading your old car at $4,000 will leave $8,000 to borrow and finance.

Other financial considerations become important. They include the loan amount, source, and monthly payment, plus interest expense, increased insurance costs, sales taxes, registration and license fees and depreciation. Without knowing all this you bought a car anyway, to learn the financial details afterwards.

Dream Becomes Reality:
Real Life 101, Borrowing and Paying

Borrowing and paying back, "Real Life 101," leads you to your local lending institution. Their new car loan rates are 10 1/2% on a 3-year loan, 11.25% for 4-years and 11.75%, 5-years. To pay it off quickly and save interest you choose the first option.

You can estimate the $8,000 loan yourself. Their quoted 10 1/2% compound interest rate, is roughly about double an easier-to-compute simple interest rate at half, 5 1/4%. Multiply that by 3 (years), then by $8,000. That's $1,260 interest (0.0525 x 3 x 8,000), for a total loan of $9,260, or a monthly payment of about $257 for 36 months.

That's not all. You pay 7% sales tax, $560, on the $8,000. Insurance increases $90 a half year, car licensing, $100 a year. Luckily your limited savings earning 8% cover these $750 additional unplanned up-front costs

Now that it is all done is there a way to determine the total costs of buying this new car? Are there other alternatives? What would have happened if you waited, saved to buy and bought later?

Total Cost including Depreciation: The Invisible Cost

Total three-year, out-of-pocket costs to buy the new car (over keeping the old one) are $10,652 which include $9,252 loan payments ($257/month, 36 months), $560 additional sales tax, $540 more insurance (6 x $90) and $300 additional licensing cost ($100 x 3).

Your first year costs expressed on an average basis are $300 a month. This is the $257 loan payment, added to sales tax ($15.56), license ($12.50) and insurance ($15), expressed monthly. Purchase costs of the new car, not including operation, maintenance or upkeep, are $10 a day for a 30-day business month. That is what you would save by NOT buying the new car.

Most purchased items lose value, that is, depreciate with time. A two or three-year old Neatcar V6 convertible costs thousands less than a new one. As a car gets older, it is worth less money. We can estimate the lower value.

Assume a car depreciates 25% the first year (has 75% value left), then 20% more the next year (80% value left) and each year thereafter. First year new car depreciation of $3,000 ($12,000 x .25), drops car value to $9,000, x 0.8 = $7,200 end of second year, x 0.8 = $5,760 car value, end of third year. Subtracting from the original $12,000 gives total 3-year depreciation of $6,240 (average $173 per month).

Add 3-year, out-of-pocket costs of $10,652 to depreciation's invisible cost ($6,240); total new car purchase cost is $16,892, $469/month, over $15 a day.

Think of that. Every day you DON'T BUY a new car saves you $10 out-of-pocket, over $15 including depreciation. Can it pay to hang onto a car just a little longer?

Three Years Later: Same Song, Second Verse.

Here is what happens at the end of three years, assuming you decide to replace the car with another brand new one. You again negotiate as effectively to buy the brand new model Neatcar V6 convertible at the same price adjusted for three years inflation, 4% a year, $13,498 ($12,000 x 1.04 x 1.04 x 1.04). Your previous car has depreciated to $6,240, requiring a loan of $7,258 for the difference.

You start all over again. You have gained $742 over the $8,000 you borrowed three years before. After paying out all that money, you have made little if any headway to build your financial future. With your additional monthly expense of $300 you have saved very little, even with annual pay increases.

Wait! It was all a bad dream, a dream car and a financial nightmare. Wake up to basic finance to make better decisions. Take better action to control your brighter future.

Waking Up to the Financial Realities of Your Life

In your dream you determined major buying and decision criteria to evaluate the cost of your options. Feeling confident you can afford the car, you also establish you have $300 a month to keep the present car going. That is the *economic criteria* to keep or trade cars.

The *non-economic criteria* is "I don't like the old car," or "I feel the old car is unreliable or unsafe," or "Because I want or I deserve a new car." These are good reasons as long as they are *not* treated as "no-cost decisions" which ignore the financial differences in your life if you decide to buy the new car.

You have only so much money. If $300 a month goes into new car expenses, it is $300 *unavailable for other purchases, savings or investing.* Statisticians call this "mutually exclusive," that is, if you spend the money on one thing, it is no longer available for something else. If you use your money to buy the car, it is gone.

What happens if you decide NOT to buy the car now, but instead, wait and save for a future new car purchase? Deciding so, you set aside $100/ month for repairs, replacement and upkeep necessary to keep the present car operational and safe. You might need a paint job or transmission overhaul. You might want a stereo, sound system or air conditioner installed, "goodies" above and beyond normal maintenance and upkeep for your pleasure to continue to own and operate the car. Now you save the remaining $200 a month towards the purchase of a new car in three years. To evaluate that alternative and make a better financial decision, there is a valuable tool to determine the time value of money, the five-function financial or investment calculator.

The Math Miracle Calculator, Bizwhiz:
A Five-Function Marvel

What long ago required a computer taking up a room, or more recently, a large corner of a small office, is a hand-held financial calculator for under $40 at electronics, office and variety stores. Learn to use this five-function mathematical marvel, the business whiz electronic computing machine we will call "Bizwhiz" for short. Using Bizwhiz for financial calculations, you will find one answer based on three of four inputs of data.

There are five important mathematically-related functions to choose from: present value *pv*, future value *fv*, number of periods *n*, interest *i*, and payment *pmt*. Only four of the five functions are used at one time. Here they are:

1. *Present value,* pv, is the initial value of money, or its value "today."

2. *Future value,* fv, is the later value at the end of a specified time period.

3. *Number of periods,* n, must be consistent with the interest rate value, eg., *3* years at 10%, or 36 months at 0.83% interest. (That's 10%/12 months)

4. *Interest,* i, is usually expressed on a yearly basis, such as 12.7% per year, from a savings or lending financial institution.

5. *Payment,* pmt, must be consistent with number of periods and calculated interest. If the payments are in months, the number of payments n, and interest i, must also be monthly-based.

Current or projected interest rate information can be obtained by contacting a lending institution's financial officers, your bank's loan officer or reading your newspaper business section. Use consistent time periods. For monthly payments, divide the annual loan interest such as 14% by 12 for monthly interest of 1.17%.

Fun With Figures: Putting Bizwhiz to Work

Here are some typical four-function, five-button calculation examples to try:

What will $1,000 invested at 6% be worth at the end of three years? Entering pv = 1,000, i = 6, n = 3, fv calculates to be *$1,191.02*.

What monthly payment would be required to pay back $2,000 in 1 ½ years, with interest at 18%? Enter pv = 2,000, n = 18 (1 ½ x 12), and i = 1.5 (18/12), pmt = *$127.61*.

Suppose at the end of four years you want to have $10,000 to make a down payment on a house. How much money must you put in the bank today at 7% interest? With fv = 10,000, n = 4, i = 7, pv = *$7,628.95*. What regular monthly payment would do the same thing? With fv = 10,000, n = 48 (4 x 12), and i = 0.583 (7/12), pmt = *$181.13/ month*. At what interest rate would that payment produce $11,500? For n = 48 periods, monthly payment, pmt. of $181.14 and future value, fv, of $11,500, i = 1.144%, or *13.72%* per year.

Your "dream car" loan can be done on Bizwhiz. What is the monthly payment on a loan of $8,000, 10.5% interest, 36 months? At monthly i = 0.875%, pv = $8,000, n = 36, pmt = *260,* very close to our previous rough estimate of *$257*.

Finally, you want to know if you can afford to buy a house. You have saved $10,000 for a down payment and can possibly increase from your monthly rent of $550 to a house payment not over $650 a month. Your dream home is listed at $80,000. You can get a loan for $70,000 at 9% fixed rate interest, for a 30-year loan.

The monthly interest rate is 9%/12, or 0.75%. With your $10,000 down payment you need a $70,000 loan. With n = 360, i = 0.75, pv = $70,000, pressing "pmt" gives the answer, a payment of *$563* per month. Seems like you can really afford to buy that new home. But are you financially ready for home ownership?

In phasing from renting to buying a home, your new monthly payment is for principal and interest. That is "PI" but that's not all there is. "PITI" is a real estate term meaning principal, interest, taxes and insurance. These days with property taxes costing hundreds of dollars a year, plus property and liability insurance, total monthly house purchase expenses can be hundreds of dollars more than a simple and misleading comparison between rent and house payments. On the plus side, property taxes and mortgage interest are tax-deductible. Take it all into account.

That is your short course on the five buttons of Bizwhiz. Now, how to use, analyze, decide and act with your new financial knowledge?

A fundamental problem is how to start saving money. Begin early and save regularly. Let it grow both in payments to yourself and return on all you have saved. How does one get started, especially with all the demands on after-tax income?

The Nightmare Becomes a Dream come True By Waiting and Saving

We have already posed a common dilemma: to borrow and buy a new car now, or wait, save and buy later? Comparing savings vs costs helps make informed decisions.

What if you decide *not* to borrow-and-buy, but to wait-and-save? What financial consequences influence a wait-or-buy decision? Assume a combined savings and investment rate of 8% interest (i, 0.67%/month). The previous analysis showed your raise made available an extra $300 a month. What if you allocate $100 a month to keep your old car operational and safe for three years, and save the remaining $200 a month? For the additional $100 a month you can buy new tires and battery, install a CD player, or do major needed repairs or overhaul.

Let's put Bizwhiz to work. Saving $200 a month (pmt) for 3 years (n, 36 months), the new car savings fund grows not to $7,200 (3 x 12 x $200), but to $8,112 (fv). The extra $912 is interest earned and accumulated on each successive $200 monthly payment. During that time you have spent (or made available to spend) $3,600—$100 a month, for upkeep of the older car.

Now calculate the value of the money not withdrawn from your savings but which stayed in the bank and collected compound interest because you delayed purchase of the car. At the end of three years these amount to $1,649.28. The up-front $750 not drawn out of savings for sales taxes, insurance and license fees grows to $953.81 (pv = 750, i = .67, n = 36, fv = *953.81*) earning $203.81 in interest. The next two $100 additional annual payments not spent for license plates grow to $208.00 (pmt = 100, i = 8, n = 2, fv = *$208.00*). The next five $90 semi-annual payments not paid for insurance grow to *$487.47* (pmt = 90, i = 4, n = 5, fv = 487.47).

The combined 3-year savings are $9,761.28 ($8,112 + $1,649.28).

What if you buy a new car at the end of the three years? The old car has depreciated to $2,048. Value retained is 100% - 20%, or 80% a year for three years ($4,000 x .80 = $3,200, end yr 1; x .80 = $2,560, end yr 2; x 0.80 = $2,048, end yr 3 (reducing its market value by $1,952). With inflation the negotiated new car price has risen to $13,498 ($12,000 x 1.04 x 1.04 x 1.04).

The difference in trade-in this time is $11,450 ($13,498 - 2,048). Bizwhiz shows payments of $372 (pv = 11,450, i = 0.875, n = 36, pmt = 372). By waiting the three years with disciplined regular saving, *Power of ONE*, you are $1,690 shy of paying cash for your new car if you want to part with all of your saved money.

Your options are open. You can keep what savings you wish, take out a loan, not buy for another year or two, or buy an older car and all the while continue to make payments to yourself for your future financial well-being. You have choices. You are in control.

Some people spell this P-e-a-c-e—o-f—M-i-n-d . Over a lifetime, you reward yourself with more security in the form of savings, fewer and lower payments and credit costs, and more options because you have more economic freedom. You are a personal "freedom builder!"

This knowledge and these techniques can be used to plan the rest of your life. Few people do this, or even know how to do it. It is relatively simple, not easy but not hard either, with personal discipline and a little bit of luck. You are in control, enjoying life now, and preparing for rich, rewarding future years.

Who needs to Worry about Retirement? No One, with Planning and Preparation!

No one need worry about retirement. The way not to worry about retirement is to PLAN, then ACT for retirement. The earlier and better you plan, the better off you are during your entire lifetime.

One prominent person in my life said there were two things no one told him: 1) He was going to grow old, and 2) He had to prepare for when he quit working, or "retired." Both are obvious, but we rarely think about them. By applying good mathematics, logic and finance, hard work, smart work, planning and discipline, retirement can be the most rewarding time of life, preceded by blest and abundant living.

Two things are always true for the living: 1) You are not getting any younger, and 2) You won't live forever. If there is anything you want to do "someday," get started now. It may be attending trade school, going back to college for a degree or advanced degree, writing a book, taking a trip or starting a business. Perhaps it is getting a better job or living in a new location.

It may be starting early to prepare for a more carefree retirement. How does one go about that?

Retirement and Lifetime Financial Planning

Planning for retirement is one activity people usually start in the middle—the middle of their life. We are essentially on "automatic pilot" in our basic education and first job. We go to school, go to work, graduate, perhaps get married, get a new job, start a family, and begin buying things and paying for them. There is never enough money to buy all we want. The realities of life and basic economics impose necessary, sometimes severe discipline on our finances.

The investment cycle is somewhat like a product curve, first dipping, then slowly accelerating as we grow and mature in our work, from ages 20 to 40. It takes off in a growth phase as our responsibilities as well as earning, spending and savings grow, ages 40 to 60. Beyond 60, the investment cycle levels out then tapers as we spend less to live, and work and earn much less.

While getting through school into the work-a-day world, you give financial planning little thought. You get health insurance for peace-of-mind and protection, and life insurance to begin building an estate. You are quite involved in the pulse beat of accelerating life activity. One day, you celebrate your 30th or 40th birthday and realize time is a-flying, and you ought to be doing some careful long-range planning.

Along the way, you have prepared for financial uncertainty. For one thing, a "go to blazes" fund is essential. That is where you save at least three, even better, six months of emergency, readily-available money should your employer tell you to "go to blazes," or a job doesn't work out and that is what you could tell them. Get your 6-month "cash stash" saved and available, the earlier the better. This is quite important and worth the sacrifice. It is called "personal security" and "peace of mind."

You have learned about buying and making payments, establishing and preserving credit. You are more into saving and investing, better prepared for emergencies such as job lay-offs or medical disabilities. It is difficult to save a lot of money, and you are nervous as to what is "a lot," and uncertain as to what is "too much" and what is "not enough."

Three Money Goals and Lifetime Financial Planning

There are three money goals: How much to make, how much to save and how much to end up with. The first is set by your job. The second leads directly into the third, how much to *accumulate* for later life and retirement, and how well off you will be when you get "there." Setting goals is powerful. Written down, goals are mighty motivators. Monitoring and repeating written goals turns them into reality, to gain more personal control over and success in your life.

One way to set a goal is to earn your age in thousands. If you are 40, earn $40,000 a year. As inflation takes its inevitable toll, use a multiplier such as 1.1 for 10 percent over your age in thousands. The important thing is to set a goal and achieve it. Obviously the more money you make, the more you have to enjoy, spend, save or invest. Money is power and it is powerful.

To plan for retirement you must think about retirement. Consider your present pay and what you think you will need when you retire. When do you want to retire? How will you want it to be?

Consider these factors: your present monthly income, when you want to retire and whether you want to retire making *more, less* or *the same* income in current dollars, unadjusted for inflation. You will not have the same wants, needs, responsibilities, even tax liabilities. (You may not be as active, say in skiing, but you plan to do more local, national, even international travel). What hobbies and activities will you pursue?

You will need one more not too pleasant bit of information. When we say we are doing "whole life planning," when does that end? At death. When will you die? No one knows, but actuarial tables provide a valuable approximation.

Look at the accompanying "Expectation of Life" table[4]. For your current age, race and gender, find your expectation of life, to determine statistical age at death. For example, as a white, 40-year old female, your expectation of life is 41 years. Statistically, you will live to age 81 (40 + 41). A black, 47-year old male's expectation of life is 25.2 years; so actuarially he will live to be 72.2 (47 + 25.2).

Getting Down to LFP Specifics—YOU

Get out your pencil and fill in the following spaces. It may be the best thinking and planning you have done in a long time. Record your "lifetime financial planning" vital statistics, starting with an easy question:

How old are you? Present age, PA: _____ years old.
Present monthly income, PI? $ _____ per month.
Age you plan for retirement, RA?____ years of age.
Projected retirement monthly income, RI? $ _____ per month.
Expectation of life from table, based on age, gender and race,
EL: ____ years.
Add PA to EL to get statistical age at death, DA: ____ years of age.
Calculate years after retirement, YAR (DA - RA) ____ years.
Calculate working years before retirement, YBR (RA - PA)____ years.

This thinking and planning is very important for your LFP. Some examples will show how to determine the appropriate LFP levels of savings.

Lifetime Financial Planning (LFP) for Retirement: Four Examples

Here are four examples of lifetime financial planning (LFP) for retirement, 37-year-old Marilyn Gimer, 48-year-old Flora Nubb,

4. *1998 Statistical Abstract of the United States,* "Expectation of Life and Expected Deaths by Race, Sex and Age: 1995," p 95

EXPECTATION OF LIFE AND EXPECTED DEATHS

AGE IN 1990 (years)	EXPECTATION OF LIFE IN YEARS					EXPECTED DEATHS PER 1,000 ALIVE AT SPECIFIED AGE [1]				
	Total	White Male	White Female	Black Male	Black Female	Total	White Male	White Female	Black Male	Black Female
At birth	75.8	73.4	79.6	65.2	73.9	7.57	6.98	5.55	16.22	13.74
1	75.4	72.9	79.0	65.3	73.9	0.58	0.57	0.44	1.10	0.82
2	74.4	72.0	78.1	64.3	73.0	0.43	0.41	0.33	0.79	0.66
3	73.4	71.0	77.1	63.4	72.0	0.33	0.31	0.26	0.60	0.53
4	72.5	70.0	76.1	62.4	71.0	0.27	0.26	0.21	0.49	0.42
5	71.5	69.1	75.1	61.5	70.1	0.23	0.23	0.18	0.43	0.34
6	70.5	68.1	74.1	60.5	69.1	0.21	0.22	0.16	0.40	0.28
7	69.5	67.1	73.1	59.5	68.1	0.20	0.21	0.15	0.36	0.24
8	68.5	66.1	72.2	58.5	67.1	0.18	0.19	0.14	0.31	0.21
9	67.5	65.1	71.2	57.5	66.1	0.16	0.17	0.13	0.25	0.21
10	66.6	64.1	70.2	56.6	65.2	0.15	0.15	0.12	0.20	0.21
11	65.6	63.1	69.2	55.6	64.2	0.16	0.16	0.13	0.20	0.23
12	64.6	62.1	68.2	54.6	63.2	0.21	0.22	0.16	0.32	0.26
13	63.6	61.2	67.2	53.6	62.2	0.31	0.35	0.21	0.59	0.31
14	62.6	60.2	66.2	52.6	61.2	0.45	0.54	0.28	0.95	0.36
15	61.6	59.2	65.2	51.7	60.2	0.61	0.74	0.35	1.37	0.43
16	60.7	58.3	64.3	50.8	59.3	0.75	0.94	0.42	1.77	0.50
17	59.7	57.3	63.3	49.8	58.3	0.87	1.09	0.47	2.11	0.57
18	58.8	56.4	62.3	48.9	57.3	0.94	1.20	0.48	2.36	0.62
19	57.8	55.4	61.3	48.1	56.4	0.98	1.26	0.47	2.54	0.67
20	56.9	54.5	60.4	47.2	55.4	1.01	1.32	0.45	2.72	0.72
21	55.9	53.6	59.4	46.3	54.4	1.05	1.38	0.44	2.91	0.77
22	55.0	52.7	58.4	45.4	53.5	1.08	1.42	0.43	3.07	0.84
23	54.1	51.7	57.4	44.6	52.5	1.10	1.43	0.44	3.17	0.92
24	53.1	50.8	56.5	43.7	51.6	1.11	1.43	0.46	3.25	1.02
25	52.2	49.9	55.5	42.9	50.6	1.12	1.42	0.48	3.30	1.12
26	51.2	48.9	54.5	42.0	49.7	1.13	1.41	0.50	3.37	1.23
27	50.3	48.0	53.6	41.1	48.7	1.17	1.44	0.53	3.49	1.34
28	49.3	47.1	52.6	40.3	47.8	1.23	1.53	0.56	3.69	1.45
29	48.4	46.2	51.6	39.4	46.9	1.32	1.65	0.60	3.94	1.57
30	47.5	45.2	50.6	38.6	46.0	1.42	1.79	0.64	4.21	1.70
31	46.5	44.3	49.7	37.7	45.0	1.51	1.92	0.68	4.49	1.83
32	45.6	43.4	48.7	36.9	44.1	1.61	2.04	0.73	4.76	1.97
33	44.7	42.5	47.7	36.1	43.2	1.70	2.14	0.79	5.02	2.12
34	43.8	41.6	46.8	35.3	42.3	1.79	2.23	0.85	5.28	2.27
35	42.8	40.7	45.8	34.5	41.4	1.89	2.32	0.92	5.55	2.43
36	41.9	39.8	44.9	33.6	40.5	1.99	2.42	0.99	5.84	2.60
37	41.0	38.8	43.9	32.8	39.6	2.10	2.53	1.06	6.18	2.78
38	40.1	37.9	42.9	32.0	38.7	2.22	2.66	1.13	6.56	2.97
39	39.2	37.0	42.0	31.2	37.8	2.34	2.79	1.20	6.99	3.18
40	38.3	36.1	41.0	30.5	36.9	2.47	2.94	1.28	7.45	3.40
41	37.3	35.3	40.1	29.7	36.1	2.62	3.10	1.37	7.92	3.63
42	36.4	34.4	39.2	28.9	35.2	2.76	3.27	1.47	8.40	3.86
43	35.5	33.5	38.2	28.2	34.3	2.92	3.43	1.59	8.88	4.10
44	34.6	32.6	37.3	27.4	33.5	3.07	3.60	1.72	9.37	4.34
45	33.8	31.7	36.3	26.7	32.6	3.25	3.80	1.87	9.88	4.60
46	32.9	30.8	35.4	25.9	31.7	3.46	4.02	2.04	10.43	4.89
47	32.0	29.9	34.5	25.2	30.9	3.70	4.30	2.24	11.02	5.21
48	31.1	29.1	33.5	24.5	30.1	4.00	4.64	2.47	11.67	5.56
49	30.2	28.2	32.6	23.7	29.2	4.35	5.04	2.75	12.38	5.95
50	29.3	27.3	31.7	23.0	28.4	4.74	5.49	3.05	13.15	6.37
51	28.5	26.5	30.8	22.3	27.6	5.16	5.99	3.39	13.97	6.84
52	27.6	25.6	29.9	21.6	26.8	5.62	6.52	3.75	14.82	7.35
53	26.8	24.8	29.0	21.0	26.0	6.11	7.10	4.12	15.68	7.93
54	25.9	24.0	28.1	20.3	25.2	6.64	7.73	4.52	16.58	8.58
55	25.1	23.2	27.3	19.6	24.4	7.21	8.41	4.96	17.48	9.26
56	24.3	22.4	26.4	19.0	23.6	7.84	9.17	5.44	18.48	9.99
57	23.5	21.6	25.5	18.3	22.8	8.58	10.07	5.99	19.73	10.82
58	22.7	20.8	24.7	17.7	22.1	9.45	11.14	6.62	21.32	11.78
59	21.9	20.0	23.9	17.0	21.3	10.42	12.36	7.33	23.17	12.83
60	21.1	19.3	23.0	16.4	20.6	11.50	13.70	8.11	25.29	14.01
61	20.4	18.5	22.2	15.9	19.9	12.62	15.11	8.93	27.45	15.24
62	19.6	17.8	21.4	15.3	19.2	13.77	16.59	9.79	29.36	16.40
63	18.9	17.1	20.6	14.7	18.5	14.92	18.12	10.67	30.84	17.44
64	18.2	16.4	19.8	14.2	17.8	16.11	19.73	11.59	32.02	18.42
65	17.4	15.7	19.1	13.6	17.1	17.35	21.43	12.57	32.99	19.34
70	14.1	12.5	15.4	11.0	13.9	26.18	32.69	19.52	48.22	29.73
75	11.0	9.7	12.0	8.8	11.1	39.26	49.26	30.73	65.70	41.08
80	8.3	7.2	8.9	6.8	8.4	60.15	75.57	49.53	89.94	59.43
85 and over	6.0	5.2	6.3	5.1	6.2	1,000.0	1,000.0	1,000.0	1,000.0	1,000.0

[1] Based on the proportion of the cohort who are alive at the beginning of an indicated age interval who will die before reaching the end of that interval. For example, out of every 1,000 people alive and exactly 50 years old at the beginning of the period, between 4 and 5 (4.74) will die before reaching their 51st birthdays.

Source: U.S. National Center for Health Statistics, *Vital Statistics of the United States*, annual; and unpublished data.

21-year-old Jack Walden and 35-year-old Tom Bush. Age makes a great difference in using the "confounding of compounding" of money. The longer it works for you and the more there is of it, the greater your savings will grow and be when you retire. The later you wait the harder you save.

LFP Example I: Marilyn Gimer

Take the case of Marilyn Gimer, a real "miracle worker." She was a housewife and mother the first part of her adult life; rejoined the workforce, learned much, worked hard, and did well. She began as a secretary and worked her way up to corporate manager of adult education and training.

At age 37, she performs her LFP for retirement with this information: How old? _37_. At what age do you want to retire? _64_. What is your present salary? _$3,000 per month_. At what monthly income do you wish to retire? _$2,500 per month_. What is your "Expectation of Life" according to the table? _43.9 years_. What is your actuarially-predicted age at death? _80.9 years old_.

Marilyn has no savings. After investigating the safety of her company's savings and investment plan she decides that is how she will prepare for retirement. She wants to know how much to save; specifically, what percentage level of her pay she should save. Her company's policy through the employee benefit program will match her savings for the first 2% and they will allow her to save up to 10%. What is best for Marilyn? It is possible not only to determine what is best, but with Marilyn's working and retirement criteria, determine what is *required* as well?

We begin at retirement age. If Marilyn retires at 64 and lives to be 81, she must have the necessary retirement savings to fund $2,500 a month for 17 years. Back to Bizwhiz, we arrive at the "nest egg" that must be available the day she retires. Assume her savings will earn 7% annual interest after taxes. Marilyn will receive a payment of $2,500 a month for 204 months. With 7% interest, 0.58% a month, she will need to begin retirement with $298,558. Bizwhiz was programmed: i = .58, n = 204, pmt = 2500, pv = *298,558*. Note pv is used because it is the "today value," present value, on hand at day one of retirement. The day Marilyn retires, the "present value" of her savings must be $298,558.

The first half of the mystery is "how much must be there to sustain Marilyn in her retirement?" Know also this assumes the money that remains during the retirement years continues to work for Marilyn each month, earning 0.58% a month ($1,783 interest the first month). But the remainder of the $2,500 will reduce the balance remaining every month, finally reaching zero at the end of the 81st year.

The second half of the mystery is "what must Marilyn do starting today?" She must set up a regular savings program that assures her of having the necessary $298,558 ("future value") when she retires. Starting at age 37 to retire at 64, Marilyn will have 27 years to save in 324 monthly payments to her savings. Knowing she must end up with $298,558 and receiving the same earned interest of 0.58% (7% a year), Marilyn calculates her savings requirement to be $314/ month, which is 10.5% of her monthly salary. Here is how you get the answer with Bizwhiz: i = 0.58, n = 324, fv = 298,558, pmt = *314*, which is 10.5% of Marilyn's monthly pay of $3000.

With her company savings plan matching her first two percent, she can either reduce the amount saved to 8.5% for as long as she has her job, or save the calculated amount as a cushion but round to 10% in line with the plan upper limit.

Marilyn was lucky she started to save early. This enabled her to use the "magic of compounding" to help make her money grow. Suppose she were 44 years of age at the beginning of her program. With the same expectation of life, she'd have 20 years to save (240 payments). Her monthly savings requirement would jump to *$576* a month, 19.2% of her monthly income, a much greater burden, and 9.2% above her employer's savings plan limit. If she were 50 with 14 years to save (168 payments), she would have to put away *$1,055* a month, a near-impossible 35% savings rate.

Start early, get regular and stay reliable to make saving easier and less burdensome. Pay yourself first.

LFP Example II: Flora Nubb

What if you already have savings? That can reduce the load. Young grandmother Flora Nubb is 48 when she does her lifetime financial planning analysis. She is a department manager making $4,000 a month and wishes to retire at 62, bringing in $3,000 a month. She has already saved $110,000 invested at 6% a year. How much should she save in dollars, and what percent of earnings?

Flora learns from the "Expectation of Life" table, actuarially she has 33 more years to live, to age 81. She will live 19 years after retirement, requiring 228 monthly payments of $3,000. Her retirement savings on the day she retires must be $407,563. For Bizwhiz, i = .5, pmt = 3000, n = 228, pv = *407,563*.

Before Flora can determine her savings requirement she must estimate the value of her already existing savings value upon retirement. Her $110,000 earning 6% for 14 years will be worth $254,268 at retirement. For Bizwhiz, pv = 110,000, i = .5, n = 168, fv = *254,268*. That is $254,268 Flora will not have to save from current monthly income, reducing those needs to the difference, $153,295 (407,563 - 254,268). Her "pay yourself first" habit is paying off.

To save $153,295 will take monthly savings of $584 (i = .5, n = 168, fv = 153,295, pmt = *584),* 14.6% of monthly pay. Obviously that is more than the employer's savings program allows, requiring savings outside her company, perhaps even a different strategy.

What difference does it make WHEN one decides to retire? Suppose "Granny Flo" decides to retire later at age 65. That changes everything. She will need less money on which to retire and have longer to save for it. Her existing savings will have three more years to earn interest and compound it. Here is how it works out:

Flora will plan on 16 years of retirement at $3,000 a month. Total savings required at retirement drop to $369,714 (i = .5, n = 192, pmt = 3,000, pv = *369,714).* Her existing savings of $110,000 will grow to $304,277 (pv = 110,000, i = .5, n = 204, fv = *304,277),* Flora will have to save the difference with a future value of $65,437 in 17 years. That will require a monthly savings of $185 (i = .5, fv = 65,437, n = 204, pmt = *185),* 4.6% of her pay.

Working longer increases the length of time she has to save and decreases the amount of time she has to plan for. This greatly reduces the amount of savings required, $185/4.6%, instead of $584/14.6% in this example.

Looking at it another way, if you wish to retire earlier you will have to start earlier, to save more faster, and give up some present consumption to do so.

LFP Example III: Jack Walden

Starting early with modest aspirations makes saving almost painless. Jack Walden, a frugal, basic, 21-year-old college graduate starts his career out of college at $2,000 a month with no savings. He plans to retire at age 60 with a retirement of $2,500 a month.

Jack's expectation of life, male, age 21, is 53.6 years, actuarial age at death, 75. He will work and save 39 years and be retired for 15 years. At retirement he will need to have in savings $296,259 (i = .5, pmt = 2,500, n = 180, pv = *296,259).* To accumulate that amount, Jack will begin saving at $159 a month (i = .5, fv = 270,351, n = 468, pmt = *159),* or 7.95%.

LFP Example IV: Tom Bush

Tom Bush performs his LFP at age 35. Working on construction, his work year and income fluctuate unlike regular salaried or non-seasonal workers. Tom checks his last three tax forms to find his average annual pay was $42,000, working nine to ten months a year. He wants to retire at 62 with $3,000 a month. Though Tom has no savings he believes he can earn 8% interest in his new program. Tom's expectation of life for a black male is 34.5 years to age 70. Because of his irregular work periods his Lifetime Financial Plan is done on a yearly basis. He will need to have available $206,879 (n = 8, pmt = 36,000 (12 x 3,000), i =

8, pv = *206,879)*. So he must save $2,368 (n = 27; i = 8; fv = 206,879; pmt = *2,368)* a year, or 5.6% of average annual income, hence, of each paycheck. Because of his varied and less predictable work schedule, added to personal on-the job risk and hard physical labor in the elements, Tom may want to increase savings somewhat for added peace of mind.

LFP Example V: YOU
Real Life Financial Planning for a Power of ONE

Once again record your "lifetime financial planning" vital statistics. In light of the preceding four examples consider carefully and write down your answers to these questions:

Present age, PA: _____ years old. Planned age at retirement, RA? _____ years old.
Present income, PI? $ _____ /month.
Planned retirement income, RI? $_____/month.
Expectation of life from table, EL:_____ years.
Statistical age at death, PA + EL = AD:_____ years of age.
Years after retirement, YAR (AD - RA) _____ years.
Working years before retirement, YBR (RA - PA)_____ years.

Question 1: How much money will you need? (YAR, in months) n =_____, i (monthly) = _____, pmt RI =_____, pv = _____. (Use consistent units!)

Question 2: What is the retirement value of your current savings? Savings value at retirement: pv = $_____ , n (months) = _____, i (monthly) =_____, fv = $_____. Subtracted from Question 1, pv = _____ = final fv.

Question 3: How much to save? (YBR, months) n =_____, i (monthly) = _____, final fv = $_____, pmt PI =_____; divide by present income, PI = _____% of present income.

That is your new monthly Lifetime Financial Plan savings goal and percentage saving rate. That wasn't so hard, was it?

The Unknowns: Inflation, Interest and Social Security; Percentage, not Dollar Savings

We have simplified this analysis to leave out what we do not know. We do know there will be inflation, but not how much. We do not know what interest rates will be, nor effects on interest of taxes and inflation. We do not know what taxes will do, but suspect they will increase.

The main gain from this analysis is the LFP retirement perspective for long range planning, and the earliest possible start of regular savings— right now. The analysis provides knowledge of how much money you will need and what percentage of savings are required.

Do whatever you must to reach and maintain your savings goal. For instance if it calculates to 7.5% per month and you have never saved anything, start small but start. Begin at a half percent (or even a dollar a week, but begin), increasing it by a half percent every several months to finally reach, say, 8% or 9% to make up for the slow start. Put part or most of every raise into savings, to gradually work up to your desired savings level.

There is an implicit assumption that your pay will progress at a rate at least equal to inflation. If it does and you continue to save at the same rate, you will have taken inflation into account. If it is your guess you are not keeping up with inflation, save at a slightly higher rate.

In times of high inflation, interest rates are higher, during stable periods, lower. Use what information you have, what you know and what you think will be. The values used as examples serve only to demonstrate the technique, but are *not* projections of future interest rates. Part of your LFP is to find the highest safe return possible for your savings and investments consistent with the risk involved.

What about Social Security? There is no trust fund, per se. It is a pay-as-you-go system, and the government uses excess revenues to shore up and hide government deficits or indicate surpluses with their all-inclusive budget. Since the Social Security system is subject to political folly and economic foibles, it is even more dangerous to predict outcomes years, even decades in the future. So it is not taken into account for these analyses. If you think you will get it, lower your savings rate.

The other consideration is how much buying power will future Social Security dollars possess? We do not know. We can't find out. Make your own guess.

There are other variables to consider on how and where to save in many books, courses and newsletters about such topics. Research them carefully and continually. A trip to the library is here in order.

Learn your own risk characteristics, timid or bold, conservative or opportunistic, risk-averse or risk-seeking. Usually the more stable and solid an investment, the lower the rate of return; the higher the risk, the higher the opportunity and rate of return. There is no "sure thing."

Do not make the mistake of thinking there is anyone who cares more about investing your hard-earned money and preserving your precious life savings than you. No matter how you manage your savings and investments, *hold yourself completely responsible* for their safety, return, liquidity and availability.

Targets to Shoot At

Decide your own earning, savings and investing levels. If you have taken the time, incurred the expense and made the effort to get advanced or continuing education you can rightly expect to be compensated more than those who do not. There are no guarantees but education "ups the odds." You pick the work you do, the place you work, the people with whom you work. All of these influence your potential success and income.

Hold yourself totally accountable for how you manage your work, your career and personal life and your money. That puts you in control. You decide how hard you work, whether you take courses, which ones and to what end. Since those decisions require your time, money, energy and sacrifice, know what you expect as a return and what you are willing to do for the potential rewards.

Another important topic is the "delusion of affluence." Suppose you are 45 years old and have $120,000 saved and a house nearly paid for. That seems like a lot of money and a comfortable situation, but is it? In an absolute sense it would seem that way, especially if it took you some 20 or 25 years to accumulate it. Does it mean you can quit saving? No. In a relative sense, you are only part way there. It is a part of a bigger picture of working, earning, saving, investing and living. These savings are only the *beginning* of your retirement. Both you and your savings must work hard to provide you with your perfect retirement at that perfect future right time.

A popular bank series of television commercials showed money required for various situations. It included $232,000 to raise a child, and $45,000 for a college education. That's out-of-pocket expense, not including the "opportunity cost," perhaps $20,000/year *not earned*, while the student attends college for a total college cost over $120,000. A more recent study[5] showed the middle class cost to raise a child through age 21 with four years of college and foregone wages was $1,455,581, which includes $996,567 on foregone wages for one parent not to work to raise the child.

Finally the first ad showed a retired couple in San Francisco in their motor home followed by their estimated lump sum required for retirement, $415,000. They were among those few fortunate, but very smart people, who did their Lifetime Financial Planning for their retirement. Are you that smart?

Do not let a seemingly big number fool you. It is big, perhaps, compared to nothing, or to the little with which you started, but it is quite small compared to how much it must be. On the way, it is security and an emergency fund for unanticipated problems or situations such as loss of a job, personal tragedy, family or medical emergency. Such a savings cushion from personal discipline provides P-e-a-c-e—o-f—M-i-n-d. What is that worth to you? Only you know, but it is probably substantial.

5. "The Real Cost of Raising Kids," by Phillip J. Longman, *U. S. News & World Report,* March 30, 1998, pp 50-58

A Net Worth Statement, Cash Flow, and a Budget

Personal financial planning is worth a professional approach to a demanding and sometimes complex topic. You are in control. You get the information. You make the decisions. But knowing where you are, where you are going and how to get there can be very powerful.

Find, read, then study, internalize and *use* one or several books on managing personal finances, financial or estate planning. Perhaps you will want to find and employ a professional financial planner, one who works with you to sort out your finances and circumstance, asks the tough questions and teaches you how to get in control of your financial present and future.

With tax considerations getting ever more complex and costly, knowledge plus timely guidance help you keep more of your hard-earned money. Know and use the big difference between an income tax specialist to fill out tax forms, and a tax advisor to plan tax strategy. The first helps you record the past; the second helps shape the future. You can change the course of the future but the past is permanent, especially concerning tax policy.

Set aside a regular time to review and assess where you are financially. Choose your birthday or New Year's Day, a half-hour a week or hour a month to help target your financial situation in time to create, build, or improve it. Know your net worth, income, outgo, spending plan or budget. These are rewarding ways in which to spend your financial control time.

A personal net worth statement is a worthwhile place to start. Get the appropriate forms, advice and help from a bank or other lending institution. They routinely have customers fill out net worth statements for both persons and businesses as basic documents upon which to assess and make loans. The net worth statement records on one sheet all you own and all you owe. For instance, in the left-hand column you record the total value of your assets—house and car(s), clothes, furniture, collections, cash values of life insurance policies, cash, savings and investments. In the right column you record your liabilities—house mortgage and car payments owed, credit card balance and all other debt obligations you have incurred. The difference is your Net Worth.

It is possible, even likely, early in life to have a negative net worth, that is, to owe more than your total assets. As time goes by you earn more, save some and incur less expense. Your net worth goes positive, grows and accelerates. Net worth is an instant photo, a snapshot in time of where you are financially. Figure out where you want to be, financially, then prepare a budget to get you there.

A budget is a cash flow document of money-in, money-out. View your own cash activity in the recent past to learn exactly how you are spending your money, how much you earn and from what sources. A month's worth of information is a good start, recording money received for one or several jobs, income from interest, dividends, rentals or other sources, and money out for house and car payments, food, clothing, transportation, utilities, insurance, recreation, education, etc. Add up both and find the difference. Hopefully, as much comes in as goes out.

Turn your cash flow into a budget, a future spending plan, and hold yourself to it. "Pay yourself first" starts here. Decide as above how much and where to save, make a deposit to a savings account even before you write one check to pay one bill. Make other payments according to your payout plan, or budget. Then work hard to control your expenditures, improve your income, increase your net worth, to where your discipline and financial control put you in control of your life. Your LFP works and makes you a continuing financial success!

Life is a Journey, Not a Destination.
So is Success and Financial Management

Life is a journey, not a destination. So is Lifetime Financial Planning. You will find happiness not so much in being there, but in going there and getting there. But what if when you get "there," there is no "there" there? Remember, you reap your rewards along the way, not somewhere near the end.

Get your financial affairs in order. You are almost "there," becoming an even more powerful *TOTAL Power of ONE in America.*

Questions for Review

1. What is the first rule of saving? Why is it so important? What percent of wages and salaries do taxes take? What is the "economic freedom concept?" What is the "Day Freedom Dies?" How do we know that? What two important lessons about freedom come from this? With so much of earnings going to taxes why do people work?

2. What percent of your income do you keep after taxes? What is your "first assignment"? Your "greater assignment"? What does "wisely use the remainder" mean? How can a person be powerful with weak finances?

3. What is the short range "uncontrollable"? Short range "controllable"? Why are they important? How are we programmed to buy and consume? Why is it important to "curb buying impulses"? What is a smart way and a dumb way to use other people's money (OPM)? Discuss "when you owe you are not in control." What is the AIDA sales formula? What is it designed to do?

4. What does "time value of money" mean? Which is more valuable, money today or a year from today? Why? What is it called to invest both principal and interest? Why is regular saving a "money power multiplier?" What three things turn savings into "large savings."

5. Describe how upon receiving a raise, you might decide to shop for and buy a car.

6. What is the powerful word that can save lots of money and make price and terms variable, not fixed? What phrase describes "the real price of something"? Describe how bargaining lowers price.

7. What other house- and car-buying financial considerations are applicable and important? How are they significant, sometimes unexpected? What is depreciation? Describe how it affects car value/price. Describe the difference between uneconomic and economic criteria to buy. Does it make any difference if you buy now or wait? Describe the alternatives of buying immediately or waiting and saving? What all must be done? Determining you could pay off a new car, describe what could be done with the money by not buying now.

8. Name and describe the five financial functions of Bizwhiz, the business investment calculator. Explain how to use three to get an answer. What would the monthly house payment be for a loan of $60,000, interest 12%, 30-year, fixed rate loan? How much interest is paid? Would PITI make the payment bigger or smaller? What is PITI? Describe by example how to use Bizwhiz to determine amounts saved by paying yourself first on a regular basis.

9. When is the best time to plan for retirement? Why? What two things in life are always true for those living? What is "lifetime financial planning" (LFP) and how does it work? Name three personal monetary goals. How can you use your age, planned age of retirement and projected age of death, to determine accurately and objectively how much to save, in dollars and percent?

10. What is the "delusion of affluence?" Regarding the economic facts of life, how much does it cost to raise a child? Go to college? Be "set" for retirement? What is net worth, cash flow, budgeting, spending plan? Why should you know tax requirements even though you have professionals fill out your return?

Our plans miscarry because they have no aim. When a man does not know what harbor he is making for, no wind is the right wind. —Seneca

We must ask where we are and whither we are tending. —Abraham Lincoln

Nothing is more terrible than activity without insight.   —Thomas Carlyle

Money is a terrible master but an excellent servant.   —P. T. Barnum

Annual income twenty pounds, annual expenditure nineteen nineteen six, result happiness. Annual income twenty pounds, annual expenditure twenty pounds ought and six, result misery.   —Charles Dickens

Chapter 23

THE TRIANGLE + APPROACH TO PERSONAL WELLNESS
Diet, Exercise, Relaxation, Plus!

Physical fitness is not only one of the most important keys to a healthy body, it is the basis of dynamic and creative intellectual activity. The relationship between the soundness of the body and the activities of mind is subtle and complex. Much is not yet understood. But we do know what the Greeks knew: That intelligence and skill can only function at the peak of their capacity when the body is healthy and strong; that hardy spirits and tough minds usually inhabit sound bodies. —President John F. Kennedy

Magic Formula for Personal Wellness: Tough Mind. Sound Body. Hardy Spirit.

Our "intelligence and skill" can only function at peak capacity "when the BODY is healthy and strong;" when "HARDY SPIRITS and TOUGH MINDS usually inhabit SOUND BODIES." There is a magic formula for success. To be personally powerful we must be physically, mentally and emotionally powerful.

LIVING Each Day of Life
with Knowledge, Discipline, Action, Repose

Three clichés are profound in their impact on developing one's life power:

"May you live all the days of your life."
"If I knew I'd live this long, I'd have taken better care of myself!"
"Start early and avoid the rush!"

All this adds up to *"Start NOW!"*

Personal Wellness can be developed and maintained with knowledge, information and disciplined action, plus repose. These essential components are summed up in the Triangle+ of Fitness: Exercise, Diet and Relaxation, Plus.

Fitness: A Body, Mind and Spirit Built to "Take It"

Fitness is not just physical. It is mental, emotional and spiritual as well. Fitness has to do with toughness, stamina, durability—the condition of being "in shape for life."

There is no one best answer. It is natural to look for *THE Answer.* Some find it jogging or bicycling, some in a grapefruit or cheese-and-egg diet. Others find it in aerobic dancing, yoga, hiking, tennis, massage, or in a sauna or hot tub.

More extreme and considerably less desirable are the use of harmful substances which affect emotions and behavior—mood-altering drugs and pills—some legal, some not. Some seek *THE Answer* in a bottle, in the form of alcohol, or in wisps of smoke, inhaling tobacco smoke, or the taste and stimulation of chewing tobacco. Avoid illegal mind- or mood-altering drugs, dope, whether "uppers" or "downers," smoked, snorted, inhaled or injected. Drugs are NOT *THE Answer* to anything.

THE Answer turns out in fact to be many things in combinations, some changing over time. We deal with one universal fact. We get older every day. When that happens other things happen also. We *deteriorate* or *rejuvenate* depending on the beliefs, values, knowledge and lifestyle we have adopted *on purpose, by accident* or *through neglect.*

Don't Take Life for Granted. What's a "TAB"?

A handicapped person offered a wholly different perspective on life. Interviewed on public radio, she explained to the interviewer how people react differently towards another's state of physical being. She described a nerve condition she has. Sometimes she can walk normal and upright, other times she is on crutches, and sometimes she is confined to a wheelchair. She told of an experience while in a normal state of walking. She met a young man who asked her for a date, which she accepted.

When he came to meet her she was in her wheelchair. He took one look at the wheelchair, turned around and left.

"The TAB just couldn't take it," she said. "TABs treat the handicapped differently."

"TAB, What's a TAB?" the interviewer asked.

She answered, "Temporarily Able-Bodied."

I realized then how very much we take for granted. We have our health and life, our faculties and capabilities, our very being. We think it is normal, natural, owed to us, that we are whole, complete and operational. All systems are "go." We had better think again. Life is transitory. Our whole existence may be "temporarily able-bodied." We are all TABs who had better appreciate what we have, all we have, how temporary it might be and what we can accomplish. We will more faithfully care for our precious gifts of health, fitness, wellness, and wholeness.

Know the Uncontrollables. Control the Controllables

A number of factors have to do with how long we live and how well we live, some controllable, some uncontrollable.

The *non-controllable factors* are who we are, including our age, sex, heredity, background and race.

More *controllable factors* are how we are, what we do and how we do it: diet, exercise, blood pressure awareness, smoking and body weight.

The more we learn, know and work on the controllable factors, the better chance we have for a fuller, better, more powerful and healthy life—mentally, physically, emotionally, spiritually.

Routine behavior, diet, exercise, relaxation, work and activities can be helpful or harmful. As with most other things, knowledge, understanding, up-to-date information, application, action and discipline help us make the most of our lives on planet Earth.

The "Triangle+ of Fitness" makes it as easy as one-two-three, in the forms of diet, exercise and relaxation, plus the "plus." Fitness added to related criteria helps achieve overall personal "high-level wellness" which we seek in becoming a TOTAL *Power of ONE.*

Fitness is overall toughness. You are in shape for life. Your body handles demands placed on it because you are in good physical shape. You have a regular regimented exercise program. You pay attention to what you allow to enter into your body: food, liquids, medications and drugs, even how you breathe.

Diet, Nutrition, Eating Habits and Uncommon Sense

Diet is common sense, learning, remembering, applying and living what you have known most of your life about food, nutrition and eating habits. Eat regular, modest meals with variety and balance. When you know and use all this it makes uncommon sense.

Include the basic four food groups: *meat,* fish, fowl, meats and beans, for protein; *fruits and vegetables* for fiber, vitamins and minerals; *grains,* breads, cereals, pasta, rice, for starches and carbohydrates; and *dairy products,* milk and milk products, low fat, for calcium, vitamins and vital nutrients. Go heavier on the carbohydrates, fruits and vegetables, lighter on sugars and fats.

Think more in terms of *nutrition,* the content and properties of the food, than strictly of *diet,* how much, what, when and how often to eat.

We can "get mathematical" to better understand properties of food, especially how we can easily become overweight, and just as easily, lose and control weight. Mother Nature wanted a way for us to store energy efficiently, so she invented fat which stores energy most compactly at 9 calories per gram, over twice that of protein and carbohydrates (including starches and sugars) with 4 calories per gram. Alcohol, in between, has 7 calories per gram.

In her interesting, useful and readable book Jane Brody[1] makes weight loss and weight control straightforward and logical. In the human body a pound of fat amounts to 3500 calories. If you take in 3500 extra calories you do not burn or eliminate, you gain one pound of fat to store that energy. It may not sound important, but over time it can have major consequences.

Suppose each day you consume only 120 calories more than you metabolize. That is two slices of bread, five ounces of milk, eight ounces of soft drink or beer, or just over one tablespoon of butter. Each month you will gain one pound, 12 pounds a year, 60 pounds in five years. It works just the opposite too. You can lose the same amount by consuming 120 calories *less* a day, or by burning it off with exercise.

How much food energy do you need? It depends on your age, sex, weight and level of activity. Just to stay alive requires a certain amount of energy, called your Base Metabolic Rate. To barely exist, the average adult male at 155 pounds needs 1600 calories a day; average adult female at 128 pounds, 1400. Greater physical activity requires more calories.

On a daily basis, if you are relatively inactive, you need only 12 calories per pound of body weight to sustain your body weight. If you are lightly active, you need 15 calories, moderately active, 20, and very active, perhaps 25 calories per pound. We are all different but predictable.

Cholesterol and Fat:
Full, Long Life; or Early, Unpredictable Death?

Increasingly, evidence accumulated over the years shows the detrimental effects of excess cholesterol and fat in the diet. Cholesterol is absolutely necessary for a healthy life. In the body the liver

---

1. *Jane Brody's Nutrition Book* by Jane E. Brody, W. W. Norton and Co, Inc: 1981

manufactures sufficient quantities of cholesterol. However, excessive intake of cholesterol and fat, along with high calories, elevates cholesterol levels in the blood.

Blood tests can routinely indicate cholesterol levels. "What is your cholesterol number?" is a popular question. Know the answer. Over 200 may indicate a need to discuss diet and exercise with your doctor. A high reading makes more important the levels of triglycerides, high density lipo-proteins (HDL) and low density lipo-proteins (LDL). HDL are "good" in that they contain or even reduce serum cholesterol levels; LDL, just the opposite. Their ratio is used as an indicator for heart health.

Medical studies show that over long periods of time, cholesterol and fat can accumulate in the veins and arteries, restricting the flow of essential, life-giving blood. If the blood flow is severely restricted or completely blocked off, serious damage, even death, can result.

Narrowing or blockage of the heart arteries results in both oxygen and nutrients starvation, and literal death of heart muscle. The blockage is called a *myocardial infarction.* It results in death of part of the heart muscle, *coronary thrombosis,* a "heart attack." If extensive enough or in a critical area of the heart, it is fatal. It is obviously important to take care of blood vessels, vital life fluid conduits, especially those serving the heart.

Heart Attack First Symptom: Death

Following a heart attack, a doctor told a friend, "You were lucky. In about half of all heart attacks, the first symptom is death."

Early on it is important to establish healthy living and eating habits to minimize these risks. Now is a good time to start.

In another part of the body, the brain, artery blockage risk takes a different form—stroke. With high blood pressure—*hypertension,* and hardening of the arteries (arteriosclerosis), the risk of having a stroke increases.

Stroke happens most commonly when a part of the brain is restricted or starved for oxygen and nutrients (ischemia) caused by hardening of the arteries and fat build-up. Another cause of a stroke occurs when a blood vessel bursts in the brain, resulting in cerebral hemorrhage. The third, vascular stroke, is caused by small clots, *emboli,* formed in the heart or other parts of the body, breaking away and traveling to the brain.

Strokes have diverse effects depending upon which part of the brain is affected. Strokes can result in partial or extensive paralysis, inability to speak, blindness, loss of memory or mental abilities.

Restrictions or blockages of blood flow to the extremities, arms and legs, can result in possible gangrene and partial amputations.

These potentially dangerous problems of the arterial system/heart/ lung/brain/muscles are related to long term excessive fat intake and build-up, resulting in restricted or clogged arteries. It is possible and desirable early on to get more calories for life from non-fatty foods and less from fatty foods. In the average American diet, it is normal to get 35% to 40% of calories from fats. Recognize fat intake as a controllable and reduce calories from fat to no more than 25% to 30% of your diet, or less. That provides a net long term positive effect, deterring vascular-related diseases in later life. Consider the importance of these powerful concepts.

High Blood Pressure, Hypertension: "The Silent Killer," Detectable, Treatable

The "silent killer," high blood pressure, or *hypertension,* affects over 20% of the population. One doctor said no other physical condition presents so many problems, is so puzzling, and so potentially dangerous. It is related to a variety of afflictions including strokes. Untreated high blood pressure is like a bomb with a long slow fuse. Yet it is detectable and readily treatable, another good reason for an annual visit with your doctor for a health check-up and discussion.

Blood pressure is expressed in two numbers, one over the other. The first measures the pressure within the arteries while the heart is pumping, *systolic,* over the pressure while the heart is resting, *diastolic.*

"Normal" is 120 over 80, systolic over diastolic.

Of some 65 million Americans with high blood pressure (about one in four people), almost half do not know they have it, therefore, do not treat it. Untreated, hypertension leads to deadly health complications— heart attack, stroke and kidney disease. For example, a 35-year-old man with average health and normal blood pressure 120/80 can expect to live to age 76. With high blood pressure of 150/100, his predicted life span drops to age 60.

The good news is that high blood pressure can be detected with no pain and little inconvenience. The pressure cuff and *sphygmomanometer* have become so commonplace they are even found in supermarkets. You can get at least an indication of your blood pressure while you shop!

Treatment for hypertension consists not surprisingly, of what we discuss here: reducing and controlling weight, restricting daily sodium (salt) intake, regular exercise, limiting alcoholic beverage intake, eating foods low in unsaturated fat, moderate intake of caffeine and reducing stress. In addition medications are prescribed to help control and contain this disease.

Know what high blood pressure is, what it does, and how important and simple it is to measure. Know yours. Keep it right. You will live longer and be healthier.

A Practical, Information-Based Approach to Weight Control: Read the Label!

Read labels carefully as you become more aware and sensitive to the importance of daily fat intake, both the amount and type. "Cholesterol-free" does not mean a food item is acceptable. It must also be low in fat, and have little or none of the "bad fats"—coconut, palm and palm kernel oils, highly saturated vegetable shortening, or chocolate. These are essentially cholesterol-free, but very "fatty." Just the opposite are shellfish—shrimp, crab and lobster, which are high in cholesterol but low in saturated fat.

In a day an individual may consume around 30 teaspoonfuls of fat, equivalent to eating 1 1/4 sticks of *margarine.* That is as much as getting 44% of your total caloric intake as fats. This should be reduced to half that amount, no more than 15 teaspoonfuls per day, still a lot of fat.

Especially *consider fast foods.* A popular "triple cheeseburger" with french fries has 19 teaspoons of fat; a small burger, 3; cheeseburger, 4; french fries, 3; and the bigger burgers with cheese, 10. The deep fat-fried fish sandwiches have 5 teaspoonsful while fried chicken ranges from 1 to 5 teaspoons per piece.

Knowing that intake of both cholesterol and fats, especially saturated fats, should be restricted, where do you start? Start at the label!

Learn the fat content of various foods and limit fat intake by reading labels. Then select foods with lower fat content and "de-select" foods that are less desirable.

When I first began reading labels carefully one of my favorite soups was cream of chicken with mushroom. Reading that label almost shocked me. One serving had 26 grams of fat in it. I compared it to cream of celery, cream of potato, tomato and vegetable soups that were around 3 to 5 grams per serving.

I learned to read the label even more carefully, because of the words "per serving." A serving turned out to be half the contents of the can, meaning the fat content was lots higher, double in fact the number on the label! That is when I realized how much fat I unknowingly consumed in some fairly common foods I liked and ate. What fat content do you think a can of chili has per serving? Per can? How to find out? Read the label! You will be surprised.

Your body can turn fat, protein and carbohydrates almost interchangeably into whatever it needs, except for "essential amino acids" which come mainly from meat. You can manipulate your taste preferences or change food availability to foods that are better for you, rather than worse. Knowledge and understanding updated with pertinent information, then action, help you live a more complete, fulfilling, and long life.

Heart: Pump of Life

Ever wonder how your heart works? It has four chambers, two inlets, two pumps, two valves and two outlets. The inlets collect blood. Powerful heart muscles pump the blood. Valves direct blood flow, then outlets distribute the blood flow and pressure. But wherefrom, whereto?

The right side of your heart, the *right atrium,* collects spent blood from the body, then forces (pumps) it through the one-way *tricuspid valve* into the *right ventricle.* When full, the right ventricle contracts (pumps) to force spent blood into and circulating throughout the lungs. There, blood releases carbon dioxide and waste gases, and picks up oxygen.

The oxygen-enriched blood is collected by the *left atrium,* then forced (pumped) through the one-way *mitral valve* into the left ventricle. From there it is pumped via the *aorta* into the body and circulated to all the organs and tissues "for life," to return back to the heart. The trip takes a minute or two depending on your state of activity.

Blood: Liquid of Life

Blood is a complex liquid that literally brings life to the body—feeds, repairs, strengthens, protects and maintains it. About half the blood consists of cells, the other half is a fluid called plasma. White cells protect against foreign substances and infection, part of your immune system. Red cells exchange gases, transporting oxygen to the body and removing exhaust carbon dioxide. In the plasma are lipoproteins which help transport the major fats of the blood—cholesterol, triglycerides, cholesterol esters and phospholipids, all important to life, but in excess, potentially dangerous.

Blood is distributed by the heart to the body, heart first 5%, head 15%, chest 3%, liver and accessory circulation 30%, kidneys 25% and limbs 22%. These vary considerably based on body activity. Blood is diverted from the internal organs to the muscles and extremities in times of intense physical exertion such as running, and, if frightened or under stress, the "fight or flight" survival response is activated.

The heart can pump the body's 6 to 8 liters of blood at up to 28 liters per minute in a high-performance runner, or at five liters a minute while at rest. Depending on the heart's condition and exercise level it can pump as high as 150 ml per stroke, about double that pumped at rest. Normally the blood returns to the heart still about 70% oxygenated. Additional capacity is available by releasing more oxygen to active tissues and returning to the right atrium with only 25% oxygen.

Between rest and high activity, the heart combines higher blood volumes pumped with more oxygen released to give over a 15 times difference in oxygen-supplying capability. What a magnificent, capable, versatile "pump of life!"

Two other fascinating parts of this miracle are the fleshy mitral and tricuspid valves that withstand continuous pounding and pressure for a lifetime, in most cases. Beating 70 times a minute for 70 years pounds heart valves 2 and 1/2 billion times! Some of our best artificial heart valve materials wear or pit in just three or four years.

What a body! What a system! What a heart! It is worth understanding, appreciating and caring for this marvelous, muscular, miracle "machine."

Arteries and Veins: Conduits of Life

It is important to emphasize the influence the amount of cholesterol, fats and calories have on the interior condition of the veins and arteries. Continuing high fat intake can deteriorate the arterial system's ability to smoothly and efficiently circulate blood to vital parts—heart, brain and kidneys, to the detriment of your well being. Choose, shape and control well your lifestyle of diet, nutrition and eating habits. Care for these blood conduits to bolster their good health and yours.

Losing and Controlling Weight the Smart, Easy Way: Diet and Exercise

Weight loss and weight control depend in part on your knowledge of foods, eating habits and diet, and discipline of what, how often and how much you eat. The other part is metabolism, *burning off the calories*, with work, activity and exercise. Together, diet and exercise control not only your weight, but level of fitness and overall wellness as well.

By developing an appropriate, custom-designed regimen of diet and exercise, you need never be concerned about overweight and worry little or not at all about a heart attack. You will have done all you can do, and worry will hurt, not help.

First learn and prepare, then *monitor* what you eat, how much and how often. That begins with *control* of cholesterol, fat and caloric intake, which determine how much excess turns into body fat. Then *exercise* to condition your whole system, and burn off whatever is needed to lose or control weight. Get where you want to be, weightwise, then stay there.

The secret to weight loss is moderation. You need lose no more than a pound of fat a week. It is gradual, possible and safe, amounting to a net difference of 3500 calories, 500 calories a day. Reduce weight partly with less food, or more correctly, less calories, say, by avoiding a pat of butter, soft drink or dessert every day. Feel full though, by eating instead, fresh fruits and vegetables, more fiber, less fat, salt and sugar. Drink adequate liquids—some recommend 6 to 8 cups of water a day.

CHART METHOD OF WEIGHT LOSS AND CONTROL

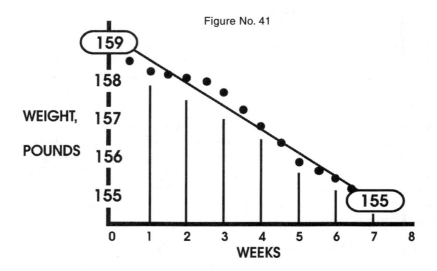

Figure No. 41

Fat Fighter Tool: Make a Chart

A simple way to monitor, measure and motivate weight loss is with a chart. As an example, suppose you wish to lose four pounds in seven weeks. Make a horizontal line with 8 major week lines, one inch apart for Sundays, and 7 minor in-between lines on the half inch, for Wednesdays. On the vertical, show 5 pounds a half-inch apart. You weigh 159 pounds and are committed to be 155 pounds. Show one mark from the top as "159" and four marks lower as "155." Circle those two weights on the first and last weeks, respectively, with a line drawn from one to the other.

Weigh and plot the weight on the chart the same time of day each Sunday and Wednesday, say upon getting up, or right after a bath or shower. You will get a sense of how well you are losing weight, whether you must exercise harder and eat lighter, or can indulge a few extra calories while maintaining your activities. Monitoring your goal helps inspire you to achieve that goal.

Diet is one part of weight control. The other half is activity—work and exercise.

Health, Fitness, Performance and Exercise

Health is a flourishing condition, overall physical well-being; freedom from disease and/or debilitating physical problems; the condition of being sound in body, mind and spirit. Fitness is the capability to do what you have to do and to do more if needed, with no serious after-effects.

Performance is how well and how much you can do. Exercise is physical activity, usually carefully formulated, organized and accomplished, and integrated routinely into your life style.

Health is improved by well-balanced living, work, diet, activity, exercise, relaxation, and control of stress. High level fitness is gained and maintained with regular and proper exercise. The key word in all of this is BALANCE. Do it all, but none too much. "Moderation in all things," to which you may want to add, "including moderation."

Work is what we do for a living. The nature of work can make you feel tired, even exhausted, doing a repetitive job eight or more hours a day. The danger here is to assume you have received sufficient physical stimulation or demand just because you feel tired. A barber, dentist or hair stylist stand long hours on their feet. Feeling tired they go home and rest. Yet they are probably more in need of aerobic exercise than others with more physically demanding work.

Before starting any fitness or exercise program schedule a physical examination and discuss your personal fitness and exercise program plans with your doctor. That will give you a good starting point, something important to discuss and work on together, and the knowledge that you are in shape to get and stay in super shape.

Measured Aerobic Exercise: Getting Back to the Heart of It All

Heart-rated fitness has become a simple but powerful formula for creating a personal exercise and fitness program. Three good books in their explanation and application are helpful. They are:

- *Total Fitness in 30 Minutes a Week,* by Lawrence E. Morehouse, Ph.D., and Leonard Gross, Simon and Schuster, New York, 1975.

- *The Official YMCA Physical Fitness Handbook,* by Clayton R. Myers, Popular Library, New York, 1975.

- *Aerobics* by Dr. Kenneth Cooper, Bantam Books, New York, 1976, and Cooper's follow-on books

Continually seek more enlightening knowledge and helpful information updates. Look for the latest.

These books, and more recent advances and studies have made exercise much more a science than art. It is measurable, safe, predictable and suitable to individual custom design. Overall you can make personal wellness a lifetime assignment providing lifetime benefits.

Aerobic exercise has evolved to a balanced, measurable and beneficial approach to personal wellness. Some exercises that are not aerobic, including weightlifting, isometrics (pitting one set of muscles statically against an opposing set of muscles) and sprinting.

Aerobic exercise steadily supplies elevated amounts of oxygen to exercising muscles over a prolonged period of time after suitable warm up and preparation. Aerobics is a rhythmic, repetitive, dynamic activity which can be continued for two or more minutes without huffing and puffing afterwards.

Examples of aerobic activity are walking, jogging, running, bicycling, swimming, cross-country skiing, handball and the like, where many and large muscles are regularly and continuously exercised. Warm-up includes slow, then increasing activity, stretching and enhanced breathing.

The Pulsebeat of Life: Aerobics Barometer

Is there a way to measure all the factors that go into exercise—type, duration, frequency and intensity? Is there a simple way to know that what you are doing is what you ought to be doing? Yes there is. Check your pulse rate. In any given state of activity your pulse indicates the sum total physical stress on your system. The static or resting pulse rate is a fundamental indicator of your basic level of fitness.

For instance, in the morning, before or just after you get up, but before you eat breakfast or drink coffee, measure and record your resting heart rate by taking your pulse. Do so by placing one hand palm up, laying the other wrist in it palm up, and gently curling the three fingers of the lower hand on the outside wrist artery to feel the pulse. Pulse rate is the number of heartbeats per minute. Count it for 10 seconds and multiply by six (or 15 seconds, multiply by four; or with very rapid pulse rates, for 6 seconds and multiply by 10).

For example you count 13 beats in 10 seconds measured with a sweep second hand or digital watch. Thirteen times six is 78, your resting pulse rate.

Not for self-diagnosis but for a preliminary physical conditioning indicator, from 50 to 60 show excellent physical fitness; 60 to 70, good fitness; 70 to 80, fair fitness; higher, poor fitness. These guidelines are slightly higher for women; that is, for women, 55 to 65, excellent, etc.

Pulse-Rated Fitness

Exercise physiologists have described a simple, self-applicable method to determine physical fitness criteria. Called "pulse-rated fitness" it begins with basic characteristics of the heart itself. The maximum pumping capability of the heart is described by the simple formula of subtracting one's age from 220. For example, if you are 40 years old, your heart's maximum estimated pumping rate is 220 - 40, or 180 beats per minute.

It has also been found that because of characteristics of the blood and heart, essentially the same efficiency is available at 80% to 90% of that rate. Knowing all this helps you custom-design exercise criteria based on your age and condition. Here are some approaches suggested by exercise physiologists.

The "target zone" concept establishes boundaries to begin an exercise program and to limit it. One says to start at 70% of maximal heart rate and work up to 85%. A more moderate approach suggests 60% and 75%, respectively.

Another method is based on maximal and resting heart rates, aiming for 60% of their difference. Suppose our 40-year-old had a resting heart rate of 75. His target exercise heart rate increase would be 180 (220 - 40), less 75, or 105, times 60%, 63. That, added to the resting heart rate of 75 establishes a target exercise heart rate of 138.

Since moderation is important, another approach to the "target zone" concept at 60% to 75% gives us another place to start. The starting point is 60% of 180, or 108. We wish to build up over time to the top of the target zone, 75%, or 135. Both techniques are usable and close. This one, however, gives a beginning target, 108, and a program target, 135. We gain guidance and understanding through custom-designing and monitoring our own program.

Start slow, moderate and smart, in partnership with your doctor.

Set Up Your Personalized
Physical Fitness Exercise Program

"Instant Fitness" can be accomplished by vowing here and now, instantly, to gain and maintain personal, lifetime, physical fitness. Set aside your fitness time, every other morning, evening, whenever is best for you, a special 20 or 30-minute period suitable to your personal lifestyle. Make it as routine as brushing your teeth, and be as devoted to it as you are to eating or sleeping. Should you have to give up either, it is probably still a valuable trade-off.

You will consider *frequency*, *duration, type* and *intensity* of exercise. Frequency is first because you must make time in your schedule and life to accomplish your purpose.

Frequency. Beneficial results are more assured by at least three times a week. More than five show no additional gains but take valuable time. Say your work and life schedule indicate Monday, Wednesday and Friday mornings, 5:30 to 6:00 am are best for you. You may feel that a four-day routine, Monday, Tuesday, Friday and Saturday, is better. This is the first consideration and decision you must make.

Duration. Why 30 minutes? Initially, you will use the time more for information and learning, gradually easing more into exercise. When you are in the half-hour exercise mode, you will warm up and stretch 5 minutes, exercise 20 minutes and cool down for 5 minutes. At first, spend more of your time learning about exercise, reading books and articles about your body, its activity and stimulation, condition and performance.

Type. Only you know what type of exercise is best for you. If you prefer being alone you might want to jog early in the morning. If you enjoy social as well as physical stimulation, aerobic dancing, group walking or weight lifting would be worth considering. There are also bicycling, swimming and skipping rope. If performed *regularly,* some sports, handball, racquetball, even tennis, may be right for you.

If you consider something like bowling or golf, think again. They are not "aerobic"; that is, they are not "rhythmic, repetitive, dynamic," continuing motions performed over a prolonged period of time after suitable warm-up and preparation. One doctor said to obtain any aerobic benefit from golf one would have to run full out carrying the caddy on your shoulders between holes.

Intensity. Recent studies have debunked the "no pain, no gain" philosophy which says you have to hurt and be miserable to get any good out of exercise. Lighter, more moderate activity is better. If you are in doubt start out walking regularly, slow, deliberately, then speeding up over time. Initially you can map out a course on flat ground, then include some hills to climb as you become better conditioned. As you become more fit, you can lengthen your course, or phase into jogging or running, depending on your goals and personal preferences.

One of the better aerobic activities is skipping rope. It is easily measured by a count of skips, easily timed, and can be done indoors with homemade or inexpensive purchased equipment. It also helps develop balance and build coordination. It is better than walking alone because in addition to upper and lower leg motions, it involves the hands and arms, hence, one's chest, shoulders, back and stomach.

If you have the luxury of a handy swimming pool, swimming is very effective since it involves so many large muscle groups working hard together in the resistance and support of the water.

All of these—walking, jogging, running, rope skipping, bicycling and swimming—have additional advantages. They coordinate arms, legs and other muscles to give you more grace and confidence. They are good for your mind as well, helping flush out waste products that can slow down your thought processes. Some studies even show exercise increases mental creativity, along with increased energy, stamina and endurance.

Another popular form of exercise is weightlifting where you start with light weights, low repetitions and sets of repetitions and work up to heavier, more demanding efforts. Then, cross-training, probably the best of both worlds, is to combine aerobic, "cardio" exercise with weight training.

Starting, Getting Going, Keeping Going

You have decided to get fit. You are going to exercise using heart-rated aerobic fitness concepts and pulse-rated fitness criteria. First, how do you feel? Are you in reasonably good overall condition? Do you have any physical drawbacks, reservations or questions? This may be a good time and reason for a thorough physical examination and relevant conversation with your doctor.

Get proper equipment needed for the exercise and program you select. For instance if you choose walking, get lightweight, properly cushioned, good-fitting walking shoes. Do not buy the cheapest shoes at the biggest sale. This is not a good place to save money. Your preventive personal fitness program will likely save money on illnesses you don't have, doctor visits you don't make and medications you don't buy.

Fitness is an investment in life so spend prudently what you have to spend to do this most important job right. Besides when you so spend your hard-earned money, to get your money's worth, you use what you buy. That accomplishes your goal to become "fit for life."

Dress appropriately for your exercise. Sit still for a moment, relax, physically and mentally let go. Take your resting pulse rate before major activity. Do necessary fitness-related reading to give breadth, understanding and direction to what you are doing. Get mentally as well as physically ready for your new life program. Determine to stick to it.

Warm-ups help keep you from getting stiff and sore, sometimes from actually hurting yourself. Do stretching exercises, slow running in place or calisthenics you have found helpful in the past. You are your own coach. Limber up the direct muscles affected such as your calves and thighs, as well as waist, back, chest, arms, shoulders and neck.

Start simple, where you are, how you are, with what you have. If you normally walk during the course of work, you may decide to add to it. To incorporate your additional walking into your schedule you get up at 5:30 am instead of your usual 6:00. Begin a regular, three- or four-day-a week program starting Monday morning. Walk around the block first, then extend that to several or many blocks, amounting to several miles.

Keep records, simply pen and paper, giving the date, starting pulse rate, ending pulse rate, period of concentrated exercise and type of exercise, plus any relevant notes:

9/23/99 78 110 22.5 min. "flat walking" 1.6 miles, felt really good!

You will find over time the same exercise results in lower pulse rates. Your heart becomes better conditioned and more efficient. You must work harder to approach your upper target pulse rate. In this example, walk faster, even farther. Include some hills or carry a back pack with some weight in it. Do what you have to do to place more exercise stress on your developing system. Over a period of 3 to 6 months get your exercise pulse rate to the top of your selected target zone.

Know you have made a personal commitment and it is a good one. "Once begun, half is done." When considered a routine part of life, rather than a strange extra-activity, you can do it and keep on doing it. You are building for life in a way you control and that makes a positive difference. Isn't that what being a *TOTAL Power of ONE is* really all about?

The Third Dimension of the Triangle of Fitness: Relaxation

Working hard is important. "Resting hard" is equally important. Your physical fitness program equips you to better handle stress, mental and emotional as well as physical. You are tougher and more resilient. As important as is all this toughness, so too is gentleness and quiet. Conquer the quiet as well. It places you even more in control, makes you more capable of handling stress and adversity.

Relaxation can be consciously induced. Find a quiet comfortable place free of interruptions. Sit or lie placidly, motionless. Direct the thoughts of your mind to the condition of your body. You can "think-talk" your body into being very calm and relaxed:

> From the tip of my toes to the top of my head I'm becoming more and more relaxed. I'm very relaxed, free from the cares of the day. My toes are very relaxed. They hang limp and lifeless, connected to my deeply resting ankles, legs and knees. All are quiet, relaxed. My thighs and hips lay quietly, solemnly. My stomach and abdomen let go and are limp. My chest and neck relax, feeling like water flowing over a flat rock. It's very calm, deeply calm, very relaxed. My neck and head let go and flow into my pillow. My throat, tongue and scalp, even my eyes are very relaxed. To the top of my head I am deeply resting, peaceful, flowing, quiet. I think thoughts of quiet places, a gently waving field of grain, tall slender trees bobbing back and forth in a gentle breeze, small waves lapping the shore of a quiet deserted beach. I am deeply relaxed, rested, quiet, peaceful.

After doing this several times, a strong mental suggestion can more quickly duplicate the entire sequence. Key-in a trigger phrase. In the relaxed state say, "I can instantly relax as much as I am now by lying down quietly and saying to myself, 'Relax, Relaxed.' I repeat it and mean it. I become even more relaxed adding the words, 'Deeper, deeper.'" Confirm, validate, and emphasize with "I am very, very relaxed. It is so. I am relaxed."

Such a relaxing exercise done once or twice a day can be as beneficial as your personalized fitness program. During especially trying, tense times, you have developed a tool to dissipate tension and produce instead, a constructive, creative frame of mind and being.

The idea and techniques of self-communication are now possible. Once deeply relaxed you can tell yourself whatever you feel necessary to help accomplish goals, realize dreams and ambitions, develop a vision. Reinforce positive thoughts and eliminate or de-emphasize negative attitudes. Get rid of old habits. Acquire and program new ones. Tell yourself what you need to hear to be what you want to be. You are in an open-minded, reflective, suggestible state called "alpha" where your brain waves have slowed down to between 8 and 13 cycles per second. You can learn better and faster, so use this alpha state to program your mind for success, peace and happiness.

The idea of transcendental meditation is another method to eliminate destructive tension and stress. Rather than paying large sums to receive a special code word, a *mantra*, you can select your own word to get into the desired quiet state. The meditative state differs from the above suggestible state in that it is passive, rather than active. You think of nothing, or only one thing, rather than of many things. A popular code word is "Om." Another is, not surprisingly but appropriately, ONE. Here, in the meditative state, you use ONE to get the power. It can symbolize a higher being, a higher, better or even best idea, or be merely a focal point of a meaningless tool to help think about little or nothing. In this reflective, meditative state, metabolism is reduced, blood pressure drops and physical and mental quiet result. Proponents recommend this meditative, reflective state twice a day, 20 minutes each. Once a day, or as designated by you, may be more suitable.

These are tools to help with your overall personal wellness. Pick and choose what fills your needs, now and in the future.

The "Final Dimension" of the Triangle of Fitness: *PLUS*

Personal wellness is enhanced but not guaranteed only with diet, exercise and relaxation. They are tools, but are limited, helping mostly with the dimensions of the physical, mental and emotional. Going beyond those gets you to the holistic and the spiritual.

Developing the holistic side of life is the PLUS dimension, the "extra added attraction" that makes it all so much more powerful and real, more meaningful and effective.

Here are a number of related thoughts, suggestions and approaches to round it out and make it fit. It is a synergism where the whole is much more than the sum of the parts because of their additive interaction.

Our world today places much emphasis on consumption and importance on satisfaction, especially instant gratification. Do not be afraid to sacrifice or delay. Don't avoid being "uncomfortable." Know "if it feels good, do it" is often not right. Our base nature requires a sensibility and personal discipline that makes it almost always right to be a bit uncomfortable and suspicious if you are too comfortable, or things feel too good.

Getting involved with drugs or addicted to toxic substances is injurious; chemical abuse or alcohol dependency is undesirable and unnecessary. You can, should and must say "NO!" You do not have to smoke or chew tobacco, take drugs, use steroids, or snort, smoke, eat, inject or inhale any harmful substance. If you do not ever start, you do not suffer lifelong damage, you don't get hooked, you do not have to experience withdrawal, you don't have to quit. Better, just don't start.

Through it all you remain a fully functioning, responsible, responsive, exemplary, beautiful person, a fully-equipped, totally committed, complete human being, stretching to be all you can be, serve all you can serve, achieve all you can accomplish, become all you can become.

Smoking. Don't smoke. Do not start. If you smoke, quit.

Alcohol. Drinking alcohol to excess is not a requirement. If you choose to drink do so in moderation. Don't drink and drive a car. Get professional help if drinking disrupts, controls or adversely affects your life, family, job and relationships.

Drugs. Don't do drugs. Don't sniff, snort, smoke, or inject foreign and dangerous substances into your body. Steer clear of drugs. Do not take uppers, downers, mellowers or hallucinators. Leave alone marijuana, cocaine and crack, angel dust, PCP, LSD, heroin and other such harmful substances, old, new or brought back.

Legal prescription drugs may be as dangerous as, or even more dangerous than illegal drugs. If they are too much perceived as "safe" they too can be abused.

Learn to face and deal with reality. Sometimes we are stronger together. Communicate needs and problems better with those in your support system and be a helpful and accessible part of theirs. Peer pressure is strong, especially in teenagers and impressionable young adults. Start early to "program" them for the inevitable temptations, to say "no" gracefully but firmly and never start. If a road must be taken, make it the high road. Rather than follow others, show them how to act.

Entertainer Sammy Davis, Jr., told of how he was encouraged to kick the drug habit by his friend, singer and actor, Frank Sinatra. He said Sinatra talked to him about his drug and alcohol problems like a son[2]:

> "Look," Frank said, "God put you here for a lot of reasons that you and I don't even know about. He gave you a talent, and you're abusing it. And I'm watching my friend go down the tubes. I loved you when you were nothing. I'll love you when you go back to

2. Dotson Rader, "My Second Chance," *Parade.* 9/24/89, p 6

being nothing. But you're cheating yourself, and you're cheating the people. . . . Stop it! Stop whatever it is you're doing, because it's taking the edge off you and taking that brilliance away from you. You're cheating yourself. You're cheating your friends, and you're cheating your public!"

Drugs dumb you down and numb you up. They keep you from being all you can be, from doing all you can do. You know what a miracle you are and what a precious gift life is. Care for both of these blessings and do not let either be interfered with by drugs or other toxic chemicals. You can control and must prevent such invasions of your mind, body and spirit.

Don't start drugs. Don't do drugs. If you're into drugs, get out.

AIDS. Acquired Immuno Deficiency Syndrome (AIDS) has shocked an unshockable society. AIDS is communicable and terminal. According to Dr. C. Everett Koop, then-United States Surgeon General, AIDS can be spread by having sex—oral, anal or vaginal—with someone who is infected with the AIDS virus. A blood disease, it is also spread by sharing infected drug needles. Much like its predecessors—gonorrhea, syphilis, herpes and other venereal diseases—AIDS is spread through promiscuous sexual behavior as well as by sharing drug-related paraphernalia. AIDS can be prevented by abstaining from sex, having sex with one mutually-faithful, uninfected partner and by not injecting drugs.

Back. Love your back. A sore, aching back is one of the costliest, most painful yet common maladies of us humans. It is easy to take for granted till it is too late, to use and abuse your back, then lose use of your back. Take a "Love Your Back" course at a local health clinic or hospital. Learn how to sit, stand, twist and lift, to preserve this marvelous yet delicate mechanism. One personal note from a "bad-back author"— me—is to get Dr. John Sarno's book, *Healing Back Pain*, Warner Books: 1991, read it, apply it, believe it, live it. It works.

Seat belts. When you drive or ride in a car wear your seatbelt. It is one cheap and simple insurance for a longer, more productive life. Tell your mind you do it because it puts you more in control of your car and life.

Basics. Develop a strong life faith by studying history, philosophy, religions and the great thinkers. Read, study, and know the basics, including the *Bible, Torah* or other books of faith, to learn and apply great spiritual and human truths. Read America's freedom documents.

Make continued learning a lifelong pursuit. Know how much easier, more effective, efficient and available knowledge is. Buy, listen and learn from cassette tapes, of the great thinkers of history and writers of our time. Gain information, inspiration and great ideas learning while you drive and in quiet moments of your day. Learn more to earn more to enjoy life more, to give back more to life. Get to know, love, care for and serve people and relationships. That is what life is really all about.

I saw a thought-provoking bumper sticker that said, "What if the hokey-pokey *is* what it's all about?" No, it's a lot more and can be dealt with, with focus.

Prioritize. Take a few moments from time to time to look at what your life is like. What are you doing? Why are you doing it? Is there something else you should or could be doing? Is there a good reason not to be doing something else? Consult your inner self to see what you really want from life. What can you give to life? What can you become by life?

Whatever it is, know you have all the resources and capabilities to do it or be it or become it. Apart from the "clutter of your life," what is the "essence of your life," the purpose of your existence, the single thing that if you were to die tomorrow, you would want to come of your life? A personal mission statement is often helpful in determining priorities and activities. The urgent and important are always in conflict.

Realize life is never complete and you will never finish all you would like get done. Pick and choose that thing that is the most important to you. Then go for it. Get it started. Get it done!

Two more books by one author are well worth mentioning, getting, reading and applying. One is *The 7 Habits of Highly Effective People* by Stephen Covey, 1989, Simon & Schuster, and *First Things First*, by Covey, A. Roger Merrill and Rebecca R. Merrill, 1994, Simon & Schuster.

With your thorough knowledge of business, economic, and political systems, ideas worth knowing, truth, character, and the like, combined with a *personal wellness* brought on by your own desire and action to be the best you can be, you will be a more powerful, more TOTAL *Power of ONE* who will make a profound difference for all the world to see, benefit by, and enjoy.

Questions for Review

1. Discuss "physical fitness is not only an important key to health but the basis of dynamic and creative intellectual activity." What is fitness? What is personal wellness and what are its three parts?

2. Why is there no "one best answer" to becoming physically fit? Explain "We deteriorate or rejuvenate depending on our beliefs, values, knowledge and life style, adopted on purpose or by accident." What is a "TAB?" How is it possible we are all "TABs?" What are the uncontrollables of fitness? The controllables?

3. What does diet include? How can one "get mathematical" about food, diet and nutrition? What are caloric values per gram of fat, protein, carbohydrates, starches and alcohol? How can a small daily imbalance in caloric intake result in major weight changes over time? What percentage of American caloric intake commonly

comes from fats? What is a better target level? How does one get to that level?

4. Why is knowledge of both fat and cholesterol content of foods important? What three vegetable fats are particularly to be avoided? What vital body system is affected by fat accumulation? What health problems can result? What is a myocardial infarction? A coronary thrombosis? What happens to a heart starved for oxygen or nutrients? In about half of all heart attacks what is the first symptom? Explain how the human heart works.

5. What is a stroke and what are three main types? How can potentially dangerous arterial system problems affect the kidneys? What is the "silent killer?" What is a sphygmomanometer? Does it hurt to use? What is "systolic" and "diastolic?" How common is hypertension? What is blood? What do fat and cholesterol have to do with veins and arteries?

6. How can one use diet and exercise to lose and control weight the smart, easy way? How can reading food labels help? How many food calories equal a pound of fat? To lose one pound a week how many calories a day must one restrict or burn up?

7. Explain "pulse-rated, aerobic fitness." What exercises are "aerobic"? Why? How does one use pulse as a meter to monitor body response to activity? Explain how to set up a custom-designed aerobic fitness program. What is a "target zone" and how is it used? How should you include your doctor in your new life fitness plans? Name the four characteristics of exercise. What is "cross-training"?

8. Why is "resting hard"—relaxing—as important as working hard? Describe how to consciously and effectively relax. How can you "key-in a trigger phrase" to make relaxing effortless and fast? Contrast relaxing with alpha mind state and meditative modes. What is the brain wave frequency of alpha?

9. Personal wellness goes beyond the physical, mental and emotional to the holistic and spiritual. Explain. Why do physical and material things frequently disappoint even when indulged to an extreme? What are specific "danger activities and substances" and how should they be handled? What relationship do the following have to each other: the back, seatbelts, smoking, AIDS, drugs, alcohol?

10. How does one "develop a strong life faith?" Why is it important to make continued learning a lifelong pursuit? How can you use not only books but audiotapes and videotapes to gain information, inspiration and great ideas? What is "what life's really all about?"

Contrast the "clutter of your life" with the "essence of your life."
Why is it important to "prioritize?"

This life, therefore, is not righteousness, but growth in righteousness; not health, but healing; not being, but becoming; not rest, but exercise. We are not yet what we shall be, but we are growing toward it.

—Martin Luther

Chapter 24

MULTIPLY YOUR POWER OF ONE TO THE POWER OF ONE MORE

This is a valuable POWER CHAPTER. It brings together what you have learned, to make happen what you will accomplish. True power comes from people, through people and from beyond people. We know one person can make a difference—an enormous difference. But when we involve others we *multiply,* not proportionally, but geometrically, or as a mathematician would put it, exponentially.

If one person convinces four people to support a point of view it becomes 16 times more powerful than a singular *Power of ONE,* because of their personal contacts, influence and interactions. Convincing ten people multiplies the power 100 times.

For example we have set up a new information/organization/action website called SuperCitizen.com with the action formula "2 hours, 2 days, 2 more." That means you make a commitment to communicate the message to your email list within two hours, take whatever action within two days and invite at least two more people to the website every day. How powerful is all this? If each email list has 10 people who keep the commitment to communicate within two hours, in half a day over one million people get the message! That is power.

The important question is how to convince one more, then many more? The important answer is we change the world one person at a time. We begin with one more.

The *Power of ONE is* the power to make a difference. But the power does not end with you. It STARTS with you.

You have gone through a metamorphosis, a transformation, a total and lasting change, *Power of ONE.* You will never be the same. You know how very important you are. You know what you can do. You know how to do it. You know how very important it is to get it done. You have learned the magic of turning knowledge, information and understanding into action. Now you put it all together to learn how to make it work more quickly, more powerfully, more lastingly, more predictably. How? By involving other people.

You are learning "people magic"—communication, persuasion, inspiration, along with patience, tolerance, forgiveness and understanding. Keep in mind others' lack of information and awareness about these new dimensions of knowledge and understanding. We develop ways to help people get more into these important parts of life and of their own lives.

We are all in this together. When we think in a "big picture" perspective, on a present and future rather than past basis; on a societal, national, even global level, we *think BIG!* If we are to survive, grow, thrive, have abundance and experience freedom, personal power and prosperity, we cannot do it alone. We must do it together, all together.

In America all this goes back to the basics. We have made a deal with each other. It is called the U.S. Constitution. Our deal was made a long time ago, and we choose to keep it. We can change it—within the law. Our nation's "birth certificate," the Declaration of Independence, says clearly:

> . . . whenever any Form of Government becomes destructive of these ends, it is the Right of the People to alter or to abolish it, and to institute new Government, laying its powers in such form, as to them shall seem most likely to effect their Safety and Happiness. Prudence, indeed will dictate that Governments long established should not be changed for light and transient causes. . . .

This country has survived well over two centuries, the longest existing constitutional form of government. It has proven itself worthy of hard work, to enjoy, maintain and strengthen, and to "pass it on." Indeed, prudence dictates we not change it for "light and transient causes." We first assure our country and government operate as a balanced Republic, as so carefully crafted.

None of this works if the people, you and yours, do not know and understand the Constitution, meet their responsibilities, and all the while, articulate and enforce their rights. Responsibilities not carried out are waived. Rights not defended are lost.

The whole concept of republican rule by democratic majority requires an aware, knowledgeable, informed and involved electorate. THAT STARTS WITH YOU. It is your country and you must be "there" to keep it on track. You, therefore, must *be involved. You* must *get others involved. You* teach them what you know, so they *get involved and INVOLVE OTHERS.* Getting more people more involved is called MULTIPLICATION. Put that one word on a piece of paper and place it where you read, think and write, so you never forget. It becomes a central part of all you do.

MULTIPLICATION

The Magic of Multiplication: The Involvement Process!

Multiplication. How does one get others involved? First, think back to when and how you began to get involved. That is our simple six-word formula that works, called the Involvement Process, or "The Six Be's":

The Involvement Process

Be *AWARE.* Be *INFORMED.* Be *INTERESTED.*
Be *CONCERNED.* Be *INVOLVED.* Be *ACTIVE.*
In that order.
"The Six Be's"

The Involvement Process makes you an even more powerful person and helps you with your new lifelong assignment and adventure.

The citizen fun has just begun!

#1: Be AWARE

We are bombarded with messages, information, advertisements. As a defense mechanism we learn to mentally tune them out to avoid "information overload." Then we tune out too much. We want to "tune in," once again, and BECOME AWARE. We can handle so much more, both knowing and caring. Let the information in. Put it to work, first with you, then with one other.

Turn on all five senses and beyond. Listen, sense, perceive, look, feel.

Know that important things are happening. People are for knowing, places for going, facts for knowing, interest for showing, things for seeing, events for watching, activities for experiencing. Life is for living, doing, feeling, being. Get into the pulse-beat of life. There is a rhythm, an action, ongoing cycles, events, trends, emerging issues, exciting changes.

The citizen fun has just begun!

BE AWARE !

#2: Be INTERESTED

As you develop a healthy awareness of what is happening around you, find out more about it. The more interestED you become, the more interestING you become. Watch television with open eyes, ears and mind. Target more informational, educational, and less recreational television. When you are tuned in, turn on. Gather information, evaluate relevance, then what to do with it, if anything. Hear the sound around you. Listen to the radio. Listen to people. Listen to inspiring and informative cassette tapes and compact discs, CD's. Listen to nature. Listen to the "wee small giant within" that knows so much and so well what needs to be done.

The citizen fun has just begun!

BE INTERESTED!

#3: Be INFORMED

Being more aware and interested, you are ready to really "get into it" and become more informed. It is an exciting, never-ending process that expands your mind, magnifies your being, amplifies your life. You are really alive. You know what is going on around you, the who, what, when, where, why, how and how much. Life takes on new dimensions and new excitement because you are growing and becoming. You know what is happening.

How to get informed? Regularly gather current information. When you have a basic knowledge and understanding, current information makes you very powerful both personally and with your circle of friends and acquaintances. Here are ten ways to stay informed:

1. Subscribe to and thoroughly read at least one, better two or three newspapers daily. One will be local, your town paper, and the other(s) regional or national, such as the *Wall Street Journal, USA Today,* perhaps even an occasional *New York Times.* People often say about a newspaper, "I just won't read that paper because it is so liberal, conservative, biased, unfair, etc." Those are not good reasons not to read the paper. The important point is that many, many people read them and form their opinions and positions from them. That is how you get to know opposing viewpoints better, truth seeker, as well as be aware (that word again) of sources, topics and content of information.

2. Subscribe to at least one, preferably two or three weekly magazines, mostly news, plus others in your special area of interest or expertise such as photography, computers, internet or investing. Examples are *Business Week, Newsweek, Industry Week,* etc. Check them out at your newsstand for what is best for you; more importantly, *what*

you will read, not just subscribe to. Monthly magazines use the longer time span to provide more in-depth analysis, greater scope, more penetrating and comprehensive treatment of topics, issues and events.

3. Television and radio provide opportunities to better know our world. Some say they do not watch TV at all because it is so bad. That woefully restricts one from valuable information and programming seen by and influencing others. Use these valuable communication and information media with discretion and selfishness. Carefully schedule your time to fulfill your needs for both information and entertainment, and monitor impressions others receive.

4. Share your views, opinions, concerns and information with others. They will appreciate it and grow by it. So will you. Stay away from who's right and who's wrong. Be more interested in *what's right* and *what's wrong.* Even with strong opinions, approach such discussions strictly as such—discussions. Not arguments. Never arguments. Arguments do not work. Concentrate on getting more information to get closer to the truth. Sharing information in discussions helps you approach the truth faster. Arguments lead you farther away and can damage friendships and relationships, too precious to risk needlessly in pursuit of more information and truth.

5. Read a book a week, fiction and non-fiction. Books teach about life. Nothing beats a book, the highest form of literature, for well thought out, developed and documented information combined with knowledge, theory, charts, explanations and sources of information. Since we humans are the highest form of life, are we worth anything less than the highest form of literature?

6. Make cassette tape learning a habit. Use a suitable, affordable cassette player to get new knowledge from this "electronic teacher." The intellectual giants of the ages are available to you, almost effortlessly. You will receive truly valuable information on topics not taught in school and not otherwise so conveniently available; contemporary topics such as super selling, persuasion and negotiation, personal organization, the art of relaxation, time management, etc. The acknowledged experts and wisdom of the ages are yours at the push of a button. Think of the valuable use of otherwise wasted time traveling in a car. Share that time instead with the great thinkers, philosophers and teachers. It is better to learn from OPE (other people's experience) than from YOM (your own mistakes). Let them make the mistakes that fail and fabricate the formulas that work, then tell you about it, so you can apply them, succeed and prosper faster.

7. Clip and save newspaper and magazine articles of special interest to you. Carefully classify and file them for future reference. One day when you decide to write an article or compose a speech, the research is done and conveniently available. Such continuing, active reading teaches you and keeps you current.

8. Take formal courses: adult education, university or college, specialized schools or courses of instruction. Learn by mail, seminar and local adult education class. Find a mentor. Never stop learning. Adopt a new language and culture. Learn more about economics, politics, public policy, Americana. Get more into political and economic systems. Learn finance, sales, real estate, statistics, negotiation, computers, advanced mathematics, self-knowledge and mastery, the arts and music. Especially, appreciate the people with whom you share these pursuits. These may be the most valuable rewards of your continuing education. Extend your new knowledge by first learning, then teaching, and formally or informally sharing what you have learned and value highly.

9. Review and thoroughly learn political tools and techniques, the legislative process and procedures, reporting and influence methods. Learn how ideas and concerns are turned into programs and law; how regulation can sometimes protect, other times backfire with unfairness and undue burdens to result in higher costs, lower quality and reduced production. Be sensitive to contemporary trends, and be thoughtful about emerging issues that prompt or influence lawmaking in national and state legislatures.

10. Follow local, regional and state politics, candidates, elected and appointed officials. Know their problems and panaceas, philosophies and positions. Follow closely and compare their stated positions and actions. Meet with them and talk to them. They are happy to share their viewpoints and appreciate yours, as well as your interest and input.

The citizen fun has just begun!

BE INFORMED!

#4: Be CONCERNED

Trying to be concerned is like trying to sleep or be happy. It happens by itself as a result of everything else you do. Once you have become aware, leading to being more interested and getting better informed, your new and continuing knowledge becomes a part of you. Your awareness becomes concern because once you know, you feel. You are concerned and involved, directly and vicariously.

You relate the situations and events of the day to yourself, your family and future, your community and nation. You consider beyond your generation to that of your children and those to come. With knowledge comes understanding and with understanding, concern. Concern is an emotional response to what you know and what you learn. It is a caring, and a feeling of keen interest and personal involvement.

When you successfully travel from "aware" to "interested" and become "informed," you will feel concern. And you will be "concerned."

The citizen fun has just begun!

BE CONCERNED!

#5: Be INVOLVED

The formula works. You are concerned. In fact, you are upset, even inspired. Things are not right. Someone must get in there and help straighten it out. Who best to do it? Someone must get involved and make the difference that needs to be made. Who is more qualified, ready, willing and able? You, that's who. So guess who is going to get involved? You.

Here is where multiplication becomes not only desirable but necessary. When you come to realize all that must be done, and the time, energy and commitment limitations on one person—you, you realize how important it is to get others involved. Many hands make light the work. One cannot do everything. But each one can do something. Choose one or two major involvements and do them well. Take friends with you and get the help and support you need. Prepare for eventual letting go to others who also become their own *Power of ONE* to make a difference by getting involved. Here are six initial areas to consider:

1. Suppose your chief concern is the education your children receive. You get involved by joining a parent-teacher association or school advisory committee at their school(s). Attend school curriculum, book and budget hearings. Get to know school leaders, teachers, officers and members of the school board by first name. Learn, study and know school finance and public education issues. Offer your considered opinions, ideas and concerns. Be the toughest lover of learning you can be. As in business, insist the citizens and students get more and better for less. The productivity imperative works even in education.

2. Local, county and state governments offer similar opportunities to get involved. Meet and know your elected federal officials, state legislators, mayor and city council members, etc. Attend planning meetings, zoning hearings, or city council meetings. Watch your local papers for meeting times and places, issues and agenda.

Then be there. Try it a time or two to pass on your experience to others.

3. Attend town meetings or group-sponsored gatherings, such as a service group's sponsorship of a "meet the candidates night." Ask questions, offer suggestions and opinions. Share your concerns. Tell them what you think—after you think and know what you think! Listen to others and learn from them.

4. Form your own group of people interested in public issues. Create an educational forum for you and others to learn from each other, the state constitution, or how laws are made. Invite selected experts to teach and liven up your meetings.

5. Join an existing community service group such as Rotary, Lions, Optimists, Kiwanis and others to become involved in their community projects and youth activities.

6. Become involved in your political party. You will meet great people, learn new techniques and ideas, serve fellow citizens and help make an important difference. At a minimum, attend your neighborhood political caucus, held early in April or May each even-numbered election year. That is where America's political process begins, with the people and the party. The caucus builds to the county, state and national levels, resulting in the selection of our powerful national policy shapers and policy makers, including the President, Senators and Congressional Representatives.

With all this, become acquainted with your local media—newspapers, radio and television, and their people—editors, columnists and reporters. Get to know them by name, and they, you. Contact them in person, by phone or letter, but respect their time and deadlines. Congratulate them for a job well done, thank them for a community service rendered, supply them with information, tips and opinions, and occasionally, correct their stories and information. Their vital job well done builds a better community, and your helping them helps you too.

You are only one, but you are doing what one can do. You are only one, and you are representing the concerns of many. You are only one, and you are serving, not just yourself, but your fellow human beings and, in the larger sense, many yet to come.

The citizen fun has just begun!

BE INVOLVED!

#6: Be ACTIVE

Human beings, as individuals and in groups, make things happen. They identify and explore problems, determine and evaluate alternatives, make decisions and implement them with directed action.

Feel comfortable making your concerns known. There are many ways to be active and to represent yourself, friends and neighbors, your family, community and country.

You can write letters to the editor for publication in your local newspaper, even national weekly magazines. Publicly share your opinions and concerns. Help to inform and influence others to think, care and get involved. Ignore the temptation to think it may not be published, therefore why waste the time? If it is not published it may prompt publication of another letter on the same topic because of the many who wrote including you. Your letter may alert the editors to a new issue that is gaining prominence. There is a 100 percent certainty it won't be published if you don't submit it!

Contact personally, call, or write letters to your elected representatives and appointed officials. You will be pleasantly surprised at the impact of such contact. Citizen input is vitally needed to help guide their decisions. Such letters are read, evaluated and answered. Public servants and elected officials serve at your pleasure. If they don't do the job, they can be voted out of office, "fired" by those not served, served inadequately or unsatisfactorily. And they know it.

Consider running for public office. Yes, YOU, *Power of ONE,* consider running for public office. Whether at the local, state or national level, there are numerous opportunities for service of concerned, well-informed people. Consider city council, county commissioner, state legislator, federal representative or senator. The governorship? Presidency? Why not? For practice there are boards and commissions for environmental control, traffic, zoning, planning and alcoholic beverage control. Pick your place and time to serve, then serve. Get ACTIVE.

Shoot down the balloons. New public policy is tested with trial balloons: "2% sales tax increase slated for improved day care." Depending on response to this there may or may not be a 2% sales tax increase or improved day care. You help shoot down the trial balloon or keep it up by your response or lack thereof.

VOTE! Yes vote and vote intelligently with knowledge, information and concern, and get others to do so as well. But voting is just the bare beginning, not the living end. We have been taught all our lives, "Vote!" But we many times hear it "Only vote."

It is not enough to "only vote" every 2, 4, or 6 years. In between time is when the damage is done if we don't *speak up* and *speak out* for what we believe. Contact elected and appointed officials. Learn their positions, offer opinions, suggest actions. Get involved. That is how the American system works. That is how we carry high our Torch of Freedom.

We must let elected officials know we are here and we care. So we write letters to newspaper editors and to Congress. We "talk it up." We seek to influence the political process in the many ways we can. Vote. But don't let it stop there. Let it *start* there.

The citizen fun has just begun!

BE ACTIVE!

An Interview with an Expert Tells the Story: A Half Hour a Day for the USA

Bill Ellis was co-author of the book *MORE*[1]. A portion of a promotional interview cassette tape[2] gave the following ideas of what can be done:

Interviewer: Mr. Ellis, your book advocates the involvement of citizens in all facets of our government. What ways can you suggest for the average citizen to become more involved with present government?

Mr. Ellis: Adam, we are saying that waking up once a year to vote won't do much of anything. The professional politician knows that the day after the election we all go back to sleep again and they can continue with the status quo operation. The only way we will win back freedom in a sound dollar from big government will be by huge numbers of us shedding our dangerous indifference to apply intensive, clamorous, insistent citizen pressure on those who presume to be speaking for us in governing. We need to be involved daily. Ideally we should each spend a half-hour a day for the USA. Like the old Greeks who spent a half-day on Public Square politicking and then a half-day making a living. That won't happen here, but practical, I should think, would be one hour a week.

Interviewer: What should this person do with that one hour a week?

Mr. Ellis: Get involved first in local government—at the very least attend council meetings and some of the other government committee meetings—zoning boards, roads committee, parks committee, and then recruit a group from your neighborhood to attend city council meetings, not just when the neighborhood is protesting a new bridge, but all the time so council knows

1. Armington, R. Q., and Ellis, William D., *MORE: The Rediscovery of American Common Sense,* Regnery Gateway, Chicago: 1984

2. "Interview #36 with Bill Ellis P-I,"- Fallout USA Productions. Heritage Building. 214 Massachusetts Ave., N.E., Washington, DC 20002

that your neighborhood is watching. And then get other precincts to do the same. Now let's face it. There is an insider group in town, people who serve on quasi-governmental agencies, school boards, library boards, park boards. Getting active on those boards puts us citizens in the inner circle impinging on influencing government. Local government must pay attention to them, be concerned about their opinions on legislation. These jobs are stepping-stones to government. A little farther out on the perimeter but still influential are the hospital boards, the youth organizations, Red Feather Welfare Agency boards. Add also the PTA's, Young Democrats and Young Republicans. An hour a week in all these things gives us a voice in local politics and government. Human beings are political. To make the Constitution work, we've got to roll up our sleeves and get our hands dirty in plain old human politics. If we don't, the "ins" will ignore the "outs." Shouldn't we spend at least as much time per week for a free republic as we spend on racquetball? I'd really like to see every young person coming out of college commit him- or herself to a half hour a day for the USA. It'll command the respect of good politicians and scare the hell out of the bad ones.

The Involvement Process:
Secret to Beginning Something Bigger and Better

The Involvement Process, the starting point, is "the Six B's": Be *Aware,* Be *Interested,* Be *Informed,* Be *Concerned,* Be *Involved,* Be *Active,* in that order. It really works, with yourself and with those around you, in getting people more motivated and involved.

In applying this not-so-secret formula, first truly believe it is important and that it makes a difference. Guess what? It does. What you believe or choose to believe is true.

Consider this question: What do you think the enemies of freedom and America want you to believe? How do they want you to act? What difference do they want you to make?

Here is what makes it easy. We really have but half the job. The six facets of the Involvement Process seem overpowering but they are not. Your job with others is *only the first three,* not all six. Doing those well prompts the next three as an internal emotional response in others. They pass from you, the initiator of "Aware," "Interested," "Informed," to others, taking on "Concerned," "Involved" and "Active."

It gets back to the basic *Power of ONE* creed:

The Power of ONE
I am ONE.
I am only ONE.
But I will do,
What ONE can do.

Never forget your mighty ONE-power. There is always so much you can do, so much more you can do, and such a big difference you can make, just knowing, believing and acting your big belief.

The citizen fun has just begun!

The Involvement Process in Action: An example.

"Did you hear the city is raising water and sewage fees by $4 million?" (aware)

"No, that sounds like a big jump." (more aware)

"You bet it is. It's a 10.8 percent increase." (informing)

"Oh really. How much has population increased?" (curious, interested)

"Not very much. In fact, it's up only 2 percent." (informed)

"You're kidding! Why do they want more money for less or the same water and services?" (curiosity and emerging concern)

"I don't know, but I found out that budget has doubled in the last five years. That's over 14% a year growth." (more information)

"Get serious! That doesn't even make sense. More money, less service. Fourteen percent a year? My pay hasn't increased a third of that. Who's going to pay all that dough anyway?" (more interested, getting more information and more concerned)

"I am and so are you. On an average home like mine, water and sewage fees will increase about $72 a year. Yours will probably be more." (more information)

"My property taxes are already sky high. An additional $72 is $6 more a month groceries and gasoline I can't buy. This may be the straw that breaks this camel's back. What can we do?" (concern, turning into emotion, emerging into involvement, action)

"The budget hearing is Monday night and I'm going to be there. Do you want to go with me?" (involved, merging into action)

"You bet! I've got a few things to tell them, and I've never even talked to a group before. It's time I get more involved in what's going on. We need more productivity—doing more and better for less—in government anyway. I think we've got to be sure we get what we're paying for." (active)

The citizen fun has just begun!

THE INVOLVEMENT PROCESS: IT WORKS!

The GREATs Work Great.
Why and How People are Moved to Action.

Why does the Involvement Process work? Because when people know, people care. People are great. They are created great. They can live great. They can contribute great.

People do not do something for nothing. We do something for something, for a reason. The better the reason the bigger the action. What moves us to action are "The GREATS."

The GREATS include a great *love,* a great *hate,* a great *fear,* a great *anger,* a great *ambition,* a great *greed,* a great *dream,* a great *passion* for justice, equity, fairness and the like. We *dream big dreams* and *work hard* to make our dreams come true. Dreams are magic stuff. What is your dream? If it is "dream stuff"—peace, love, harmony, success, happiness and the like, you can make it happen! If it is material stuff—cars, big house, electronics, etc., you can make it happen!

When you dream a big dream you *will* make it happen.

How to make your dreams come true is what counts. You can only get back big when you give big. Work big. Play big. Sell big. Tell big.

When you give, you get. When you give big, you get big. That is how free enterprise in America works. You please big, serve big, give big, get back big. Your service is great and your GREATs are great.

Put your GREATs to work. Develop a great vision. Tap into the GREATs to get your drive, ambition, motivation, inspiration, action.

We do not so much create GREATs as awaken them. By acquiring knowledge, information, ideas and ideals, it is possible to nudge the slumbering giant within. That is what the Involvement Process does. Finally, keep in mind the three ways to move people to action:

1) Take something away from them
2) Tell them they can't do something, or
3) Overtly put power over them.

Big government, for example, does all three. When unfair laws are enacted, or oppressive taxation imposed, people are ripe to react. Knowledge of government growth, power and control activates these three triggers, to turn on the GREATs.

The Power of IDEAS. The Power of INFORMATION.
Applying the GREATs.

Why does the Involvement Process work? It works because we are human beings, with all the blessings and curses of being human. We seem selfish because we are programmed to survive. Because we have the human spirit, our dreams go beyond survival to prosperity and abundance. Especially in America we know these things are not dreams.

They are challenges and opportunities waiting to become reality. We know our faith, determination and vision can turn them into reality.

We want MORE. All people want more. But it is more complicated than that. We are daring enough to *want more for less,* and to the limit, to *want something for nothing.* Generally we know that is not probable, and if possible, usually not fair. So we work for what we want, expecting we will get more and better if we work harder and smarter. We live and let live.

What works is the *Power of IDEAS,* and for us, the power of shared ideas. Some have the idea that goodness is good. Others disagree and act differently. We act how we believe. Some believe in God. Others don't. Some believe in a final accounting for our actions. Others think there is no reward or punishment. They act how they believe. Some think the individual is responsible and is therefore self-governing. Others think less of the individual, believing the answer is government, or the state to control individuals. These ideas all manifest themselves in our actions, organizations, institutions, policies and laws.

The magic of the GREATs happens when people find out what is going on, what is happening to them, through another power, the *Power of INFORMATION.* It is a link between the power of ideas and our values and belief systems.

A Cultural Arts Tax Teaches Real Life, Modern Day Fabian and Democratic Socialism

Here is another example using The Involvement Process for a public vote on a Cultural Arts Tax in Colorado, in the November, 1988 election.

By the Colorado Constitution[3] legislation referred to public vote by the state general assembly is a referendum and must be publicized the same as an amendment to the Constitution. It requires that such bills "shall be published in two issues of two newspapers of opposite political faith in each county in the state. This publication shall be made at least one week apart and not less than three nor more than five weeks before the election. . . . " This constitutional provision was not followed.

The issue was a "sleeper" for 18 months until ten days before the election where, by a more accommodating law, the legal publication was a very small part of a near full page of nine propositions and numerous candidates for public office, in two languages, English and Spanish. Notification of the Cultural Arts Tax was lost in the milieu of the legal notice.

This whole situation left the proponents in total control of the timing and content of the information release, and in a power position regarding

3. *Colorado and United States Constitutions,* Department of State, 1560 Broadway. Suite 200, Denver, CO 80202, Art V, Sec 1, C13, and Art XXIII. $6

the use of people and propaganda to sell the issue by emphasizing benefits and contriving the need while avoiding mention of the cost or principles involved.

Since narrow, special interests wanted to get the estimated $13 million a year "for the arts," they compressed the campaign time, emphasized the benefits, exaggerated the need, and trivialized the cost in their well-planned and executed promotion. With 18 months to prepare an effective campaign strategy they were in the enviable position of no opposition and having raised nearly a million dollars to convince an unsuspecting public in a "glitz blitz" propaganda campaign. We join a *Power of ONE* speaking to a fellow citizen:

Power of ONE: What do you think of the upcoming cultural arts tax vote?

Fellow Citizen: Seems pretty good to me. They say it'll cost 'less than a cup of coffee a month,' about 57 cents per Colorado citizen. That's not much, I guess, for better arts.

Power of ONE: The 57 cents is an interesting number. That is what proponents estimate the cost to be for the 0.1% increase in the sales tax. What I find more interesting is that we already pay about 7.7% sales tax, 77 times the proposed sales tax increase. Using their numbers, that amounts to $43.89 a month per person, over $500 a year, or $2,000 sales tax for a family of four. It is probably not really that much, but does it seem like our sales taxes are high enough?

Fellow Citizen: I never thought of that. But maybe they really need the money.

Power of ONE: Some five or six years previous they were struggling. The arts in Colorado reduced their annual deficit from about $7 million to less than $2 million three years ago. They began to charge admission and are now essentially self-supporting. Doesn't it seem like that's the right direction to go?

Fellow Citizen: Then why do they seek public funding after over a century of self-funding?

Power of ONE: Because like many others they have learned to work the system and play the people. They want to remove the risk from their financing. So they foist a one-sided, little-discussed special interest scheme on an unsuspecting public and get them to vote for it. By investing $1 million one time they receive $13 million a year forever, indexed for inflation with the added bonus to seek "small increases" directly from the legislature. Why do you think they were willing to invest money, time and effort so carefully to assure public funding forever?

Fellow Citizen: I don't know. I can't figure out why government is getting into the arts. It seems like it is a threat to freedom of expression— if someone criticizes a public official, for instance, will their funding be affected? With government money, always, comes government control. Will they get into other areas too?

Power of ONE: Probably. They will try as long as people don't understand. This is such a good example of Fabian and Democratic Socialism. Fabian Socialism is where those in power tell the people this is good for them because it assures a badly-needed program, takes the risk out of it and spreads the cost of it over the whole people. It becomes Democratic Socialism when they are confident enough they have convinced the people to vote themselves another tax increase 'for their own good.' Through their ignorance and gullibility why do people in effect help special interests pick their own pockets?

Fellow Citizen: But isn't it taxation for a good cause?

Power of ONE: It seems so. But people don't know how much they are already *really taxed* "for their own good." It is difficult to understand the effect of the $13 million of goods and services not bought as a result of the money being channeled into the arts. Also it adds a bigger burden to an already heavy tax load. From 1990 to 1997 America's annual per-capita taxation rose $2,619 per-person, $855 state-and-local, $1,764 federal. Total per-capita taxation was $9,135, which calculated to be $29,141 for the average family size of 3.19. Median family income in 1997 was $44,568.

Fellow Citizen: Wait a minute. That's a tax on the family of 65%! Do you mean a family actually keeps only one-third of its income, while the government takes almost two-thirds? What we don't need is another or higher tax. I for one will vote against the cultural arts tax. I earn the money and it's my money. I will support the arts I want to support when I want to support them. When government takes more of my money in taxes than I get to keep, taxation has gone too far.

Power of ONE: This reminds me of the dedication in Friedrich Hayek's book *The Road to Serfdom*[4] which says "To the socialists of all parties." Those politicians that initiate and legislate such tax law and public subsidies just don't understand, or they do. They think themselves to be free enterprise, free marketeers and moderates, some even 'conservative Republicans.' Why do they kid themselves to the detriment of future citizens burdened by unbearably heavy, excessive, unnecessary and continually rising taxes?"

Fellow Citizen: I think they just don't understand. They let noble motives override good judgment with oppressive taxation.

Power of ONE: Yes, but taxpayers under those burdens are the very ones who don't get involved in their system to keep it on track. Why do they instead choose not to get involved and let others corrupt the system and jeopardize the future?

4. Hayek, Friedrich A., *The Road to Serfdom: A classic warning against the dangers to freedom inherent in social planning,* University of Chicago Press. Chicago: 1944

Fellow Citizen: Yeah, that's the way I used to be, but not any more. It is time to take our country back and I accept that assignment here and now.

The citizen fun has just begun!

Uncovering the Magic of Enriching and Stimulating Minds

Re-read the preceding paragraphs to learn secrets of enriching and stimulating minds. Here are guidelines:

Is it better not to give answers? Is it more effective not to give opinions or conclusions? Aren't they subject to instant rebuttal, perhaps silent, internal and unyielding? The question is, whose opinion is it—yours or theirs? If they hear your opinion what do they do with it? If they form their own opinions how do they handle it?

Here are three approaches that work:

1. Ask questions. They make people think.
2. Present evidence and information. They stimulate interest.
3. Create doubt, a framework for thinking, probing and exploring.

Make your "case" so good you do not have to tell them your opinion. They will get one of their own based on the knowledge and current information they acquire from you and others. Their opinions may turn out remarkably close to yours! The risk is worth the result.

The KIMAX Revelation. The KIMAX Response.

Another way to move yourself or others to action is with the KIMAX Revelation and the KIMAX response.

The KIMAX Revelation is: *You Count! You matter! You make a difference!*

The KIMAX Response is a formula for success. KIMAX is an acronym which stands for *K*nowledge, *I*nformation, *M*otivation, *A*ction, and e*X*cellence, in that order. Whether you wish to buy a car, get football tickets, go to college, get a job, or woo and win a mate, the KIMAX response helps make it happen. Here is how it works:

Get the *Knowledge.* It takes time, effort and sacrifice to acquire knowledge and understanding, to think and analyze. No pain, no gain. One example is where you take the time to regularly read books. Another is when you choose to take a formal college course or pursue a high-risk career experience. While others are having fun you are working, taking tests, spending time for studying, reading and research. You can tell you are doing good because you have incurred risk of failure and given up something for it—time, energy, money, effort. Knowledge is worth it. Get the knowledge.

Get the *Information*. Read newspapers and magazines lavishly and regularly. Update your knowledge with current articles, factual data and information. You will get more and better ideas and make better decisions. You will also develop a higher level of concern so necessary for motivation to action, and enthusiasm for working with and involving others. Get the information.

Get the *Motivation*. Go beyond thinking to feeling—strongly. Things are not right or fair. Serious short or long term consequences are imminent. "Something must be done." Someone must do something! Guess who that someone is, *Power of ONE!* This is the more difficult part. Motivation does not come from *without,* but from *within.* Something inside you rebels against what is, preferring what could be or should be. It is based on finding out more, knowing more and feeling more. Put your "GREATS" to work. Here are some examples.

One "motivator" is to recall your "parent tape" that says "Work hard, save and get ahead." Then review some pertinent concepts and information. Recall how the 1970 average weekly salary of $298 dropped to $261, inflation-adjusted, 27 years later, that we have less, not more leisure time, that more of us work. We work more and harder, make less and have less time to ourselves. Why? That could be motivating.

Here is another motivator. We are stealing from our children's future To pay interest on the 1986 deficit of $220 billion will require a high school graduate to pay $12,000 taxes over their 40 to 45 year working lifetime. That's a car. To pay interest, not principal, on the national debt, will require $120,000 taxes in their working lifetime. That's a house.

We have stolen a house and a car from our children! We have been having a party. They aren't even invited. But they get the bill!

That's motivating. Take *Action*. Think different. Act different. Be different. Make a difference.

Seek *eXcellence*. One never knows who is watching, but they are watching. Actions, always, speak louder than words. Whatever you do, do it with EXCELLENCE. You are a model for others on what to do and how to do it. When you know they are watching, particularly impressionable children and young adults, make it exemplary watching for them. Be a master model. Show them how to speak responsibly, honorably, honestly, and how to act morally, ethically and with integrity. In a word, do all you do with EXCELLENCE.

You can create your own success with KIMAX.

Reach Out to One More,
Many Times to Reach Many More

Learn the importance of reaching out to accomplish a lot more good through others. We are all so different yet so much alike. We all want the best for our children and ourselves. We all have not only a great capacity for self-service, but for other-service. The greater good can and must become a part of all our lives.

Someone left us a better world and we want to do the same for those to come. It first of all starts with you. You have complete control over yourself. You can do what you want to do and not do what you don't want to do. If something is to be done, you can be the first to do it, then share it with others, one at a time.

Our alikeness indicates you will find others like you who know the importance of getting involved and active, and do likewise. Your world will begin to change for the better as you begin and continue to involve "one more" not for your reasons, but for their very own good reasons.

Power of ONE, it is already a better world because you are here and doing something about it, with knowledge, care and concern. Involving each new person multiplies your speed, impact and momentum. You magnify your *Power of ONE* with the *Power of ONE More.* Congratulations on being a world changer, *Power of ONE!*

Questions for Review

1. How is the *Power of ONE* related to the power of many, beginning with the power of one more? How do we enlist the power of one more? Why?

2. Discuss "…the power does not end with you. It STARTS with you." What one word means getting more people more involved?

3. Discuss and explain the Involvement Process. Why is it called "The Six Be's"? Why must they be "in that order"? Discuss each "Be" in detail, who, what, why, when, where, and how?

4. Describe ten ways to get and stay informed. How does that lead to interest, then concern? What is next after concern?

5. What types of involvement and action are possible by dedicated, aware citizens? How does one get started? Discuss "Give a half hour a day to the U. S. A."

6. Concerning the Involvement Process what does it mean to say, "We really have only half the job."

7. Describe by example how sharing information and asking and answering questions makes the Involvement Process work.

8. What are "The GREATs" and why are they important in human motivation? How do you "put your GREATs to work?" What does it mean to say "We don't so much create GREATs as awaken them"? Discuss the Power of Ideas and the Power of Information.

9. How are both Fabian and Democratic Socialism used to increase taxes and public funding of non-government projects and programs? How does the dedication read in Friedrich A. Hayek's book *The Road to Seldom?* What does it mean? How can stories and explanations about increasing taxes make people more aware, interested, informed, concerned, involved and active?

10. What is the KIMAX Revelation? The KIMAX Response? Describe the 5-word, 5-part success formula. How can you make it work for you? What does it mean to "Recall your 'parent tape' that says 'work hard, save and get ahead.'" Does it work? Why? Why must we "reach out"?

Do more than exist—live.
Do more than touch—feel.
Do more than look—observe.
Do more than hear—listen.
Do more than listen—understand.
Do more than talk—say something.
—John Hoarse Rhodes

Ode

We are the music-makers,
    And we are the dreamers of dreams,
Wandering by lone sea-breakers,
    And sitting by desolate streams.
World-losers and world-forsakers,
    On whom the pale moon gleams:
Yet we are the movers and shakers
    Of the world for ever, it seems.

With wonderful deathless ditties
    We build up the world's great cities,
And out of a fabulous story
    We fashion an empire's glory:
One man with a dream, at pleasure,
    Shall go forth and conquer a crown;
And three with a new song's measure
    Can trample an empire down.

> We, in the ages lying
>> In the buried past of the earth,
> Built Ninevah with our sighing,
>> And Babel itself with our mirth;
> And o'erthrew them with prophesying
>> To the old of the new world's worth;
> For each age is a dream that is dying,
>> Or one that is coming to birth.
>>>> —Arthur William O'Shaughnessy

from Edwards, K. Morgan, *More Than Survival: The Need for a Moral and Spiritual Revolution,* Abingdon Press, New York: 1961

> "'Your task—
> To build a better world,' said God.
> I answered, 'How?
> The world is such a large, vast place,
> So complicated now.
> And I so small and useless am.
> There's nothing I can do.'
> But God,
> In His great wisdom said,
> 'Just build a better you.'"
>>>> —Dorothy James

With good conscience our only sure reward, with history the final judge of our deeds, let's go forth to lead the land we love, asking His blessing and His help, but knowing that here on earth God's work must truly be our own.   —John F. Kennedy

You gain strength, courage and confidence by every experience in which you really stop to look fear in the face. . . . You must do the thing you think you cannot do.   —Eleanor Roosevelt

And ye shall know the truth and the truth shall make you free.
                                    —John 8:32

Some look at things as they are and say "Why?" I dream dreams that never were and say "Why not?"   —Robert F. Kennedy

America was built into the greatest country the world has ever known, not through government control, regulation and handouts; but rather through individual imagination and initiative. It has been the individual and not government that built this nation, and it will be the individual that will save it for future generations.   —Robert W. Miller

The only thing necessary for the triumph of evil is for good men to do nothing.   —Edmund Burke

Chapter 25

MULTIPLY YOUR POWER OF ONE MORE TO POWERS OF MANY MORE

We change our world one person at a time. As we help more people to understand and comprehend, the power multiplies, not proportionally, but geometrically, exponentially. That means small changes portend big changes that result in ever-growing changes if we keep up everlastingly our hard work and good works. That is why starting out seems fruitless and discouraging, the key word being *seems*. Soon the *more* become *MANY*.

We get our timescape in order, more historically rather than in a current or contemporary frame of reference. Certainly we are not looking at geologic time, in millennia or centuries. As well we are not working for the day, week, month or year. We are building for the age. Set your sights long, your expectations high and your timetables open. Inhibit your propensity to expect immediate, tangible results. Do not waste precious time and energy on such unnecessary worry.

To get people to change, first do your homework and know you are right. Acquire the necessary knowledge, information and understanding. Share them with others, and get them to multiply in their own way, once informed, convinced and inspired. Use "gentle pressure relentlessly applied" on yourself and others. Why? Because it is that effective and that important.

The Greatest Speech: One Out of 50,000

Mr. Charles Malik once served as Lebanon's ambassador to the United States and later as president of the U. N. General Assembly. Syndicated columnist James J. Kilpatrick writes[1] of Malik's memorable speech delivered June 11, 1960, in Williamsburg, Virginia, on the topic, "Will the future redeem the past?"

Malik launched into a discourse of "a life-and-death struggle between international communism and the rest of the world, especially the United States of America." He placed himself wholly on the side of the West "despite its many imperfections, mistakes, failures and sins."

Malik stated that Communism started from zero in 1917 and was rigidly controlling one-third of mankind. He asked the rhetorical question: "Was this phenomenal development inevitable?" He posed the same question of the Korean War, the retreat of freedom in southeast Asia, and communist activity in Africa and the United States, 21 questions in all. Then he came to the crux, with voice soaring, questioning these communist gains:

> If only people rose to the occasion, if only they were not overwhelmed by their softness and apathy, if only they overcame their greed, if only they were morally strong, if only they were not selfish and narrow, if only they were not petty and spiteful and stupid, if only they were big, if only they knew what was at stake, if only they were not hypocritical, if only they trampled underfoot the wide and easy way!

That is not only quite an indictment, but an opportunity as well. Malik articulated the problem of getting people knowledgeable and involved. We have the solution, the means, the know-how and the assignment. All we need do is to begin to help people change their lives and future in ways we have discussed.

People-Change Made Easy: Telegraph Your Punches.

The Change Process is an important concept. It is how to promote and implement change more smoothly and effectively.

To effect change it would seem one should quietly, almost secretly, gather the necessary information, analyze it, arrive at logical conclusions and make suitable recommendations. Write it down, print it up and prepare for action. Then tell the world, "We're making a BIG change." Guess what? It doesn't work. It scares people. Change, especially sudden and drastic change *really* scares people. The Change Process is a better way.

1. James J. Kilpatrick, "Great speech outlives obscure speechmaker," *Rocky Mountain News,* 1/14/88, p 51

The Change Process is simply, in the vernacular, to "telegraph your punches." Let people know and be a part of what's going on *while it's going on*. *Don't wait till it's all done* to involve those who will be affected.

Involve people from the start for two reasons: You will get 1) their good ideas and 2) their support, as they feel a part of controlling and directing the change. Describe the nature of the problem. Tell them what you know about the problem. Solicit their ideas, suggestions and opinions. Level with them. Let them know how the problem is being studied and that something is going to be done about it. INVOLVE THEM. The magic part of the change process is the *ongoing PROCESS of communication, interaction and involvement.*

Share ideas. Communicate with them regularly, personally and by the written and spoken word. Let them know the direction things are going, the shape things are taking, and what will likely be tried.

Take the threat out of change. Phrase new things as an extension of the old, the "tried and true," rather than the untried and unknown. It is a modification of what we are already doing, or close to the way we are already doing it. It is "temporary." We can go back, modify, try something else or try another way. Make it exciting to anticipate, something to look forward to. Turn a threat into a treat by getting the "h" out of it.

The Change Process of involving people in change makes good sense. Use it. You are on an exciting journey—take the people with you.

The Magic of MASO: MULTIPLY AND SO ON!

Getting other people involved is no simple task. It is hard work. It is frustrating. It is disappointing and sometimes seems discouraging. But it is very important. Because of the involvement process, the magic of the "Six Be's," it builds like an avalanche. The more you do of it, the more you get involved, the faster a momentous and important difference can be made.

The whole concept of involving others can be put into one word: MASO. That means "Multiply And So On." It is the magic of multiplication and involving other people. But it means more. It means teaching them how to get involved, how to make a difference. It means showing them what to do and how to do it, where to get information and how to use it.

MASO: Multiply And So On!

It is not enough only to "multiply." "And so on" is just as important, perhaps even moreso because therein lies the magic of multiplication. "And so on" means to get others to get others to get others also to get others, and so on. It means you send out a letter, report, clipping, chart or news article to friends. You ask them to make ten copies and share them with others who will also make 10 copies, "and so on." It means you call five people, ask each of them to call five people, who will also ask those five people each to call five people, "and so on." Same for email. As the chain letter puts it, *don't break the chain!*

Let us fit all this into MASO. Most concerned Americans know something is wrong and something should be done about it. But what? What can one person do to make a difference? Lots. Can one person make a difference? Yes, definitely. How? By starting with that one person, you, and employing the ideas of MASO, Multiply And So On.

One person *CAN* make a difference. The secret is to *Know, Believe* and *ACT* on that notion. *YOU* can make a difference. Use your *Power of ONE* and get others to do likewise.

Trounce Tyranny with the MASO "FREEDOM TOOLS"

Andre Codresque, poet and immigrant from Romania, was interviewed on public radio. He said, "The two greatest tools against tyranny are the typewriter and the mimeograph machine." We, who are blessed to live in the United States of America, can modernize and paraphrase that to read:

The two greatest tools against tyranny
are the *computer* and the *copier!*

We have both, in abundance! USE these "Freedom Tools!"

Use the COMPUTER (or typewriter) to compose and record your thoughts about the issues of the day, your opinions and suggestions (or demands) of just what should be done, what you want or what you expect. Send them to newspapers and magazines for publication, airing, or to influence their editorial policy.

Use the COPIER to share copies with friends. Then get them also to use the COMPUTER (or typewriter) and the COPIER to share these messages of freedom also.

Use the MAIL to distribute and extend your ideas, suggestions, convictions and considered solutions, for others likewise to get involved.

Use the TELEPHONE to follow up and reinforce your messages of freedom with your friends, neighbors, relatives, co-workers and citizens, concerned Americans. Contact your local phone company to learn how to use the power of three-way calling.

Use EMAIL and the INTERNET in what I call "communication with a click." It is the most efficient, least expensive communication ever. Create and use your personal and "issues" email lists. As events unfold and controversies emerge, as you get information and action, share them with your lists. Think of the power you have. Suppose each person on your list has one citizen email list of 10 people and so do the others, and a "communication with a click" speeds information along every two hours. In half a day your message will reach 1 million people!

Call a RADIO or TV STATION to get an issue on the air in front of tens of thousands of listeners or viewers. Ask questions, offer information and insights. More often I realize that the saving grace of this Republic will be in the people—Powers of ONE, and their use of talk radio for information and the Internet for communication.

Get TOGETHER. Call a meeting. Get your close friends and theirs together to share ideas and concerns about the pressing issues of the day. Volunteer to do parts of what must be done. Get others involved. Make assignments. Take assignments. Complete assignments. Let the world know you are there and you care.

Share YOURSELF. What more profound statement can you make about who you are and what you believe and support, than to take time to visit, explain, listen and share concerns for a better present and future for our children? You are the best there is. You are a knowledgeable, aware, informed, interested, concerned, involved, active and capable *Power of ONE.* They see it. They feel it. They are impressed, motivated and inspired by all you are and all you do. They join in and help make the difference worth making, taking the risk worth taking. And that is what it is really all about, isn't it?

Start a NEWSLETTER. Occasionally share concerns, issues and events with friends. Make it a sort of citizen concerns correspondence club.

Finally, *Share the message of MASO* and teach others the magic of MASO.

You can make a difference. *Choose and use your weapons:* Computer, typewriter, copier, mail, telephone—and three-way calling, audiotapes and YOU. Newer technologies may include the videocassette recorder (VCR), computer disk, email, fax machine, Internet and phone answering systems. Stay current on state-of-the-art for dispensing and disseminating information.

Multiply. Involve your family, friends, neighbors, relatives, fellow employees and citizens, voters and taxpayers.

The Magic of the WHAT Formula!

"Contact my elected representatives? Write a letter to the editor? I have never done that. How do you do that?" So say your friends in frustration, asking what to do, how to do it, and probably looking for some encouragement to do it.

Tell them about the simple, easy four-part WHAT Formula: What, So What, Now What and What Next? It works for both kinds of letters—to the editor and to the Congress and public officials.

What? State what is wrong, accurately, concisely, courteously.

So What? Tell why it is wrong, your opinion, your information.

Now What? Give your good ideas, what you think should be done to correct it.

What Next? Multiply. Share letter with others. Get others to do likewise.

Make it a simple "3-by-3 letter"—three paragraphs, three sentences each, for a short letter, a "4-by-4 letter" for a longer one. Most Americans can string nine or sixteen sentences together. And those are relatively long for letters to the editor.

Pointers for Letters to the Editor

A letter to the editor is to inform and persuade many people, the subscribers and readers of the publication. A letter to the editor is a powerful tool, the next-best read part of the paper, second only to the front page. Politicians, elected and appointed officials, even newspaper editorial page editors, columnists and reporters watch these letters closely. These are the people speaking. One letter may represent thousands, even millions of people with the same opinion. Or a new issue or idea may be making its way into the public forum.

You can once again be quite powerful, *Power of ONE,* with these letters. After reading them you can act and react. You can contact the author with congratulations. You can respond to the issue or the letter. You can clip and mount the letter, add your own comments and share them with appropriate elected officials, and all of your contacts. You can apply all the powerful MASO concepts.

I have discussed writing letters to the editor with friends. They will bring up a topic they think should be addressed. Sometimes they will ask me to write the letter. I tell them they should do so. Sometimes they will say "Oh, I've never written a letter to an editor before." I respond, "That is your very first line and a most powerful statement." It is like being a virgin. You can only say it once and that is why it is so important and powerful to use. In effect you are saying "I am ___ years old and have never written a letter to an editor. But this topic is so important, I am so concerned and emotional about it, that I am doing what I have never dared to do before." That is powerful prose!

People have told me, "Okay, Fred, I'll submit a letter for you."

"Don't send one for me. I'm not worth it. Send it for you. You are worth it."

"What do you mean, you are not worth it?"

"Because I might leave town or collapse or worse. You must continue to send your letters because they are important, the issues are important, and most important, you are important."

Here are a few tips for writing and submitting such letters. "Be ABC": accurate, brief, courteous. Stick to one subject. Type and double-space for easy editing by the paper. Include your address, phone number and signature. Double check before sending. Prior to publication the editor will likely call to verify you wrote the letter.

For MASO, once your letter is published, mount the clipping artfully on a piece of paper. Be sure to include its source—publication, date, page number, and your name, address and phone number. Then make copies and share it generously with friends, personally and in correspondence.

A final "secret" to such letters is to present your case but not your conclusions. Give the information you have—facts, data, and quotes—but without declaring your opinion. People naturally argue with or discount what others say. *End the letter instead with a question.* We are programmed from birth to answer questions, aren't we? If the answer is your own answer, you don't argue with it. You defend it.

Here is an example. You have provided data that shows taxes have risen dramatically. They have gone up faster than inflation, faster than population; in fact, lots faster than both combined.

Don't TELL, "Vote no on this proposal." ASK, "Do you think this proposal deserves taxpayer support?" ASK, "Do you think taxes have risen about enough?" ASK, "Is it time to slow this tax roller coaster to oblivion?" Give your information, your experience.

There are risks but there are rewards. The risks are believing in people, having confidence in your ability to adequately provide them information, and trusting them to use it wisely. Those are also the rewards.

Pointers for Letters to Congress and Other Public Officials

Letters to Congress are a little different. You wish to persuade one person. You are not asking questions as much as telling them you are concerned about something and you want something done about it. Rather than concluding these letters with questions, end them with clear, direct answers or opinion. "I unequivocally oppose this tax increase!"

Limit these letters to a single issue or topic. It is easier for their staff to tabulate and classify a continuing stream of letters on many topics and coordinate fast responses to them if each one is single stated and single minded.

The advent of the personal computer and desktop publishing has brought their own problems. It is common for lobbying organizations to get citizens to send thousands or millions of letters and to coordinate the mailing of as many return postcards to the Congress. Such mass-produced communications do not have the same impact as a personal letter. Here we go back to the past. A legible, hand-written note or letter may have many times the impact of the more high-tech letters. Use your own stationery, preferably with your letterhead. Obviously handwriting distinguishes you from all the machines.

If you are a member or the leader of a group, mention that. There is power in numbers, "The 845 members of the Lincoln Log Homeowners

Association wish to convince you to re-zone the adjacent area from 'heavy industrial' to 'light commercial.' Sincerely, Pat Citizen, President"

Finally, if you do not get an answer, or get back a form letter or one that obviously answers a different question, write on your original in a bright color, "You didn't answer my question with this form letter. Please respond." Then send a copy of it back. If it happens again, put another "angry-red-crayon-comment" on it, plus "CC's," courtesy copies to "all God's children"—your mayor, Governor, state and county officials, Secretary of State or Treasury, and local and national newspapers, and send it again to all of them. Public officials do not like to be exposed or embarrassed.

Always when appropriate, express commendation and appreciation for a stand courageously taken and gratitude for a job well done.

Cottage Citizenship and the Freedom "Tithe-Tithe" Pledge

Another way to involve others is in Citizen Cottage Meetings. These have to do with each person taking control of the direction of our community and country. It consists of small, informal, neighborhood meetings to discuss, learn, share and react to issues that affect our current freedoms, our community and nation, and our children's education and future.

Invite a dozen friends and neighbors to get together to discuss issues and share expertise. Bring articles of interest from local newspapers and highlight how issues affect those in the group. Decide on courses of action, each taking responsibility for some specific action and reporting back at the next meeting. Share your good ideas with others outside the circle and encourage them to do likewise. Meet regularly and briefly to maintain momentum , interest and impact.

The "Freedom Tithe-Tithe Pledge" is a pledge to yourself and your family to defend, preserve and strengthen freedom. It is an unconditional pledge of 1% of your income to groups and individuals actively engaged in monitoring government growth, condemning wrongful and illegal elected official actions, and restraining tax increases. Many people agree to paycheck deductions of two hours pay a month, most of which is used for political lobbying and influence-peddling that directly and negatively affects your net income and purchasing power. The way to fight back is to do likewise. Routinely budget a half-hour of pay and time a week to your unconditional 1% freedom pledge.

Form Your Own Great American FAN Club.
Welcome to the Club!

The Great American FAN Club brings it all together. Here is how it works. FAN stands for *Freedom Action Network.* From what you know about freedom and how we are losing it, examine and verify your internal guidance, sense of urgency, commitment and inspiration. Then take action with YOUR network, your circle of friends and acquaintances; then get them to do likewise, with MASO. It is informal and unorganized (disorganized?), but it works when you work, keep working and get others to work for freedom too.

This American FAN Club is great because you and those who are your friends are great Americans. It is a club because it is loosely organized for the purpose of building a better country and future with concerned and involved people working separately, yet together. "Join the Club! Welcome to the Club!" That is what you tell your friends in starting up and keeping going.

"Now that we're organized, what'll we do?" There are lots of things to do together. To get it started compose a cover letter introducing the idea of the FAN Club. Here are some starter working paragraphs of such a cover letter:

To: Great American FAN Club Members

From: _____

Date: _____

Subject: Freedom Action Network (FAN)

I have designated an informal Freedom Action Network (FAN) of people whom I respect and care for, and who I know are concerned and willing to TAKE ACTION. You are one of these really special people.

My extended thoughts for a later date are for each one to *form his or her own Great American FAN Club* composed of friends and acquaintances that also care and are willing to help make a positive difference. Ask each one to do the same thing for further multiplication and impact, knowing each of us is strong and we are stronger together. I call it "working together separately." Most already have such a listing. Setting up your own American FAN Club focuses "Positive People Potential."

Here is the issue I propose we initially address and what each should begin doing to have the desired happy ending that protects our future and freedoms: . . .

[Prepare your one-page information and suggested action sheet entitled something like: "ACTION PLAN: A FUN Way to Let [your state] Officials Know Informed, Concerned [State] Taxpayers go beyond Alive-and-Well to INVOLVED and ACTIVE!" You will want to supply the initial response information needed to get started, indicated by a double-star (**), such as address and telephone number, where or how to contact them. Here is an activist information letter to accompany your cover letter that tells what you are doing and why:]

American FAN Club (Freedom Action Network)

ACTION PLAN: A FUN Way to Let Elected State Officials
    Know We Support (or Oppose) _____ !

1. Read at least one local and national newspaper for stories, editorials, letters-to-the-editor, articles, etc. Learn of trends, issues, emerging public concerns. Respond especially to "trial balloons" sent up for public acceptance or protest. Similarly monitor radio and television news and information.

2. Contact elected and appointed officials at address**, phone**, including Governor _____, state and/or national senators, representatives, majority leaders, committee chairs (all**), etc. Name names, give contact information.

3. Here are some possible themes: *Your* idea or theme; government and tax growth, home foreclosures, homeless, unemployment, business failures, protecting the environment, personal bankruptcies, inflation, interest rates, recession, etc. Thank them for their public service, praise their positions with which you agree. Be respectful, polite, sincere; ABC—accurate, brief, courteous.

4. Suggest in your own words your ideas, opinions, criticisms. Ask questions.

5. Make and send copies to other newspapers, etc. (MASO)

6. Make 7 copies, share 5 with local friends, 2, out-of-town. (More MASO)

[Here put in your own hints, wishes or requests to state specifically what each person should do. For instance, if you are suggesting a letter-to-the-editor campaign, use the "What Formula" to explain how to write the letters and attach a fact sheet or several example articles with information about the topic or issue you are addressing.]

This will be the most effective "citizen fun" you have had in years, costing some time and money, perhaps 3 hours, and a well-invested $10 or $20 for postage and printing, each time you "address the club." It is cheap entertainment to promote public official appreciation of voters, citizens and taxpayers, those who pay the bills. You pay now or pay later.

Now, the money is an investment. Later it is a tax. Make this your best investment ever. Have some citizen fun!

As this works out perhaps some of us will later be leaders split off from this FAN Club starting another to spread this new "citizen fun that has just begun."

Remember the guidelines for your group:

1) Don't give answers, ask questions,

2) Present evidence and information that lead to your conclusions, and

3) Create doubt for the public to fill, by thinking.

4) Have fun!

If you can fit your whole communication on one sheet, to sides, it will be easy for your network to reproduce and pass along to their networks, and theirs and theirs, etc. Set deadlines too, to add to the impact on the receiving end. Have fun! Work together separately.

One effective communication is to have FAN club members make a hundred or more copies of relevant articles and share them by mail or in person, to get the word out. What are your good ideas for communicating and preserving freedom through people? Have fun!

Good luck, Great American, with your Great American FAN Club. You and your good friends and citizens are worth it. Have fun!

The Constitutional Equivalent of "Throw the Rascals Out!"

The U.S. Constitution provides for public officials to be brought to justice. Article I, Section 2, Clause 5 says, "The House of Representatives . . . shall have the sole Power of Impeachment." That means they can cause an investigation into the behavior of elected public officials. They would possibly do so with one, or several, but not the entire House. If done, Section 3, Clause 7 provides, "The Senate shall have the sole Power to try all Impeachments," Clause 8, "Judgment in Cases of Impeachment shall not extend further than to removal from Office, and disqualification to hold and enjoy any Office of honor, Trust or Profit under the United States: but the Party convicted shall nevertheless be liable and subject to Indictment, Trial, Judgment and Punishment, according to Law." Can you imagine the senate "trying" itself?

If all else fails, the founding fathers wove into the U.S. Constitution a means of correcting abuses of this Republic. Found in Section 2, Clause 1, "The House of Representatives shall be composed of Members chosen every second Year by the People of the several States, . . ." and Section 3 for the Senate, "one third may be chosen every second year. . . ." Likewise, from Article II, Section 1, "The executive Power shall be vested in a President of the United States of America. He shall hold his Office during the Term of four Years ... ."

These are the Constitutional equivalent of "Throw the rascals out!" This fits perfectly with the Declaration of Independence provision "That whenever any Form of Government becomes destructive to these ends, it is the Right of the People to alter or abolish it. . . ."

"Throw the rascals out" does not do it all. When the taxpayer and citizen finally finds out what kind of public servant an elected official truly is, it may be too late. Legislation is already passed, taxes are already raised and spent. Changing public servants every two, four or six years may be inadequate. It is much like William Shakespeare put it:

> The evil that men do lives after them; the good is oft interred with their bones. (Julius Caesar, III, 1)

If some of the present flagrant, destructive abuses continue, such drastic action may be in order in election years 2000, 2002, 2004, 2006, 2008, 2010 and beyond. It is a powerful, peaceful, lawful, effective way to motivate incumbents. We use ballots instead of bullets.

Don't Just Vote—V-O-T-I !

We can go beyond philosophy or perceived need, to *action* as we have stressed repeatedly. There is one way to discipline those in Congress for flagrant abuses of power, damaging our freedoms, families and future. That is by discreetly and judiciously using the power of the people granted by these provisions of the U.S. Constitution. It is simply summed up:

V-O-T-I: VOTE   OUT   THE   INCUMBENTS!

V-O-T-I may well become a national act of patriotism. We do all we can do to contact and communicate with our elected representatives by letter, phone, fax, email and personally, along with more blatant advertising, publicity and promotion. We continually *remind* them of what our expectations are. If the targets are missed we simply Vote-Out-The-Incumbents, *ALL of them!* By doing so the citizens make the most powerful political statement possible. It is the equivalent of a revolution, only with ballots, not bullets; brains, not blood; actions, not apathy.

Keep a primary goal in mind: To *slow government growth,* get its finances in order, reduce the tax and regulatory burdens and get back in balance. The goal is *NOT* to vote out anybody. We communicate fairly, firmly, directly and regularly with our elected representatives to relay exactly what we expect. If they meet the criteria they retain their jobs and the privilege to represent us.

We ask of them discipline, honor and integrity to inhibit extravagant, uncontrolled spending, cruel abuse of power and ever-burgeoning government to perhaps forever preclude such an ultimate act as voting out all incumbents. Certain issue areas as defense, education, social reform and environmental protection may be considered high priority. Let them know they must meet the criteria and you mean business. If their biggest job is truly keeping their job, they will listen and respond.

Use good sense. If you have a Senator or Representative doing a very good job, while exercising V-O-T-I, vote to keep the good one there doing the good deeds. Likewise if a candidate is decidedly the worse of two evils, support instead "the better of two evils," then closely communicate with and guide him or her.

Carefully monitor congressional action to get true surpluses, reduce taxes, control spending, then forge a continuing surplus to reduce the national debt. For starters, as the present administration has articulated, reduce the national debt held by the public (about $3.6 trillion of $5.5 trillion, end of 1999) to ZERO. If they do not demonstrate positive progress and good faith, it is truly time to get tough and "throw the rascals out," all of them if necessary, in the way the Founding Fathers provided for us.

Remember your secret weapon, Citizen *Power of ONE:* V-O-T-I !

VOTE OUT THE INCUMBENTS !

A Yardstick for V-O-T-I
GOAL 25-25: The Two Percent Solution

Our quest is for relatively smaller, less government. Two goals— government at one-fourth our economy, taxes at one-fourth of our income—bring together our desire for better balance between the public, government sector and private, enterprise sector. Both goals are backed by logical, doable historical analysis and consistent people poll conclusions. Our government has performed admirably at or below 25% of output, GDP (gross domestic product) from 1776 into 1960 when its social programs began to balloon out of proportion. A 1995 national poll by *Reader's Digest* showed people consistently supported taxes at no more than 25% of income.

GOAL 25-25: The Two Percent Solution brought it all together. Surprisingly, it involves no cuts or even a freeze. With their Constitution the Founders put together such an economic and political success system that even shackled by big government, just by controlling its growth its bounty would sustain it. GOAL 25-25 shows that by limiting federal tax growth to 3% and spending to 2%, 1999's $3.66 trillion national debt held by the public can be paid off in 13 years. By similarly holding state-and-local spending and tax growth to 2%, in the same time both government size in the economy and taxes from income will be at 25%, an economic miracle.

This is very much a "Citizen" GOAL 25-25, because governments cannot do it by themselves. Being government and bureaucratic they grow automatically in survival mode. They will respond, though, to citizens, if only to maintain their survival and jobs, if citizens prevail.

Two key needs are regular reports and a method of determining progress from the reports. For state-and-local government, the report is the after-the-fact annual publication of the *Economic Report of the President* (February) and *Statistical Abstract of the United States*, (November). Use the same references for the federal government plus the monthly reported "Government Finances." Here's how this looks:

GOVERNMENT FINANCES, through May, 2000

WASHINGTON (AP) -- Figures on government spending and debt (last six digits are eliminated). The government's fiscal year runs Oct. 1 through Sept. 30.

Total public debt limit July 10	5,577,845
Statutory debt limit	5,950,000
Total public debt outstanding	5,622,950
Operating balance July 10	37,417
Interest Fiscal 2000 thru May	226,370
Interest same period 1999	222,674
Surplus fiscal 2000 thru May	120,319
Total surplus fiscal 1999	124,360
Receipts fiscal 2000 thru May	1,318,490 /1
Receipts same period 1999	1,179,136 /2
Outlays fiscal 2000 thru May	1,198,171 /3
Outlays same period 1990	1,138,419 /4

--Denver Post, p. 7C, 7/12/2000

Calculate YTD Government Receipts (Tax) Growth:

$$\frac{1,138,490 \ /1}{1,179,136 \ /2} = 1.11818 = \underline{11.82\% \ increase}$$

Calculate YTD Government Receipts (Tax) Growth:

$$\frac{1,198,171 \ /3}{1,138,419 \ /4} = 1.05249 = \underline{5.25\% \ increase}$$

Both analyses fail the Citizen GOAL 25-25 test. Tax growth is set at 3%, spending, 3.0% first year, dropping 0.2%/year to 2.0% in 2003. Send your Congress Repr. and two Senators a "Government Financial Performance Appraisal" with your "heads up" letter. Mention your V-O-T-I, "not negotiable" stance. Tell them this abysmal fiscal performance is completely unacceptable.

Note the valuable and abundant information supplied. On a monthly basis Joe and Jane ("super") Citizen can quickly and accurately calculate GOAL 25-25 progress and report. How to calculate growth of federal receipts and spending is shown following the concise report as presented, in this case, in the business section of the *Denver Post*. Sample calculations show increase of tax receipts at 11.8%, considerably above GOAL 25-25's required 3%; of spending increase, at 5.25% likewise above the required 2%. This prompts a postcard or brief letter to your federal representative and both senators cheering or booing their performance. If the latter, a mention or reminder of "VOTI," vote-out-the-incumbent, is in order.

At the slightest note of progress be quick and lavish in your praise. For instance if the following report shows significant progress in either or both numbers, in your communication heap praise, gratitude, thanks and appreciation on them for doing a good job, encouraging them to keep up the good work.

You will have to appraise the state-and-local 2% growth target performance after-the-fact, with the latest *Economic Report of the President*, to learn of prior year(s) performance. For instance check the latest (February, 2000) edition, page 404, Table B-83, "State and local government current receipts and expenditures, 1959-1999." For complete years 1998 and 1997, in billions of dollars you would find receipts (tax) growth of 6.08% (1070.4/1009) and outlays (spending) growth of 4.81% (1028.7/981.5). You might take note of the previous values for 1997/ 1996, respectively, 5.06% and 4.53%. Slightly different data are available from the *Statistical Abstract of the United States*. The 1999 edition shows similar results on state-and-local spending for recent years through 1997, page 316, Table 510, "State and Local Government Receipt and Current Expenditures ... 1980 to 1997." They too are in the wrong direction from GOAL 25-25.

Next, your action is to make up a brief letter with the data and trends and send it to all kinds of local public officials—state senators and representatives, county commissioners, superintendents of schools, city managers and mayors, heads of commissions and authorities. Don't forget special tax districts for recreation, transportation, sports stadiums, law enforcement, water and sewerage and others. With your data and GOAL 25-25 remind them of their performance, the public trust they serve, the integrity of their office towards citizens and taxpayers, and their fiduciary responsibilities with the public purse. Tell them the "productivity imperative"—to do more and better for less—you work and sweat under in your job and business, and that the hard-earned money taken from you for their stewardship bears for them the same financial responsibilities for their respective productivity in their jobs.

The pen is mightier than the sword, and so are today's communication tools—computer, copier, telephone, fax machine, email, Internet, websites, public meetings, even face-to-face, eyeball-to-eyeball get-togethers. This Power of ONE you wield must be used regularly and often. Beyond, remember to head towards the Power of ONE More, and the Power of Many More. Share this information, your concerns and action with others. Motivate and inspire them to do likewise by emulating your citizen activity.

The rest is simple and fun. In *each communication* with your public officials remind them of the upcoming critical spending, tax and debt reduction targets. "PS With your 2006 re-selection or de-selection only one year away please meet or beat the GOAL 25-25 targets by September 30, 2006. Make your commitment—and that of your colleagues, to gradually reduce the growth of government taxing, spending and debt—as firm as is mine to V-O-T-I—Vote Out The Incumbent, to highly encourage you all to meet these critical goals. This is not negotiable." For any election year the targets are violated, *Vote Out The Incumbents* regardless of who they are (and hopefully you will have let them know repeatedly in the months preceding).

Remember, the whole purpose is *to achieve government fiscal responsibility* based on a moderate, reasonable, long-term program to control spending growth to two percent. The purpose is NOT to vote out the incumbents. V-O-T-I serves only as a handy citizen tool and motivator. Even all of this may be an exercise to begin truly cutting government size as the discipline is imposed, to a level one-half or two-thirds of today's relative size in terms of government spending as a percent of national output, GDP, gross domestic product.

You will be part of a citizen revolution using the U.S. Constitution provisions for giving adulation and approval or expressing discontent and disapproval of the performance of your government(s) and their impact on America's freedoms and future.

Will you do it, *Power of ONE?*

The True, Invincible Power of ONE, From the Power of Many

True, the Power of ONE seems limited, and perhaps it is. But in a larger context it is invincible. Using these methods and techniques to get information, then getting that information to many, then many more with the magic of multiplication, the action must be done and will be taken. Bryce Courtenay, author of the fiction book *The Power of ONE* set in South Africa, puts it this way:

> Changes can come from the Power of Many,
> But only when the many come together to form
> That which is invincible—The Power of ONE.

Network Building for Life

Get your own business cards, or visiting cards, with your contact information thereon—mailing address, email address, telephone and fax numbers, website, cellphone, etc. Trade them with others for theirs. File them alphabetically and/or set up your "special people" quick reference files. Set up your Email Citizen Action List for those whom you have found to be what might be called "SuperCitizens," the best-of-the-best who will make the difference that must be made. Make notes of personal characteristics, spouse and children's names, birthdays and anniversaries, special interests or experience areas, hobbies, pets or pet peeves, areas of expertise, etc. A short pencil is better than a short memory. Contact manager programs are available for doing this on a computer.

People are all-important. Only people make this planet work. We must understand how to live together cooperatively and work together competitively to have a life worth living and a future worth building.

Your influence is only as big as the people you know, the respect they have for you and your continuing growth of contacts and credibility. Strive to meet more people and get to know them better. Join or attend groups, purposely and assertively introduce yourself to others and they to each other. Draw a bigger circle and include you and many others in it.

Build your network. Put your network to work. Keep your network working!

Use your *Power of ONE* to multiply your *Power of ONE More* to the larger *Power of Many More*, building to "that which is invincible—The Power of ONE."

Questions for Review

1. Explain how, as we change our world one person at a time, the change we make is not just proportional but geometric, or exponential.

2. What is "The Change Process" and how does it work? Give two reasons why it is important to involve people in change early in the process. Give three pointers to help people accept, even support change.

3. What is MASO? Why is it "magic"? Why does it work? Why is "and so on" different from "multiply"?

4. Romanian poet Andre Codresque said we have two tools to fight tyranny. What are they? What is different about those tools in the abundance of America? What are their updated names and how do you use them?

5. Name additional "tools" both in ways of communication and actions. Who are the various people who care and who can benefit and grow by MASO? What is the 4-part "What Formula" and how does it work?

6. What are some "secrets" of writing letters to the editor of a publication to make them more stimulating and effective? Why is it better to conclude with a question than with an opinion? Why give evidence and information that convinced you, rather than your conclusion? Discuss a different approach in writing letters to the Congress.

7. What is "The Great American FAN Club" and how does it work? What does "FAN" stand for? Give five action steps a FAN Club member can take. What is the "Freedom Tithe-Tithe Pledge"?

8. What is the Constitutional equivalent of "throw the rascals out?" Explain "Don't Just VOTE—V-O-T-I." How can this concept motivate elected federal officials to be more responsive to the people? Describe and explain a "yardstick for V-O-T-I" in terms of federal, state-and-local government taxing and spending, deficits and surpluses, debt and debt interest, and curing these "Congressional Diseases."

9. What is the perplexing and exasperating part of "deficits" versus true deficits, "surplus" and true surplus? How can you tell that you have true surplus? Explain how a timetable to eliminate the public debt over a period of 13 years can use V-O-T-I to make it work. Why is it reasonable, responsible and necessary?

10. How is it that changes from the Power of Many are related to "the invincible Power of ONE"? Describe the importance and method of "Network Building for Life."

One man awake
Can awaken another.
The second can waken his next door brother.
The three awake can rouse the town,
By turning the whole place upside down.
And the many awake, make such a fuss,
They finally awaken the rest of us.
One man up with dawn in his eyes ...
            ... Multiplies!
            —Helen Kromer, from "For Heaven's Sake"

I see us ... not in the setting sun of a dark night of despair ahead. I see us in the crimson light of a rising sun, fresh from the burning, creative hand of God. I see great days ahead. Great days made possible by men and women of will and vision.   —John Steinbeck

The politician ... has developed on the American scene largely because of an abdication of the rank and file citizen in the exercise of his duties and responsibilities ... To the problems which beset us there can be but one answer—citizen participation in political activity, including financing. A theory which has for too long furnished an excuse behind which lazy citizens have hidden is that inspired leaders always appear on the national horizon in times of great stress ... However, many nations of the world have had great leaders and today are in oblivion ... The answer lies in our determination that all of us shall become politicians, rather than leaving it to the greedy, the hypocritical, the corrupt and selfish who have little regard for the chastity of American citizenship.
                    —Fred M. Betz, Sr.

The political machine triumphs because it is a united minority acting against a divided majority.

                    —Will Durant

Each time a human being stands up for an idea ... or acts to improve the lot of others ... or strikes out against injustice ... he or she sends out a tiny ripple of hope. In crossing each other from a million different centers of energy and daring, those ripples build a mighty current which can sweep down the most terrible walls of oppression and injustice.
                    —Robert F.Kennedy

> Changes can come from the Power of Many,
> But only when the many come together to form
> That which is invincible—The Power of ONE.
>   —Bryce Courtenay, author *The Power of ONE*

If the people lead, the leaders will follow. —Anon.

Chapter 26

THE JOY HAS BEEN THE JOURNEY
To TOTAL Power of YOU in America!

Go back to page 37 and read Chapter 26.

Yes, we did produce a near perfect Republic. But will they keep it, or will they, in the enjoyment of plenty, lose the memory of freedom? Material abundance without character is the surest way to destruction.
—Thomas Jefferson

I touch the future. I teach. —Christa McAuliffe

Bibliography

Freedom

United States Constitution, Bill of Rights and remaining amendments—get a copy and read it.

Declaration of Independence—get a copy and read it.

Your own State's Constitution—get a copy and read it.

The Mainspring of Human Progress by Henry Grady Weaver, Foundation for Economic Education, Irvington-on-Hudson, NY: 1953

America, United States of America

The Miracle of America by W. Cleon Skousen, National Center for Constitutional Studies, Washington, DC: 1981

The Making of America: The Substance and Meaning of the Constitution by W. Cleon Skousen, National Center for Constitutional Studies, Washington, DC: 1985

The Majesty of God's Law: It's Coming to America by W. Cleon Skousen, Ensign Publishing, Salt Lake City, UT: 1996

Economics

Economics in One Lesson by Henry Hazlitt, Arlington House, Conn: 1979

Free to Choose by Milton and Rose Friedman, Harcourt Brace Jovanovich, New York: 1980

Human Action by Ludwig von Mises, Regnery Gateway, Chicago: 1966

An Inquiry into the Nature and Causes of the Wealth of Nations by Adam Smith, Modern Library, NY: 1937

The Way the World Works by Jude Wanniski, Simon & Schuster, New York: 1983

Education

The Bible

The Lessons of History by Will and Ariel Durant, Simon & Schuster, New York: 1968

The People Puzzle: Understanding Yourself and Others by Morris Massey, Prentice Hall, Reston, VA: 1979

Economic and Political Systems

The Five Thousand Year Leap: 28 Great Ideas that are Changing the World by W. Cleone Skousen, Washington, DC: 1981

Libertarianism in One Lesson by David Bergland, Orpheus Publications: 1984

Call It Conspiracy by Larry Abraham, Double A Publications, Wauna, WA: 1985

An Overview of our World by John F. McManus, John Birch Society, Appleton, WI: 1971

Selected Works by Karl Marx and Friedrich Engels, International Publishers, New York: 1980

Socialism by Ludwig von Mises, Liberty Classics, Indianapolis: 1981

The World in the Grip of an Idea by Clarence B Carson, Arlington House, New Rochelle, NY: 1979

Democracy in America by Alexis de Tocqueville (translation by Richard D. Heffner) Mentor, New York: 1956

The Law by Frederic Bastiat, Foundation for Economic Education, Irving-on-Hudson, NY: 1950

The Road to Serfdom: A classic warning against the dangers to freedom inherent in social planning by Friedrich Hayek, University of Chicago, Chicago: 1944

Government

A Call for Revolution: How Washington is Strangling America—And How to Stop It by Martin L. Gross, Ballantine Books, New York: 1993

Government Is Too BIG and It's Costing YOU!: How to Change America by James P. Gills, M. D. and Ronald H. Nash, St. Lukes Cataract and Laser Institute, Tarpon Springs, FL: 1996

Constitution: Fact or Fiction by Dr. Eugene Schroder, Buffalo Creek Press, Cleburne, TX: 1995

Why Government Doesn't Work by Harry Browne, St. Martin's Press, New York: 1995

The Federalist Papers by "Publius"—Alexander Hamilton, James Madison and John Jay, Mentor Books, New York: 1961

The Foundations of the Constitution by David Hutchinson, University Books, Secaucus, NJ: 1975

The General Theory of Employment, Interest and Money by John Maynard Keynes, Harcourt, Brace & Co., New York: 1936

The Incomplete Conquest: Governing America by Theodore J. Lowi, Holt, Rinehart and Winston, New York: 1981

The Miracle on Main Street by F. Tupper Saussy, Spencer Judd, Sewanee, TN: 1980

Our Ageless Constitution by W. David Stedman and LaVaughn G. Lewis, Editors, David Stedman Associates, Asheboro, NC: 1987

The Phoenix Phenomenon, by Fred Holden, Phoenix Enterprises, Arvada, CO: 1984

Health, Fitness and Exercise

Aerobics by Dr. Kenneth Cooper, Bantam Books, New York: 1976

Jane Brody's Nutrition Book by Jane Brody, W. W. Norton & Co., Inc. New York: 1981

The Official YMCA Physical Fitness Handbook by Clayton R. Myers, Popular Library, New York: 1975

Total Fitness in 30 Minutes a Week by Lawrence E. Morehouse and Leonard Gross, Simon & Schuster, New York: 1975

Personal Growth, Personal Organization

The Seven Habits of Highly Effective People by Stephen Covey, Simon & Schuster, New York: 1989, and, with A. Roger Merrill and Rebecca R. Merrill, *First Things First*, Simon & Schuster, New York: 1994

You Can Negotiate Anything: How to Get What You Want by Herb Cohen, Lyle Stuart, Secaucus, NJ: 1980

Regular Current Information-Periodicals

Newspapers such as YOUR daily newspaper, the *Wall Street Journal, USA Today, Los Angeles Times, San Francisco Chronicle, Chicago Tribune, New York Times, Washington Times, Washington Post, Denver Rocky Mountain News, Denver Post,* etc.

Weekly news magazines, *Newsweek, Business Week, Insight, Time, Industry Week, U. S. News & World Report,* etc.

Human Events, weekly conservative magazine, 1 Massachusetts Ave NW, Washington, DC 20001, 1/800/787-7557

New American bi-weekly magazine, American Opinion Publishing, PO Box 8040, Appleton, WI 54913

Economic Statistics

Budget of the United States Government, Federal Government

Economic Report of the President, Federal Government

Statistical Abstract of the United States, Federal Government

The World Almanac & Book of Facts, Newspaper Enterprise Association

About the Author

Fred Holden was Director of Economic Affairs for five years leading Adolph Coors Company's award-winning Employee Economic Awareness Program. He had a staff of 10 people whose only job was to teach Coors employees and others *economics*, then to share that technology with other corporations and organizations. Following a year as Director of Public Affairs Research, Fred left the corporate world to write this book which has gotten him on over 620 talk shows nationwide.

Holden's goal is to get *TOTAL Power of ONE in America* in the heads, hands, and hearts of 20 million Americans. "The Great American Book" is an ideal candidate for businesses, corporations and organizations to adopt, promote, sell, give and boost to get out the real "rest of the education story." To create better understanding, appreciation and support of business, he created a "Business as Teacher" consortium for economic understanding with the theme, "The education solution. A new burst of freedom." He offers sizable discounts on the Custom Legacy Edition of 300 or more books. With the great price and book, the CEO/president gets the Front Page for his or her special message to stakeholders—employees, clients, customers, prospects and friends.

Since 1987 Holden has been listed in Heritage Foundation's *Annual Guide to Public Policy Experts* in the areas of U. S. Government spending and taxation, state and local public finance and economic education. For five years he was a Senior Fellow-Budget Policy at Colorado's nonpartisan think tank, Independence Institute, and on Denver's *Rocky Mountain News* Board of Economists.

Holden has worked since 1996 to form a national movement of citizens to get Congress to substitute a revenue-neutral national retail sales tax for the complex, expensive, wasteful, intrusive and invasive federal income tax and its collection arm the Internal Revenue Service. NRST—"the choice tax"—is voluntary, anonymous, and discretionary, in a word, private. In 1999 he teamed up with website expert Bruce Douglas to create http://www.supercitizen.com, to build awareness, knowledge and support for NRST.

For 15 years Holden was a member of Colorado and National Speakers Associations, and Denver and National Associations of Business Economists. He was on the speakers bureau, 1987 Commission on the Bicentennial, U.S. Constitution, served on the Roosevelt Center for American Policy Studies' 1986 deficit reduction national task force, and twice on the Washington DC-based Committee for a Responsible Federal Budget.

With a BS Chemical Engineering, University of Colorado, he worked nine years in aerospace for Hercules Incorporated, plus two years, chemical intermediates manufacture in plastics laboratory and data processing supervision in Utah, Maryland and New Jersey.

In 15 years at Coors in Golden, CO, after earning his MBA he served in resource planning and development, public relations, and 3 ½ years as facilities engineering manager.

Holden in 1984 published *The Phoenix Phenomenon,* a book that analyzed the growth of government from 1948 to 1982, and its detrimental effect on America's standard-of-living and quality-of-life. He has lectured in 15 colleges and universities. He knows and communicates the immense *Power of ONE* in over 1,000 speeches to audiences all over America, especially concerning freedom, government, taxes and citizenship. He has published some 500 articles in newspapers and magazines, including *Chemical Engineering, Wealth Building* and *Colorado Business.* He has been listed in *Who's Who in the World* since 1980, *Who's Who in Finance & Industry* (1977), *Who's Who in the West* (1982), and *Who's Who in America* (1993).

He lives in Arvada, a suburb of Denver, Colorado, where he and his wife Dottie raised their three daughters, Lori, Sheri and Tami and enjoy (Sheri's) grandboys, Jake, Ben and Ross.

Holden believes the critical balance towards less government must be restored, that we must all get more involved to: 1) Work with youth in schools to teach them: a) How to make a living, b) How to live, and c) How to understand life; 2) Restore, preserve and strengthen the family; and 3) Help kids learn that drugs, crime, gangs, violence, sex and suicide are not viable solutions to teenage problems.

For a free copy of "Have a Heart: Talk to Kids, Listen to Kids, Let's STOP the Teen-icide!" send a self-addressed, stamped business envelope to TOTAL Power, PO Box 1900, Arvada, CO 80001.

Index

Expense
   company
       definition of 201
   employee
       definition of 201
Expenses 200

F

Fabian socialism 292
   creeping 290
Face of God 41
Failure 70
Falling downs 108
Far left 289
Far right 289
Fascism 25-26, 28, 281, 286-
   287, 289, 298, 345
Fascist Scale 294
Fat 496
Father of Boredom 69
Fear 78
Feather, William 196
Fed. *See* Federal Reserve Bank
Federal Correction Center 359
Federal Reserve Bank 19, 28,
   123, 124, 125, 366, 453
   definition of 366
Federal Reserve Note 122,
   123
Federal Reserve System 369
Federalist Papers, The 353,
   361
Feulner, Edwin J. 380
Fiat money 124, 125
Financial planning
   lifetime 32
   pay yourself first 32
First Amendment 95, 253, 262
First assignment
   definition of 59
First magic number 88-89
First most priceless treasure
   57, 67. *See also* freedom
First Things First 512
Fiscal responsibility 127
Fitness 493, 495
   definition of 495
Five-P's 166
Flourish or Perish 47-48
Flynn, Trisha 160
Food on the shelves 216
Force of law 329
Foreign oil cartel 193

Forstchen, Bill 87
Fortunate five percent 113
Fortune 500 213
Fortune 213
Founding Fathers 28, 51, 136,
   158-160, 261, 276, 282,
   290, 291, 292, 329, 332,
   334, 336, 342, 352, 353,
   368, 453, 549
4x4 letter 542
Four food groups
   dairy products 496
   fruits and vegetables 496
   grains 496
   meat 496
Fractional banking 126
Frameworks 9
   for living 9
   for thinking 9
Franklin, Benjamin 9, 20, 151,
   155, 159, 282, 347, 374,
   389
Free enterprise 19-20, 129-
   130, 133-150, 165, 179,
   193, 243, 247, 249, 286,
   346, 397. *See also*
   American free enterprise
   system
   competition 19
   customer sovereignty 19
   definition of 19
   economic freedom 19
   economics 113
   free markets 19
   ingredients of 136
   limited government 19
   mystery of 170
   private property 19
   self-interest motives and
       incentives 19
   triangle model 19
   two definitions 148
Free Enterprise Economic
   System 134
Free enterprise society 142,
   190
Free market 19, 144-146, 216,
   397
Free market system 148, 286
Free society 61
Free-market society 112
Freedom 9, 15-16, 29, 57-67,
   93, 97, 129, 134, 162,
   188, 193, 263, 378, 393,
   470

and responsibility 162
   as greater job 15
   as greatest gift 16
   as your most priceless
       treasure 63-64
   begets choices 163
   blessings of 162
   change process 9
   contrived ignorance of 28
   dangers of 162
   deductions of 66
   definition of 158, 306, 310
   destiny of 465
   documents of 17
   economic 141
   economics 9
   experiment in 148
   ingredients of
       honesty 165
       honor 165
       principle 165
   involvement process 9
   magic of 170
   miracle of 44, 96
   of choice 162
   private property 346
   to work 130
   torch of 15
   with responsibility 69, 163
Freedom Action Network 545-
   547
Freedom builders 35, 53, 480
Freedom builders building
   freedom builders 38
Freedom documents 17, 28,
   33, 58
Freedom fighters 53
Freedom of expression 95
Freedom of religion 95
Freedom of speech 95
Freedom of the press 95
Freedom Tithe-Tithe Pledge
   544
Freedom to peaceably
   assemble 95
Freedom to petition 95
Freedom to work with risk
   138
Freedom with responsibility
   69
Freedomism 286
Freedoms
   economic and political 112
   individual 112
French revolution 377

TOTAL POWER BOOK ORDER

(Please Print Plainly)

I WANT *TOTAL POWER* NOW!

Please send _____ copies of *TOTAL POWER OF ONE IN AMERICA* to:

Name_____ Date _____

Address _____

City, State, Zip _____

Quantity_____ x $29.95 . . . . $_____

    (Colorado, add 7.41% Sales Tax, $2.22 per book) . . . . _____

Include $5 postage and handling per book . . . . _____

(**FAST** Delivery, **Add per book** 1st Class-$4.00) . . . . _____

                       TOTAL . . . . $_____

Enclose Check (to *TOTAL POWER*), M/O or Credit Card Information:

Charge to my Credit Card: ❑ Visa   ❑ MasterCard

Card No. _____

Expiration Date_____ Signature _____

Mail Order TODAY! No Risk Guarantee!
TOTAL POWER, Box 1900, Arvada, CO 80001
If not satisfied return book in good condition for full refund.